American First Ladies

American First Ladies

Editor

Robert P. Watson, Ph.D.

SALEM PRESS, INC.
Pasadena, California   Hackensack, New Jersey

Editor in Chief: Dawn P. Dawson
Managing Editor: Christina J. Moose
Manuscript Editor: Elizabeth Ferry Slocum
Assistant Editor: Andrea E. Miller
Research Supervisor: Jeffry Jensen
Photograph Editor: Philip Bader
Production Editor: Cynthia Breslin Beres
Layout: James Hutson

Cover photos: AP/Wide World Photos; Library of Congess; PhotoDisc

∞ The paper used in these volumes conforms to the American National Standard for Permanence of Paper for Printed Library Materials, Z39.48-1992 (R1997).

Library of Congress Cataloging-in-Publication Data
American First Ladies / editor, Robert P. Watson
   p.cm.
   Includes bibliographical references and index.
   ISBN 0-89356-070-7 (alk. paper)
   1. Presidents' spouses—United States—Biography. 2. Presidents' spouses—United States—History. 3. Presidents' spouses—United States—Social life and customs. 4. Washington (D.C.)—Social life and customs. I. Watson, Robert P., 1962-

E176.2.A4 2001
973'.09'9—dc21

2001042903

PRINTED IN THE UNITED STATES OF AMERICA

Contents

Publisher's Note

American First Ladies is a response to the increasingly visible role First Ladies have played in U.S. government as well as the increasing interest in women's achievements from the birth of the United States to the present time. The book is designed to meet the needs of college and high school students and those seeking information about U.S. history and women's history.

Users of this one-volume reference will find it a useful supplement to other publications, notably Salem Press's *The American Presidents*, to which *American First Ladies* is a companion piece. Who, then, are the First Ladies? Included are forty-four biographical essays on women who were married to or served as hostesses and partners of American presidents. Additionally, nine topical essays cover various facets of White House life, including managing the Executive Mansion, championing social causes, and influencing government policy.

American First Ladies contains a number of useful tools to help readers locate their areas of interest. To supplement the text, four appendices have been included. A Chronological List of First Ladies summarizes vital information on each First Lady from 1789 up to the twenty-first century. A list of U.S. presidents, also in chronological order, is followed by the appendix of seventy Libraries, Museums, Historic Sites, and World Wide Web Sites. Special care has been taken to include visitor information for any place referred to in the text as being on display or open to the public. Web sites of interest to presidential scholars as well as those interested in specific historical figures have been in-

cluded. The volume closes with a Bibliography, listing 134 sources for further study, as well as a comprehensive Subject Index.

Written with the needs of students and general readers in mind, the articles contained in *American First Ladies* present clear discussions of the individuals and topics, explaining any contemporary issues or historical references that may be unclear. Distributed throughout the book are more than one hundred photographs and drawings, complementing the verbal portraits of the First Ladies, their lives, and times.

Each biographical article is formatted to help readers find specific information they may be pursuing. Birth and death dates and locations appear at the beginning of each essay on a First Lady. The text is further divided into sections, including Early Life, dealing with family and educational background; Marriage and Family, discussing the First Lady's relationship with the president; Presidency and First Ladyship, covering the First Lady's years in the White House; and Legacy, which varies widely by the individual but always provides additional insights into those activities and accomplishments for which the First Lady was known, both during and after her time in the White House.

A key feature of the volume is its boxed sidebars: one hundred essays-within-essays. A sidebar on each president will assist the reader in placing the First Lady's biography in a historical context. Additional sidebars recount anecdotes about every First Lady, highlighting some event or quality for which she is particularly well known or with which she is associated. Topical essays include sidebars describing examples of White House renovation attempts, campaign efforts of First Ladies, and the like.

Reference works such as *American First Ladies* would not be possible without the help of experts in the field. More than fifty contributors, including historians, political scientists, and other academicians, have lent their knowledge and insight to the this project, and Salem's editors wish to extend their gratitude to them. We are particularly grateful to the project's editor, Robert P. Watson, Ph.D., whose guiding hand shaped this project and its contents at every step of the way. The names of all the contributors, along with their affiliations, are listed at the beginning of the book.

About the Authors

Editor **Robert P. Watson**, Ph.D., is Editor of the journal *White House Studies* and has written or edited nine books. His books on First Ladies include *The Presidents' Wives: Reassessing The Office of First Lady*, *First Ladies of The United States*, and the forthcoming *The Presidential Companion: Readings on the First Ladies* and *Martha Washington*. He also served as Project Director of *Laura Bush: The Report to the First Lady*.

Carole Elizabeth Adams, Ph.D., is Associate Professor of History at the University of Central Florida.

Jeffrey S. Ashley, Ph.D., is Assistant Professor of Political Science at Eastern Illinois University. His research interests include natural resources policy, American Indian politics, public administration, the presidency, and First Ladies. He is the author or coauthor of several articles and two books and is writing a full-length biography of Betty Ford.

Jean Baker, Ph.D., is Elizabeth Todd Professor of History at Goucher College. She is the author of *Mary Todd Lincoln: A Biography* and *The Stevensons: A Family History*.

Jean Becker, Chief of Staff to former president George Bush, helped edit *Barbara Bush: A Memoir* and complied President Bush's book *All the Best, George Bush: My Life in Letters and Writings*. She was a veteran newspaper reporter when she became Barbara Bush's Deputy Press Secretary in 1989.

Cynthia D. Bittinger is the Executive Director of the Calvin Coolidge Memorial Foundation in Plymouth, Vermont. She also teaches Vermont History and Women in U.S. History at the Community College of Vermont.

Mimi Bogard is a Library Media Specialist with the Sandy Valley Schools in Magnolia, Ohio, and Docent with the National First Ladies' Library.

Patricia Brady, Ph.D., is Director of Publications at the Historic New Orleans Collection. She is the editor of *Nelly Custis Lewis's Housekeeping Book* and *George Washington's Beautiful Nelly* as well as the author of a biography of Martha Washington.

Pamela T. Brannon, Ph.D., is Adjunct Professor in the Organizational Management program of Warner Southern University and the Political Science program of Florida Atlantic University. Her research interests include First Ladies, public administration, and race and diversity issues.

Susan Roth Breitzer is a doctoral candidate in History at the University of Iowa. Her research and writing interests include U.S. social, political, cultural, and labor history. She is the author of a biography of Eleanor Roosevelt for the PRESIDENTS' WIVES series.

Mary M. Cain is President of the Canton Community Clinic in Ohio and a Docent and Researcher with the National First Ladies' Library.

Colton C. Campbell, Ph.D., is Assistant Professor of Political Science at Florida International University (the State University of Florida at Miami). He is coeditor of six books and has published articles in *Congress & the Presidency*, *The Journal of Legislative Studies*, and *Talking Politics* as well as numerous chapters in various books on Congress. He is cowriting a book titled *The Congressional Impeachment of Bill Clinton*. He served as an American Political Science Fellow in 1998-1999 in the office of U.S. senator Bob Graham.

Virginia A. Chanley, Ph.D., is Assistant Professor of Political Science at Florida International University. Her research interests include public opinion, the presidency, and First Ladyship. Her research has been published in journals such as *Public Opinion Quarterly* and *Political Behavior*, and she is writing a biography of Rosalynn Carter.

Jean M. Choate, Ph.D., is Associate Professor of History at Coastal Georgia Community College.

Robert Dewhirst, Ph.D., is Professor of Political Science at Northwest Missouri State University.

Sina Dubovoy is an independent scholar and writer in Bethlehem, Pennsylvania.

Anthony J. Eksterowicz, Ph.D., is Professor of Political Science at James Madison University. He is the coeditor of *Public Journalism and Political Knowledge* published by Rowaman and Littlefield, and coeditor with Robert P. Watson of *The Presidential Companion: Readings on the First Ladies*.

Raymond Frey, Ph.D., is Associate Professor of History and Dean of the Faculty at Centenary College.

Frances Hughes Glendening, J.D., M.P.A., is First Lady of Maryland. As chairwoman of Maryland Women of Achievement, Inc., she is spearheading a history book project of a similar title. Twice-named to the Top 100 Women of Maryland list by the *Daily Record*, Francie Glendening also serves as a senior legal and policy adviser to the Chairman of the Federal Election Commission in Washington, D.C.

Myra G. Gutin, Ph.D., is Professor of Communications at Rider University. She is the author of *The President's Partner: The First Lady in the Twentieth Century*.

Tom Lansford, Ph.D., is Assistant Professor of Political Science at New England College and a fellow at the Frank Maria Center for International Politics and Ethics.

Bryan Le Beau, Ph.D., Professor of History, is the John C. Kenefick Faculty Chairman in the Humanities and Chairman of the Department of History at Creighton University. He is the author of several books, including *America Imagined: Currier and Ives*, published in 2001 by the Smithsonian Institution Press.

Mary Linehan, Ph.D., is Assistant Professor of History at Spalding University.

Pierre-Marie Loizeau, Ph.D., teaches Languages and American Civilization at Universite de Nantes in France.

James McCallops, Ph.D., is Assistant Professor of History at Salisbury State University.

Dale C. Mayer is an Archivist at the Herbert Hoover Presidential Library.

Anne Moore is an administrator with the President Benjamin Harrison Home.

David Murphy is a senior political science student at American University and served as a White House Intern in spring of 2000.

Barbara Bennett Peterson, Ph.D., is Emeritus Professor at the University of Hawaii; Adjunct Fellow, East-West Center; and a Professor at Oregon State University. She is Associate Editor for the American National Biography's twenty-four-volume series published by Oxford University Press, which won the Dartmouth Medal in 1999. Dr. Peterson has published more than seventy professional journal and encyclopedic articles in the field of historical biographies and eight books.

Mary J. C. Queen is a Docent and Lecturer with the National First Ladies' Library and a member of the board. An alumna of Ohio Wesleyan University, she is a history scholar specializing in the First Ladies of Ohio.

Lawrence J. Rifkind, Ph.D., is Associate Dean of the College of Arts and Sciences at Georgia State University.

Stephen Robar, Ph.D., is Assistant Professor of Political Science at the University of Pittsburgh-Bradford. In addition to his work in the area of American politics and policy, which includes work on presidential character and collaborative policymaking, he is the Codirector of the Environmental Studies Program.

Craig Schermer is a Consultant and Historian with the National First Ladies' Library.

John Shaw, Ph.D., is Professor Emeritus at Hiram College.

Valerie A. Sulfaro, Ph.D., is Associate Professor of Political Science at James Madison University. Her research areas include public opinion and electoral behavior, with a focus on the role of information in candidate and issue evaluations.

Clinton P. Taffe is the Administration and Operations Manager of the Board of County Commissions, Leon County, Florida. Assigned to the LeRoy Collins Leon County Public Library System, he oversees policy, planning, budget, and public relations.

Elizabeth Lorelei Thacker-Estrada earned her Master of Library and Information Studies degree at the University of California at Berkeley and is a Department Manager at the San Francisco Public Library. She is researching and writing the first book-length

scholarly biographies of Abigail Powers Fillmore and Jane Means Appleton Pierce and contributed to the publication *Laura Bush: The Report to the First Lady*.

Anne Toplovich is the Executive Director of the Tennessee Historical Society and has contributed articles to regional journals and *The Tennessee Encyclopedia of History and Culture*. She is the author of a book-length biography of Rachel Jackson, to be published in 2003.

Gil Troy, Ph.D., is Professor of History at McGill University in Montreal. He is the author of *Mr. and Mrs. President: From the Trumans to the Clintons*, published in 2000 by University Press of Kansas.

Patricia Foltz Warren is a retired educator and Docent and Researcher with the National First Ladies' Library.

Claudia Pavone Watson is an Administrative Assistant at the journal *White House Studies*.

Paul M. Zall, Ph.D., is a Research Scholar at the Huntington Library and Professor Emeritus of English and American Studies, Harvard University and California State University, Los Angeles.

Foreword

Certainly, First Ladies occupy a unique position in the political and cultural realm of the nation. They are not elected, they receive no salary, and their duties are not outlined by the Constitution, yet, despite the ambiguity of their post, first ladies have become an integral part of American history. They occupy a role which has evolved according to the customs of the day and the personalities of the women who fill it.

Emily Oland Squires, Maryland State Archives

The role of First Lady originated with Martha Washington, wife of the first president of the United States, but it has been reinvented and revised multiple times during the 225 years of the presidency. Mrs. Washington was referred to as Lady Washington, a title eventually becoming First Lady. Over time, the title was adopted by governors' wives as well as the wives of U.S. presidents. Interestingly, apparently none of the male gubernatorial spouses has accepted the title of first gentleman. In fact, typically they claim no title as spouses of female governors.

There is significant evidence many First Ladies throughout U.S. history have not embraced the role willingly. Rather, they made the best of it as loving, supportive wives and as civic duty dictated. Several wives actually complained they felt imprisoned as a private citizen in a support role for a publicly "owned" man.

Even from the beginning, most presidents' wives were outspoken, and many were highly political themselves. During the United States' infancy, Abigail Adams and Dolley Madison did much to advance women's status, and they proved their worth as first-rate First Ladies. In the twentieth century, Bess Truman seemed to speak for all her predecessors when she said, "We are not any one of us happy to be where we are, but there's nothing to be done about it except to do our best—and forget about the sacrifices and many unpleasant things that bob up."

In short, there is nothing either a First Lady or first mate (as some call male spouses) is required to do; rather, they have the choice of what they wish to do or not do, feel compelled to do, what they undertake, and what they avoid. There has been a wide range of involvement in activities and approaches to the "job" ever since the United States' initial First Lady assumed the role.

Many First Ladies have made the most of the position and have contributed vastly to the growth and well-being of the United States. We have witnessed a few instances during contemporary times where national First Ladies have used the opportunity as training ground for their post-presidency careers. Prime examples are Ambassador Eleanor Roosevelt and Senator Hillary Rodham Clinton, whose tenures as successful First Ladies undoubtedly contributed to their success as nationally prominent public servants.

Still, there are differing points of view even about the necessity or desirability of having a First Lady. On January 9, 2000, the CBS television program *Face the Nation* dedicated itself to this debate, pointing out: "Modern First Ladies have been supported by enough paid staff to operate major [public relations] firms, which they've become." The program suggested the Clintons took this role to another level when then-President Bill Clinton asked the First Lady to shape health care policy. Countless advisers and critics warned he was committing the ultimate management blunder—hiring someone he could not fire. Yet the day she left the White House, Hillary Rodham Clinton's high popularity among Americans nearly equaled her husband's. All in all, there are nearly as many varying opinions of a First Lady's role as there are different personalities of the women themselves.

State First Ladies

Like national First Ladies, state First Ladies have a variety of concerns. Although the governors' spouses have common interests, each spouse's experience is unique. In addition, a number of state First Ladies have long-standing careers as teachers, lawyers, business professionals, journalists, librarians, doctors, professors, and entrepreneurs. Most also have children and grandchildren, whose privacy they fiercely seek to protect, to ensure as much normalcy as possible as the children mature under the public eye.

Some First Ladies take a leave of absence from their professional careers during their tenure as First Lady, to fully explore this "experience and privilege of a lifetime," as Hillary Rodham Clinton characterized her eight years in the White House. Juggling home, family, and public functions while making a personal impact as First Lady is all-consuming. When a full-time job is left intact, as some First Ladies have chosen to do, time management becomes a formidable task. The demands are great, and the opportunities for involvement are endless. For those choosing to be active partners, the trick is to know when to accept requests and invitations and when to forgo them, because

countless worthwhile organizations hope to engage a First Lady in their causes. These organizations view the First Ladies as highly visible volunteers who can help them gain access to those in power to affect policy or obtain much-needed funding.

There are several distinct phases of the spouse's role. The first phase is the campaign trail. Campaigning is an exciting, busy, and sometimes harrowing experience. It is full of ups and downs—minute to minute, hour to hour, and day to day. My experience with the two Glendening campaigns was somewhat different from that of most spouses of candidates. My position at the Federal Election Commission prevented me from campaigning independently on behalf of my husband, although I could accompany him to most events. By federal law (the Hatch Act), my campaign activities were limited; however, this did not make campaigning any easier. In fact, it made it more difficult to provide the support I wanted to give.

For me, an additional phase ensued because the election was so close. In our case, the opponent challenged the election results, both through an official recount and, subsequently, in court. When this was behind us and we were victorious, I was ready to become an active First Lady. In fact, my husband had been an elected county executive for twelve years in local government. During this time, not only had I been extremely active in certain community organizations, but I cochaired all of his transition efforts. As a result, I was immediately appointed cochairperson of the governor's transition team, helping to select personnel, develop management policies, and lead the transition. The next phase is the actual "move in, create something, go forward" period.

Unfortunately, a dearth of information exists at the state level about the busy women behind powerful men. While conducting research on the Internet recently, I found it disheartening (and a bit humorous) to see "goddesses" listed as an information link for the general search entry of "states' First Ladies." Besides Maryland, Illinois was the only other state listed with information pertaining to First Ladies, but the site listed did not include biographical information. In both states, the small number of official First Lady portraits represents only a fraction of the women who performed the duties of First Lady or official hostess during each governor's administration. Actually, in Maryland, only about one-fourth of the them (fourteen in total) were featured officially in portrait. Contrast this with Maryland's governors: There are fifty-five official portraits of them, with only three governors inexplicably missing from the collection.

At the same time, this is a new century and a new millennium. We entered it with a controversial, yet popular former national First Lady now ensconced in Washington, D.C., as a U.S. senator.

Similarly, a former state First Lady, Missouri's Jean Carnahan, was sworn in beside Hillary Rodham Clinton as her colleague. These are interesting times. With more female members of the U.S. Congress and more female governors than ever before in history, it behooves women in leadership positions to support women's rights actively, speak out, maintain diaries, and write and save letters, papers, and the like to provide documentation and insight about their contributions and points of view. Books such as *American First Ladies* will assist us in this endeavor.

Women's History Projects: The Example of Maryland

Unremittingly, I am passionate about ensuring women have their rightful place in history. In fact, I am a lifelong women's history crusader, having begun as a teenager when I first discovered what sociologist Clarice Stasz Stoll meant by "history's collective forgetfulness about women." I remain determined to provide adequate information about my role and con-

tributions, and more important, to uncover the countless women of achievement in Maryland history. As Maryland First Lady, I direct my efforts within three distinct categories. First, I sponsor and support a number of women's history projects within my home state. Second, as chair of the National Governors' Association Spouses' Committee, I promote similar activities for First Ladies and other women of achievement among the states. Third, as an active member of the new National First Ladies' Library (NFLL), I help to implement the extraordinary vision of NFLL founding president Mary Regula to chronicle the lives of our national First Ladies and women of achievement.

Upon becoming Maryland First Lady, as a women's historian, I was curious about what my predecessors had accomplished. Two motivating forces led me to delve into the history of Government House, the official governor's residence, built in 1869. First, I wanted to know about the women who had lived there before me. Second, I was eager to use this information to help develop my agenda as the First Lady of Maryland. Sadly, I found virtually nothing chronicled about the women who stood beside Maryland governors before me. Yet, after digging for quite some time with the help of State Archivist Dr. Edward Papenfuse and his staff, we uncovered inspiring information proving many of the women made meaningful contributions to the well-being of the state and nation.

Maryland, the Old Line State, was extremely influential at the time of the United States' birth. In fact, Annapolis served as the nation's capital from November, 1783, to August, 1784. It was here George Washington resigned his commission as commander-in-chief of the Continental Army, and the ratification of the treaty with Great Britain officially ended the American Revolutionary War. Even before Maryland gained statehood, women played important official roles. Beginning with Ann Jennings Johnson in 1777, Maryland has had fifty-four First Ladies or official hostesses (the title reserved for women who are not actually governors' spouses). While there is much chronicled about most Maryland governors, we found very little compiled information about the women who served as First Lady or official hostess spanning Maryland's history. In fact, when I first arrived in Annapolis, there was not even a list of the names of these women.

As Government House evolved from a Victorian structure to a Georgian redesign in the 1920's, so too evolved the roles of the women who lived there. We conducted an exhaustive search of both the mansion and the state archives. The search eventually produced fourteen portraits. With these in hand, we gathered facts about the past and began recording the future.

Since 1995, we have worked extensively to piece together and chronicle the lives of the First Ladies and official hostesses of Maryland. In March of 1995, when adequate information and data had been collected, we unveiled my first art exhibit, titled "Portraits of First Ladies and Official Hostesses of Maryland," at Government House. This exhibit brought long overdue attention to both the collection and the women, subsequently attracting significant interest among descendants of these women and prompting several donations of artifacts and historical data. This resulted in a second, expanded exhibition five years later, in March of 2000, titled "Lady of the House: First Ladies and Official Hostesses of Maryland, 1777-2000," which included numerous personal items loaned by family and friends.

Another long-term archiving project is a forthcoming book and accompanying Web exhibit titled *If These Walls Could Speak: The Official Residences and Public Lives of Maryland's First Ladies and Official Hostesses, 1777-2000*. The project is directed by Dr. Papenfuse and will provide the most comprehensive, accessible information about Maryland First Ladies and official hostesses ever assembled. *If These Walls Could*

Speak will be a lasting tribute to Maryland's First Ladies and official hostesses and will serve as a definitive resource to help us trace their evolution in history. Simultaneously, I am spearheading a book project titled *Women of Achievement in Maryland History*.

To ensure my activities are recorded properly, from the onset, my talented staff and I began collecting my speeches, event programs, news clippings, and letters. In 1995 we began carefully arranging them into a compendium of all activities centered around my agenda. In celebration of Women's History Month, 2000, I turned over the first eleven books to the Maryland State archivist, who graciously accepted them for the State Archives, saying, "I wish all First Ladies would do this. I hope other Maryland women of achievement and future First Ladies not only will continue this project but . . . will strengthen and institutionalize it." I was inspired to document my activities, in part, by former Maryland First Lady Helen Avalynne Tawes (First Lady 1959-1967), who said with much candor in 1961: "A governor's wife comes here and she works like a dog. I just feel that they get so little credit; some recognition would be nice." Interestingly, Helen Tawes instituted the custom of official portraiture for First Ladies and commissioned portraits of four of her predecessors, in addition to her own, by one of Maryland's—and the United States'—most illustrious portraitists, Stanislav Rembski (1896-1998).

Spouses' Leadership Committee at the National Governors' Association

This fairly new, dynamic arm of the National Governors' Association (NGA) has evolved to play an active role in shaping the national political agenda and assuming a leadership role promoting volunteerism in a bipartisan way. Most governors' spouses are active volunteers in their states, though their levels of involvement are wide-ranging. Typically, forty members of this spouse organization attend the annual winter conference held in Washington, D.C. This is a large majority of gubernatorial spouses, who have joined together to pursue common interests and share information about initiatives in their home states.

First Ladies lead by example, and as Laura Welch Bush said in an interview with *Today Show* host Katie Couric, "It is not our dresses we want citizens to know us for." Laura Bush has been active in her home state of Texas, as well as the spouse organization, for several years, sharing many issues of importance with other active state First Ladies, including early childhood education, which she actively is pursuing on a national policy level. At the NGA, spouses do not limit themselves. For instance, the spouses simultaneously supported Habitat for Humanity's "First Ladies' Build" project in nearly every state as well as women's health, literacy, and other vital current issues.

The NGA Spouse Program has evolved over the years, just as the lives and roles of women have evolved. Although the NGA was founded in 1908, the governors' spouses did not formally meet until many years later. In the early years, when the governors gathered for their meetings, their spouses would accompany them, attending only the social events with their husbands. As the First Ladies of the states became familiar with one another, they began to meet informally for coffee or lunch while the governors were involved in business meetings.

During the 1976 winter meeting of the NGA, then-First Lady of Iowa Billie Ray hosted a spouses' luncheon meeting, with the chief of protocol from the U.S. Department of State appearing as guest speaker. Following this luncheon, the First Ladies visited Happy Rockefeller, the wife of then-Vice President Nelson Rockefeller, for tea at the vice president's residence. This was the beginning of the first organized spouse sessions. Since then, sessions have been held regularly during the winter meetings in Washington, D.C. In 1979 the official program was expanded to include spouse

sessions during the annual meeting held during the summer. A full-time NGA staff member dedicated to serving the spouses' organization was added in the mid-1980's. The program agendas for the annual winter and summer NGA meetings are affected by the Spouses' Leadership Committee chair. Typically, when a member becomes chair of the committee, he or she chooses an issue or initiative as a focus for the spouses' organization.

Not surprisingly, an early Spouses' Leadership Committee chair was Hillary Rodham Clinton, then-First Lady of Arkansas. In written remarks welcoming new members of the committee in 1987, she said:

> During the past decade, the role of the spouse and the nature of our programs have changed measurably ... the role of the spouse has become increasingly involved and visible, and in recognition of that fact, we have attempted to be responsive. With the assistance of NGA staff, we now regularly receive informative resource materials on major issues and legislation.

The National First Ladies' Library
The National First Ladies' Library (NFLL) was established to fulfill an informational void which long has frustrated academicians and history buffs alike. The library is the first central repository of information documenting the contributions of U.S. First Ladies. The library is located physically in Canton, Ohio, in the former family home of Ida Saxton McKinley, wife of President William McKinley. The virtual library is located on the Internet at *www.firstladies.org*. The library's scholarly centerpiece is a comprehensive, annotated bibliography of books, manuscripts, journals, diaries, and other materials by and about the First Ladies. It was developed by First Lady historian and author Carl Sferrazza Anthony. As a historic first, the First Ladies bibliography at NFLL is more complete than any bibliography about U.S. presidents.

As an NFLL founding vice president, my role is to further the mission to actively support and increase public awareness of First Ladies' contributions and legacies. History must properly record spouse contributions at the state level. This is becoming increasingly critical for two reasons. First, as governors assume the presidency more often, their spouses ascend to the role of national First Lady. Seventeen state governors and three territorial governors have become presidents of the United States, and four of the six most recent presidents were governors. Their national prominence, as well as that of their "running mate" spouses, were built on successes and experiences at the state level. For this reason, we should record gubernatorial and First Lady information together. In doing so, we more accurately portray the American story.

Second, and equally important, as a society and nation, we cannot permit this enormous gap in our history to continue. We must make every effort to chronicle the countless significant contributions women have made to our social, political, and economic order. By doing so, we ensure a complete historical perspective that serves as an inspiration and a road map for those who come after us. The book you are about to read fully documents the lives of U.S. First Ladies and, much like the NFLL, goes a long way toward fulfilling this important mission.

Life as a First Lady
Spouses on both the national and state levels have played an integral part in American history and the politics which have defined it. Because of the inherent ambiguity in the nature of the post, the First Lady (or first spouse) has the privilege of bringing her (or his) own personality, values, and customs as well as personal interests to the position with distinct tailoring. The role requires constant balancing of multiple priorities, but in its greatest fulfillment, it can bring the administration's agenda into citizens' daily lives, promoting the goodwill of government for the people.

Perhaps more than their spouses, First Ladies know the joy of bipartisanship. They can reach out to the citizenry and exemplify volunteerism and citizenship. They are active community volunteers who can use their notoriety and bully pulpits effectively in this way. If CBS had asked me to participate in their *Face the Nation* program in 2000, I would have said First Ladies perhaps are more necessary than ever in helping define the role of today's women and emphasizing the need for everyone to work together for the mutual benefit of our children and our children's children. This reason alone should be enough to support First Ladies' efforts. In fact, sometimes First Ladies are more popular than their elected spouses. As one Mississippian opined, former Mississippi First Lady "Pat Fordice has been a better First Lady than her husband has been a governor."

As more women assume high elected office, the pressure will be on their spouses to live up to the proactive, achievement-oriented women who have institutionalized the spouse role as American tradition. By then, I suppose we will have disposed of an actual title for the spouse of a president or governor, and the title First Lady slowly will die and eventually be archived forever. Until then, and by any label, there is much to contribute as the spouse of a president or governor and many ways spouses can lead based on a strong sense of patriotism. It is a great honor to serve as Maryland First Lady, and I will hold these days dear for the rest of my life. In the meantime, I intend to record my own history, accurately reflecting my sentiments as well as my contributions. Simultaneously, I encourage other Maryland women—and all women—to document their contributions by saving their own letters, journals, and the like. After all, we are women charting our own course of history at the dawn of a new millennium.

It is my distinct privilege to contribute to

this book. The editor, Robert P. Watson, a scholar well known for his work about First Ladies, has assembled a capable and diverse set of contributors. *American First Ladies* certainly will help us all better understand the roles of the presidential spouses and hostesses. It is precisely the type of vital project for the recognition of women's contributions I long have championed. I hope you find these essays on American First Ladies to be both insightful and inspiring. Their stories are fascinating, and their accomplishments helped shape the course of the United States.

Frances Hughes Glendening
Maryland First Lady

Introduction

American First Ladies are among the most popular and well-known figures in the world. Indeed, the First Lady is easily recognizable to many grade school students, and the American public can more readily identify their First Lady than they can the most senior members of Congress or even the vice president. Add to that the fact that the First Lady often tops the Gallup Organization's annual poll to determine the United States' most admired women. What emerges is a clear picture of one of the most prominent American public figures. Yet, this familiarity and popularity tell only part of the story, and it would appear that we know less about the presidential spouses than would initially seem to be the case.

In truth, little is known about many early First Ladies, especially those serving prior to the twentieth century. Moreover, the public remains uncertain about what roles and duties it expects First Ladies to perform. The serious study of the institution began only at the close of the twentieth century. The First Ladyship is a vastly more complex and powerful office than it is often depicted as being in textbooks and the media. For instance, even though the First Lady emerged over the course of the twentieth century as one of the most powerful positions in the United States, it must be remembered that this person is unelected, unappointed, and unpaid for service. In short, First Ladyship is an intriguing institution, one that has been home to a group of no less intriguing individuals.

Further consideration of the First Ladies of the sort encompassed in this encyclopedia is necessary if one is to gain an adequate understanding of the office and its occupants. Also, the reader should rest assured that he or she will gain a full appreciation for the trials and tribulations of the presidential spouses, which have earned them their rightful place in American history.

Perhaps the First Lady is worth our attention if for no other reason than she has been a part of the presidency since the United States' founding. To be sure, the existence of the First Ladyship even predates the completion of the White House. During the inaugural presidency of George Washington, the White House was under construction, and the Washingtons were forced to serve from a private residence in New York City, then later from a home in Philadelphia. Although the title of First Lady was not used until much later in the next century, Martha Washington did serve her country in the capacity of presidential spouse. In this role, Lady Washington presided over official state affairs and appeared with her husband at public events. George Washington's two terms as president ended in 1797, with the presidential residence in the city bearing his name still unfinished.

Abigail Adams, wife of the second president, was the first spouse to actually reside in the White House. She and her husband, President John Adams, moved into the newly completed building in 1800, only four months before the end of his term in office. Although

Abigail and John Adams did live in the White House, they were like many other early presidential couples who did not enjoy the mansion as the grand structure it is today. Only six rooms in the building were completed in 1800, and Mrs. Adams complained that the original design of the Executive Mansion failed to consider such concerns as practicality and livability. Abigail was even forced to hang her laundry in the East Room and had a difficult time keeping the building warm and dry in the cold Washington winter. Many other pre-twentieth century presidential couples found the Executive Mansion to be inadequately staffed, and the first couple also had to pay for entertainment, staff support, and building upkeep out of their own pockets.

The presidential wives' service also predates the use of the term First Lady. The title was not originally a part of the office. In fact, the first few presidential spouses were known by a variety of titles. Martha Washington, for instance, was widely known as Lady Washington, and Dolley Madison was occasionally called Lady Presidentress. Later, in the late 1850's, Harriet Lane, the niece of bachelor President James Buchanan, was nicknamed the Democratic Queen. Some newspapers of the day also referred to her as Lady of the White House.

The exact date of origin of the title remains unclear, but a reference to Dolley Madison, the woman who helped make the office popular, might mark the initial use of the title. While delivering the eulogy after Dolley Madison's death in 1849, President Zachary Taylor spoke of her as "our First Lady for a half-century." The term did not immediately catch on and would not appear again until the Civil War, when the wife of Jefferson Davis was described by journalists as the "First Lady of the Confederacy." A decade and a half later, in the late 1870's, newspapers spoke of Lucy Hayes as "the First Lady of the Land," in reference to a nationwide tour she completed with her husband. However, it was not until the twentieth century that the title really became commonplace.

Even though the title First Lady is widely accepted today and has even been used to describe spouses of male political leaders around the world, governor's wives, and women of prominence in theater, the arts, and even commerce, some First Ladies did not like the moniker. Jackie Kennedy so disliked the title that she forbade her staff from using it. Rosalynn Carter opted simply for "Mrs. Carter" when in the company of the White House staff.

Who Can Be Considered a *First Lady*?

To date, only two bachelors have been elected to the presidency. James Buchanan and Grover Cleveland hold this distinction; however, Cleveland married Frances Folsom during his presidency. In total, First Ladies have served in thirty-seven of the first forty-two presidencies, so the institution of the First Ladyship has certainly been a part of the American presidency for most of the nation's history. Moreover, five spouses died prior to their husband's service as president: Martha Jefferson, Rachel Jackson, Hannah Van Buren, Ellen Arthur, and Alice Roosevelt. Even though these women did not preside over the White House, they are still deserving of our consideration because they were influential forces in the lives and careers of their husbands in the period before his election to the presidency. For instance, Rachel and Andrew Jackson had been married for thirty-seven years before her untimely passing during the brief interim between Andrew Jackson's election and inauguration as president. Likewise, Ellen Arthur passed away just prior to her husband's selection as vice president; Ellen and Chester Arthur had been husband and wife for twenty years at the time of her death. After Alice Lee Roosevelt's death, Theodore Roosevelt remarried, and his second wife, Edith, was with him during his presidency.

Three First Ladies died while serving in the White House: Letitia Tyler, Caroline Harrison, and Ellen Wilson. All three of these presidential wives appear to have had close relationships with their husbands throughout their married lives, including the period that they were in the White House. All three widowed presidents would later remarry. In fact, presidents John Tyler and Woodrow Wilson remarried while still serving as president, so they each had two different First Ladies during their White House years.

The majority of First Ladies outlived their husbands. Only two presidential widows, Frances Cleveland and Jackie Kennedy, would later remarry. These two were considerably younger than their first husbands. A total of three presidential spouses had previously been married and widowed before marrying their second husbands, men who would go on to be presidents. Included in this group are early mothers of the nation Martha Washington, Martha Jefferson, and Dolley Madison. Each of these three women brought children from their previous marriages into their second marriages. There have been five divorces associated with the presidency, three involving eventual First Ladies: Rachel Donelson (Jackson), Florence Kling (Harding), and Betty Bloomer (Ford). These women were divorced when they married their second husbands. President Ronald Reagan had been married to actress Jane Wyman before marrying Nancy Reagan. Wyman herself had previously been divorced before marrying Reagan.

At times, when the president's spouse was either deceased or too ill to carry out her duties, the president received the assistance of "surrogate" White House hostesses. This was true for presidents Thomas Jefferson, Martin Van Buren, and Andrew Jackson, all of whom lost wives prior to their inaugurations. Typically, young female relatives were called upon to preside over the social events of the White House. Oftentimes, these young nieces, daughters, and daughters-in-law lived at the White House. Some First Ladies, including Letitia Tyler, Jane Pierce, and Anna Harrison, were limited by poor health and also sought the services of a female relative to assist them in managing the White House's social affairs. Such examples of surrogate hostesses being called into duty point to the importance of the institution within the White House as one responsible for social events.

The Second-Toughest Job in the United States?

Not only have First Ladies been a part of the presidency since the inaugural administration of George Washington, but presidential wives have made many important contributions to their husbands' lives and presidencies. In so doing, they helped shape the very course of American history. Indeed, many presidents found the First Lady's presence, service, and counsel to be invaluable and a source of their own success in the White House.

Although the office is not a job per se, and the president's spouse is not mentioned in the Constitution, First Ladies have fulfilled many social and political functions in the White House. For example, the First Lady often presides over White House social events, oversees the upkeep of the Executive Mansion, makes obligatory public appearances, and supports her husband's political agenda.

Initially, and perhaps because of the sex roles present in society, many a First Lady has found herself responsible for running the White House. In addition to being a political landmark of the United States, the White House is the private residence of the first family. Although no distinct job description existed for First Ladies, the office evolved to be responsible for the social affairs of the White House to the extent that the First Lady has become the United States' de facto social hostess. She is expected to preside over everything from formal state dinners for visiting dignitaries to afternoon receptions for women's social clubs. In so doing, First Ladies manage a large White

House domestic staff and such details as menu selection, seating arrangements, guest lists, and entertainment for a wide variety of state affairs that demand careful attention to detail and protocol.

Some First Ladies also functioned as the chief White House preservationist, archivist, or tour guide. Not surprisingly, the wear and tear on the building has required many First Ladies to supervise elaborate renovations and restorations of the furniture, rooms, and historical pieces found in the White House. Some First Ladies have consulted historians and architects in their efforts to achieve historically accurate restorations. Most First Ladies have been responsible for selecting the White House's official china sets and furnishings. Thanks to the efforts of First Ladies, the White House remains a living museum of American history, replete with historic period collections and political memorabilia from the nation's past.

First Ladies are now expected to campaign for their husbands, and many function as presidential booster, spokesperson, and surrogate, traveling with and appearing on behalf of the president. Several First Ladies have traveled internationally. Rosalynn Carter even met with heads of Latin American states in the official capacity of presidential envoy. Other First Ladies, from Martha Washington to Mary Lincoln to Barbara Bush, have met with U.S. troops during times of war and have visited soldiers in military hospitals.

The nature of American politics and society has required the wives of politicians to appear in public with their husbands and, at a minimum, give the appearance of supporting his campaign and political office. Nowhere in American politics has this been more prevalent than in election years, with the prospective president and First Lady spending upward of a year making constant campaign appearances together. Most recent First Ladies have also been asked to make public speeches while on the presidential stump. This campaigning does

not stop after the election. Once in office, First Ladies often continue to lobby for their husbands' programs and make public appearances on behalf of the president's public image and popularity. Indeed, many First Ladies have become quite adept at campaigning. Lady Bird Johnson and Rosalynn Carter campaigned alone and on behalf of their husbands. Barbara Bush and Bess Truman were fixtures next to their husbands on the campaign swing and were often met with more enthusiastic applause than that which greeted their husbands. Even in the nineteenth century, such First Ladies as Ida McKinley and Frances Cleveland appeared on their husbands' campaign paraphernalia.

First Ladies have gone above and beyond the call of duty by making speeches, fulfilling a demanding schedule of travel and public appearances, and even serving as the president's political adviser. This is especially true in more recent times, when First Ladies have functioned as political partners. It is not uncommon for recent First Ladies to assist the president in making staffing and political appointments, serving on presidential task forces, attending cabinet meetings, and speaking on his behalf at political rallies. At their husbands' urging, First Ladies Rosalynn Carter and Hillary Rodham Clinton led, respectively, high-profile mental health and health care reform task forces. Other First Ladies, such as Eleanor Roosevelt, were called upon to testify before Congress as expert witnesses on policy matters. Mrs. Roosevelt also prompted her husband to appoint a woman to his cabinet: President Franklin D. Roosevelt selected Frances Perkins as his secretary of labor, the first woman to serve as a cabinet secretary. As far back as the 1840's, Sarah Polk served as James K. Polk's personal secretary, editing his speeches, giving him political advice, and organizing his official papers.

The First Lady has also become a public leader in her own right. Beginning with Jackie Kennedy, First Ladies have emerged as advocates of important social issues and have become identified with a particular social cause or pet project. Pat Nixon advocated volunteerism, Lady Bird Johnson initiated a nationwide beautification and conservation program, Nancy Reagan became the leading spokeswoman for the "Just Say No" to drugs campaign, and Barbara Bush embraced adult literacy as her cause. To be sure, the public has grown to expect First Ladies to champion social issues and perform a wide array of functions within and beyond the White House. At this challenge First Ladies have generally succeeded. They have led large, public campaigns on behalf of a wide array of important social issues and, in so doing, emerged as leading spokespersons for these issues and generated public interest in and support for these causes.

Ironically, First Ladies are subject to criticism for their political activism, even if this activism is in response to public expectations. The American public has yet to determine its preference regarding the parameters of involvement for First Ladies in political activities. Public opinion polls reflect this uncertainty, revealing that the public is divided as to the exact roles and responsibilities it deems appropriate for First Ladies. It seems that if First Ladies are too active they are criticized, and if they are too inactive they are criticized. For instance, First Ladies have been condemned simultaneously for being too active and too passive, too old-fashioned and frumpy yet too excessive and uppity, and for having either too many socials or not enough socials. Martha Washington was thought to be too old, whereas the public was concerned that Julia Tyler was too young. Betty Ford was criticized for being too outspoken, whereas others complained that Pat Nixon was too reserved and unwilling to speak her mind. Harriet Lane was too happy, and Jane Pierce was too depressed. Nancy Reagan was criticized for saying that her life began when she met her husband, and Hillary Rodham Clinton was attacked for having a career inde-

pendent of that of her husband. In fact, so prevalent is public criticism that it would appear that about the only thing all First Ladies have in common, besides being married to someone who is the president, is that they all have been criticized for their actions in the White House.

The most common basis for such public condemnation is that a First Lady is too powerful. This criticism dates all the way back to the second First Lady, when Abigail Adams found herself under attack from her husband's political enemies because of her apparent interest in politics. The president's political opponents resorted to calling Mrs. Adams by the monikers Her Majesty and Madame President, nicknames meant to be negative because of her perceived influence. Eleanor Roosevelt was also subjected to accusations of having too much power, and her high profile inspections of public facilities were followed by both her admirers and her critics. More recently, Nancy Reagan was called Queen Nancy and the Dragon Lady by those who questioned her perceived power in the Reagan White House, while Hillary Rodham Clinton's role as her husband's policy adviser was rebuked by her husband's critics.

The criticism First Ladies have faced has come not only from the presidents' political opponents but from the press and larger public alike. At times, the attacks have transcended all notions of decency and have been highly personal and painful. For example, political satirists of the day depicted Margaret Taylor as something of a hick, smoking corncob pipes, while Eleanor Roosevelt was drawn with oversized buck teeth by insensitive cartoonists. Incredibly, even First Lady Ida McKinley's epilepsy and Julia Grant's crossed left eye were sources of criticism.

A First Lady's actions, even when performed under noble circumstances, also invite controversy. Lou Hoover and Eleanor Roosevelt were attacked in the southern press for inviting African American guests into the White House. Betty Ford was ambushed by the media for her frank views on social problems of the day. To her critics, Betty answered that "Being ladylike does not require silence." While some First Ladies endured these criticisms and relentless public introspection better than others, most did, in fact, persevere. First Ladies can take solace in the fact that, despite the criticism, most of them have been enormously popular. Recent public opinion polls often show that the president's spouse enjoys higher approval ratings than the president, and she is typically shown to be included among the United States' most admired women.

Presidential Partners

Of course, it is not only in the public limelight that the First Lady's influence has been exercised. Rather, it appears that the presidential spouse has wielded considerable influence behind the scenes. She is, after all, the president's wife, and of all the presidential aides and advisers, none knows the commander-in-chief as well as the First Lady or has the access to the president that the First Lady enjoys. Unlike most presidential aides and advisers, the First Lady has generally been at the president's side long before his presidency or even his political career. The First Lady is family, and her influence extends beyond any formal jurisdiction such as a job title or description. This influence also goes beyond the confines of the office and working day.

The majority of First Ladies served as their husbands' most trusted confidante. Many presidential marriages were healthy and involved a shared interest by husband and wife in the husband's career. As opposed to the notions of a single-income family or dual-career family, first families often lead what can be described as co-career marriages, wherein the spouse is an intimate part of the political career. White House wives have subordinated their own careers and interests to the co-career or "team." Even those First Ladies reluctant to participate in politics or public service have often found

that they are forced into a political role, or at least the symbolic and social roles associated with being a political wife.

A total of twenty-seven presidential couples were married at least twenty years *before* entering the White House. First couples such as Andrew and Eliza Johnson, Benjamin and Caroline Harrison, the Eisenhowers, and the Carters all spent more than three decades together as husband and wife prior to the time they spent in presidential service. Others, such as George H. W. and Barbara Bush, the Washingtons, John and Abigail Adams, and William and Anna Harrison, spent in excess of four decades together as husband and wife. Even those First Ladies who died prior to their husbands' election to the presidency had spent many years with him and often were major forces in his life and pre-presidential political career. This behind-the-scenes, "pillow" influence is hard to gauge but has the potential to have a profound influence on presidents and presidential decision making.

What has emerged is an institution with great influence. The First Lady has become one of the United States' most recognizable and influential public figures. Several presidential spouses have played central roles in their husbands' political careers and presidencies and have been so intimately involved in all facets of the public office that they can best be described as "presidential partners." Abigail Adams, Sarah Polk, Helen Taft, Florence Harding, Eleanor Roosevelt, Rosalynn Carter, Nancy Reagan, and Hillary Rodham Clinton all functioned as full partners in their husbands' presidencies. Each of these First Ladies campaigned for their husbands, supported their spouse's careers, offered political advice, edited political speeches, embraced and promoted their husband's policies, and served as the president's most trusted, closest political ally and confidante.

Because the Constitution is silent on the issue of the First Lady and relatively few legal parameters exist regarding the duties of the office,

First Ladies have had little in the way of formal guidelines to follow in determining their approach to the office. Yet this does not mean that First Ladies have been free to function in a manner solely determined by themselves. First Ladies must formulate their approach to the office with consideration to the fickle winds of public opinion and major events of the day. Of course, because the First Lady derives her legitimacy through marriage, she must be mindful of the particular preferences of the president. There is also historical precedent to consider, as many early First Ladies contributed to the shaping of the office. The actions of all previous First Ladies continue to frame the nature of the role. However, the lack of legal guidelines and the wide array of styles, actions, and duties of First Ladies throughout history have forged an office that is still evolving and allows for a considerable degree of discretion by each particular First Lady. Each must consider her own talents and vision for the office in defining her particular First Ladyship. First Ladies can assume a number of roles in their husbands' administrations. Among them appear to be a core set of unwritten responsibilities, including social hosting, management of the White House, social activism on behalf of a pet project or issue, and general political and public support of the president, which may include public speaking, campaigning, and making public appearances.

The First Lady has emerged in the twentieth century as an institution of the White House and of the American political system. Modern First Ladies have a sizable staff to serve them. Although many early First Ladies were active and wielded political influence, the "Office of the First Lady" is a twentieth century development, dating to the First Ladyship of Edith Roosevelt (1901-1909). In response to the overwhelming amount of mail the First Lady received, she requested the assistance of an aide. Isabella Hagner James, a clerk in the Department of War, was reassigned to the First Lady, becoming the first permanent, non-domestic staffer working directly for the First Lady. In recent times, the First Lady's staff has grown to include roughly twenty employees who serve the First Lady in such capacities as press relations, scheduling, correspondence, and special projects.

The First Lady's staff offices are usually located in the East Wing, opposite the presidential offices in the West Wing of the White House. This has led some political observers to comment that while the West Wing contains the brain of the American body politic, and the East Wing contains the heart. However, with the advent of a presidential partnership, a fusion of the two wings has occurred. In fact, First Lady Hillary Rodham Clinton even relocated her office to the West Wing. In so doing, she symbolically and physically completed this joining of the Office of the President and Office of the First Lady. Indeed, beginning around the time of Jackie Kennedy's service, the First Lady has enjoyed a staff, office space, and budget that exceed that appropriated for many of the so-called top presidential advisers.

Historically, spousehood was one of the few avenues to political power for women. Fortunately, women have made significant progress in virtually all sectors of American society and today serve in nearly every public office except the presidency. Still, the position of political spouse, especially presidential spouse, remains an avenue to political power. First Ladies have responded by using the office to advance a host of issues and causes and have made many important contributions to the United States. Spouses have shared power with the president to the extent that the First Ladies have at times operated as "the power behind the throne" of the presidency.

A Legacy of Service

The First Ladies represent a somewhat diverse group of intriguing women. While it benefits our understanding of the presidency and the history of the United States to consider them, they are fascinating individuals in their own right. Their accomplishments are impressive, and their importance throughout American history is only now beginning to be fully appreciated.

First Ladies have served without pay and often at great personal expense. A few were reluctant political spouses who dreaded the prospect of living in the White House. The White House is, after all, an intimidating place, and one can count on losing any semblance of private life or normal family life while there. Several presidential spouses had little training to prepare them for the challenges of the presidency, and others were barely out of their teenage years. The trials and tribulations of the White House are difficult for even those in peak physical condition. Yet several wives of the presidents suffered from poor health prior to entering the White House, and others were well into their later years, often far beyond the average life expectancies for the day and age.

There are other challenges in serving one's country in this capacity. Four First Ladies lost their husbands as a direct result of presidential service. Mary Lincoln, Lucretia Garfield, Ida McKinley, and Jackie Kennedy all lost husbands to assassination while in office. The husbands of Anna Harrison, Margaret Taylor, Florence Harding, and Eleanor Roosevelt suffered from poor health while in office and died before

completing their full presidential terms. Eliza Johnson, Pat Nixon, and Hillary Rodham Clinton endured the ugly and highly public turmoil surrounding the impeachment or attempted impeachment of their husbands, and most First Ladies endured the intense public scrutiny and hostile political attacks on their spouses that seem to come with the office.

Still, First Ladies have endured. Most have succeeded. They have served largely without proper recognition. As a group, the First Ladies have generally been a capable lot, and considering their responsibilities, they have generally discharged their duties as well as, if not better than, the presidents. Their stories deserve to be told. It is time to recognize their accomplishments and for the First Ladies to assume their proper place in American history.

The essays that follow profile each of the First Ladies, beginning with Martha Washington, the first presidential spouse. There are also essays on major topical areas associated with the institution of the First Lady which offer the reader a larger, conceptual understanding of the office. The contributing authors have been selected to write for this encyclopedia because of their expertise on the subject and are recognized as leading scholars in this field of study. I hope you enjoy learning about those individuals who have served as American First Ladies.

Robert P. Watson, Consulting Editor

Martha Washington

Martha Dandridge Custis Washington

Born: June 2, 1731
    New Kent County, Virginia
Died: May 22, 1802
    Mount Vernon, Virginia

President: George Washington
    1789-1797

Overview: Martha Washington remains one of the most admired women in U.S. history. As the wife of George Washington, her status as heroine of the early Republic is assured. Yet, to most people, Martha remains a distant figure about whom little is known in detail outside her marriage to "The Father of His Country." Nevertheless, Martha not only was a complex and intriguing person in her own right but also accomplished much as a partner in her husband's public career, as his lifelong hostess, supporter, and confidante. As the spouse of the new nation's first president, her actions framed the First Ladyship.

Early Life

Martha was the first of six children born to John and Frances Dandridge. She was born on June 2, 1731, at Chestnut Grove, the two-story Dandridge family home in New Kent County, Virginia. Her father, a county clerk, owned a successful five-hundred-acre plantation on the edge of the Pamunkey River in eastern, Tidewater Virginia. The family was prosperous, and Martha's upbringing put her in contact with members of the Tidewater aristocracy. Although the Dandridges were not among the upper echelons of the colony's elite families, they were a part of what has been described as Virginia's "lesser aristocracy."

    Martha's paternal lineage, the Dandridges, can be traced to the Oxfordshire region of England in the sixteenth and seventeenth centu-

Martha Washington. *(Library of Congress)*

ries. By the late seventeenth century, however, several sons and grandsons of the farming family had done well for themselves. In the year 1715, two descendants of the Dandridge clan decided to pursue their dreams in America. The two—William Dandridge and his younger brother John—found success in Virginia as merchants and landowners. John Dandridge later married Frances Jones, whose family came from a line of well-respected preachers. Unlike her husband, John, Frances had been born in the colony. Her grandfather, the Reverend Rowland Jones, had emigrated from England to establish a ministry in Virginia.

Not much is known about Martha's childhood, but it appears that her youth was happy and normal for a girl of her time and social class. Martha had brown hair and hazel eyes, and she grew to a height of approximately five feet. She was considered to be of average attractiveness. Unlike the popular image of her in her later years as the plump and matronly First Lady, donning her signature white bonnet, Martha seems to have been quite vivacious and spirited as a youth. She liked horses and was said to have been a proficient horseback rider. At age fifteen she was a society belle who had been to the governor's palace in Williamsburg. Given her family's status and her father's involvement in civic affairs, Martha would have been exposed to politics while growing up. She would also have had ample experience with the art of social hosting during her family's visits to Williamsburg for the social season.

Like most girls raised in the eighteenth century, Patsy, as she was nicknamed, did not have the benefit of a formal education. Her education was at home and might have been supplemented by traveling tutors who frequently lent their services to affluent families in the region. Stressing practicality, Martha's education focused on domesticity and the social graces, the two pillars in the lives of girls of her social standing. She learned to embroider and sew, studied music and played the spinet, danced, and was taught to cook and manage a household. Little else is known about young Martha's education, except that it also involved religion. Her father was a church elder and her mother came from a line of preachers. Consequently, Martha was an active churchgoer and was raised in a Christian home.

Martha enjoyed reading and was a reasonably astute observer of the events of her day. Surviving letters from her adult years show her to have been a phonetic speller, which was normal for colonial times. Martha was so self-conscious about her poor grammar that, later in life, she often asked George Washington to pen on her behalf those letters requiring formality. Her upbringing instilled in Martha strong principles, as Lady Washington became much admired for her proper manners and resolve. Possessing simple tastes, she was always a plain dresser and one to whom frugality and prudence were second nature. Yet, she carried herself with dignity and, although guarded about her privacy, many of her contemporaries were moved to comment on Martha's charm and warmth. Regardless of her lack of a formal education, Martha's youth seems to have prepared her well for the challenges she faced throughout her life.

Marriage and Family

It can safely be assumed that young Martha Dandridge would have attracted many suitors. While still a teenager she caught the eye of Daniel Parke Custis, one of the colony's most eligible bachelors and son of one of its wealthiest citizens. Daniel Custis had been born in 1711, which made him twenty years Martha's senior. Because both worshiped at St. Peter's Church and lived in the same county, however, Custis likely knew Martha from her youth. In fact, Custis was a deacon of the church. The Dandridges were members of the congregation and, as a child, Martha frequently played at the church.

At the time Martha and Daniel courted, the

Custis family reigned much higher on the social ladder than did the Dandridges. Daniel's notoriously difficult and domineering father opposed the union, in part because he deemed Martha's family not wealthy enough for his son, who, in his late thirties, had still not married. Daniel's father even threatened to remove him as heir to the Custis tobacco fortune. That Daniel Custis still courted young Martha suggests something impressive about her. That the teenage Martha was able to calm the elder Custis's reservations about the marriage implies she was a confident young woman. Martha and Daniel were married in 1749 at the Custis family home, known, ironically, as the White House. The marriage produced four children: Daniel Parke II (1751-1754), Frances Parke (1753-1757), John Parke (1754-1781), and Martha Parke (1755-1773).

Sadly, Martha's first two children died in infancy. These years must have been trying times for Martha, as her father, two of her children, and her husband all died within a few years of one another. Daniel Custis had often been sick and passed away during their eighth year of marriage. In 1757, Martha, then twenty-six years old, found herself a widow with two infant children. Both her father and her father-in-law had died a few years prior to her husband, leaving Martha in charge of one of the largest, most prosperous plantations in the colony. To add to her challenge, Daniel Custis had, for unknown reasons, failed to prepare a will, and a complicated lawsuit hung over the family business. Martha endured, maintaining her late husband's business affairs in England and overseeing the plantation. She was wise enough to accept the counsel of the colony's most celebrated attorneys and political leaders throughout this ordeal. Martha deserves credit, as the legal matter was resolved and the plantation profited. A year after her husband's death Martha was mistress of one of Virginia's largest and most prosperous plantations, two mansions, an abundant slave labor force, and thousands of

acres of the colony's choicest land. She was arguably the wealthiest woman in Virginia.

It was around this same time that fellow Virginian George Washington entered Martha's life. Washington had recently achieved the rank of colonel and was making a name for himself. Given the prevailing social expectations of the time, it would thus seem that George was a great catch for Martha, as young widows were expected to remarry. Martha, who was a few months older than her suitor, was likewise a good spouse for young Washington. George was a highly ambitious young man who had been unlucky in love and long dreamed of becoming a gentleman planter like the wealthy neighbors whom he so admired. The exact details of their meeting remain unknown, although it is likely that Martha and George knew of each other through their mutual Tidewater society connections and may even have met in Williamsburg. One story, given by Martha's grandson years after her death, suggests that when George was traveling to Williamsburg on business he encountered a neighbor by the name of Chamberlayne, a prominent citizen of the region, who invited George to join him for dinner. Washington is said to have declined, but on Chamberlayne's insistence the young colonel dined with Chamberlayne and his other guest, the widow Custis.

By 1758 the two were courting. George and Martha married on January 6, 1759, at the White House, the home she had inherited. Under the laws governing marriage and property, George secured for himself not merely a bride but a vast fortune and extensive land holdings, and he began his life as a gentleman planter. The union was a productive although childless one, with the newlyweds sharing many similar interests. Both were dependable, worked hard, valued a solid reputation and social appearances, and refrained from many of the social vices so common among the aristocratic class. So too did they value their home and family life, despite

George Washington

As a young man, George Washington dreamed of becoming a British army officer. His own military career began in his early twenties, and in 1753 he was made a major in the Virginia militia. Two years later he was promoted to the rank of lieutenant colonel. Though marred by early mistakes, Washington's record as an officer was lauded when he distinguished himself during General Braddock's disastrous campaign against the French in 1755. With Braddock mortally wounded and his troops in disarray, Washington showed remarkable calm and courage, rallying the soldiers and minimizing their losses. He emerged from the battle a hero but found himself once again passed over by the British in his bid to join their officer corps. Washington returned to civilian life, marrying and farming at Mount Vernon. The general was not forgotten when, during the meetings of the Continental Congress, Washington was selected to lead the revolutionary militia. In the face of seemingly insurmountable odds, he led the colonials to victory over the world's greatest military power.

At the pinnacle of his career, Washington could easily have gained control over the new nation, but he transferred power to the civilian government. After presiding over the Constitutional Convention of 1787, the hero of the revolution was again called to service as the new nation's first president, a duty which, at age fifty-seven, after a lifetime of service to his countrymen, he accepted reluctantly:

My movements to the chair of government will be accompanied by feelings not unlike those of a culprit who is going to the place of his execution, so unwilling am I, in the evening of a life nearly consumed in public cares, to quit a peaceful abode for an ocean of difficulties .... He was about to navigate uncharted waters. Fearful of a new monarchy, soured by the failures of the Articles of Confederation, and wary of government in general, the disparate peoples of the thirteen colonies looked to Washington's administration to chart a course toward the new republic's democratic ideals.

Washington was astute politically and felt his burden morally. When presented with various forms of address, from "His Most Benign Excellency" to "His Highness, the Protector of Liberties," he supported the simple "Mr. President." After two terms in office and at the height of his popularity, Washington relinquished power, assured that the United States' experiment in popular democracy would succeed. His outgoing advice, known as the Farewell Address, warned against "foreign influence" and domestic factionalism at the same time that it supported Federalist causes—thereby, in some ways, functioning as the first campaign speech by an incumbent president on behalf of his hoped-for successor, John Adams. Nearly unheard of in the annals of history, Washington's act of relinquishing power—not once but twice—was arguably his greatest legacy to a nation and a world waiting to see whether the fledgling republic was truly committed to the ideals stated in its Declaration of Independence and its newly framed Constitution.

their frustration at not having children together. Martha's two surviving children, John Parke, who was known as Jacky, and Martha Parke, nicknamed Patsy, were raised as if they were George's children.

Shortly after their wedding, the Washingtons moved into Mount Vernon, the home George was renting from the widow of his deceased half brother and would soon own. Their beloved Mount Vernon would become the centerpiece of the Washingtons' lives for the four decades of their marriage. Whatever passion the Washington marriage may have lacked was made up for in mutual respect and a working partnership built around Mount Vernon. George and Martha's strengths and weaknesses complemented one another as they worked together to turn the estate into one of the colony's most thriving businesses.

Although Martha's main interest was always her children and grandchildren, she was a gifted hostess and, with her husband, an efficient comanager of the estate. Over the years, Mount Vernon would regularly host the leading citizens of the colony and, later, the young nation, and it was Martha who served as hostess. Ever humble, Martha once described herself as "an old-fashioned Virginia housekeeper, steady as a clock, busy as a bee, and cheerful as a cricket." She enjoyed what has been referred to by Washington scholars as the "golden years" at Mount Vernon, the period between the Washington marriage and the start of the Revolutionary War, when her husband and children were at home and Martha played host to and baked her famous "great cake" for their many guests.

This period of tranquillity and happiness was interrupted by the tragic death of Martha's daughter, Patsy, of an epileptic seizure in 1773. Patsy had long suffered from the affliction, and Martha's continuing efforts to find a cure had proved fruitless. Still in mourning, Martha was unable to attend her son Jacky's wedding to Eleanor "Nelly" Calvert of Maryland the year after Patsy's death. Martha did find happiness in her four grandchildren: Elizabeth "Eliza" Parke (1774-1781), Martha "Patty" Parke (1777-1854), Eleanor "Nelly" Parke (1779-1852), and George Washington "Wash" Parke (1781-1857). Mount Vernon was always a house full of children, and Martha welcomed the regular visits of her neighbors' children and those of her relatives.

Perhaps because of the sudden deaths of her first two children and first husband, Martha constantly worried about the health of those she loved, especially the children. The many letters she exchanged over her lifetime with friends and relatives reflect her fears. In them, Martha dwells on everyone's health, gives details of the illnesses of those around her, and discusses antidotes and cures. Not surprisingly, she was stricken with grief after her remaining daughter's death from an epileptic seizure. Because of her fears, Martha was overly protective of Jacky, her youngest and sole remaining child. She therefore prevented Jacky from participating in the Revolutionary War until the end of the conflict, when it was agreed that Jacky would simply join George Washington as the general's aide. Ironically, shortly after joining his stepfather in 1781, Jacky contracted a severe fever in camp and died.

The golden years of tranquillity and happiness at Mount Vernon were shattered by the momentous events of the American Revolution. George Washington had been serving as a member of the House of Burgesses in Virginia and had gained recognition as an able military officer in the years before the Revolutionary War. He was therefore among those chosen to represent Virginia at the meetings of the First and Second Continental Congresses in 1774 and 1775, where he was picked by the delegates to command the colonial forces in June of 1775.

The war separated Washington from his home for eight years, until he resigned his commission on December 23, 1783. Despite the interruption of her cherished family life at Mount Vernon, Martha was solidly behind the revolutionary cause. Indeed, as a symbolic public gesture, Martha adopted the practice of wearing clothing made in the Colonies during the wartime period. She also made several long and often difficult journeys to join her husband at his headquarters in such places as Cambridge in Massachusetts, Valley Forge in Pennsylvania, Morristown in New Jersey, Newburgh in New York, and Annapolis in Maryland. These travels afforded Martha the rare opportunity both to see more of the fledgling nation than most women of her day and to demonstrate her commitment to the revolutionary cause.

As the war wound down, Martha dreaded the thought of a home without any children, so she adopted the two youngest of her four grandchildren. George and Martha certainly had the financial means to do so, the two children were still infants, and the practice of relatives adopting children after an untimely death of one of the parents was common. Little Nelly and Wash came to live at Mount Vernon, while the oldest two grandchildren stayed with their widowed mother, who later remarried. Martha was very close to the two grandchildren and raised them as her own.

Against seemingly insurmountable odds, the continental militia and their commander succeeded in defeating the world's most powerful military, propelling Washington to the status of hero. Both the general and his wife were eager to return to private life and the comforts of Mount Vernon.

Presidency and First Ladyship

After only a few short years in retirement, the hero of the revolution was again called into service. The Articles of Confederation, ratified in 1781, had proven ineffectual for the challenges facing the new Republic. Changes were needed, and a new approach to governance was put forward. Because the public was suspicious of power in the hands of government, the advocates of the Constitution needed someone of Washington's stature to lead the discussion and, in 1787, the drafting of this new system. Once again, duty would take George away from his wife and private life. Martha was understandably uncomfortable with her husband's return to public affairs. So, too, was she concerned about his health, moaning, "I think it is much too late for him to go into public life again." Still, as she would do many times in her life, Martha placed her interests behind the call of duty.

Washington, the most widely respected man of his time, was chosen to assume the new position of president, which he did in 1789.

As neither the capital city of Washington, D.C., nor the White House had yet to be built, the inaugural presidency commenced in the temporary capital of New York City. As George had gone on before her, Martha departed from Mount Vernon in the company of her two grandchildren and a few attendants to join the president in New York. The trip was marked by much fanfare, as crowds turned out at each

Martha at War

George Washington's role in the Revolutionary War is well known. Less celebrated are Martha's contributions to that struggle. In one of his letters to Martha, George expressed his reservation about being selected commander-in-chief and questioned his own fitness for the challenge. During the critical hours of the revolution, however, he drew assurance from his wife. Martha traveled each winter of the war to join George at his headquarters. In camp, she also assisted with his wartime correspondence; from her surviving letters, it is clear that he confided to her the details of his campaigns.

Visitors to camp frequently noted that she occupied herself with sewing, knitting, mending soldiers' uniforms, and tending to the sick and dying. She became a favorite of the troops. One soldier remarked in his diary, "Mrs. Washington combines in an uncommon degree great dignity of manner with the most pleasing affability."

town to greet her, shouting "Long live Lady Washington!" So too was she celebrated by cannonade salutes and soldiers on horseback who escorted her to and from the towns along her journey. Once, while stopped in Philadelphia, Martha went shopping. Her presence attracted huge crowds, who followed her around the city. The trip from Mount Vernon to New York was even covered by newspapers, marking perhaps the first time in the continent that a woman was the focus of reporters' attention.

Although she appeared surprised by the outpouring of adulation, her response was vintage Martha: Largely unaffected by her treatment, she responded with humility. It was also during this trip that Martha made what was perhaps her first and only public speech. Recognizing the crowd, Martha is said to have stood in her carriage and thanked them for their appreciation. Her journey marks a point of self-awareness for Martha, for it was during this trip that she pondered the roles and expectations of the president's spouse. The institution of the presidency was a new and experimental office without precedent. Even the title by which the president would be called remained uncertain, and mixed expectations about the office and the Constitution stirred among the public. In fact, when Washington took the oath of the presidency, two states had yet to ratify the Constitution. Yet, while much uncertainty remained over the exact nature of the presidency, the duties of the presidential spouse had not even been considered. Martha worried about how she would be received and what she would be expected to do. The leaders of the revolution, the American public, and foreign powers all seemed divided in terms of their expectations for the presidency. On one hand, a level of diplomatic protocol modeled on the regal courts of Europe was expected. Yet, others favored democratic simplicity, which they saw as more befitting the new experiment in popular governance. The result was a precarious situation, bound to complicate protocol,

the burden of which fell to Martha as the social hostess.

Here, both President and Lady Washington deserve credit for fashioning ceremonies associated with the office that somehow managed to find balance between the two seemingly irreconcilable approaches. Martha's social events struck a balance between formality and informality, pomp and practicality. Her socials helped lend legitimacy in the eyes of European diplomats and monarchs to both the new Republic and the presidency, while embracing an entirely new and American way of entertaining political guests. In spite of a lengthy and tiring trip to New York City, Martha found herself hosting on her first full day in the new capital. This set the tone for what would be a busy eight-year tenure and set a precedent for the presidential spouse that exists to the present time. Although she had not traveled to Europe and had no experience in the courts of Europe's monarchs, Martha came to the office well prepared for the social tasks before her. As mistress of Mount Vernon, Martha had decades of experience hosting the leading citizens of the land. Moreover, she was acquainted with the standards of social etiquette. Lady Washington's social receptions or "levees," were held on Tuesdays and Fridays and were popular and well attended. Letters written by guests at these functions praise Martha's abilities as a hostess and speak fondly of her as a person. In fact, Abigail Adams, an astute and demanding judge of character who was destined to be the second First Lady, said of Martha that she felt "much more deeply impressed than I ever did before their Majesties of Britain." As the wife of the president, Martha hosted visiting dignitaries, met the demands of meeting an endless flow of ladies "calling" on the wife of Washington, and initiated the practice of holding an open house at the president's residence on New Year's Day, a tradition that would continue at the White House until 1933. The Washingtons worked hard at making the inaugural presidency work,

Martha Washington's reception. *(Library of Congress)*

and they took their responsibilities quite seriously.

The demands of the presidency were considerable. George and Martha were no longer young, and the president experienced health problems during this time. Martha wrote home to friends and family, "I have not had one half hour to myself since the day of my arrival." In their free time, Martha and George attended the theater, dined out in the capital city, and visited friends; Martha indulged her fondness for waxworks and ventriloquists. She continued to attend church regularly, and the family found time to ride in their carriage. Martha's two adopted grandchildren, Nelly and Wash, lived with her during the two terms of the Washington presidency, and George and Martha attempted to secure a good education for them. After a year in New York City, the Washingtons

moved to Philadelphia. The relocation of the president's home suited Martha, who much preferred Philadelphia and had numerous friends in the city.

Martha's contributions to the presidency and the young nation go beyond serving as hostess. The four-decade-long Washington partnership, a marriage built on mutual respect, strong values, and duty, served them well during the presidency. Both George and Martha also seem to have been cognizant of the historic magnitude of the presidency. When George Washington suffered from severe illness while in office, Martha calmed him and demanded the president be allowed rest and quiet. Martha's warmth and disarming, homespun manner balanced the president's aloofness and formality. It is clear that George and Martha Washington represent the first in what would become a long line of presidential couples who shared a working partnership.

Through it all, Martha somehow managed to remain rather unaffected by all the pomp and pageantry. She had never been attracted to public life and served only out of a strong sense of duty to her husband's career and her country. In fact, during the presidential years Martha was much the same person she had always been. She was still an early riser and continued her practice of going to bed early. During social events she would announce that she always retired early and preceded her husband to bed; with that announcement, Lady Washington would excuse herself from her guests.

Nor did Martha enjoy the presidential years, referring to them as her "lost days" and a "burden." She appears to have been an unusually strong and resilient woman who took great challenges in stride. This was the woman who traveled long distances to join George at his winter encampments, dealt with the nearly consecutive deaths of her father, her first two children, and her first husband, and dismissed any threats to her safety during the war.

Nevertheless, she often complained of her unhappiness during the presidency. She was an intensely private individual who valued, above all else, her family and home life and who, like George, longed to return to Mount Vernon. Writing to family, she pined that she would "much rather be at home."

A simple and hardworking grandmother, Martha even dismissed her famous levees as "empty ceremonies of etiquette" and failed to join her husband on the dance floor during her socials. Indeed, the celebrated Lady Washington literally counted the days to when her family could return to Mount Vernon. Herein lies another illustration of the sacrifice Martha made in the name of duty. She disguised her feelings when in public and, as she had done her

whole life, dedicated herself with resolve to her husband's presidency, her country, and her sense of service and duty.

Legacy

The peaceful retirement for which George and Martha had longed was not to be: Mount Vernon would receive a steady flow of well-wishers and admirers. The Washingtons did have two years together at their beloved Mount Vernon. After catching a chill while out riding around his farms, George Washington passed away on December 14, 1799. His death drained Martha of much of the enthusiasm she had for life. The once cheerful Lady Washington was reduced to an extended period of mourning, much of it passed in isolation in an upstairs bedroom at Mount Vernon. Martha never again entered the master bedroom at the estate and, in an act that historians still bemoan, burned nearly all of the letters she and George had exchanged.

Still, even the general's death did not bring an end to Martha's public life. Despite her grief, she granted audience to those of her countrymen who came to pay their respects. Martha distributed mementos of her deceased husband's life, such as his signature clipped from his letters, and, against her own wishes, acquiesced to the wishes of Congress for an elaborate funeral for Washington. She died roughly two years later, on May 22, 1802, of "severe fever."

Martha Washington's image on this 1886 $1 silver certificate makes her the only First Lady—and one of the few women—to appear on U.S. currency.

17

Martha Washington lived in the shadow of her husband's greatness. However, she emerged as the most famous woman of her time. She can be credited with shaping the office of the First Lady. In particular, her actions forged a precedent for three roles still identified with the office: public figure, the nation's social hostess, and confidante and supportive partner to the president. Martha's legacy is one of duty and sacrifice. Perhaps no other woman of her time better exemplified these characteristics, and accordingly, she did so in the service of her husband's career and her country. As not only the wife of Washington for four decades but his confidante and supporter, her legacy is interconnected with that of Washington himself. In the words of her obituary, to the foremost man of his times Martha Washington was truly a "worthy partner."

Suggested Readings

Fields, Joseph, ed. *Worthy Partner: The Papers of Martha Washington*. Westport, Conn.: Greenwood Press, 1994. A collection of all of Martha Washington's known letters, with an informative overview of her life.

Freeman, Douglas Southall. *George Washington*. 7 vols. New York: Scribner, 1948-1957. This multivolume work is widely considered to be the definitive account of the United States' first president.

Thane, Elswyth. *Washington's Lady*. New York: Dodd, Mead, 1954. One of the very few works on Martha Washington; lacks citations.

Washington, George. *The Diaries of George Washington*. Edited by Donald Jackson and Dorothy Twohig. 6 vols. Charlottesville: University Press of Virginia, 1976-1979. Multiple volumes of Washington's meticulous and dry diaries, which read somewhat like a farmer's almanac.

Wharton, Anne Hollingsworth. *Martha Washington*. New York: Charles Scribner's Sons, 1897. A lively, if somewhat romanticized, account of Martha Washington.

Robert P. Watson

Abigail Adams

Abigail Smith Adams

Born: November 22, 1744
  Weymouth, Massachusetts
Died: October 28, 1818
  Quincy, Massachusetts

President: John Adams
  1797-1801

Overview: Abigail Adams was the wife of American president John Adams and the mother of another president, John Quincy Adams. She also established herself as one of the most respected intellects and champions of women's rights of her time. She had no formal schooling, but by availing herself of the few options available to women, she achieved a remarkably broad and sophisticated education. Her voluminous letters, not only to her husband but also to the leading figures of her time, open an important window on the eventful years in which she lived.

Early Life

Abigail was the second of four children born to William Smith and Elizabeth Quincy Smith. Her father, a Congregational minister, was descended from a prosperous family of merchants. Her mother came from one of Massachusetts's oldest and most prominent families of landowners, public officials, and merchants.

Elizabeth Smith exercised close supervision of her children. As she fell victim to more than her fair share of the illnesses of the day, Abigail became the special object of maternal watchfulness, in response to which Abigail occasionally voiced her disapproval in the privacy of her personal letters. From their mother, Abigail and her sisters learned a patient submission to their duty in whatever life brought them. Nevertheless, the Smith household was hardly a gloomy one. William Smith's good nature bal-

Abigail Adams. *(Library of Congress)*

anced any severity on the part of his wife, and Abigail was especially close to her Grandmother Quincy, whom she described as a "merry and chatty" woman.

Smith softened the harder edges of his New England Congregational Calvinist Puritanism by accentuating its positive contributions to daily living. That is the faith his daughter embraced when she formally became a member of the Weymouth church in 1759.

Consistent with practices of the day, Abigail received no formal education, but she enjoyed her father's substantial library and the informal tutoring of educated relatives and friends, under whose guidance she became conversant with classical and contemporary literature and history. Particularly influential in her early years was Richard Cranch, who became acquainted with the family when she was eleven. Although self-taught, the English-born Cranch developed a passion for scholarship and mastered the classical languages and a substantial body of biblical and secular knowledge. By the time he married Mary Smith, Abigail's older sister, he had infected Abigail with a zeal for life and literature.

John Adams, a twenty-seven-year-old lawyer from Braintree (now Quincy), Massachusetts, became a regular visitor to the Cranch home in 1759. By the end of 1761, John began to think seriously about Abigail, then seventeen, whom he described as "a constant feast . . . Prudent, modest, delicate, soft, sensible, obliging, active," and physically passionate. It became family lore that the Smiths considered the struggling lawyer an unworthy suitor for their daughter, but the record suggests that at least William Smith welcomed John's petition for his daughter's hand and that his wife offered no strong objection.

Marriage and Family

Abigail married John Adams on October 25, 1764, a month before her twentieth birthday. They established their home in his hometown of Braintree. Soon after their union, John stated his expectations of her:

> You who have always softened and warmed my heart, shall restore my Benevolence as well as my Health and Tranquility of mind. You shall polish and refine my sentiments of Life and Manners, banish all the unsocial and ill natured Particles in my Composition, and form me to that happy Temper, that can reconcile a quick Discernment with a perfect Candour.

For her part, Abigail enjoyed being out from under her mother's watchful eye, but when her husband was away on business, she suffered from loneliness, especially for her sisters. The Adamses' first child, Abigail, called Nabby, was born on July 14, 1765.

John Quincy Adams, John and Abigail's second child, was born on July 11, 1767. A daughter, Susanna, followed at the end of 1768 but died thirteen months later. A second son, whom they named Charles, was born in May, 1770, followed by Thomas Boylston in September, 1772. In the meantime, Abigail's husband became ever more deeply involved in the American independence movement. The family moved to Boston just before the birth of their last child so that John could be closer to his clients and political interests, and Abigail took advantage of her new home to meet a number of influential Bostonians. Among her new acquaintances was Mercy Otis Warren, who, as a mother of five and an aspiring literary figure, became a lifelong friend, correspondent, and inspiration.

By the early 1770's, John Adams had become a leading political figure in Boston. In August, 1774, he departed Boston for Congress in Philadelphia, the first of his several prolonged absences from his family. Although she regretted his absence and dreaded the prospect of war, Abigail supported the position her husband and others of like mind were taking. In a letter to Catharine Macaulay in 1774, she wrote

John Adams

John Adams was born in Braintree (now Quincy), Massachusetts, in 1735. John, a lawyer and political theorist, first gained public attention during the Stamp Act crisis of 1765, when he published a number of essays collectively printed as *A Dissertation on the Canon and Feudal Law* (1765). He stressed the need for an educated, politically active populace as essential for the maintenance of a free government. He argued that the Stamp Act "divest[ed] us of our most essential rights and liberties," since the colonies were not "in any sense" represented in the British Parliament.

The most famous of Adams's cases was the Boston Massacre trial. With Josiah Quincy, he defended British captain Thomas Preston and seven soldiers accused of murder for their role in the March 5, 1770, incident. By their actions, Adams and Quincy showed that the resistance leaders stood for justice even in partisan cases. Six soldiers were acquitted, and two were convicted of manslaughter, for which they were branded on the thumb and released.

The Massachusetts General Court elected Adams to the First Continental Congress in 1774. He insisted that Parliament had no power over the colonies and that the United States owed only a conditional, contractual allegiance to the king. Adams's principal contribution to the Second Continental Congress was his insistence on independence. "John Adams was our Colossus on the floor," Thomas Jefferson remarked. Adams was selected for the committee to frame the Declaration of Independence, but he yielded to Jefferson to compose the document—both because of Jefferson's more graceful prose style and in order to deemphasize New England's leading role in the independence movement.

In 1779 Adams wrote the new state constitution for his native Massachusetts; it became a model for the other states. In 1780 he sailed for France to negotiate peace with England. When the peace treaty was signed in 1783, Adams was appointed minister to England. Adams returned to the United States in 1788, whereupon he was elected vice president, to serve under President George Washington. Adams was reelected in 1792, and in 1796 he became president, defeating Thomas Jefferson by three electoral votes.

Problems with France dominated the Adams administration. Soon after he took office, France dismissed the American ambassador and began seizing American ships trading with England, with whom it was at war. Adams sent a mission to France, but his envoys were not even admitted to see the Directory—then ruling revolutionary France in place of a king—because they would not pay a bribe. The XYZ affair, as it came to be known, resulted in undeclared naval warfare with France before the incident was settled. Adams also signed the Federalist-sponsored Alien and Sedition Acts, which Congress passed in 1798. The acts extended the waiting period for U.S. citizenship from five to fourteen years, permitted the president to deport "alien enemies," and authorized imprisonment and fines for critics of the administration. Adams broke ranks with the Hamiltonians, causing a feud within the Federalist Party. As a result, the Federalists were defeated in the presidential election of 1800, with Jefferson receiving seventy-three electoral votes to Adams's sixty-five. Adams left Washington, D.C., a bitter man, refusing to attend his successor's inauguration. Before leaving office, Adams appointed a large number of Federalist judges in an effort to stave off the "abyss" opening before the nation.

Adams lived the remaining quarter-century of his life in Quincy. He died during the presidency of his son, John Quincy Adams, on the fiftieth anniversary of his signing of the Declaration of Independence. His last words were "Thomas Jefferson survives," a reference to his ally in independence, from whom he had become alienated as a result of the politics of the early republic, but with whom he reconciled in his final years. He did not know that Jefferson died on the same day in Virginia.

that "the only alternative which every American thinks of is Liberty or Death." The colonies did not desire independence unless Britain forced it on them, she explained. Connected "by blood, by commerce, by one common language, by one common religion as Protestants, and as good and loyal subjects of the same king," they earnestly wished that "the three fold cord of Duty, interest and filial affection" would not snap. "'Tis the Gordean knot. It can never be untied, but the sword may cut it."

John returned home in November, 1774, but returned to Philadelphia and the Second Continental Congress the following April. Only one week before he left, shots were fired at Lexington and Concord. More than a year before the Congress voted independence, Abigail predicted it:

> 'Tis thought we must now bid a final adieu to Britain, nothing will now appease the Exasperated Americans but the heads of those traitors who have subverted the constitution, for the blood of our Brethren cries to us from the Ground.

With the actual coming of independence, Abigail began to think about, and to force John to consider, the role of women in the new republic. John did not deny Abigail's reasoning that, in theory, women were included among the governed whose consent gave moral legitimacy to government. He held that their delicacy, domesticity, and primary concern for their children, however, made them more valuable as a private influence on husbands and sons than in any public capacity. Abigail did not quarrel with this position: An educated and enlightened wife and mother would be an important instrument for the inculcation of those virtues essential for the survival of the very tenuous, even experimental, republic. Toward that end, however, the republic had to produce learned women.

On July 9, 1777, Abigail gave birth to their last child, a little girl who died soon following her arrival in the world. Devastated by her second loss, Abigail's despair was lifted only upon John's return, for what he thought would be the final time, in November. Their anticipation of domestic bliss, however, quickly vanished when John was notified that the Congress had appointed him as one of its three commissioners to France. Abigail was deeply troubled and considered accompanying John to Europe. The difficulties of ocean travel during the winter and in time of war, however, convinced both of them that she should remain behind. Instead, John took John Quincy with him. Abigail stayed behind with Nabby and the two younger boys.

John and John Quincy did not return to Braintree until August, 1779, and then, within weeks, Congress summoned John to be its minister plenipotentiary to negotiate peace with Great Britain. In November, 1779, he and Abigail parted again; this time he took Charles and John Quincy. John and Abigail would not see each other for three years. When, in the fall of 1783, following peace, Congress appointed John Adams, John Jay, and Benjamin Franklin to a new commission to negotiate a commercial treaty with England, John urged Abigail to join him, and she accepted. In June, 1784, Abigail left Braintree to join her husband.

Abigail and John spent a year in Paris and three years in London, the experience of which expanded Abigail's political, social, and cultural knowledge of the world. It also deepened her republican sensibilities and commitment to the better education of American women. Abigail learned to feel at home in French society, but she was not impressed by the majority of the French, voicing her disapproval of what she held to be their ostentatious dress, idle chatter, and loose morals. A notable exception was the Marquise de Lafayette, wife of a hero of the American Revolution, whom Abigail found friendly and unaffected. Abigail came to enjoy the theater and opera but was shocked at the immodest apparel of French dancers. She was

A Truth of No Dispute

On March 31, 1776, Abigail Adams wrote a letter to her husband, John Adams, who was in Philadelphia attending the Second Continental Congress. She had recently learned that he was serving on a committee that would draft the Declaration of Independence. Understanding the significance of this appointment, she used the opportunity to approach him with some of her ideas about American independence and American women. She wrote:

> I long to hear that you have declared an independency, and by the way in the new Code of Laws which I suppose it will be necessary for you to make I desire you would Remember the Ladies, and be more generous and favourable to them than your ancestors.

She continued with more specific observations: "Do not put such unlimited power into the hands of the Husbands. Remember all Men would be tyrants if they could."

"If particular care and attention is not paid to the Ladies," Abigail continued, "we are determined to foment a Rebellion, and will not hold ourselves bound by any Laws in which we have no voice, or Representation." As writer Edith Gelles has pointed out, Abigail did not mean to organize a revolt but rather to employ humor in such a manner as to allow her to propose a subject that was likely to be dismissed by the men of Philadelphia. She could then proceed to raise the subject of women's civil and social subordination, writing:

> That your Sex are Naturally Tyrannical is a Truth so thoroughly established as to admit of no dispute. But such of you as wish to be happy [will] willingly give up the harsh title of Master for the more tender and endearing one of Friend.

also scandalized by the crime and prostitution in the streets of Paris.

With a year in Paris behind her to bolster her, Abigail entered London society with confidence. She found English society no more to her liking than French society. By her own estimation, it suffered from too much formality and not enough of the sincerity and warmhearted social intercourse on which she had thrived in her homeland. Paying and receiving calls were required of her as the wife of the American minister to England, but in gatherings of women, Abigail felt alone. At mixed parties, she preferred the conversation and attention of the men, and her closest friends were Americans living in London.

The Adams family returned home in 1788. In 1789 John was elected vice president of the United States, and Abigail found herself divid-

ing her time among the farm in Braintree and the U.S. capitals of New York and Philadelphia. Abigail's political philosophy had changed from her experience abroad, as had John's, and their philosophies continued to mirror each other. She no longer believed that the masses could become enlightened or that American republicanism could bring about a universal moral revival. All people throughout history displayed the same fundamental needs and were driven by the same passions. She wrote to her daughter: "I am sometimes led to think that human nature is a very perverse thing, and much more given to evil than good." To preserve American freedom, enlightened and virtuous leaders had to preside over the government. Ideally, though, an elite of virtue and wisdom, not of wealth or heredity, should govern.

Abigail's attitudes toward women changed as well. She now regarded women in general as no more capable of enlightenment than men. No mass reformation of American women would preserve the republic. Hope lay, instead, in attaching equal importance to the education of both sexes so that both might "move with honour and dignity in their proper sphere." The proper sphere for women was considered to be marriage and motherhood, and conjugal fidelity stood highest in the "ranks of female virtues." The future of the country depended on creating homes with loving, educated, devout parents and girls of sufficient virtue to be wives and mothers to patriots. Abigail believed that women in the United States enjoyed a situation relative to men more favorable than that experienced by women at any other time and place. "Consequently there is more conjugal Fidelity and domestic happiness here than is to be found anywhere else," but women had to make use of that situation to better the nation. In 1790, she wrote:

> Tho' as females we have no voice in Legislation, yet is our happiness so blended and interwoven with those who have, that we have every reason to rejoice in the improvement of science and the advancement of civilization which has proved so favorable to our sex, and has led mankind to consider us in a much more respectable light than we deserve.

For most of her husband's second term in office as vice president, illness forced Abigail to live in Braintree. This spared her the agony of witnessing firsthand the quarreling of former allies in the cause of independence over differences in political philosophy and the running of the new nation.

Particularly difficult for Abigail was the growing estrangement between John and his friend Thomas Jefferson. The two disagreed on nearly every issue: the power of the federal government versus that of the states, Secretary of the Treasury Alexander Hamilton's plan to fund the federal debt, and even what the United States' proper position should be on the French Revolution.

In 1794, largely as a result of the years he had spent abroad with his father, John Quincy Adams was named minister to the Netherlands. Two years later, when George Washington announced that he would not accept a third term in office, it became clear that John Adams would be his successor. Abigail let her feelings be known to her husband concerning the prospect of being First Lady. She doubted that she had the "patience, prudence, discretion" of Martha Washington, who had gracefully avoided all controversy. Abigail's outspokenness, she feared, would prove detrimental to her husband as president. "I should say that I have been so used to a freedom of sentiment that I know not how to place so many guards about me, as will be indispensable, to look at every word before I utter it, and to impose a Silence upon My Self when I long to talk." John responded: "I have no concern on your Account but for your health. A Woman can be silent, when she will."

Presidency and First Ladyship

Abigail served as First Lady from 1797 to 1801, during her husband's single term as president. It was a tumultuous period, during which her husband became embroiled in highly contentious international and domestic political controversies. Abigail supported John's policies and became an ardent Federalist, though no friend of her husband's greatest Federalist foe, Alexander Hamilton. In the process, Abigail was criticized for her partisanship, as well as for the influence she allegedly had over her husband.

The experience of being the president's wife confirmed in Abigail her view of the role of women in republican America. She had no illusion that women would soon be permitted the vote, and she was content to see them participate in the political process only through private influence on their husbands and sons. At the same time, she insisted that the separate roles of the sexes were coordinate and of equal importance. While First Lady, she wrote:

> I will never consent to have our Sex considered in an inferior point of light. Let each planet shine in their own orbit, God and nature designed it so. If man is Lord, woman is Lordess—that is what I contend for, and if a woman does not hold the Reigns of Government, I see no reason for her not judging how they are conducted.

John was not only willing that Abigail should be his "fellow Labourer," even in his capacity as president; he insisted on it. "I never wanted your Advice and assistance more in my life," he wrote soon after his inauguration. Two weeks later he pleaded, "The Times are critical and dangerous, and I must have you here to assist me." He needed her to manage the presidential household and to meet his social obligations, to be sure, but he also wanted the confidence that he gained from her critical support. Being well aware of her responsibilities to John and his office only deepened Abigail's anxiety, but she nevertheless hastened to his side.

Abigail's greatest satisfaction came from her private role as confidante of, and counselor to, the president. She was intensely concerned with the issue that dominated his administration: relations between the United States and France. That issue divided nearly everyone in Philadelphia, including, once again, John Adams and Thomas Jefferson. By the summer of 1798, Abigail wanted Congress to declare war on France as a means of rallying the American people against foreign subversion. However, John delayed asking for a declaration of war because he lacked sufficient support in Congress to make any war effectual. In time, Abigail grew closer to her husband's position that not only was Great Britain no bulwark against the

French Revolution, its jealousy toward American prosperity, even in independence, would lead it to promote continued friction between the United States and France. The answer, both Adamses agreed, was not to follow the more extreme Federalist lead of establishing stronger ties with Great Britain, but rather to render the United States "independent of foreign attachments" altogether.

At the same time, Abigail watched with concern the growing power of Alexander Hamilton, who proved to be Adams's rival within his own party. She perceived Hamilton to be a man driven by ambition without the check of virtue she saw in her husband. She also supported the Federalist-led congressional action known as the Alien and Sedition Acts. The former she saw as a necessary response to the threat "foreigners" posed to the country. The latter would serve to muzzle the most objectionable Republican editors, who, she believed, were libeling her husband. John Adams had not asked Congress for this legislation, but he signed the bills with little hesitation.

By 1800 the Hamiltonians sought to replace Adams as their president. By May, Abigail realized they presented a threat and that the odds did not favor John's reelection. She wrote to John Quincy Adams in Europe: "If the people judge that a change in the chief Majestracy of the Nation is for its peace, safety and happiness, they will no doubt make it." She voiced her confidence not only in John's conduct regarding U.S. diplomatic difficulties with France and England, but that in matters generally, history would vindicate the wisdom of his administration.

Abigail expressed little bitterness at the defeat of her husband, except against Hamilton and Vice President-elect Aaron Burr, to whose intrigues she attributed John's removal from office. She accepted the election results with more resignation than disappointment. She had few regrets because, at her age and with her poor health, she felt she would be happier in

Braintree, now called Quincy. She felt no resentment against Jefferson, the victor. Instead, she hoped that his administration would be "as productive of the peace, happiness, and prosperity of the nation as the two former ones." She left immediately for home; John followed on the morning of Jefferson's inauguration, without attending the affair. For the first time in thirty-six years of married life, John and Abigail Adams did not have to anticipate another long separation from each another.

John and Abigail returned to private life in Quincy. They lived comfortably in retirement but not with great wealth, for John's commitment to public service had left him little opportunity for pecuniary gain. The last quarter-century of her life had severely tested Abigail's inner strength. Chronic illness had plagued her for much of that time and equally painful absences from her husband even more. Her separation from John Quincy proved difficult, ameliorated only by his distinguished service to the nation (she would not live to see him become president). Her daughter, Nabby, would fight an unsuccessful battle with cancer, finally succumbing in 1813.

John divided his time between the farm and his books, enjoying "a tranquility and a freedom from care" he had not known before. Abigail was more restless but consoled herself with the thought that labor in the garden would yield flowers and fruit rather than the crop of "calumny" and "ingratitude" harvested from public service.

Abigail initiated a correspondence with Thomas Jefferson, showing that she still cared about him, despite his estrangement from her husband. Following Abigail's letter expressing regret at the death of Jefferson's daughter Polly in 1804, Jefferson replied with a long, warm letter expressing his continuing esteem for the Adams family. In attempting to explain why political differences had broken their friendship, he opened the door for Thomas and Abigail to at least attempt to clear the air

of years of disharmony. John knew nothing of the correspondence until, after five months or writing, Abigail showed John the letters. John merely noted that he had nothing to say about them. It would take eight more years for John Adams and Thomas Jefferson to renew their friendship. In 1818 Abigail contracted typhus fever and died on October 28. She was buried in the First Church in Quincy. John died on July 4, 1826, fifty years from the date he signed the Declaration of Independence.

Legacy

Perhaps Abigail Adams's greatest legacy was her letters, which her grandson Charles Francis Adams began publishing in 1840. These letters provide an invaluable source of information on the revolutionary era and years of the early republic, on subjects ranging from family life to life at the courts of Europe, and from American politics and religion to the role of women in the early republic. They also give a personal view of the life of one of the United States' earliest female figures of strength, intelligence, and insight.

Abigail had conversed with statesmen of Europe and the United States, and she wrote long letters of political commentary. She developed a keen sense of the liabilities of being female in a male-dominated society. She denounced the potential for tyranny in the legal subjection of wives to husbands, and she believed a woman should be free to make a prudent choice of a mate and to limit the number of children she bore. Refusing to accept the widely held views on the inferiority of the female intellect, she added her influence to the growing demand for the education of young women. Her acceptance of the doctrine of separate spheres for men and women fixed the boundaries of her feminism. Within those limits, however, she maintained that the private political role of women in a republic was as important as the public role of men.

Abigail Adams was not an original thinker;

she wrote no books and led no reform movements. Her greatness lay in her example. She demonstrated that an intelligent, spirited woman, given the opportunity, could lead a rewarding life and make a significant contribution to her country. As her son John Quincy Adams put it: "Her life gave the lie to every libel on her sex that was ever written."

Suggested Readings

Adams, Abigail. *Letters of Mrs. Adams, the Wife of John Adams*. Edited by Charles Francis. 2 vols. 4th ed. Boston: Little, Brown, 1848. The first edited selection of Abigail Adams's letters, published by her grandson.

Akers, Charles. *Abigail Adams: An American Woman*. Boston: Little, Brown, 1980. An accessible, detailed portrait, which examines the status of women and situates Abigail Adams's life in the social context of her times.

Butterfield, L. H., et al., eds. *Adams Family Correspondence*. 6 vols. Cambridge, Mass.: Harvard University Press, 1963-1993. Intended to be the most complete published collection of Abigail Adams's letters, with additional volumes planned.

Gelles, Edith B. *First Thoughts: Life and Letters of Abigail Adams*. New York: Twayne, 1998. Gelles treats a limited number of periods in Abigail Adams's life, which were best documented by her personal letters, thereby revealing Adams's personality and character in her own words.

_____. *Portia: The World of Abigail Adams*. Bloomington: Indiana University Press, 1992. Gelles takes a critical view of the "Abigail industry" and seeks to define Adams on her own terms.

Keller, Rosemary. *Patriotism and the Female Sex: Abigail Adams and the American Revolution*. New York: Carlson, 1994. A study of Abigail Adams's views on women, republicanism, and the role of women in the new republic.

Levin, Phyllis. *Abigail Adams*. New York: St. Martin's Press, 1987. Provides an overview of Abigail Adams's life, largely organized around her marriage and family.

McCullough, David. *John Adams*. New Yrok: Simon & Schuster, 2001. Biography highlights John Adams's integrity and brilliance.

Nagel, Paul C. *The Adams Women: Abigail and Louisa Adams, Their Sisters and Daughters*. New York: Oxford University Press, 1987. An interesting comparative study of the first generations of Adams women.

Withey, Lynne. *Dearest Friend: A Life of Abigail Adams*. New York: Free Press, 1981. A biography which highlights the relationship of Abigail and John Adams.

Bryan Le Beau

Martha Jefferson and Patsy Jefferson Randolph

Martha Wayles Skelton Jefferson

Born: October 19, 1748
    Charles City County, Virginia
Died: September 6, 1782
    Albemarle County, Virginia

President: Thomas Jefferson
    1801-1809

Martha "Patsy" Washington Jefferson Randolph

Born: September 27, 1772
    Albemarle County, Virginia
Died: October 10, 1836
    Washington, D.C.

President: Thomas Jefferson
    1801-1809

Overview: Martha Wayles Jefferson was Thomas Jefferson's true love and companion during the forming of the United States. Their happy marriage produced seven children, but only two survived. Martha was left weakened, and after ten years of sharing her life with Thomas at Monticello, she died in 1782. So devastated was Thomas by the loss of his wife that he burned all things that reminded him of her, including their correspondence. Consequently, Martha remains an obscure and unknown figure, and history is left with more questions than answers about her life. The Jeffersons' eldest daughter, Martha Washington Jefferson, was called Patsy. She ably helped her father entertain at the White House during his presidency.

Early Life

Martha Wayles was born to John Wayles and Martha Eppes Wayles in Williamsburg, Virginia, in 1748. Martha's father was a prominent lawyer who owned a large plantation. She had a privileged upbringing and expressed an inclination for and love of music; playing the harpsichord and piano brought her particular en-

Martha Jefferson *(Courtesy of Craig Shermer, National First Ladies' Library)*

Martha "Patsy" Washington Jefferson Randolph, daughter of Thomas and Martha Jefferson. *(Courtesy of Craig Shermer, National First Ladies' Library)*

joyment. Several accounts of young Martha describe her as a widely admired woman. Given her family's social status and her beauty, it is not surprising that she was said to have many suitors for marriage.

On November 20, 1766, she married Bathurst Skelton, a successful lawyer from the region. A year after their wedding, they had a son who would die by the age of four. Bathurst, too, would soon die, and in 1770 Martha found herself widowed and the heiress to a large fortune.

Marriage and Family

At age twenty-two, Martha was courted by Thomas Jefferson, a twenty-eight-year-old lawyer and a member of the House of Burgesses in Williamsburg. As they would throughout their

marriage, the two spent many hours together enjoying music. He played the violin while she played the harpsichord. The courtship was brief, and on New Year's Day of 1772, Martha and Thomas were married. The event took place at Martha's plantation home, known as The Forest. The newlyweds moved to Jefferson's home in a rural region farther west in the Virginia colony. The mansion, Monticello, was Jefferson's pride and joy. An architect, he had designed the home himself. To accommodate his new bride, who was far away from home and not accustomed to living in such a remote area, he ordered a fortepiano to be brought to the mansion.

The small amount of evidence that exists of Martha's life suggests that her marriage to

Thomas was a happy one in spite of the adversities they faced together during subsequent years. Of the six children born to Martha, four (three of them born to Jefferson) would die in infancy. Their first child together, Martha Washington, was born in 1772. Jane Randolph was born in 1774 but died at age two. Later, in 1777, a son was born, but he did not survive infancy. Another daughter, Mary, was born in 1778. By now Martha's difficult pregnancies and tragic losses had weakened her health. Lucy Elizabeth was born in 1780 and died two years later. Their last daughter, also named Lucy, was born in 1782 and would die in 1785. In poor health, Martha did not survive this last childbirth, dying shortly after giving birth.

In addition to the tragedies of losing so many children, the Revolutionary War began only three years after Martha married Thomas. During the war a British invasion near Monticello in 1781 forced Martha to flee twice from the area, and it is likely that she was not in a condition to travel, as she was frail and had an infant child with her.

Martha's fragile health always worried Jefferson, who did not want to leave her side. Although he served in Virginia's House of Delegates and as Virginia's governor, he did not accept an appointment as commissioner to France, in order to be close to his frail wife. When Martha died in 1782, she was thirty-three years old, and only two of her children—both daughters—would survive past infancy. Her daughters Martha Washington, who was nicknamed Patsy, and Mary, who was also called Maria, both lived to adulthood.

Thomas Jefferson was deeply affected by the loss of his beloved wife. Patsy recalled seeing her father in a stupor as never before after his wife passed away. Sinking deep into depression, he stayed in seclusion for three weeks, pacing back and forth in his room. He kept a lock of his Martha's hair, as he did of the four children who had not survived. It is also believed that he had promised Martha he would never remarry. So distraught was Jefferson that he appears to have destroyed all of his wife's correspondence.

Presidency and First Ladyship

Nineteen years had passed after Martha's death when Thomas Jefferson was inaugurated as

Martha's Homecoming

Martha Jefferson, raised in Charles City County, Virginia, was used to the social scene of the nearby town of Williamsburg. This was where she had met her first husband, Bathurst Skelton, whom she married in 1766. When she was widowed as a young woman, Martha inherited great wealth and a large plantation near Williamsburg. It is clear from what little is known about her life that she enjoyed social life and was used to a much more populated community than that which she would live in after she married Thomas Jefferson.

After her second marriage in 1772, she moved to Jefferson's new mansion, Monticello, located in an isolated, rural part of the colony far west of the Tidewater region of Virginia. This certainly was a major transition for Martha: moving from the populated political and social capital of the colony to a remote area of Virginia with a new husband in the middle of winter.

They reached Monticello in late January in the midst of a snowstorm and found the house without food or a fire in the fireplace and with all of the servants asleep. In spite of these inconveniences, the long trip, and the drastic change in Martha's life, she was happily in love and, according to Jefferson's personal papers, the new couple "toasted their new home with a leftover half-bottle of wine."

Thomas Jefferson

Thomas Jefferson was born on April 13, 1743, in Albemarle County, Virginia, the son of a prominent Virginian descended from Welsh ancestors. His mother, Jane Randolph, was also from an influential family. Jefferson was educated at the College of William and Mary. As a young man, he practiced law as the winds of revolution blew across the land, and at age twenty-six he entered public life as a member of the House of Burgesses. Jefferson's career was highlighted by his service as a delegate in the Continental Congress, where, at the age of thirty-three, he drafted the Declaration of Independence. He later served as governor of Virginia, in a diplomatic capacity in France, and as President George Washington's secretary of state.

Jefferson was a passionate man, known more for his skill as a writer than for his orations. As the United States' third president, he purchased the Louisiana Territory and sent Captain Meriwether Lewis and Lieutenant William Clark on their famous western expedition to explore the new nation beyond the eastern seaboard. Jefferson spoke several languages and mastered several of the arts and sciences. He spent his final years contemplating Greek philosophy and the new experiment in popular democracy his hand had helped create. He died on July 4, 1826, the same day as fellow founding father and second U.S. president John Adams. It was also the fiftieth anniversary of the signing of the Declaration of Independence.

president on March 4, 1801. He was the first widowed president and the first chief executive to start the presidency in the new "federal city," Washington, D.C. Martha (Patsy), the Jeffersons' eldest daughter, served as First Lady, presiding over the White House social affairs during the winter seasons of 1802-1803 and 1805-1806.

Patsy was a highly capable hostess, having received a well-rounded education at schools in Philadelphia and, later, in Paris. When Thomas served as a diplomat in Paris in 1784, Patsy joined her father in France, where she was sent to an elite Parisian convent school. There, in addition to receiving a solid formal education, she considered becoming a nun. A concerned Jefferson immediately diverted his daughter's interest by giving her a secular education instead. She also participated in social affairs of the European courts.

Patsy married her cousin Thomas Mann Randolph in 1790 and had ten children. One of her sons was the first child to be born in the President's House and was named after James Madison, Jefferson's secretary of state. As only

the third First Lady in the young republic, Patsy had to shun the extravagances of the royal parties of Europe and to host in a less ostentatious manner, one befitting the new democracy and her father's famous political ideology. She therefore stopped the practice of hosting "levees," the weekly socials for ladies of the capital city, and changed the dress code for her social functions to a less formal standard. Patsy appears to have done an admirable job as hostess and was said to resemble her mother in appearance and her father in intellect. When she was unable to preside over the social affairs of state, Dolley Madison, the wife of James Madison, hosted for Jefferson.

Legacy

Martha Wayles Jefferson never became First Lady, but she did witness her husband's thriving political career. Although scholars cannot be sure because of the limited documentation that exists, it appears that Martha was not directly involved in her husband's writing and work during the American Revolution and founding of the United States. She did, never-

Monticello, home of Thomas and Martha Jefferson. *(Library of Congress)*

theless, provide a home where Thomas could find solace and happy moments with his family. As did most of the other presidential spouses, Martha lived with her husband during the important formative years of his political career. Martha and Thomas Jefferson supported each other through the difficult times of the founding of the United States, including his drafting of the Declaration of Independence. The loss of four children and her frail health may have brought stress to their lives, but in spite of this they were known to be content with each other.

One intriguing aspect of Martha's legacy is that no verifiable portrait or likeness of her is known to exist. Given her family's social standing and that of her first husband, Bathurst

Skelton, as well as the custom of the period for affluent Virginia families to have portraits painted of each member, it is probable that Martha sat for several portraits during her lifetime. These might have been destroyed by the depressed Jefferson after her death, along with her correspondence. The result is that, despite the fame Thomas Jefferson achieved as one of the most admired public figures in U.S. history, his wife remains one of the most obscure of all presidential spouses.

Suggested Readings

Brodie, Fawn M. *Thomas Jefferson: An Intimate History.* New York: Norton, 1974. Provides personal insights into the social and family life of the third president.

Eckenrode, Hamilton J. *The Randolphs*. New York: Bobbs-Merrill, 1946. Story of Martha "Patsy" Jefferson's husbands family in early Virginia.

Jefferson, Thomas. *The Family Letters of Thomas Jefferson*. Edited by Edwin Betts and James A. Bear. Columbia: University of Missouri Press, 1966. Insights into the lives of Thomas and Martha Jefferson, through Thomas Jefferson's correspondence.

Smith, Margaret Bayard. *The First Forty Years of Washington Society*. New York: Ungar, 1965. A reporter who was a friend of Thomas Jefferson and his daughter Martha Randolph provides an account of their presidential years.

Whitton, Mary Ormsbee. *First First Ladies, 1789-1865: A Study of the Wives of the Early Presidents*. New York: Hastings House, 1948. Includes one of the very few accounts of Martha and Thomas Jefferson and their daughter.

Claudia Pavone Watson

Dolley Madison

Dolley Payne Todd Madison

Born: May 20, 1768
     Guildford County,
     North Carolina
Died: July 12, 1849
     Washington, D.C.

President: James Madison
     1809-1817

Overview: Over many years, Dolley Madison developed tactics and strategies befitting a practical politician that set the model for successful First Ladies—and presidents—ever after. She established an office not even mentioned in the Constitution and made it integral to the presidency. By relieving the president of social chores and using her interpersonal skills, she helped James Madison's administration achieve more national unity than those of his three predecessors put together.

Dolley Madison, engraving from an original picture by Gilbert Stuart. *(Library of Congress)*

Early Life

The woman who would become a national icon was registered at birth by the Quaker New Garden Monthly Meeting as "Dolley," the name she retained all her life. She also considered herself a lifelong Virginian, though she was born in what is now Greensboro, North Carolina, where her parents, John Payne and Mary Coles Payne, were searching for opportunities for a merchant-farmer. By the time Dolley was eleven months old, they had returned to Mary's ancestral plantation, Coles Hill, in rural Hanover County, in eastern Virginia.

When Dolley was seven, her family moved to a plantation of their own: Scotchtown, the former home of her mother's cousin Patrick Henry. The mansion, said to have been Virginia's largest, proved useful for the growing Payne brood, which would number four boys and four girls. Its attic was large enough for a ballroom, but since pious Quakers frowned upon dancing, the door was kept locked. Nevertheless, Dolley could teach other youngsters the latest steps.

With her brothers and sisters, she went to an old field school, that is, a school set up by neighbors in a field lying fallow. An itinerant tutor would teach rudimentary reading, writing, and arithmetic. For more advanced schooling, Dolley attended coeducational classes in the Quaker meeting house at Cedar Creek.

At the same time, she was learning the arts of homemaking and hospitality. Slaves would do the menial work, but she learned to train and supervise them, preserve and prepare food, and receive regular or random guests, in or out of visiting season, as a good Virginia housewife should. Oval-faced and fair, with jet black hair, sky-blue eyes, and a tilted nose, she would wear close-fitting bonnets and gray gowns with elbow-length sleeves and square necklines but no jewelry.

When she was fifteen, postwar agricultural depression forced her father to abandon farming and try manufacturing cornstarch in Philadelphia, then the nation's capital and largest city. After six years, he had accumulated so much debt that the Quakers read him out of meeting (expelled him from their community). At that time in Philadelphia, yellow fever had become a fact of city life. Open sewers, pools of stagnant water, and piles of rotting garbage bred disease-bearing mosquitoes. The Paynes' eldest son succumbed at age twenty-one from the perennial Philadelphia fever. That, coupled with his bankruptcy, led John Payne into a depression so deep he no longer left the house. Mary Payne supported the family by boarding government officials, one of whom was the New York senator Aaron Burr.

Meanwhile, life in Philadelphia proved a finishing school for Dolley. The city, as capital, commercial center, and cosmopolitan seaport, set the national taste for fashion and style. The prevailing influence during Dolley's adolescent years was French, but after the French Revolution fashion trends became more British and, in democratic eyes, more aristocratic. In the course of Dolley's youth, some of her friends split from their religious community to form a more liberal meeting of Free Quakers, but she remained conservative.

Marriage and Family

In 1790, Dolley married John Todd, a rising young Philadelphia lawyer from a respectable, middle-class Quaker family. They could afford a fine three-story home at Fourth and Walnut Streets. Within a year, she gave birth to a boy, Payne, and brought her ten-year-old sister, Anna, to live with them as a daughter. Having given birth to another baby boy two years later, she seemed content to live happily ever after as middle-class wife and mother.

About that time, Dolley's sister Lucy wed George Steptoe Washington, a young nephew of the president, and made a home for their mother and two youngest siblings, Mary and John, at Harewood, a plantation near what is now Charleston, West Virginia. The location was close enough for occasional visits and far enough to avoid Philadelphia's fatal fevers.

The summer of 1793 brought the worst fever epidemic in years. Up to mid-August, burials averaged three to five per day. By month's end, they rose to twenty-four per day. Dolley joined the exodus to suburban Gray's Ferry with her babies, sisters Anna and Mary, brother John, and their mother. Her husband stayed behind to nurse his stricken apprentice, and her in-laws stayed behind to nurse their son. The apprentice and both elder Todds died within two weeks. Her husband lived to join the little family at Gray's Ferry for a month before he, too, died. On the same day, their two-month-old baby, sickly from birth, also died.

James Madison

A measure of James Madison's modesty is the fact that he is less familiar than his wife, Dolley. Although five feet six inches, the same height as his wife, she seemed to tower over him. Her opposite in personality, he struck strangers as a colorless little man who would be more at home in a library than in the White House, and they were right.

His Virginia planter parents had sent him to boarding school at age eleven. After seven years studying the classics and foreign languages, he went to Princeton (then College of New Jersey), where he completed three years' work in two. He had returned for another year to study religion and ethics when the Revolutionary War broke out. Too frail for fighting, he served during the war as a delegate to the Virginia convention of 1776, then the state assembly and governor's council. In 1780 he became a delegate to the Continental Congress.

Returning home at the end of the war, he entered the Virginia House of Delegates. In the turmoil following the war, Madison was a strong voice advocating the replacement of the Articles of Confederation by a constitution that would provide for a stronger central government. Later called the Father of the Constitution, he played a major role in drafting the Constitution and then easing its acceptance. No orator, he persuaded by conversation and his classic Federalist essays. He argued for a government responsive to the people's will, confident that a representative democracy would balance political power and human interests. This was the same argument he would use as he became leader of Congress and, finally, president in 1808.

The problems he inherited as president tested his principles. New England was talking about seceding, old England was interfering with American ships at sea, and his own party had split into factions. In the interest of party unity, Madison's appointments represented all factions and interests without regard to merit, even in military appointments. Meanwhile, tensions between Britain and the United States had long been simmering over the rights of American ships on the high seas.

The United States declared war but was ill-prepared to fight on land. Though Secretary of War John Armstrong ignored the president's warnings that the British would attack Washington, D.C., leaving the city undefended, the fighting throughout the War of 1812 was inconclusive and both sides signed the Treaty of Ghent in 1814 to restore prewar conditions. The Americans' victory at the Battle of New Orleans in January, 1815 (word had not yet reached the United States of the treaty, signed in Belgium) was so resounding that a U.S. triumph was proclaimed both domestically and abroad. This mollified would-be separatists in New England, and Madison was lauded in Washington upon leaving the presidency.

Dolley Todd was left far from home with only nineteen dollars. She appealed for funds from the babies' nurse in Philadelphia, but once back at home, she found no relief. Her late husband's brother James tied up her legacy for two years, even selling his brother's books, meant for baby Payne's future. It was after Aaron Burr introduced her to the "great little Madison," that the famous congressman from Virginia, James Madison, came to Dolley's rescue, persuading James Todd to pay Dolley her fair share.

Though James and Dolley were the same height, he had been rheumatic since childhood and so slight as to appear shorter than she, who carried herself like a queen. James, at forty-three, conducted a breathless four-month courtship of the twenty-six-year-old widow. On her wedding night, she took time to send a letter to her best friend, Eliza Lee, who had been a bridesmaid at her first wedding, announcing that she was now "Dolley Madison! Alass! Alass!"

Because they married at her sister Lucy's estate, on September 15, 1794, before an Episcopalian clergyman, Dolley's Pine Street Meeting disowned her for marrying a non-Quaker before "a hireling priest." She gradually set aside traditional Quaker simplicity for more fashionable French gowns befitting the wife of the congressional leader—though retaining her Quaker caps until becoming First Lady.

Bucolic Montpelier, the Madison family's Virginia plantation, became Dolley's new home in 1797 and gave her full range for her role as Virginia housewife. The region's first brick house, the small mansion was named Montpelier for its spectacular ninety-mile panorama of the Blue Ridge Mountains. The Madisons, junior and senior, shared the four rooms until the death of James's father in 1801, when the younger Madisons added a wing so that the widow could have privacy from the constant stream of visitors.

While her husband spent hours in his study, Dolley made sure they lived well and within their means, furnishing the home with fashionable furniture from France, bought secondhand, and entertaining sometimes thirty guests at a time with homegrown, abundant meals. Even in prosperous years for agriculture, the Madisons realized no profit from ten acres of corn and tobacco.

In addition to James's rheumatic fevers, he suffered recurring bouts of malaria. The only time Dolley left his side for any length of time was when he sent her to spend a summer in Philadelphia to cure an abscessed knee. Even then, he spent most of the summer by her bedside. When Thomas Jefferson became president in 1801 and asked James to be secretary of state, Madison acceded only after weeks spent recovering his own health.

Because Jefferson and Burr, the vice president, were widowers and Jefferson's two daughters could not afford to live in Washington, D.C., Dolley played First Lady for his two terms, along with Jefferson's daughter Patsy.

Other cabinet wives helped, but as the wife of the secretary of state, Dolley assumed the risky role of hostess under Jefferson's policy that ceremony was undemocratic. At their first banquet, Jefferson openly snubbed the British ambassador's wife, Elizabeth Merry, by escorting Dolley to dinner—not Mrs. Merry, as protocol demanded.

Jefferson offered the Madisons a home in the White House, but after three weeks they moved to one of the few brick houses in town. Located on F Street, it was three stories high with plenty of rooms for eleven-year-old Payne, twenty-year-old Anna, and the hundreds of guests attracted to Dolley's abundant dinners and informal receptions, including exclusive receptions for women that rivaled the all-male affairs at the White House.

From 1804 through 1809, there followed in seemingly endless succession a series of deaths in the family: two beloved nieces, still toddlers; their mother, sister Mary; Mrs. Madison's mother; two brothers; and sister Lucy's husband. All this came during a time of political tempests, both foreign and domestic. Britain, again at war with France, harassed American ships at sea because the United States was friendly with France; the northeastern states talked of secession over the embargo on foreign goods; and members of Madison's own party tried to block his election as president.

Presidency and First Ladyship

When Dolley assumed the role of First Lady in her own right in March, 1809, her first goal was to cool the political heat. She did so by refashioning the role of First Lady with a keen sense of public relations. Jefferson still inhabited the White House, so the reception for James's inaugural was at the Madisons' home. That wintry afternoon, it took a cold half-hour just to get in to shake the new president's hand. At his side, Dolley glowed in a plain, American-made cambric dress with no jewelry except her gold engagement ring of diamond roses.

That night, four hundred guests attended the inaugural ball. Some stood on benches, just to see Dolley enter to the Marine Band's rendition of "Madison's March." She dressed down in a plain, pale buff velvet gown with no trimming. In place of the afternoon's bonnet, however, she wore a velvet and white satin turban, topped in the latest Parisian style by two towering white feathers.

With Benjamin Latrobe as interior designer and French-born Jean Pierre Sioussat as butler and master of ceremonies, Dolley set about refurbishing the twenty-three-room White House as a palace fit for an American president. She started with the drawing room for her Wednesday receptions. Jefferson had brought a few spare pieces from his home, Monticello, but from Montpelier Dolley brought her French furniture. With funds from Congress, she redecorated with large lamps illuminating sunflower yellows and reds, red velvet cushions, and superb red silk curtains, which cost four dollars per yard.

Dolley's sisters Anna Cutts and the widowed Lucy Washington came to live with her, and rumors of promiscuity among the women of the White House caused a minor scandal. The president's ally Postmaster General Gideon Granger, Jr., accused Congressman Samuel Hunt of spreading such rumors. Hunt challenged him to a duel. Dolley made a great point of publicly inviting Hunt to lunch, and the duel was called off. Still, the president's enemies forged ahead. Their Georgetown newspaper advertised a fake book that claimed Madison's impotence was the cause of Dolley becoming the model for "the insatiability of democratic women."

Nevertheless, Dolley's informal receptions showed off her remarkable skills as a hostess. With the hospitality of a Virginia housewife, she made each guest feel like the most important person in the room. No matter how naïve or sophisticated, young people particularly fell under her spell. On his first visit, twenty-three-

year-old Elbert Gerry, Jr., spoke for all: "She treated me more like a son than a stranger." New Yorker Frances Few saw her as "all things to all men," telling people what they wanted to hear. "I do not think it possible to know what her real opinions are," she said and yet found it impossible to be with her and not be pleased.

At formal dinners, Dolley would seat the president's secretary at one end of the table and herself at the head, so that James sat in the middle of his guests, the better to converse with the greatest number. So smoothly did she maintain her policy of nonpartisanship at receptions and dinners that one congressman remarked, "You cannot discover who are her husband's friends or foes."

Her friend Benjamin Latrobe insisted that she was a closet Federalist, applying pressure to appoint favorites of her own. She did have her network of cabinet and congressional wives to exchange information, but nobody knows the extent to which pillow talk influenced James's decisions. She made sure that every day, no matter how full the schedule, she would visit him to impart a cheerful story or news.

Aware of intrigues playing all around them, she had to be circumspect even in correspondence. "I could tell you many curious things . . . but I must not trust my pen." Yet it was her pen that assured her place in the pantheon of national heroines. She herself was responsible for publicizing the dramatic story of how in 1814, at the height of the War of 1812, she rescued George Washington's famous Lansdowne portrait by Gilbert Stuart when the British burned down the White House. A woman who takes time on her wedding day to write a letter to her best friend would surely be capable of penning a running account of the action as it was happening. In the form of a letter to her sister Lucy, she told how she refused to leave the White House, waiting for the president to come home from the front and fearing for his safety. With dramatic immediacy she told how, the next day, finally persuaded to flee, she insisted on rescuing official papers, valuable articles, and Washington's portrait, even as troops advanced unimpeded up Pennsylvania Avenue.

The account was not published until 1836, by which time she had so endeared herself to the nation as to overcome intimations of exaggeration. Perhaps she had forgotten that the portrait was only a copy of Stuart's original by the landscape artist William Winstanley, but she surely knew its value as a national icon.

Her own adventures were dramatic enough without embellishment. She and James had planned to meet at a tavern in Maryland, but in a night filled with tempestuous rain and fear of marauding troops, she stopped to rest, missing him in the darkness by just five miles, then arriving at the tavern only to find that she had missed him again. Finally, she disobeyed his order to stay until he sent for her, commandeered a carriage, and raced home

Dolley Madison escaped the flames of the White House, shown in this 1814 scene depicting the British invasion of Washington, D.C., during the War of 1812. *(Bettman/CORBIS)*

through crowds of refugees. Their cheers encouraged her to think that she was thus sustaining the nation's morale in this, its darkest hour.

She returned about noon on August 27,

Dolley's Heroics

In 1848, when a would-be robber set fire to Dolley Madison's Washington, D.C., house, she escaped safely, then sent a servant to retrieve a trunk full of James Madison's papers. The newspapers, in reporting the facts, also recounted the story of how, during the War of 1812, she had bravely rescued George Washington's portrait and fled in the night when the British burned down the White House. Now they relished how, as the flames died, she went back upstairs to bed, still barefoot in her black velvet nightgown.

When questions arose about the story of her White House heroics, she had the press reprint her earlier account with a statement: "I acted thus because of my respect for General Washington, not that I felt a desire to gain laurels." In fact, she enjoyed reliving the event, confessing, "I was so unfeminine as to be free from fear. . . . If I could have had a cannon through every window, but alas!" A neighbor recounted how she had defiantly escaped the White House through two files of British soldiers. The legend of Dolley Madison was solidified in her own time.

1814, to find Washington gutted. The War, Navy, and Treasury buildings, along with the arsenal and Navy yard, were destroyed; the White House was a burned-out shell. The Madisons took up temporary quarters in the fashionable Octagon House, which was large enough to restore the Wednesday receptions as an act of defiance, another boost to local morale.

In public, she and the president made a great show of returning to normality, but in private Dolley suffered from depression. Visitors were surprised at her violent outbursts against the British and her complaints against Americans who were blaming her husband for the devastation and even refusing to visit her. Intimates said she had moments of uncontrolled sobbing, the immediate reaction to seeing her lovely White House in ruins and a delayed reaction to the trauma of pursuing James in the dark of dreadful night.

Compounding her anxiety, reports from abroad said that Europeans had been treating her son, Payne, who was part of the peace mission, as an American crown prince and leading him into a life of drinking and gambling all night long. Worse, wandering in the field of battle had done frail James's health no good. The Madisons were forced to move from the dampness of Octagon House to a smaller place in the Seven Buildings. One town house there served as James's executive office building, with the adjacent house having to do as Dolley's White House for the rest of their two years in Washington.

By Christmas, the enemy seemed to have given up. Dolley celebrated Andrew Jackson's victory at the Battle of New Orleans in January, 1815, with a gala open house and the peace treaty in February with receptions on a scale unseen in years. Now she complained in a different key: "Such overflowing rooms I never saw before—I sigh for repose."

As she stood at the door receiving soldiers on their way home, all tossed their hats in the air, cheering wildly. Good times had come again. Her receptions remained the hub of the social whirl. As Madison's term came to a close, former president John Adams marveled that Madison had somehow managed to establish "more Union, than all his three Predecessors." When Georgetown held a gala farewell ball, it was to honor Dolley in her own right. Even the conservative press praised the retiring First Lady for perfecting the principle expressed by "We are all Federalists, we are all Republicans," referring to the two political factions of the time.

Retirement at Montpelier, only ninety-three miles away, could have been a romantic idyll. Dolley was surrounded by spectacular scenery, a library of nine hundred books, and a collection of fine art acquired during forty-three years of public service and diplomacy. She was also surrounded with visitors; ninety attended the Fourth of July picnic of 1820. "I am," she said, "less worried here with a hundred visitors than with twenty-five in Washington." She would have liked to travel, and she missed keeping up with the latest fashions, but James's illness kept her close to home.

Besides her husband's health, her chief anxiety was for her son Payne. At twenty-six, he had led a life of reckless wandering so that she seldom knew where he was. Her letters had gone unanswered so long that she wrote to the postmaster, asking if they had been delivered. She had, however, heard from his many creditors, and both she and James, unknown to each other, had been keeping him out of debtors prison. Payne finally returned home, living on land he purchased nearby.

Without Dolley knowing, her husband had paid an estimated twenty thousand dollars to cover Payne's debts—and she did know he had paid about a third more. At retirement, they had owned the five-thousand-acre Montpelier estate plus one thousand acres in Kentucky. The continual drain to cover Payne's debts led to selling off lands, mortgaging half the Montpelier estate, and selling those of their slaves who consented to be sold to a kindhearted neighbor.

From 1830 on, as James suffered severe arthritis and the ophthalmia that she had suffered for years made Dolley give up reading, they began a Herculean task of organizing his papers. They put Payne to work as a copyist alongside three hired clerks and Dolley's brother John. As a legacy for her and for the United States, they hoped that Congress would buy James's records of the Federal Convention of 1787, at least, and that a commercial publisher would print the remainder of Madison's public papers. They burned their personal correspondence.

James died at breakfast on June 28, 1836, at the age of eighty-five. Drained, Dolley took to her bed for the next six months. Payne's demands on New York publishers ruined hopes for commercial sale of the papers, but through such friends as Senator Henry Clay, Congress paid her thirty thousand dollars for records of the convention. At age seventy, she returned to their Washington house at Lafayette Square and H Street, there to take on the role of venerated national monument.

For a few years, Montpelier provided a retreat from Washington summers, but Payne continued to drain her resources, both emotional and financial. Fur magnate John Jacob Astor gave her a mortgage on the Washington house, and she had to rent out Montpelier until 1844, when her brother-in-law William Madison sued the estate, forcing her to sell it. Her appeals to Payne to help make decisions went unanswered.

By the mid-1840's, Payne had become a chronic alcoholic and deadbeat. Whatever his mother gave him, he spent on liquor, marked cards, and women. She asked him to help decide what to salvage from Montpelier for Lafayette Square, and he thereupon sold the furnishings—along with assorted loot and papers from her safe deposit box. Loving not wisely

but too well, she insisted only that he return the silver service, then eventually allowed him to pawn it anyway. When Congress paid twenty-five thousand dollars for some of Madison's papers Payne had not purloined, the funds were put in trust so that he could not get his hands on them so long as she lived.

Although Payne was keeping her penniless, Dolley kept up appearances appropriate to a relic of the revolution. One of the first things she did with the payment from Congress was to take a party of friends on a pleasure cruise along the Potomac River before returning to her diurnal course of the past dozen years, paying and returning visits, enjoying homage with Elizabeth Schuyler Hamilton, Alexander Hamilton's widow, as the last of the Founding Mothers and in her own right, eldest First Lady of them all.

Few officials, foreign or domestic, visited the White House without a pilgrimage across Lafayette Square to Dolley Madison's comfortable, two-story home on the corner of H Street. New Year's Day visits to a president were considered incomplete without a visit to Dolley Madison. For presidents from Martin Van Buren to James Buchanan, she was both constant visitor and confidential consultant. After her twenty-two-year-old cousin, Angelica Singleton, wed Van Buren's son and acted as First Lady for the widowed president, Dolley became a featured fixture in the White House.

After mourning the loss of his first wife, President John Tyler reinstituted public receptions as "a Virginia notion," to bring all people together. With a nod to Dolley Madison, he told the New York *Herald*, "It Americanizes them." When he wed Julia Gardiner, Dolley, who tutored the new First Lady, found her own ideas of hospitality discarded for imitation imperial glamor. Making guests wait until all were assembled before making her grand entrance, Julia Tyler would greet guests from an elevated armchair with her hair shaped to resemble a crown and with six maids of honor on each side, dressed as elegantly as she was, in grotesque contrast to Dolley's elegant but democratic style.

Dolley still rode around town in her old-fashioned chariot so disreputable that some wag tagged it with a sign reading "This is gentility." She remained a model of gentility in poverty with a glamor all her own. At nearly eighty, she looked much younger, still attending parties and receiving company. With her niece Annie Payne as adopted daughter and constant companion, she presided over Washington as dowager First Lady.

As pilgrims venerated the tall, handsome octogenarian in a shabby old gown of black velvet or brocade, short-waisted, puff-sleeved, with a muslin handkerchief tucked into the low waist, and a stiff quilling of net to cover the scragginess of her neck, they could not see the depth of her poverty. She would wear basic black to hide the fact that her once overflowing wardrobe now stood emptied. Friends declined her wine, knowing the wine cellar was bare. Her old slave Paul Jennings, now free and a civil servant, would deliver food baskets to her and occasionally give her small sums from his own pocket.

She kept up appearances, joining ninety-two-year-old Elizabeth Hamilton at the laying of the cornerstone for the Washington Monument. Both had chaired the drive to raise funds for the monument, founded orphan societies, and had devoted their lives to guarding their husbands' fame, but Elizabeth seldom visited or entertained and almost never went out in society. Dolley, by contrast, seldom missed a social event. In the freezing January cold, she attended a wedding party where guests marveled at her consumption of oysters, ice cream, chicken salad, jelly, tongue, and champagne.

Not long afterward, she stood for three hours on the receiving line at President James Polk's reception, this time in a white satin gown that revealed shoulders and arms youthful as ever and in one of her favored turbans, also fringed with white satin. The fatigue was too much for her to last till midnight. Polk's successor, Zachary Taylor, knowing she was too weak to attend his inauguration, crossed Lafayette Square to seek her blessing. At eighty-one, a stroke had left her too weak to attend even the inauguration balls.

Confined to her bed, she slept peacefully through her final days, with Annie Payne her constant nurse, relieved by Dolley's best friend and bridesmaid Eliza Lee and other friends. Just two days after dictating her will, between 10:00 and 11:00 on the night of July 12, 1849, Dolley died.

President Taylor, along with hundreds of Washingtonians, mourned at services in nearby Saint John's Episcopal Church, which Dolley had joined after James's death. She who had followed long processions as a refugee from Philadelphia's yellow fever and marauding British troops was now followed by a procession reported to be the largest yet seen in the city. The Washington *National Intelligencer* spoke for the nation: "She touched all hearts by her goodness and won the admiration of all by the charms of dignity and grace."

Years later, after Virginians raised an obelisk over James Madison's grave in the Montpelier burying grounds, Dolley Madison's remains were removed from the Congressional Cemetery in Washington to lie near James's with a small stone of her own, inscribed: "To the Memory of DOLLEY PAYNE wife of James Madison." It was half-hidden by the obelisk, just as her inner thoughts were hidden with the destruction of her intimate letters. What remains is the image that she forged.

Legacy
Dolley Madison brought the First Ladyship out of the shadow of the presidency and gave it a life of its own. Counting two terms as Jefferson's hostess, she served sixteen years, longer than any president served in his office before or since. It was no accident that, when they were

displaced by fire in 1814, the Madisons had to set up an executive office house for James separate from her temporary White House. While he took care of governing, she took care of everything else.

By force of personality, she fused the political concerns of Abigail Adams with the ceremonial concerns of Martha Washington, creating a First Lady who cared for people rather than party. Her extraordinary sense of public relations enabled her to sustain a neat balance between the rhetoric of democracy and the ritual of royalty, the formula for successful First Ladies. If she is now known more for having served ice cream in the White House than as the first modern First Lady, it is a sign of how well Dolley did her job.

Suggested Readings

Arnett, Ethel S. *Mrs. James Madison: The Incomparable Dolley.* Greensboro, N.C.: Piedmont Press, 1972. Arnett, a regional historian skilled in research, offers reliable coverage of Dolley Madison's early life.

Brant, Irving. *James Madison.* 6 vols. Indianapolis: Bobbs-Merrill, 1941-1961. Standard biography of the president; the last four volumes include the most authentic information about Dolley Madison in the context of American and European history.

Clark, Allen C. *Life and Letters of Dolly Madison.* Washington, D.C.: W. F. Roberts, 1914. While not up to modern editorial standards, provides a large selection of letters by and about Dolley Madison, her family, and friends, with interesting appendices.

Cutts, Lucia Beverly. *Memoirs and Letters of Dolley Madison, Wife of James Madison, President of the United States.* Boston: Houghton Mifflin, 1886. Edited by her grandniece.

Hunt-Jones, Conover. *Dolley and the "Great Little Madison."* Washington, D.C.: American Institute of Architects Foundation, 1977. A succinct treatment of Dolley Madison's life, lifestyle, and material culture, with full illustrations of fashions in costume, art, and furnishings at Montpelier and the White House.

Paul M. Zall

Elizabeth Monroe

Elizabeth Kortright Monroe

Born: July 30, 1768
New York, New York
Died: September 23, 1830
Oak Hill, Virginia

President: James Monroe
1817-1825

Overview: Although probably one of the most well-known public figures of her time, Elizabeth Kortright Monroe, wife of James Monroe, is almost unknown today. She received both harsh criticism and high praise during her time in the White House, and the changes she made in the role of the First Lady drastically revised public expectations for future generations of presidents' wives. Her beauty and manners were widely discussed in Washington, D.C., and European circles, as was her courage in Paris during the French Revolution. The Parisians called her *la belle Americaine*.

Elizabeth Monroe. *(Library of Congress)*

Early Life

Elizabeth was born in New York on July 30, 1768, the second of five children of Hannah Aspinwall Kortright and Captain Lawrence Kortright. The Lawrence Kortrights were part of an old, socially prominent New York family, descended from ancestors who emigrated from Holland to the Dutch colony of New Amsterdam in 1633. The family's wealth was based on farming and real estate.

Lawrence Kortright made his own fortune as a merchant and a privateer in the British army during the French and Indian War (1754-1763). As part owner of several vessels authorized by the Crown to wage legal piracy against French ships, he accumulated considerable wealth and property in New York City. However, he lost most of this fortune during the American Revolution when he sided with the Loyalists.

Elizabeth and her brother, John, and her sisters Hester, Maria, and Sarah were raised in New York City. Hannah Aspinwall Kortright died when Elizabeth was nine, and Hester Kortright, her paternal grandmother, raised the young girl. Hester had a reputation of being a strong and independent woman and seems to have played a significant role in forming Elizabeth's character.

Little is known about Elizabeth's early years and education. During that time, generally three events were marked in a woman's life: birth, marriage, and death. Elizabeth was probably educated at home, in the domestic skills required for marriage. Growing up with wealth and social position enabled her to become a self-confident, cultured, and sophisticated young woman. She was attractive and slender, five feet in height, with dark hair and blue eyes. She retained her youthful beauty throughout her life.

James Monroe

In the famous painting *Washington Crossing the Delaware*, James Monroe is shown immediately behind General George Washington, clutching the flag as the boat makes its perilous way across the ice-strewn river. In some ways, this picture is a metaphor for Monroe's career: a sturdy participant in great events who has not always received recognition for his contributions. Severely wounded at Trenton, he stayed with the Army through Valley Forge and the Battle of Monmouth. In 1780 he returned to Virginia to study law with Thomas Jefferson.

Monroe divided the next thirty years between a sporadic law practice and a number of government positions. He held elective office as governor of Virginia twice, a member of Congress under the Articles of Confederation, a Virginia state legislator, and a United States senator. He served in diplomatic posts as well. He had an unsuccessful tenure as ambassador to France from 1794 through 1796, where his revolutionary zeal was contrary to the wishes of President Washington's administration. However, his good relations with the French later served him well as he negotiated the Louisiana Purchase with Napoleon in 1803. He also served as the ambassador to Great Britain from 1803 through 1807. Under President James Madison, Monroe held two cabinet posts: secretary of state and secretary of war. The latter was an effort to restore morale in Washington, D.C., after it had been attacked and burned during the War of 1812.

Monroe's own tenure in the White House, from 1817 through 1825, was marked with foreign policy success. The first start was made on the disarmament of the border with Canada, and the remaining problems with Britain from the War of 1812 were resolved. Florida was purchased in 1819. Finally, and of the greatest significance, he espoused the Monroe Doctrine, pledging to keep the Americas free of European encroachment.

Domestically, the Era of Good Feelings, as the years of Monroe's presidency were known, and the unity that began with his first term dissipated throughout his second. Political competition and sectional hostilities that had merely gone underground came to light again. The necessity for the Missouri Compromise between slave and free states in 1820 gave a glimpse of the passions that would ultimately lead to Civil War.

As the last revolutionary hero who became president, James Monroe was a transitional figure. A reticent man who has to be defined by his actions, his main interest was in the realm of statecraft and the implementation of policies and ideas. A fundamentally decent man, he was the Virginia governor who put down a slave rebellion, yet the capital of Liberia was named Monrovia after him by freed slaves who returned to Africa. His diplomatic successes helped to point the new country toward the West.

Marriage and Family

Elizabeth met James Monroe, a man of modest means, in 1785 when he was attending the Continental Congress as part of the Virginia delegation. They married the next year, on February 16, 1786, and honeymooned on Long Island, New York. She was seventeen and he was twenty-seven.

Despite the differences in their ages and backgrounds, Elizabeth and James had a very successful marriage. They were devoted to each other, and in spite of financial concerns that plagued them throughout James's public service, they traveled together whenever they could. They lived in the major cities of the northeastern United States and in Paris and London. Elizabeth's beauty and manners were assets to James's career.

They had three children: Eliza Kortright Monroe, born in 1786; James Spence Monroe, born in 1799; and Maria Hester Monroe, born in 1803. Eliza received a French education, married successful lawyer George Hay in 1808, and became a social hostess for her mother at the White House. James Spence contracted whooping cough and died in 1800 at the age of sixteen months. Maria Hester, educated in Philadelphia, became the first child of a president to be married in the White House when she wed Samuel L. Gouverneur in 1820.

Elizabeth's role as a public figure changed as James's career developed and flourished. In Virginia, their first home together, he was a state legislator, a representative to the constitutional ratifying convention, a senator, and then governor. In Paris, where James had two assignments separated by seven years, Elizabeth was the wife of the United States minister to France, then the wife of the successful negotiator of the Louisiana Purchase. In London, she was the wife of the minister to Great Britain. Back in Washington, D.C., Elizabeth became the wife of the secretary of state, who also, for a short time, held the position of secretary of war.

Paris was a personal success for the Monroes, especially Elizabeth. She became known as a successful hostess, in spite of food and fuel shortages that followed the French Revolution. The entire Monroe family learned to speak French, and Eliza was enrolled in a fashionable school. Elizabeth and James developed a lasting enjoyment of French decorative arts, furniture, and social customs. This appreciation, together with Elizabeth's beauty and grace, won them favor with their host country. The French called Elizabeth *la belle Americaine*. Their favorable impression of the minister and his wife enabled James to secure the release of several Americans who were in prison as suspected enemies of the French Revolution. The successful conclusion of the Louisiana Purchase agreement placed James in the national spotlight at home in the United States and would help to secure his position as a candidate for the presidency.

Presidency and First Ladyship

James Monroe became the fifth president of the United States and served two terms, from 1817 to 1825. During this time, the President's House literally became the "White House," as it was painted and restored after the War of 1812. Elizabeth and James brought in fifty-four pieces of carved and gilded French Empire furniture made by a Parisian cabinetmaker, and they had the house decorated in French style. Eight of the fifty-four pieces remain today.

Not only did the Monroes introduce French decorative arts to Washington society, Elizabeth introduced formal European social customs, which were not well received. Most notably, she broke with her predecessors' custom of making initial calls on all the new congressional wives. Her health may have played a major role in this decision: She had been sickly throughout her life with rheumatism, headaches, and fevers. Some felt that she used her illness as an excuse to refrain from following local custom. Washington wives retaliated by boycotting White House invitations. A cabinet

The Prisoner's Release

Although Elizabeth shunned public life while living in the White House, she placed herself in the spotlight in Paris to save a friend. When the Monroes arrived in Paris in 1794, the city was in turmoil at the height of the Reign of Terror. One hundred government officials had been beheaded in the five days before the minister's arrival. Thomas Paine, whose publications contributed to the Americans' victory in the Revolutionary War, had been imprisoned for his unsuccessful bid to banish, rather than execute, King Louis XVI. James Monroe was able to save Paine, but he needed Elizabeth's help to save the Marquise de Lafayette, wife of a French nobleman who had fought in the American Revolution.

Madame Lafayette had been imprisoned with her mother and grandmother, and she had seen both of them taken to the guillotine. James hoped to raise public sentiment so that she would be released. Elizabeth, with only her servants to accompany her, was driven in the minister's official carriage through the streets of Paris to the prison, drawing a substantial crowd. Once there, she asked to speak to the prisoner. Madame Lafayette, thinking she was being called to her death, broke down when she saw Elizabeth. The crowd was so moved they spread word of the meeting. Soon informal conversations between James and the French government produced Madame Lafayette's release. Elizabeth's courage had saved her.

meeting held in 1819 discussed social etiquette in the city, and Elizabeth received approval for her decision.

Additional criticism came to Elizabeth for her refusal to open Maria Hester's wedding to the public. Only family and close friends were invited, and the rest of Washington felt snubbed. In an attempt to reconcile their European tastes with the American public, Elizabeth and James held events that were known as "drawing rooms": Every two weeks while Congress was in session, the White House was open to visitors who wished to meet the first family. Records of those events discuss Elizabeth's youthful looks, her hairstyles, her manners, and her French dresses. She was both admired and envied. When she was unable to attend these gatherings, her daughter Eliza Hay stood in for her.

Legacy

Elizabeth's health declined throughout James's second term. Her last public appearance was on New Year's Day, 1825. That year the Monroes retired to Virginia and lived quietly for the next five years. Elizabeth died on September 23, 1830; James died the following year, on July 4.

Elizabeth Kortright Monroe dramatically reduced the social obligations of future First Ladies. She zealously guarded her daily schedule and her family's privacy, even at the risk of disappointing the American public. Some social customs she developed remain a part of White House protocol.

Suggested Readings

Ammon, Harry. *James Monroe: The Quest for National Identity*. Charlottesville: University Press of Virginia, 1990. The definitive biography of James Monroe, with a large amount of material on his life with Elizabeth Monroe.

Boller, Paul F. *Presidential Wives: An Anecdotal History*. 2d ed. New York: Oxford University Press, 1999. Contains a short chapter on Elizabeth Monroe, including her part in freeing Madame Lafayette from prison.

Gould, Lewis L., ed. *American First Ladies: Their Lives and Their Legacy*. New York: Garland, 1996. Contains a lengthy chapter on Elizabeth Monroe, which is informative and filled with details.

McCombs, Charles Flowers. *Imprisonment of Madame de Lafayette During the Terror.* New York: The Library, 1943. Information on Elizabeth Monroe's role in freeing Madame Lafayette.

Watson, Robert P. *The Presidents' Wives: Reassessing the Office of First Lady.* Boulder, Colo.: Lynne Rienner, 2000. An analysis of the development of the First Lady's role and its influence on presidential politics.

Wooten, James E. *Elizabeth Kortright Monroe.* Charlottesville, Va.: Ash Lawn-Highland, 1987. A slim biography of Elizabeth Monroe.

Pamela T. Brannon

Louisa Adams

Louisa Catherine Johnson Adams

Born: February 12, 1775
     London, England
Died: May 15, 1852
     Washington, D.C.

President: John Quincy Adams
     1825-1829

Overview: The only First Lady born outside the United States, Louisa Adams was a refined and intelligent woman who endured a difficult marriage to the son of the country's second president. Her skills as a social hostess helped boost John Quincy Adams's prominence in Washington, D.C., contributing to his election to the presidency in 1824. Her strong views against slavery are thought to have influenced her husband, who became a leading voice in Congress for abolition.

Louisa Adams. *(Library of Congress)*

Early Life

Louisa was born in London in 1775 to a British mother, Catherine Nuth Johnson, and an American father, Joshua Johnson. She was the second child in a family of nine children. Her father was a successful tobacco importer who had moved to England from Maryland. Johnson's brother, Thomas, was one of the signers of the Declaration of Independence and a justice on the U.S. Supreme Court. When Louisa was three, Joshua Johnson again moved to pursue new business ventures; this time the family went to France. It was there that Louisa was raised, attending a convent school and an elite boarding school.

President George Washington later appointed Louisa's father as U.S. consul to England, and the family returned to the city of her birth, where they lived near the famous Tower of London. Louisa's upbringing was comfortable and defined by privilege. She enjoyed an impressive formal education, excelled in writing, and learned to speak French, Latin, and Greek. This intelligent young woman was known for her love of books, theater, and music.

Louisa and John Adams's relationship would be a troubled one, defined by ups and downs throughout its duration. Both Louisa and John had courted prior to meeting each other; John's relationship with a woman named Mary Frazer would have ended in marriage had his parents not voiced their disapproval. John never appeared to have the deep love for Louisa that he demonstrated for earlier romantic interests. Their courtship was interrupted on more than one instance, and John remained hesitant throughout the affair, apparently concerned about financial security and his formidable mother's displeasure with Louisa as a potential daughter-in-law.

Marriage and Family

Despite a rocky courtship, John and Louisa were married on July 26, 1797. An unlikely couple, the two shared few interests. He was impulsive, demanding, and aloof, whereas Louisa was warm, sensitive, and somewhat shy. John did not appreciate his wife's outspokenness and independence of thought. His political career was the dominant factor in their marriage, taking them on numerous diplomatic postings in Europe. Much of their early life together was spent living outside the United States.

Soon after their marriage, Adams accepted a position in Berlin. When Thomas Jefferson became president in 1801, however, Adams was recalled. Back in the United States, Adams pursued a legal career before being elected to the Massachusetts senate. Following his ambition, he pursued higher office. Although he was unsuccessful in his bid for a seat in the U.S. House of Representatives, he was later elected to the U.S. Senate.

Louisa's first child, George Washington Adams, was born in 1801, followed by John II in 1803. Louisa did not enjoy living in Massachusetts, so she welcomed the opportunity to join her husband in the nation's capital, which she found more agreeable. In Washington, D.C., Louisa lived with her sister Nancy and her recently widowed mother, whose company she enjoyed.

John Quincy Adams

The sixth president, John Quincy Adams, was also the son of a president. Born in Braintree (later called Quincy), Massachusetts, in 1767, he grew up under the influence of his intellectual father and formidable mother. Not surprisingly, his passions were politics and the intellectual life. What Adams lacked in warmth and charm, he made up in discipline and experience. Educated at Harvard University, he gained valuable insights serving as his father's secretary during the elder Adams's diplomatic assignments in Europe and political work in Washington, D.C.

John Quincy became a diplomat, gaining his first posting at age twenty-six as the minister to the Netherlands and was soon after offered a position in Berlin. He also served in both the Massachusetts senate and the U.S. Senate before returning to Russia and France for diplomatic assignments and then as secretary of state under President James Monroe. Adams's presidency was marred by doubt cast from his narrow and controversial victory in 1824 in the electoral college, after failing to carry the popular vote, won by his opponent Andrew Jackson. He nevertheless promoted a series of infrastructure projects, including roads and canals to connect the young nation. Adams is also known for his staunch position against slavery when, after his presidency, the people of Massachusetts returned him to Washington as a U.S. representative. It was during an impassioned session on the House floor in 1848 that Adams collapsed of a stroke and died two days later.

The Journey to Paris

While serving as the wife of the U.S. minister to Russia, Louisa Adams distinguished herself in several ways. John Quincy Adams had been appointed to the post in 1809 by the new president, James Madison. Adams accepted the assignment without consulting his wife and departed without her. She later joined him, after making a trans-Atlantic voyage in the company of only her maid, a niece, and her newborn son, Charles. Although lonely in Russia, she impressed members of the diplomatic community with her grace and warmth and was a favorite of Tzar Alexander I, her occasional dance partner while in court. Enduring brutally cold winters and with limited funds, Louisa's unhappiness was exacerbated by the death of a baby daughter.

John again abandoned his wife when he was called to Paris in 1814 to help negotiate the treaty ending the War of 1812. Louisa spent several lonely months in Saint Petersburg before receiving word to join her husband in Paris. Departing in February—the middle of winter—she traveled with her young son, a nurse, and two male servants. The trip was harrowing; the small party struggled against the weather, the sheer distance of the journey, and threats posed by defeated soldiers in the final days of the Napoleonic Wars. Louisa held her party together when their carriage became stuck in the mud and lost their way; she also quickly thought to cry out *"Vive Napoleon!"* when Napoleonic loyalists threatened the travelers.

Arriving in Paris after more than five weeks on the road, Louisa's display of courage earned her the respect of her demanding mother-in-law and the newfound admiration of her husband. In a marriage otherwise marked by difficulty, the trials of this period improved John's view of his wife as well as the state of their marriage.

In 1809, President James Madison appointed Adams as his minister to Russia, and Louisa again joined her husband abroad. Her voyage to Russia was made more difficult because she traveled with her young son Charles Francis, who was only two when the family crossed the Atlantic. The Russian winters did not agree with Louisa, and the death of her daughter Louisa Catherine in 1812, only a year after her birth, scarred Louisa for life. She remembered her time in Russia as difficult and lonely, although she was a popular figure at the Saint Petersburg court.

Louisa was frail; several difficult pregnancies and the birth of five children had further weakened her. In addition to suffering from her physical weakness, she often felt lonely in her marriage, because her husband neglected her as he pursued his political career. Louisa's unhappiness was further exacerbated by the financial problems they faced during John's diplomatic career. The pay for ministers was often insufficient to cover the high costs of entertaining, an expected part of a diplomat's duty.

Presidency and First Ladyship

In 1817, Adams was named secretary of state in the administration of President James Monroe, and the Adamses finally returned to the United States. For perhaps the first time in their married life, Louisa began to take a more active interest in her husband's career, distinguishing herself through the social events she hosted in Washington. Adams believed he deserved the presidency, but neither did his personality endear him to official Washington nor did he feel he had to work to attain the office. Thanks to his wife, who hosted important and well-attended socials to build support for his candidacy, Adams emerged as a leading candidate. On one occasion, standing in for First Lady Elizabeth Monroe, Louisa presided over a grand ball on

January 8, 1824, with one thousand guests in attendance to celebrate General Andrew Jackson's victory at the Battle of New Orleans, the last battle in the War of 1812. John Quincy Adams was elected president that November.

The presidency was a challenge for both John and Louisa from the outset, when John failed to receive the majority of the popular vote, winning the electoral college in a contest plagued by rumors that he cut a deal with influential House leader Henry Clay. John later appointed Clay as his secretary of state. The Adamses' marriage suffered alongside the difficulties of governing, and John's already foul disposition worsened. He failed to heed his wife's advice not to read the negative stories about him in the press, which only further angered him. By 1826 John and Louisa were taking separate vacations and barely speaking to each other. Louisa also began to distance herself from the functions of the White House, finding solace in books and enjoying playing music in her room in the building's private residence.

The First Lady was only too happy to leave the White House, but the event was dampened by the death in April, 1829, of her firstborn son of an apparent suicide. Louisa blamed the death on John, whom she thought was too critical of the boy.

Legacy

After leaving the White House, Louisa found solace in her books and music, composed poetry, and was a prolific writer. She was the first First Lady to write her memoirs, titled *Adventures of a Nobody*, which gave testimony to the bouts of depression she suffered despite her obvious talents and charm. She also wrote a play, *The Metropolitan Kaleidoscope*, which drew on her life experiences, for it was a story of a harsh politician consumed by ambition and his suffering wife. *Narrative of a Journey from St. Petersburg to Paris, 1815*, which she penned in 1836, was a remembrance of her bold trip to join her

husband in Paris. It would be published years after her death by her grandson Brooks Adams.

The mercurial nature of the Adamses' marriage improved in the years after John's presidency. Adams's retirement was ended when he was elected to the U.S. House of Representatives, and both John and Louisa seemed to find in his service the opportunity to pursue social reform. It appears that her strong views against slavery shaped her husband's convictions, and he became a leading voice in Congress for abolition. Louisa also opposed the brutal Indian removal policies of the United States government, and her progressive views on the rights and role of women continued to develop. Even as a young girl, Louisa had expressed an interest in women's issues and always believed that women were as intelligent as men, a progressive idea for a woman of her day. Louisa's views and actions mark her as an early human rights advocate in the White House. She died in Washington in 1852, four years after the death of her husband.

Suggested Readings

Adams, Louisa Catherine. *Adventures of a Nobody*. In *The Adams Papers*. Boston: Massachusetts Historical Society, 1755-1889. Papers are owned by the Adams manuscript trust and deposited in the Massachusetts Historical Society. Her memoir gives testimony to her depression during her White House years.

_____. "Diary." In *The Adams Papers*. Boston: Massachusetts Historical Society, 1755-1889. Louisa's diary covers the period in her life from December, 1819, to January, 1824.

_____. "Narrative of a Journey from St. Petersburg to Paris in February, 1815." In *The Adams Papers*. Boston: Massachusetts Historical Society, 1755-1889. Contains a foreword by Brooks Adams, Louisa's grandson, and chronicles her treacherous trip.

Corbertt, Katherine. "Louisa Catherine Adams: The Anguished Adventures of a Nobody." In *Women's Being, Women's Place: Female Identity and Vocation in American History*, edited by Mary Kelley. Boston: Houghton Mifflin, 1979.

Shepherd, Jack. *Cannibals of the Heart: A Personal Biography of Louisa Catherine and John Quincy Adams*. New York: McGraw-Hill, 1980. A helpful biography of Louisa Adams's life, including her public role as First Lady.

Robert P. Watson

Rachel Jackson

Rachel Donelson Robards Jackson

Born: June 15, 1767
    Pittsylvania County, Virginia
Died: December 22, 1828
    Nashville, Tennessee

President: Andrew Jackson
1829-1837

Overview: Rachel Donelson Jackson became one of the most famous women in the United States because of her marriage to Andrew Jackson. Divorced in an age when divorce equaled scandal, she became the target of attacks during Jackson's campaigns for the presidency in the 1820's. One of the first pioneers in middle Tennessee, Rachel ably ran their Hermitage plantation near Nashville during Andrew's many absences while raising an adopted son and several wards left to their care by family and friends. The central focuses of Rachel's life, however, were her devotion to Andrew and her Presbyterian faith.

Early Life

Rachel Donelson was born in 1767, in Pittsylvania County, Virginia, the ninth of eleven children. Her parents, Rachel Stockley Donelson and John Donelson II, were members of prominent colonial families in Maryland and Virginia. Donelson was a planter, iron manufacturer, surveyor, and land speculator who made a fortune in frontier land deals. He served as a member of the Virginia House of Burgesses from 1769 to 1774, negotiated Indian treaties, and supported the colonies' separation from Great Britain.

In the 1740's, Donelson moved his family to the western Virginia frontier. Rachel grew up on a plantation with a large log house, receiving a basic education at home and learning the skills that a farm mistress needed to maintain a

Rachel Jackson. *(Library of Congress)*

household. In 1779, when Rachel was twelve, Donelson again moved his family, this time to the Cumberland settlements in what would become Tennessee. The settlers' harrowing journey from December 22, 1779, to April 24, 1780, on flatboats down the Tennessee River to the Ohio and then up the Cumberland, included an outbreak of smallpox and attacks by Cherokee warriors.

The Donelsons established a rough camp and planted crops on their land near Nashville, but Indian attacks sent them to Manskers Station for shelter in July, 1780. That November, the warfare between the Indians and pioneers drove the Donelsons to the larger communities in central Kentucky and a new plantation near Harrodsburg. However, in 1785, Donelson determined that his family would return to Tennessee.

Marriage and Family
By 1785, Rachel was a vivacious young woman known for her accomplished horseback riding and love of dancing. The seventeen-year-old girl had met Lewis Robards, ten years her senior, and did not wish to return to Tennessee.

On March 1, 1785, the dark-eyed, dark-haired Rachel married Lewis, and they moved in with his widowed mother. Rachel's family moved back to Tennessee; during John Donelson's journey to join his family in September he was murdered. Rachel's marriage soon failed, and in 1788 she went to her mother's home near Nashville. Widow Donelson had a number of boarders, among them Andrew Jackson. Rachel and Andrew became friends, and after they thought Rachel was divorced, they married. Robards, however, did not actually divorce Rachel until 1793, and the Jacksons were remarried in January, 1794.

Despite the circumstances of their marriage, the frontier settlement seemed to take small notice. Andrew was named attorney general for the territorial district in 1791, and when Tennessee became a state in 1796, he was elected to the U.S. Congress. In 1794, Andrew acquired the Poplar Grove farm, and in 1796 he bought additional acreage, where they built Hunter's Hill, an elegant frame house. In 1804, financial difficulties led them to sell this plantation, and they then bought the nearby farm and log house that Jackson called the Hermitage.

Rachel's Divorce

Rachel Donelson's marriage to Lewis Robards in 1785 quickly turned dark as his jealousies emerged. By 1788, the couple had separated, and Rachel moved to her mother's home, where she met Andrew Jackson. Rachel reconciled briefly with Lewis when he moved to Nashville, but his rages continued, now fueled by Rachel's friendship with Andrew. Lewis abandoned Rachel in May, 1790.

Fearing Lewis's return, Rachel left for Natchez, Mississippi, with family friends and Andrew Jackson. Historians disagree as to whether Lewis asked the Virginia legislature for the right to sue for divorce on the grounds of desertion and adultery before or after Rachel fled to Natchez. The Jacksons said they married in Natchez in August, 1791, after getting news that Rachel had been divorced. However, no record has ever been found of the marriage, and Lewis did not actually divorce Rachel until September, 1793, long after Rachel and Andrew had returned to Nashville. When they learned of their dilemma, Rachel and Jackson had a marriage ceremony performed on January 18, 1794.

The question of their marriage's legality would always be a cloud in their lives, and it became a major issue in Jackson's campaign for the presidency in 1828.

Rachel managed the household work of the farm, overseeing the production of food and clothing for the couple and their slaves. Although Rachel bore no children in either of her marriages, she raised at least eleven wards left to the Jacksons' care. In December of 1809 the Jacksons adopted the infant son of her brother and sister-in-law, whom they named Andrew Jackson, Jr. In the fall of 1813, they took in a Creek boy named Lincoyer as their son.

In 1802 Andrew became major general of the Tennessee militia, and he spent much of the next twenty years on military campaigns against the Spanish, Indians, and the British. While he was gone, Rachel managed the household and plantation. On occasion, she would join Andrew on campaign and at government posts, notably in Florida and in New Orleans. She was there when the city celebrated General Jackson's spectacular triumph after the Battle of New Orleans in January, 1815.

Although Andrew's duty often took him from home, Rachel took little pleasure in traveling. By 1820 she was quite stout and often in ill health, and she came to resent Andrew's absences. In 1821 Andrew resigned his military

Andrew Jackson

Andrew Jackson was born on March 15, 1767, in the Waxhaw settlements of South Carolina, the son of Andrew and Elizabeth Hutchinson Jackson. Widowed just before her son's birth, Elizabeth managed to send Andrew to an academy for a formal education, intending him to be a Presbyterian minister. Andrew, though, was a warrior from age thirteen, when he joined his brothers Hugh and Robert in fighting the British. His mother and brothers died in service in the Revolutionary War, leaving the orphaned Andrew a fierce American patriot.

Jackson became an attorney, planter, merchant, and politician in Tennessee, and his career was helped by his marriage to Rachel Donelson, daughter of one of the most highly regarded and largest families in the region. Jackson was elected major general of the Tennessee Militia in 1802. His military success in defeating the southern Indians and negotiating for their lands, in limiting the influence of the Spanish in Florida, and, most of all, in crushing the British at the Battle of New Orleans in January, 1815, left him a national hero. By 1822, the tall, thin Jackson, with his bushy hair and intense blue eyes, was nominated for U.S. president.

In the 1824 election, Jackson won a plurality of the popular and electoral votes over four other candidates, but an alliance between candidates Henry Clay and John Quincy Adams resulted in the election of Adams by the U.S. House of Representatives. Over the next four years, the Jacksonians organized the new Democratic Party and developed a platform of reform. In November, 1828, Jackson won the presidency in a resounding victory. However, during the campaign Rachel became the target of slander, and Jackson blamed the attacks for hastening her death that December.

During his two terms, Jackson worked tirelessly to battle corruption in the federal government and to establish respect for the United States among foreign powers. Among his greatest challenges were facing down the nullifiers of South Carolina, who threatened to leave the Union over tariff policies, and breaking the Bank of the United States, which he felt held too much power over U.S. citizens. When he left the presidency, the executive office had become equal in power to the Congress.

After his retirement to the Hermitage, Jackson continued to influence U.S. politics, including the elections of Martin Van Buren and James K. Polk. He remained a voice for the common man until his death on June 8, 1845.

The Hermitage, home of Andrew and Rachel Jackson. *(Library of Congress)*

commission and the governorship of Florida, planning to retire from public life. His friends, however, urged his candidacy for U.S. president. Rachel wrote a niece,

> I do hope they will leave Mr. Jackson alone.... He has done his share for his country. How little time has he had to himself or his own interests in the thirty years of our wedded life. In all that time he has not spent one fourth of his days under his own roof.

Rachel hoped that she and Andrew would settle into a quiet life, enjoying the new brick mansion and formal garden they had built in 1819. From 1821 to 1823, Andrew was a gentleman farmer, and these were likely the couple's happiest days. Nevertheless, in October, 1823, Jackson left for Washington, D.C., as a U.S. senator, and he returned as a presidential candidate in June, 1824.

Presidency and First Ladyship

In November, 1824, Andrew learned that he had received more of the popular and electoral vote than the other candidates for president but had not gotten the majority needed for election. He and Rachel left for Washington, D.C., so he could be present as the House of Representatives chose the new president. They arrived in December. Andrew and his supporters were stunned when the House elected John Quincy Adams.

In April, 1825, Andrew and Rachel returned to Nashville, and the following month they entertained the Marquis de Lafayette, who had fought in the American Revolution. The war hero's meeting with the Hero of New Orleans added to Jackson's immense popularity. In October, the Tennessee General Assembly officially nominated Jackson for president, and he began to direct his election campaign from the Hermitage.

The 1828 campaign became especially nasty as Adams' supporters attacked Jackson for his "theft" of Rachel from her first husband. Although Rachel's friends tried to shield her, she wrote a friend in July, 1828:

> The enemies of the General have dipped their arrows in wormwood and gall and sped them at me. Almighty God was there ever any thing to equal it. . . . To think that thirty years had passed in happy social friendship with society, knowing or thinking no ill to no one—as my judge will know—how many prayers have I offered up for their repentance.

An additional blow to Rachel that summer was the death of her son Lincoyer, despite her best efforts to nurse him.

In November, Jackson won the presidency in a resounding victory. As her family and friends celebrated Andrew's election, Rachel was reported to say, "For Mr. Jackson's sake, I am glad, but for myself I had rather be a doorkeeper in the house of my Lord than to live in that palace in Washington." Although she had reservations, Rachel agreed to leave for Washington on December 23.

After a shopping trip to Nashville to prepare for the inauguration, Rachel returned disturbed. She had overheard gossipers talking about her backwoods ways and her "bigamy." She told her niece:

> Listening to them, it seemed as if a veil was lifted and I saw myself, whom you have all guarded from outside criticism and surrounded with flattering delusions, as others see me, a poor old woman. I will not go to Washington, but stay here as often before in Mr. Jackson's absences.

Rachel's words proved prophetic, for on December 20, 1828, she suffered a heart attack. Andrew was constantly at her side, but he left her for a short while on the evening of December 22. As her maid helped her prepare for bed, Rachel collapsed. She died before Andrew could return to her.

Legacy

On Christmas Eve, 1828, ten thousand people attended Rachel's funeral at the Hermitage. In her garden, she was laid to rest in the white dress she had planned to wear to Andrew's inauguration as president. Newspapers across the United States reported the death of the First Lady-elect, extolling her goodness but also reporting the rumors that had caused her pain. The tablet Andrew placed on Rachel's grave stated in part, "A being so gentle and so virtuous slander might wound, but could not dishonor."

Although Rachel's niece Emily Donelson and her daughter-in-law Sarah Yorke Jackson would share duties as White House hostess, President Andrew Jackson never forgot his devotion to Rachel or the treatment she received. Later, his defense of another maligned woman, Peggy Eaton, would tear his cabinet apart. He looked at Rachel's portrait each night, and when he was at the Hermitage, he visited her grave each evening until when, in June, 1845, Jackson was laid to rest beside his beloved Rachel.

Suggested Readings

Burke, Pauline Wilcox. *Emily Donelson of Tennessee*. 2 vols. Richmond, Va.: Garrett and Massie, 1941. With illustrations and bibliographical notes.

Caldwell, Mary French. *General Jackson's Lady*. Nashville, Tenn.: M. F. Caldwell, 1936. The first full-length biography of Rachel Jackson includes previously undocumented anecdotes.

Moser, Howard D., et al., eds. *The Papers of Andrew Jackson*. 5 vols. Knoxville: University of Tennessee Press, 1981-1996. The first five volumes include correspondence to and from Rachel Jackson through 1824; more are planned.

Remini, Robert V. *Andrew Jackson*. 3 vols. Baltimore: Johns Hopkins University Press, 1977. Reprinted in 1998 with new introduction. The definitive biography of Andrew Jackson, with significant insights into Rachel Jackson and their marriage.

Sawyer, Susan. *More than Petticoats: Remarkable Tennessee Women*. Helena, Mont.: Falcon, 2000. Written for young adults, primarily an account of Rachel Jackson's divorce and remarriage.

Ann Toplovich

Hannah Van Buren and Angelica Singleton Van Buren

Hannah Hoes Van Buren

Born: March 8, 1783
    Kinderhook, New York
Died: February 5, 1819
    Albany, New York

President: Martin Van Buren
    1837-1841

Angelica Singleton Van Buren

Born: February 13, 1816
    Sumter County,
      South Carolina
Died: December 28, 1878
    New York, New York

President: Martin Van Buren
    1837-1841

Overview: Hannah Van Buren, the wife of President Martin Van Buren, did not live to take the position of First Lady. Hannah died eighteen years before her husband was elected to the presidency. Martin Van Buren did not remarry, entering office without a spouse. President Van Buren's daughter-in-law, Angelica Singleton Van Buren, acted as hostess in the Van Buren White House. Angelica was the wife of Abraham Van Buren, Hannah and Martin's eldest son.

Early Life

Hannah Hoes was born and grew up on the banks of the Hudson River. Her family was of Dutch descent. Hannah was born a few months after her future husband, Martin Van Buren, who grew up in the same community. The Van Burens were also of Dutch descent, and the Hoeses and Van Burens had a history of inter-

marriage. Hannah was the granddaughter of Martin's mother's brother, and Hannah's brother courted one of Martin's sisters at the same time that Hannah and Martin were courting.

Relatively little is known about the life of Hannah Van Buren. Her family owned land and farmed in the village of Kinderhook in Co-

Hannah Van Buren. *(Library of Congress)*

Angelica Singleton Van Buren, wife of Hannah and Martin Van Buren's son Abraham. *(North Wind Picture Archives)*

lumbia County, New York, some thirty miles from Albany. Hannah's ancestors came to the American colonies from the Netherlands, and the first Hoes was born in the Kinderhook region as early as 1630. Hannah attended the same village school as Martin Van Buren. In the late 1700's, the education of girls did not go beyond the local school. Daughters usually remained close to home, as Hannah did.

Martin became interested in the law, and he worked as a clerk to a local attorney before going to work at the age of nineteen for a noted New York law office. Within two years, Martin was licensed to practice law and returned to Kinderhook as a lawyer.

Marriage and Family
Hannah has been described as the sweetheart of Martin Van Buren's youth. A portrait of her

from around the time of her marriage suggests that she was an attractive young woman. The couple waited until Martin had established himself as a lawyer before they married in February of 1807, when Hannah was twenty-four years old. The couple made their home in Kinderhook, where their son Abraham was born late in 1807. Martin's position as a lawyer took the couple to live in Hudson, where he was appointed as an attorney for the county.

In Hudson, Hannah and Martin had three more children. Their sons John and Martin were born in 1810 and 1812, respectively. A boy born after 1812 died in infancy. In 1816, Martin became the attorney for the state of New York. The family moved to the state capital, Albany, where Hannah and Martin's fifth and final son was born in January of 1819. In Albany, the Van Buren household was composed of Hannah,

Martin Van Buren

Martin Van Buren was born in 1782 in Kinderhook, New York. His family was of Dutch descent and had been residents in east central New York from the 1630's. One of nine children, Martin attended the Kinderhook Academy, only staying in school because of his promising intellect.

Van Buren's early career was that of a lawyer with judicial aspirations. Van Buren's political career began when he was appointed surrogate for Columbia County, New York, and as the local meeting chairman for the Democratic-Republican Party. Van Buren rose quickly through successive New York state and federal offices, including state senator, U.S. senator, governor, secretary of state, vice president of the United States, and eighth president of the United States.

Van Buren was an astute political operator. As a member of the Democratic-Republican Party, he led the Albany Regency, one of the first patronage political machines. Van Buren was known for rewarding his followers with appointments to state and county public offices. Remarking on his ability to make deals and use political processes to gain his ends, Van Buren was known as the Fox of Kinderhook and the Little Magician. He was also known as one the most powerful politicians of his time.

Van Buren's loyalty was most apparent in his relationship with President Andrew Jackson, who described Van Buren as "a true man with no guile." Van Buren resigned the governorship of New York to be Jackson's secretary of state. As the leader in Jackson's so-called Kitchen Cabinet, Van Buren was one of Jackson's closest advisers. In 1832 Jackson supported Van Buren to be his vice president, and in 1836 Jackson supported Van Buren as his successor.

Van Buren's presidency is generally regarded as one of the least important and least effective in U.S. history. The roots of Van Buren's problems can be tied to the Panic of 1837 and increasing tension between proslavery and abolitionist factions. The Panic of 1837 was the worst economic downturn the United States had known up to that time. The depression was made worse by the fiscal, tax, and tariff policies of the Van Buren administration. As president, Van Buren had a mixed record on slavery. He opposed the westward expansion of slavery but opposed abolition in the District of Columbia and supported states' rights within the existing slave states.

Van Buren served one term, losing his 1840 reelection bid to William Henry Harrison. Van Buren lost the 1844 Democratic presidential nomination over his refusal to accept Texas's admission to the Union as a slave state. In 1848 Van Buren ran for president on the abolitionist Barnburner ticket with support from the Free-Soil Party. After running a distant third, he retired from politics. The former president died in 1862.

Martin, their four surviving sons, Martin's law partner, and three apprentice lawyers. Letters from the time indicate that family relatives were frequent visitors to the household.

Hannah was religious throughout her life, following her family's loyalty to the Dutch Reformed religion. In the absence of a Dutch Reformed Church in Hudson or Albany, Hannah joined Presbyterian churches that were most closely associated with the Dutch Reformed faith. Hannah became a parishioner of the Reverend John Chester, who first became pastor of her church in Hudson. Chester moved to a church in Albany prior to the Van Burens' move, and Hannah again joined his church. Chester encouraged members of his congregation to help the less fortunate, and he began a Sunday school to teach poor children to read. Chester was progressive for his time, and many women in his church were unsupportive of his efforts. Hannah Van Buren, however, was among those who supported the pastor.

In 1818 Hannah became ill. The Albany winters of 1818 and 1819 were particularly cold and wet, and this may have contributed to Hannah's poor health. She did not leave her house after September of 1818, and the birth of her last child in January, 1819, further weakened her. Hannah died a few weeks later, on February 5, 1819. She was buried in the cemetery at the Reverend Chester's Presbyterian Church.

Relatively little is known about the relationship between Hannah and Martin Van Buren. Hannah died many years before Martin became president, and his autobiography does not mention Hannah. At that time in history, it was considered an insult to refer publicly to a lady. Van Buren's autobiography reflects this, and it focuses on public affairs and politics alone. Biographies of Martin Van Buren reveal little of Hannah beyond her marriage and early death.

Presidency and First Ladyship
Martin Van Buren entered the White House a widower with four unmarried sons. The little that is known of Hannah suggests that she may not have enjoyed being the wife of a president and that the Van Buren White House may have been different if she had lived to be First Lady. Hannah's obituary describes her as "modest and unassuming, possessing the most engaging simplicity of manners, her heart was the residence of every kind affection, and glowed with the sympathy for the wants . . . of others." It goes on to say that she had "no love of show, . . . no ambitious desires," and "no pride of ostentation." The public likely desired some amount of ostentation on the part of the First Lady, however, and the woman who served as hostess in the White House during the Van Buren administration was very different from Hannah.

Shortly after Van Buren's inauguration in 1837, former First Lady Dolley Madison brought Angelica Singleton, her young and attractive cousin from South Carolina, to dinner at the White House. Soon thereafter, the twenty-one-year-old Angelica was married to President Van Buren's eldest son, Abraham. Angelica came from a wealthy family, and she had attended a prestigious school in Philadelphia. President Van Buren became very fond of Angelica, and he was happy to have her act as lady of the White House. At the same time, Angelica's husband, Abraham, served as the president's private secretary.

The first event at which Angelica played hostess was the New Year's open house of 1839. The *Boston Globe* account of the event describes Angelica as "a lady of rare accomplishments . . .

American Royalty?

Angelica and Abraham Van Buren traveled to Europe in the spring of 1839, which made Angelica the first lady of the White House to travel to Europe during her tenure as First Lady. British and French royalty received Angelica and Abraham, unsure as to whether the couple should be met as American royalty. Newspapers in the United States closely followed the trip to Europe, detailing Angelica's appreciation of the royal lifestyle.

After Angelica admired the gardens and parks of the European royalty, the party in opposition to Van Buren's Democratic Party, the Whigs, accused her of proposing congressional appropriations for gardens at the White House. With the Democrats held responsible for the economic depression of 1837, Van Buren was defeated in his 1840 bid for reelection. A portrait of Angelica hangs in the Red Room of the White House, and she has been described as receiving White House visitors on a "throne" in the Blue Room.

vivacious in her conversation," and "universally admired." Angelica enjoyed public life and sought the guidance of her cousin Dolley Madison, who had considerable experience in Washington social life and as First Lady. Hannah, who had come from a less privileged background and who did not seek public attention, would likely have been less comfortable assuming the role of First Lady. Angelica, however, was very happy in her position as lady of the White House. She and Abraham lost a daughter who was born at the Executive Mansion, but they later had other children.

Legacy

Acting in the role of First Lady, Angelica Singleton Van Buren helped to establish the place of the First Lady in U.S. history. She was very popular with the press and the public, making a positive impression both as hostess in the White House and in representing the Van Buren administration abroad. Angelica and Abraham took a honeymoon trip to Europe after she had taken on the responsibilities of First Lady, making her the first sitting hostess of the President's House to travel in Europe. In 1842 the first engraving of all of the presidents' wives or hostesses, from Martha Washington to Angelica Singleton Van Buren, was produced. Angelica's tenure as lady of the White House demonstrated that someone other than a presi-

dent's wife could successfully serve in the role of First Lady.

Suggested Readings

Anthony, Carl Sferrazza. *First Ladies: The Saga of the Presidents' Wives and Their Power*. Vol. 1. New York: William Morrow, 1990. Details important events and the impact of presidential wives throughout U.S. history.

Boller, Paul F. *Presidential Wives: An Anecdotal History*. 2d ed. New York: Oxford University Press, 1999. Includes a brief account of what is known about the life of Hannah Van Buren.

Holloway, Laura Carter. *The Ladies of the White House: Or, In the Home of the Presidents*. Reprint. New York: A. M. S. Press, 1976. Describes the lives of Hannah Hoes Van Buren and Angelica Singleton Van Buren, focusing on Angelica's time as hostess in the Van Buren White House.

Lynch, Denis Tilden. *An Epoch and a Man: Martin Van Buren and His Times*. 1929. Reprint. New York: Kennikat Press, 1971. Includes a brief account of the life of Hannah Van Buren.

Whitton, Mary Ormsbee. *First First Ladies, 1789-1865: A Study of the Wives of the Early Presidents*. New York: Hastings House, 1948. Includes details of the married life and family background of Hannah Hoes Van Buren.

Virginia A. Chanley

Anna Harrison

Anna Tuthill Symmes Harrison

Born: July 25, 1775
    Wolpack Township,
      Sussex County, New Jersey
Died: February 25, 1864
    North Bend, Ohio

President: William Henry Harrison
    1841

Overview: The life of Anna Harrison gives insight into the founding and early progress of the United States. One of the earliest pioneer women to live in the Ohio and Indiana Territories, she was motherless at one year old, and her father fought in the Revolutionary War. She left the settled eastern community where she spent her first nineteen years to travel across the Appalachian Mountains and down the rivers to the new Northwest. This western land had dense, forbidding forests, areas of dank swamplands, and hostile Indians. Alongside her father and her husband, William Henry Harrison, she faced the trials and tribulations of the Western movement. Although Anna's tenure as First Lady was brief, her life was one of intelligence, courage, and strength.

Anna Harrison. *(Library of Congress)*

Early Life

The future wife of President William Henry Harrison was born Anna Tuthill Symmes. Her parents were Mr. and Mrs. John Cleves Symmes, who were married at Southold, Long Island, New York, in 1760. Two years later they had a baby girl they named Maria. John Symmes and his wife moved to Flatbrook, New

Jersey, a village by the Flatbrook River near Morristown. While living there, Symmes was assigned to a post at the New Jersey garrison for the Continental Army. When her second baby arrived on July 25, 1775, Mrs. Symmes was in very poor health. Exactly one year after Anna's birth, her mother died, on July 25, 1776. Maria was fourteen years old, and she and her father cared for baby Anna. The American Revolutionary War was under way, and at this time the British troops were gaining ground; some were moving south through New York State while others were moving north along the coast. Symmes feared for the safety of his young daughters. Determined to get his family to Long Island, out of the path of battle, he disguised himself as a British soldier and carried Anna on horseback. He cautiously maneuvered around the enemy's camps until he reached the home of his daughters' grandparents.

The Henry Daniel Tuthills were well established and respected in the Southold community. In this tranquil and very comfortable setting, Anna was well loved. The Tuthills were devout Presbyterians. Each day was filled with devotions, religious training, and educational pursuits. At her grandmother's side, Anna learned the joy and importance of being a good cook and gardener. She attended the Clinton Academy, located near East Hampton. Later she studied at Miss Isabella Graham's Academy, a boarding school in New York City. At these institutions she received an excellent classics education. These early years provided Anna with inner confidence, a strong work ethic, and social grace. In times of sorrow and tragedy, her religious faith sustained her.

The Revolutionary War ended in 1783, and Symmes settled in New York City, where he was appointed to the Continental Congress (1785-1787). It was during this time that he heard about land speculation of the Western territory. These were the lands later to become Ohio and Indiana. Symmes bought one million acres between the Great Miami and the Little Miami Rivers, both of which flow into the Ohio River. On February 19, 1788, the U.S. Congress appointed him judge of the Northwest Territory. It was a goal of the newly formed government to promote settlement; the judgeship gave Symmes the legal authority to divide the land into parcels for sale to homesteaders. In the next few years, Symmes's acreage was reduced to 311,682 because he could not raise the money to pay for more than that amount of land. He built a cabin at North Bend, in what is now Ohio. His second wife, Mary H. Halsey, of whom little is known, died two or three years after their marriage. Symmes was lonely and returned to New York City, eager to see his daughter. In the same year, 1788, Maria Symmes married Major Peyton Short and moved to Lexington, Kentucky, near Fort Harrod. While visiting in New York and New Jersey, Judge Symmes met and married Susanna Livingston, daughter of New Jersey governor William Livingston. Symmes collected his young daughter Anna and, with Susanna, returned to North Bend. Susanna and Anna became very close companions and remained dear friends throughout their lives.

Maria Symmes Short invited Anna and their stepmother to spend the winter months at Lexington. Judge Symmes agreed this would be good for the two women. At Lexington they could have some social life and conveniences which were not available to them at North Bend. Another advantage was that they would be safe from any Indian attacks. The year was 1795 and Anna was twenty years old. She had developed into a poised and gracefully beautiful woman with a serious manner despite her youthfulness. She was about five feet, one inch tall and had a slender figure, lustrous dark hair, and large brown eyes. Her skin was smooth and fair. She had a dimpled chin and full lips.

At this time a group of soldiers had been sent to Lexington for a well-earned rest from the fighting that was being waged from Fort

William Henry Harrison

William Henry Harrison, the seventh child of Benjamin Harrison V, a signer of the Declaration of Independence, and his wife, Elizabeth Bassett Harrison, was born on February 9, 1773, at Berkeley, the family home on the James River near Williamsburg, Virginia. He was raised a devout Episcopalian. From his early youth, Harrison planned on being a doctor, so he attended Hamden-Sydney College. After his father died, however, Harrison was left penniless. A close friend of his father suggested he continue his education and training through military service. Harrison respected the military as his chosen field of endeavor. His dedication to his duty to his country enabled thousands of homesteaders to move West.

He married Anna Tuthill Symmes, with whom he had ten children. One child, James Findlay, died after the first year of life. Eight children grew to adulthood but died before Harrison became president. The only surviving child was John Scott.

Harrison had an excellent background for the times in which he lived. He served as secretary of the Northwest in 1798, territorial delegate to Congress from 1799 to 1801, territorial governor of Indiana from 1801 to 1813, United States congressman from 1816 to 1819, U.S. senator from 1825 to 1828, and minister to Colombia from 1828 to 1829. His name became well known and admired by the public when he led the Army to a successful win at the Battle of Tippecanoe. From that time on, he carried the nickname Old Tippecanoe or Old Tip. The Battle of Thames secured his status as the great general of the West. It was these events that brought him to national prominence. He was elected the United States' ninth president.

Detroit to the Ohio River. Among this group of men was Lieutenant William Henry Harrison from Virginia. He was a seasoned soldier who, upon his arrival as a young novice from the East, had been assigned to General Arthur St. Clair's Fort Washington. Under St. Clair's loose command, William learned that a young soldier confined to the fort life could easily fall into heavy drinking and dueling. Quickly, William decided to spend his time reading military tactics books and English literature.

At a social gathering at Lexington, William and Anna were very attracted to each other. Near the close of the winter season, William was sent back to war, as an aide to General Anthony Wayne. Anna waited anxiously for her sweetheart to return. This "waiting" for her William would become a big part of her life. The fighting came to a temporary close, and William headed back to North Bend with three hundred dollars of borrowed money and two packhorses. He had one thought in mind, to marry Anna Symmes. He asked permission of Judge Symmes and received a resounding no for an answer. The judge wrote his dear friend Robert Morris in New Brunswick, New Jersey:

> A Mr. Harrison, son of the late Governor Harrison of Virginia, and presently a captain in the army and aide-de-camp to General Wayne has made Nancy [Anna] the offer of his hand, but he has not yet received an answer from me, tho' I know not how to state objections, save that as yet, we are all too much strangers to each other. The young man has prudence, education and resources in conversation, about 300 [dollars] property but what is to be lamented is that he has no profession but that of army.

Marriage and Family

When the judge left on a business trip, Anna and William eloped on November 25, 1795. To date, Anna Harrison is the only First Lady of the United States to have eloped.

Again Judge Symmes wrote to Robert Morris: "If I knew what to make of Captain Harrison, I could easily make proper arrangements for his family, but he can neither bleed, plead, nor preach and if he could just plow, I would be satisfied." Symmes and William, over time, began to meld their shared interest in Anna. Also, William proved that he could distinguish himself in battle and as a leader of men. General Wayne had high regard for Harrison.

On September 29, 1796, the Harrisons' first child, Elizabeth Bassett (Betsy), was born. They were at North Bend while William commanded Fort Washington at Cincinnati. John Cleves Symmes Harrison was born in 1798. The growing family needed their own home, so William bought 169 acres of his father-in-law's property. On it, Anna and William built a log cabin. Harrison had been appointed territorial delegate to the United States House of Representatives. Anna had not been East since she left New York City and must have been excited, as the wife of Delegate Harrison, to participate in that city's society. Anna, William, Betsy, and John then went south to Richmond, Virginia, to visit some of William's family; Anna had never before met any of her husband's relatives. While in Richmond, she had her third child, a baby girl, Lucy Singleton, in 1800.

When at the new capital of the United States of America, Harrison was appointed governor of the Indiana Territory as well as superintendent of Indian affairs. The Harrisons and their three children moved from North Bend—near Cincinnati and Fort Washington—to Vincennes, Indiana, in 1801. Grouseland, the home-fortress they built there, was in the middle of Indian territory. Most of the local Indians had been given supplies by the British. Tecumseh, their leader, had organized the tribes to fight as one, when necessary.

Many an Indian council meeting took place at Grouseland, where Anna cooked and served meals to soldiers, dignitaries, and Indians alike. At Grouseland, their family increased to nine children with the births of William Henry (1802), John Scott (1804), Benjamin (1806), Mary Symmes (1809), Carter Bassett (1811), and Anna Tuthill (1812). William wrote to President Thomas Jefferson, thanking him for his renewal of commission:

> I received the new commission and I beg you to receive my warmest thanks for this additional proof of your confidence and friendship. The emoluments of my office afford me a decent support and I will hope—enable me to lay up a small fund for the education of my children. I have hitherto found, however, that my nursery grows faster than my strong box.

Anna took full responsibility for her children's education and religious teachings. She handled the gardening and management of the animals and land. She was a careless bookkeeper, however, whose finances were never quite balanced. From the beginning of her marriage, there always seemed to be some debt. In her other endeavors, Anna was praised. Guests in her home spoke of her delightful manner, entertaining skills, and beauty.

During the war years, Anna had to be prepared mentally, emotionally, and physically to protect her children against rogue Indian raids. Each time her husband said goodbye, she knew it could be the last time she and her children would see him or that he could be returned wounded. Many wives returned to the eastern states, including her dear stepmother, and Anna could have too. It was not frowned upon, the West being understood to be no place for a lady. She stayed, however, believing in her husband's duty to his country. In 1811 William and his troops defeated the Shawnee leader Tenskwatawa, known as the Prophet, at the Battle of Tippecanoe.

The War of 1812 erupted, and William was promoted to brigadier general of the regular Army. Anna was sent to safety in Cincinnati, along with their nine children. She also took her ailing father, whose home had recently burned to the ground. Anna found the two years she spent in Cincinnati especially enjoyable. The Presbyterian Sunday school her children attended and the beautiful church music reminded her of her childhood on Long Island.

When the war ended, William returned a hero from the Battle of the Thames. The family went back to North Bend. In 1813 Symmes named his son-in-law executor of his estate. The judge died the following year. The Harrisons moved their plain little house from its original 169-acre plot to a new location and

The Matriarch of the New Northwest

Anna Harrison's husband, William Henry Harrison, was assigned by President Thomas Jefferson the job of organizing northern Louisiana after the Louisiana Purchase agreement was completed. Harrison did not want to leave his family again and asked to be relieved of this duty, but the president said no.

Harrison, his wife, and three children settled at Grouseland, the home they built in Vincennes, Indiana, in 1801. Anna and William modeled their house after Berkeley, the Harrison family plantation in Virginia, but the façade was where the resemblance ended. Grouseland was the first home to be built of brick in all the region. It had four chimneys and was two and one-half stories high. The brick walls were eighteen inches thick. Upper stories of the house were loopholed for defense, and the attic windows were broad enough to accommodate sharpshooters. Sturdy double doors were added. In the cellar, a powder magazine was surrounded by huge masonry. Upstairs, a trap door led to a rooftop lookout station. There were secret passages running from closet to closet that led to the cellar, to ensure escape in case of surprise attack. From the cellar there was a tunnel to the bank of the Wabash River. With William's frequent absences, this fortress was Anna's home for herself and the children. The constant threat of Indian raids or attacks by rogue Indian snipers worried her deeply.

When William was home, and also during his frequent absences, Anna's duties continued as teacher to her children and minister of religion. A change in the routine came only rarely, when a circuit rider stopped by. The news the rider brought was as welcome as the chance to offer hospitality; both lessened the loneliness of frontier living.

Anna also had guests when an impending battle brought soldiers, many accompanied by their wives, to Grouseland. William took every musket, all the gunpowder, and every recruit to meet the enemy. The wives were left for Anna to manage. She tended one woman with ague and high fever as well as those with other ailments. Anna cared for her children and the soldiers' children, and she prepared all the meals. She posted some wives as lookouts. Nearby homesteaders, alone in open space, were easy targets for the Indians. Their houses were burned, and family members were carried off by the attackers. If the Indians had learned about all the women at Grouseland, unprotected and with no real weapons, an attack would almost certainly have ensued. When a communique was received at Grouseland, Lydia Bacon, a soldier's wife, took note of it, saying, "Oh what a day was that, we heard of the Battle. . . . all break into tears." Anna's feelings must well have been expressed in the same manner. The war-weary soldiers returned, took their wives, and left for their own homes. Anna, tending and caring for her husband, openly thanked the Lord for William's safe return.

The only place of Anna's Western residences to survive, Grouseland still stands, with bullet holes as evidence of battle. The building is open to the public today.

expanded it to twenty-two rooms. They called it The Bend. That year, their last child was born, a son. He was named James Findlay, after their close friend General James Findlay. The city of Findlay, Ohio, is named for General Findlay.

Anna hoped to have her husband remain near home, but her hopes were short-lived. William was elected to Congress in 1816. Upon leaving Washington, D.C., he was elected to the Ohio state senate (1819-21). In 1824 he returned to Washington as a United States senator. While William was away, James Findlay died, at less than three years of age. Between 1820 and 1847, Anna saw the deaths of all their children, save one, John Scott. It was this son who was the father of President Benjamin W. Harrison (1889-1893). Anna Harrison is the only First Lady who had a grandson elected to the presidency of the United States.

Presidency and First Ladyship

While General Harrison, the "War Hero of 1812," was being touted for the presidency, Anna, at this time in her life, just wanted to be home with her husband at The Bend. Pa and Nancy, as they affectionately called each other, were not only partners, they had a lifelong love. They did not seek any political reward for his military service. However, the new nation beckoned, and the slogan of Tippecanoe and Tyler Too was heard everywhere from the Atlantic seaboard to Indiana State.

William Henry Harrison became the ninth president. Anna did not accompany her husband to Washington, D.C. She planned to join him as soon as she recovered from influenza and completed the packing. A number of his relatives did accompany him, including Jane Irwin Harrison, the widow of their son William.

At sixty-five, Anna was the oldest wife of a president to date, and he, at sixty-eight, was the oldest president. During Harrison's hour-long inaugural address in the bitter cold of March, 1841, he developed a serious cold and flu and died one month after taking office,

making his administration's term the shortest in U.S. history.

Legacy

The last twenty years of Anna's life were spent at North Bend. Diligently, through letters and friends, she pursued the right to have franking (free postal service) and a pension of twenty-five thousand dollars as the wife of a former president. An avid reader and correspondent, she kept in close contact with friends and relatives. Anna always maintained her interests in current events, especially political matters, criticizing the direction of the Democratic Party on national policy. Her contact with family was illustrated well when she wrote her grandson Benjamin Harrison, president of the United States from 1889 to 1893, that he should serve in the Civil War. Anna followed the news of the Civil War closely. She opposed slavery, as did all her family.

Born during the Revolutionary War, in 1775, she died at the close of the Civil War, in 1864. During her lifetime she witnessed both the formation and the preservation of the Union. A woman who had left the comfort and security of New York, where she was in the top echelon of society, had lived in a cabin in North Bend, with only a fireplace for heat and no conveniences at all. There were almost no women at North Bend, and none of her background; only fur traders, adventurers, and soldiers from Fort Washington. For a dignified, educated, and cultured lady, Anna defied most preconceptions. Though she spent her entire adult life as a pioneer wife on the edge of the rough and dangerous wilderness, the roughness never became part of her manner. As a mother, she kept her children close and guided their education and religion.

Without the wives and mothers who were her contemporaries, the plains states and lands west of the Mississippi River would not have been settled until much later.

Suggested Readings

Anthony, Carl Sferrazza. *First Ladies: The Saga of the Presidents' Wives and Their Power.* Vol. 1. New York: William Morrow, 1990. A unique glimpse at the changing role of the First Lady.

Boller, Paul F. *Presidential Wives: An Anecdotal History.* 2d ed. New York: Oxford University Press, 1999. Boller devotes a chapter to every First Lady from Martha Washington to Hillary Rodham Clinton.

Cleaves, Freeman. *Old Tippecanoe: William Henry Harrison and His Time.* New York: Charles Scribner's Sons, 1939. Focuses primarily on William Henry Harrison's experiences in Indiana and early history of the region.

Goebel, Dorothy. *William Henry Harrison: A Political Biography.* Philadelphia: Porcupine Press, 1974. Originally published as part of the Indiana Library's Historical Collection. Includes bibliography

Green, James. *William Henry Harrison: His Life and Times.* Richmond, Va.: Garrett and Massie, c. 1941. Illustrated.

Healy, Diana Dixon. *America's First Ladies: Private Lives of the Presidential Wives.* New York: Atheneum, 1988. An entertaining yet insightful look at the women who would be First Ladies.

Whitton, Mary Ormsbee. *First Ladies, 1789-1865: A Study of the Wives of the Early Presidents.* New York: Hastings House, 1948. The biographical chapter on Anna Harrison gives a detailed sense of the environments in which she lived.

Mary J. C. Queen

Letitia Tyler

Letitia Christian Tyler

Born: November 12, 1790
     Cedar Grove, Virginia
Died: September 10, 1842
     Washington, D.C.

President: John Tyler
     1841-1845

Overview: The Tyler White House was distinguished by two First Ladies. First Lady Letitia Tyler suffered a stroke two years before her husband assumed the presidency, leaving her unable to serve as hostess at the White House. Letitia's daughter-in-law, Priscilla Cooper Tyler, served as lady of the White House in Letitia's place. Letitia died in 1842, and in 1844, President John Tyler married Julia Gardiner. The Tyler presidency ended in early 1845, with Julia thus serving as First Lady for a period of eight months. Despite this short tenure, Julia left her mark on the First Ladyship.

Letitia Tyler. *(Courtesy of Craig Shermer, National First Ladies' Library)*

Early Life

Letitia Christian was one of six daughters born to Colonel Robert Christian and Mary Brown Christian. The Christians were a wealthy Virginia plantation family. Letitia adopted the conventions of Southern agricultural society of the time and learned how to successfully manage a household and be attentive to the concerns and interests of the man of the house. In the tradition of the time, the lady of the plantation acquiesced to the wishes of her husband.

Letitia is described as very attractive in both physical beauty and character, and she received several offers of marriage. Some of these offers would have made her much wealthier in marriage than her choice of John Tyler did. Initially,

John Tyler

John Tyler was born in 1790 on a Virginia plantation. He was educated at the College of William and Mary and graduated in 1807. He then studied law and became an attorney.

In 1811 Tyler was elected to the Virginia state legislature. In 1816 he was elected to the U.S. House of Representatives. Tyler was an ardent supporter of states' rights and a strict constructionist in his interpretation of the Constitution. During his tenure in Congress, Tyler opposed the rising power of the federal government. After numerous defeats, Tyler resigned his seat in the House in 1821. In 1823 Tyler was again elected to the Virginia state legislature. In 1825 he was elected governor of Virginia. The following year he was elected to the U.S. Senate.

In 1824 he had supported the election of John Quincy Adams. Tyler, however, came to oppose Adams' subsequent proposals for federal regulations on commerce and agriculture, switching his support to Andrew Jackson in the next presidential election. Tyler again became disaffected with his presidential choice when he believed that the Jackson administration sought to expand federal power at the expense of states' rights.

Dissatisfied with all factions within the Democratic Party, Tyler joined the Whig Party. The Whigs were an unlikely coalition of groups united to oppose Jackson but were bitterly divided over issues of nationalism and states' rights. In 1840 the Whigs selected William Henry Harrison as their presidential nominee and Tyler as the vice presidential nominee. The subjects of the popular slogan Tippecanoe and Tyler Too were successful, and Harrison was sworn in as ninth president in March, 1841. A month later, however, Harrison died of pneumonia.

At that time the constitutional procedure for vice presidential succession was unclear. Many argued that Tyler should be the interim president until new elections could be held. Tyler held that he succeeded Harrison and had himself sworn in as the tenth president. Although both houses of Congress passed resolutions recognizing Tyler as president, critics referred to Tyler as His Accidency, and many continued to question the legitimacy of his presidency.

Most of Tyler's tenure involved running feuds with Congress over limiting federal power. Tyler's two lasting achievements, clarifying vice presidential succession and convincing Congress to annex Texas by joint resolution rather than by means explicitly specified in the Constitution, were departures from his strict Federalist ideals.

After leaving office, Tyler returned to farming and practicing law in Virginia. When Virginia succeeded from the Union in the Civil War, Tyler was elected to the Confederate Congress at Richmond. He suffered a stroke, however, and died before taking office.

Letitia's parents were not pleased with her attachment to John. Robert Christian was a strong supporter of Federalist principles, whereas John followed his father's support for the Democratic-Republican principles of Thomas Jefferson. It was several years before Letitia's family gave their support to her marriage to John.

Marriage and Family

After several years of courtship, Letitia married John in 1813. They were both twenty-three.

John's father was governor of Virginia, and John's plan was to follow his father's career path as lawyer and politician. At the age of twenty-one, as a rising young lawyer, John had been elected to the Virginia House of Delegates. John was the second son in his family, and he and Letitia began married life in a modest farm home. In 1816 John was elected to the U.S. Congress. After three years in Congress, he sold their first home and bought a larger farm home known as Woodburn, the first in a succession of

The First Lady Behind the Scenes

First Lady Letitia Tyler entered the White House largely paralyzed by a stroke and unable to assume the public duties of the First Lady. Behind the scenes, however, Letitia helped to direct her daughter-in-law, Priscilla Cooper Tyler, who performed the role of hostess in the White House until the time of Letitia's death. Priscilla had been an actress before her marrying the president's son, and her acting experience helped her assume the position of lady of the White House.

As recounted in Robert Seager II's book *And Tyler Too*, Priscilla provides a description of her mother-in-law shortly after they met for the first time in 1839:

[She] must have been very beautiful in her youth, for she is still beautiful now in her declining years and wretched health. . . . she is gentle and graceful in her movements, with a most peculiar air of native refinement about everything she says and does. She is the most entirely unselfish person you can imagine. I do not believe she ever thinks of herself. Her whole thought and affections are wrapped up in her husband and children. . . . The room in the main dwelling furtherest removed and most retired is "the chamber," as the bedroom of the mistress of the house is always called in Virginia . . . here Mother with a smile of welcome on her sweet, calm face, is . . . always ready to sympathize with me in any little homesickness which may disturb me. . . . Notwithstanding her very delicate health, Mother attends to and regulates all the household affairs, and all so quietly that you can't tell when she does it. All the clothes for the children, and for the servants, are cut out under her immediate eye, and all the sewing is personally superintended by her. All the cake, jellies, custards, and we indulge largely in them, emanate from her, yet you see no confusion, hear no bustle, but only meet the agreeable result.

plantations that he and Letitia would inhabit.

Their first child, Mary, was born in 1814, followed by Robert, John, Letitia, Elizabeth, Alice, and Tazewell. The couple had two other children, both of whom died in infancy. Following the deaths of her last two children, Letitia's health was poor. Despite her failing health, she remained actively involved in the lives of her family, raising her children, overseeing the household, and providing counsel to her husband.

Throughout their married life, Letitia successfully took charge of the responsibilities of maintaining a home and plantation. From Congress, John went on to become governor of New York, followed by his return to Washington, D.C., as a senator. During John's years in the House and Senate, Letitia remained primarily at their home in Virginia. Without her support for his public life and attention to their eco-

nomic affairs, John would have been unable to devote himself so completely to his political career.

Letitia was a religious woman. One of her daughters wrote that among her earliest memories of her mother was being taught the alphabet from the family Bible. In her later years, Letitia kept a Bible on a table by the side of her armchair. Although she wholeheartedly supported her husband's pursuits, Letitia shunned public life for herself. During John's tenure as governor of Virginia, she performed duties that were required by custom, but she only once went to Washington in the years before John succeeded to the presidency, upon the death of President William Henry Harrison.

Presidency and First Ladyship

John unexpectedly became president after President Harrison died, barely a month after his inauguration. John took the oath of office and moved into the White House within ten days of Harrison's death. Partially paralyzed by a stroke in 1839, Letitia entered the White House as an invalid. Although she was unable to take on the public duties of First Lady, she continued to oversee the affairs of her household.

Letitia's daughters were either married with their own homes or too young to assume the full responsibility for entertaining at the White House. Letitia's daughter-in-law Priscilla Cooper Tyler, aged twenty-four, had been an actress before her marriage. Letitia and Priscilla got along very well, and Priscilla was happy to play the role of lady of the White House, taking advice from Letitia. Letitia also supervised other household affairs at the White House, delegating responsibilities to her daughter Letitia.

First Lady Letitia Tyler's only public appearance at the White House was for the wedding of her daughter Elizabeth in January, 1842. In September, 1842, Letitia became the first First Lady to die in the White House. A period of mourning at the Executive Mansion followed, during which the usual social activities there were curtailed. Daughter Letitia took over management of the household for her father.

Early in 1843, the period of mourning ended and John again began to greet visitors at the White House. In February, the president invited guests onboard the war steamer *Princeton* for a day's outing on the Potomac River. An explosion on the *Princeton* resulted in the death of five men, including the father of young Julia Gardiner. After Letitia's death, President Tyler had developed an attraction to the young woman, and he reportedly carried a fainting Julia off the steamer that day. Shortly thereafter, Julia accepted a marriage proposal from the president, although the engagement was not made public. It was not until after their wedding on June 26, 1844, that President Tyler and Julia Gardiner Tyler announced their marriage

to the public. Julia's beauty and vivaciousness were remarked upon widely before her marriage to John. Marriage did not change her outgoing nature, though she was clearly devoted to her husband.

Julia served as First Lady in the White House for the final eight months of the Tyler presidency. Her family background and her education at a fashionable New York finishing school prepared her well for a public role as First Lady. She presided over lively dinner parties at the White House and received praise for her conduct as First Lady. Some proposed that Julia behaved in too regal a manner in her position, but public support for her appears to have been greater than public criticism of her. In private, some of Letitia's children did not approve of their father's new wife, valuing Letitia's more reserved nature and criticizing what some saw as pretension and vanity in Julia. Publicly, however, Letitia's children followed their mother's dutiful nature, and they did not openly criticize their father's choice of a bride.

Legacy

As an invalid, First Lady Letitia Christian Tyler had little influence on the office of the First Lady, although she did continue the established tradition of having a surrogate take the place of the First Lady in the absence or inability of the First Lady to serve. Julia Gardiner Tyler made more of a mark as First Lady. Julia was instrumental in beginning the tradition of playing "Hail to the Chief" to honor the public appearance of the president. Julia was a strong advocate for her husband's political views, and she was instrumental in helping President Tyler gain support for the annexation of Texas to the Union.

Suggested Readings

Boller, Paul F. *Presidential Wives: An Anecdotal History.* 2d ed. New York: Oxford University Press, 1999. Summarizes the lives of Letitia and Julia Tyler and identifies interesting anecdotes about the lives of each of the presidential wives.

Coleman, Elizabeth Tyler. *Priscilla Cooper Tyler and the American Scene: 1816-1889*. University: University of Alabama Press, 1955. Details the life and times of President John Tyler's daughter-in-law, who served as hostess in the White House from 1841 to 1844.

Holloway, Laura Carter. *The Ladies of the White House: Or, In the Home of the Presidents*. Reprint. New York: A. M. S. Press, 1976. Holloway includes information on Letitia Tyler that is based on family memories.

Seager, Robert. *And Tyler Too*. New York: McGraw-Hill, 1962. A biography of both John and Julia Gardiner Tyler.

Whitton, Mary Ormsbee. *First First Ladies, 1789-1865: A Study of the Wives of the Early Presidents*. New York: Hastings House, 1948. Includes the highlights of the life of First Lady Letitia Christian Tyler and contrasts Letitia Tyler with John Tyler's second wife, First Lady Julia Gardiner Tyler.

Willets, Gilson. *Inside History of the White House*. New York: Christian Herald, 1908. A good source for information on Letitia Tyler and her daughter Letitia Tyler Semple.

Virginia A. Chanley

Julia Tyler

Julia Gardiner Tyler

Born: May 4, 1820
    Gardiners Island, New York
Died: July 10, 1889
    Richmond, Virginia

President: John Tyler
    1841-1845

Overview: Julia Tyler was an atypical First Lady for her time. She set a regal standard for the White House, thus elevating the presidency, by all appearances, to one of American nobility. As the wife of John Tyler, the first vice president to ascend to the presidency upon the death of an incumbent, Julia blazed her own trail. She was young and flirtatious, had courtly manners, and used her looks and tenacity to gain public and legislative support for both her and her husband's causes. She remains today as one of a select few First Ladies whose beauty, poise, and stature drew the attention of the entire nation.

Julia Tyler. *(Courtesy of Craig Shermer, National First Ladies' Library)*

Early Life

Julia's father, David Gardiner, was a descendant of English immigrants who had come to America and settled in Connecticut in 1635. Her grandfather Lion Gardiner had purchased a 3,300-acre island off the eastern tip of Long Island, New York, which bore the family's name: Gardiners Island. Julia Gardiner was born the third of four children on May 4, 1820, to David and Juliana Gardiner. She was the Gardiners' first daughter, and she grew up in the posh surroundings of East Hampton, Long Island.

A Yale College graduate, Julia's father practiced law in New York, managed the family's extensive property holdings, and was later elected to the New York state senate. Juliana McLachlan Gardiner, Julia's mother, was the daughter of a wealthy brewmaster. She was known to have been highly opinionated and exerted a dominating influence over the lives of her husband and children.

In 1835 Julia began her formal education at boarding school. She attended Madame N. D. Chagaray's Institute in New York City. Her major studies of interest were arithmetic, history, English composition, French literature, and music. Brought up to believe in her own social superiority, she also internalized her father's deep fear of monetary insolvency. Julia was considered quite beautiful for her day. Short and slightly plump, with dark eyes and black hair, she was high-spirited and adept at flirtation, which, along with her family's social prominence, would serve her well in her adult life.

Julia was learned in social propriety, but as an adventurous young lady, she pushed the bounds of propriety by posing for a Bogarty & Macamly dry goods and clothing store lithograph advertisement in 1839. This was the first time a lady of New York's upper class had personally endorsed a retail establishment. The well-to-do Gardiners were so embarrassed by Julia's overt impropriety that, in 1840, they took her away from New York City until things settled down. Julia's travels included a year-long excursion to Europe, where she found herself attracting a number of prominent suitors before her return home in the late summer of 1841.

In 1842 Julia's father took her to Washington, D.C., for the winter season. The Gardiners' wealth granted Julia access to the elite circles of Washington society. It was through attending these social gatherings that Julia would eventually be invited to the White House and introduced to the recently widowed President John Tyler.

An 1840 lithograph shows Julia Gardiner, four years before she married President John Tyler, carrying a placard which reads, "I'll purchase at Bogert and Mecamly's . . ." *(Library of Congress)*

Marriage and Family

Julia's flirtatious nature attracted prestigious suitors

from the U.S. Congress and Supreme Court. However, she was most taken by President Tyler; at fifty-four, he was thirty years her elder. In 1844 they both attended a social event aboard the warship USS *Princeton*. During the firing of a new cannon, the gun exploded, killing several guests, including Julia's father, Senator Gardiner. After this tragic incident Julia grew closer to the president. After several proposals she finally agreed to marry him. They were wed in a quiet ceremony in New York City at the Church of the Ascension on June 26, 1844. Her bridesmaid was her sister, Margaret, and the best man was her brother Alexander. Several of John's seven children from his first wife, Letitia Christian Tyler, were hurt and angered by his marriage to twenty-four-year-old Julia, and it took many years for some of them to accept her as their stepmother. After a short honeymoon at the Tylers' Virginia estate, Sherwood Forest, the couple quickly returned to Washington and the White House.

By all accounts, their marriage was a loving one. They enjoyed music, and John, a well-trained violinist, was often accompanied by Julia on guitar. They also were avid animal lovers, maintaining a menagerie of pets at Sherwood Forest. Julia Tyler was a wealthy Northerner who had embraced the southern lifestyle, complete with its grandiose, slave-run plantations. She and her northern relatives consistently were at strained relations as the Civil War grew nearer, and she freely talked of her acceptance of states' rights, slavery, and secession. Her marriage to John gave her prestige and a broader social life both in the North and in the South.

One known drawback to their marriage was that John was quite jealous of Julia's flirtations. Even after her marriage, Julia continued to flirt with powerful and prestigious gentlemen who she felt could benefit her own causes as well as those of her husband. Though she did openly use her looks and position for her own devices, there is no evidence that she was

ever unfaithful to her husband. Their romantic life flourished, as their seventh and last child was born when John was a spry seventy years old.

Presidency and First Ladyship

Julia Tyler, as the new First Lady, took Washington by storm in dazzling style. She viewed the office of president as royalty and was determined that it should be represented as such. With only eight short months remaining in the president's term, Julia wasted no time in elevating the appearance and prestige of the White House. Although carrying on the official mourning period for her late father, she wore extravagant gowns in the mourning colors of white and black. She also wore jewelry, including one strand of jewels about her forehead that gave the appearance of a crown.

Mrs. Tyler also took her brief role as First Lady as an opportunity to brighten the White House walls. She was one of the first to begin extensive renovations to portions of the dark and dilapidated structure. She worked both to brighten the house physically and to make it the social centerpiece for Washington, if not the nation.

She hosted a number of opulent balls and invited huge crowds of the United States' most prominent persons to attend. Once the word was out about her social masterpieces, she began to drastically shorten the guest lists, making the mystique of her invitations even more sought-after. She introduced the polka at her balls; this dance, which the president had forbidden his children to try, was all at once the forbidden rage of the nation.

Extremely conscious of public impression, Mrs. Tyler made history with the "hiring" of a press agent as well as befriending many news correspondents who would write her praises in their news releases. She was insistent upon coverage of her events in the newspapers catering to the social set, and she was not above writing her own reviews and getting them into print.

John Tyler

John Tyler attended the College of William and Mary and became a lawyer after having studied with Edmund Randolph, the first U.S. attorney general. Tyler passed the bar examination in 1809. During the War of 1812, he joined the militia and was assigned to help defend Richmond, Virginia, but saw no action.

His political career began in earnest with his election to the Virginia House of Delegates in 1811. During his tenure he led the efforts to censure U.S. senators from Virginia for supporting legislation for the Bank of the United States. Tyler left the House of Delegates in 1816 after his election to the U.S. House of Representatives. There, he led the opposition to the Missouri Compromise; an act of legislation that he later reflected as having set the United States on its course toward the Civil War. He resigned his seat in 1821.

Later, in 1823, he was again elected to the Virginia House of Delegates. He served in this capacity until 1825, when he was elected governor. In that office, Tyler tried unsuccessfully to garner support for issues surrounding education, transportation, and state infrastructure improvements. He served as governor until 1827, when he was elected to the U.S. Senate. His service in the Senate was similar to his earlier service in the House of Representatives. Seemingly always on the opposing side of issues, he resigned his seat in protest in 1836.

Tyler was an unsuccessful candidate for the vice presidency in 1836. He was again elected to the Virginia House of Delegates (1838-1840). The Whig party chose him to run for vice president in 1839, which he won. Upon the untimely death of President William Henry Harrison in 1841, Tyler became the tenth president of the United States. He was the first vice president to ascend to the presidency upon the death of an incumbent.

As president, Tyler opposed almost all major legislation from his own Whig party. All but one of his cabinet members resigned during the course of 1841. Tyler opposed the re-creation of the Bank of the United States. He signed the Preemption Act (1841), which provided squatters the right to buy federal lands; the Webster-Ashburton Treaty (1842), which set the boundary between the United States and Canada; the Treaty of Wanghia (1844), by which China granted access to certain ports; and the Annexation of Texas Joint Resolution of Congress (1845). The state of Florida was formally admitted into the Union in 1845.

Tyler was a strong states' rights advocate who supported the right to own slaves. He opposed federally funded activities for national infrastructure improvements and armed intervention into issues within the states and territories. He was also a strict believer in the separation of church and state. Strong-willed but often in poor health, he was more often than not on the minority side of legislative policy arguments.

That Julia could be seen as young and daring was no doubt an attribute that attracted the president. The ever-so-young Mrs. Tyler drove around Washington in a carriage pulled by fine horses. Julia received her guests seated in a large, formal chair on a raised platform, as though imitating a queen, surrounded by several elegantly dressed "ladies-in-waiting." She was also the first incumbent president's wife to pose for a daguerreotype, the earliest form of photography.

Legacy

A glamour girl of her day, Julia Gardiner Tyler brought to the White House definite views on how the world should regard the president and the First Lady of the United States. Julia was considered by many to be the most beautiful

First Lady up to that time. She brought style, elegance, and a heightened sense of regality to the White House. Like many of the First Ladies before her, she was devoted to her husband as a spouse, a working partner, and a confidante on legislative issues. She sought publicity to impress both her admirers and her critics. By elevating herself in the eyes of her peers, she also elevated her husband.

It was she who made the playing of "Hail to the Chief" a regular part of the introduction of the president at public appearances. She also helped her husband win legislative battles while in office and even continued to promote his contributions to the country long after his death.

After leaving the White House, John and Julia had seven children: David Gardiner "Gardie" Tyler (1846-1927), John Alexander "Alex" Tyler (1848-1883), Julia Gardiner Tyler (1849-1871), Lachlan Tyler (1851-1902), Lyon Gardiner Tyler (1853-1935), Robert Fitzwalter "Fitz" Tyler (1856-1927), and Pearl Tyler (1860-1947). The Tylers raised their children as Episcopalians although, in 1872, Julia and her youngest daughter converted to Roman Catholicism.

Julia also believed in the supernatural and in the prescient power of her dreams. In January, 1862, John Tyler—the only past U.S. president to serve in the Confederacy—was preparing to take his seat in the Confederate Congress. Julia joined her seventy-one-year-old husband in Richmond, Virginia, days before the two had planned to meet because she had dreamt that her husband was very ill. Upon arrival, Julia did indeed find him gravely ill. He died only two days later.

Following her husband's death, she was left with seven children to raise and educate, and her land holdings were in great debt. After the Civil War she was forced to sell one of her estates to the federal government for a fraction of its value, but she managed to maintain and even rebuild the war-ravaged Sherwood Forest. Julia also spent a number of years fighting for her right as a past First Lady to receive a pension. Because she was a Confederate sympathizer, Congress did not look favorably on this issue. She did finally win a five-year battle for a pension of five thousand dollars annually, which was equal to that received by the other living former First Ladies in 1882.

Julia spent the later years of her life trying to keep the memory of her husband's accomplishments alive. She died in 1889 following a stroke

Julia's Texas

Julia Tyler made the president's ambitious push for the annexation of Texas into her own political campaign. She used her well-honed flirting skills and social clout to sway legislators to favor the annexation. When the joint resolution was first published, Julia quickly distributed copies within Washington and sent more to New York.

Word of her lobbying efforts soon made its way around the country. One of the first cartoons ever to link a First Lady with a political issue was printed concerning the Texas annexation. It depicted the president standing at a fork in the road with one way leading to reelection and the other, which he was shown favoring, being a path marked Texas, down which Julia could be seen strolling. When the debate made it to the floor of the House, it was the stunning Julia who made an appearance in the visitors' gallery.

The passage of the Texas Annexation Resolution was as much Julia's work as that of the president. The president was so taken by his wife's devotion that he gave her the gold pen he used to sign the proclamation. She attached the pen to her necklace and wore it for all to see and admire.

and was laid to rest next to John in Hollywood Cemetery in Richmond, Virginia.

Suggested Readings

Anthony, Carl Sferrazza. *First Ladies: The Saga of the Presidents' Wives and Their Power*. Vol. 1. New York: William Morrow, 1990. A unique glimpse at the power and prestige in the evolving role of the First Lady.

Boller, Paul F. *Presidential Anecdotes*. 2d ed. New York: Oxford University Press, 1999. A collection of concise historical chapters on the presidents and their families.

Caroli, Betty Boyd. *First Ladies*. Expanded ed. New York: Oxford University Press, 1995. A look at the varying roles each First Lady to date has undertaken, along with vital statistics.

DeGregorio, William A. *The Complete Book of U.S. Presidents*. 4th ed. New York: Barricade Books, 1993. A detailed compilation of brief family and political histories of the presidents.

Gould, Lewis L., ed. *American First Ladies: Their Lives and Their Legacy*. New York: Garland, 1996. An enjoyable, informative, and objective combination of biographical sketches and histories of the First Ladies.

Healy, Diana Dixon. *America's First Ladies: Private Lives of the Presidential Wives*. New York: Atheneum, 1988. An entertaining yet insightful look at the women who would be First Ladies.

Seager, Robert. *And Tyler Too: A Biography of John and Julia Tyler*. New York: McGraw-Hill, 1963. A lengthy but detailed look at the lives and times of John and Julia Tyler.

Truman, Margaret. *First Ladies*. New York: Random House, 1995. A colorful yet warm glimpse into the changing roles of the First Lady, as seen from the author's own experiences as a president's daughter.

Watson, Robert P. *The Presidents' Wives: Reassessing the Office of First Lady*. Boulder, Colo.: Lynne Rienner, 2000. A statistical and research-oriented assessment of the roles and the long-ranging impacts of the First Ladies as presidential partners.

Clinton P. Taffe

Sarah Polk

Sarah Childress Polk

Born: September 4, 1803
Rutherford County, Tennessee
Died: August 14, 1891
Polk Place, Nashville, Tennessee

President: James K. Polk
1845-1849

Overview: Sarah Polk was First Lady of Tennessee when James K. Polk, her husband, served as governor (1839-1841) and First Lady of Washington, D.C., when he served as president of the United States (1845-1849). She was well respected for her intelligent political advice, her wit and charm, and her acumen in dealing with political factions. She established a role for herself as her husband's closest political adviser, serving as his secretary, thus establishing an example of a First Lady of great strength and political influence.

Early Life
Sarah Childress was born in Rutherford County, Tennessee, to Joel Childress and Elizabeth Whitsitt Childress. The county seat of Murfreesboro was nearby. Her father, born in Campbell County, Virginia, had moved his family to Sumner County, Tennessee, in the 1790's. Murfreesboro served as the capital of Tennessee from 1819 to 1825, when the capital was transferred to Nashville. Sarah was the middle child, with an older brother, Anderson; an older sister, Susan; and three younger siblings: John Whitsett, Benjamin, who died in infancy, and Elizabeth, who also died in infancy. From an early age, Sarah learned the arts of mediation and diplomacy. She became a beauty, with long, dark brown curls and

Sarah Polk. *(Library of Congress)*

83

James K. Polk

James Knox Polk developed friendships early in his career which assisted him in making his way toward the presidency. His Irish family name had originally been Pollock but had been changed through years of mispronunciation to Poll'k and finally to Polk. He was a close friend of Andrew Jackson and received the nickname "Young Hickory" and followed his mentor's politics and viewpoints.

Polk remained close friends with Felix Grundy, the famed lawyer with whom he had read and studied law. Polk began his law practice in Columbia, Tennessee; with Grundy's support, Polk became the clerk of the Tennessee state senate in 1821. Jackson and Grundy aided Polk in his election to the Tennessee House of Representatives in 1823, and Polk supported the presidential aspirations of Jackson. Polk's marriage in 1824 to Sarah Childress combined the political forces of two of Tennessee's formidable political families which supported the Jacksonians. By 1825, Polk was ready for the national scene and was elected in that year to the first of his seven terms as a congressman in the House of Representatives from Tennessee. He was an avid campaigner, earning respect as the "Napoleon of the Stump."

Polk rewarded Jackson's early political confidence in him by serving ably as the speaker of the House from 1835 to 1839, during Jackson's presidency. The Democratic Party primed Polk to run for governor of Tennessee in 1939, which he won, reuniting their power base in the state. Former Whig victories and contentious rivalries during the Jacksonian era involving issues such as the tariff, the re-charter of the Second Bank of the United States, and the question of states' rights to nullify an act of the federal government had splintered the Democratic base, which Polk rebuilt temporarily. The Whigs, however, came back to win the gubernatorial elections of 1841 and 1843.

Afterward, Polk turned his attention once again to the national scene, winning the Democratic nomination for president for the election of 1844. Polk was nominated as a compromise candidate and emerged as a dark horse. His friend, historian George Bancroft from Massachusetts, put Polk's name forward at the nominating convention after Martin Van Buren and his Michigan opponent, Lewis Cass, could not win the necessary two-thirds majority vote to gain the nomination. Polk won the election and named Bancroft his secretary of the Navy.

Polk boldly took the political position of the expansion of the United States to annex Texas and Oregon. His slogan was "Fifty-four Forty or Fight," which meant that he would risk war with Britain to gain the United States' expansionist goals of Manifest Destiny—to extend the United States' boundaries in the Pacific Northwest with Canada to that latitude. Polk also campaigned for the immediate annexation of Texas, knowing war with Mexico would likely result. His rival, Henry Clay, the Whig nominee, was more cautious, less daring; his attempt to keep the Texas issue from becoming a campaign issue failed.

Polk was swept to victory on the expansionist sentiment of American enthusiasm for extending U.S. boundaries from ocean to ocean. Polk delivered on all of his campaign promises and goals. He would settle the Oregon boundary dispute with Britain through the Oregon Treaty of 1846. He would win the Mexican War (1846-1848), opening the way for Western settlement of U.S. citizens and agricultural prosperity. He helped stabilize the finances of the United States with Congress's passage of legislation in 1846 ensuring a treasury independent of the government. Finally, Polk reduced tariffs on trade to stimulate more free trade worldwide, winning a larger share of the world's markets for the United States.

Polk was an expansionist and an internationalist who understood the political mood of Americans. He was also an individual who enjoyed the confidences of strong political friendships and capitalized upon them to the advantage of the United States.

brown eyes, and she wore immaculate silk and satin clothes from the finest dressmakers in the area.

Sarah received a genteel education, first with tutors at home, then at the local Bradley Academy, then at Abercrombie's Boarding School, which was a private school in Nashville. She then attended the Moravian-run Female Academy in Salem, North Carolina. Sarah was educated in Greek and Roman literature, grammar, writing techniques, world history, and home economics. Respectability, manners, and breeding were the watchwords of her family upbringing.

Living in Tennessee's capital allowed her to mingle with politicians and visiting dignitaries. Her parents were well-to-do land investors and plantation owners, and her father was appointed the first postmaster of Murfreesboro in 1813. The Childress children were close to their cousins, whose uncle Judge John Childress often hosted General Andrew Jackson at their home at Roxeby. Sarah's family also supported the Jacksonian Democrats in the territory of Tennessee, which became a state in 1796. They supported General Jackson's military forces during the War of 1812 by providing military uniforms.

Sarah's father died in 1819 while she was at the Moravian Female Academy, and she returned home to aid her widowed mother while her brother Anderson settled the estate. Each surviving Childress child inherited one-fourth of the family estate when he or she reached the age of twenty-one, and they all continued to provide for their mother. Hence, Sarah became a wealthy young woman in her own right before she was married, and she learned to manage her own resources, a skill she would bring to the governor's mansion as well as the White House. Her upbringing taught her to be frugal but to enjoy the finer appointments of a household. As First Lady, she always did things elegantly but took care not to be lavish. Simple elegance served her husband's best interests, and

this image later was well appreciated by the public.

Marriage and Family

Sarah's highbred gentility dictated that she marry for position as well as for love, and she found a perfect match in James K. Polk, born November 2, 1795, near Pineville, North Carolina. His family had moved, like the Jacksons and Childresses, to Tennessee when he was young, and he grew up in Columbia in a prosperous home. James was the eldest of ten children born to Samuel and Jane Knox Polk. James, like other highbred young plantation gentlemen, received the finest education. He graduated from the University of North Carolina in 1815 and passed the bar examination in 1820, after reading law under the famed Felix Grundy, who then headed the Tennessee bar. In 1821 James became a clerk in the Tennessee state senate when a position there opened just after James had completed his education. The doors continued to open for James throughout his political life.

He was introduced to Sarah by her brother Anderson, who had met James in school. James, at once smitten by her refinement, loveliness, and wit, visited her family, courting her. In a large, country-style wedding at her home, Sarah became Mrs. James K. Polk on January 1, 1824. The couple settled into a big home in Columbia, Tennessee, while James worked as the Tennessee state senate clerk and as a young, bright lawyer who enjoyed politics.

Young James had successfully managed his family plantation interests, and the newlyweds managed their vast cotton plantations together. Polk was elected to the U.S. House of Representatives in 1825, a year after his marriage, and he and Sarah lived part time in Washington, D.C., when Congress was in session. Polk was both friend and adviser to Andrew Jackson during the election of 1828 and planned the celebration trip from Tennessee to Washington for Jackson after his victory. James and Sarah also returned to Tennessee with Jackson at the end of his second term as president, signifying their close and lasting friendship as well as their ability to work well together.

For fourteen years the Polks enjoyed the highest social and political circles of Washington, where Sarah developed a network of valuable political friendships. James Polk was elected Speaker of the House in 1835 and served there until 1839, his last four years in a congressional seat before he returned to Tennessee to serve as its elected governor. His position as Speaker allowed his wife to make political contacts, which would later help him attain the presidency. In 1839 Polk was elected governor of Tennessee, but because the capital shifted over the years (to Knoxville, Kingston, Murfreesboro, and later to Nashville), there was no permanent governor's mansion. Hence, while serving as governor in Nashville, James and Sarah rented a palatial home on Cherry Street, called Craighead, which served as the official residence. During Polk's governorship, Sarah began to accept more clerical and advisory duties, and she often forced him to rest and not indulge in late hours of overwork.

Because of James's busy schedule with public affairs, Sarah managed most of the family estates and plantations, traveling to oversee their plantation in Mississippi as well as their Tennessee properties. Polk's salary as governor was two thousand dollars per year, and their rent was five hundred dollars. Sarah efficiently managed their household expenses. They entertained both Democrats and Whigs, as Tennessee was considered a swing state, and Sarah utilized her grace and charm to convert Whigs to Democratic views. During Polk's governorship, the state capitol building of Nashville was perched on a high hill in the center of the city, surrounded by a park, and decorated with an equestrian statute of native son President Andrew Jackson. The capitol, with its fine view overlooking the city, served as Nashville's political center. The Polks fended off barbs from the *Nashville Whig* newspaper during his ad-

ministration, but James would lose the gubernatorial elections in 1841 and 1843.

Presidency and First Ladyship

In 1844 Polk received the Democratic nomination for the presidency. His campaign slogan captured the issue of Oregon statehood: "Fifty-four Forty or Fight," meaning he believed that all of Oregon territory, from the forty-second parallel north to fifty-four degrees, forty minutes, should be annexed.

Sarah read the newspapers of the day, attended sessions of the legislature, became knowledgeable of significant bills and their process of passage, and discussed politics at very high levels. She was a joiner and a mixer who enjoyed people and was very loyal to her many friends in various factions. In turn, they were loyal to the Polks.

Sarah Polk became First Lady on March 4, 1845, when her husband was inaugurated at the Capitol in Washington, D.C. She exercised great power behind the scenes, serving as her husband's personal assistant, opening mail, answering letters, and writing speeches. She encouraged philanthropic projects such as the construction of the Washington Monument. In her busy and dedicated role as the president's special assistant and secretary, Sarah acted as a political partner to her husband.

James set her to work, and one of her tasks was to select articles from the newspapers that she thought the president should read immediately or attend to especially; hence, she included articles which benefitted her political agenda and philanthropic charities. In this manner she was able to guide part of the president's attention to needy causes and issues beneficial to women and children. This was especially important during the Mexican War, when the president's main concern was the direction of successful military activities, but local and domestic issues influenced support for his policies and resources. Washington civic leaders as well as local politicians respected Sarah as a channel to her husband and often sought her political counsel.

Sarah, as First Lady, decided not to redecorate the White House as an economic measure and brought in her own slaves to operate the household, boarding them in the basement of the mansion to further save public funds. This was a period when abolitionists denounced the injustice of slavery, but the Polks were rooted in their old cotton plantation values and ideas from Tennessee, where the "employment" of household slaves was viewed by many as gracious as well as frugal. Slavery existed throughout the South but would be abolished in 1863, when the Polks' slaves were emancipated.

Sarah was as careful with her husband's image as she was with household finances. She allowed no hard liquor to be served at White House functions and no dancing parties or balls. Sarah Polk, as First Lady, encouraged serious business of state and diplomatic exchange. The White House, to Sarah, was to be a sacred shrine of the public's trust, always morally upright, and she never compromised her views. Sarah believed "to dance in these rooms would be undignified, and it would be respectful neither to the house nor the office."

Because of her moral stands, Sarah was called the Spanish Madonna, or the Prim Madonna. "How indecorous it would seem for dancing to be going on in one apartment, while in another we were conversing with dignitaries of the republic or ministers of the gospel. This unseemly juxtaposition would be likely to occur at any time, were such amusement permitted," she said. Her "Puritanism" was reflected in her attendance at the Presbyterian Church, which her husband also attended. The Polks had no children, but Sarah engaged in many philanthropic projects to support children and the needy, such as her fund-raisers for the Washington Orphans' Asylum. Her maternal instincts also manifested themselves in the special attention she paid to the children of her siblings.

Sarah loved to dress up, displaying her special gowns, luxurious velvets, long trains, turbans, and hats with ostrich feathers and always displayed perfect taste, whether at a White House reception or at church. She often patterned herself after former First Lady Dolley Madison, who was her close friend, with whom she worked on projects such as raising funds to erect the Washington Monument. The ladies would later accompany President Polk as he laid the cornerstone for the Washington Monument in 1848. Dolley was approaching eighty and Sarah was forty-one as she entered the White House. Their relationship was similar to a mother-daughter relationship, as Sarah had lost her own mother years before.

Dolley was in Washington to lobby for the U.S. government's purchase of her husband's presidential papers, which she would accomplish in May, 1848, during the Polk administration. Hence, the partnership and friendship was mutually beneficial. The two First Ladies enjoyed riding around Washington, D.C., in a carriage, pointing out projects and discussing plans to improve the city. It was more becoming for ladies to travel together in public rather than to be out alone on the streets, and they believed the fresh air improved their health. Sarah considered Dolley's advice invaluable, as Dolley was an icon, famed for saving the portrait of George Washington as the British marched on the capital during the War of 1812.

Careful of her own image and decorous behavior, Sarah was careful not to attend too many receptions alone as First Lady. Her judgment proved flawless in matters of decorum. She found it rewarding to attend functions such as teas and daytime parties with her respected friend Dolley when the president could not escort her. On one occasion Sarah had refused to attend a party without her husband where two bachelors, James Buchanan and William Rufus King, would be present. She refused to attend horse races or card parties because her appearance there, she felt, would lower the stature of the First Lady.

Sarah was a very humble person, in addition to being dignified. She believed that God had destined her for greatness, and she never shirked her responsibilities. Sarah did not allow her husband to work on the Sabbath, and on one occasion an Austrian diplomat was not received when he called on a Sunday; it was recommended to him that he return the next day. Piety was popular and widely respected in these times, even though Sarah was sometimes called "Sahara Sarah" for her anti-hard liquor policies. Closely guarding her place in history, she stood firmly by her moral choices, to the pride of her husband.

She had also learned the lessons of history: Just as the Jacksonian reception had admitted everyone, the Polk inaugural reception had been open to all. The *Nashville Union* often attested to her virtue, stating, "The example of Mrs. Polk can hardly fail of exerting a salutary influence," praising her for shunning "the follies and the amusements of the world." Congressman Franklin Pierce relished discussing politics with her more than he did with other men, he bragged, and Sarah took pleasure in discussing the issues of state with men. It was a compliment to her that they admitted her to their circles and confidences—both Democrats and Whigs.

She had only one issue on which she departed from her husband's viewpoint: She supported the National Bank, favoring paper money during the Jackson presidency. Her husband supported Jackson, calling the Bank a "hydra of corruption," and sought to encourage the use of only hard currency. "The separation of the moneys of the Government from banking institutions is indispensable," Polk said, "for the safety of the funds of the Government and the rights of the people." Sarah traveled the campaign trails with her husband and was feted everywhere, always publicly supporting his viewpoint and prefacing her comments with, "Mr. Polk believes . . ."

James K. Polk's administration and the ten- ure of Sarah Polk as First Lady are credited with significant accomplishments. First, Polk concluded the settlement of the Oregon boundary along the forty-ninth parallel. This settlement with Great Britain allowed the region of the Oregon Country to eventually become states of the Union, and it allowed for the border between the United States and Canada to remain a peaceful and unfortified one, rooted in goodwill and political friendship. Polk related that he had desired an amicable settlement of the question of joint occupancy of the Oregon Country "in the spirit of moderation which had given birth to new discussion . . . . " Polk protected migrants to the Oregon Country with a series of frontier blockhouses and forts to protect the settlers from Indian raids. He also arranged for armed guards of mounted riflemen to protect them along the Oregon Trail to settle the newly acquired lands.

A second important foreign-policy issue was the successful conclusion of the Mexican War (1846-1848) and the settlement of the boundaries of the United States in the southwestern regions of the United States. During the war, Sarah was praised for her patriotic sentiments, and she entertained gallant diplomats and military officers at her dinner table, lobbying for military support. President Polk successfully ended the war with Mexico by signing the Treaty of Guadalupe Hidalgo on February 2, 1848. By this treaty, the United States greatly enlarged its area, incorporating regions of Texas, California, New Mexico, Arizona, Nevada, Colorado, and Utah. Throughout the Mexican War, James commented on his wife's sagacity and hard decision making. Sarah contributed her own views in political speeches that she edited for the president and exerted her diplomacy in issues of patronage and appointments to political offices.

In 1848 Polk also formally recognized the overthrow of the French monarchy and the establishment of the French Republic based on "republican" principles close to the American

Ahead of Her Time

During the presidency of Andrew Jackson, the issues of the National Bank of the United States and the use of hard specie versus paper currency were raised. James K. Polk, as a congressman from Tennessee during the Jacksonian era, naturally supported Jackson's attack on the Bank and the decision not to support its re-charter. The Jacksonians favored a "hard money" policy, or the use of gold and silver coinage over paper Bank notes. Sarah Polk, however, favored the use of paper money and voiced her own opinion in the matter.

On one occasion, the Polks were traveling to Washington, D.C., and had stopped en route overnight. The next morning, as the journey was to resume, Polk asked his wife for some extra money from their locked trunks, believing he did not have enough to cover the day's expenses. Sarah unlocked the trunks and rummaged through the clothes, searching for bags of coins. "Don't you see," she exclaimed, "how troublesome it is to carry around gold and silver? This is enough to show you how useful banks are." She found the bags of money, dispensing some to her husband for their needs. Later, while they were riding in the carriage, Polk told their traveling companions jokingly about Sarah's viewpoints. Several members of the party happened to agree with Sarah on the matter of the National Bank and were delighted by the tale and by her sharing of their sympathies.

Hence, Sarah was bold enough to voice her own opinion on the matter of the National Bank and the expediency of using paper money, taking a stand in a controversy that stirred the United States for a number of years. Her husband retold the story often, with great mirth, of how she had stood up to him, and even though he disagreed, he respected her viewpoint. Polk's male friends joked that she could not carry enough money (gold and silver) for shopping, but she saw the matter differently. Paper money could be more easily carried, secured, and accounted for, she believed.

Even though the Second Bank of the United States was not re-chartered during Polk's presidency, eventually banks became part of the American way of life. Practicality and efficiency, as Sarah Polk had realized, ultimately won the day for the proliferation of local, state and federal banks and the circulation of paper currency. President Polk himself recognized the need for fiscal stability, establishing an independent treasury in 1846 during his presidency, which created sub-treasuries throughout the United States to disburse federal funds. In 1863 the National Bank Act would provide for the federal charter of a system of banks known as national banks and in 1913 the Federal Reserve System was created and, with its federal depositories, acted as banks for public revenues, thus institutionalizing Sarah's thoughts on the Bank.

model. Earlier, in February of 1847, Polk had concluded an important treaty of "peace, amity, navigation and commerce" with the Latin American state of New Granada, ensuring the safe passage of U.S. ships across the Isthmus of Panama. In return, the United States guaranteed New Granada independence and sovereignty. This treaty laid the foundation for future U.S. involvement in Central and South America, especially in planning a canal later under Theodore Roosevelt. Hence, the Polks were enthusiastic builders and expansionists for the United States' interests abroad and domestically.

After leaving the White House, the Polks returned to Nashville to Polk Place, a mansion they had purchased for their retirement. However, James died three months later, on June 15, 1849, and Sarah was to remain a widow for forty-two years. She invited her great-niece Sarah Polk Jetton, her husband, and their daughter Saidee to live with her at Polk Place. Sarah enjoyed her golden years surrounded by family and became a southern icon. During the

Civil War, as battles raged through the South, military commanders of both sides, Union and Confederate, paid their respects and never harmed her home or her family. In her later years following the Civil War's end, the representatives of the Tennessee legislature made an annual visit to Polk Place. The widowed Sarah was granted a pension of five thousand dollars per year after Congress passed a bill in 1882 authorizing similar payments to all living widows of former presidents.

Sarah enjoyed many accolades in her later life. She was named an honorary vice president of the Daughters of the American Revolution and participated in the July 4, 1888, opening of the Cincinnati Centennial Exposition through a special telegraph sent to her in Nashville. After a fulfilling life of leadership, Sarah Polk died at eighty-eight. James had been buried at Polk Place, and upon her death she was also interred there. Later, both were reburied at the state capitol in Nashville.

Legacy

Sarah's legacy was in laying the foundation for a wife to be her husband's key adviser and political confidante, something Edith Wilson would later carry further. Sarah established a basis for a woman to participate fully in political debates, exchange views, and contribute her own agenda and style, though hers was carefully couched in her husband's best interests. A southern woman of considerable energy, style, grace, wit, and charm, she could gently cajole a gentleman friend to support her husband's policies and politics. She positioned herself and her husband, as governor or president, as a couple working for worthy causes, especially the public interest.

She supported and encouraged the work of Frances Willard and the Women's Christian Temperance Union, entertaining Willard in her home and offering political words of advice in the 1880's. Beauty and brains was an apt description of Sarah Polk. Her social breeding was a tremendous aid to her husband, as a gracious handshake or word of warm welcome to the White House was a prelude to political agreement and personal friendship. She understood image and its uses long before modernists became interested in the concept. Frugality was another of her significant traits, especially with the public's money, and she was personally generous with her own money for charities she supported, such as orphanages or the construction of public monuments. Shrewd and astute, she was well educated, well versed on current issues, and extremely dedicated to seeing her own and her husband's job done well in public office.

Suggested Readings

Anthony, Carl Sferrazza. *First Ladies: The Saga of the Presidents' Wives and Their Power.* Vol. 1. New York: William Morrow, 1990. A unique glimpse at the power and prestige in the evolving role of First Lady.

Bergeron, Paul H. *The Presidency of James K. Polk.* Lawrence: University Press of Kansas, 1987. Has been called the best available one-volume history of James Polk.

Caroli, Betty Boyd. *First Ladies.* Expanded ed. New York: Oxford University Press, 1995. A look at the varying roles each First Lady has undertaken, along with vital statistics.

DeFiore, Jayne Crumpler. "Sarah (Childress) Polk, 1803-1891, First Lady: 1845-1849." In *American First Ladies: Their Lives and Their Legacy,* edited by Lewis L. Gould. New York: Garland, 1996. One of the book's informative biographical sketches and histories of the First Ladies.

Nelson, Anson, and Fannie Nelson. *Memorials of Sarah Childress Polk.* New York: A. D. F. Randolf, 1892. Reprint. Spartanburg, S.C.: Reprint Company, 1974. This book was reprinted from the 1892 edition in the Tennessee State Library and Archives in Nashville.

Polk, James K. *The Diary of a President.* Edited by Alan Nevins. New York: Longmans,

Green, 1952. Annotated, with a bibliographical note.

Sellers, Charles G. *James K. Polk: Continentalist, 1843-1848*. Princeton, N.J.: Princeton University Press, 1966.

_____. *James K. Polk: Jacksonian, 1795-1843*. Princeton, N.J.: Princeton University Press, 1957.

_____. "Polk, Sarah Childress." In *Notable American Women*, edited by Edward T. James et al. Vol. 3. Cambridge, Mass.: Harvard University Press, 1974. Biographical dictionary profiles well-known and obscure women who contributed to American society.

Barbara Bennett Peterson

Margaret Taylor

Margaret Mackall Smith Taylor

Born: September 21, 1788
        Calvert County, Maryland
Died: August 18, 1852
        Pascagoula, Mississippi

President: Zachary Taylor
        1849-1850

Overview: Born and raised in Maryland plantation society, for thirty-five years Margaret Taylor followed her husband, Zachary Taylor, from one wilderness Army fort to another, making a comfortable home for her family wherever they lived. Just as the Taylors had begun planning their retirement to a southern plantation, Zachary's heroics in the Mexican War thrust him into the national spotlight and then the presidency. Margaret, who did not want to serve as First Lady, delegated her official duties to her daughter. When Zachary fell ill and died the year after entering the White House, the grief-stricken Margaret retired to Mississippi for the remaining two years of her life.

Margaret Taylor. *(Courtesy of Craig Shermer, National First Ladies' Library)*

Early Life

Margaret Mackall Smith was born September 21, 1788, on a plantation near St. Leonard's, Maryland, in rural Calvert County between Chesapeake Bay and the Patuxent River. Peggy, as the family always called her, was the younger daughter of Major Walter Smith, a state militia commander during the American Revolution, and Ann Mackall Smith. The Smiths were members of the plantation gentry and enjoyed a comfortable social and economic position but were not among the grandees of planter society.

Little is known of Margaret's childhood or education, but they were probably similar to those of other southern planters' daughters: a grounding in the basics by an itinerant tutor or her mother, with a heavy emphasis on household and domestic management as well as the social graces, in preparation for her presumed future as a planter's wife. Eligible men in her neighborhood, however, must have been scarce or incompatible; the slender, attractive Peggy remained unmarried at the age of twenty-one.

For a woman who was not rich herself, choosing an acceptable husband—a man of similar social class with stable financial and professional prospects—was a matter to be taken quite seriously. Young women of marriageable age frequently went to visit relatives or friends in larger towns or resort areas, such as spas, where dances, parties, and promenades gave single people a greater opportunity to encounter one another, while their families assessed the financial advisability of any prospective union. The nineteenth century view of matrimony was decidedly practical.

In 1809 Peggy came West for an extended visit with her elder sister Mary and her husband, Samuel Chew, who lived in the vicinity of Louisville. By this time, Kentucky had mostly outgrown its frontier past. Plantations were well established, and towns such as Louisville enjoyed many of the amenities of the eastern seaboard, including brick houses, shops, churches, a newspaper, and a very active social round. Among the ambitious young men of Louisville was Zachary Taylor, four years Peggy's senior and the third son of a prominent local family.

The Taylors, originally from Virginia, had come to the area in 1785 and by this time owned several thousand acres of prime farmland as well as town property. Zachary had decided to pursue a military career, receiving his commission as first lieutenant in the regular Army in the spring of 1808. Serving in Louisiana, he had become ill and was sent home in the fall of 1809 to recuperate. It was probably then that he met Peggy Smith. He wrote of her: "I am confident the feminine virtues never did concentrate in a higher degree in the bosom of any woman than in hers," and he never looked at another woman.

Marriage and Family

Margaret and Zachary were married the following summer, on June 24, 1810, with the groom receiving 324 acres of land as a wedding present from his father. During the first year of their marriage, the newlyweds lived in Louisville, where their daughter Ann Mackall was born, and Zachary was promoted to captain. With the outbreak of the War of 1812, he was posted to the Indiana territory, the first of many frontier assignments. Throughout his military career, Taylor generally served at outposts in the Western territories of Wisconsin, Michigan, or Minnesota as well as serving hardship duty in the backwoods of Louisiana and Mississippi. Not being a West Point graduate counted against him, but much more damaging to his career was the lack of significant "interest," that is, influence, brought to bear in Washington on his behalf to gain rapid promotions and plush assignments.

For thirty-five years, Peggy accompanied her husband to one wilderness fort after another, unless active warfare threatened her life or those of their daughters. Ann Mackall had been followed by Sarah Knox (always called Knox), Octavia Pannill, and Margaret Smith. Discomfort, loneliness, or primitive conditions could not deter Peggy. In an era when officers on Western duty were seldom joined by their wives, being with Zachary was Peggy's primary concern, even though their children had to be sent back East to be educated. With the addition of such comforts as mahogany dining room furniture, Peggy made each post a home, entertaining officers and travelers graciously and impressing them with her composure and quiet charm.

Life was tenuous in the nineteenth century, on or off the frontier. On a family visit in Louisiana, Peggy and her daughters contracted one of the region's endemic fevers; the two youngest girls died, and their mother's life was in danger. Zachary was distraught, writing "At best her constitution is remarkable delicate. . . . my loss will be an irreparable one." Peggy did recover,

Zachary Taylor

Until he was nearly sixty, no one would have dreamed that Zachary Taylor would become president. A professional soldier who was also a planter, Taylor served at hardship frontier posts, and promotions were slow in coming; indeed, once early in his career, he resigned briefly in protest. He finally reached the rank of general in his late fifties.

The Mexican War changed everything. Sent to Texas in 1845 to press U.S. territorial claims, Taylor became a national hero when he led his army to strategic victories at Palo Alto, Resaca de la Palma, Monterrey, and Buena Vista. When he returned to the United States in 1847, the Whig party began courting him as a presidential candidate. Taylor was not only a genuine hero, but he lacked political baggage. He had never been active in politics and had never even voted. Many Whigs preferred him to their longtime party leaders, such as Henry Clay, who had already been rejected by voters. Taylor's most formidable opponent for the nomination was the other hero of the Mexican War, General Winfield Scott. Although inexperienced, Taylor was shrewd. Once he decided to pursue it, the nomination was his.

When Taylor was inaugurated in 1849, his views were still largely unknown in Washington. The explosive issue that dominated his presidency was the extension of slavery into the new Western territories. Philosophically, the question was the legality of owning human beings; politically, the issue was the balance of power between slave and free states. Ultimately, the fate of the Union depended on the resolution of this issue. Although a planter and slaveholder, Taylor was staunchly pro-Union and opposed the extension of slavery into free territories.

Among other issues during his presidency were conflicts with Indians in Florida and the Southwest, both of which Taylor brought to speedy conclusions, frontier peace being his goal. Foreign affairs were an area in which the president was completely unversed. Disagreements with France, Portugal, Spain, and Germany were made much of by the press of the day, but in retrospect, none were of any lasting significance. Taylor's staunch favoring of his nation's Manifest Destiny, a popular notion that the country's territory should stretch across the continent, showed itself in his opposition to Cuban filibusters and dissension with the British over Nicaragua, where expansionists hoped that the United States would one day build a trans-isthmian canal.

Zachary Taylor's legacy was very much unfinished. An unknown quantity upon his inauguration, in slightly more than a year as president, Taylor had begun to emerge as a strong executive in the mold of Andrew Jackson. His untimely death in 1850, during a period of national crisis, leaves only speculation as to what effect his leadership might have had on the coming of the Civil War.

but she never shared her husband's robust constitution, causing her family to worry about the state of her health throughout the rest of her life.

During the long years of Western exile, two more children were born: Mary Elizabeth (Betty) and Richard, their prized only son. The Taylors began to make plans for their retirement. While serving in Baton Rouge, Taylor had begun to purchase plantations in Louisiana and Mississippi, which were put in the hands of managers while he was away on active duty. They lived in Peggy's favorite home, the old Spanish commandant's house in Baton Rouge. A simple four-room cottage with galleries all around, it sat on a bluff on the Mississippi River. Open and breezy, it was surrounded by gardens and trees. It exactly suited the lifestyle they had evolved over the years, intimate and unpretentious, with room for family and close friends but no provision for grand entertainments or unwanted guests.

All three of their daughters married military officers, despite their parents' wish for them to enjoy comfortable civilian lives. Given the family circumstances, however, the Taylors could hardly have expected anything else: All eligible bachelors the girls met were Army men. They approved Ann's choice of assistant surgeon Robert Crooke Wood and Betty's, nearly twenty years later, of Lieutenant Colonel William W. S. Bliss, her father's adjutant and most trusted adviser. For reasons still unclear, they adamantly opposed the courtship of their second daughter, Knox, by Lieutenant Jefferson Davis. The young couple eventually prevailed, but the Taylors refused to attend the wedding ceremony at an aunt's house in Louisville where, of the immediate family, only the Woods were present. Within less than three months, the newlyweds contracted malaria while visiting Davis's sister in Louisiana, and Knox died. The estrangement between the Taylors and Jefferson Davis continued for many years, but they were eventually reconciled. They came to look on him as another son-in-law, and his second wife, Varina Howell Davis, was considered a daughter of the family.

The life trajectory of "Old Rough and Ready," as the broad-shouldered, bandy-legged Zachary Taylor was known by his soldiers, was completely changed by the Mexican War. Despite assiduous attention to duty and success in battle, promotions had come slowly and grudgingly during nearly forty years in the Army. Then, in 1845, General Taylor was posted to Texas to press U.S. claims there against Mexico, and his signal victories at Palo Alto, Resaca de la Palma, Monterrey, and Buena Vista suddenly shot him into national attention. On his return to Louisiana in 1847, he found himself a hero and was widely touted as a possible presidential candidate.

An apolitical man who had never voted in his life, Taylor hesitated at first to have his name put forward by the Whig Party, perennial losers in presidential elections, who wanted a hero to capture the White House for them. Peggy Taylor, like many First Ladies before and since, was horrified to see her husband's candidacy assume inevitability just when she had expected a quiet retirement. She prayed nightly that her husband would not become president.

When Zachary was handily elected in 1848, Peggy refused to accept the corollary that she also had a position to fill. Pleading poor health (very much exaggerated) as an excuse, she delegated all White House ceremonial functions to her daughter Betty Bliss, a delightful and efficient young woman who thoroughly enjoyed serving as her father's hostess on formal occasions.

Presidency and First Ladyship

The position of First Lady—unofficial, undefined by law, and unelected—is inherently laden with ambiguity and contradictory expectations. Whatever her own wishes, the American public regards the president's wife as the hostess of the nation. First Ladies have always been criticized for perceived social shortcomings, but such sniping was initially kept more or less private. When the capital of the United States was moved to the raw, unfinished village of Washington, D.C., in 1800, society there was predominantly masculine and informal, as the wives of legislators stayed at home.

By 1849, though still lagging behind established cities, Washington was indubitably the center of national political power. European diplomats, longtime congressmen, and successful military officers and their families came to be semi-permanent residents of the city, and the older area of Georgetown was home to a resident population of wealthy and socially prominent merchants, bankers, developers, and professionals. These Washingtonians saw the capital as their city and its social life as their concern. The occupants of the White House, particularly Westerners, were seen as outsiders whose tenure would be brief. The president and his lady should, they believed, adapt to the city's society, not attempt to lead it.

When the Taylors arrived in the capital, the rules of society were almost as rigid as those of any European court. Society doyennes decided who would, or would not, be received, sometimes precipitating a political crisis by their actions. Frontier representatives were sneered at for their perceived gaucheries. The ritual of paying calls—sometimes as many as fifty in a day—was an essential way of occupying time for women and some men. Fortunes were spent on houses and their furnishings, gowns, servants, food and drink, hothouse flowers, and all the other appurtenances of social status seeking. The favored adjectives of the day were "choice," "rare," "select," or "exclusive," the old democratic ideals forgotten. After years of developing a simple and satisfying lifestyle, Peggy simply had no interest in joining this social scene or allowing herself to be patronized by society matrons. She was perfectly capable of serving as the president's hostess—she had, after all, trained Betty Bliss—but she did not care to do so.

Brief as it was, Taylor's presidency was filled with violent controversy: The Union groaned under the pressure of pro- and antislavery forces as they battled over the question of extending slavery into the Western territories. Although he was a plantation owner and slaveholder, Taylor was as pro-Union as his predecessor Andrew Jackson. The newspapers of the day were viciously partisan, without any pretense of fairness. Democratic papers commonly portrayed Taylor as an illiterate, dialect-speaking hick. Beginning with the divorced Rachel Jackson, newspapers had also begun to make a habit of attacking First Ladies. The refined and quiet Peggy Taylor was lampooned as a weatherbeaten, pipe-smoking, backwoods crone who was kept out of the limelight to avoid embarrassing the White House. As the object of such scurrilous attacks, it is no wonder that she did not care to mix with capital politicians.

Far from being a recluse, Peggy led a very active private life, constantly surrounded by her family and favored visitors. A devout Episcopalian, she attended services nearly every day at

Peggy Taylor's White House

In the private quarters of the White House, Peggy Taylor created a warm haven where her husband could forget presidential cares in the company of family and friends. Delegating the official role of hostess to her twenty-five-year-old daughter, Betty Bliss, Peggy declined joining the social whirl of the nation's capital.

During the Taylors' residence, the newly wed Betty and her husband and an attractive teenage niece, much courted by young men of Washington, D.C., lived with them. Their older daughter Ann Wood and her husband stayed there for months at a time, as did their children, the Taylors' four beloved grandchildren, who ranged in age from nineteen down to a cheerful little girl of eleven, called Dumple. The house also rang with the sounds of laughing voices and running feet of visiting nieces, nephews, and youthful family friends.

Peggy held sway over her chosen realm from a bright and cheerful sitting room at the head of stairs, overlooking the mansion gardens. The few visitors invited there considered themselves quite honored. Among her guests were her former son-in-law Jefferson Davis with his second wife, Varina; Daniel Webster; and George W. P. Custis and Nelly Custis Lewis, Martha Washington's now-elderly grandchildren, all of whom left admiring accounts of their visits. Washington society circles considered Peggy Taylor a failure, but her family and friends adored her and the lively home she created at the White House.

the nearby Saint John's Episcopal Church and was active in the Sunday school movement. The private quarters of the White House were full of comings and goings, and the Taylors' grandchildren, nieces, nephews, and other young people kept things lively. Sympathetic friends such as Varina and Jefferson Davis, Daniel Webster, and Martha Washington's grandchildren, George W. P. Custis and Nelly Custis Lewis, were frequent and welcome visitors.

Despite a serious illness the year before, President Taylor's final sickness and death were completely unexpected. On July 4, 1850, a broiling hot day, he attended the lengthy ceremonies marking the inauguration of the Washington Monument. Back at the White House, he bolted raw fruit and perhaps vegetables and washed them down with icy milk and water. Soon he was suffering from cholera morbus, a term in those days for acute indigestion and diarrhea. At first the indisposition seemed minor, but five days later the president was dead.

Peggy gave way completely to her grief. In the intervening days before the funeral on July 13, the sobbing widow had the undertaker remove the ice from Zachary's body and lay it out several times for repeated farewells. Funerals were primarily masculine affairs in the nineteenth century, and many widows including Mrs. Taylor did not attend the public ceremonies. Despite Millard Fillmore's thoughtful offer, as the new president, to await her convenience, Peggy left the White House the evening of the funeral and never again mentioned the presidential mansion, even as she apportioned keepsakes to friends and supporters. Four months later, she met with her daughters and son in New Orleans to divide Zachary's considerable property. Peggy then retired to East Pascagoula, Mississippi, where she lived with the Blisses until her death on August 18, 1852.

Legacy

Peggy Taylor was very much an anomaly among First Ladies. Although there have been reclusive presidential wives who did little public entertaining, their reasons—severe illness or chronic depression—have been indisputable. Peggy's health was not robust, but she led an active social life with family and friends, while declining to serve as the official hostess of the White House. Zachary Taylor had chosen to become president; Peggy Taylor chose not to serve as First Lady.

Suggested Readings

Bauer, K. Jack. *Zachary Taylor: Soldier, Planter, Statesman of the Old Southwest.* Baton Rouge: Louisiana State University Press, 1993. An account of Zachary Taylor's career with perceptive consideration of Margaret Taylor as First Lady.

Dyer, Brainerd. *Zachary Taylor.* Baton Rouge: Louisiana State University Press, 1943. Solid account of Zachary Taylor's career.

Farrell, John J. *Zachary Taylor, 1874-1850, and Millard Fillmore, 1800-1874: Chronology, Documents, and Bibliographical Aids.* Dobbs Ferry, N.Y.: Oceana, 1971. Guide for further research.

Hamilton, Holman. *Zachary Taylor.* 2 vols. Indianapolis: Bobbs-Merrill, 1951. The most detailed work on Zachary Taylor, which also contains the most complete account of Margaret Taylor's life.

Nevins, Allan. *Ordeal of the Union: Fruits of Manifest Destiny, 1847-1852.* New York: Charles Scribner's Sons, 1947. Considers Zachary Taylor's career in context of the Civil War.

Patricia Brady

Abigail Fillmore

Abigail Powers Fillmore

Born: March 13, 1798
        Stillwater, New York
Died: March 30, 1853
        Washington, D.C.

President: Millard Fillmore
        1850-1853

Overview: Abigail Powers Fillmore rose above her humble upbringing and lack of formal schooling to become the caring and cultivated woman who established the permanent White House library. During her tenure, the Executive Mansion became a magnet of culture, attracting authors, entertainers, and statesmen. Abigail supported the political career of her husband, Millard Fillmore, a self-made man as well as a "wife-made man" who owed much of his rise from a log cabin to the White House to his intelligent and capable spouse.

Early Life

Abigail was born on March 13, 1798, in Stillwater, Saratoga County, New York, the youngest child of the Reverend Lemuel Powers, a Baptist clergyman, and Abigail Newland Powers. Her father passed away in 1800, leaving his widow with five sons and two daughters to support. In 1804 the family resettled in what was then the frontier of Sempronius in central New York. In the library her father bequeathed to his family, Abigail developed a lifelong love of books. At sixteen she became a schoolteacher, one of the few paid occupations open to women of the time and the most common profession among First Ladies before marriage.

Abigail Fillmore. *(Library of Congress)*

Abigail was tall and erect, with light blue eyes and fine auburn hair that fell naturally in ringlets. She met student Millard Fillmore, two years her junior, at the New Hope Academy and encouraged him in a course of study. Millard purchased a subscription to a circulating library that Abigail had probably helped establish near her home in 1817 or 1818.

Marriage and Family

The young couple began their courtship in 1819 but delayed marriage while Millard studied law, which would enable him to support a family. Members of Abigail's family, although poor, were proud of their descent from the prominent Leland family and had reservations about her marrying the son of an impoverished farmer. Nevertheless, Abigail and Millard, the first presidential couple to rise from poverty, married on February 5, 1826, in Moravia, New York.

Abigail continued to work for wages after marriage, which was unusual for women at the time, while Millard established his legal practice in East Aurora in western New York. She became the first First Lady to earn a living before and after marriage. On April 25, 1828, she gave birth to their son, Millard Powers Fillmore. In 1830, the family moved to Buffalo,

Millard Fillmore

Millard Fillmore was born on January 7, 1800, in Locke Township (now Summerhill), Cayuga County, New York. Millard overcame his backwoods origins to become an attorney, a New York State assemblyman, a U.S. congressman, the state comptroller of New York, and, in 1849, the vice president of the United States.

Fillmore became president when Zachary Taylor died on July 9, 1850. He came to power during a heated congressional session over slavery and its expansion into western territories. Several southern states were threatening to secede. Congress debated and finally passed the Compromise of 1850. This compromise included measures to admit California to the Union as a free state, establish the boundary of Texas, organize the territories of Utah and New Mexico, abolish the slave trade in the District of Columbia, and strengthen the Fugitive Slave Law.

Throughout his political career, Fillmore had supported humane legislation. As an assemblyman, he successfully sponsored a bill eliminating imprisonment for debt. As president, he signed legislation abolishing flogging in the U.S. Navy and supported reformer Dorothea Dix's crusade for better treatment of the mentally ill. Fillmore detested slavery and favored gradual emancipation. His like-minded wife, Abigail, reportedly advised her husband not to sign the Fugitive Slave Act, which reinforced the Fugitive Slave Act of 1793 and required the return of runaway slaves who had escaped from a slave state into a free state or territory. Though she warned him that it would ruin his political career, he signed the law in the belief that it would preserve the Union.

The compromise, which would avert civil war for a decade, was initially popular. Ultimately, though, the controversial Fugitive Slave Act and the publication of the book *Uncle Tom's Cabin* by Harriet Beecher Stowe in 1852 strengthened opposition to slavery in the North. The president, probably the only Whig candidate who could have won the election in 1852, was denied the nomination by his party.

In 1856 Fillmore became the presidential nominee of the Native American or "Know Nothing" Party but lost the election. He ended his days as a philanthropist in Buffalo, New York, where he died on March 8, 1874. One of the lasting legacies of his presidency was his decision to authorize Commodore Matthew Perry to open Japan to Western trade.

New York, where daughter Mary Abigail Fillmore was born on March 27, 1832.

Abigail lived in Washington, D.C., from 1837 to 1842, when Millard was a U.S. congressman. There she listened to House and Senate debates, read newspapers, participated in boardinghouse discussions, and left her calling card at the homes of government officials and foreign dignitaries. While separated from her children, she wrote to them and encouraged them in their lessons.

Presidency and First Ladyship

Vice President Millard Fillmore became president of the United States when Zachary Taylor died in July, 1850. Fifty-two-year-old Abigail, who was not in Washington when her husband unexpectedly became president, was not able to close her house and move to Washington until October of that year.

Well read and well informed, Abigail had long exerted a strong influence on her husband and his political career. Millard was heard to say he never took any important step without her counsel and advice. Inconvenienced by the absence of books in the White House—which did not even have a Bible—the new president sought funding for a library. The president and

his cabinet needed law books during meetings, and Millard wanted to please Abigail by creating a more habitable home. In Buffalo, the Fillmores had amassed an impressive personal library. The president, a Whig, confronted a contentious Democratic majority in Congress wary of strengthening the executive branch of government. Initial library legislation failed, but a second attempt in late September, 1850, yielded an appropriation from Congress for two thousand dollars.

For the new library, located in what is now the Yellow Oval Room, Abigail ordered mahogany bookcases and light, informal "cottage" furniture. She has been credited with selecting many of the books for the library's collection, including works of Charles Dickens and William Makepeace Thackeray, several histories, and other standard titles. The library was also a sitting room, where family members would read aloud to one another and greet visitors. From her home in Buffalo, Abigail brought a piano and harp, creating a music room as well as a library. Here her family enjoyed singing old-fashioned melodies and new Stephen Foster songs.

During this period of history, the wife of the president did not take public stands on issues

The Salon in the White House

In the comfortable library she established upstairs in the Executive Mansion, Abigail Powers Fillmore presided over a presidential salon in the heart of Washington, D.C. Family members, friends, and prominent literary and political guests gathered in the library, where Abigail enjoyed "the conversation of the cultivated society which Washington, D.C., at that time" afforded. One evening, which a guest recalled "with more than ordinary pleasure," Abigail arranged musical entertainment for Secretary of State Daniel Webster and other cabinet officers and their wives. Along with a singer and a harpist, the Fillmores' daughter, Mary Abigail, "played the piano with much skill and exquisite taste."

Abigail's sociable entertainments not only brought culture to the White House, but they helped to establish and expand the circle of power and influence of her husband and family. In the White House library, the domestic and social roles of hostess and entertainer played by the Fillmore women were political duties as well.

but did act on behalf of specific causes and individuals. In February, 1852, Abigail donated money to a Sunday school for poor children in Washington, D.C. That same year, she appealed to a physician to examine Helen De Kroyft, the blind novelist, as a personal favor. The doctor, who had been recommended to Abigail by reformer Dorothea Dix, operated on the author and restored her sight. In December, 1852, De Kroyft thanked Mrs. Fillmore in an open and enthusiastic letter published in newspapers. This letter prompted others to write to the Fillmores, requesting information and referrals.

Historically, the quiet and reserved Abigail has been portrayed as a passive invalid who turned over almost all of her hostessing duties to her daughter. However, contemporary reports depict Abigail as an active hostess, present at weekly morning receptions and evening levees whenever her health permitted. When Abigail missed an event, it was often due to an ankle injury, which she sustained first in 1842 and again in 1851. Proud of her husband's success and reluctant to disappoint the public, she would rest her ankle during the day in order to be able to stand through evening receptions. Sometimes Mary Abigail literally had to stand in for her mother as hostess.

The Fillmores entertained many prominent guests. In December, 1850, the celebrated diva Jenny Lind, known as the Swedish Nightingale, and her famous manager, P. T. Barnum, visited the White House at the invitation of the Fillmores, who attended both of Lind's concerts at the National Theater. From late December, 1851, through early January, 1852, Louis Kossuth, the Hungarian revolutionary, was in Washington. He visited the Executive Mansion on more than one occasion and attended a banquet hosted by the Fillmores. On February 28, 1853, Washington Irving, the American author of *The Legend of Sleepy Hollow*, and William Thackeray, the English author of *Vanity Fair*, were guests at a dinner President and Mrs. Fill-

more held in honor of the president-elect, Franklin Pierce.

Abigail attended the Pierce inauguration on a cold and blustery March 4, 1853. She shortly came down with a severe cold which developed into bronchial pneumonia. On March 30, 1853, she died at the Willard Hotel in Washington. Millard mournfully stated, "For twenty-seven years, my entire married life, I was always greeted with a happy smile." To honor her memory, the new president suspended his cabinet meeting and ordered public offices closed. The Senate promptly adjourned. Abigail's body was transported back to Buffalo and was buried at Forest Lawn Cemetery.

Legacy

Abigail was a resourceful and competent woman who might have achieved more as First Lady if not for declining health and a brief White House tenure. Even though Abigail did not long survive her husband's term of office, the library in the White House has endured. The Lincolns and other presidential families cherished the library, which continued to function as a music room, a parlor, and even as an early "oval office." During the Franklin D. Roosevelt administration, the library was secured in its present location on the ground floor, where it is the first room featured on the White House tour. A historic room in a famous house, the library has served every first family since the Fillmores.

Suggested Readings

Ellet, Elizabeth F. *Court Circles of the Republic: Or, The Beauties and Celebrities of the Nation, Illustrating Life and Society Under Eighteen Presidents, Describing the Social Features of the Successive Administrations from Washington to Grant*. Philadelphia: Philadelphia Publishing, 1872. The "first historian of American women" discusses Abigail Fillmore.

Fillmore, Millard. *Millard Fillmore Papers*. Edited by Frank H. Severance. 2 vols. Buffalo, N.Y.: Buffalo Historical Society, 1907. Millard Fillmore mentions his wife in his description of his early years and in other papers.

Hoganson, Kristin. "Abigail (Powers) Fillmore." In *American First Ladies: Their Lives and Their Legacy*, edited by Lewis L. Gould. New York: Garland, 1996. One of the few scholarly works focusing on Abigail Fillmore.

Holloway, Laura Carter. *The Ladies of the White House: Or, In the Home of the Presidents*. Reprint. New York: A. M. S. Press, 1976. One of the earliest sources devoted to First Ladies confirms Abigail Fillmore's involvement with the library.

Scarry, Robert J. *Millard Fillmore*. Jefferson, N.C.: McFarland, 2001. The first comprehensive biography to draw upon Fillmore family papers long believed to have been lost.

Wharton, Anne Hollingsworth. *Social Life in the Early Republic*. Philadelphia: J. B. Lippincott, 1902. Describes the activities of Abigail Fillmore and her daughter during the Millard Fillmore administration.

Whitton, Mary Ormsbee. *First First Ladies, 1789-1865: A Study of the Wives of the Early Presidents*. 1948. Reprint. Freeport, N.Y.: Books for Libraries Press, 1969. Features a romanticized yet informative account of Abigail Fillmore.

Elizabeth Lorelei Thacker-Estrada

Jane Pierce

Jane Means Appleton Pierce

Born: March 12, 1806
      Hampton, New Hampshire
Died: December 2, 1863
      Andover, Massachusetts

President: Franklin Pierce
      1853-1857

Overview: Jane Pierce, one of the most tragic First Ladies, eschewed the political life and wished that her husband, Franklin Pierce, would not seek public office. Her White House tenure demonstrates how a very reluctant and bereaved First Lady coped with her duties, often by relying on surrogate hostesses. Jane possessed many of the traits associated with the ideal for women of her time. She was delicate and spiritual, and she desired to remain in her own domestic sphere, away from the often coarse political world of her husband.

Early Life

Born March 12, 1806, in Hampton, New Hampshire, Jane was the third of six children of the Reverend Jesse Appleton and Elizabeth Means Appleton. Jane's father was a Congregational minister and president of Bowdoin College in Maine. Following his death in 1819, the family went to live with her mother's wealthy relatives. Petite, dark-haired Jane was both well educated for her day and devout.

Marriage and Family

In 1826 Jane met Franklin Pierce, a student of her brother-in-law at Bowdoin. Although Franklin was the son of a Revolutionary War hero, her family objected to her marrying him. While he was a Democrat, the Appletons were Federalists, and they did not consider his tavern-owning family their equals. After a long

Jane Pierce. *(Library of Congress)*

courtship and his election to the U.S. Congress, the gregarious Franklin finally married shy Jane on November 19, 1834, in Amherst, New Hampshire.

Franklin whisked Jane away from the shelter of rich relations to the roughness of Washington, D.C. Legislators of the time lived in boardinghouses, and this "mess" life challenged frail Jane. Living conditions were often crude and uncomfortable, and politics dominated everyone's lives. During the miserable, hot summer months in Washington, Jane's health suffered. She was often sickly and melancholy, even before a series of tragedies beset her and her husband.

In 1835 Jane left Washington to stay with her mother and other relatives. The Pierces' first son, Franklin Pierce, Jr., was born in February, 1836, but he lived only three days. The next year Jane returned to Washington with Franklin following his election to the Senate. Two more sons were born: Frank Robert in September, 1839, and Benjamin in April, 1841.

Jane came to oppose Franklin's political pursuits. The heavy drinking of other politicians, she felt, aggravated her husband's problems with alcohol. Jane observed, "Oh, how I wish he was out of political life! How much better it would be for him on every account!" In 1842 she persuaded Franklin to resign from the

Franklin Pierce

Franklin Pierce was born on November 23, 1804, in Hillsborough, New Hampshire. He attended Bowdoin College in Brunswick, Maine, graduating in 1824. Authors Nathaniel Hawthorne and Henry Wadsworth Longfellow were fellow students. Pierce studied law and was admitted to the bar association in 1827. He became a member of the New Hampshire House of Representatives in 1829 and its speaker in 1832. In 1834, he was elected to the United States House of Representatives, and two years later he was the youngest man elected to the Senate to date. Beginning in 1842, he temporarily relinquished his political career and practiced law in Concord, New Hampshire.

In 1847, during the Mexican War, he earned the rank of brigadier general. He was nominated for president in 1852, on the forty-ninth ballot to break a stalemate at the Democratic Convention. He defeated Whig candidate General Winfield Scott to become, at age forty-eight, the youngest president up to that time.

Although Vice President William Rufus Devane King died just a few weeks into the administration, Franklin Pierce is the only president to date who retained the same cabinet throughout his tenure. During the Pierce administration, the United States negotiated the Gadsden Purchase of forty-five thousand square miles of land from Mexico. The most serious event of his presidency was his signing of the Kansas-Nebraska Act on May 30, 1854. This act essentially repealed provisions of the 1820 Missouri Compromise, which had provided that one free state be admitted to the Union for every slave state admitted. Under the Kansas-Nebraska Act, the question of whether to allow slavery in those two territories was left up to "popular sovereignty." The act brought proslavery and antislavery settlers, including John Brown, into conflict in what became known as Bleeding Kansas.

Although Pierce intended to preserve the Union, under his administration the country veered closer to civil war. The political fissure between the northern and southern states widened and the sectional, antislavery Republican Party was formed. In 1856 Pierce became the only president elected to office who was not renominated by his party. He died in Concord, New Hampshire, on October 8, 1869, and is buried beside his wife and sons in Old North Cemetery.

Letters and the Law

During the conflict over slavery in so-called Bleeding Kansas, Jane Pierce played a role in rescuing the leader of the free state settlers in Lawrence: She interceded with her husband to free Charles Robinson from prison. Dr. Robinson had been indicted in 1856 for treason by proslavery courts. His wife, Sara Tappan Doolittle Lawrence Robinson, was a distant relative of the Lawrence family of Massachusetts and therefore kin to Jane Pierce.

Jane received a letter from Mrs. Robinson, who feared her husband was certain to be tried, convicted, and hanged. Jane showed Franklin this letter as well as one from her aunt Nancy Means Lawrence petitioning for Dr. Robinson's release. President Pierce telegraphed orders satisfactory to the wishes of his wife's aunt, whose good opinion he valued "more than that of all the politicians." As a consequence, Dr. Robinson was eventually freed. In an era when women had few legal rights and could not vote, this incident illustrates that they could and did exert influence through family and other private connections. The event also reveals Jane's antislavery sympathies.

Senate and come home to Concord, New Hampshire, where he would be close to his family and away from bad influences. According to Nathaniel Hawthorne, his friend and campaign biographer, Franklin left the Senate to practice law and thereby provide a better living for his growing family. In 1843 the Pierces' son Frank died of typhus fever.

In 1846 President James K. Polk asked Franklin to join his cabinet as attorney general, but Franklin declined, stating, "Besides you know that Mrs. Pierce's health while at Washington, was very delicate." Jane even objected to Franklin's running for governor of New Hampshire, an office his father had held. As governor, Franklin could have gained the executive experience he lacked prior to becoming president. Not wishing to become First Lady, Jane fainted upon learning that Franklin had been nominated as a dark horse candidate for president. Benjamin wrote his mother, "I hope [Father] won't be elected for I should not like to be at Washington and I know you would not either." Despite Jane's prayers to the contrary, Franklin won the presidential election in November, 1852.

His happiness was short-lived. The Pierces saw their last surviving son killed in a railroad accident on January 6, 1853, just two months be-fore Franklin took office. Benjamin, the sole fatality, was killed by a violent injury to his head when their car went off track and hurtled off a ledge.

Presidency and First Ladyship

Following the shock of Benjamin's death, Franklin immersed himself in his public and political duties as president of the United States, while Jane went into deep mourning. Seeking comfort in religion, Jane read her Bible and Henry Thornton's *Family Prayers*. She also wrote letters, including notes to her dead son. The minister's daughter urged White House staff to attend religious services, and Pierce's private secretary later admitted that he went to church out of respect for her.

Jane has been referred to as the Shadow in the White House. Reportedly, she sequestered herself in upstairs rooms and carried out few social or public duties. However, she did venture out for carriage rides and to go sailing on the Potomac River. She enjoyed visits from her relatives and from friend Nathaniel Hawthorne, the celebrated author of *The Scarlet Letter*, who escorted her on a visit to Mount Vernon.

Jane relied on her friend and widowed aunt, Abigail Kent Means, for companionship. Both

Aunt Means and Varina Davis, the wife of Secretary of War Jefferson Davis, acted as White House hostesses, particularly during the first years of the Pierce administration. Several of Jane's contemporaries testified that she bravely discharged her duties at dinners and receptions, although her heart was not in performing the public requirements of her position.

Initially she avoided crowded public events, such as evening receptions, but did appear at private dinners, where she could be quite charming. At a March 24, 1854, dinner, Mrs. Pierce impressed Elihu Burritt, a well-known peace proponent of the day, with her questions regarding international affairs. At a dinner the Pierces held the following month, the guest list embodied the political tensions of the time. Senator Stephen A. Douglas of Illinois, who escorted Mrs. Pierce, would soon see his Kansas-Nebraska bill become law, providing for self-government in those two territories and leading to the migration of proslavery forces. Also present was Jane's cousin Amos Lawrence. He would heavily finance the New England Emigrant Aid Company in its quest to establish free-soil settlers in Kansas. Lawrence, Kansas, an antislavery stronghold, was named in his honor.

Gradually, Jane became more socially active. On New Year's Day, 1855, after two years of mourning, she publicly received guests alongside her husband. Her grief still evident, Jane never recovered from the deaths of her children, particularly the violent death of Benjamin.

After leaving the White House in 1857, the Pierces took an extended tour of Europe, returning to the United States in 1860. Jane died at the age of fifty-seven on December 2, 1863, in Andover, Massachusetts, and is buried in Concord, New Hampshire.

Legacy

In early 1853, Jane not only lost her last child but also, at least temporarily, lost her faith in her husband. She learned that, despite his claims to the contrary, Franklin had sought the nomination for president. Modern historians have often placed the responsibility for their estrangement, and even his failings as president, on her. Although devastated by the events of her life, Jane Pierce has been depicted as contributing, however innocently, to the start of the Civil War by hurting her husband's performance in office. She has been portrayed as a vindictive, even insane, woman who blamed Franklin for their son's death and deliberately shut herself away from her husband.

However, in an 1853 letter to her sister, Jane indicated that Franklin's presidential duties kept them apart. She regretted that they could not share their grief. Varina Davis confirmed that Mr. Pierce's "society was the one thing necessary to [Mrs. Pierce], and he was too overworked to give her much of his time." Evidence indicates that greater mutual support would have benefitted both Jane and Franklin as well as his presidency. Very much a lady of her era, Jane was highly regarded by many of her contemporaries.

Suggested Readings

Bell, Carl Irving. *They Knew Franklin Pierce (and Others Thought They Did): A Sampling of Opinions About the Fourteenth U.S. President Drawn from His Contemporaries*. Springfield, Vt.: April Hill, 1980. Includes descriptions of Jane Pierce by historian Elizabeth Ellet and Jessie Benton Fremont, the wife of John C. Fremont.

Boas, Norman F. *Jane M. Pierce (1806-1863): The Pierce-Aiken Papers: Letters of Jane M. Pierce, Her Sister Mary M. Aiken, Their Family, and President Franklin Pierce, with Biographies of Jane Pierce, Other Members of Her Family, and Genealogical Tables*. Stonington, Conn.: Seaport Autographs, 1983.

_____. *Jane M. Pierce (1806-1863): The Pierce-Aiken Papers Supplement*. Mystic, Conn.: Seaport Autographs, 1989.

Cottrell, Debbie Mauldin. "Jane (Means Appleton) Pierce." In *American First Ladies: Their Lives and Their Legacy*, edited by Lewis L. Gould. New York: Garland, 1996. A chapter-length biography of Jane Pierce.

Davis, Varina. *Jefferson Davis, Ex-President of the Confederate States of America: A Memoir by His Wife.* 2 vols. New York: Belford, 1890. The future First Lady of the Confederacy was a confidante of Jane Pierce.

Means, Anne M. *Amherst and Our Family Tree.* Boston: privately printed, 1921. This history of Jane Pierce's family includes descriptions of her in their letters.

Nichols, Roy Franklin. *Franklin Pierce: Young Hickory of the Granite Hills.* 1931. Rev. ed. Newton, Conn.: American Political Biography Press, 1998. Jane Pierce is mentioned throughout this comprehensive biography of her husband.

Whitton, Mary Ormsbee. *First First Ladies, 1789-1865: A Study of the Wives of the Early Presidents.* 1948. Reprint. Freeport, N.Y.: Books for Libraries Press, 1969. Includes a sentimentalized but insightful account of Jane Pierce.

Elizabeth Lorelei Thacker-Estrada

Harriet Lane

Harriet Rebecca Lane

Born: May 9, 1830
      Mercersburg, Pennsylvania
Died: July 3, 1903
      Narragansett Pier, Rhode Island

President: James Buchanan
      1857-1861

Overview: Harriet Lane assumed the role of White House hostess for the only bachelor president in American history, her uncle James Buchanan. She exerted a great influence on her female contemporaries and was one of the most popular First Ladies in the nineteenth century.

Early Life

Harriet Rebecca Lane was born on May 9, 1830, in Mercersburg, Pennsylvania, the youngest of four children. After her mother's death in 1839 and the death of her father a year later, she had no hesitation when it came to choosing her guardian: "Nunc," alias James Buchanan, her favorite uncle.

Buchanan was flattered to be in charge of his niece's education. He encouraged her to read a great deal, introduced her to the classics of British and American literature, and stimulated her interest in history and politics. She was allowed to attend his conferences and meet his friends, and she became familiar with political conversation.

Although Harriet was mature for her age in some ways, she was also boisterous, and Buchanan sent her to a boarding school, run by the Misses Crawford, two severe women who imposed strict discipline and tolerated no lapses in behavior. In her letters to her uncle, Harriet

Harriet Lane, niece of James Buchanan. *(Courtesy of Craig Shermer, National First Ladies' Library)*

complained, according to Laura Carter Holloway Langford, of "early hours, brown sugar in tea, restrictions in dress, stiff necks and cold hearts." After that period of chagrin, she attended other private boarding schools in Lancaster, Pennsylvania, and in Charles Town, Virginia, from which she was graduated with honors.

Aware of her talents, Buchanan was concerned that his niece should also develop a sense of gentility suitable to a fine, respectable young lady. Therefore he chose the venerable Visitation Convent in Georgetown, Washington, D.C., as her finishing school. With the nuns, Harriet blossomed into a bright and self-confident young woman.

When she was eighteen, she moved to Wheatland, a vast country home in Lancaster County, Pennsylvania, her uncle had recently acquired, where she became a gracious hostess as if it were second nature to her.

In April, 1854, Harriet went to London, where Buchanan had been appointed minister to Britain's Court of St. James by President Franklin Pierce. More lovely and charming than ever, she soon became a favorite of England's Queen Victoria, who decreed that she be called Dear Miss Lane, a title that granted Harriet a status equivalent to that of an ambassador's wife. In the brilliant circles in which she moved, she received much attention and many compliments as well as numerous offers of marriage. She even fell in love with a former lord chancellor, Sir Fitzroy Kelly, but she com-

James Buchanan

James Buchanan was the fifteenth president of the United States and served during the tumultuous pre-Civil War years. He was born on April 23, 1791, at Cove Gap, Pennsylvania, the second of eleven children. He received a good education and, in 1809, graduated with honors from Dickinson College in Carlisle, Pennsylvania. He then studied law and was admitted to the bar association in 1812. In August, 1814, he volunteered to join a cavalry company and fight the British, who had burned Washington, D.C., in the War of 1812. After the war, Buchanan occupied a seat in the Pennsylvania legislature for two years before resuming his law practice in Lancaster. In 1819 he was engaged to one Ann Coleman, but the romance broke up, and he never married.

Buchanan returned to politics and was elected as a Federalist to the U.S. House of Representatives in 1821. During his ten years of service in the House, he switched to the Democratic Party and supported Andrew Jackson. In 1831 President Jackson appointed him minister to Russia. On his return, Buchanan was elected to the Senate, where he served until 1845, when President James Polk asked him to become secretary of state. After a four-year break from political life, caring for nephews and nieces in his Wheatland mansion, he was made minister to Great Britain by President Franklin Pierce.

On Buchanan's return from London in 1856, his conciliatory position over the 1854 Kansas-Nebraska Act helped him win the Democratic nomination and the presidential election. He supported the Supreme Court's 1857 Dred Scott decision that Congress could not outlaw slavery in U.S. territories and recommended that Kansas be accepted to the Union as a slave state. Despite his efforts at compromise, he failed to prevent the North-South divide from widening. The secession crisis that Buchanan had striven to prevent came with the election of President Abraham Lincoln in 1860. Five weeks after Buchanan left Washington, Fort Sumter fell and the Civil War began.

Buchanan spent his retirement at his home, Wheatland, and in 1866 published his memoirs, in which he defended the policies of his administration. He died on June 1, 1868.

plied with her uncle's advice not to marry a man forty years her senior. Harriet and James always acted as a team, and she made a point of respecting his opinion in all circumstances.

Conscious of her role in diplomacy, Harriet contributed to the promotion of the United States through her introduction of American Indian art at a time when English interest in Oriental and African cultures was becoming fashionable. She wanted to reveal the Indians' creative talent and spiritual life. With the Industrial Revolution at its height, Harriet also became active in social work. She emphasized the need to improve the living and working conditions of English laborers and vigorously supported the reform movement.

Marriage and Family

Although men had admired her since her teens, it was not until October, 1864, that she announced her engagement to Henry Elliot Johnston, a handsome gentleman she had met in Bedford Springs, Pennsylvania, in 1849. She was almost thirty-six when, on the cold, snowy morning of January 11, 1866, her uncle the Reverend Edward Y. Buchanan of the Oxford, Pennsylvania, Episcopal Church, declared Henry and Harriet husband and wife. After a honeymoon in Cuba, they settled in Henry's house in Baltimore. On November 21, 1866, a son was born, James Buchanan, named in honor of the former president. Harriet gave birth to a second son, Henry Elliot, Jr., two years later.

Her Uncle James's death on June 1, 1868, caused Harriet inconsolable grief. She had lost her best friend, her moral guide, her second father. Fortunately, the next ten years of parenthood brought Harriet great satisfaction. Life was easy and comfortable, as Henry was a prosperous banker and the family traveled extensively in the United States and abroad. Summers were spent at Wheatland, the estate she had inherited from her uncle. In the 1880's, sadness and sorrow gained the upper hand as one tragedy followed another. On March 25, 1881,

her fifteen-year-old son Buchanan died of rheumatic fever. On October 13, 1882, his brother, Henry, died of the same illness at the age of thirteen. Tragedy befell Harriet again on May 5, 1884, when her husband died suddenly of pneumonia.

Though grief-stricken, Harriet was by nature resilient, and instead of living in the past, she decided to work for the future. She sold both Wheatland and her Baltimore home and moved to Washington, D.C., where she devoted herself to philanthropic causes. She died of cancer on July 3, 1903, at Narragansett Pier, Rhode Island.

Presidency and First Ladyship

After the dismal years of the Millard Fillmore (1850-1853) and Franklin Pierce (1853-1857) administrations, Washington society was longing for a more lively and exciting White House. Their wishes came true with the election of James Buchanan in 1856. The new leader of the country, however, was not the cause of the joyful atmosphere that prevailed in the capital. It was his niece Harriet Lane who stole the show and was the center of attention. At the age of twenty-seven, she was installed in 1600 Pennsylvania Avenue as one of the youngest First Ladies in American history. Beautiful, gracious, and spirited, the new hostess of the White House became the talk of the town and soon won the hearts of many Americans across the country.

Her knowledge of politics and diplomacy, combined with her grace and dignity, helped her to perform her social duties with tact and style. According to one congressman's wife, "White House functions rose to their highest degree of elegance." Harriet brought gaiety back and the press dubbed her "Our Democratic Queen." The song "Listen to the Mockingbird" was dedicated to her. A U.S. steamboat was christened the *Harriet Lane*, and many baby girls were given her name. Harriet also became a trendsetter in youth-conscious Amer-

Stones That Stayed

As First Lady, Harriet Lane retained a character trait from her childhood years: her mischievous side. Because of her popularity, she was offered many gifts by her admirers, but her uncle James Buchanan had always advised her against an excessive display of luxury. She respected his opinion in all matters but still found hard to resist a splendid bracelet, set in part with real diamonds. Fearing James's reaction, she asked him innocently if she could keep some "pebbles" someone had sent her. The president saw no objection to keeping such an insignificant gift. Harriet later commented, "Diamonds are pebbles, you know!"

ican society, and her stiff, full skirts and "low-neck lace bertha" became all the rage in the capital.

Behind the young beauty there lay a strong personality and an astute politician who was well informed on the intricacies of the time. The president confided in her "in all matters political and personal," according to Sarah A. Pryor. Like Buchanan, Harriet believed in the triumph of moderation over extremism. She kept supporting him when his political friends started to abandon him, and she defended him against accusations of inertia or treason. Leaving the White House was a relief for both of them.

Legacy

Though not by definition, Harriet Lane was truly a First Lady in the eyes of Americans, and it was in her honor that the expression appeared for perhaps the first time in a magazine, *Frank Leslie's Illustrated Newspaper*, on March 31, 1860.

Harriet left a valuable legacy of social and cultural service. Because of her interest in art, she instituted concert evenings at the White House and regularly invited artists to her receptions. She also supported the movement to create a national gallery. After her death in 1903, her own vast collection was bequeathed to the Smithsonian Institution and formed the basis of the National Gallery of Art, which prompted one official to call her the First Lady of the National Collection of Fine Arts.

Since her years at the convent, she had always pleaded the cause of the American Indians and celebrated their culture. She used her proximity to power to improve their living conditions, increasing educational and medical assistance available to them. In gratitude, the Chippewas called her Great Mother of the Indians, and Harriet became a popular name for their babies.

After the death of her two sons, she decided to create the United States' first hospital for children, the Harriet Lane Home for Invalid Children, in Baltimore. This pediatric institution is still in service today, as part of the Johns Hopkins Hospital, and has acquired a worldwide reputation. As a devout Episcopalian, Harriet also began planning the Saint Albans choir school in Washington, D.C., which was founded in 1909.

According to historian Lloyd C. Taylor, Harriet Lane "was the first of the modern First Ladies to capture the imagination of her contemporaries." Her celebrity was not determined by the vagaries of public opinion; it was the result of her natural sense of communication and her political perspicacity as well as her influence in humanitarian reform and promotion of the arts.

Suggested Readings

Anthony, Carl Sferrazza. *First Ladies: The Saga of the Presidents' Wives and Their Power*. Vol. 1. New York: William Morrow, 1990.

A must-read on First Ladies, including a valuable chapter on Harriet Lane.

Holloway, Laura Carter. *The Ladies of the White House: Or, In the Home of the Presidents*. Reprint. New York: A. M. S. Press, 1976. Despite its pompous style, this includes precious testimony of a contemporary of Harriet Lane.

Peacock, Virginia Tatnall. *Famous American Belles of the Nineteenth Century*. Freeport, N.Y.: Books for Libraries Press, 1970. A general portrait of Harriet Lane.

Shelley, Mary Virginia, and Sandra Harrison Munro. *Harriet Lane, First Lady of the White House*. Lititz, Pa.: Sutter House, 1980. This is juvenile literature but is the only modern book on Harriet Lane.

Taylor, Lloyd C. "Harriet Lane: Mirror of an Age." *Pennsylvania History* 30 (January-October, 1963): 213-225. This is the best article of historical value that has so far been written on Harriet Lane.

Pierre-Marie Loizeau

Mary Lincoln

Mary Todd Lincoln

Born: December 13, 1818
    Lexington, Kentucky
Died: July 16, 1882
    Springfield, Illinois

President: Abraham Lincoln
    1861-1865

Overview: Mary Lincoln continues to be one of the most controversial First Ladies in U.S. history. As the wife of Abraham Lincoln, the most admired of American presidents, Mary Lincoln serves as a tempestuous counterpoint to his depressed personality. Full of verve, wit, and high temper, she was as ambitious as Lincoln was for his political success. She redecorated the public rooms of the White House and, in the process, overspent the budget for its repair. As First Lady, she was admired as an elegant social hostess. A devoted mother, she outlived three of her four children. After her husband's assassination, her surviving son, Robert Todd Lincoln, had her institutionalized for behavior that most historians believe displayed nervousness and instability but not insanity.

Mary Lincoln, circa 1861. *(Library of Congress)*

Early Life
Mary Todd was born on December 13, 1818, in Lexington, Kentucky, into a distinguished Kentucky family. Her grandfather Levi Todd had been one of the founders of Lexington, and among her uncles and earlier relatives were generals, planters, and political leaders. Her father, Robert Smith Todd, was a successful slave-owning cotton manufacturer and banker as well as an aspiring Whig politician who served in the Kentucky legislature. Her mother's fam-

113

ily, the Parkers, were equally distinguished and affluent. Both sides of the family had been among those ambitious settlers who flooded into Kentucky in the 1790's in order to take advantage of the state's fertile land and the commercial opportunities that arose in its leading city, Lexington.

Mary was the third daughter of Robert Smith Todd and Elizabeth Parker Todd's seven children. When Mary was six years old, her mother died of puerperal sepsis, the post-birth bacterial fever feared by nineteenth century women and called childbed fever.

The loss of her mother was the beginning of a series of tragic losses for Mary. She and her older sisters disliked her new stepmother, whom her father had married in 1828. A diligent and intelligent student, Mary excelled at both John Ward's local seminary and later at a boarding school in Lexington. There she learned French, as well as the school's curriculum of every branch of "good education," which included rigorous training in the traditional studies of reading, writing, and arithmetic as well as the home arts of embroidery and sewing. After twelve years of schooling, she was eager to leave Lexington, mostly because of her hostility to her stepmother. While she en-joyed the social life in town, where women dressed formally to pay afternoon calls, she sought associations with those who were interested in politics and literature. Even in these early years of her life in Kentucky, neighbors and friends remembered this energetic, vivacious young woman's interest in politics.

In 1838 Mary traveled to Springfield, Illinois, to live with her older sister Elizabeth, who had married Ninian Edwards, an aspiring Whig politician and a political ally and friend of Abraham Lincoln. Like Mary Todd, Abraham was a newcomer to Springfield. While her sisters had encouraged her to come, Abraham had settled in the prairie town on his own because it was the new capital of Illinois. As a lawyer and ambitious Whig assemblyman, he benefited from his associations with clients and politicians there. Soon Mary and Abraham were courting. Physically, they were very different. Mary was five feet, four inches tall, plump, brown-haired, and graced with an appealing, round face. Abraham was six feet, four inches tall, with black hair and a long, narrow face. No doubt Abraham was attracted by Mary's wit and lively conversation, as were several other leading politicians, including Stephen A. Douglas.

A Lifelong Interest in Politics

When Mary Todd was a young girl living in Lexington, Kentucky, one of her neighbors was the well-known Whig politician Henry Clay, who ran for president three times. One day, according to her relatives, young Mary rode her pony through Ashland, Clay's estate. When Clay told her that he might be moving to the White House, she responded that she, too, expected to move to Washington—as a president's wife.

This story reveals Mary's interest in public affairs at a time when women were supposed to remain in private life. Mary Todd Lincoln, like few other American women, sought a role in one of the central preoccupations of nineteenth century men. She wrote patronage letters for her husband, offering her advice. In May, 1860, when Abraham Lincoln was nominated for president by the Republican Party, reporters traveled to Springfield to learn more about "Honest Abe." In the simple Lincoln home, they found Mrs. Lincoln to be a well-informed spouse who, since her childhood, had enjoyed talking about politics.

Abraham Lincoln

Abraham Lincoln was ambitious as a young man and intended to better himself. Growing up on isolated farms in Kentucky and Indiana as the son of a farmer, he had less than two years of formal education and was largely self-taught. When he moved to the small community of New Salem in 1832, his horizons broadened. When the Illinois capital moved to Springfield, Lincoln followed. Having been accepted into the Illinois bar association, he immediately combined the law and politics. After an initial defeat, he was four times elected as a Whig to the Illinois legislature. By the 1850's he was well known in Illinois for his support of internal improvements as well as his principled stand against the extension of slavery into the territories. He was also sufficiently self-confident to have senatorial ambitions, although he was twice defeated for an Illinois senate seat. Meanwhile, his legal practice flourished.

By 1856 Lincoln had become a member of the newly created Republican Party. Lincoln now emerged as a powerful spokesman of a party whose bedrock position was to prevent the extension of slavery into the territories absorbed into the United States as a result of the Mexican War. As a result of the Kansas-Nebraska Act, which provided for self-governance in the territories; the struggles in so-called Bleeding Kansas; and especially the 1857 Dred Scott decision by the U.S. Supreme Court that made slavery legal in all the territories, slavery seemed to be nationalized. Lincoln found this an appalling prospect which would destroy the democratic experiment based on freedom and liberty that the founders had created.

In a series of debates with U.S. Senator Stephen A. Douglas, Lincoln made history. Douglas argued for popular sovereignty and the right of white citizens to decide whether they would have slavery in their communities. In powerful speeches which gained him a reputation beyond the boundaries of his state, Lincoln, who despised slavery, argued that slavery must not be nationalized. As a result of his eloquent enunciation of an important northern principle, in the Republican nominating convention of 1860 he became his party's second choice for president. He was elected in 1860 in an unusual election in which four candidates ran.

Abraham also appreciated her interest in politics, which was unusual among women of this time. She found in him a man who would treat her with tolerance and understanding, and she certainly sensed in him the ambition that would lead him to the White House. Her family, the Edwardses, and Mary's sister Frances Wallace, who also lived in Springfield, objected to the match, believing Abraham Lincoln was not as wellborn as their sister. Despite the family's objections and a disruption in their courtship occasioned by Mary's anger at Abraham's tardy arrival for a dance, twenty-four-year-old Mary Todd married thirty-three-year-old Abraham Lincoln on November 4, 1842. He gave her a ring inscribed Love Is Eternal.

Marriage and Family

Like most nineteenth century American women, after marriage Mary was soon absorbed in childbearing and raising and caring for her home and husband. Mary Todd Lincoln became pregnant almost immediately with her first son. Named after her father, he was born in August, 1843. Soon her second son, Edward Baker Lincoln, followed, but Eddie suffered from tuberculosis and died in 1850. In a pattern that suggests the Lincolns controlled their fertility, only after Eddie's death did Mary become pregnant again. William Wallace Lincoln was born in 1850, and because, as his mother said, he needed a playmate, Thomas Lincoln, called Tad, was born in 1853.

Abraham and Mary Lincoln with sons Robert and Tad. *(Library of Congress)*

As the family grew, and with the financial help of Mary's father, the Lincolns moved from the boardinghouse they first inhabited to a small cottage and finally to their famous Springfield home on Eighth and Jackson Streets. Because Lincoln's law practice took him to the courtrooms in counties throughout the Eighth Judicial District in central Illinois, Mary was responsible for running the house. In the nearly twenty years in which the Lincolns lived in Springfield, Mary was well-known as an energetic housekeeper who worked hard to keep a clean, well managed home. Like other middle-class women in Springfield, at various times she employed domestic servants to help with the endless tasks of cooking, cleaning,

sewing, and the dreaded Monday chores of washing and ironing. Yet Mary did most of the domestic labor in her household.

Like her husband, she was a permissive parent who was very much engaged with her children and who was ambitious for their success. Rarely did the sons of even Illinois's wealthiest families venture across the prairies to eastern universities, but both Abraham and Mary Lincoln wanted their sons to attend the best schools in the United States. Accordingly, in 1859, Robert left for Harvard University, where he failed his entrance exams and spent a postgraduate year at Phillips Exeter Academy before his admission to Harvard in 1860.

By the 1850's Abraham Lincoln's political

ambitions focused on a United States Senate seat. Earlier he had been elected as a Whig to Congress, where he served from 1847 to 1848. In an unusual decision that attests to her interest in politics, Mary and the boys accompanied him and lived in a Washington, D.C., boardinghouse. In 1855 and again in 1859, Lincoln was defeated for election to the Senate. During this dry spell in his political career, Mary played a supporting role in his efforts. She entertained important state officials, wrote patronage letters, and perhaps most important, bolstered the spirits of her husband.

In May, 1860, Lincoln became the presidential nominee of the Republican Party. When delegates and reporters traveled to Springfield to inform him of his nomination, they found a talkative, intelligent informant in his wife. They also complimented her home as tasteful and graceful. In an age in which Americans were beginning to foster a celebrity culture, Mary Lincoln became public property—and became subject to praise and blame from the press in her new role as First Lady.

Presidency and First Ladyship

In February, 1861, the Lincoln family traveled to Washington to take up residence in the White House. By this time, seven southern states had seceded from the Union, and the future of the republic was in doubt. In these turbulent times, as the train carrying the new president moved through the Midwest into New England and the Middle Atlantic states, crowds flocked to the stations in order to hear him and to see his family, in an age before photographs introduced the people to their leader. Everywhere Mary Lincoln appeared, cheers were heard from a crowd that sometimes saluted "Mrs. Abe." In Baltimore, however, the triumphant journey turned sour when rumors reached the presidential party of an assassination plot in that city. Within five weeks of their moving into the Executive Mansion, the Civil War began.

Once settled in the White House, Mary began to redecorate—a task that she believed necessary and important as a statement of the power of the Union. In previous administrations the White House had been neglected; its furniture and upholstery were dingy. The atmosphere of the White House became important during the Civil War, when the mansion played an essential role as a symbol of a powerful Union.

Mary, with the characteristic personal bravery that kept her in Washington even as other political wives returned home to safer sanctuaries, soon undertook her own campaign to improve the interior of the White House. She traveled to Philadelphia and New York in the spring of 1861 to choose new fabrics for the public rooms, and she ordered fancy wallpaper from a Paris house. She changed the dusty rugs and hired Washington cabinetmakers to revarnish and fix the broken furniture that she, Willie, and Tad found in the attic. She also ordered a new, 190-piece set of Limoges china.

In the process she overspent the budget granted by Congress to the commissioner of public buildings. She also irritated her husband, who was furious at what he called her flub-a-dubs. Moreover, some newspapers accused her of trying to behave in the manner of a European queen. Unfairly and incorrectly, she was also accused of supporting the Confederacy, even of being a spy, because of her Kentucky heritage and the fact that her half brothers were fighting in the Confederate Army.

Eventually, even her enemies had to agree that the restored public rooms of the White House were elegant. It was in the East Room and the Blue Room that Mary Lincoln presided over her receptions and soirees. Handsomely gowned in dresses and shawls which were often lent by shops that wanted advertisement of their wares, she was widely acknowledged as poised and sociable. According to servants, the White House was opened during the Lincoln years more often and to more Americans than in any previous administration. In March, 1865, more than two thousand Americans pushed into the White House to enjoy what became the last Lincoln reception.

Intensely interested in politics, Mary sometimes interceded with her husband's cabinet officers in order to gain various civilian and military posts for her family and friends. Once Secretary of State William H. Seward encouraged her to mind domestic affairs, but this First Lady believed that an interest in public issues was, in fact, her business. Her interest in matters beyond the usual fare of women is documented in the telegrams that Abraham sent her while she was away. They frequently mentioned military news which the president knew she would be interested in reading.

In the summers the Lincolns moved to the Old Soldiers Home outside Washington, where the air was considered cleaner and fresher. Mary, who traveled more than any other First Lady up to this time, also visited New England. When in Washington, she was, like many other women, a frequent visitor to the Army hospitals, and she helped raise money to aid newly freed slaves who moved into Washington during the Civil War.

The White House was also home to a family with young children. In this era, with her husband's office on the second floor, Mary and the children had to step over the patronage seekers lining the halls in order to get to the seven rooms of the family quarters in the West Wing. With maternal sensitivity, Mary understood that Willie and Tad were isolated from other children and so she worked hard to find playmates for them. She was also concerned about her husband as he struggled to find a general and strategy. For the most part, recreation outside the White House took the form of visits to the theater or afternoon carriage rides around Washington.

The White House, for all its glories as a center of power during four years of war, soon held sorrow. In February, 1862, eleven-year-old

Abraham and Mary Lincoln greet Union generals, cabinet members, and others at their last reception, 1865. *(Library of Congress)*

Willie died of typhoid fever. Both his parents were desolate. While the president could absorb Willie's death into a larger perspective of the sorrows of the time, his wife was unable to do so. Mary's fierce mourning rendered her incapacitated for months. Then in 1865, shortly after Lincoln's second inaugural and just as the war was ending, she saw her husband murdered as they watched the play *Our American Cousin* in Ford's Theatre.

Legacy

Again devastated by the abrupt loss of a loved one, Mary moved to Chicago with Tad. Later she traveled to Europe with Tad, who, after their return from Germany in 1871, died an agonizing death from pleurisy, the third of her sons to die before her. In 1875 Robert Lincoln had his mother committed to an insane asylum, and after her successful battle to be released, she moved to France. She returned the year before her death in 1882 to live with her sister Elizabeth Edwards in Springfield.

Her legacy as a First Lady involved her commitment to making the White House a statement of power and glory during a threatening period of American history. Ahead of her time, she turned the president's home as well as his public entertainments into symbolic statements of his authority and, through him, the power of the nation. It was a role that would bring future First Ladies acclaim, but in Mary's time it was an unusual obligation for First Ladies, who usually stayed out of the limelight. No one since Dolley Madison had taken such pains to fix up the White House and turn it into a place where the American people—soldiers, politicians, and others—could meet the leader of the nation. Given her interest in public affairs, Mary Lincoln also represented a new kind of First Lady—one who was concerned with affairs beyond domestic life.

Suggested Readings

Baker, Jean H. *Mary Todd Lincoln: A Biography.* New York: W. W. Norton, 1986. A largely sympathetic biography that looks at Mary Lincoln's life from her perspective.

Brooks, Noah. *Washington, D.C., in Lincoln's Time.* 1895. Reprint. Chicago: Quadrangle Books, 1971. Edited revision with new commentary by Lincoln biographer Herman Mitgang.

Helm, Katherine. *Mary, Wife of Lincoln.* New York: Harpers, 1928. An engaging biography that includes family perspectives on Mary Lincoln.

Randall, Ruth Painter. *Mary Lincoln: Biography of a Marriage.* Boston: Little, Brown, 1953. Based on excellent research, Randall's book discusses the Lincoln marriage with sympathy and understanding.

Schreiner, Samuel A., Jr. *The Trials of Mrs. Lincoln.* New York: Donald A. Fine, 1987. An account of Mary Lincoln's later years. With index.

Turner, Justin, and Linda Leavitt. *Mary Lincoln: Her Life and Letters.* New York: Alfred A. Knopf, 1972. Although Mary Lincoln's letters continue to surface, this compendium serves as an excellent introduction to her life.

Jean Baker

Eliza Johnson

Eliza McCardle Johnson

Born: October 4, 1810
      Leesburg, Tennessee
Died: January 15, 1876
      Greeneville, Tennessee

President: Andrew Johnson
      1865-1869

Overview: Eliza McCardle Johnson became First Lady in 1865 when her husband, Andrew Johnson, assumed the presidency after the assassination of Abraham Lincoln. Born into poverty in east Tennessee, Eliza helped lift her family into the prosperous middle class, but much of her life was spent as an invalid. Although she lived in the White House during her husband's term, she appeared in public only four times. Her story carries as much tragedy as it does triumph.

Eliza Johnson. *(Library of Congress)*

Early Life

Born in Greene County, Tennessee, on October 4, 1810, Eliza was the only child of Sarah Phillips McCardle and John McCardle, a Scotsman who was an innkeeper at Warrensburg and later a cobbler at Greeneville. John died while Eliza was a child, and she and her mother made quilts for a living. Although poor, Eliza received a basic education at Rhea Academy.

A modest, retiring girl, Eliza first met Andrew Johnson in September, 1826. Legend tells that she was the first person he spoke to when he arrived in Greeneville and that she told her friends to mark Andrew as her future husband. Johnson moved briefly to Rutledge, Tennessee, but he returned to Greeneville in the spring of 1827. A brunette with hazel eyes, sixteen-year-old Eliza married eighteen-year-old Andrew on May 17, 1827, in Warrensburg. Mordecai Lincoln, a cousin of Abraham Lincoln, performed the ceremony. Of all the presidential couples, the Andrew Johnsons were the youngest to wed.

Marriage and Family

The newlyweds rented a house with two twelve-foot-square rooms on Main Street in Greeneville. Andrew used the front room for his tailoring business, while the couple lived in the rear. Andrew had taught himself to read, but Eliza encouraged him to gain more education. Though she was a devoted Methodist, she never convinced Andrew to attend church regularly with her.

Eliza bore their first child, Martha, on October 25, 1828, and their son Charles on February 19, 1830. Andrew's shop became a popular gathering place for working men to discuss politics, and in 1829 Andrew was elected as town alderman. As he prospered, the couple bought a brick house across the street in 1831. There, Eliza had two more children: Mary on May 8, 1832, and Robert on February 22, 1834. By 1837, Andrew employed several tailors and purchased his first slaves, eventually owning as many as nine.

Elected state representative in 1837, Andrew left for Nashville, the capital, leaving Eliza as manager. When Andrew became a U.S. congressman in 1843, Eliza oversaw the family, house, tailor shop, real estate holdings, and a farm. In 1851 the Johnsons purchased a larger

Andrew Johnson

Andrew Johnson was born in Raleigh, North Carolina, on December 29, 1808, the son of poor, landless workers Mary McDonough Johnson and Jacob Johnson. His father died when Andrew was three, and at age ten, Andrew was apprenticed to a tailor. He had no formal education and taught himself to read and write. He eventually set up a tailor shop in Greeneville, Tennessee, where he met and married Eliza McCardle. A Democrat, Johnson never forgot his early poverty, and he would always be a champion of the working class.

These laborers elected Johnson to his first office as alderman in 1829, and he rose to state representative in 1835, U.S. congressman in 1843, and governor of Tennessee in 1853. In 1857 Johnson became a U.S. senator, and he was one of the few southern statesmen to remain with the Union when the Civil War began. Abraham Lincoln rewarded Johnson's service as military governor of Tennessee by placing Johnson as vice president on the 1864 campaign ticket. However, Lincoln's assassination in April, 1865, thrust Johnson into the office of president.

In the first months of his administration, President Johnson extended amnesty and pardons to all Confederates (with a few exceptions) who would take an oath of allegiance to the Union. He appointed provisional governors for former Confederate states, allowing them to hold elections and constitutional conventions. When Congress reconvened in December, 1865, Johnson claimed he had restored the Union. Congress countered by passing civil rights bills, including the Thirteenth Amendment, forbidding slavery, and the Fourteenth Amendment, giving African American men the right to vote. Tension grew as Johnson vetoed bill after bill, and in 1867 he suspended Secretary of War Edwin Stanton in defiance. Congress retaliated in 1868 by impeaching Johnson for violating the Tenure of Office Act, and the president escaped conviction by only one vote in the Senate.

After leaving Washington in March, 1869, Johnson found it impossible to retire quietly. He began campaigning for a return to office and in 1874 was elected once more to the U.S. Senate. Johnson saw his election as vindication for his policies on the Union, and when he died in 1875, he was buried wrapped in the American flag with his head on a copy of the Constitution.

brick house, which was filled by their family, along with Eliza's and Andrew's mothers. Mary married Daniel Stover in April, 1852, moving to his farm, and Eliza had her fifth child on August 5, 1852, Andrew, Jr., nicknamed Frank. After Frank's birth, Eliza showed increasing signs of tuberculosis, which would make her an invalid for the remainder of her life.

Elected governor of Tennessee in 1853, Andrew lived mostly in Nashville. Martha helped her ailing mother until she married attorney David Patterson in December, 1855. In 1857 Andrew was elected U.S. senator. In early 1860 Eliza, Frank, and Robert visited Andrew briefly in Washington, D.C., to give him support in his efforts to preserve the Union. In April, 1861, Andrew returned to Tennessee, encountering violent anti-Union mobs along the way. Eliza remained firm in her antisecession support. Some observers felt that Andrew drew more counsel on his public policies from Eliza and Martha than from anyone else.

By June, however, Tennessee had seceded from the Union. Andrew returned to Washington. Their sons Robert and Charles joined the Union military, as did Daniel Stover. David Patterson, now a judge, was imprisoned by authorities of the Confederate States of America (CSA). Eliza and Frank joined Martha's family at the Patterson farm, as the Johnson house and slaves were seized by the Confederates. Eliza remained there for months, reviled as a Unionist, especially when Andrew became military governor of Tennessee in February. In October, the CSA authorities suddenly gave Eliza thirty-six hours to leave Confederate territory. She managed to move her children and grandchildren through enemy lines to Nashville, arriving there on October 12.

Although Eliza had reached Andrew, her tuberculosis made her so ill that she traveled to a resort in Indiana, seeking relief. Eliza returned to Nashville in better health, but a heavy blow fell in April, 1863, when Charles died after a fall from his horse. To add to her worries, Frank was showing signs of tuberculosis, as was Robert, who had become an alcoholic. Andrew was elected vice president of the United States in November, 1864; in December, Daniel Stover died of consumption, the name used to refer to tuberculosis and its effects. When Andrew left for his inauguration in March, 1865,

Eliza's Escape Through the Lines

In October, 1862, as the Civil War raged, Eliza was suddenly given thirty-six hours to leave Confederate territory. Quickly gathering her children Charles, Frank, and Mary, and three grandchildren, she fled Greeneville, Tennessee, by train. Her destination was Nashville, the capital of Tennessee, of which her husband, Andrew, was military governor. Traveling through the Rebel-held cities of Knoxville and Chattanooga and then to the Confederate line at Murfreesboro, a total of 275 miles, Eliza and her family arrived at 9:00 on a rainy night, only to be refused permission to cross the lines to Nashville. They were sent back to Tullahoma, where they found shelter in a cold, vacant house, with no furnishings, food, or heat. Eliza comforted them by producing candles and matches and giving the children supper from her lunch, which she had saved.

The next day they returned to Murfreesboro, where Confederate Brigadier General Nathan Bedford Forrest sent Eliza's party under a flag of truce to Nashville. Eliza finally reached her husband on October 12. A witness to the reunion said, "The great joy of this long and sorrowfully separated family may be imagined. . . . Even the governor's Roman sternness was overcome, and we wept tears of thankfulness."

Eliza remained in Nashville with the widowed Mary and her children, hoping to return to Greeneville soon.

Presidency and First Ladyship

An assassin's bullet fired on April 14, 1865, catapulted Andrew and Eliza Johnson into the White House: President Abraham Lincoln's death on April 15 left Andrew as the new president.

In August, Eliza arrived in Washington, and the entire extended family would remain in the White House throughout Andrew's term of office. Ever modest, Eliza chose a small bedroom in the northwest corner of the second floor. She took most of her meals in her rooms, and Andrew would visit her each morning before going to his office. Eliza's routine seldom varied. She read newspaper and magazine articles from around the country, giving Andrew good news in the evening and bad in the morning. After Andrew's morning visit, she would inspect the upstairs rooms, giving special attention to his quarters and wardrobe. Her grandchildren would visit her after their classes each day. Eliza never felt comfortable in the role of First Lady, saying, "It is all very well for those who like it, but I don't like this public life at all. I often wish the time would come when we could return to where I feel we best belong."

Eliza's illness prevented her attending all but a few of the social functions required of the president. In August, 1866, she received Queen Emma of the Sandwich Islands (now Hawaii) and other guests, and Queen Emma gave Eliza a hand-carved ivory basket that still adorns the Johnson house in Greeneville. The following February, Eliza attended two receptions. One guest commented that she was "a very amiable, unassuming woman [and] acts her part so modestly and so well as to win the affections of all who see her." Eliza always dressed elegantly in rich fabrics; as a former tailor, Andrew took great pride in the quality of his family's wardrobes.

When Andrew was impeached in February, 1868, Eliza never wavered in her support. She upheld Andrew in staying the course he felt best for the nation and following his conscience, regardless of the outcome. The ordeal weighed upon her, however, and Eliza told a visitor, "But for the humiliation and Mr. Johnson's feelings, I wish they would send us back to Tennessee—if it were possible, give us our poverty and peace again, so that we might learn how to live for our children and ourselves. I have not seen a happy moment since I came to this house." When Andrew was acquitted of charges in May, 1868, Eliza exclaimed, "I knew he'd be acquitted. I knew it."

Eliza attended one last gala, for Andrew's sixtieth birthday, on December 29, 1868, a ball for three hundred children of Washington dignitaries. The party was such a success that children's balls became a regular feature of the capital's social scene.

Legacy

Shortly after President Ulysses S. Grant's inauguration in March, 1869, Eliza and Andrew traveled home, greeted by a large crowd in Greeneville. Mary had their house ready, the war's damages repaired. That spring, Mary married William R. Brown and settled into a home across the street. New tragedy struck, however, when Robert committed suicide on April 22. Further trouble came when the Johnsons saw that Mary's marriage was unhappy. Andrew wrote Brown, "Rather than have anything like [separation] happen in my family, I would sooner have everything I have sunk in the depths of Hell." After Andrew's death, the couple would divorce.

Eliza had longed to return to her home, but Andrew longed only to leave it again. He began making speeches around the United States and, in the fall of 1874, was once again elected senator from Tennessee. He left for Washington that winter. Andrew returned in the spring of 1875, but in July the old political warrior headed for

Ohio to help in a campaign. He stopped at the Stover farm on July 28 to visit Eliza, who was staying with Mary. There, Andrew suffered a series of strokes, and he died on July 31. His funeral was attended by all of his family and virtually the whole town, except for Eliza, who was too weak to go. Andrew left no will for his estate, worth as much as $200,000, and Eliza was left once more as administrator. Too ill to attempt a settlement among the children, Eliza stayed with Mary at her farm.

Eliza passed away on January 15, 1876, and was laid to rest next to her husband on Monument Hill in Greeneville, a property Andrew had bought years before. In 1906 this land was designated a national cemetery and, in 1942, the home Eliza so longed for while First Lady became a national monument.

Suggested Readings

Brabson, Fay Warrington. *Andrew Johnson: A Life in Pursuit of the Right Course.* Durham, N.C.: Seeman Printery, 1972. Includes biographical material on Eliza Johnson.

Graf, Leroy P., Paul Bergeron, et al., eds. *The Papers of Andrew Johnson.* 16 vols. Knoxville: University of Tennessee Press, 1967-2000. The full collection of Johnson's correspondence, including some letters sent to Eliza Johnson and references to her.

Thomas, Lately. *The First President Johnson: The Three Lives of the Seventeenth President of the United States.* New York: William Morrow, 1968. Includes insights into the relationship of Andrew and Eliza Johnson.

Sawyer, Susan. *More than Petticoats: Remarkable Tennessee Women.* Helena, Mont.: Falcon, 2000. Written for a young audience, the profile of Eliza Johnson includes legends and anecdotes.

Smith, Gene. *High Crimes and Misdemeanors: The Impeachment Trial of Andrew Johnson.* New York: William Morrow, 1977. A detailed account of the Johnsons during the months of the impeachment trial.

Trefousse, Hans L. *Andrew Johnson: A Biography.* New York: W. W. Norton, 1989. This scholarly, full-length biography of Andrew Johnson includes insights from the Johnson papers.

Ann Toplovich

Julia Grant

Julia Boggs Dent Grant

Born: January 26, 1826
    White Haven,
       St. Louis County, Missouri
Died: December 14, 1902
    Washington, D.C.

President: Ulysses S. Grant
    1869-1877

Overview: As the wife of the Union's most accomplished Civil War general, Julia Grant was already in the public eye before Ulysses S. Grant assumed the presidency. An energetic and optimistic woman, Julia played a crucial role in her husband's success, providing a loving family circle and offering support to her husband in all circumstances. During his presidency, she deftly made the Executive Mansion a family home, while bringing her warmth and enthusiasm to public occasions. After her husband's death, she worked to promote his memory, supported charities and the cause of women's suffrage, and enjoyed her family.

Julia Grant. *(Library of Congress)*

Early Life

Julia Boggs Dent was born on the Western frontier at her family's farm near St. Louis, Missouri. Although she had four older brothers, she was the first daughter born to Frederick Dent and Ellen Wrenshall Dent, and throughout her life she remained her father's favorite. Three sisters followed after her birth, although one died in infancy.

Colonel Dent came from a prominent Maryland family but had left home as a teenager and made his fortune in the fur trade. He married Ellen Bray Wrenshall of Pittsburgh, Pennsylvania. The couple soon moved to St. Louis, an

125

increasingly important fur-trading center. Dent established a firm there and began to acquire property, placing the family within the social elite of St. Louis. After a few years, however, the appeal of country life grew on him, and the family settled at White Haven, a farm he had purchased near St. Louis, where the colonel lived the life of a slave-holding gentleman farmer.

Julia grew up the beloved daughter of her parents and the indulged sister of her brothers, and like them, Julia attended the local one-room schoolhouse. At age ten she was enrolled at the Mauro Academy for Young Ladies in St. Louis, where she enjoyed singing and reading—including poetry, mythology, and the works of William Shakespeare. Graduating in 1843, Julia visited White Haven, then returned to St. Louis to enjoy the winter season's balls and entertainments, although she later wrote, "I was the shyest of little girls, and if I had any admirers, I am sure I did not know it."

Julia wore a braid until she was sixteen, when she put her thick, dark hair into a chignon, a sign of adulthood. She was a petite woman, barely five feet tall, with beautiful, delicate hands. Her face was rather plain and she suffered from strabismus, an eye problem now easily corrected, but then afflicting many. One eye at times lost focus and turned in, giving her a cross-eyed appearance and making reading difficult. Late in her life, Julia confided to a friend that her eyes had always made her feel ugly. When she sought an operation to correct the problem, however, Ulysses Grant insisted that he loved her as she was and declared surgery unnecessary.

Marriage and Family

While Julia visited St. Louis, her parents were welcoming Lieutenant Ulysses Grant to White Haven; he was a West Point friend of their son Fred, stationed near the farm. Once Julia returned home, Ulysses' visits became more frequent. Both Julia and Ulysses were accomplished on horseback, and the pair enjoyed long rides through the countryside. In later life, Julia referred with fondness to that period of her life and to her "handsome lieutenant," who had clearly come to love her. Nevertheless, she refused his offer of his West Point ring and mused that although it might be fun to be engaged, she did not know about marriage. Julia's hesitation was allayed by her mother's vision of fame in Ulysses' future, for the family believed that Ellen Dent had second sight. Further, Julia believed that she had inherited the gift, and when a dream involving the lieutenant came true immediately, she seems to have felt destined to become his partner.

The couple became secretly engaged in the spring of 1844, when Ulysses was posted to Louisiana. When he approached Julia's father a year later, the colonel voiced scepticism about his daughter becoming an Army wife. Though he doubted the young man's future prospects, he permitted the couple to correspond. In 1845 the outbreak of war with Mexico further postponed their marriage until August 22, 1848, when the war had ended and Ulysses returned from Mexico. Rejecting her father's suggestion that she remain at White Haven while her husband returned to the Army, Julia and Ulysses Grant traveled to Army posts at Sackets Harbor, New York, and at Detroit.

Julia was determined to build a life for herself and her husband, and participated actively in the social life of Detroit and Sackets Harbor. Their first child, Frederick Dent Grant, was born in 1850. While she was pregnant with their second child, Ulysses received orders for California, and the couple agreed that the difficult journey would not be possible for Julia. Several weeks after his father set sail for the Isthmus of Panama in 1852, Ulysses S. Grant, Jr., or Buck, was born. The child was more than a year old before Ulysses learned of his birth.

The posting to California marked a turning point in the young couple's fortunes. Julia and her sons went to White Haven to live with her

Ulysses S. Grant

Ulysses S. Grant's reputation is undergoing a serious reevaluation, which also affects popular understanding of Julia Dent Grant. From a view of the wartime general as a butcher and a drunk, clearly inferior to Robert E. Lee, a new picture is emerging. General Grant is now recognized by many historians to have been a master strategist and outstanding military leader, not only the best officer in the Union Army, but the best general on either side of the Civil War.

Similarly, Grant's political role after the war and during his presidency is also being revised. Scholars have pointed out that President Grant sought equal civil rights for the African American population emerging from slavery and was in many ways hampered by policies established during Andrew Johnson's presidency. People of color were always welcomed at the Grant White House, and social reformer Frederick Douglass remained a firm supporter.

The corruption that dogged his administration certainly existed, and President Grant too frequently turned a blind eye to improprieties engaged in by subordinates and relatives whom he trusted and to whom he felt loyalty. American political life had been rife with patronage and corruption for decades, however, and the Civil War heightened opportunities for favoritism, nepotism, and bribes as the government issued land grants and military contracts and sought to harvest cotton in occupied areas. For too long, historians evaluated Grant as postwar partisans had, accepting as true the criticisms made by white Southerners or by members of the northern elite who were hostile to the self-made men important in political and economic life after the war.

parents, while her husband faced enormous trials en route to California. Crossing the Isthmus of Panama, Lieutenant Grant was responsible for troops and dependents. Corruption, disorganization, lack of transport and supplies, and disease dogged their trip, which took much longer than expected. Ulysses was heartily glad that Julia and the children had not accompanied him. Nor was California much better. Gold Rush inflation and failed business attempts meant that the lieutenant could not afford to send for his family, and orders arriving in 1853 directed him to Fort Humboldt, a small, isolated fort, commanded by an unsympathetic officer. Having been promoted in 1854, Captain Grant resigned his commission. Military officers afterward circulated the rumor that he resigned to avoid a court-martial for drunkenness on duty, a charge that, although never substantiated, haunted him throughout his life.

In 1854 Ulysses returned to Missouri to farm sixty acres of wooded land that Colonel Dent had given Julia as a wedding present. He built a

log homestead, dryly dubbed "Hardscrabble," and, with Julia, immersed himself in farming. Their two youngest children were born: Ellen in 1855 and Jesse in 1858. A fall in agricultural prices and lack of cash for investment meant that the only sure "crop" in these years was the wood being cleared for planting. Ulysses sought help from his prosperous father in Illinois, but the old man always set terms designed to separate him from Julia, as the two did not get along. Jesse Grant disapproved of the Dents' slave-holding and also regarded Julia as a spendthrift and an overindulgent mother.

An attempt at real-estate management with a Dent relative in St. Louis went awry. The failing health of Ulysses' brother Simpson, however, finally led their father to relent toward his eldest son and invite him to work in the family leather business in Galena, Illinois. In 1860 the Grants moved to the flourishing river town, where Ulysses clerked and traveled through the North, purchasing skins, and expecting that he would eventually become a partner in the

Ulysses and Julia Grant and son Jesse at their vacation cottage, circa 1872. *(Library of Congress)*

during the Civil War, Julia was unusual in the amount of time she spent in the field and was almost captured by Confederate raiders on at least one occasion. Ulysses told Julia that she gave him a quiet domestic sphere, a respite from the pressures and responsibilities of military leadership. While at the front, Julia took up the duties of a commanding officer's wife, visiting troops and Army hospitals. She also continued her maternal duties, for her younger children Nellie and Jesse usually accompanied her, and she took responsibility for their education. At the same time, she encouraged the children's independence and sent eleven-year-old Frederick to the field with his father, whose worries about the boy's safety she rejected.

firm. The couple lived quietly in their family circle, spending evenings listening to Ulysses read or to Julia sing. It was a family filled with love and very tolerant of childish mischief in an age when parents were advised not to "spare the rod."

Within the year, however, sectional turmoil brought on the Civil War and ended the Grants' new life. Captain Grant became involved in efforts to raise troops, became a colonel of volunteers, and then almost immediately a brigadier general. Over the summer of 1861, Julia remained in Galena and shared women's support efforts, sewing and knitting items for the troops. When her husband wrote, asking her to join him in Cairo, Illinois, she too began new private and public duties as the wife of an increasingly important Union general. Although other officers' wives visited their husbands

By the time of the Civil War, both newspapers and photographs had become powerful sources of popular information. Ulysses' victory at Fort Donelson in early 1862 catapulted him into the public eye. Julia and her children, as well as General Grant, became a focus of attention which made them celebrities. Modest for herself, Julia was proud of her husband's popular recognition. Looking back after his death, Julia commented that she "rested and was warmed in the sunlight of his loyal love and great fame." After the war ended in 1865, the attention continued, for President Abraham Lincoln's assassination made Grant important as commander in chief of the U.S. Army and adviser to President Andrew Johnson. Julia enjoyed life in the capital and entertaining at their home on I Street.

Presidency and First Ladyship

Ulysses Grant was sworn in as president in March, 1869, with high expectations placed upon him as the man to reconcile the United States—North and South, freedman and white citizen, Republican and Democrat. Julia continued her role as the president's confidante and supporter, creating in the White House a sphere that mixed the private, domestic life that her husband cherished with the public dimensions of office. The new ambiance created by Mrs. Grant was homey and welcoming, yet lively, sociable, and moderately elegant as well. Observers who expected a return to formal etiquette and high fashion found the First Lady's approach disappointing. For most, however, the Grant White House symbolized post war democracy, represented in particular by the First Lady's weekly receptions, at which all were welcomed, including working women, immigrants, and African Americans.

In planning her social duties, Julia wisely drew upon the services of Julia Fish, an experienced political spouse and the wife of Secretary of State Hamilton Fish. At the same time, Julia invited the wives of dignitaries to receive along with her at public receptions. This made the First Lady appear less regal and haughty, allied important Washington wives to her and her husband, and spread the burden of formal and extensive entertaining. Such deft maneuvering was, however, not always the case when the First Lady moved from social to more directly political activities. Insiders recognized that Julia was an important informal adviser to the president and often tried to win her support for people and policies. Many indeed felt that her husband listened too closely to her views, for emotional ties and loyalty were important criteria for Julia. When clear evidence linked the wife of Secretary of War W. W. Belknap to a kickback scheme, for instance, Julia nevertheless pleaded the secretary's case. Her support of women's suffrage was more measured, centering upon discussion among guests at the Executive Mansion and private contributions.

The White House was very much a family home during the Grants' tenancy. Nellie and Jesse played in the rooms and appeared during levees and meetings. The children's friends and cousins had the run of the house. Old Colonel Dent, now a household member, regularly sat in the main hall and conversed with visitors. Julia's brother Fred served as a secretary to the president, receiving guests and attending to their wants. When official events were not

Singing Julia's Praises

From cabinet wives to journalists, commentators praised Julia Grant as a sociable and unaffected First Lady who sincerely enjoyed entertaining and who did not mind deferring to others in order to smooth relationships.

Early in her husband's presidency, Julia described herself as being a simple frontier woman to Maria Lydig Daly, descendant of a prominent New York Dutch family. This allowed Mrs. Daly to explain the intricacies of opera to her guest, unaware that Julia had attended plays and musical evenings as a young woman in St. Louis.

On the other hand, persons who questioned the probity of the Grants were not tolerated. At about the same time that she denied familiarity with opera, Julia Grant received an anonymous news clipping dealing with a purported presidential scandal. Learning that the clipping had been sent by the wife of Secretary of the Interior Jacob D. Cox, the First Lady no longer welcomed Mrs. Cox socially, and her husband soon found himself replaced in office.

scheduled, the family ate together in their private dining room early in the evening and then spent time together. Relatives and friends were frequent White House visitors, overflowing the inadequate guest rooms and remaining for weeks and months at a time.

Legacy

Ulysses left the presidency determined to return to private life and to travel, which he had always enjoyed. Julia was less happy to leave, for the White House had been the family home longer than any other place during their marriage. The general had expected to undertake his travels as a private citizen, but this was not to be. Sailing for England, the couple found at their first port of call that neither privacy nor anonymity awaited, for they were received as visiting dignitaries. Thus began a year and a half of cheering crowds, interviews, and entertainment by officialdom and royalty in Europe and Asia as well as renewed celebrity back home in the United States. Julia took it all with aplomb, enjoying both the time with her family and the opportunity to meet new people. Her warmth and personal engagement rarely flagged; one of her granddaughters was later told by an Ottoman vizier that during the Grants' visit, "your Grand Mother was more interested in us little boys than in the men of importance, and one day she put her hand on my head and said, 'For you I see a great future.'"

The Grants completed their travels in 1879 by visiting the American West. Although Julia hoped that her husband would be nominated again for the White House, Ulysses refused to stand after the Republican convention appeared to deadlock. The couple finally entered private life, living in New York City, only to make headlines once again in 1884 when the financial firm of Grant and Ward, which their son Buck had convinced his father to join, went spectacularly bankrupt. Deeply humiliated and anxious about the welfare of his family, Ulysses sold off as much personal property as possible, including such prized possessions as swords given to him in honor of Civil War victories. To earn some income, he accepted magazine offers to write about the war, embarking on yet another career.

More bad fortune was to come: In the midst of financial ruin, Ulysses was diagnosed with throat cancer, clearly caused by his heavy cigar smoking. Under sentence of death but desperately seeking an income, he decided to write his memoirs. His friend author Samuel Clemens, better known as Mark Twain, who had recently established a publishing firm, offered the general a substantial advance and royalties for his work, freeing him from his financial burden. *Personal Memoirs*, the two volumes which have since become a classic, brought $450,000 to Julia and provided her with a substantial widow's income.

Devastated by her husband's death in 1885, Julia remained for a time in her New York home, shared by her son Fred and his family. She began to write her own memoirs, which helped her to recover from Ulysses' death. She also spearheaded efforts to select a site for Grant's tomb and to raise funds for its construction. Julia also continued her work for women's suffrage, helping to raise money for the National Woman Suffrage Association. She became friendly with Varina Davis, widow of the Confederate President Jefferson Davis, a sign of the shift in personal and popular understanding of the Civil War. In 1894 Julia moved back to Washington, D.C., where she lived quietly until 1902, when she died after an illness.

Suggested Readings

Grant, Jesse R. *In the Days of My Father, General Grant*. New York: Harper and Brothers, 1925.

Grant, Julia Dent. *The Personal Memoirs of Julia Dent Grant (Mrs. Ulysses S. Grant)*. Edited by John Y. Simon. Carbondale: Southern Illinois University Press, 1975. Julia Grant's insightful memoir shows the romance in her relationship with Ulysses S. Grant.

Grant, Ulysses S. *Personal Memoirs of U.S. Grant*. Introduction by James M. McPherson. New York: Penguin Books, 1999. Considered one of the best autobiographies of any major military leader; focuses mainly on his military career.

Ross, Ishbel. *The General's Wife: The Life of Mrs. Ulysses S. Grant*. New York: Dodd, Mead, 1959.

Simon, John Y., ed. *The Papers of Ulysses S. Grant*. 24 vols. Carbondale: Southern Illinois University Press, 1969. The set, in which Grant's own words show his humor, pathos, and unique personality, contains all known correspondence written and received by him.

Carole Elizabeth Adams

Lucy Hayes

Lucy Ware Webb Hayes

Born: August 28, 1831
    Chillicothe, Ohio
Died: June 25, 1889
    Fremont, Ohio

President: Rutherford B. Hayes 1877-
    1881

Overview: Lucy Hayes was the first wife of a president to be called First Lady on a frequent basis. The troops commanded by her husband, Rutherford B. Hayes, during the Civil War referred to her as Mother of the Regiment because of the care and concern she showed to all soldiers. During her White House years, she was known by her many admirers for her generosity and charity. To those who disagreed with the Hayeses' stand on temperance, she was known as Lemonade Lucy.

Early Life

The daughter born to Dr. James Webb and his wife, Maria Cook Webb, on August 28, 1831, was christened for her paternal grandmother, Lucy Ware Webb. The Webbs had two older children, Joseph, aged four, and James, aged three. Born in the old capital of Ohio, Chillicothe, Lucy's father had a sizable practice and although he had served in the War of 1812, he preferred a medical career to a military one. Though born a Southerner, Dr. Webb was an avowed anti-slavery man, and Maria Webb, whose family came from New England, was equally so.

In the terribly hot summer of 1833, Dr. Webb set off for Kentucky to free the fifteen to twenty slaves left to him by his aunt in her will, but as he arrived a cholera epidemic was sweeping through the region. Working long hours to save the victims, Dr. Webb, weakened and over-

Lucy Hayes. *(CORBIS)*

worked, contracted the disease. As did his parents and brother, Dr. Webb died in the epidemic, before his wife could reach him.

When questioned about the poverty she faced, Maria Webb shrugged. When again asked why she did not sell the slaves her husband had intended to free before his death, Maria replied, "I will take in washing to support my family before I would take money for the sale of a human being." This made a deep impression on Lucy; for the rest of her life, she had a deep respect and love for her mother and the memory of her father.

Like many women of the time, Maria Webb took in boarders or cleaned other people's homes for a living. Staying on in Chillicothe, Maria leaned heavily on her stern but loving father, Isaac Cook, a former state legislator and supporter of public schools. Lucy loved her grandfather and often visited his farm, Willow Branch. His firm Methodist faith was to be a lifelong influence on Lucy; when he asked her and her brothers to take a temperance oath, they complied. Lucy often went riding with her brothers and cousins, climbed trees, and helped her mother with the household chores.

Maria, like her father, believed in education for her daughter as well as her sons. As both Joe and James would one day be doctors like their father, Maria saw to it that Lucy received a good, thorough education. Lucy attended a variety of local schools, including the Chillicothe Female School, an elementary school. One of her early teachers, Miss Baskerville, did not believe in recess or in any form of levity during the school day. Aside from a short lunch break, Lucy and her classmates spent all day at their desks. Once, when Lucy brought her cousin Joe to school as her guest, Miss Baskerville got angry with him for some minor infraction and proceeded to whip him. Lucy flew at her in a rage, yelling, "I brought him to school to visit and you shan't touch him!" Miss Baskerville, amazed at the normally cheerful Lucy's rage, said nothing.

Another time at school, some of the girls were cruelly picking on two German-speaking girls, making fun of their dress and speech. It was Lucy who took the newcomers aside, brought out her dolls, and showed the girls the clothes she had made for the dolls. Thus, Lucy's generous and cheerful nature crossed the barriers of both language and culture.

All her life, Lucy loved reading but disliked writing and arithmetic. (One time, as a young housewife, Lucy attempted to keep the household accounts, but after reading them, her husband took over that duty himself.)

In 1844 the Webb family moved to Delaware, Ohio, where Maria saw her two sons into the Methodist school, today known as the Ohio Wesleyan University, where they began their medical training. She enrolled Lucy in the preparatory department, extending the education her daughter had received in Chillicothe. Intent on furthering her education, Lucy took courses at the college level and got several credits while there. It was here that Rutherford B. Hayes saw her for the first time and in his diary, which he kept all his life, noted Lucy's "bright eyes" and her sunny nature. He was twenty-four to her fifteen, and romance would have to wait.

It was shortly after this that Maria, not wanting her daughter to be swept off into an early marriage, moved Lucy to the "Queen City" of the Ohio River, Cincinnati. Lucy enrolled in the Cincinnati Wesleyan Female College, one of the first colleges to grant degrees to women. Along with about four hundred other women, Lucy studied, wrote, flirted, and enjoyed herself. Pretty, with black hair, parted "Madonna-like" in the middle, sparkling hazel eyes, and a merry laugh, she was well liked. In 1850, in spite of her dislike of writing, she was elected to the exclusive Young Ladies' Lyceum. There she studied rhetoric, geometry, astronomy, literature, trigonometry, and the sciences. She had to write long essays every two weeks, which sorely tried her patience, but she nonetheless did well in school. She also became an excellent speaker, which stood her in good stead when she gave speeches for the Methodist Missionary Society toward the end of her life. Upon Lucy's graduation from college, she delivered a dissertation on the effects of Christianity on the economy.

The day of her election to the Young Ladies' Lyceum, Lucy saw Rutherford again. His mother, Sophia Birchard Hayes, and Maria Webb had known each other in Delaware and had both secretly hoped their children would fall in love. At the wedding of a friend that fall, Rutherford noted Lucy's beauty and felt such a peculiar feeling in his chest that he gave her the surprise from the wedding cake: a gold ring. She kept it always and used it as her engagement ring when he proposed to her the next summer. Upon their engagement, she felt that she was "too light" a personality for his more serious nature, but they shared a love of life as well as great common sense. Above all, each adored the other. Rutherford's only complaint, then and later, was Lucy's slowness to answer letters. He wrote two to her one, which was exactly what she suggested he do. At this time his sister, Fanny Platt, with whom he had always had a close relationship, also began a correspondence with Lucy, leading to a close friendship.

Marriage and Family

At two o'clock in the afternoon of December 30, 1852, in the parlor of the Webb home in Cincinnati, Lucy Ware Webb became Mrs. Rutherford Birchard Hayes. She was twenty-one years old; he was thirty. It would prove to be an unusually happy and contented marriage. Lucy's wedding dress, which can still be seen at Spiegel Grove, was of white brocade satin with gold fringe and was, as would become her trademark later in life, high in the neck and modest in cut. At five in the afternoon, the young couple boarded a train for Columbus, where Rutherford was to argue a case before the Ohio Supreme Court. They then spent a monthlong honeymoon staying with Fanny, Rutherford's sister.

The first years of the Hayeses' marriage were spent in Cincinnati. Like many couples in the United States in the mid-nineteenth century, they would move a number of times before settling in a permanent home. Part of their early years were spent in Columbus, but they stayed primarily in Cincinnati, where they were close to not only Mother Webb but Mother Hayes as well. In November, 1853, Lucy gave birth to the first of her eight children, a son. Both Lucy and Rutherford wanted to wait to name their child, thinking that the child's personality would help them determine a name. This greatly upset Mother Hayes, who was never known for her patience or sense of humor, so Lucy named the baby Puds. Of course, this was not the final name; after several other ideas, they settled on Birchard Austin, or Birchie for short.

Shortly after Birchie's birth, the Hayeses bought their first home; as Lucy had forgotten to pack the silverware, they all ended up using little Birchie's child-size knife to cut their food. In March, 1856, another son was born and christened James Webb, but his parents found the name did not suit him and changed it to Webb Cook Hayes. Though Lucy loved all of her children, her secret favorite was Webb, who later called his mother "my best friend" (when he was not referring to her as "the old lady," a nickname she often called herself). Webb proved to be an engaging child but was stubborn in his refusal to learn his letters. He would climb on his mother's lap, smile, cajole, whine—anything but learn to read. Ironically, he was later to be his father's White House secretary.

These years before the Civil War were difficult ones for presidents Fillmore, Pierce, and Buchanan and the people of the United States. It was Lucy's strong antislavery views that changed Rutherford's lukewarm stand on abolition and issues associated with it. Her influence can be seen in his taking cases involving runaway slaves who had crossed the Ohio River into Cincinnati. As his fame grew in this regard, Lucy's concern for the former slaves grew as well. Within a month of their moving into their first home, she was appalled to find an abandoned black child on her doorstep. Lucy also remained in touch with the former slaves of her family, freed by her father's desire, and often employed them, most famously Aunt Clara and her daughter, Winnie Monroe, who served Lucy in the White House. Lucy encouraged Winnie's daughter Mary Monroe to attend Oberlin College. When Winnie died in Washington after the Hayeses had left the White House, it was Lucy who paid her funeral expenses.

Shortly after Webb's birth in the summer of 1856, Rutherford suffered the loss of his beloved sister, Fanny, who died giving birth to twin daughters, who also died. Before Fanny's death, she had suffered from a severe depression which led to a short stay in an asylum. She had recovered, only to die in childbirth. Her temporary bout of depression touched on a secret fear of both Rutherford and Lucy: insanity. Both had a deep horror and fear of it, for mental illness had been noted in both their families. In the years to come, Lucy would take a deep interest not only in the treatment of the mentally ill but also in the creation of better hospitals for their care. This would be especially evident when Rutherford was governor of Ohio.

Fanny's death had another effect on Lucy's political development. Fanny had been an ardent supporter of women's suffrage and Lucy, who was lukewarm on the subject, accompanied Fanny to several meetings. Though the meetings fired Lucy's spirits, with Fanny gone and her own family continuing to grow, her interest in the women's movement fell by the wayside.

In the summer of 1858, Lucy gave birth to her third son, Rutherford Platt Hayes, after she developed a severe case of rheumatism, accompanied by severe headaches which plagued her

for the rest of her life. With the presence of her mother and her unmarried brother, Joe, Lucy often had help raising her children; so much so, that Birchie, Webb, and Ruddie pitied their Platt cousins because they did not have an Uncle Joe. With the addition of a new baby, the Hayeses enlarged their house, improving the kitchen and adding an extra bedroom for paid servants. One Christmas, Rud and Lucy were surprised to find a Christmas tree put up for them by a German servant of theirs.

The Hayeses were fond, loving, and practical parents. They rarely had to discipline their sons, but the children's high spirits sometimes led to a whipping—by Rud, not Lucy. Lucy's tenderness extended especially to old people, as her mother-in-law, Sophia Hayes, often referred to herself. She who was not prone to high praise once complimented Lucy on her tender regard for the elderly, calling it "a rare and excellent trait of character." Lucy would often take in motherless nieces and cousins and once, years later, when she heard of the illness of a young employee in Fremont, brought him home to Spiegel Grove to nurse back to health.

Rud's uncle Sardis Birchard was an extremely successful businessman who had a huge influence on the lives of his nephew and his family. In the late 1850's he had bought twenty-five wooded acres, which he called Spiegel Grove. The brick home he built there in time became home to Rud and Lucy and the site of the first presidential library. Often during the hot summers of the Civil War, Lucy would send her older boys to Uncle Sardis's in upper Sandusky, which later became Fremont, Ohio.

The fall of 1860 saw the election of President Abraham Lincoln and the splitting of the Union. In February of 1861, Lucy accompanied her husband to Indianapolis to escort Lincoln, who had just been joined by his wife, Mary, and her two younger sons, to Cincinnati. Lincoln was on his way to Washington to be sworn in as president. When Lucy heard the news of Fort Sumter on April 12 through 14, 1861, she exclaimed that if she had been in a regiment of women, the fort would never have surrendered. She proudly—and fearfully—saw Rud off to war as commander of the Twenty-third Ohio Volunteer Infantry, in which her brothers also served as surgeons. Often when she visited Rud, they would walk from campfire to campfire, talking, joking, and sympathizing with the men under his command. It was not long before Lucy became known as the Mother of the Regiment, or Mother Lucy. Of concern to Lucy was the treatment of the former slaves. She wrote, "If a contraband [runaway slave] is in Camp, don't let the 23rd Regiment be disgraced by returning [him or her] or anything of the kind."

In December of 1861, her fourth son, Joseph, named for her brother, was born. In spite of her periodic fears of Confederate raids on Cincinnati and missing her husband, Lucy kept up her spirits, but even she had some dark moments. Confined with three active boys and a colicky baby, Lucy once commented to her husband that "drilling a regiment would be play." She often wrote—overcoming a lifelong distaste for writing letters—to her brother Joe, as well as to Rud, and once said, "It is a hard thing to be a woman and witness so much and yet not do anything." She told her brother to be ever kind to the wounded and sick and often went herself to the hospitals when visiting the regiment.

On September 14, 1862, the Union forces, including the Twenty-third Ohio, had pursued the Confederates to South Mountain, near Burkittsville, Maryland. Lucy was about to embark on one of her greatest trials. As the regiment engaged the enemy, Rud, not known for profanity, swore at his men to take the hill. As they advanced, he was hit in the left arm. His elbow was shattered, but he managed to stay on the field until ordered off. Lucy's brother Joe treated Rutherford and managed to save his arm. The wounded man was then transferred to the home of strangers in Middletown, Maryland, where he had his orderly send off three

telegrams to Lucy. Because the orderly did not have enough money, the first was not sent. When Lucy got the second message, "I am here, come to me. I shall not lose my arm," it was mistakenly marked "Washington, D.C."

Leaving her children to the care of Maria and Lucy's oldest friend, Eliza Davis, Lucy took off for Washington with her brother-in-law, Mr. Platt, Fanny's widowed husband. Arriving there, Lucy frantically searched the hospitals, which knew nothing. Figuring that Baltimore might be another possibility, she boarded another train and headed east. That, too, proved fruitless. Returning to Washington, Lucy traveled to the hospitals again and upon leaving the patent office, which was serving as a military hospital, she saw the number twenty-three on several uniforms and cried out, "Twenty-third Ohio!"

"It's Mrs. Hayes," someone called out. Upon learning her husband was in Middletown, Lucy and Mr. Platt took a train and arrived late at night to find Joe Webb waiting for them: He had come every night for a week in the hope that Lucy would arrive. One can only imagine her relief when she saw her husband's face. He joked, "Here's my wife who visits Washington and Baltimore before she visits her wounded husband!" Lucy did not find it funny, then or later when he repeated it in the White House. Rutherford's relief in Lucy's presence was evident in his letters home to Uncle Sardis, though he noted, "She visits the wounded and comes back in tears." She often read to the men, laughed with them, soothed their fears, and closed their eyes.

While traveling, little Joe, who had always been sickly, caught a fever and died. As Lucy was sick herself, the little body was shipped home to Cincinnati for burial, which was taken care of by Lucy's friend Eliza Davis. Lucy said later that this event had shown her what the meaning of friendship was all about. In September of 1864, Lucy gave birth to her fifth child, a boy whom Lucy hesitantly asked her husband if she could name for his commander, General George Crook. Rutherford agreed, and George Crook Hayes was christened.

Lucy, like all others, was overjoyed when peace came at long last in April, 1865, though she and Rud grieved for the loss of President Lincoln. When peace was announced, Rutherford, despite his abstemious modern-day image, told his daughter years later that "he went on a 'toot.'" That he would do so showed how relieved he was at the war's close. At the Grand Review on May 23, 1885, Lucy joined her husband on the reviewing stand. She later said that while she was pleased to know that slavery was forever dead, she grieved for all the boys, especially those of the Twenty-third Ohio, who would never come home.

Taking his seat in the House of Representatives (though elected, he had not left the Army until the fighting was done), Rutherford divided his time between Washington and Cincinnati. These few years gave Lucy a taste of what entertaining in Washington would be like. She was not entirely happy at the thought of living in the capital, though she loved attending the debates in Congress and would always wear a large, checkered shawl so Rud could see her. This fascination with politics would stand her in good stead in Columbus as a governor's lady.

Back in Cincinnati in April, 1866, Lucy was horrified to discover Birch had come down with scarlet fever, which then afflicted all of her children, killing little George in late May. The loss of her favorite grandchild took a heavy toll on Maria Webb, and on September 14, 1866, Lucy, who had a beautiful voice, sang "Nearer My God to Thee" as she closed her mother's eyes. Sophia Hayes, her mother-in-law, died the following month. Lucy later referred to 1866 as her worst year.

It was the era of Reconstruction, and in 1867, after the terrible race riots in the South, Lucy accompanied her husband to Memphis and New Orleans to see the devastation for herself. That same year Rud was elected governor of Ohio,

and Lucy became the proud mother of a daughter, who was quickly named for the much lamented Fanny. Little Fanny became a special favorite of her father, who when he left for the office would hear her call out, "Bye-bye." Fanny's birth was followed in 1871 by the arrival of the eleven-pound Scott Russell, whose birth took a heavy toll on his mother's strength. Fanny and Scott were to be Lucy's younger family, while the three older boys were already almost in college. Webb had absolutely no idea his mother was expecting, and the last baby's birth was a total surprise to him. Two years after Scott came Lucy's last child, born in August of 1873. At first named Nibs, his name became Manning Force. Manning never thrived, and his death, on Lucy's birthday in 1874, was grievous but not unexpected. Despite the loss of three children, Lucy could look back and write to Webb, "With all our changes and sorrows, a happy and blessed family we have been and are."

Presidency and First Ladyship

When Rutherford Hayes was sworn in as governor of Ohio, Lucy made it her business to find a home in Columbus, to entertain and raise a family. These were normal duties of a Civil War-era matron, but she did more. She visited insane asylums, schools, reformatories, and orphanages, both for her own concerns and as the wife of the governor. Remembering the dead and wounded from her ghastly visits to wartime hospitals, Lucy had a special concern for the orphans left by the war. She was able to get state funding for an orphanage after lobbying for its passage in the eleventh hour. She shared Rutherford's concern for education; it was he who signed the charter for Ohio State University. Lucy often attended the debates at the state capitol, even joking to Webb that she was becoming "quite the politician."

Concern about their growing family, lack of a real home, and a need for rest made a third term as governor less than desirable for both

Rutherford B. Hayes

Rutherford B. Hayes, was actually one of the United States' better presidents. He was a man of honor and common sense, and one who loved books and learning. As governor of Ohio, he signed the charter for Ohio State University and after his White House years would serve on the committee for the Ohio State Historical Society and many other educational charities.

Hayes attended Kenyon College in Ohio, and after graduating as class valedictorian in 1842, he studied law at Harvard University. He received his degree in 1845 and joined the Ohio bar association.

After his marriage to Lucy Webb in December, 1852, Hayes settled in Cincinnati, where Lucy's abolitionist views influenced her more moderate husband into taking cases involving African Americans. He served as Cincinnati city solicitor from 1858 to 1862, then during the Civil War as commander of the Twenty-third Ohio regiment, rising to the rank of major general. Elected to the U.S. House of Representatives in 1865, he served there for two years and in his tenure fostered the modernization and expansion of the Library of Congress.

Elected governor of Ohio in 1868, he would serve two terms until 1872 and be elected to a third in 1876 but gave up the governorship for the presidency. As governor, he protected the rights of African Americans, trimmed state debts, tried to appoint to office men by reason of merit and not party, and improved schools, insane asylums, and prisons.

He was nominated in June, 1876, for the presidency by the Republican Party and faced Samuel J. Tilden of New Jersey. This turned out to be one of the most contentious elections in U.S. history. Reform was the key issue for both the Republican and Democratic parties, but after the scandals of Ulysses S. Grant's administration, it was harder for the Republicans to appear honest. The result was so close that, though Tilden carried the popular vote, Hayes tied him in the electoral college vote. The House of Representatives would end the deadlock but not until Hayes agreed to end Reconstruction, bring one Democrat from the South into his cabinet, and foster better education and railroads in the South.

In a hardworking administration, R. B. Hayes stood for reform, hoping to end the ancient spoils system, and for bringing federal troops out of the South, as he had promised. This action was seen by some as a tragedy in the long run, ensuring the denial of the right to vote for African Americans and prolonging the hatred engendered by the Civil War for another hundred years. He sought better treatment of the American Indians and encouraged the Timber and Stone Act of 1878, by which trees cut down on public lands had to be paid for by timber firms.

It was in the area of civil service that Hayes made his real mark. In 1877, he issued an order barring all federal employees from political activities. He called for a civil service commission, but Congress failed to act; it would take the assassination of President James A. Garfield to get the Pendleton Civil Service Act passed. Hayes encouraged the use of competitive examinations in the Interior Department and the Post Office. He fired Chester A. Arthur from the position of collector of New York for widespread corruption. In doing so, Hayes drew on himself the hatred of the boss gangs of New York.

In foreign affairs, President Hayes vetoed Congress's attempt to exclude all Chinese immigration to the United States. Further to the South, Hayes worked on Europe's attempt to create a canal in Panama, and his stand would lead to American intervention under President Theodore Roosevelt.

That Hayes's administration was one of great honesty surprised many, coming after such a prolonged election. He expanded the presidency by his visibility and open-handedness.

husband and wife. The Hayeses held their last reception in Columbus in January, 1872. The arrivals of Fanny and Scott had necessitated a larger home, and Uncle Sardis's offer of Spiegel Grove met their needs most handsomely. Though saddened by Sardis's sudden death in 1874, Rutherford, looking back on his years as governor, wrote his beloved Lucy, "My life with you has been so happy, so successful, so beyond anticipation that I think of you with a loving gratitude that I do not know how to express."

He contemplated his retirement only until necessity and politics brought him back again for a third term as governor. Upon his election, the *Ohio State Journal* wrote, "Mrs. Hayes is a perfect queen of a woman, and demonstrated as of old that she is equal to any emergency."

However, the Hayeses would not long enjoy Columbus. At the Republican National Convention in Philadelphia the name of Rutherford B. Hayes was brought forth, and on the seventy-seventh ballot he was nominated for the presidency. Afterward, Lucy found herself the center of press coverage: They commented on her bearing, her "Madonna-like" hairstyle, and her educational background. Lucy handled it all like a professional. The appearance of the Hayeses at the Ohio Day celebrations at the Centennial Exposition sparked the reaction of an appreciative crowd, to which Lucy, writing to Ruddie, then eighteen, said, "It was one of the happiest days in your mother's life. The expressions of pleasure and joy at your father's appearance touched the old wife who had known his merits for many years."

The presidential contest of 1876 between Rutherford and Samuel J. Tilden was one of the most intensely partisan in U.S. history. In that time, campaigning was done through the newspapers, and the candidates stayed home to greet well-wishers. Lucy enjoyed it all, and though shots fired through her window dampened her usual good spirits, her enthusiasm remained. On the evening of November 7, 1876, the Hayeses went to bed uncertain of the elec-

tion's outcome. Fearing Rutherford had lost, their only regret was their fear that the South might force the nullification of the Fourteenth and Fifteenth Amendments, which granted civil and voting rights to African Americans. However, nothing had been decided. Though Tilden had won the popular vote, electoral returns from South Carolina, Florida, Louisiana, and one vote from Oregon were in dispute. Hayes needed all to win, and Tilden needed only one. Congress appointed an electoral commission to decide the election. That decision would not come about until March, 1877, because of delaying tactics by both parties, so when the Hayeses boarded the train for Washington, they thought they might be returning by the same train. During a stop, Lucy was deluged with little white cards and demands for her autograph. In spite of her dislike of writing she obliged, only to discover that it had been a prank of Webb's.

On March 2, 1877, several hours after the commissioner awarded the election to Hayes, the family was roundly cheered as they entered Washington. Because the election had been contentious, President Ulysses S. Grant insisted on a private swearing-in ceremony for Hayes in the Red Room of the White House on March 3. On the following day, Inauguration Day, the newspaper noted Lucy's striking looks, her confidence, her handsome family, and her college degree. After the luncheon given for them by Julia Grant, who was extremely unhappy to be leaving, the Hayeses took possession of their new home.

In reports of the women's movement and all the changes it brought about, Lucy Hayes is often overlooked, if not actively criticized for not supporting the suffrage movement. Lucy, the first college graduate among U.S. First Ladies, was a firm believer in higher education, often visiting schools and colleges but never making speeches. She followed Julia Grant's policy in allowing African American servants to take time off work to pursue an education. She did not support the cause of universal suffrage, though, and gave two reasons: first, because her husband did not, and second, because illiteracy among women was still high. What good would voting be, she reasoned, if a woman was denied a chance at an education and was even viewed as being incapable of reasoning? The more the suffrage activists pushed Lucy for a statement of support, the more she resisted; neither she nor her husband ever supported women's suffrage.

However, according to accounts written at the time, Lucy was loved and admired. She had the ability to make others feel cared for and valued. As she grew older, Lucy became more thoughtful, kinder, and more loving of those who needed her help, but by the same token, she grew less confrontational and more fearful of fights or arguments. The deaths of three children, the loss of her mother, and the election and its attacks on her husband had drained her of some of her earlier zest. With that went her championing of causes.

There is one exception, however. Her name is forever linked to the banning of alcohol from the White House, for which she earned the nickname of Lemonade Lucy, though she was never publicly referred to by that name in her lifetime. It must also be noted that Lucy herself did not ban alcoholic beverages—her husband did. He had made it a part of the Republican campaign platform. Rutherford B. Hayes had a broad reformer's streak in his nature, which led him not only to ban liquor from the White House but also to try to reform the hiring of federal employees. He wanted to eliminate a system of granting jobs in return for favors, believing that hires should instead be based on merit, no matter what party one voted. As far as liquor was concerned, Lucy agreed wholeheartedly, for she had taken the temperance oath from her own grandfather when she was a girl. Lucy's temperance stance, however, was balanced by her own good sense and humanity. She felt that what people did in their own homes was their business. If the White House was to be her home, she was happy that no liquor would be served there.

As soon as the Hayeses announced their policy of banning alcohol, the State Department protested. The Grand Dukes Alexis and Constantine, sons of Czar Alexander II of Russia, one of the Union's allies in the Civil War, were expected at a White House reception in mid-April, 1877. Because the Grand Dukes and their staff would expect to be served wine, the president and his wife yielded. This was the only occasion upon which wine was served at the White House during the Hayes years.

Lucy's stand on liquor won her the support of the Women's Christian Temperance Union, which later donated a portrait of Mrs. Hayes in a red velvet dress to the White House. Others, however, were very unhappy with the ban. One of those who made a practice of secretly bringing flasks of whiskey in their coats was heard to say, "Water like wine flowed at the president's house." Cartoons were even drawn of Lucy, ridiculing her; yet she abided by her husband's wishes, which were in accordance with her own principles.

During Lucy's four years in the White House, there was an ever-increasing use of the title First Lady. While in earlier times it had been used to refer to her predecessors, including Mary Lincoln, its first consistent usage was in Lucy's time. Her charm, her expressive face, and even her childlike joy, which found expression in her jumping up and down, won even her husband's enemies to her. When a comment was made to the president about her influence, Hayes remarked, "Mrs. Hayes may not have much sway with Congress, but she has a lot with me." Once when she went home to Fremont, a newspaper said, "In the absence of Mrs. Hayes, the president will run the country."

Loving history as she did, Lucy was appalled at the gaps in the presidential portrait gallery in the White House. She corrected it by hiring an Ohio artist to paint portraits of the

Lending a Hand

Much of Lucy Hayes's time was spent in charity work, visiting hospitals, schools, and orphanages. No one who came begging at the White House for food or money was turned away. In one month, President and Mrs. Hayes gave away nine hundred dollars in handouts to the homeless. One of Lucy's household rules was if she was not home while someone came begging, Tom Pendel, the White House doorman, was to write down their name and address so Lucy could go to the needy person's home and drop off something.

Her generosity extended to friends and associates as well. When the veterans of Rutherford Hayes's Twenty-third Ohio Volunteer Infantry came to the White House to be photographed with their old commander, one of them, a newly promoted sergeant, was bemoaning the fact that he did not have his new sergeant's chevrons on his uniform yet. Grumbling good-naturedly, Lucy got down on her knees, bustle and all, to sew the chevrons on his uniform. No one could have been happier than that sergeant.

missing presidents, such as William Henry Harrison and Zachary Taylor. Perhaps one of her most lasting gifts to the White House was the full-length portrait of Lady (Martha) Washington to accompany the full-length portrait of George Washington by Gilbert Stuart. Both paintings hang today in the East Room.

During her tenure in the White House, Lucy saw the installation of the telephone, an appliance which was demonstrated to her by its inventor, Alexander Graham Bell. Late one night, she was awakened by her husband to dress and come downstairs to meet an inventor and see his invention. She obliged and an hour later shook hands with Thomas Alva Edison, who introduced her to the phonograph.

Lucy Hayes's White House glowed with good spirits, which were evident at Eastertime because it was she who returned the Easter Egg Roll to the White House from the Capitol Building. Lucy's china was another contribution to the White House. Loving the flowers, animals, and scenery of the United States, she hired artist Theodore R. Davis to design a set of uniquely American china that would reflect this beauty. The results were certainly striking, to say the least, and drew some fire for their realistic depiction of animals and birds. One senator told

Lucy that he did not want to see at the bottom of his dish what he had had for dinner. Some of the dishes are truly works of art, and others are almost distasteful. To this day, anyone who has seen the Presidential China Collection will remember the Hayes china.

Lucy invited a crowd to her first Thanksgiving dinner in Washington, including all the White House secretaries and their families as well as the telegraph operator. It took three turkeys and a roast pig to feed all the guests. After dinner, ten-year-old Fanny and six-year-old Scott played blindman's buff. Christmas was similarly festive, with Lucy giving gifts to all the staff members.

On December 30, 1877, Rud and Lucy celebrated twenty-five years of marriage, with their original minister presiding and Lucy wearing her original wedding dress, let out a good bit, as her weight had increased to 160 pounds. The celebration would become one of Lucy's happiest memories.

While visiting the South with her husband as part of an attempt to heal the wounds caused by the 1876 election, Lucy made it a point to call on former First Lady Sarah Polk in Nashville, Tennessee. Julia Tyler, another former First Lady, would be invited back to the

White House to stand in a reception line with Lucy. Lucy was also friendly with Julia Grant, Lucretia Garfield, and Caroline Harrison, who had entertained them in Indianapolis, as well as Ida McKinley, who had entertained them in Canton. When family friends the Herrons were invited to the White House to christen their baby daughter, seventeen-year-old Helen Herron was so impressed that she determined to return as First Lady. She did so, as Mrs. William H. Taft.

In 1880 President and Mrs. Hayes spent seventy-two days traveling from Washington, D.C., to San Francisco. For the first time in history, a presidential couple traveled the width of the continent, which inspired the press to use the title First Lady of the Land. They rode on train, wagon, and stagecoach. At one point Lucy donned her husband's pants, hat, and shoes to go down in a mine. They stopped to see Sarah Winnemucca, a Paiute Indian who had been vaccinated against smallpox at the White House along with Lucy and other guests. Winnemucca made a plea to President Hayes to gather all people together to one place where they could all live in peace. Lucy was so moved, tears could be seen on her cheeks.

Having seen California, including Los Angeles, the Hayeses headed back to Washington for the 1880 election. Rutherford had stuck to his resolution to run for only one term and was pleased when the Republican candidate, James A. Garfield, won handily. Lucy's last White House reception, on February 24, 1881, saw the house lit beautifully, with every room open to provide room for the two thousand guests.

"Out of scrape, out of a scrape," Rutherford chuckled to himself as he watched Garfield take the oath of office. Wearing a large, white bonnet, her face beaming, Lucy made her last appearance as First Lady. Her last act as First Lady was to slip away from the luncheon she had provided for James and Lucretia Garfield to look over the rooms to make sure everything was in its place. It was time to say goodbye. The

doorman, Tom Pendel, said later that never before or since did a First Lady's departure cause so many tears to flow.

Legacy

Lucy's last years were spent happily among her children and animals. Aside from her work for the Women's Home Missionary Society of her Methodist Church, Lucy made almost no public speeches or visits except accompanying her husband to New York as the guests of President and Mrs. Benjamin Harrison on the one hundredth anniversary of George Washington's swearing in as president. Aside from her usual aches and pains, Lucy suffered from high blood pressure, probably not helped by her increasing weight, and shortness of breath. Otherwise, she was generally cheerful and happy, often whistling or singing to herself.

On June 22, 1889, after she and her niece had spent the day ordering roses (her niece laughingly said maybe they should just notify the company which ones they did not want) Lucy told her to go out and watch the others play tennis. Shortly afterward, Lucy's maid found her paralyzed, a needle and thread in hand. She had suffered a massive stroke. Three days later, on Tuesday, June 25, 1889, she died, with her husband holding her.

Rutherford got up and, even while his beloved wife was being readied for her coffin, wrote in his diary about her. He closed his entry with two statements: "I consider the single most interesting fact of my life is my marriage to Lucy Ware Webb," and "She was the Golden Rule Incarnate."

Suggested Readings

Geer, Emily Apt. *First Lady: The Life of Lucy Webb Hayes.* Kent, Ohio: Kent State University Press, 1984. Well-researched, balanced portrait of Lucy Hayes.

Gould, Lewis L., ed. *American First Ladies: Their Lives and Their Legacy.* New York: Garland, 1996. An enjoyable, informative, and objective combination of biographical sketches and histories of the First Ladies.

Holloway, Laura Carter. *The Ladies of the White House: Or, In the Home of the Presidents*. Reprint. New York: A. M. S. Press, 1976. Further subtitled *Being a Complete History of the Social and Domestic Lives of the Presidents from Washington to the Present Time, 1789-1882*, this book includes twenty-five leaves of plates.

Hoogenboom, Ari Arthur. *Rutherford B. Hayes: Warrior and President*. Lawrence: University Press of Kansas, 1995. Author of the first new biography in fifty years makes the case of appreciating Hayes' limited options and the choices he made.

Klapthor, Margaret Brown. *The First Ladies*. 9th ed. Washington, D.C.: White House Historical Association with the cooperation of the National Geographic Society, 1999.

Mayo, Edith P., ed. *The Smithsonian Book of the First Ladies: Their Lives, Times, and Issues*. New York: H. Holt, 1996. This book's brief chapters include a biography of Lucy Hayes.

Craig Schermer

Lucretia Garfield

Lucretia Rudolph Garfield

Born: April 19, 1832
    Hiram, Ohio
Died: March 14, 1918
    Pasadena, California

President: James A. Garfield
1881

Overview: Like her husband, who rose so spectacularly from poverty to be a United States president, Lucretia Rudolph Garfield began life on a farm in Ohio's Western Reserve. She managed to educate herself widely and deeply through constant reading. Though her days as First Lady were brief and her thirty-nine years as a widow were determinedly private, she enjoyed the same national respect and admiration accorded her husband. Her influence upon James A. Garfield and his political endeavors was considerable and often acknowledged by him.

Lucretia Garfield. *(Library of Congress)*

Early Life

Lucretia was the eldest of the four children born to Zeb and Arabella Rudolph. Her father, of German stock, had been born in Virginia's Shenandoah Valley in 1803. Zeb's father, John, and his Welsh mother had bought a farm in 1806 between the tiny village of Garrettsville and the even smaller community of Hiram, in what was known as the Western Reserve in northeastern Ohio. In addition to helping his father farm their land, Zeb became a fine carpenter. In 1830 he married Arabella Mason, who lived on a nearby farm.

Arabella, born in 1810 in Hartford, Connecticut, was the daughter of Elijah Mason and Lucretia Green. Her family had moved out to Portage County in the Western Reserve in 1816.

On April 19, 1832, Lucretia, named for her grandmother, was born to Zeb and Arabella Rudolph.

Lucretia's childhood was a happy one. She was close to her two brothers, John and Joe, and her sister, Nellie; from her mother she learned the requirements of a well-organized and smoothly run household. The Rudolphs believed strongly in education. Lucretia was unusually intelligent, with refreshing common sense. People respected her for her practical insights. James Garfield, who came to know her at her first school, wrote that she had "good, practical, sound common sense," and "a well balanced mind . . . logical and precise."

In 1850 Lucretia became a student at the school newly founded by the Disciples of Christ in Hiram, the Eclectic Institute. James Garfield also entered the institute in 1850. He and Lucretia studied Greek and Latin, music, art, and religion. It was not long before James saw in Lucretia the kind of woman he might like to marry. Their courtship began in 1853.

Marriage and Family

In the winter of 1854, the two became engaged. That summer, James departed for Williams College in Massachusetts, where he studied for the next two years, earning his bachelor's degree. He and Lucretia exchanged letters regularly over those months, building their dreams and hopes of a future together as well as comparing books and ideas and experiences.

When Garfield returned to Hiram to teach and later to head the Eclectic Institute, his love for Lucretia seemed to have cooled; nevertheless, after much soul-searching, he finally decided he ought to marry her. She accepted, but she knew he was marrying her out of a sense of duty. They married in 1858. James was twenty-seven and Lucretia was twenty-six.

The marriage got off to a rocky start. Unhappy with his domestic and professional life at Hiram, James cast about for something more fitting his extraordinary talents than teaching.

He won a seat in the Ohio senate in 1859, then volunteered for the Union Army in 1861. Lucretia remained at her home in Hiram, nursing her first baby, and suffering from loneliness and neglect. The domestic scene improved after James came home ill from Tennessee. The two, with their child, spent an idyllic month isolated from friends and admirers at a retreat near Warren, Ohio.

In 1863, after James had been elected to the United States House of Representatives, Lucretia once again settled down to her life in Ohio, managing a household of college boarders as well as James's mother. Two more children were born, and James and Lucretia and their family grew closer together. In 1869 James built a home in Washington, D.C., so that the family could be united there.

During these years of the Ohio senate, the Civil War, and then the House of Representatives, Lucretia never hesitated to advise James. Her first letter to him as he left for Columbus, Ohio, as a public servant in January, 1860, made it clear that she intended to be an influence on him: "I want you to be so great and good. So worthy of the highest respect and love of all. So unimpeachable in every relation that your bitterest enemy can find no just cause for accusation . . ." Often James spoke of her influence on him and their growing family. "You have gained such an ascendancy over us all," he told her.

Presidency and First Ladyship

In 1880 James Garfield was nominated and then elected to the presidency of the United States. Lucretia, now forty-eight years old with five surviving children—they had lost two—moved her family into the White House in the beginning of March, 1881, after Garfield's inauguration. Her tenure as First Lady was even briefer than James's as president—less than three months. Early in May of that year she contracted malaria. For the last two weeks of May, she lay ill in the White House and then was taken to the New Jersey shore to fully recover her strength. James was shot on July 2, just as Lucretia was on her way back to rejoin him. He died on September 19. Thus, Lucretia served for only ten weeks as First Lady, but she was a forceful one, nevertheless.

She had not wanted James to be president. "I begin to be afraid that the convention will give you the nomination," she wrote him on June 4, 1880. She added with prophetic insight: "and the place would be most unenviable with so many disappointed candidates." Once he was president, however, Lucretia aided and abetted James in many ways as he struggled with the angry machinations of those Republicans who lost out to him at the Republican National Convention in Chicago, led by Senator Roscoe Conkling of New York. "You will never have anything from those men but their assured contempt until you fight them *dead*," she said to him. "You can put every one of them in his political grave if you are a mind to, and that is the only place where they can be kept peaceable." Lucretia's diary recorded Conkling's and Garfield's political maneuvers, suggesting that James had discussed his strategy with her before making his decisions.

James A. Garfield

James A. Garfield was the last U.S. president (with the possible exception of Chester A. Arthur) to be born in a log cabin, one built by his father in the wilderness of the Western Reserve in 1831. Educated in typical local primary schools and the newly formed Eclectic Institute at Hiram, Ohio (later Hiram College), he received his degree at Williams College in 1856. He soon came to be head of the Hiram Eclectic Institute, while at the same time participating in the Ohio legislature as a senator.

He joined the Civil War as a colonel and later became a general, but he had to resign in 1863 in order to take his seat in the House of Representatives, to which he had been elected in 1862. Having served in the House for seventeen years, he became the dark horse candidate for president in 1880, breaking the deadlocked Ulysses S. Grant and James G. Blaine forces in that divisive Republican convention.

Garfield's administration began uncertainly, with bitter rivalry between the same two Republican factions in the spring of 1881. That July, just as Garfield was bringing the various opponents under his own control, he was fatally shot by Charles Guiteau, who had become embittered because he felt he deserved special privileges for having supported Garfield in the election.

Though brief, Garfield's tenure in office provided indications that he might have been an effective president. First, the economy had long been one of his chief interests and one of his outstanding strengths. A clear accomplishment, even in those few weeks, was the successful refunding of the national debt, achieved under the leadership of his secretary of the treasury, William Windom. Another of Garfield's interests was Latin America. Encouraging his secretary of state, James Blaine, to be clear and decisive in his Latin American policy, he called for closer diplomatic ties and better trade relations.

Garfield's critics, while admiring his accomplishments, found him too ready to compromise, too naïve in assessing others' motivations. He was "soft," they said, he lacked "ego," and was not "tough minded." However as his first official biographer, T. C. Smith, wrote, "There is a place in our American public life . . . for men who lead without rancor, persuade rather than order and care less for their own personal success than for the fate of measures." Garfield, Smith concluded, should be grouped along with Benjamin Franklin, John Jay, and Abraham Lincoln "as a worthy representative" of this sort of leader.

James and Lucretia Garfield and their family, circa 1881. *(Library of Congress)*

Not only did Lucretia support James with her tough-minded insights, she also provided him with a White House he could rely on to be similar to the farm in Ohio in its domesticity. The children, so necessary to James's happiness and her own, were there—rambunctious, perhaps, but lovingly and competently managed by Lucretia. Soon after arriving in Washington, she began a serious study of the White House. She expected James to request a grant from Congress to restore the old building during their first summer there. She was among the earliest of all those First Ladies who wished to restore the old building along lines faithful to its character and history.

Lucretia was never one to care about social convention. What she hoped to bring about was a kind of "social family" at the White House, inviting not just good old friends, but artists and writers of national renown.

Legacy

Upon James Garfield's death in September of 1881, Lucretia took her family back to the farm in Mentor, Ohio, as unobtrusively as she had brought them to the White House. Now her determination was twofold: first, to honor and protect the memory of James, and second, to live the quiet, private life of a devoted mother and grandmother for her and James's beloved family. For the first of these goals, to protect James's memory, she insisted that, whenever possible, she review all books and articles published about him. At Lawnfield, the Mentor farm, she built the first "presidential library," gathering all of James's papers and books there, keeping the most valuable letters and papers in a fireproof vault. She spent months going through her husband's papers, private and public, as well as more than twelve hundred personal letters she had exchanged with him. She dated and ordered

147

Lucretia at Lawnfield

Perhaps Lucretia Garfield's greatest accomplishment was in her determination to cherish the memory of James Garfield, the United States' twentieth president, by carefully preserving and enlarging Lawnfield, the family's home and farm in Mentor, Ohio. When James bought it in 1876, the farm was run-down, with ramshackle outbuildings. After just two summers, largely under Lucretia's management, the place took shape. In 1879 she wrote Garfield these words: "Everything here now seems to give life and health. . . . it is cool, and the cleanliness and freshness surpass either previous year. The old farm bursts into gladness under each caress and grows beautiful with every touch, and I want you all here to catch the inspiration which it breathes out in grateful generosity."

In 1880 Garfield used Lawnfield for his campaigning, addressing the media and large groups of people from his front porch. After his death in September, 1881, Lucretia built a secure library on the second floor, in which to store James's many documents: the first presidential library. Lawnfield today, handsomely restored to its 1895 state, represents Lucretia's own monument to James's memory.

these documents. Not until 1912 did she allow Theodore Clarke Smith, a historian from Williams College, to begin, with her help, the first "official" biography of President Garfield.

As for the second of these decisions, she saw to it that her family lived its life modestly and out of the public eye. When various editors wished to write about, or interview, her or her children, she typically said no. As the extraordinary worldwide grief died down during the autumn of 1881, the Garfields as a family simply faded into ordinariness. Lucretia traveled, visiting friends and relatives. The two older boys grew to be substantial public figures, and the younger children married and also led productive lives.

After 1900, Lucretia, while spending her summers at the farm in Mentor, began to winter in Pasadena, California. She continued her wide range of reading, often wrote essays for a book club, and kept up with the political scene, even to the extent of voting once for Democrat Woodrow Wilson, who was a friend of her son Harry. She died peacefully in Pasadena on March 14, 1918, and was buried next to her largely forgotten husband in Cleveland, Ohio.

Suggested Readings

Anthony, Carl Sferrazza. *First Ladies: The Saga of the Presidents' Wives and Their Power.* Vol. 1. New York: William Morrow, 1990. Contains an excellent account of Lucretia Rudolph Garfield.

Comer, Lucretia Garfield. *Strands from the Weaving.* New York: Vantage Press: 1959. Family reminiscences from Lucretia and James Garfield's granddaughter.

Garfield, James A. *The Diary of James A. Garfield.* 4 vols. Edited by Harry J. Brown and Frederick D. Williams. East Lansing: Michigan Sate University Press, 1967-1981.

Leech, Margaret, and Harry J. Brown. *The Garfield Orbit: The Life of President James A. Garfield.* New York: Harper and Row, 1978. A highly readable biography with special insights into the Garfield marriage.

Shaw, John, ed. *Crete and James: Personal Letters of Lucretia and James Garfield.* East Lansing: Michigan State University Press, 1994. The story of the Garfield marriage, as told by James and Lucretia's correspondence written between 1853 and 1881.

John Shaw

Ellen Arthur

Ellen Lewis Herndon Arthur

Born: August 30, 1837
      Culpeper, Virginia
Died: January 12, 1880
      New York, New York

President: Chester A. Arthur
      1881-1885

Overview: Very little is known about Ellen Lewis Herndon Arthur. In part, this is because she did not live to see her husband serve in the White House. She died in the prime of life, just months before Chester A. Arthur would become vice president.

Early Life

Ellen Lewis Herndon (Nell to her family, friends, and future husband) was born on August 30, 1837, at Culpeper Court House, Virginia, in the house that her uncle Dr. Brodie S. Herndon had built. Her family's pedigree was distinguished, and her southern roots ran deep. In 1674, an immigrant ancestor, William Herndon, presumably English, received patented lands in Virginia. At Ellen's birth, her father, William Lewis Herndon, was a rising young officer in the U.S. Navy; her mother, Frances Elizabeth Hansbrough Herndon, was also descended from a reputable and presumably wealthy southern family.

Young Ellen was an only child, growing up in a doting, close-knit extended family. At the age of two or three, she and her parents moved to Fredericksburg, their ancestral seat, only to move again in 1842 to Washington, D.C., when Ellen was five. Her naval officer father was assigned to assist his brother-in-law, Lieutenant

Ellen Arthur. *(Library of Congress)*

149

Matthew Fontaine Maury, U.S.N., who directed the Depot of Charts and Instruments (the future U.S. Naval Observatory). Ellen grew up in the capital city, her home until she was in her late teens.

Instead of being educated at home, as girls usually were in southern families, Ellen was sent to school in Washington, D.C., although little is known about the extent of her schooling. Her family attended Saint John's Episcopal Church on Lafayette Square, where the city's most prestigious families were members and where Ellen sang in the choir. Her most notable gift seemed to be her lovely operatic singing voice, deeply admired by all who knew her.

Her personality also appears to have been a strong asset: She was called affectionate, sweet, and lovable by those who knew her. Later on, as a married woman, she remembered the names of all the kitchen and dining staff at a mansion she visited only on her birthdays. In a day and age when physical beauty was considered an unmarried woman's greatest asset, Ellen was reportedly not handsome or beautiful, as were her mother and many of her cousins. She had brown hair and fair skin, was slender, of medium height, and wore eyeglasses.

In 1853, when she was sixteen, her Uncle Maury invited her and another niece to accompany him and his two teenage daughters to Europe while he attended a naval conference in Brussels. Afterward, he and his four companions toured the capitals of northern Europe as well as London. The trip made a lasting impression on Ellen, who afterward loved travel and changes of scenery.

By 1856 Ellen had fallen in love with a prepossessing New York lawyer, Chester A. Arthur. The two met when his friend Dabney Herndon, a medical student and cousin of Ellen, introduced Chester to her at her home in New York. Chester was seven years her senior.

No two backgrounds could have been more unlike than those of Ellen Herndon and Chester Alan Arthur. If it had not been for the fact that Chester was already a prospering partner in a law firm, their union would have been unthinkable. Chester was a Northerner to the core. His birth is not well documented, but it is believed to have taken place in a rude log cabin on October 5, 1830, in remote Fairfield, Vermont. He was one of many children of William and Malvina Arthur. His father was a Baptist preacher and committed abolitionist. Chester received a good general education from his father and graduated from college in 1848. Pur-

---

Chester A. Arthur

Chester Alan Arthur, twenty-first president of the United States, was born on October 5, 1830, in Fairfield, Vermont. In 1848 he graduated from Union College in Schenectady, New York, studied law, and pursued a highly successful career as a New York City lawyer. In 1859 he married Ellen Herndon, descendant of an old Virginia family, with whom he had three children. Serving briefly as a quartermaster general in New York during the Civil War, he continued to rise in Republican Party ranks after the war. From 1871 to 1875, he headed the New York City Customhouse, a high-profile political appointment that served as a stepping-stone to his appointment as James A. Garfield's running mate in 1880. When President Garfield was assassinated in September, 1881, Arthur succeeded him and ably served out his term of office. His most notable achievement was signing the Pendleton Act in 1883, which inaugurated the Civil Service Commission and ended the spoils system of federal appointments. In failing health, Arthur declined to run for a second term in 1884 and died of Bright's disease on November 18, 1886.

suing his law career in New York City, he had never even been to the South until, at age twenty-eight, he visited his fiancé's relatives in Fredericksburg.

His courtship with Ellen lasted three years. One long, passionate love letter from Chester to Ellen has survived, revealing an interesting glimpse of the warm-blooded young woman who was to become his wife. Writing to her on

acquiesced to Ellen's choice of October 25, 1859, as their wedding day, which happened to coincide with the birthday of her father. It took place in the bride's church, Calvary Episcopal, in Manhattan. It was likely an elegant affair, with the clothes-conscious Ellen garbed in the latest bridal fashion. For two weeks afterward they honeymooned, returning to live with Ellen's mother in her Manhattan home.

A Mild and Easy Man

Of the many great sorrows in Ellen Arthur's life, perhaps the greatest occurred in 1857, when she was twenty: Her beloved father died prematurely, during a storm at sea. Commander William Herndon had attained fame in 1853 when he was assigned, at age forty, to chart the course of the Amazon River. It was ironic that, four years later, he would lose his life needlessly when the mail steamer *Central America* sprang a leak during its regular run from Havana to New York. Captain Herndon was hailed as a hero for his death at the helm of his sinking ship, after he ordered the safe evacuation of all women and children aboard. Exhaustive interviews of survivors of the disaster told a somewhat different story. An English passenger and seasoned traveler told a reporter that "Captain Herndon, although personally brave . . . was too mild and easy a man for the position he occupied" and that "the lives of all the passengers might have been preserved by proper foresight and judgment on the part of the officers."

her twentieth birthday, two years before their marriage, Chester mused, "If I were with you now . . . you would come and sit by me. You would put your arms around my neck and press your soft sweet lips over my eyes. I can feel them now." Her fiancé was over six feet tall, fair, and considered handsome by all.

Ellen's other great love, her father, was taken from her during her youth when he died tragically at sea. If Ellen had deeply loved her father while he was alive, she idolized him after his death. A group of New York citizens, as a tribute to the heroic commander, gave his widow a house in the city, at 34 West 21st Street, which she gratefully accepted.

After the tragic death of Ellen's father, Chester involved himself in Ellen and her widowed mother's legal and financial affairs. Finally, he

Marriage and Family
The Civil War erupted in the spring of 1861. No sooner had the guns of Fort Sumter fallen silent than Chester found himself on active duty with the rank of brigadier general. This appalled his southern in-laws, especially his mother-in-law, who was openly hostile to the Union. All of Ellen's male relatives fought on the Confederate side. Chester's friend and Ellen's cousin Dabney Herndon was a prisoner of war for a time in a prison camp near New York City, where Chester permitted Ellen to visit regularly. Although the couple attended President Abraham Lincoln's inauguration in 1865, Ellen remained a Confederate at heart. While Chester jokingly referred to his "little rebel wife," the strain that the war created on the young marriage may have led to his resignation from the

Army in the middle of the war. His nearly two years of active duty as assistant quartermaster general, and then as quartermaster general of New York, were frantically busy ones. Hence, the Civil War years must have borne down hard on Ellen, with an absentee husband and fears for the safety of her loved ones.

Soon after the war began, Ellen's mother made plans to leave for Europe, where she remained for the rest of her life. Chester and Ellen moved into an elegant boardinghouse. By then they were the proud parents of a baby boy, born in December, 1860, whom Ellen promptly named after her father, William Lewis. Her intense joy at his birth turned to grief when the little boy died suddenly in July, 1863, at age two. His death, wrote Chester to his brother, was sudden, due to some "affection of the brain." The effect on Ellen was devastating. "Nell is broken hearted. I fear much for her health. You know how her heart was wrapped up in her dear boy," wrote Chester.

The young mother's agony was mitigated when she found herself pregnant with a second child. Chester Alan Arthur II, called Alan, was born exactly a year after her tragic loss. With the war over nine months later, the Arthurs moved out of their boardinghouse rooms in May, 1865. Their new abode, a tastefully appointed, two-story brownstone on fashionable Lexington Avenue, would soon resonate with sumptuous dinner parties. Chester's prosperous law practice, coupled with his involvement in New York politics, made the family rich. On the day that Chester was appointed collector of the Port of New York, November 21, 1871, a daughter was born, Ellen Herndon Arthur.

In the postwar years, Ellen's interests appear to have been exclusively centered on family, fine living, fine dining, and climbing the social ladder. Her address book was crammed with the names of well-heeled and well-connected Republicans. Her husband's political ambitions had her utmost approbation, although at a cost that at times was too high for her. It seems that she never found a way to reconcile her desire for his political advancement with her need to have him at home with her and the children. The more she furthered his interests with her social calls and invitations, the more he dissatisfied her as a family man.

Legacy

Added to the strains of her marriage was another deep sorrow for Ellen, the illness and death of her mother, an expatriate living in France. The two had always been very close. Ellen made the sad voyage to visit her stricken mother in the spring of 1878, only to return with her mother's body for burial in the United States. The emotional toll affected her health in the long run. Ellen caught cold one icy night waiting for her carriage after she had sung at a charity concert. As usual, she was unaccompanied by her husband. Her immune system may have been compromised before this, because in a matter of a few days her cold developed into pneumonia. During that time her husband was away, attending to politics in Albany, New York. When he received a telegram informing him of Ellen's condition, he left immediately, but by the time he reached her side, she was in a coma. She died the next day, January 12, 1880. Apparently her illness had aggravated a heart condition, which contributed to her untimely death at age forty-two. She left behind her two children, Ellen, age eight, and Chester Alan, age fifteen.

His wife's death devastated Chester. After her funeral, which took place in the Episcopal Church of the Heavenly Rest on Fifth Avenue (she was then laid to rest in Albany), he would pace up and down his neighborhood until the early hours of the morning, pouring out his grief. Six months after Ellen's death, Chester was nominated vice president and, in the spring of 1881, moved with his children to the U.S. capital. President James A. Garfield died from a gunshot wound six months later, elevating Arthur to the presidency.

Upon being congratulated by his wife's Uncle Brodie, Chester said to him, "Honors to me are not what they once were." When his young daughter, Ellen, presented him with flowers one evening to congratulate him, he broke down sobbing, "There is nothing worth having now." The flowers might have reminded him of his wife's favorite violets; in his three-and-one-half-year term as president, fresh violets always graced his wife's photograph in the White House. Another touching reminder of his devotion to her memory and her pervasive influence on him was his regular attendance at his late wife's former church, Saint John's, where she had sung in the choir as a girl. In 1883 he donated a stained glass window in his wife's memory, asking that it be placed on the south side of the church, where he could see it from his private quarters in the White House. The inscription on the window reads "To the Glory of God and in memory of Ellen Lewis Herndon Arthur entered into life January 12, 1880."

Suggested Readings

Arthur, Chester A. *Chester A. Arthur Papers*. Washington, D.C.: Library of Congress, 1959. The papers include not only his presidential papers but also letters and many other manuscripts predating his presidency. Biographical information about Ellen Arthur is contained in the biography by John W. Herndon; includes miscellaneous Herndon notes about her.

Howe, George Frederick. *Chester A. Arthur: A Quarter-Century of Machine Politics*. Reprint. New York: F. Ungar, 1966. This biography first appeared in 1935 and is the first scholarly biography of Chester A. Arthur, which contains a little information on Ellen Arthur.

McConnell, Burt, and Jane McConnell. *Our First Ladies*. New York: Crowell, 1969. Chapter on Ellen Arthur contains a newspaper story which describes Ellen Arthur's room at the Arthur home in New York.

Reeves, Thomas C. *Gentleman Boss: The Life of Chester Alan Arthur*. New York: Knopf, 1975. A sensitive biography of Chester A. Arthur, with the fullest treatment of Ellen Arthur of any published source.

Sadler, Christine. *Children in the White House*. New York: G. P. Putnam's Sons, 1967. Information on the women of the Arthur family, specifically Ellen and Chester Arthur's daughter Nell.

Watson, Robert P. *The Presidents' Wives: Reassessing the Office of First Lady*. Boulder, Colo.: Lynne Rienner, 2000. A statistical and research-oriented assessment of the roles and the long-ranging impacts of the First Ladies as presidential partners.

Sina Dubovoy

Frances Cleveland

Frances "Frank" Clara Folsom Cleveland

Born: July 21, 1864
     Buffalo, New York
Died: October 29, 1947
     Baltimore, Maryland

President: Grover Cleveland
     1885-1889 and 1893-1897

Overview: Frances Cleveland was truly a first among First Ladies. Frances was the first woman to marry a president in the White House, the first president's wife to have a child in the White House, and the only First Lady to return to the White House for a second "term," as her husband, Grover Cleveland, was the only president elected to two non-consecutive terms. She was a beautiful and intelligent woman who graduated from college and was very interested in the issues of the day, though she remained "nonpolitical." She brought to the Cleveland presidencies a grace many feel was due to her natural goodness.

Frances Cleveland, circa 1886. *(Library of Congress)*

Early Life

Frances Clara Folsom was born on July 21, 1864, in Buffalo, New York, the only child of Oscar and Emma Folsom. She was called Frank for most of her youth. Frank was blessed with a strong family background. Her father was one of six children from a wealthy family; her grandfather, Colonel John B. Folsom, owned a mill and lived in a stately home in Folsomville, New York, just east of Buffalo. Her mother's roots were also pedigreed. Emma Harmon came from the prestigious Harmon family of Caledonia, Vermont, who were early benefactors of the University of Rochester in New York.

Frank enjoyed a young girl's life; she did well in school, and summers were largely spent in recreation with her family. However, just after her eleventh birthday, her father was killed in a carriage accident in Buffalo. Although Oscar Folsom was a lawyer, he left no will. He did leave an insurance policy of $5,000 and an estate worth $250,000, of which his partner, Grover Cleveland, acted as executor. Cleveland began to look after Frank and her mother. Without any indication of their future relationship, Frank began calling Cleveland, her future husband, Uncle Cleve.

Frank's education began at Madame Brecker's French Kindergarten. She attended Miss Bissel's School for Young Ladies and attended the Medina Academy for Boys and Girls until 1879. Frank finally attended Central School in Buffalo, where she was popular both with teachers and among her fellow students. When she left in October, 1881, no longer interested in school, her family became concerned and obtained certification of her completed studies. In February, 1882, at age seventeen, Frances was admitted with advanced standing to Wells College in Aurora, New York, one of the first liberal arts colleges for women in the United States. She would become only the second First Lady to earn a college degree, following Mrs. Rutherford B. Hayes.

Frances loved college. As a student, she had diverse academic interests. Although she was not a bookworm, she did have a decidedly literary taste, reading the classics often, and did well even in those subjects which did not really interest her. She never missed a lesson while at

Grover Cleveland

Grover Cleveland, a rising star in the Buffalo, New York, legal community, was elected sheriff of Erie County in 1870. He preferred life in the saloons to that in the country club, and it was not until January 1, 1882, that he became mayor of Buffalo, gaining office on a reform platform and making the most of his reputation for honesty and integrity. Indeed, it was his timely and successful implementation of a reform administration, as well as a divided Republican Party, that propelled him to the New York governorship on January 1, 1883. He served two years as governor before being elected president in 1884, after a campaign in which issues of character and integrity took center stage.

During the campaign, Cleveland had been charged with fathering an illegitimate child, calling into question his honesty and integrity. He admitted paying for the child's support, claiming that his doing so had prevented the humiliation of a married friend whose family would have otherwise suffered. Cleveland was elected largely because James G. Blaine, the Republican nominee, had problems of integrity larger than Cleveland's. In addition, the Mugwumps, a break-off faction of the Republican Party, largely supported Cleveland.

Cleveland's presidencies came at the height of "Gilded Age" politics, and he was the only Democrat to be elected—and then reelected—between the Civil War and World War I. Historians are divided, however, as to the legacy of Cleveland's administrations. Many feel he was a "Bourbon" Democrat, interested in maintaining the economic status quo; a Whig follower who believed in the supremacy of Congress; or a social conservative who did not care about the working class. They point to his breakup of the 1894 Pullman strike, coddling of the railroads and large monopolies, refusal to help drought-stricken Texas farmers, and mishandling of tariff reform. Others, however, note his efforts to professionalize bureaucracy; clean up public corruption within Tammany Hall, the executive committee of the Democratic Party; and institute civil service reform. His seemingly nonpartisan view of the president as neutral arbiter, his efforts to preserve Western lands, and his opposition to imperialism in an age of jingoism are also cited.

college and was always prepared for class. She was considered a first-class English scholar and was very interested in the arts, especially playing the piano, painting, and photography. She enjoyed the social sciences, and her friends adored her for her storytelling ability. She would often tell a story relating to her own life or would simply spin one about her girlfriends.

Social codes were closely monitored on the Wells campus; Grover Cleveland was forced to ask Frances's mother and the principal for permission to write to her. Grover, nonetheless, was constantly lavishing attention, gifts, and flowers on Frances throughout her days at Wells. Even so, it is unclear just when the relationship between the two turned to romance; in fact it was thought that the object of Cleveland's affection was Frances's mother. After graduating in 1885, Frances spent the summer at the Folsom farm with her grandfather. That September, before she left on a trip to Europe, a graduation gift from her family, she received a formal letter from Grover—who was by now governor of New York—proposing marriage.

Marriage and Family
Grover's wedding to Frances, the first of a president to be held in the White House, was a newspaper spectacle. The press accounts were numerous and narrative, with detailed reporting of the wedding and honeymoon. Even so, the press was barred from the actual ceremony. Grover's sister Rose, a direct woman, told reporters the wedding would be "a very private affair." This infuriated the newspapers and encouraged them to produce more stories and even to make them up.

On the day of the wedding, June 2, 1886, crowds gathered long before the ceremony. They covered the lawn and peered into the windows, thus affording them a view of hundreds of potted plants and fresh-cut flowers. The ceremony, which Grover had specified should be simple, lasted only ten minutes. Grover had also decided to strike out the word obey and in-

sert the word keep. The president was forty-nine when he married. Having taken her vows just seven weeks before her twenty-second birthday, Frances Cleveland became the youngest woman ever to become First Lady.

The couple planned to honeymoon at Deer Park, a resort in Maryland's Blue Ridge Mountains. Grover wanted to avoid reporters, and the couple managed initially to elude the press. However, upon arrival they found that the newspaper reporters were already there, and the newlyweds awoke the next morning to a swarm of newsmen, many of whom had camped out around the honeymoon cottage or were up in the trees with binoculars. Once the crowds were controlled, however, the honeymoon was quite an arcadian affair—Grover fished, and Frances took long walks, enjoying the air and scenery. She was reported to have drunk the pure mountain water using only her hands, indicating just how comfortable she was among the beauties of nature.

The Clevelands, notwithstanding their disparity in age, were a very close couple. Grover openly displayed his love for his wife and she displayed hers for him. The campaign of 1888, for example, was a nasty one with ugly charges that Grover abused Frances. She wrote a letter, widely circulated in public, indicating that she could "wish the women of our country no greater blessing than that their homes and lives may be as happy, and their husbands may be as kind, attentive and considerate, and affectionate as mine."

Grover was determined to keep Frances far away from the scrutiny of the press. During the first Cleveland administration, the couple spent a great deal of time at Oak View, an old country farm near Georgetown in the District of Columbia that Grover had bought before their marriage. During Cleveland's second administration, they rented a house called Woodley and spent as much time as possible at Gray Gables, their home on Cape Cod, Massachusetts, which they had purchased during their

Frances Cleveland, center, with the wives of her husband's cabinet members, circa 1897. *(Library of Congress)*

years in New York between the two Cleveland administrations. Their first child, Ruth, was born in New York. By the time the Clevelands moved back into the White House, Frances was expecting their second child, Esther, who was the first presidential child to be born in the White House. Their third daughter, Marion, was born on Cape Cod during the second term. It was not until after their White House years that their two sons—Richard, born in Princeton, New Jersey, and Francis, born at Gray Gables—became part of the family.

Early in Grover's second term in the White House, he was diagnosed with cancer of the mouth. The operation he required, which would remove part of his jaw, was kept secret to avoid alarming the public in the midst of the Panic of 1893, the aftermath of a stock market collapse. The surgery was successfully performed on a friend's yacht, and Frances proved adept at answering questions and allaying suspicion that arose from the president's five-day absence.

Frances cried as she left the White House for the second time, in March of 1897, as did many

members of the staff. She had always taken a personal interest in their lives and had given them birthday and Christmas gifts each year. Grover and Frances thought about returning to New York but decided that a small town would be better for the children. At the urging of Andrew West, Dean of Princeton University, they chose to relocate to Princeton. They named their new home Westlands in his honor. In 1904, after thirteen-year-old Ruth's death from diphtheria, they bought a four-bedroom cottage in Tamworth, New Hampshire, later remodeled to twenty-seven rooms with thirteen bedrooms. It was named Interment.

Grover Cleveland suffered minor ailments for several years, but in the spring of 1908 he became seriously ill. He and Frances went to Lakewood, New Jersey, where he had found the climate beneficial; however, when he felt no better, he asked to be taken home. He returned to Westlands, where he died on June 24, 1908, leaving an estate in excess of $250,000. Frances sold some small properties but retained the houses at Princeton and Tamworth. She was remarried to Thomas Preston, a professor at

An Open-Door Policy

Though she was accustomed to a comfortable station in life, Frances Cleveland "showed a genuine concern for women who worked," and "helped a struggling friend, who taught music to support herself, by obtaining several pupils for her," according to writer Carl Sferrazza Anthony.

Word of her Saturday afternoon receptions at the White House perhaps did more to endear her to the public than any other act. These receptions for working women, however, were not popular with everyone. Shortly after she began them, one Washington official asked her to stop, saying an afternoon at the White House was not appropriate for "clerks from the department stores and others—a great rabble of shop girls." Frances became extremely angry. "Indeed!" she said, "And if I should hold the little receptions . . . other than Saturday, they couldn't attend, because they have to work all other afternoons. Is that it?"

The First Lady gave strict orders that the Executive Mansion should be open every Saturday to "any store clerks, or other self-supporting women and girls who wished to come to the White House." She meant what she said, and opened White House reception areas and her Saturday receptions to African Americans, according to scholar Robert P. Watson, possibly making her the first First Lady to integrate the White House in this manner.

Wells and Princeton, in 1913. She never accepted the five-thousand-dollar annual pension awarded to presidential widows.

Presidency and First Ladyship

Frances enjoyed performing her social responsibilities as First Lady and was good at it. She enchanted everyone she came in contact with, and Washington, D.C., society was amazed by her poise. Her handling of receiving lines was impressive, and it was said that she never made a false step. While people admired her grace and beauty, it was her naturalness and cordiality that won their hearts. Americans from all walks of life accepted Frances as the ideal First Lady, and she served as a model for her successors.

Frances made both the White House and herself available to people of all stations. People were able to move throughout the White House freely and often made themselves at home in the East Room. Except for a few private rooms on the second floor, the White House was truly the people's house. The most conspicuous examples of Frances's democratic and earnest interest in people were her weekly receptions for working women. Held every Saturday afternoon, these receptions won her the respect of lower- and middle-class women; she made the events a part of both of her terms as First Lady.

Frances was such a celebrity that her clothing and grooming habits became the object of public scrutiny. After one newspaper described her as wearing a dress that was "cut low in the neck . . . the arms bare from the shoulder to the elbow," the Women's Christian Temperance Union demanded that she stop wearing such gowns. While Frances was a supporter of the temperance movement, she continued to wear the clothes she preferred. When the newspapers reported that she was not fond of the bustle and had stopped wearing it, the bustle quickly became part of fashion history.

Fan clubs, called Frances Cleveland Influence Clubs or Frankie Clubs, sprang up across the United States. During the 1892 presidential campaign, against the wishes of Grover Cleveland, Frances's picture appeared beside his own on many campaign posters. No other First Lady had been thus featured on campaign material.

Advertisers also began to take advantage of Frances's popularity and began to use her name and image without her permission to sell candies, liver pills, soaps, ashtrays, and even ladies' undergarments. One magazine advertiser claimed that she owed her beautiful complexion to the use of arsenic pills. A bill was introduced in Congress in 1888 in order to make such false claims a crime, but it did not pass.

Legacy

Even though her popularity brought with it a great deal of attention, Frances did not feel that it was proper for women to speak in public. Because of that, it has been said that she was totally nonpolitical. The reality could not be further from the truth. Frances, though not political in the traditional sense, had her own viewpoints on issues. While it is true that she politely declined to support many of the causes that sought her sponsorship, two important points have been overlooked. First, while Frances did not feel that it was proper for women to speak in public, she did not feel this applied to all women. Rather, she was likely speaking for herself. Second, her popularity itself translated into political influence. Though Frances personally avoided the issue of women's suffrage, her popularity made her a visible role model for women.

Frances Cleveland's legacy is defined not so much by the many firsts that history ascribes to her but by her thoroughly democratic perspective on society and the role of the White House in it. She firmly believed that the White House was the people's house and that those who served in it had an obligation to the people.

Suggested Readings

Anthony, Carl Sferrazza. *First Ladies: The Saga of the Presidents' Wives and Their Power.* Vol. 1. New York: William Morrow, 1990. A unique glimpse at the power and prestige in the evolving role of the First Lady.

Crook, William H. *Memories of the White House: The Home Life of Our Presidents from Lincoln to Roosevelt.* Boston: Little, Brown, 1911.

Hoover, Irwin Hood. *Forty-two Years in the White House.* Boston: Houghton Mifflin, 1934. A former White House chief usher recalls his experiences with and opinions of the Clevelands.

Sadler, Christine. *Children in the White House.* New York: G. P. Putnam's Sons, 1967.

Severn, Sue. "Frances (Clara) Folsom Cleveland." In *American First Ladies: Their Lives and Their Legacy,* edited by Lewis L. Gould. New York: Garland, 1996. Biographical chapter in collection of histories of the First Ladies.

Stephen Robar

Caroline Harrison

Caroline Lavinia Scott Harrison

Born: October 1, 1832
      Oxford, Ohio
Died: October 25, 1892
      Washington, D.C.

President: Benjamin Harrison
      1889-1893

Overview: Caroline Harrison brought friendliness, courtesy, and gracious dignity to the White House and was a social asset to the reserved President Benjamin Harrison. She was a loving, supportive wife and a devoted caregiver to her close-knit family. She was also committed to performing her duties of First Lady, and yet she made time for her personal artwork. Known for her thoughtfulness, she gave regularly of her services to charity.

Early Life

Caroline Lavinia Scott was born on October 1, 1832, in the quiet college town of Oxford, Ohio. Her parents, Mary Neal Scott and John Witherspoon Scott, provided a secure home environment of culture and refinement, imbued with Christian and intellectual education. Although Dr. Scott was an ordained Presbyterian minister, he was employed for most of his life as a professor of mathematics and sciences. An advocate for women's education, he established the Oxford Female Institute in 1849.

While she was First Lady, Caroline told a reporter at the White House that she remembered a happy childhood in Oxford, enjoying a close relationship with her parents and siblings: an older sister Elizabeth, a younger sister, Mary, and two younger brothers, John and Henry. Caroline was an active, fun-loving child. Her father, although known to his students and col-

Caroline Harrison, circa 1889. *(Library of Congress)*

leagues as being buoyant and genial, was anxious about Caroline's lively behavior. In a letter to his wife he wrote, "Tell Caroline she must try and act the lady now, and leave off her romping and venturesomeness." He complained of her mirthfulness when he thought she should have been solemn.

Caroline's talents in art and music were nurtured from childhood. Her aunt Caroline Neal often visited the Scott family in Oxford and gave her niece Caroline many hours of instruction and guidance in drawing. Examples of fifteen-year-old Caroline's artistic ability are contained in an unpublished book at the Harrison Home: *Floral and Poetical Album, by Caroline Scott at Pleasant Hill, Ohio in 1847*, composed of selections of poetry on death, carefully penned in fine dainty script, and embellished with charming floral and landscape illustrations in pencil and watercolors. Caroline inherited her musical talent from her mother, who taught her to play the piano. Sometimes they delighted children by making exquisite little dolls dance to the music of their piano playing. By the age of nineteen, Caroline was an accomplished musician.

When she met Benjamin Harrison, Caroline was an attractive young woman. She was five feet, two inches tall, with large brown eyes, thick brown hair, and tiny hands and feet. She was vivacious and optimistic, with a keen sense of humor. While Ben was a student at Farmer's College in Cincinnati, Ohio, he frequently visited the home of his mathematics and physics teacher, Dr. Scott, and there became acquainted with Caroline. When Dr. Scott moved with his family back to Oxford, Ben transferred to Miami University, also located in Oxford. Caroline enrolled as a student at Oxford Female Institute, where her father served as principal.

Ben and Caroline began to spend many evenings together, often on buggy and sleigh rides. Caroline had a busy senior year at the Institute, where she taught in the music department, and earned her degree in language, music, and art

on June 22, 1852. The following year she went to Carrollton, Kentucky, to teach music and sewing in a girls' school. In the meantime, Ben was an honors student at Miami. Upon his graduation from the university, he went to Cincinnati to read law with the prestigious Bellamy Storer law firm. He soon was concerned and distressed about Caroline, who was becoming ill from exhaustion and overwork. That August, even though Ben was not earning an income, he and Caroline decided to marry within two months.

Marriage and Family
On the morning of October 10, 1853, in the parlor of the Scott family home in Oxford, Ben and Caroline were married in a simple ceremony officiated by Dr. Scott, attended by family members and a few close friends. Caroline wore a gray traveling dress, and Ben wore a black suit with a satin vest and a frock coat. Following a wedding breakfast, the newlyweds traveled to the home of Ben's father, John Scott Harrison, in North Bend, Ohio, where they lived until Ben completed his law training. After Ben was admitted to the bar association in 1854, he and Caroline moved to Indianapolis, Indiana.

They both endured hardships during their first year in Indianapolis. Because Caroline was pregnant and ill, she went to her parents' home in Oxford, where she gave birth to a boy, Russell, who was born on August 12, 1854.

Active church membership was of primary importance to both Ben and Caroline. They regularly attended services at the First Presbyterian Church. While Ben taught young men's classes and served as deacon and elder, Caroline played the organ, taught children's classes, and became superintendent of the primary department of the Sunday school. Most of the family's social life was centered on church activities, to which Caroline contributed generously her time. Her vivacious, friendly leadership influenced and attracted a following of the younger women.

Benjamin Harrison

Benjamin Harrison was born in 1833 near Cincinnati, Ohio. His father, John Scott Harrison, was the son of former president William Henry Harrison. Benjamin Harrison became a lawyer; however, his initial years as an attorney were a struggle. He became discouraged sitting alone in his office waiting for clients. He was forced to borrow money to pay for food, lodging, and medical care for his wife. To augment his income, he worked as court crier for $2.50 a day.

His financial outlook brightened in March of 1855 when William Wallace, an established Indianapolis lawyer, invited Ben to become a partner in his firm. Ben worked diligently to advance the practice, and the Harrisons never again experienced poverty. In Indianapolis, Harrison joined the newly formed Republican Party.

For his success and bravery in 1864 at the Civil War Battle of Peach Tree Creek near Atlanta, he attained the rank of brigadier general. Ben's presidential ancestry and his reputation as an outstanding lawyer and Civil War general were used to launch his political career. He served one term as a Republican U.S. senator from Indiana, from 1880 to 1886, and was elected president in 1888. Though he lost the popular vote, he carried the electoral college. He was the last Civil War general to become president.

His term was notable for promoting an expansion of shipping and in the U.S. Navy's forces but was marred by struggles over tariffs and a declining economy. The McKinley Tarriff Act, passed in 1890, raised duties on most imports, while that same year the Sherman Antitrust Act made illegal "every contract, combination . . . or conspiracy in restraint of trade or commerce." During Harrison's administration, huge sums were spent on business subsidies, and populist opinion felt that the government's policies heavily favored the nation's wealthy elite. Growing discontent among farmers and other Americans paved the way for Harrison's defeat in 1892 to former president Grover Cleveland. During the campaign, neither candidate did much active campaigning, out of respect for Caroline Harrison's poor health. She died before the election.

After his return to private life, Harrison, now widowed, married the widowed Mary Dimmick, his late wife's niece, in 1896. A sought-after public speaker, he died of pneumonia in 1901.

On April 3, 1858, the Harrison family increased with the birth of a daughter, Mary. These were good, secure years for the young couple. Ben was concentrating his efforts to increase success in the law practice, and Caroline was busy with domestic responsibilities, church, and charity work.

The Civil War interrupted their contented family life. In 1862, while Caroline stayed at home with two small children, Ben departed Indianapolis as commander of the Seventieth Volunteer Regiment from Indiana. He survived many battles without injury or serious illness and returned when the war was over.

In Indianapolis, prosperity followed the traumatic war period. Industry and new businesses caused the city to grow quickly, drawing an influx of job seekers. Ben established partnerships with different attorneys, and his law practice prospered. In 1875 the Harrisons moved into their newly completed, stately sixteen-room house on North Delaware Street.

Caroline quickly established a daily schedule for the family and the household staff. At 6:00 A.M. she was usually at the market, selecting meats and vegetables. The meals were served regularly, with breakfast at 7:30, followed by prayers led by Ben, lunch at 1:30 P.M., and dinner at 6:30 P.M. The Sabbath was strictly observed; no work was done, two meals were served, and the evening was usually spent quietly at home. Social responsibilities increased at the Delaware Street home. Visitors were received on Thursday afternoons for Caroline's calling days, and guests were often entertained with dinner parties and receptions. A remembered social event was a lawn party for President and Mrs. Rutherford B. Hayes on October 3, 1879, following a parade headed by presidential dignitaries.

In spite of her full calendar, Caroline found time for her own work. One of the rooms on the north side of the second floor of the home was used as an art studio, where Caroline produced floral compositions in watercolors and painted china. She took lessons from the gifted artist Paul Putzki, who had moved to the city from Chicago. For several years her work was entered in the Indiana Exposition, where she won prizes. Caroline enjoyed playing the piano, creating fine needlework, and reading the classics, history, and contemporary writing. A leader in Impromptu, a local literary club, Caroline became well known for her portrayal of scenes from the works of author Charles Dickens. She also increased her charity work as a board member for the local orphanage.

July 4, 1888, marked the beginning of Ben's campaigning for U.S. president. He became known as a front porch campaigner, giving more than eighty speeches at his front door to the multitudes of eager supporters gathered in the front yard. Caroline prepared refreshments and welcomed hundreds of well-wishers into the home. The morning after the election, Ben learned that he had lost the popular vote, but had won the election through the electoral college.

Presidency and First Ladyship

Strong winds and torrential rain prevailed on Harrison's inauguration day on March 3, 1889, but did not dampen the spirits of the incoming Republicans. A crowd of twelve thousand gathered at the Pension Office Hall for the Inaugural Ball. At 10:30 P.M., Ben and Caroline descended from the balcony to lead the grand promenade to the music of the Marine Band and its director John Philip Sousa. Caroline's elegant inaugural ball gown, styled by New York artists, received approval. The gown was made of silver-gray satin, and the skirt featured alternate panels of brocade with a burr oak leaf design and apricot crepe covered with lace. Beads of gold, silver, crystal, and pearls trimmed the dress. To support Ben's platform favoring high tariffs to protect American industry, the fabric and gown were made in the United States. The oak leaf pattern, designed by Mary Williamson of Lafayette, Indiana, was manufactured into the fabric by Logan Silk Mills in Auburn, New York. Because of an injury she had received by catching her hand in a door, Caroline did not attempt to shake hands but carried a floral bouquet.

Ben and Caroline continued their thoughtful and affectionate relationship throughout the White House years. Ben did not hesitate to discuss with Caroline plans of his administration or affairs of the state, and he valued her advice.

Four generations of Harrisons lived together at the White House; eleven people occupied five rooms, sharing one bathroom. Caroline organized her close-knit family with a domestic schedule similar to the one she had in her own home, including morning family prayers. She usually supervised the care of the grandchildren. Their grandson Baby McKee became nationally famous through reporters who wrote feature stories about him, ignoring the Harrisons' requests for privacy. It was for the grandchildren that the first elaborately decorated Christmas tree was set up on the second floor of the White House on December 24, 1889. After dinner, both Ben and Caroline were trimming the tree and stuffing gifts in the branches.

Caroline became the first First Lady to plan and supervise a major White House renovation project. She made creative plans, with the help of architect David Owen, for major architectural changes for the White House and enlisted the enthusiastic support of Senator Leland Stanford. "Caroline Harrison's work on the President's house represents not only the first major effort to give the house new functions, but also the first to bring it in historic perspective," according to the White House Historical Association. The formal plans were rejected by Congress, and instead thirty-five thousand dollars was allocated to renovate the historic building.

The First Lady was determined, as she said, to "see the family of the president provided for properly, and . . . get the present building put into good condition." After inspecting the dilapidated White House, she supervised the cleaning and refurbishing of the entire house, from attic to basement. In her White House diary, Caroline notes the problem of infestation of rats: "The rats have nearly taken the building so it has become necessary to get a man with ferrets. They have become so numerous and bold they get up on the table in the Upper Hall and one got up on [Harrison's private secretary] Mr. Halford's bed."

Two private bathrooms became available for the first time on September 16, 1891. One bathroom was exclusively for the president and First Lady, with new white tile and porcelain-lined marble tub. The other bathroom, called the double bath, had several tubs and basins and was shared by everybody else. The black, dirty basement, with damp floors and moldy walls, housed the laundry, kitchen, and living quarters of the servants, as well as storage areas for wood and coal. Five layers of rotting wood floors were removed and replaced with crushed brick and cement. The kitchen was completely remodeled.

The Edison Company hired Ike Hoover to install the first electric lights and electric bells throughout the White House beginning on May 6, 1891. The chandeliers, built for gas, were converted to either electric or gas fixtures, and the candle wall brackets were replaced with electric lamps. While he was working on the installation, the electrician sometimes felt surrounded by the friendly and curious Harrisons. They were afraid to turn the lights on and off for fear of electric shock, and at first they did not use the lights in their private rooms. Because

A New World Design

While unearthing and cleaning forgotten artifacts in the White House, Caroline found several pieces of porcelain, which she gathered together. After researching and repairing a group of china from past presidents, she made plans for a first permanent display.

In 1891 Caroline was inspired to design the Harrison White House china. One of her sketches, a pencil drawing of corn stalks around the rim of a plate, is preserved in the Harrison Home collection. In a letter to her daughter Mary, she describes her American symbolic design for the plate. "I take the Lincoln china set for a guide. Instead of . . . spots on the border, I have 44 stars. . . . Corn is indigenous to the North American soil. I think they will be right pretty." Caroline asked the artist Paul Putzki to execute a finished design, adapted from her sketches and ideas.

After several china makers had duplicated samples of her plate design, Caroline selected Tressemannes & Vogt in Limoges, France, to produce the Harrison china. Six dozen soup bowls, dinner plates, breakfast plates, and tea plates were ordered on October 21, 1891, and received on January 21, 1892. Caroline was pleased with her china. The Washington, D.C., firm of M. W. Beveridge, importers of French china, supervised the orders for Tressemannes & Vogt. The William McKinley and Theodore Roosevelt administrations continued to use and reorder the Harrison china.

electricity was not entirely dependable, it was for a time a supplement to gaslight. The entire White House was illuminated with electric lights on September 15, 1891.

One of Caroline's successful social events was the opening in 1892 of the new Blue Parlor, redecorated and installed with electric lights, for the annual New Year's Reception. Each room extravagantly displayed hundreds of flowers and decorative plants grown in the restored conservatory. Caroline had added numerous exotic plants to the collection, including orchids.

Caroline was aware of the popularity of her predecessor Frances Cleveland, who had given the White House social events a youthful and stylish flair. However, *The Washington Post* wrote, "Mrs. Harrison has mastered the art of entertaining. . . . She has a friendliness of manner that is proof against criticism." Caroline's events were praised for "an air of genteel gaiety" and beautiful floral decorations.

In her diary she wrote, "One feature of entertainment which I was very pleased with—that was the lack of stiffness which generally characterized all such dinners & I believe all felt at ease and at home." Dancing became a regular part of Harrison public receptions, with daughter Mary and other young relatives helping Caroline as hostesses, although illnesses and deaths caused cancellations of many events on the social calendar.

Caroline organized cultural classes, such as French language classes, at the White House for Washington, D.C., women. Caroline persuaded her Indianapolis art teacher to move to Washington, where he instructed weekly classes in watercolor and china painting at the Executive Mansion. A room in the attic became Caroline's art studio. Literary society meetings were also regularly attended.

Caroline was interested in improving the status of women. When Johns Hopkins Medical School in Baltimore, Maryland, asked her to help with fund-raising, she accepted on the condition that women be admitted on the same terms as men. She served as president of the Washington committee, recruiting the support of influential women from the capital. The committees of women together raised $100,000.

As First Lady, Caroline's charity work continued. She served as director of the Washington City Orphan Asylum and worked on the board of the Garfield Hospital. Her frequent contributions of hand-embroidered cloths and hand-painted china for bazaars brought high sales with recognition of her name. In October, 1890, Caroline was appointed the first president-general of the National Society of the Daughters of the American Revolution. The First Lady's acceptance of this position brought before the public her personal and official approval of the new patriotic and educational enterprise.

Caroline was deeply hurt and distressed by political attacks on her husband and herself and was shocked by slurs on Ben's integrity and partisan lies. She was criticized for being overly domestic; cleaning the White House was not considered an appropriate task for the First Lady. When department store founder John Wanamaker gave the Harrisons a sixteen-room house on the New Jersey shore, journalists called it a political bribe. Caroline was particularly dismayed at the ridicule of her grandchildren in national newspapers.

In the winter of 1891-1892, while she tried to fulfill her social obligations, Caroline was frequently ill with bouts of bronchial infection. In March she developed catarrhal pneumonia, followed by hemorrhages of the lungs. That July, on the advice of their family physician, she was taken five hundred miles by train to Loon Lake in the Adirondack Mountains. Ben rented a three-bedroom cottage with a scenic view of the lake. Boughs of evergreen were hung across windows and doorways because of the theory that the fragrance of the sap would enhance healing of lung problems. After initial improvement, Caroline's condition deteriorated.

The medical diagnosis was finally announced as tuberculosis, with little hope of recovery.

Surgery was performed to drain the fluids from the pleural cavity of the right lung, and repeated two days later. From the time Ben arrived at Loon Lake in August after Congress recessed, he was at Caroline's bedside constantly, helping with the nursing care. On September 20, she was brought back to the White House, where she died after a painful struggle on October 25, 1892. Following funeral services at the White House and at the First Presbyterian Church in Indianapolis, she was buried at Crown Hill Cemetery in Indianapolis.

Legacy

Caroline Harrison should be remembered for her charm and grace as official White House hostess and as a supportive wife. The annual tradition of the decorated Christmas tree at the White House was begun by the Harrisons in 1889, for their grandchildren. Caroline should be remembered for bringing public attention to the need to preserve the historic White House and its collections. She organized the presidential china collection and designed the Harrison White House china, which was used by three administrations. Caroline's enthusiastic interest in china painting increased the popularity of the art form across the United States at the end of the nineteenth century.

Caroline also provided leadership and influence to the National Society of the Daughters of the American Revolution. The organization has continued to uphold and enlarge upon its original goals.

Suggested Readings

Carpenter, Frank. *Carp's Washington*. New York: McGraw-Hill, 1960. Contains information based on a prominent journalist's interview with Caroline Harrison.

Hoover, Irwin Hood (Ike). *Forty-two Years in the White House*. Boston: Houghton Mifflin, 1934. The chief usher when electricity was installed at the White House for President Benjamin Harrison records a chapter of his experiences with and opinions of the Harrisons.

Klapthor, Margaret Brown. *Official White House China, 1789 to the Present*. Washington, D.C.: Smithsonian Institution Press, 1975. Detailed descriptions and illustrations of various administrations' official White House china.

Sievers, Harry Joseph. *Benjamin Harrison*. 3 vols. Indianapolis: Bobbs-Merrill, 1968. An accurate biography of Benjamin Harrison; contains details illustrating Caroline Harrison's political acumen.

Whitcomb, John, and Claire Whitcomb. *Real Life at the White House: Two Hundred Years of Daily Life at America's Most Famous Residence*. New York: Routledge, 2000. Includes information about the Harrisons at the White House.

Anne Moore

Ida McKinley

Ida Saxton McKinley

Born: June 8, 1847
    Canton, Ohio
Died: May 26, 1907
    Canton, Ohio

President: William McKinley
    1897-1901

Overview: Ida McKinley died only nine blocks north of her birthplace, yet the news of her death saddened the entire world. William and Ida McKinley were the most popular couple since Abraham and Mary Lincoln. The McKinleys' hallmarks were their love for each other, their Christian beliefs, and their seemingly faultless characters. Ida's passions were "my dear William," kind acts extended to children, and roses of any color (except yellow). William McKinley's were Ida's whereabouts and well-being, roses he would clip and bring "Idy" after early morning walks, cigars, and brass bands. They were the Gilded Age and the New Millennium, the twenty-fifth "first couple."

Early Life

Ida was the oldest of three children of James Saxton and Katherine Dewalt Saxton. Her paternal grandfather, George Dewalt, was among the first settlers of Canton, Ohio. In about 1820, he built and operated one of the finest hotels and stagecoach stops in northern Ohio. The three-story hotel, complete with kitchen and full dining facilities, was set on the public square at Market and Tuscarawas Streets. George's father, Philip Dewalt, predated his son's efforts, constructing a two-story brick building at Cleveland and Tuscarawas Streets, which housed his tavern. Buying one of Canton's first platted lots, Philip paid seventy-one dollars for this prime land in the newly opened Ohio territory. Ida's maternal grandmother,

Ida McKinley. *(Library of Congress)*

Christina Harter Dewalt, was the sister of Isaac Harter, who began the Harter Bank in 1854. Both Ida's mother, Katherine, and her grandmother Christina were known as devout Presbyterians and good keepers of house and hospitality.

Previous to its founding in 1805, Canton was the Indian territory surrounding the Tuscarawas and Nimishillen Rivers. Ida's paternal grandparents were numbered among early Canton pioneers. Her grandfather John Saxton came West with a wagon and a printing press, publishing his first issue of the *Ohio Repository* within two weeks of his arrival in Canton in March, 1815. The *Ohio Repository* was one of the state's first newspapers, founded in a town of five hundred, described by John Saxton as "a beautiful eminence which rises in the midst of an extensive plain." John Saxton, a Whig, was close friends with Horace Greeley, a Whig nominee for president and the famed publisher of the weekly *New Yorker*; the *Log Cabin*, a campaign paper used to get William Henry Harrison elected president; and Greeley's most successful newspaper, the *Tribune*. Greeley, famous for his passionate orations against slavery, was a frequent guest of John Saxton.

John Saxton was one of twelve who founded Canton's first public school, the Academy, and he was a Canton Township trustee. John Saxton became moderately wealthy; however, his son James chose to make his living by buying and selling land and founding the county's largest bank. This proved to be a good choice, and James Saxton became the second-wealthiest man in Canton by 1870. Only one man was wealthier: Cornelius Aultman, a multimillionaire and one of the world's top producers of mowers and reapers. Ida's uncle Joseph Saxton was numbered among the United States' top twenty inventors in 1867. Ida's ancestors not only were among Canton's pioneers but also were national figures on many levels of interest.

The McKinleys were cousins of Aultman's half brother Lewis Miller, and Miller's daughter was the second wife of inventor Thomas Alva Edison. Cornelius Aultman, Lewis Miller, and Jacob Miller were the founders of Mount Union College. In 1896 Aultman was chairman of William McKinley's election campaign. Lewis Miller invented the "Sunday school" method of graded instruction and was a chief founder of the famous Chautauqua Assembly in New York, a revered national movement of instruction which combined the teaching of Christian principles and the arts.

Ida Saxton McKinley's father acquired the now-famous Canton landmark the Saxton House, which was built by her grandfather George Dewalt in 1841 in Federal style. Her father acquired the Dewalt house in 1869, and in 1870 substantially remodeled the house, adding to both floors and giving the house an imposing, Victorian appearance, with a value of more than $100,000. The house was grand, inside and out, and the contents at its opening were valued at more than seventy-five thousand dollars. William and Ida McKinley lived in the Saxton House, at 331 North Market Avenue, from 1876 through 1890, when William was a congressman. Ida was born in a two-story, commercial-looking building at 226 South Market Avenue, which would also be the site of the McKinleys' wedding reception on January 25, 1871. The Saxtons were rich, and while that brought luxuries and privileges into their lives, the family's values were strong: love for family, devotion to God, and service to humankind. Hence, Ida could never resist befriending any young person, regardless of rank or race, even though her ideals could have been compromised by the loss of both her daughters.

Not much is known about Ida until 1868. She attended two "girls' seminaries"—the word "college" was almost exclusively associated with men. Nonetheless, Ida was more educated than most women of her day as well as many of the men. Her father was quite uncon-

William McKinley

William McKinley was born to middle-class parents in Niles, Ohio, in 1843, the seventh of nine children.

William attended Allegheny College but returned home, ill. He secured a job as a teacher, earning twenty-five dollars per month. He enlisted in the Ohio infantry at the beginning of the Civil War in 1861. Four years later, McKinley mustered out as a major, with a commendation signed "A. Lincoln."

Returning to Ohio, McKinley studied law. In 1867 he was lured to Canton by its bustling population of seven thousand. He became a "working man's attorney" and earned the admiration and backing of industrialist Marc Hanna. Less than three years after arriving in Canton, he was considered an up-and-comer, despite the fact that he was a member of the minority Republican Party.

McKinley's accomplishments were markedly modern-day. He vigorously pursued fair trade among nations and was the first president to significantly engage in foreign affairs. Without seeking congressional authority, McKinley sent U.S. troops to rescue American missionaries caught up in the Boxer Rebellion in China. He established the Open Door policy with China. He advanced civil service reforms started by other presidents. He forwarded funding the best canal route through Nicaragua or Panama and securing one million dollars for the feasibility investigation. He worked to annex Hawaii, stating, "We need Hawaii as much and a good deal more than we did California."

He was the president during the United States' shortest war (April 20, 1898 to Aug. 12, 1898), the Spanish-American War. McKinley, a decorated veteran, was so against the talk of war that some in Congress spoke of impeachment. Finally, with the February, 1898, sinking of the USS *Maine*, all resolution attempts were abandoned, and the United States went to war eagerly, the newspapers of the day having worked the citizenry into a patriotic frenzy.

The United States prospered under McKinley, maintaining U.S. interests abroad and, for the first time, becoming a world power. Still, many would say that McKinley's chief legacy was that of a strong character. He loved his wife, family, and country, in that order, and served them all well.

On January 1, 1900, the diplomatic corps and the everyday citizenry prepared for the annual tradition: New Year's Day Open House at the White House. Ida McKinley took her place beside her husband for the onslaught. Electricity was somewhat of a novelty, and little electric lights decorated the White House. Two thousand guests were already waiting in line. Guests of the day would include Chinese Minister Wu Ting Fang, inventor Alexander Graham Bell, scientist Samuel Langley, the cabinet members and their wives, and congressmen. Most of the crowd, however, was made up of everyday citizens, numbering 3,354, and the president shook hands with every one of them. McKinley believed that no one should be turned away from shaking the hand of the president.

Holding a somewhat dubious record, McKinley could shake twenty-four hundred hands in an hour, often to his detriment. He was shaking hands at the 1901 Pan-American Exposition in Buffalo, New York, when he was assassinated. The hand-shaking event had been canceled twice, with McKinley returning it to the schedule.

Another hand-shaking story was told by U.S. Representative Joseph Cannon of Illinois. When McKinley was Ohio governor, he campaigned by train with Cannon. McKinley had already made a dozen speeches championing protectionism. He was eating lunch on the train when the crowd clamored for him. He stepped out onto the platform and spoke for ten minutes. While trying to return to the train car, the crowd grabbed hold of McKinley's hands, pulling him down a line of hands. It was obviously painful, and a reporter called to Cannon. Cannon put both arms around McKinley and pulled hard, finally freeing him from the grasp of the crowd. Cannon said, "Hey, this is my district, Mack, and I would like to do a little talking myself."

ventional in that he determined all three of his children were to be educated equally. The young Ida Saxton was educated at Miss Sandford's School in Cleveland and the well-known Miss Eastman's seminary in Media, Pennsylvania: Brooke Hall. Ida was no keeper of the house—a life with servants precluded that—but her teachers reported never hearing an unkind word from the young woman who would become First Lady.

Her father's unconventional aspirations did not end with his children's education. Most of the wealthy men who were graduating from the nation's foremost colleges capped their scholastic years with a "Grand Tour" of Europe, a trip lasting six to twelve months. This was seen not as a graduation gift but as another year or so of studying abroad, seeing firsthand what they had read about in books. Ida and her sister, Mary, nicknamed Pina (pronounced Piney), were sent on a Grand Tour of Europe for eight months, thus "finishing" their education. Both Mary and Ida worried about the "grand cost": two thousand dollars per woman in 1869. Ida took charge of the finances, and the women journeyed frugally throughout Ireland, Scotland, England, France, Switzerland, Germany, Italy, and Belgium.

Touring, which was predominantly walking, was focused on seeing museums, landmarks, cathedrals, and the homes of famous authors and artists. The women met Vinnie Ream, an American woman living in Italy who was commissioned to do a sculpture of Abraham Lincoln for the Capitol. Studies were foremost, but Ida did slip away, unchaperoned, to the theater. She was a lifelong lover of staged dramas. The young women twice visited Paris, making sure it was the last stop so they could shop. Souvenir gathering along the way was prohibited by the necessity of carrying only one small bag. Only being able to carry a few belongings, they washed their clothing nightly in hotels and inns and referred to their dresses as "water-proof."

They came home as self-confessed "conquerors" with their "loot"—various textiles for the making of dresses, furs, gemstones, lace, silver jewelry, a Swiss music box for their adored "Ma," presents for the members of Ida's all-boys Sunday school class, and more. Upon their return, Mary had a beau waiting to court her; however, while in Italy, Ida had learned that the twenty-eight-year-old man who had been sending her letters every other week had died suddenly of a brain inflammation (a common reference to, usually, meningitis). She was devastated and could only gaze and weep at the card case with the inscribed "W," which she had purchased as a gift to him. Research reveals that Mr. W was John W. Wright of Canton, formerly of Kentucky. Upon her return to Canton, no mention was again made to Mr. Wright. Ironically, he was a major in the Confederate Army and subsequently a lawyer. Surely Ida could not have guessed that in 1871 she would marry a major (but from the Union Army), one who would also be a lawyer.

Also upon Ida's return, she was the first woman in Canton to cut her hair short, shunning hairpins or ornaments, occasionally donning a modest hat.

Again her father would make an unusual request of his oldest daughter—that she become an actress. She was recruited to help raise funds for the building of the new Presbyterian Church. The Saxtons were the most generous donors to this project, as the foremost Presbyterian family. Ida would, of course, be expected to contribute her talents. The church fund-raiser was held at Schaefer's Opera House. More than twelve hundred people crammed into the opera house in their finery to see the latest Victorian rage—a tableaux of a staged series of scenes from history, some depicting early U.S. themes and some scenes from European history (since Victorians were enamored with all things European). Ida was named the actress of the year. It was not much of a title, because the trick was to not speak or move. She did not know that she would be the first bride married in the church she helped build.

In 1870, her father again asked the unconventional: that she go to work. At that time, teaching school or working as a shop matron or dressmaker were the only acceptable women's jobs outside the home. Ida's father insisted she work in his bank as a teller and bookkeeping clerk. Often she would be required to run the bank in her father's absence. This venture gave rise to rumors all over town that the Saxtons had seen "reverses" in their finances. "No," her irritated father would say, "I have seen girls left stranded by sudden losses . . . she can be taken care of at home now, but I may be poor some day. . . . I want her to be able to support herself. . . . above all, I don't want her to marry solely to be supported." This was quite unconventional for a Gilded Age man. Ida's response was, "Media [Brooke Hall Seminary] has taught me something besides a little Latin."

Local newspapers described Ida as possessing "piquant" features, auburn hair "and lots of it," and "languorous blue eyes under a marble brow." She loved reading, social gatherings, traveling, and, as a young girl, athletic pursuits such as horseback riding.

Marriage and Family

Ida's banking transactions for Major William McKinley, a lawyer, ultimately led to their courtship, composed of conversations over banking transactions, socials held in local homes, and weekly encounters while "the major" was on his way to teach Sunday school at the Methodist Church and Ida was on her way

"The Major" and "Idy," circa 1896. *(Library of Congress)*

to teach at the Presbyterian Church. In 1870 her father would announce her engagement to the only man in town he trusted.

Actually, Ida and William had met shortly after the Civil War hero came to town from Poland, Ohio. It was at a chance meeting at Meyer's Lake Park in 1867; the introductions were performed by William's sister Anna, who was a teacher and school principal.

On January 25, 1871, with one thousand guests in attendance, the wedding was the social event of the era. Ida was one of Canton's wealthiest and most beautiful women, and William was the popular attorney and community leader who had just been elected county prosecutor. The "major" and the "belle" would marry in front of a standing-room-only crowd, none of whom were disappointed by the grandeur. After the 7:00 P.M. wedding and 8:00 reception, the newlyweds departed on a 10:00 train for a honeymoon trip to the East. During William McKinley's first presidential campaign, he gave Ida a twenty-fifth anniversary party in Canton. She wore her white lace wed-

No Prouder Soldier

During the "War with Spain" (the Spanish-American War, 1898), the White House was turned into a "war room." President William McKinley often went sleepless, working with the War Department to await and return dispatches, seeking an end to the war at the earliest possible date. Ida McKinley tried to function as in normal times, keeping up with an extensive schedule of visitors that was further complicated by war-related visitors. Patriotism ran high, and the president's first call for men was 125,000. One million responded.

One such volunteer was a fifteen-year-old boy who had managed to enlist in Tennessee and was stationed at Camp Alger, Virginia. It is unknown why he was visiting the White House, but Mrs. McKinley had only to look at his young face, and she beckoned him into the Blue Room to talk with her. The young soldier was bashful, but she was insistent. She asked him many questions and made him feel at ease. When the boy was ready to depart, she wished him well and gave him some bananas. There was no prouder soldier that day.

Such acts were not uncommon for Ida Saxton McKinley. A reporter who interviewed Mrs. McKinley stated, "She has a keen interest in people. They are more to her than the position. It is the individual, not the class, for which she cares." The reporter queried Mrs. McKinley, "What are your chief preferences?" Mrs. McKinley responded, "Children."

ding gown. During the extravagant dining, the former governor and soon-to-be president pronounced her beautiful, although the years had not really been kind to the former belle of Canton. Hundreds of well-wishers heard McKinley say, "She is ever happy when surrounded by friends, children, and roses."

The couple traveled throughout the United States, with William constantly giving speeches on behalf of the Republican Party. They never vacationed, unable to think of a place to go they would like better than Canton, Ohio. Often, McKinley's cabinet officers would have to spend part of their summers in Canton, excepting the summer of 1898, during the Spanish-American War. Ida and William were seldom parted, except for her shopping trips to Chicago. Ida's cousin, by this time, owned the largest department store in the city. However, William would write his wife during those short absences, ending his letters, "Always your lover." In Washington, D.C., or Columbus, Ohio, he would stop as many as a dozen times to check to see what Ida was doing. Most often, what she was doing was crocheting. In the

White House she made three thousand pairs of slippers, giving them to children and Civil War veterans, Union or Confederate. During her lifetime she crocheted more than ten thousand pairs of slippers. Occasionally, she would make silk ties for her "precious William." Often, in meetings and gatherings, she would be seated, and William would stand beside her, his hand gently resting on her shoulder.

As if from a storybook, the January union would produce their first child on Christmas Day, 1871. Katie, who was named for Ida's beloved mother, Katherine, had blue eyes and golden curls. Six months after Katie was born, Ida was pregnant again. Little Ida would be born within weeks of her grandmother Katherine's death on April 1, 1873. The strain of the birth and the sudden loss of Ida's mother contributed to an extremely difficult labor. Within four months, baby Ida had died of cholera. After Ida arose from her sickbed, epilepsy, phlebitis, migraines, and stomach ailments would plague her for the remainder of her life, at times returning her to bed, and fostering descriptions of her as an invalid. In 1876 four-year-old Katie died of heart disease. Canton's most idyllic couple had become Canton's most tragic couple, with more trials to come. Many of the late nineteenth century medical treatments given Ida would be considered heresy by today's standards. Many of these practices actually contributed to the creation of the so-called invalid, such as alternately giving her stimulants and laxatives in an hourly rotation.

Still, Ida and William always maintained a heavy schedule. At the holidays, the McKinleys would often hold their celebrations away from the family, exchanging small gifts and taking time to remember their girls. Suffering from phlebitis and often severe swelling of her legs, Ida walked with a gold-topped wooden cane or the arm of a man, usually her husband. On at least two occasions, her "falling sickness," today known as epilepsy, and phlebitis forced her into a "rolling chair," but never for long.

Presidency and First Ladyship

William McKinley's contributions to the United States were well established by the end of his second term as Ohio's governor. It would have been relatively easy for the couple to retire to Canton and live off that legacy, but the nation would not hear of it.

Gerrymandering and his role as the champion of the protective tariff had cost him the 1890 election in his last congressional race. Still, the McKinley Tariff Bill of 1890 was considered a major victory for him and for the U.S. economy. It was his June, 1890, speech on the McKinley Tariff which rooted him in the people's hearts. He had, with its passage, created about one-half million jobs and saved another one-half million jobs—a feat by even today's standards. From his first speech in Congress until the end of his life, he was a strong protectionist. "It is our duty and we ought to protect sacredly and assuredly the labor and the industry of the United States as we would protect her honor from taint or her territory from invasion," stated McKinley. When he returned to Canton,

seventy-five thousand people would spontaneously gather outside the Saxton House to pay tribute to this deed which so protected U.S. dinner buckets.

McKinley, who won two terms as governor of Ohio (1892-1896), was an American hero and the favored candidate for president. Cleveland industrialist Marc Hanna spent 1895-1896 in grass-roots campaigning among state Republican leaders to assure the McKinley nomination met with no last-minute snags. The only undercurrent was that the question of a sound currency must be settled along with the selection of a new president. The East favored the gold standard; the West preferred silver.

The June, 1896, ballot at the St. Louis Republican Convention was not even close. McKinley received 661 votes and his closest competitor received 84. At home, William was in one parlor with the men, pencil in hand, noting the state's votes as they were wired to him. The upstairs wire operator called down to the guests, "Ohio, forty-six for McKinley." McKinley arose, walked across the hall to the ladies' parlor, and kissed his wife and mother. "Ida," he said, "Ohio's vote has just nominated me."

The popularity of McKinley's selection immediately gave birth to the Front Porch of 1896. The news spread rapidly and special trains were immediately dispatched to Canton to congratulate McKinley. Between 5:00 P.M. and midnight, more than fifty thousand gathered on and around the McKinleys' front porch. The presidential election of 1896 was decisive. There were about fourteen million potential votes, and McKinley's tally topped seven million, easily beating William Jennings Bryan. McKinley would go on to beat Bryan a second time in 1900 by even a larger margin in both the electoral and popular vote. By the time William was elected president, in 1896, there was scarcely a blade of grass left on the McKinley lawn.

Soon Ida would be sitting next to her William at some official White House event or traveling by train to some political stump. Her illness and the couple's closeness gave rise to a new tradition at the White House: the First Lady being seated or standing by the president at formal occasions. Previously, First Ladies had been relegated to the end of a long dining table or another part of the White House, serving tea to womenfolk. Ida's legacy in protocol says the first couple preside at major events side by side, as equals.

For Victorians, any illness in any woman made her "delicate." Victorians, too, were very much lashed to rules and protocol, especially for mourning. Commonplace was the keeping of shrines in the most prominent living areas. Ida kept two small rockers, adorned with mementos from her daughters, in every favorite parlor over which she presided. Often, when holding a small child, she would burst into tears. Still she constantly sought out young people of all ranks and races. Children, it was said, were attracted to her skirts like magnets. Canton's youngsters often followed after her carriage, calling "Auntie McKinley, Auntie Mc-Kinley," and she would stop and present them with a kiss or a token. The string of events to follow would characterize her personal life as tragic, while the McKinleys' public life would seem always golden—a type and shadow of the era they lived in, the Gilded Era.

Among the personal tragedies would be then-Governor McKinley's cosigning of a $15,000 bank loan for a friend, which would leave him unwittingly indebted $130,000 and produce financial ruin. Other tragedies were the suicide of William's brother David, which left two orphaned children; the murder of Ida's brother George and the converging of the world's press upon that disaster; the death of the president's closest confidant, "Mother Mc-Kinley" (Nancy Allison McKinley), who did not live to see her son's second inaugural; and their long desire for a home of their own, one that the salary of public life would not support. The couple never lived off Ida's independent wealth. In their thirty years of marriage, they predominantly lived in hotels. For a few years at the beginning of their marriage and then a few years at the end, they owned homes and kept house. Ironically, their marital years would begin and end in the same house, at 723 North Market Street in Canton.

The couple's final tragedy was their separation by an assassin's bullets. The twenty-fifth president was shot twice in the abdomen while visiting the Pan-American Exposition in Buffalo, New York, on September 6, 1901. He died on September 14. Three funerals commemorated his life and death: one in Buffalo, one in Washington, D.C., and one in Canton. Forty-five days after McKinley's death, the confessed murderer, twenty-three-year-old anarchist Leon Czolgosz of Detroit, the son of Polish parents, would be put to death in the electric chair in Auburn State Prison, New York. A crew sent by Thomas Edison would film the funeral and the execution of the assassin.

The four months preceding William's death were the happiest that William and Ida had known. From June through September each year, Canton had been the summer White House. Cabinet officers did not see the attraction that Canton, Ohio, held but were obliging. Spending summertime in Canton enabled the president to engage in his favorite pastimes, such as dining on fresh vegetables from his Minerva, Ohio, farm and visiting his groom and favorite horse, Midnight.

Although the widowed Ida was begged to return to the Saxton House, now owned by her sister, Mary, she preferred to stay on, alone, at 723 North Market Street, cared for by a maid and nurse. Her friends tried in vain to encourage her to travel to visit friends; however, her days were dominated by daily visits to Westlawn Cemetery to see the graves of William and the girls. Seldom would she leave her home, except to attend small, local tributes to her "dear William."

Often she would wonder aloud to friends why she had not been taken before her husband

and girls. Much to most everyone's surprise, Ida's health improved after leaving the White House. At the entreating of President Theodore Roosevelt, she even began to look forward to the September, 1907, opening of the national memorial to her husband. Ida Saxton McKinley died of a stroke on May 26, 1907, just three months before the dedication of the national memorial. It had pleased her that a "penny campaign" had been conducted among American children to help fund the building of the memorial, which was dedicated by President Roosevelt and Ida's sister, Mary Saxton Barber.

Legacy

Ida's legacy was that she supported her husband unwaveringly. Detractors knew better than to criticize him in her presence, for she would immediately exhibit anger, a tendency much unlike her William. It was said that McKinley only ever lost his temper twice: once when he saw a black maid mistreated and the other time when a so-called friend cost him $130,000.

McKinley sought and gained Ida's opinion on every matter. While he was a perpetual student of domestic topics, it was she who was the avid reader of the world's news, keeping track of even the smallest story.

Ida and William were matched in their passion to serve the underprivileged. They found the high infant mortality rate of the Philippines intolerable, and they would send aid to cure the ills of the people and feed them. The concept of foreign aid was a first for this U.S. president.

Although McKinley was a longtime proponent of women's suffrage and black suffrage, Ida supported these tenets long before their marriage, she being a product of her own time in Canton, Ohio. They were both opposed to slavery. McKinley's first public speech was in support of Ulysses S. Grant's presidency, his second for women's suffrage, and his third for black suffrage.

McKinley was passionate about healing the wounds from the Civil War, and he made it a point to speak to and embrace veterans from both sides, thus endearing him to both the Union and Confederate soldier. Ida, too, felt strongly about veterans, and many of her pairs of crocheted slippers were blue or gray gifts.

Ida encouraged William's life of public service and supported him in it. In light of their early losses, William felt duty-bound to love and care for her in every way. He never deferred any kindness he could extend to her. The McKinleys were among the most devoted and loving couples ever to occupy the White House.

Suggested Readings

Gould, Lewis L. *The Presidency of William McKinley.* Lawrence: Regents Press of Kansas, 1980. A scholastic account of the twenty-fifth president.

Halstead, Murat. *Life and Distinguished Services of William McKinley.* Chicago: M. A. Donohue, 1901. Available at most libraries; Halstead was the foremost author of historical accounts at the turn of the twentieth century.

Heald, Edward Thornton. *Condensed Biography of William McKinley.* Canton, Ohio: Stark County Historical Society, 1964. An overview of William and Ida McKinley.

Leech, Margaret. *In the Days of McKinley.* New York: Harper & Brothers, 1959. Probably the most entertaining account of the McKinleys.

Olcott, Charles, *The Life of William McKinley.* 2 vols. New York: Houghton Mifflin, 1916. A thorough and accurate examination of William McKinley's life and accomplishments and his life with Ida McKinley.

Mary M. Cain

Edith Roosevelt

Edith Kermit Carow Roosevelt

Born: August 6, 1861
      Norwich, Connecticut
Died: September 30, 1948
      Oyster Bay, New York

President: Theodore Roosevelt
      1901-1909

Overview: Edith Kermit Roosevelt—for many decades held up as the ideal First Lady—was a reluctant presidential spouse who successfully negotiated the difficulties of balancing official duties as a president's wife with her own desires to maintain her privacy and put her family duties first.

Edith Roosevelt. *(Library of Congress)*

An intensely private woman, she nonetheless became the role model as Theodore Roosevelt's wife and a semipublic figure of First Lady. Her sense of privacy has made her a somewhat shadowy historical figure, often obscuring her role in shaping the "office" of First Lady.

Early Life
Edith Kermit Carow was born in 1861 to Gertrude Tyler Carow and Charles Carow, of the shipbuilding Carow family, whose business had suffered under Edith's alcoholic father. She could trace her American ancestors, who included Puritan theologian Jonathan Edwards, back to the 1630's. As a child, Edith was very well read, even bookish. She also had a reputation for inscrutability that became one of her lifelong personal trademarks. Nonetheless, she developed a close friendship with Corinne Roosevelt, Theodore Roosevelt's younger sister, that only disintegrated after her marriage to Theodore. Edith received her formal education at the prestigious Miss Comstock's School.

Marriage and Family

Edith Carow's courtship and marriage to Theodore Roosevelt had many elements of a Victorian romantic melodrama. She and Theodore, who was three years her senior, had been around each other since they were young children. Although they had made no plans, there was an unspoken understanding that they would someday marry. That understanding was broken after a quarrel. Soon after, Theodore courted and married a beautiful, aristocratic Boston debutante named Alice Hathaway Lee. Edith, however, remained in his social circle and even attended his wedding. Alice Hathaway Lee Roosevelt died of Bright's disease in 1884, shortly after the birth of her daughter, Alice. Although the grieving Theodore at first avoided Edith, after an awkward chance meeting they soon resumed what had been broken off and became engaged by November, 1885. They then arranged to travel separately to England and were married there in 1886.

Once she and Theodore had settled into married life, they did not look back. Edith insisted on raising Theodore's daughter Alice as her own, in part to reduce the influence that Theodore's sister Anna Roosevelt Cowles (who had cared for the infant Alice) held over him. Theodore and Edith's own five children included four sons: Theodore, Jr., born in 1887; Kermit, born in 1889; Archibald, born in 1894; and Quentin, born in 1897; and a daughter, Ethel, born in 1891. The Roosevelts' family life was very happy overall, with Theodore very much involved in his children's lives. Edith was a strict but loving mother, who took much effort to treat Alice as well as or better than her own children. However, she developed the closest lifelong relationship with her second son, Kermit, her clear favorite among her children. Edith also had an intimidating streak and could command husband or children by a simple measured tone of voice.

For all of his devotion to family, when duty called, Roosevelt had little compunction about

Alice Hathaway Lee Roosevelt, first wife of Theodore Roosevelt. *(Library of Congress)*

leaving his wife's side to fulfill it. For example, Roosevelt organized the First Volunteer Cavalry, called the Rough Riders, while Edith, though not deathly ill at the time, was recovering from surgery to remove a tumor. During Roosevelt's rise to public prominence, money troubles were a periodically recurring theme in their marriage. This may have had more to do with Edith's ingrained fears of financial instability than the state of the family fortunes. Although some of her economizing measures, such as making her own toothpaste, were more symbolic than anything, they were based on her awareness of the tension between maintaining financial solvency and living in the style expected of people of the Roosevelts' social class.

Following their marriage, Edith remained an important, if sometimes unintended, influence on Theodore's career trajectory. In 1894,

Theodore Roosevelt

Theodore Roosevelt, often regarded as the creator of the modern presidency, was born in 1858 to Theodore Roosevelt, Sr., and Martha "Mittie" Bulloch Roosevelt. Theodore's formal education included the prestigious Groton School and Harvard University. During his Harvard years, he met and courted his first wife, Alice Hathaway Lee. During his brief marriage to Lee, he launched his political career as a New York State assemblyman in 1882. After Alice's sudden death in 1884, Theodore seriously considered giving up politics and retreated to his remote ranch in the Dakota Badlands. The time he spent there, however, helped him return to the East more mature and seasoned, and his return to public life came not long after his second marriage, to Edith Kermit Carow in 1886.

Roosevelt restarted his public career with an appointment to the United States Civil Service Commission in 1887. A few years later, in 1894, he accepted an appointment to the board of police commissioners, where he built his reputation as a reformer. In 1896, after helping William McKinley win the White House, Theodore was appointed assistant secretary of the Navy. In this post, he agitated for going to war over Cuba, then organized and commanded the First Volunteer Cavalry, better known as the Rough Riders, in 1898. Following his triumphal return from the Spanish-American War, Theodore Roosevelt was elected New York State governor. During his tenure as governor, he launched a series of economic reforms that won him both acclaim and political enemies. In 1900 he became President McKinley's running mate. During his short tenure as vice president, he weathered the expected official inactivity. Then McKinley was shot on September 6, 1901, and died a week later.

At the beginning of his presidency Theodore Roosevelt was called His Accidency. Before his first term was complete, however, he achieved a variety of accomplishments in both domestic and foreign affairs, ranging from negotiating the treaty that jump-started the building of the Panama Canal to establishing his reputation as the "trust buster." When Roosevelt handily won a term in his own right in 1904, he immediately announced that he would not seek another, a statement he soon regretted.

Nonetheless, he served out an even more successful second term, in which his accomplishments included negotiating the end of the Russo-Japanese War in 1907. By 1912 the growing dissatisfaction with his successor William Howard Taft prompted Roosevelt to break his word and run again. Failing to win the Republican nomination from the incumbent Taft, Roosevelt ran on the quickly formed Progressive (Bull Moose) Party ticket. In the end, he split the Republican Party, enabling the Democratic candidate, Woodrow Wilson, to win. His political career ended, Theodore Roosevelt died seven years later.

for example, he planned to run for mayor of New York, but Edith was opposed to it. He chose not to run and Edith, in a comparatively rare display of deep emotion, expressed remorse at what she saw as her failure as a wife. Later, Theodore disregarded Edith's opposition to his successfully seeking the vice presidential slot on the 1900 Republican ticket, on the basis of the comparative inconsequentiality of the vice president's job. Edith, while continuing to raise her large family, adjusted herself to the social demands incumbent upon the wife of a public official, albeit on her own terms. She cleverly avoided the uncomfortable task of shaking many strange hands by holding a bouquet in public receiving lines. Similarly, she assiduously avoided having her picture taken or distributed for publicity purposes. Although she was never happy with Theodore's decision to accept the vice presidential slot, she dutifully supported her husband. Then, on September 13, 1901, President William McKinley died from an assassin's bullet.

Presidency and First Ladyship

Edith, coming into the role of First Lady unexpectedly and somewhat reluctantly, made a quick enough adjustment to allow her to do things that would leave a visible stamp on the role. For example, to maintain control of the flow of information to the public, she hired Belle Hagner as her social secretary, setting a precedent for subsequent First Ladies. Hagner took on responsibility both for correspondence and for doling out photographs and information to the many reporters who were hungry for news about the young and vigorous first family. Despite the increased demands on her as First Lady, Edith was determined that her young children should have a normal upbringing, which meant shielding them as much as possible from the prying eyes of the press. She set aside time each day for her children and frequently wrote to her sons who were at boarding school.

Edith Roosevelt's greatest accomplishment as First Lady, supervising the renovation and refurbishing of the Executive Mansion (which was only renamed the White House during Theodore Roosevelt's administration), grew out of her desire to create the private space necessary to maintain a semblance of normal family life. Although others had previously proposed additions to the Executive Mansion in order to deal with this long-recognized problem, Edith and Theodore Roosevelt were the first to overcome earlier objections on aesthetic grounds. Although it was Theodore who contracted and publicly dealt with the architectural firm McKim, Mead, and White, Edith's influence was evident throughout the project. For example, the creating of a third floor within the mansion and the building of the West Wing for office space created a clear division for the first time between public and private areas in the White House. In her supervision of the redecoration, she also permanently set the expected mode of interior decoration of the public rooms, transforming them from the earlier ornate Victoriana to the spare, elegant Federalism that is now familiar to visitors and tourists. Finally, Edith was instrumental in shoring up the status of the White House as a public museum and monument as well as an executive office and residence. She followed Caroline Harrison's efforts to preserve and display former administrations' White House china. Her other significant accomplishment in this area was to designate space for display of First Lady portraits.

In the traditional hostess role, Edith not only excelled but also was a shaping force in Washington, D.C., society. She introduced high culture to the White House entertainment scene with her musicales, which featured performers such as Pablo Casals (who would perform at the White House again during the Kennedy administration). As First Patron of the Arts, Edith also influenced Congress to appropriate funding for what would become the National Gallery of Art.

Her high standards, however, had a darker side. In addition to barring blacks and middle- or working class people from her social events, she also excluded those whose moral and sexual behavior transgressed her strict personal code of conduct. To help ensure that her standards were understood within official Washington society, she held regular meetings with wives of cabinet officers to help establish social rules. Her other purpose for these meetings was to establish standards for White House entertainment and to disseminate information on her entertainment style to Washington hostesses, with the expectation that they were not to try to upstage the First Lady.

As much as she was greatly admired for her acumen as hostess, she did not escape the sometimes petty criticism of the way she played her semipublic role. The most famous criticism was of her decidedly economic attitude toward clothing and her unwillingness to spend what it took to remain at the height of fashion. A snide critic wrote that "the wife of the President, it is said, dresses on $300 a year and looks it." Edith, however, was proud enough of her economies to clip and save the offending article. It should also be noted that the role she played in her husband's administration was not always limited to the accepted traditional roles of decorator and hostess. For example, she was the first president's wife to accompany her husband on an official trip abroad, traveling with Theodore to Panama in 1906 to visit the new canal. She also served as an unofficial diplomatic go-between on occasions.

Given the social prominence of the Roosevelt family in addition to Theodore's position as president, it did not take long before the public and the private would intersect on the Roosevelts' social calendar. The first of these was the formal debut of Edith's stepdaughter, Alice. Four years later came Alice's wedding to Congressman Nicholas Longworth. The wed-

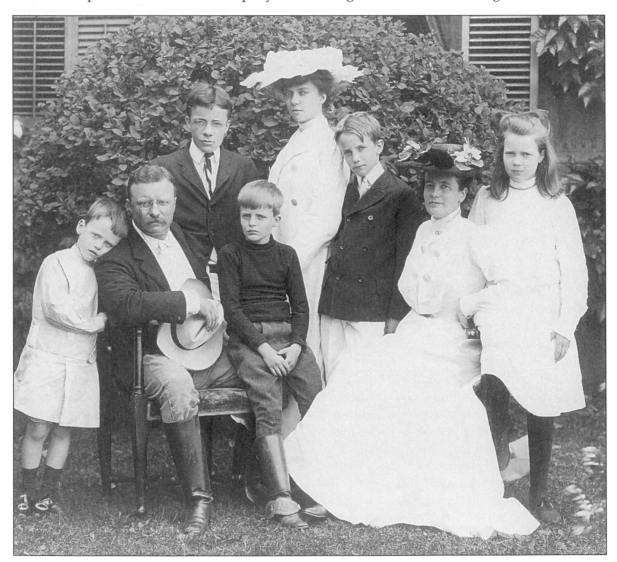

Theodore and Edith Roosevelt, surrounded by their family. *(Library of Congress)*

Edith and the American Public

Although Edith Roosevelt has long been regarded as the ideal First Lady who never made a mistake, she was keenly conscious of the one significant gaffe she committed as First Lady. During the course of the White House refurbishing, Edith ordered a small settee, which was purchased for forty dollars. When her husband's term ended, she decided to take the settee back home with her to their home, Sagamore Hill, as a treasured reminder of the family's years in Washington, D.C. Before removing it, she had prudently decided to have a reproduction made, at her own expense. However, the press soon got wind of her plans to remove the settee and reacted as if she was stealing a priceless national treasure. Under public pressure, Edith decided not to insist on her right to keep the piece. Rather, she concluded that even if the settee was to be offered to her as a gift, she would not want it because of the negative associations it now held. The incident was a stark reminder to her of the public nature of her seemingly private decisions.

ding was billed as the social event of the year and became the closest thing Americans experienced to a royal wedding, receiving detailed newspaper coverage. To prevent party-crashing, selected reporters and photographers were included in the preparations. For Edith, however, it was a source of fatigue. When Alice thanked her stepmother for the wedding, a wearied and irritated Edith responded, "I want you to know that I'm glad to see you leave. You have never been anything but trouble."

Even with the blurring of her private roles as mother of the debutante, or bride, and her public role as First Lady, Edith was careful to guard her privacy. She assiduously sought to avoid drawing what she saw as needless attention to her daily doings. This avoidance of the spotlight made Edith a diametric contrast to her publicity-courting stepdaughter, "Princess" Alice, who reveled in her celebrity status as First Daughter and made the press regularly with her style, active social life, and willingness to test the limits of proper behavior during that period.

Following the Roosevelts' departure from the White House in 1909, Edith found herself missing life there, as much as she welcomed the comparative quiet and privacy of Sagamore Hill, their home on Long Island. Although she

opposed Theodore's premature announcement not to seek a third term, when he decided to run on the Progressive "Bull Moose" Party ticket in 1912, she told him to face the fact that he would never be president again.

Legacy

Edith Roosevelt, the former First Lady, did not content herself simply with staying home and presiding over Sagamore Hill. When Theodore went on his famous post-presidential African safari, Edith traveled in Europe, accompanied by her daughter Ethel. Later, in 1913, when Theodore set off with his son Kermit on their exploration of the Brazilian wilderness along the River of Doubt, Edith traveled with him as far as Brazil, to the starting point of the expedition. She then rejoined him at the point where his party emerged from the wilderness.

The death of their youngest son, Quentin, in World War I grieved Edith deeply but affected Theodore even more. Neither did widowhood and old age easily slow Edith down. After Theodore's death in 1919, she not only continued but expanded her travels, both alone and with her daughter Ethel.

During these years, Edith also increased her participation in public life—and partisan politics. Her emergence into public life was prompted somewhat ironically by the nomination of her husband's cousin Franklin Delano Roosevelt for president. After receiving hundreds of congratulatory telegrams and letters by people who mistakenly believed her to be Franklin's wife or mother, she came out publicly in support of his opponent, Herbert Hoover, as much to distance herself from Franklin's branch of the extended Roosevelt family as for political reasons. Her subsequent public appearances included a speech in support of Hoover before a huge crowd in New York's Madison Square Garden. Although she became recognized as an accomplished political speaker late in life, she still resolutely refused to talk to the press.

Edith, in failing health by the late 1940's and having lost two more of her sons in World War II, spent her last days at Sagamore Hill, cared for by her daughter Ethel. Private to the end, she burned Theodore's letters to her, save for one bundle of love letters found at her bedside when she died in 1948.

Edith's greatest legacy was to institutionalize the role of First Lady as First Hostess and set a standard for those who followed her. She also was a pioneer among First Ladies in raising public awareness of the White House's status as a historical site and museum. Since her tenure, the role of First Lady as official First Hostess, as created by Edith Roosevelt, has shown a remarkable staying power. Although the style and scope of White House hospitality changed somewhat over the twentieth century (most no-tably in welcoming a greater spectrum of the American people to White House functions), the high standards for the hostess set by Edith have largely remained and have, as much as possible, been scrupulously followed.

Suggested Readings

Anthony, Carl Sferrazza. *First Ladies: The Saga of the Presidents' Wives and Their Power.* Vol. 1. New York: William Morrow, 1990. Places Edith Roosevelt's life in the context of the "sorority" of First Ladies.

Caroli, Betty Boyd. *First Ladies.* Expanded ed. New York: Oxford University Press, 1995. Provides a comprehensive overview of Edith Roosevelt's tenure as First Lady.

_____. *The Roosevelt Women.* New York: Basic Books, 1998. Edith Roosevelt's family versus public images.

Collier, Peter, with David Horowitz. *The Roosevelts: An American Saga.* New York: Simon & Schuster, 1994. Places Edith Roosevelt within the context of the Roosevelt family history.

Hagedorn, Hermann. *The Roosevelt Family of Sagamore Hill.* New York: Macmillan, 1954. A lively narrative of Edith and Theodore Roosevelt's growing family, primarily before and during the White House years.

Morris, Sylvia Jukes. *Edith Kermit Roosevelt: Portrait of a First Lady.* New York: Coward, McCann & Geoghegan, 1980. The definitive biography of Edith Roosevelt.

Susan Roth Breitzer

Helen Taft

Helen Herron Taft

Born: June 2, 1861
      Cincinnati, Ohio
Died: May 22, 1943
      Washington, D.C.

President: William Howard Taft
      1909-1913

Overview: Helen Taft, always called Nellie, is remembered as an especially ambitious First Lady, sometimes charged with having designs on a White House life from her youth. Certainly Nellie's frankness revealed an exceptional intelligence and drive, which fueled her eagerness to experience the diversities of life. She was, therefore, a well-suited match for William Howard Taft, whose tal-

ents as a jurist were recognized early. As his career opportunities carried him to ever higher levels of power and prestige, both at home and abroad, Nellie maintained an equitable marriage partnership with him in determining his career path and their family's experiences.

Helen Taft. *(Library of Congress)*

Early Life

Born to Harriet Anne Collins Herron and John Williamson Herron, Nellie was the fourth born of their eight daughters and three sons, eight of whom lived beyond childhood. Harriet, the daughter of U.S. congressman Eli Collins from upper New York State, came to Cincinnati as a young woman to live with her brother Judge Isaac Clinton Collins. John Williamson Herron, a Miami University (Oxford, Ohio) contemporary of Benjamin Harrison, enjoyed a successful law practice in Cincinnati, where he shared a partnership at times with Rutherford B. Hayes and Judge Collins and served as both a U.S. attorney and state senator.

William Howard Taft

William Howard Taft rose to the presidency along a path of public service. After graduating from Yale University, he returned home to Cincinnati to study law. He progressed through a series of judiciary appointments with notable ability. His only election prior to that for the presidency was in 1888, to retain his previously appointed seat on the Ohio Superior Court. Taft disliked politics; his true desire was to become a U.S. Supreme Court justice.

As a result of the Spanish-American War, the United States found itself in possession of the Philippine Islands. President William McKinley chose Taft to lead the Philippines Commission. As governor general from 1901 to 1904, Taft successfully negotiated with the Vatican to return church-held lands to Filipinos, built schools and roads, improved the economy, and instituted a limited self-government. His restrained attitude and lack of racial prejudice earned the Filipinos' confidence. Taft's work demonstrated colonialism at its best.

Theodore Roosevelt, president after McKinley's assassination, valued Taft's capabilities, though the two men were temperamentally opposite. Roosevelt saw Taft as his own worthy successor and persuaded him to join the cabinet as secretary of war. In that capacity, Taft administered Panama Canal construction, negotiated peace in a Cuban revolution, and eased Japanese-American tensions over immigration issues.

Reluctant but prodded by Roosevelt, his wife, and his brothers, Taft accepted the Republican nomination for president in 1908. He recalled the campaign as "one of the most uncomfortable four months of my life." He easily defeated newspaper editor and former congressman William Jennings Bryan.

William Howard Taft spent four uneasy years in the White House, caught in the crossfire between conservatives and progressives and enjoying little recognition of his successes. To his credit, Taft's administration aggressively prosecuted Sherman Antitrust lawsuits, strengthened the Interstate Commerce Commission, established the postal savings bank and parcel-post system, and created the Department of Labor. Two constitutional amendments were submitted to create a federal income tax and the direct election of senators.

Although he actually outperformed Roosevelt on the latter's own policies, Taft's compromise on several decisions inflamed the progressive Republicans. They berated his Latin American policy, which encouraged refinancing Nicaragua's foreign debt, and his support of the Payne-Aldrich Tariff Act was seen as protectionist because of the duties it increased. Additionally, his defense of the secretary of the interior, who had come under fire for reportedly opening federal land for sale, painted Taft as an enemy of conservation.

These alienated liberals formed the Progressive, or Bull Moose, Party after Taft received the Republican nomination for reelection in 1912. Roosevelt, now at odds with Taft, ran as the third-party Progressive candidate. With the Republican vote split, Democratic candidate Woodrow Wilson won.

Relieved to escape political life, Taft joined the Yale faculty as a professor of law. In 1921, President Warren G. Harding appointed him chief justice of the United States. Taft held his position on the Supreme Court with distinction and satisfaction until shortly before his death on March 8, 1930.

Nellie grew up in an intellectually stimulating, socially prominent atmosphere. The large Herron family required that they live in somewhat more modest circumstances than their social standing might suggest, but all of the Herron children received the highest quality education; the sons at Harvard and Yale Universities and all the daughters at Miss Nourse's school in Cincinnati.

Mid-nineteenth century Cincinnati culture was a contrasting mix of prosperous businessmen flourishing at the door to Western expansion and the rough, smog-bound life of riverfront workers laboring for them. Enriching the "Queen City" was the conspicuous German influence on local customs and arts, which provided exceptional musical training and performance opportunities. Nellie benefitted from this musical presence, displaying a lifelong talent and discipline for music, especially the piano, and believed it could become her life's work.

Because of the close friendship between the families, seventeen-year-old Nellie visited President and Mrs. Hayes in the White House, the single most notable event she cherished from her youth. Whether her remarks about wanting to live there herself were the casual response of a typical young girl's fancy or the determined statement of a goal cannot be known. Her upbringing certainly prepared her for a future as First Lady.

After completing her education, Nellie taught school and gave piano lessons. At a sledding party in 1879, she first met the recent Yale graduate William Howard Taft and the two immediately experienced a mutual attraction of quick minds and humors. By 1883, Nellie, wishing to elevate her social life, had formed a literary salon with several of her friends, both male and female, to engage in intellectual discussions. Among the group was Will Taft.

Marriage and Family

The salon occasions brought Nellie and Will closer. An engagement was announced in May, 1885, leading to their marriage in the Herron family home on June 19, 1886. Their one-hundred-day honeymoon in Europe cost just one thousand dollars, much to the pride of frugal Nellie. On the trip, Nellie did, however, indulge her love of attending musical performances until reaching the limit of her good-natured groom.

Will's career continued to quickly advance. Shortly after the 1889 birth of their first child, Robert Alphonso, Will was appointed solicitor general of the United States. Nellie was delighted to be moving to Washington, D.C. While the Tafts resided there, a daughter, Helen, was born in 1891. Nellie found life with two small children in their small Dupont Circle home to be mostly a simple routine.

The Taft family returned to live in Cincinnati after Will's appointment to the Federal Circuit Bench by President Benjamin Harrison. Nellie feared her husband, much younger than his fellow jurists and very happy in this position, would lose his youthful ambitions. During this eight-year period, she directed her energy toward the organization of the Cincinnati Orchestra Association. She garnered support from the city's music lovers, who raised adequate funds to provide financial stability for a high-quality orchestra with a capable director. The other highlight of this period in her life was the 1897 birth of her youngest child, Charles.

In 1900, when President William McKinley asked Taft to go to the newly acquired Philippine Islands to end U.S. military rule, Taft was certain the sultry climate, disease, and primitive conditions would repel Nellie. Instead, she was eager for adventurous travel in Asia. While her husband traveled ahead to make living arrangements for his family, Nellie, with her children, sister, and other ladies of the party, passed several weeks of sightseeing in Japan. There Nellie acquired great appreciation of the Asian aesthetic, particularly in the design of living spaces and gardens. When honored by an audience with the Japanese Empress, she regretted to see that the Palace in Tokyo was furnished with heavy, ornate Victorian pieces—an attempt to modernize by adopting Western styles.

Although living conditions in Manila, Philippines, equaled their unpleasant reputation, Nellie took a kind of First Ladyship role there. For more than three years Nellie, living first in a house on Manila Bay, then the Malacañang Palace, struggled to stretch a limited budget. Her social events presented a blend of local and Western customs. The palace provided a grand scene for her frequent receptions, at which everyone was welcome, regardless of race or social standing. She boldly traveled to outlying areas of the Philippines and witnessed its diverse indigenous cultures.

By 1904 an exhausted Nellie sought respite in China, only to hear that her husband had to be rushed to surgery for an abdominal abscess. Only weeks later, when Will required a second surgery, was his need to return to the States apparent. Nellie, too, was further strained by news of her mother's life-threatening stroke. Without much-needed rest, the family took leave and headed home. Sadly, the Tafts were confronted by weather delays and received word of Mrs. Herron's death before reaching Cincinnati. Nellie completely broke down, unable to attend her mother's funeral once they arrived in Ohio.

Before returning to the Philippines, the Tafts recovered from their misfortunes. At President Theodore Roosevelt's request, Will went to Rome to resolve Philippine land ownership issues with the Vatican. Nellie and the children joined him and were granted an audience with Pope Leo XIII. Upon returning for a final year in Manila, they were threatened by a devastating cholera epidemic. The Taft family was spared the disease but witnessed overwhelming death, famine, and the resulting social unrest. However, by the time Roosevelt convinced Taft to return to Washington and accept the post of secretary of war, Nellie was able to plan a lavish farewell gala, assured that the Filipinos recog-

nized the progress achieved by her husband's efforts for their benefit.

During his term in the cabinet, Nellie and Will traveled extensively on U.S. affairs and took a trip around the world. By this time, she saw the presidency within her husband's reach and actively intervened to divert Roosevelt's offer of a Supreme Court seat to her husband. She also grew distrustful of Roosevelt's promise not to seek reelection. Taking nothing for granted, Nellie hovered over her husband's nomination and campaign, and was joyfully relieved at his 1908 election. At last, Nellie Taft would be First Lady.

Presidency and First Ladyship

Once her husband was inaugurated into the presidency, Nellie turned her energies to the duties of First Lady. Because of the additions and restorations to the White House during the Roosevelt years, Nellie found the building to be in acceptable condition. She did, however, rule that formally costumed footmen should be at the doors to greet and guide visitors, and she replaced the position of steward with that of housekeeper, believing that only a woman could attend to so many domestic details.

The Tafts retained Major Archie Butt, who had served as Roosevelt's military aide. His forebodings about Mrs. Taft quickly dispelled; he liked her straightforward honesty, and the two developed a deep mutual respect. With Major Butt's help, Nellie purchased the first White House automobiles. Congress had appropriated twelve thousand dollars for such a purchase, but Nellie wanted four cars—more than the sum could cover. Ever frugal, Nellie negotiated with the automakers. She would get her four autos at a reduced price; they could advertise that their cars were used by the White House. The deal was settled.

After only two months as First Lady, Nellie experienced a cruel irony. While entertaining on the presidential yacht, she suffered a severe stroke which removed her from public life for

A newly inaugurated President William Taft is joined by his wife, Nellie, on the ride to the White House, 1909. *(Library of Congress)*

The Inaugural Ride

Nellie Taft's unprecedented ride in the coach with her husband from the inaugural ceremony to the White House was interpreted by some observers as an announcement of her position of power, surpassing that of any of her predecessors. She savored the opportunity with full understanding of breaking tradition, though that had not entirely been her intention.

Taft's inauguration departed from other precedents. First, President and Mrs. Theodore Roosevelt invited the Tafts to be overnight guests on the eve of the March 4, 1909, inauguration. In their writings, both Nellie Taft and Roosevelt aide Archie Butt anticipated the arrangement to be uncomfortable, regardless of the cordiality between the Tafts and the Roosevelts.

Secondly, President Roosevelt had announced two years earlier that he would not accompany his successor on the return to the White House. Since Taft had not yet selected any new appointees to his cabinet, he could invite no gentlemen of those ranks to ride with him. Thereon Nellie decided, since Roosevelt had already broken tradition, that she would ride with her husband. Though counseled against her decision, she held firm.

The day's icy conditions forced Taft to take his oath inside the Senate Chamber. When he departed and climbed into the coach, Nellie was at his side. Her memoirs recount feelings of elation and triumph, undaunted by the scuttlebutt that followed.

one year and affected her speech for the remainder of her life. During that year, her daughter Helen and Nellie's sisters fulfilled her social duties, with Nellie often directing events from her second-floor private quarters. Her husband devoted much of his time to her rehabilitation. Always reliant upon Nellie's advice, the president became careful not to burden her with his official problems, for fear of a setback to her health.

By spring of 1910, she was able to institute weekly garden parties, a favorite custom she continued each spring that the Tafts were in the White House. None of these, though, approached the extravagant celebration of the Tafts' twenty-fifth wedding anniversary in 1911. More than four thousand guests greeted the couple, amid glittering illumination of the White House and gardens. Perhaps Nellie especially enjoyed the occasion, aware that her husband's chances for reelection were already fading.

After the White House years, Nellie busied herself by writing her memoirs, *Recollections of Full Years*. She enjoyed observing the successes of her children and their families and became very active in the National Society of the Colonial Dames. Along with her husband, she is buried in Arlington National Cemetery.

Legacy

The particulars of Nellie Taft's legacy provide insight into her character. Her memoirs, *Recollections of Full Years*, elaborate on the happier details of her life as wife and First Lady and reveal her disappointments and sorrows in conspicuous brevity. Having long sought a prominent role in American political circles through her husband's career, Nellie perfected the habit of putting on the composed, pleasant exterior necessary to stand by a world leader.

Thoroughly proud to have realized her dream of being First Lady, Nellie was first to contribute her gown and personal endorsement when the Smithsonian Institution created

its First Ladies Collection in 1912.

As the first president of the Cincinnati Symphony Association, Nellie's goal was to secure and maintain a fine musical organization for her hometown. To this day, civic leaders and volunteers have continued that work. The Cincinnati Symphony and Pops Orchestras have earned an international reputation for consistently superlative performances. That a Midwestern orchestra can boast being among the best financed in the United States is testimony to the strong foundation initiated under Nellie's watch.

No political ambitions ever exceeded Nellie's devotion to her children. Her high expectations for their success were equally balanced by frequent indulgences and boundless love. Whether intentional or not, Nellie reared another generation of Tafts into lives of public service. Her firstborn, Robert A., earned the title of Mr. Republican in his lifetime by serving in both houses of the Ohio legislature, then advancing to a long career in the U.S. Senate. Daughter Helen, who attended Bryn Mawr College on an academic scholarship, became an outspoken proponent of suffrage and safe working conditions for women. She earned a doctorate in history from Yale University and distinguished herself in an academic career at Bryn Mawr, in time rising to the position of dean. Charles Phelps II, named for his father's brother, built a distinguished law practice in Cincinnati, served in city council, and worked for the Federal Security Agency and the State Department during World War II.

The glorious cherry blossom display in Washington, D.C., is, undoubtedly, Nellie's most picturesque gift to our nation. While living in Manila, she experienced the pleasure of the Luneta, an oval carriage path with a bandstand nearby. On warm evenings, music played as the social elite drove around to share greetings and gossip. In Washington, Nellie saw that Potomac Park could accommodate a similar function. A bandstand was erected and Marine

Band concerts scheduled. The park also offered a favorable location for Japanese cherry trees, another of Nellie's favorite memories from the East. She ordered that all domestic stock be found and planted along the Tidal Basin. The mayor of Tokyo, flattered that the First Lady was honoring Japanese custom in this way, sent another two thousand trees. The annual Cherry Blossom Festival endures as one of the most beautiful American festivities.

Suggested Readings

Anderson, Judith Icke. *William Howard Taft*. New York: Norton, 1981. Includes a valuable chapter about Helen Taft.

Anthony, Carl Sferrazza. *First Ladies: The Saga of the Presidents' Wives and Their Power*. Vol. 1. New York: William Morrow, 1990. Examines the nature of the First Ladies' influence on their husbands' career paths and presidencies.

Butt, Archie. *Taft and Roosevelt: The Intimate Letters of Archie Butt, Military Aide*. 2 vols. Garden City: Doubleday, Doran, 1930. This correspondence often recounts conversations between Helen and William Howard Taft during their White House years.

Pringle, Henry F. *The Life and Times of William Howard Taft*. New York: Farrar & Rinehart, 1939. An exhaustive biography of the president, with extensive coverage of Helen Taft.

Ross, Ishbel. *The Tafts: An American Family*. Cleveland, Ohio: World Publishing, 1964. Describes the generations of one family's public service; includes information on Helen Taft's early and later years.

Taft, Helen (Mrs. William Howard). *Recollections of Full Years*. New York: Dodd, Mead, 1914. Helen Taft's autobiography, written after William Howard Taft's presidency and before his Supreme Court appointment.

Mimi Bogard

Ellen Wilson

Ellen Louise Axson Wilson

Born: May 15, 1860
      Savannah, Georgia
Died: August 6, 1914
      Washington, D.C.

President: Woodrow Wilson
      1913-1921

Overview: Ellen Wilson is among the lesser known of the First Ladies. Woodrow and Ellen Wilson were very much in love, and she was an important partner and adviser to Wilson throughout his career in public service. As First Lady, Ellen Wilson lent her name to the cause of improving slums in the District of Columbia. Shortly before her death, Congress passed legislation, which Ellen strongly supported, to aid in the improvement of the slums. She was a poised and gracious hostess and enjoyed her public role.

Ellen Wilson. *(Library of Congress)*

Early Life

Ellen's ancestors settled in New England and New Jersey. John Hoyt had come to Salem, Massachusetts, in 1629 from Curry Rivel, Somersetshire, England. John's great-great-grandson Winthrop Hoyt (Ellen's great-great-grandfather) was born in 1739. Winthrop served in the French and Indian War. He was with Ethan Allen and his Green Mountain Boys when Fort Ticonderoga was captured in 1775. Ellen's grandfather Nathan Hoyt was born in 1793 in Gilmanton, New Hampshire. Nathan was self-educated and studied privately for his ordination into the Presbyterian ministry. In 1826, Nathan married Margaret Bliss from Springfield, Massachusetts. The young couple moved to Beech Island, South Carolina, so Nathan could pastor the Presbyterian Church of Beech Island.

In 1830, Nathan went to the First Presbyterian Church in Athens, Georgia, where he stayed the rest of his life.

Margaret Jane "Janie" Hoyt was born on September 8, 1838, in Athens, Georgia. Janie was Nathan and Margaret's sixth and last child. At the age of fifteen, Janie began to attend the Greensboro Female College in Greensboro, Georgia. Her father, Nathan, was on the part-time faculty there, and Ellen's paternal grandfather, the Reverend Isaac Axson, was president of the college.

Isaac completed his studies at Columbia Theological Seminary in May, 1834, and married Rebecca Longstreet Randolph in October. In 1836 Isaac and Rebecca moved to Liberty County, Georgia, so Isaac could copastor the Midway Presbyterian Church. The couple had a son on December 23, 1836, named Samuel Edward, called Edward.

Edward became engaged to Janie Hoyt in the summer of 1856 after his first year at the Columbia Theological Seminary. Janie and Edward were married in Athens, Georgia, on November 23, 1858. He was ordained into the ministry on May 23, 1859, at the same Presbyterian Church in Beech Island, South Carolina, Janie's father had pastored. Ellen Louise Axson was born on May 15, 1860, in a second-floor bedroom of the Presbyterian manse in Savannah, the home of her Axson grandparents. Ellen was named after her aunts Ellen Axson and Louisa Hoyt.

Almost one year after Ellen's birth, Georgia seceded from the Union. Edward Axson joined the Confederate Army and became the chaplain for the First Regiment of the Georgia Infantry. In letters to Edward, Janie described their new daughter as spirited and merry. Edward left the Confederate Army because of illness in 1863 and resumed pastoring the Madison Presbyterian Church in Madison, Georgia. He also taught at the Madison Male and Female Academy, held in the Axson home, where Ellen was first educated.

The Axson family moved to Rome, Georgia, in 1866 so Edward could pastor the First Presbyterian Church there. Ellen enrolled in the Presbyterian Church's Rome Female College when she was eleven years old. She studied philosophy, logic, natural history, botany, and algebra. She performed well in composition, English literature, and French as well as studying geometry and teaching herself trigonometry during one summer, according to a Hoyt cousin.

Ellen graduated from the Rome Female College in 1876, in the same class as her friend and childhood playmate Rosalie Anderson. Helen F. Fairchild, who had studied at the New York National Academy of Design, tutored Ellen in art. Fairchild submitted a drawing of a "school scene" by Ellen Axson to the Paris International Exposition. Ellen won the bronze medal for excellence in freehand drawing. She took graduate courses at the Rome Female College in art, German, and advanced French and was selling small crayon sketches done from still photographs at the age of eighteen. She made so much money from her drawings that she considered going with Rosalie to study art in New York. At this time, her father described Ellen as obstreperous, saying she was "entirely too much inclined to have her own opinions."

In the fall of 1881, Ellen went to visit Rosalie in Sewanee, Tennessee. While she was gone, her mother gave birth to Margaret Randolph on October 10. Ellen returned to Rome to find her mother in a puerperal fever, called childbed fever. Jane Axson died on November 4, 1881, leaving Ellen to raise her two young brothers and serve as hostess for her father. Ellen was heartbroken at the loss of her mother and said that she would never again touch a paintbrush. However, Ellen provided a still life crayon exhibit to benefit the Young Men's Christian Association in Atlanta.

Marriage and Family

Ellen had several male suitors, nearly all of whom expressed their desire to marry her.

Woodrow Wilson

Thomas Woodrow Wilson was born on December 28, 1856, in Staunton, Virginia, to Joseph Ruggles Wilson, a Presbyterian minister, and Jessie Woodrow Wilson. Wilson was named after his maternal grandfather. Wilson entered the College of New Jersey at Princeton in 1874. There, he was speaker of the Whig Society, founder of the Liberal Debating Club, and managing editor of the school newspaper. He read modern history, politics, and literature on his own. He graduated 38th in a class of 107 with a grade average of 90.3.

Though Wilson admired the Confederacy for taking up arms in the name of states' rights, he did not appreciate southern sectionalism and wanted the South to be a major player in national affairs. In 1885 he enrolled in Johns Hopkins University for graduate studies, where he studied American history, jurisprudence, constitutional history, German, and international law. By this time Wilson had settled on a career as a statesman. He published his book *Congressional Government* in 1885, stating that the United States' constitutional system lacked responsible leadership.

Wilson returned to Princeton in 1890 to teach law. The school's board of trustees made him president of Princeton University, as it was now known, in 1902. In 1910 Wilson was elected governor of New Jersey; the office would serve as a springboard to the White House. He was elected president of the United States in 1912.

Wilson took office on March 4, 1913. He devoted his first term to progressive reforms, such as a lower tariff, and signed legislation that authorized the Federal Reserve Board. His wife, Ellen, died of Bright's disease on August 6, 1914, and around that time, the Austrian archduke Ferdinand was assassinated in Sarajevo, Yugoslavia, igniting World War I. Wilson remained neutral and won re-election in 1914 with the slogan: "He kept us out of war."

The United States could not remain neutral, however, and declared war on Germany on April 7, 1917. During wartime, Wilson found time to work on the peace settlement that would follow the fighting. To that end, he went to Versailles, France, in 1918 to negotiate the peace treaty. That year he presented Congress with his plan, called the Fourteen Points, intended to foster a fair postwar settlement. Point Fourteen of the plan called for the establishment of an organization of nations whose goal would be to preserve world peace. The Senate rejected the Treaty of Versailles and voted against U.S. membership in the League of Nations, which was established in 1920. Wilson's vision of an organization of nations, including the United States, was ultimately realized with the creation of the United Nations during World War II.

While spending time in Darien, Georgia, when she was eighteen, Joe Walker fell in love with her. She turned down a proposal from Walker, but he continued to pursue her for four years thereafter. She was disgusted by the attention from a Mr. Williams and also turned down James Wright and Charles Thornwell from Rome. She also refused marriage to a missionary who offered to take her to China. She told a friend that if she ever fell in love with a man, it would be against her will, and was thus known in Rome as Ellie the Man Hater.

On April 8, 1883, she attended a service led by her father at the First Presbyterian Church in Rome. A young lawyer, Woodrow Wilson from Atlanta, was in the congregation that day and was distracted from the sacrament of Communion when he saw her. Woodrow's father, the Reverend Joseph Wilson, was a friend of Ellen's father. Woodrow was staying with his uncle James Bones, who was an elder at the church. At the time that Woodrow first saw Ellen, she had bronze-blond hair and dark brown, deep-set eyes and was five feet, three inches tall.

Woodrow visited the Axson home that afternoon and asked Edward about his daughter's "health." Edward called Ellen downstairs, and Woodrow was again distracted, this time from conversation with Edward, at the sight of her. When legal business brought Woodrow back to Rome a month later, he asked her to go riding with him one evening, and she agreed. In June, 1883, he told his mother that he loved Ellen and would ask her to marry him.

He spent two weeks in Rome in June, and his cousin arranged a picnic between Ellen and Woodrow. That September, Ellen was vacationing in North Carolina. Woodrow, by now a graduate student at Johns Hopkins University in Baltimore, was also visiting North Carolina and had planned to meet with Ellen in Morganton. However, Ellen had to rush back to Rome when her father fell ill. She arrived in Asheville on Friday, September 14, to make a train connection to Rome. By chance, Woodrow had gone to Asheville that day. As he was walking down the street, he recognized Ellen from her room window on the second floor of the Eagle Hotel. He was able to encourage Ellen to stay until Sunday, the day he would head back to Baltimore.

Woodrow took Ellen to meet his brother, mother, and sister that Saturday. On Sunday, before he left, in a hallway at the Eagle Hotel, Woodrow asked Ellen to marry him. They hugged and kissed right there in the open, and Ellen agreed to marry him.

Ellen's father passed away on March 6, 1884. He bequeathed enough money to Ellen for her to finally study at the Art Students League in New York City. Woodrow dropped Ellen off in New York, and she started classes on October 6. Ellen and Woodrow, who returned to Baltimore, kept in touch through letters and holiday visits. Their letters during this period of separation show that they missed each other and that one did not feel complete without the other.

Bryn Mawr College in Pennsylvania offered Woodrow the position of associate professor of history. He accepted and was set to begin in the fall of 1885. Now that he had a job to support Ellen, they set a wedding date and were married on June 24, 1885, in the Presbyterian manse in Savannah. The ceremony, which included no music or flowers, was conducted by Ellen's grandfather Axson and Woodrow's father. The Wilsons would have three daughters: Margaret Woodrow Wilson, born on April 16, 1886; Jessie Woodrow, born on April 28, 1887; and Eleanor Randolph Wilson, born on October 10, 1889. An Axson family friend said of the marriage, "What a pity for such a beautiful girl to throw herself away on an unknown lawyer from Atlanta."

Presidency and First Ladyship

Woodrow accepted the position of chairman of Political Economics and Jurisprudence at the College of New Jersey (now Princeton University) in 1890. By 1902 he was president of Princeton, and he was elected governor of New Jersey in 1910. Ellen enjoyed public life and gave political advice to her husband. Joseph Tumulty, Woodrow's private secretary, said that Ellen was a better politician than her husband. When Woodrow became a Democratic candidate for president of the United States in 1912, Ellen went with him on a campaign train trip through Georgia that spring. Wilson was nominated on the forty-sixth ballot at the Democratic National Convention on July 2. He delivered his acceptance speech from the porch of the Sea Girt, the governor's summer home, on August 7. Ellen and all three of their daughters were with him.

Woodrow faced Republican incumbent President William Howard Taft and Progressive Party candidate Theodore Roosevelt in the general election. Roosevelt's candidacy had split the Republican Party, and Wilson won the election on November 5, 1912. Taft sent Ellen a letter with the plans of the White House second floor, the family residence, enclosed. He suggested that Ellen ask Congress for funds to renovate bedrooms on the third floor. On March 3, 1913, Helen Taft led Ellen on an inspection tour of the White House. Inauguration Day was March 4, 1913. Ellen's attire for the day was a smoke-brown suit with black velvet trim and a black hat decorated with brown ostrich feathers.

As president, Woodrow's annual salary was seventy-five thousand dollars, in addition to a twenty-five-thousand-dollar travel allowance. Transportation, servants, flowers, and the Marine Band, which performed at all social events, were provided for the first family at government expense.

Ellen saw to it that the second-floor residence was cleaned and decorated to her liking. She also took Taft's advice and added five furnished bedrooms and bathrooms to the third floor. She set up an art studio in a White House attic; as the honorary president of the Southern Industrial Association, she allowed the group to display items for sale at the White House. Mountain crafts, such as rugs and quilts, were sold to benefit rural women. The First Lady invited cabinet and congressional wives to the White House to see and purchase the artwork.

Ellen performed her role as White House hostess with grace and poise. A White House usher said that Ellen would stay and greet guests until the very end of each event. She was a close political adviser to her husband, and she took interest in the issues of sanitary working conditions for federal government employees, child labor, adult education, and care of the mentally ill. The First Lady always looked over the president's speeches and did not hesitate to offer her input. Wilson did not mind and said, "No president but myself ever had exactly the right sort of wife!"

Charlotte Hopkins, chairwoman of the Washington, D.C., branch of the National Civic Federation, came to the White House for tea with Ellen on March 22, 1913. Hopkins's organization sought better living conditions for the poor, regardless of race or creed. She told the First Lady that there were areas in Washington in which blacks were living in alleys, in shacks that contained no electricity, plumbing, or running water. Model homes, said Hopkins, that contained electricity and running water could replace the shacks. Three days later she took Ellen on a tour of the slums and to a community of

The Rose Garden

Perhaps the most visible legacy of Ellen Wilson's tenure as First Lady is the complete redesign of the White House grounds, which she initiated and oversaw. She rejected as too expensive designs submitted by a New York landscape architect. Ellen then decided that she and the head White House gardener, Charles Henlock, could draw and complete the new layout on their own.

In early 1914, planning a trip in Princeton to get some family jewels from a bank, Ellen had Henlock accompany her so he could see some of her prior landscaping efforts. When the two returned to Washington, D.C., they drew up plans for redoing the White House grounds from the south portico to the arcade on the east grounds and to the presidential office on the west grounds. Ellen said she wanted her husband to be able to enjoy a "rose walk" from the White House to his office.

The landscaping renovations were still under way when Ellen died in 1914. Today, however, the splendid, world-renowned White House Rose Garden stands just as she envisioned it, right outside the president's Oval Office. Every time a president holds a press conference, signs legislation, or makes an announcement with the elegant Rose Garden as a backdrop, Ellen Wilson can be thanked.

A view of the White House Rose Garden, designed in 1914 by Ellen Wilson and White House gardener Charles Henlock, with the Oval Office in the background. *(AP/Wide World Photos)*

model homes; the First Lady greeted and talked with the black citizens without revealing her identity. Ellen then became a shareholder in the Sanitary Housing Company, which built the model homes.

A group of leaders from civic and charitable organizations, called the Committee of Fifty, was set up to draft legislation to clean up slum conditions. A White House tea was given in honor of the committee in June, and Ellen invited members of Congress to hear about the living conditions of the poor. The Alley Bill, which funded model homes to replace the shacks, was presented to Congress in February, 1914.

On March 1, Ellen fell at the White House. Medical examinations revealed that she was suffering from Bright's disease, a kidney condition for which no cure was known. By August 6, it was clear that she did not have much longer to live. That day she told her husband, "I would go away more peacefully if my Alley Bill was passed by Congress." Tumulty, Woodrow's secretary, delivered the news to Capitol Hill, and the Senate immediately passed the legislation. The House assured Tumulty that it would pass the Alley Bill the next day. He brought this news back to the White House; an hour later, Ellen died. President Wilson burst into tears and cried out, "Oh my God, what am I going to do?"

Woodrow and Ellen Wilson and their three daughters. *(Library of Congress)*

Legacy

Ellen Axson Wilson is not as well-known as some First Ladies; during her tenure she did not wish to make any fashion statements. She once said, "A person would be a fool who lets his head to be turned by externals; they simply go with position." Instead Ellen worked behind the scenes to read and revise her husband's speeches, improve Washington slums, and encourage cabinet members to improve the working conditions in their jurisdictions. Ellen Wilson showed that the First Lady could be an advocate for social change, a model that future wives of presidents followed.

Suggested Readings

Anthony, Carl Sferrazza. *First Ladies: The Saga of the Presidents' Wives and Their Power.* Vol. 1. New York: William Morrow, 1990. A collection of articles about the First Ladies from Martha Washington to Mamie Eisenhower.

Link, Arthur S. *Woodrow Wilson: A Brief Biography.* New York: World Publishing, 1963. A brief biography of Woodrow Wilson, written by the editor of *The Papers of Woodrow Wilson.*

McAdoo, Eleanor Wilson, ed. *The Priceless Gift: The Love Letters of Woodrow Wilson and Ellen Axson Wilson.* New York: McGraw-Hill, 1962. The love letters since the beginning of Woodrow and Ellen's courtship, up to the time Ellen died.

Saunders, Frances Wright. *First Lady Between Two Worlds: Ellen Axson Wilson.* Chapel Hill: University of North Carolina Press, 1985. A complete biography of Ellen Axson Wilson.

Truman, Margaret. *First Ladies.* New York: Random House, 1995. This book contains a critique of the role of the First Lady and brief biographies of First Ladies from Martha Washington to Hillary Rodham Clinton.

David Murphy

Edith Wilson

Edith Bolling Galt Wilson

Born: October 15, 1872
　　　Wytheville, Virginia
Died: December 28, 1961
　　　Washington, D.C.

President: Woodrow Wilson
　　　1913-1921

Overview: Edith Bolling Galt married President Woodrow Wilson following the death of his first wife, forging a union that changed the dynamics of Wilson's presidency. As Woodrow's confidante, Edith was an important resource at the Paris Peace Conference and even became an unofficial re-gent following Woodrow's stroke in 1919 while he was still in office. Her influence was readily apparent, and although she denied being any-thing more than a devoted wife, her actions be-lie the statement. Although Woodrow lived only a few years after leaving the White House, Edith continued to guard his legacy until her own death thirty-seven years later, remaining forever Woodrow's protector.

Edith Wilson. *(Library of Congress)*

Early Life

Born in Virginia on October 15, 1872, Edith was one of nine surviving children of the Bolling family. Her father, whom she idolized, was a lawyer and circuit court judge. After the Civil War, he settled with his family in Wytheville, Virginia, where Edith was born. Growing up, Edith received a rather informal education from her father and her paternal grandmother.

At fifteen, she embarked on three years of formal education before moving to Washing-ton, D.C., in 1890 to spend time with her newly married sister. Edith was fascinated by the

United States' capital. She enjoyed the opera and theater and was also exposed to high fashion, which would become her trademark. During her stay Edith, through her sister, met Norman Galt, a senior partner in Galt's, a family silversmith firm. He was immediately smitten, and they began dating. Their courtship lasted four years, and they married on April 30, 1896.

For the next twelve years, Edith remained Norman's devoted wife, supporting her husband but keeping out of his business affairs. In 1908 Norman, diagnosed with a rare liver ailment, died suddenly. Edith was left a widow

and sole owner of Galt's. Eventually she sold the business for a hefty price, which left her financially secure. The next several years she spent traveling and visiting with her relatives. On one of her trips, she befriended Alice Gertrude Gordon, who would aid in introducing Edith to the White House inhabitants. Alice was acquainted with Helen Woodrow Bones, the cousin of President Woodrow Wilson.

Marriage and Family
Because Edith steered clear of politics, she was relatively unaware of President Woodrow Wil-

Woodrow Wilson

Thomas Woodrow Wilson was born in Staunton, Virginia, on December 28, 1856. Raised in the South by his mother and stern Presbyterian minister father, Woodrow was taught piety and perfection. This produced a studious and rigid man who graduated from the College of New Jersey (later called Princeton University), the University of Virginia School of Law, and Johns Hopkins University with degrees in history and political science. He taught at Princeton for twelve years before becoming president of the university in 1902. Under his direction, Princeton tightened admission standards, revamped its curriculum, and enlarged the faculty. His actions garnered the attention of New Jersey Democrats and ultimately the electorate as he won the governorship in 1910. As governor, Wilson pushed workers' compensation and ballot reform laws through the legislature, gaining him national recognition for his efforts.

Fate smiled on Wilson when he won the Democratic Party's nomination for president in 1912. His luck continued to hold as the Republican Party split between those supporting party nominee William Howard Taft and those who joined rebellious Theodore Roosevelt's "Bull Moose" Party. Wilson campaigned on breaking up trusts, a reduced tariff, and more power to state and local governments. The split vote, however, proved to be the deciding factor as he won the election.

Having experience with domestic issues, Wilson hoped that foreign affairs would not come to dominate his tenure. Ironically, they did. Wilson had kept the United States neutral in World War I from its beginning in 1914. Yet he faced criticism from those who advocated early entry as well as those who wanted a peaceful solution to be found. He capitalized on his support of military preparedness and continued U.S. neutrality in his successful reelection bid in 1916. The German threat grew, however, and Wilson asked for a declaration of war the following year.

Wilson's administration directed the war at home and abroad. Fortunately, U.S. involvement only lasted eighteen months; armistice was declared on November 11, 1918. Wilson attended the Paris Peace Conference with the goal of lasting world peace his main focus. His idea for the League of Nations was included in the Treaty of Versailles, but the United States Senate balked. Having U.S. military committed to other nations' causes was dangerous, senators argued. Although Wilson attempted to take his cause to the people, his health, and ultimately ratification of the treaty, failed. For the remainder of his life, Wilson defended the League of Nations and encouraged the United States' involvement.

son or his family. The Wilsons had been married more than twenty-five years and had three daughters. Ellen Wilson made national headlines in 1914 for fainting during an official receiving line and was soon diagnosed with Bright's disease. Her health continued to fail until she finally passed away in August of that year. Woodrow was grief-stricken, and according to White House insiders, the pall within the Executive Mansion was stifling. That was soon to change.

"Turn a corner and meet your fate," was the expression Edith used to describe her first meeting with Woodrow in March, 1915. She and Woodrow's cousin Helen Woodrow Bones had just returned from an outing, splattered with mud and looking quite disheveled. Helen, the White House hostess since the death of the first Mrs. Wilson, assured Edith that the president was out golfing and that they would not be seen. As they exited the White House elevator on the second floor and rounded the corner, Edith and Helen came face-to-face with the president. Woodrow was captivated. He enjoyed Edith's quick wit and quickly moved to spend as much time with her as possible. They went for drives, had dinner at the White House, and corresponded. Woodrow was already in love and ready to propose. He discussed the matter with his daughters, who liked Edith and supported their father's decision. Edith requested time to consider his sudden proposal; she wondered whether the marriage would affect his presidency and if her presence would distract him.

Ultimately, after time and constant assurances of his love and need for her, Edith agreed to marry Woodrow. Their engagement was publicly announced on October 6, 1915, and Edith immediately became the subject of intense scrutiny. She refused to make herself available to well-wishers, claiming her time was limited since she wanted to be available to the president whenever he needed her. Woodrow's growing dependence on Edith concerned his advisers, who complained that he never had time for them and was increasingly turning to his fiancé for advice or consultation.

Presidency and First Ladyship

On December 18, 1915, forty-four-year-old Edith Bolling Galt married fifty-nine-year-old Woodrow Wilson in a quiet ceremony at Edith's home. Only fifty family members and intimate friends were invited to witness the event as the couple exchanged vows. It was then that Edith entered the whirlwind of presidential politics in her role as First Lady. Her wish was not to upset the pattern already established at the White House; she fired no staff and made no major changes. Instead, she arranged her schedule to fit Woodrow's. She ate meals when it was convenient for him and instructed the staff to alter their own schedules if they conflicted with the president's. Edith was admired by the staff and was always pleasant unless someone disturbed the president; then Edith made her anger felt. She also made it her priority to anticipate Woodrow's needs, especially his need for rest. This meant keeping advisers and cabinet officials from dropping in on the president. They quickly discovered that without an appointment it was very difficult to see Woodrow, as Edith would claim that he was busy and ask that they visit another time.

Major issues surfaced over the next year which illustrated Edith's devotion to Woodrow: the presidential election and World War I. With some trepidation, she ultimately supported Woodrow's successful reelection bid in 1916, though she believed that in retirement they could spend more time together, and was equally supportive of his decision to go to war with Germany in April, 1917.

The United States' entry into the war meant that Americans had to sacrifice, pull together, and unify around the cause. The White House set an example by ceasing all receptions and parties, unless they were for a visiting ally. This was not an unwelcome occurrence for Edith,

Woodrow and Edith Wilson ride to his second inauguration on March, 1917. *(Library of Congress)*

pack, with much care to her own wardrobe. She commented that, faced with constant scrutiny, it was her obligation to dress well as a representative of the people of the United States.

The conference turned out to be immensely draining on Woodrow. The political bickering among the participants, coupled with his own desire to create a new world peace based upon his Fourteen Points plan, meant that Woodrow put in eighteen-hour days in meetings with various parties as well as in his own research and writing. Edith sat in on many meetings between Woodrow and foreign diplomats. While initially put off by her presence, these statesmen soon became accustomed to her being in the room for their discussions.

Following almost six months of grueling negotiations, in which Edith was constantly concerned about Woodrow's health and the

who much preferred time alone with Woodrow to large, formal receptions. She sewed clothing for soldiers, curtailed her own shopping (she commented that she did not buy any new clothes for the duration), and worked hard to name all the new ships being commissioned into service.

With the war's end in November, 1918, controversy erupted over who should represent the United States at the Paris Peace Conference. Woodrow felt he had to go, and Edith, who never considered staying behind, began to

blinding headaches he suffered, the Treaty of Versailles was finally completed. Woodrow knew the opposition he would face from the U.S. Senate over the inclusion of provisions for the new League of Nations in the treaty. Consequently, he decided to take his case to the American people. Edith warned that he was not strong enough to handle such a grueling schedule, but he was adamant that this trip was vital and could not be delayed. Edith would later say the trip in September, 1919, was a nightmare, as the president sacrificed himself for the cause of peace. Her predictions came true as his health suffered greatly, and by the end of September, the campaign was canceled.

Back in Washington on the morning of October 2, 1919, Edith entered Woodrow's bedroom and discovered him sitting on his bed, unable to move his left arm or leg. He appeared to have suffered a stroke. Immediately, Edith barred servants from the family quarters and called in specialists, who verified the stroke and offered opinions as to Woodrow's prognosis. She was advised that Woodrow must avoid worry and disturbances. This meant he could not perform his governmental duties, so she simply stepped into that role for six weeks. It is unclear how involved Edith was in actual policy and decision making, as she disavowed any part in running the nation and called her role a stewardship. She did comment later that she felt uniquely qualified to deal with matters because, as Woodrow's confidante, she knew his feelings on most issues.

As Woodrow's strength improved, the Wilsons settled into a new routine for the remainder of his presidency. Woodrow dispensed with issues of state in the morning, followed by lunch, an afternoon nap, dinner, some form of entertainment (he liked movies) and bedtime. Feeling better by the summer of 1920, Woodrow made it clear to those closest to him that he hoped to receive his party's nomination for a third term as president. Edith and his doctor worried that another term would surely kill him. Fortunately for them, James Cox got the Democratic nomination—but lost the election to his Republican opponent. Woodrow's last official function, therefore, was to escort newly elected President Warren G. Harding to his swearing-in ceremony.

Legacy

After leaving the White House, the Wilsons settled into a comfortable routine at their new house on's Street in Washington, D.C. Woodrow made it clear he wanted to remain out of the political spotlight. He did not want to use his fame, as former presidents Theodore Roosevelt and William Howard Taft had, to influence policy. Instead, he had thoughts of finishing a book on politics or writing his memoirs. Unfortunately, his declining health prohibited any real projects of this nature. It was a rather shel-

---

Convincing Congress

By December, 1919, though Woodrow Wilson had recovered sufficiently from his stroke to devote more time to affairs of state, the Senate demanded to see the president to ascertain whether he should continue to serve in his present capacity or if Vice President Thomas S. Marshall should step in as chief executive.

Edith carefully arranged a meeting among her husband and two senators, Republican Senator Albert B. Fall and Democratic Senator Gilbert Monell Hitchcock. She had Woodrow positioned in the bed with his paralyzed face in shadow. A blanket was pulled up to his neck, covering his left arm, while his right arm was free to gesture. Edith stayed in the room and took notes to make sure no misunderstandings occurred. The president was quite animated, and except for a slight heaviness in his speech, he seemed much like himself.

As the senators were leaving, Edith overheard a comment that she enjoyed repeating. Senator Fall, a critic of her husband, bent over Wilson and said, "I am praying for you." President Wilson responded, "Which way, Senator?" The meeting proved successful; Wilson remained in office, and for Edith, a large hurdle had been cleared.

tered life he led as Edith and her brother Randolph, whom she hired as their secretary, censored all mail and news stories so as not to upset Woodrow. His moods continued to swing back and forth between anger, frustration, loneliness, and depression as his condition worsened. Edith said there were times when his eyes cleared from the confusion, and he seemed almost his old self. Yet those times were rare. The arteriosclerosis that had caused his stroke affected other portions of his body, including his eyesight. On Friday, February 1, 1924, news was released that Woodrow Wilson was ill, and at 11:55 A.M. on Sunday, February 3, the sixty-eight-year-old statesman died in his sleep.

For Edith, a new chapter began in her life. After a year of mourning, she emerged once more into the public light. She could now be seen traveling around Washington again, visiting friends and attending events to honor her husband. For the rest of her life, Edith strove to maintain control over all images of Woodrow, in order to protect him and his legacy. This protectiveness had been apparent throughout their marriage, but it became more pronounced after Woodrow's death, especially when books began to be published about the former president.

Edith was convinced to write her own recollections of life with Woodrow. Titled *My Memoir*, her book contains unflattering descriptions of some notable people. Originally, friends thought she should soften the tone in which she wrote about people, but she refused. The book caused a stir when it was published in 1939. While some people disputed what Edith said, no one could dispute her clear devotion to Woodrow. In her eyes, he was the sage of his generation, whose goals of world peace were ruined by near-sighted politicians. In her depiction, he never made a wrong decision, but sometimes external factors served to paint him as less than successful.

Edith traveled quite a bit in her later life, making frequent trips to Europe and around the world. Her devotion to her family continued unabated. Relatives from across the country frequently stopped in to see Aunt Edith, and she welcomed their visits. Her last public appearance was in October, 1961, when at the age of eighty-nine she witnessed President John Kennedy sign into law a commission, approved by Congress, to establish a memorial for Woodrow Wilson. On December 28, 1961, she planned to attend the opening of the Woodrow Wilson Bridge across the Potomac River, but her heart gave out. It would have been Woodrow's one hundred fifth birthday.

Edith Bolling Wilson never intended to ascend to the White House or to become involved in international issues, yet ultimately she wielded enormous power as First Lady. While she denied ever influencing Woodrow on matters of state, her own autobiography and the accounts of others dispute that statement. The depth of her influence, however, is debatable. Most, including Edith, argued that Woodrow was often inflexible and determined; when his mind was set, no one could get him to change. His love and respect for her, however, allowed Edith to become his closest confidante and adviser; a position which clearly contained power, even if she refused to acknowledge it. As to her alleged running the country during Woodrow's illness, she was a protective wife and stated that she only followed orders, that Woodrow made the decisions and she conveyed them to the right people. For Edith, the greatest role she played was that of Woodrow's wife.

Suggested Readings

Gould, Lewis, L., ed. *American First Ladies: Their Lives and Their Legacy*. New York: Garland, 1996. An enjoyable, informative, and objective combination of biographical sketches and histories of the First Ladies.

Grayson, Cary T. *Woodrow Wilson: An Intimate Memoir*. New York: Holt, Rinehart and Winston, 1960. Recounts the life and times of the twenty-seventh president.

Hatch, Alden. *Edith Bolling Wilson: First Lady Extraordinary.* New York: Dodd, Mead, 1961.

House, Edward. *The Intimate Papers of Colonel House.* Boston: Houghton Mifflin, 1930.

Ross, Ishbel. *Power with Grace: The Life Story of Mrs. Woodrow Wilson.* New York: G. P. Putnam's Sons, 1975.

Smith, Gene. *When the Cheering Stopped: The Last Years of Woodrow Wilson.* New York: William Morrow, 1964. Well researched; describes Wilson's life and work as well as his stroke, his disillusionment, and his last days.

Weinstein, Edwin A. *Woodrow Wilson: A Medical and Psychological Biography.* Princeton, N.J.: Princeton University Press, 1981.

Wilson, Edith Bolling. *My Memoir.* Reprint. New York: Arno Press, 1981.

James McCallops

Florence Harding

Florence Kling DeWolfe Harding

Born: August 15, 1860
      Marion, Ohio
Died: November 21, 1924
      Marion, Ohio

President: Warren G. Harding
      1921-1923

Overview: Florence Harding was among the most popular of First Ladies. Vocal in her support of women's equality, in her concern for World War I veterans, and in her campaign for humane societies, she carved out her own niche in the White House. Yet suspicion will forever cloud her accomplishments because of the sudden death of her philandering husband, Warren G. Harding, and the rumor that she poisoned him. In truth, Florence Harding was a dominant force in Warren's administration who loved her husband immensely and protected his and her own images fiercely.

Florence Harding. *(Library of Congress)*

Early Life

Florence, the first child of Amos and Louisa Kling, was born above her father's store on August 15, 1860, in Marion, Ohio. Mystery surrounded her paternal heritage, as her father attempted to hide his German, and possibly Jewish, ancestry. Florence's maternal family had a more distinguished background, having descended from prominent French Huguenots. When Louisa announced her pregnancy, the domineering Amos declared his first child would be a boy. Neighbors wondered how Amos would deal with a daughter instead. According to local residents, he simply decided to raise her as a son.

For Flossie, as Florence was called, growing up in Marion was comforting and stifling at the same time. Through various business ventures, her father was becoming wealthy and powerful. Though devoting little time to his wife and two young sons, Amos strove to "make" Flossie into a boy by providing her with an excellent education, some argue because he saw in her elements of himself. Of the three children, Florence was indeed the most like Amos. She had his temperament and his ambition. Not surprisingly, as Flossie entered her teen years, she and Amos clashed over what Florence felt were his controlling ways.

Except for a brief stint in Cincinnati to study piano, Florence spent her youth in Marion, eventually challenging her father by missing her curfew and staying out late. It is unclear exactly what she was doing those nights; however, she did become close to Henry "Petey" DeWolfe, and by January, 1880, Florence was pregnant. Dispute exists over whether Petey was truly the father, yet he took responsibility for the child.

According to legend, the couple ran off in March, 1880, to a justice of the peace. Although Florence began to use the title Mrs. DeWolfe, research reveals that they never officially married. It is unclear if Petey refused to get married or if Florence decided against it, yet they told everyone they had "tied the knot." Amos reacted bitterly, cutting off all ties with Florence. Petey attempted to support his new wife and his son, Eugene (Marshall) DeWolfe, Jr., born on September 22, 1880, but his alcoholism interfered. On December 22, 1882, Petey left Florence and Marshall with no money to pay the rent or buy food. She found a room, rented a piano, and began giving lessons. Unwilling to ask her father for help, Florence struggled to support herself and Marshall. In 1884, after Florence filed for separation and divorce from Petey, Amos offered Florence a deal: He would raise Marshall as a Kling, and Florence would be relieved of all financial burdens. Faced with that offer, Florence gave up her child.

A new chapter in her life now opened. Florence met and became interested in Warren G. Harding, the young owner and editor of the *Marion Star*. Although he was five years younger than she, Florence was immediately attracted to his dark good looks and bright blue eyes. People wondered about the pairing, but Warren seemed to genuinely appreciate Florence's quick wit, intelligence, and drive. For Florence, Warren was interesting and, although she found him somewhat lazy, he had charm and charisma which she felt could take him places. Amos was furious about the match. While it is unclear what reasons he had for disliking Harding, the reason he gave was a persistent rumor in Marion that Harding had Negro blood.

Marriage and Family

In anticipation of her marriage, Florence became involved in the financial operations of the *Star*. She was quite capable of handling the paper's finances, something Warren disliked and was glad to turn over to her. She collected money owed the paper and set the business on firm monetary ground. This, in turn, provided the capital Warren needed to complete their house in Marion; Florence had contributed to the blueprints. Eventually, on July 8, 1891, before three hundred guests in their new home, Florence and Warren wed. Reportedly, Florence was pleased, but her ambition did not wane. She claimed that next she would "make him president." She refused to wear a wedding ring because she felt to do so detracted from a woman's own accomplishments.

During the next few years, while Florence focused on managing the *Star* and the Harding finances, Warren suffered from health problems. Not long after their wedding, he had his second nervous breakdown in four years. In 1894 he checked into a sanitarium, in which he stayed for almost a year. Florence continued to run the paper, and he was quite impressed when he returned to Marion in late 1894. Acknowledging that Florence, or as he called her, "the Duchess," was essential at home and work meant, however, that he also faced jokes about his "manly wife" and questions about who "wore the pants" in the family. Perhaps that helps explain Warren's penchant for extramarital affairs. His natural desire for female companionship, coupled with his feelings of inadequacy next to Florence, made Warren seek out conquests. Three years into his marriage, he began a relationship with one of Florence's closest friends, Susan Hodder, and fathered a baby girl, Marion Louise. While it is unclear when or how Florence discovered the affair, she wrote about the betrayal in her diary and how much hurt Warren had caused her. This only made Warren work harder to keep future conquests from Florence.

A new, growing passion in Warren's life was politics. A devout Republican in the Democrat stronghold of Marion, Warren was a member of the Republican County Committee. In this capacity, he became involved in many civic activities. He belonged to several clubs and cultivated a wide circle of friends and potential supporters. When the Republican state office suggested that Warren run for the vacant state senate seat in his area, which included some Republican districts, Florence's ambition for her husband swung into full gear. She goaded and cajoled Warren to get him to run, and ultimately he was elected. Florence accompanied him to Columbus, Ohio, and shocked some observers

Warren G. Harding

Warren G. Harding was born in 1865 to farmers in Ohio. The charming, dark-haired young man became the owner and editor of the *Marion Star* newspaper. He enjoyed writing but lacked any real drive. Through his marriage to Florence Kling DeWolfe, however, he gained a powerful ally and motivator who supported his career. Politics became a fascination and love for Warren. With Florence's help and his own charismatic speeches, Warren moved from state senator to lieutenant governor to United States senator and, finally, to president in 1920.

A staunch Republican, Warren favored reduced government spending and tax cuts for the wealthy to stimulate economic growth. He chose some notable men for his cabinet, such as Charles Evans Hughes and Herbert Hoover. However, Harding's support for the forty-hour work week, his concern for women's health issues, and his attempt to balance the budget were lost in charges of corruption and scandal.

Warren contributed to the scandals through his numerous liaisons with women. In one celebrated incident, Harding allegedly stunned the press by claiming, "It's a good thing I am not a woman. I would always be pregnant. I can't say no." Payoffs and intimidation were used to quiet mistresses, but the stories surfaced anyway. In addition, Harding left governing in the hands of subordinates, some quite willing to line their own pockets with illegal money. Attorney General Harry M. Daugherty was tried but not convicted of graft and fraud. Secretary of the Interior Albert B. Fall was convicted of illegally leasing government land for private gain in the Teapot Dome scandal; he went to prison. Another administrative official committed suicide, and yet another was rumored to have been murdered.

Though Harding tried to persevere, his own feelings of inadequacy ("I am not fit for this office") were thus validated. The true extent of the corruption and scandal surfaced after his death, however. In the summer of 1923, Warren and Florence traveled west and into Alaska. Following food poisoning and some rather dubious medical care, Harding suffered a heart attack and died on August 2, 1923. This brought to an end one of the most corrupt administrations in the history of the U.S. presidency.

by her refusal to allow Warren out of her sight. In 1904 Warren was elected lieutenant governor of Ohio.

In the middle of his term, Florence suffered an attack of nephritis, a kidney infection which threatened her life. Her recuperation was extensive and meant that she could no longer keep an eye on Warren. Alone and carefree, he embarked on another romance, this time with Carrie Phillips, the wife of his friend Jim. The Hardings and Phillipses traveled together, but both Jim and Florence were unaware of the infidelity. For Warren, Carrie was the love of his life; their relationship lasted fifteen years. Florence discovered the affair in 1911 and contemplated divorce. However, she truly loved Warren and believed she could accomplish goals and be happy as his wife. Warren also chose to stay in the marriage; in Florence he had a political partner whom he trusted to protect him and his image.

Although Warren's affair with Carrie continued unknown to Florence, the Hardings began to focus on the United States Senate race in 1916. Warren had been very successful on the speakers' circuit, receiving praise for his oratory skills, and had been selected to speak at the Republican National Convention in 1912. That exposure, along with Florence's support and drive, brought Warren another election victory. Soon the Hardings departed for the nation's capital and Warren's new post in the U.S. Senate.

Presidency and First Ladyship

Washington, D.C., afforded Florence the opportunity to escape Ohio and forge new politi-

President and Mrs. Warren G. Harding. *(Library of Congress)*

cal and personal alliances. She was helped by her introduction to Evalyn McLean, owner of the famed Hope Diamond, and wife of *Washington Post* chief Ned McLean. The McLeans were well known in Washington and introduced the Hardings to other prominent and well-connected people. The friendship proved immensely important in 1920, when Warren decided to run for the presidency. His decision to run was strongly supported by Florence. Carrie Phillips, by now his former mistress, was demanding twenty-five thousand dollars from Warren for their love letters. Afraid the letters would be released to the public and War-

First Lady for Women

As a true partner to her husband, Florence Harding used her national image to draw attention to issues important to women. After the Nineteenth Amendment was ratified in 1920, granting women the right to vote, she was a strong supporter of the League of Women Voters, arguing that women's education about the political process was crucial to their ultimate success in politics. As such, she praised female politicians and sent telegrams congratulating them on their victories. Florence supported the National Woman's Party in their commission and placing of a marble sculpture of suffrage leaders Susan B. Anthony, Lucretia Mott, and Elizabeth Cady Stanton, which was unveiled in 1921 in the U.S. Capitol.

In addition, she encouraged and cajoled her husband, Warren G. Harding, into selecting qualified women for government jobs.

Florence cultivated a working relationship with the emerging female press corps, holding special news conferences just for female reporters. She visibly supported higher educational opportunities for women by inviting recent female graduates, including African Americans, to the White House. She encouraged all women to learn financial management, claiming it was key to a "partnership marriage." However, she did not support the Equal Rights Amendment, which was introduced in Congress in 1923.

ren's career would be destroyed, Florence pushed for his Republican Party nomination so he could use the Republican National Committee's funds to "buy off" Carrie. With that accomplished and the election won, Warren promised the American people a "return to normalcy" following years of upheaval during progressivism and World War I. Florence, the one-time single mother from Marion, was now First Lady.

As First Lady, Florence became nationally known. She began her tenure by opening the White House to the public, even conducting tours herself. She utilized the newsreel to document her accomplishments. This visual medium had proven very useful during the election, as Florence also tapped, for the first time, celebrities to campaign for her husband. Singer Al Jolson headed the endorsement effort, and throughout her years in the White House, Florence was often seen in the company of movie personalities. Historians argue that she was the creator of the "photo op," which she used to publicize her causes.

Unlike many previous First Ladies, Flor-

ence had been an avid suffragist and was the first woman to vote for her own husband for president. Her support of women's issues, however, transcended the vote. She championed women's equality in education, business, and politics. When Harding's administration endorsed improved health care for women and children, Florence's influence was evident. She was his closest adviser and was well known to all members of the cabinet. She convinced them to support World War I veterans as well as humane societies. She used newsreels to make her dog, Laddie Boy, a nationally recognized figure.

The Harding administration, however, was fraught with corruption. Those closest to Warren tried to protect him and his administration from scandal, but others seemed to relish the chaos. His extramarital affairs continued over the years, with Senate aide Grace Cross; Rosa Hoyle, who was said to have delivered a son by Harding; and Augusta Cole, whose pregnancy was allegedly terminated after Harding sent her to a sanitarium. He was also known to have bedded at least five other women. The most famous was twenty-two-year-old Nan Britton, who wrote about their first encounter when fifty-one-year-old Warren was a senator and she became pregnant with his daughter. Their affair continued during his presidency; they had sex in a White House closet. Florence knew about the affairs (except Nan) and worked with Warren's friends to "quiet" these women. She could not, however, stop the corruption.

While dealing with Warren's infidelity, Florence came under the influence of two people who would play large roles in her life. The Hardings had met "Doc" Sawyer in Ohio. He was a homeopathic physician who slowly worked his way into their confidences. Warren had grown up with homeopathic medicine and easily warmed to Doc. Florence, however, took time to be convinced. By the White House years, Doc had ingratiated himself into the role of physician for the first couple. The other person who gained Florence's confidence was called Madame Marcia. She had predicted Warren's presidential nomination and election but warned Florence that he would die before completing his term. Florence had become interested in the occult during her youth, when hex signs on barns belonging to farmers of German descent were a common sight. Over time, she based many of her actions and reactions on "readings" by psychics such as Madame Marcia.

In 1923, rumors were flying about possible corruption in the Harding administration. As evidence began to surface, the Hardings planned a trip to Alaska and the West Coast. Warren became weak and sickly. A military physician sent along was alarmed at the president's obvious heart trouble, but Doc Sawyer adamantly denied there was any problem. Yet along the way, Warren's condition worsened. The onset of food poisoning after ingesting tainted Alaskan crab exacerbated Warren's condition, as "Doc" gave him purgatives which strained his heart, ultimately causing it to fail on August 2, 1923. As Florence brought the body back, rumors began to circulate that Warren had been murdered. A book published in 1930 claimed that Florence had poisoned him. Florence was drained, but she was concerned about more than Warren's death. She worried about his image.

Legacy

Immediately following Warren's burial in Marion, Florence returned to Washington to collect her things. She settled into Evalyn McLean's estate with crates of government documents, the president's private papers, and other assorted items, all of which were burned. Florence wanted to destroy anything that might damage the Harding administration. She then returned to Marion, as Congress investigated corruption in her husband's administration. Settling on Doc's sanitarium grounds, Florence's health rapidly deteriorated, and her troubled kidneys began to fail. With Doc able to do little more than provide bleedings and laxatives, Florence Harding died on November 21, 1923, just four months after her husband's death.

She was an ambitious woman who defied conventions in her life and in her quest for the presidency for her husband. A true partner as First Lady, Florence was different from any of her predecessors. Not until Eleanor Roosevelt would the United States see a First Lady become more involved in presidential politics. Yet Florence is known as the wife who poisoned her husband. Though unfounded, this depiction is not so outrageous given the time in which she lived and the power she exercised. She challenged popular perceptions of the First Lady and presented an alternative role model.

Suggested Readings

Anthony, Carl Sferrazza. *First Ladies: The Saga of the Presidents' Wives and Their Power.* Vol. 1. New York: William Morrow, 1990. A unique glimpse at the power and prestige in the evolving role of First Lady.

———. *Florence Harding: The First Lady, the*

Jazz Age, and the Death of America's Most Scandalous President. New York: William Morrow, 1998. Biography portrays Florence Harding as a thoroughly modern woman.

Frederick, Richard G., ed. *Warren G. Harding.* Connecticut: Greenwood, 1992. Biography of the twenty-eighth president also covers foreign and domestic policies of the 1920's.

Murray, Robert K. *The Harding Era: Warren G. Harding and His Administration.* Minneapolis: University of Minnesota Press, 1969. Includes bibliographical references.

Trani, Eugene P., and David L. Wilson. *The Presidency of Warren G. Harding.* Lawrence: Regents Press of Kansas, 1977.

James McCallops

Grace Coolidge

Grace Anna Goodhue Coolidge

Born: January 3, 1879
      Burlington, Vermont
Died: July 8, 1957
      Northampton, Massachusetts

President: Calvin Coolidge
      1923-1929

Overview: Grace Coolidge was known to the American public as a glamorous First Lady. She was suddenly thrust into the role at age forty-four. Since her husband discouraged any interviews with the press, her public silence only enhanced her mystery and glamour. Because Calvin Coolidge was often perceived as taciturn, her outgoing nature impressed visitors and dignitaries, making for a joyous White House.

Grace Coolidge. *(Library of Congress)*

Early Life

Grace Anna Goodhue was the only child of Andrew Issachar Goodhue and Lemira Barrett Goodhue. Her mother was from Merrimack, New Hampshire, and her father was from Hancock. Andrew, at eighteen years of age, was apprenticed to be a mechanical engineer. He married Lemira in 1870 and shortly thereafter the couple moved to Burlington, Vermont, to work at Gates's Cotton Mill. They lived in mill housing, and after nine years of marriage, their daughter, Grace, was born. Her parents built their own home on lower Maple Street and moved there when Grace was two years old.

An early memory for Grace was that of an injury her father sustained at the mill. Despite the fact that she was only four years old, she remembered that a knot in the wood he was cutting flew out and struck his face so that bones of

Special Guests

Grace Coolidge took an interest in hearing-impaired children at a very early age. Her neighbors, the John Lyman Yale family, often had visits from children who were deaf, since Yale's sister was principal of the Clarke School for the Deaf. Grace pledged that teaching deaf children would be her vocation and began teacher training at Clarke soon after her college graduation. She taught at Clarke for three years, and even though Calvin Coolidge was supportive of her work, she retired after marriage to him.

What is unique to this couple is that her interest in deaf children resonated with Calvin as well. After she stopped teaching, Grace still invited children to visit with her and her children while they lived in Northampton, Massachusetts. When she was First Lady, she frequently invited Clarke School students to the White House. She also hosted author and educator Helen Keller, who was blind and deaf. The Coolidges led a major fund-raising campaign for the research department at the school and, after leaving the White House, presented two million dollars in contributions to the Clarke School for the Deaf.

his nose and jaw were broken and his eye muscles were injured. Because her father needed a quiet recovery, Grace was sent to live with Mrs. John Lyman Yale and her family. Grace grew to love this family and respected their work at the Clarke School for the Deaf in Northampton, Massachusetts.

Grace graduated from high school in 1897, and even though the population of women was small at the University of Vermont, she assumed she would attend. She took a year off for health reasons before going to college, needing exercise to overcome a slight curvature of the spine. Her father built a new home up the hill on Maple Street, and she lived there during college. When Grace entered the university, she was five feet, four inches tall and considered herself to be plump. She had thick, curly black hair, gray-green eyes, and a generous mouth. She liked her life at college. She enjoyed sleigh rides in winter and theater productions. To enhance her social life, she joined with thirteen other women to petition Pi Beta Phi, a national sorority, for a charter at the University of Vermont. The group was successful and met many times in the attic of her house.

Upon graduation, Grace did not apply to teach in Burlington but wrote Caroline Yale, principal of the Clarke School for the Deaf, to apply for a position in the teacher training class. Grace's mother agreed that Grace should teach in Northampton, which was a town of many young women, with Smith College dominating its social life.

Grace's chosen career of teaching deaf children was a challenging one, sought by few. Despite the fact that Grace taught only a few years, she had a lifelong interest in children who were deaf.

Marriage and Family

There are two versions of how Calvin Coolidge met Grace Goodhue, but the proximity of the two was helpful: They lived across the street from each other. Grace saw Calvin Coolidge stand in his window to shave with a derby hat on the back of his head (to keep down a cowlick). One story is that she laughed and he pursued her. Another is that she asked her janitor to deliver a flower in a pot to him. The next morning, the janitor brought back Calvin's calling card, asking if he might call. The two began dating; Calvin's letters of this period survive and show their shared plans and interests.

Wed on October 4, 1905, Grace characterized her marriage to Calvin as uniting people of "vastly different temperaments and tastes" and commented that her mother "was not in her usual good health" on Grace's wedding day. Actually, Mrs. Goodhue opposed the timing of the marriage and wanted the couple to wait longer. Only relatives and a few friends attended the wedding; however, the Northampton newspaper called the groom "one of the best known young lawyers of Northampton" and "prominent in Republican politics," so his visibility in this Massachusetts city was already noted.

Grace treasured the simplicity of their early years of marriage. She characterized the knotted counterpane blanket that Calvin's invalid mother made as "our most precious heirloom." They set up housekeeping in rented rooms and then in half a house. She wrote, "What matter these trappings if love is strong and life is sweet?" She also immediately agreed to a traditional marriage with one head of the household, Calvin. This was based on economics as

Calvin Coolidge

Calvin Coolidge wanted to please his father, a Vermont state legislator, by choosing a political career, despite his natural shyness. His path began at Black River Academy in Ludlow, Vermont, when he gave a graduation oration. He had found his calling. He again rose to the occasion at his graduation from Amherst College in 1895 when he gave the Grove Oration, a humorous class speech to commemorate the day. After graduation and reading the law in a politically active Northampton, Massachusetts, law firm, politics became his career. He ran for office at the local, state, and national levels.

Two events created the path to the White House for Coolidge: the Boston Police Strike and the death of President Warren G. Harding. Coolidge's strong stand as Massachusetts governor showed leadership in the 1919 Boston Police strike: "There is no right to strike against the public safety by anybody, anywhere, any time." Newspapers lauded his strong actions against the striking Boston Police who left the city unguarded, and Coolidge's popularity soared at the 1920 Republican convention, where he was chosen by the delegates after the party bosses picked the top of the ticket, Warren Harding. As vice president, Coolidge summered with his father at Plymouth Notch, Vermont, in 1923. On August 3, he received news of the sudden death of Harding. Coolidge was the successor.

His reaction to Harding's death was characteristically cautious. He led the mourning of the former president and retained Harding's cabinet. The stellar members, Charles Evans Hughes and Andrew Mellon, were fine advisers. Attorney General Harry M. Daugherty and Secretary of the Navy Edwin Denby would eventually be embroiled in the Teapot Dome scandal, along with Interior Secretary Albert B. Fall, who traded oil leases for cash gifts. Coolidge restored the dignity of the office and cleaned house by appointing a Republican and a Democrat to investigate the scandal.

Preparation for a second term and presidency in his own right was a priority. At the pinnacle of his success, with his nomination for the office in hand, his second son died of a blood blister. "When he went the power and the glory of the Presidency went with him," wrote Coolidge in his autobiography. Despite a presidential administration lauded for cuts in the budget, debt, and taxes, Coolidge was ready to retire.

He wanted his economic programs to be his legacy. A country at peace and in prosperity was a success, he thought. On leaving the presidency, Calvin Coolidge wanted to return to the people and become one of them again.

well. As she had stopped teaching, his law firm and political offices would be their sole income. She gave birth to a son, John, on September 7, 1906, soon after they moved into their two-family house.

Calvin's description of John's birth showed how much he revered his wife and their new family: "The fragrance of the clematis which covered the bay window filled the room like a benediction, where the mother lay with her baby. We called him John in honor of my father. It was all very wonderful to us." However, as Calvin climbed the political ladder, mainly in Boston, Grace was often left alone to raise the baby and make a home. She said, "I marvel at the father's confidence in my ability to cope with the problem." The Coolidges quickly added a second son to the family in 1908, so she had two boys to raise. She was the one who laid out the train tracks and built the sport roadster with John, not his father.

Grace's sorority, Pi Beta Phi, was a meaningful part of her social life. She went to their conventions and, in 1901, before the boys were born, had been president of the Western Massachusetts Alumnae Club. She traveled with her sorority sisters to Berkeley, California, in 1915 for the national convention. She enjoyed the comradeship of the tour, but this was abruptly interrupted with a telegram from Calvin announcing his race for lieutenant governor of Massachusetts. She did not finish the trip and took the next train home.

Political offices did not pay large salaries in the early 1900's, so Calvin Coolidge borrowed funds from his father and tightened his budget. He did not want to be beholden to anyone. As his political trajectory escalated, Frank Waterman Stearns, his political backer, offered the couple a house on Beacon Hill when Calvin was elected governor. They turned it down, with Grace remaining in Northampton with the boys and Calvin taking an extra room at Adams House in Boston. They had no car; Calvin took the train and public transportation to social affairs. Grace did hire a housekeeper in Northampton. Calvin also liked to buy hats for himself and Grace; buying clothes for his wife was his one extravagance.

The governorship, which Coolidge was elected to in 1918, would probably have been the pinnacle of his political career if not for the Boston Police strike of 1919. His strong stand against the striking public servants was lauded across the land, and his name appeared on the list at the Republican convention. Grace was in Boston with him when Calvin received the call from Chicago. She was surprised that he accepted the vice presidential nomination.

The 1920 victory of President Warren G. Harding and Coolidge over James M. Cox and Franklin D. Roosevelt brought a major change for Grace. Her husband had been in politics since the year their son was born, 1906, while she had been on the periphery. Only when Calvin was mayor of Northampton had she been part of the political equation. Now things would change. They moved to Washington, D.C., to live at the Hotel Willard, since no residence was provided for the vice president. The boys were to board at Mercersburg Academy, about one hour away. Grace no longer had daily responsibility for them. Now she was expected to preside over "the Ladies of the Senate," the wives and hostesses of U.S. senators. She felt more prepared to play with train tracks, but Lois Marshall, wife of the outgoing vice president Thomas S. Marshall, gave friendly guidance to Grace, which helped her break through the Washington façade. Grace's natural charm and ability to recall names and faces also helped break the ice. Frances Parkinson Keyes, a noted author and wife of a senator, wrote, "I doubt that any vice presidential hostess has ever wrung so much pleasure out of Washington or given so much in return. She is the only woman in official life of whom I have never heard a single disparaging remark in the course of nearly twenty years."

It was common to travel to cooler climes dur-

From left: Aviator Charles Lindbergh, Grace Coolidge, and Lindbergh's mother pose with President Coolidge, June, 1927. *(Library of Congress)*

ing the summers, when Washington was hot and humid. Thus, Calvin and Grace went to visit his father in Vermont in August, 1923, while Warren and Florence Harding toured the West Coast. Calvin's autobiography described the trembling in his father's voice as he climbed the stairs of the farmhouse to tell the couple of the death of President Harding. After praying, they went to the parlor, and Grace brought in an oil lamp so they could make plans. Calvin wrote a telegram to Mrs. Harding. Then Congressman Porter Dale of Vermont drove up and encouraged an immediate oath of office for the new president. Calvin turned to his father who, as a notary public, had the authority to witness such an oath. Grace produced the family Bible, and Calvin Coolidge was sworn in as president.

Presidency and First Ladyship

"This was I and yet not I, this was the wife of the President of the United States and she took pre-

cedence over me; my personal likes and dislikes must be subordinated to the consideration of those things which were required of her."A role had been thrust upon Grace Coolidge, and she admitted to having no influence over national decisions, even if they affected her personally. This obviously could have brought stress upon her as she tried to perform her obligations without really having substantial input. As a college-educated woman whose ideas were valued by many, this position must have felt submissive. However, the role of First Lady as greeter and cheerleader was something she liked; she admitted to loving the interaction with people. Just as her father greeted people at church, she greeted them at the White House. She liked making people feel at home.

A high point for Grace was a visit to the Executive Mansion from her sorority sisters, the Pi Phis. They made a gift to the White House: a portrait, by Howard Chandler Christy, of Grace in a red dress, next to the president's dog, Rob Roy. The thirteen hundred women filled the White House with joy and pride.

The low point was the death of her second son. Admiral Boone, the assistant White House physician, encouraged the boys to play tennis. He arrived one day to play and found Calvin, Jr., resting in a room, his mother watching him. When Boone examined the boy, he found an infection due to a blister from playing tennis. Fast-moving septicemia took the life of Calvin, Jr., within a few days. Grace was very religious and believed that her son would be waiting for her in heaven. She even wrote a poem, *Open Door*. Some historians believe that President Coolidge became clinically depressed at this time. Grace had to soldier on as well as look to their other son, John, now at Amherst College.

When Calvin chose not to run again for president in 1928, the family planned to retire to the two-family house in Northampton. Lacking the privacy they needed, they bought The Beeches, a gated estate. Grace plunged into community service and wrote articles. After Calvin's sudden death of a coronary thrombosis in 1933, Grace filled her retirement with her "precious four" (son John, his wife, Florence, and their children Cynthia and Lydia) and her many interests. She hiked and swam and loved baseball enough to attend games into the late innings of her own life. In the 1950's her heart began to fail. She died at seventy-eight years of age of congestive heart failure related to kyphoscoliosis.

Legacy

Grace Coolidge remains a popular presidential wife among First Ladies. This is probably due to her image as an elegant and vibrant First Lady. The Secret Service nicknamed her Sunshine. The social climate of the White House, under her guidance, exemplified tradition, such as her emphasis on holidays, and also included children and those with disabilities. International in outlook, she raised funds for victims of World War II and loaned her house to the Women Accepted for Volunteer Emergency Service (WAVES) military unit as their headquarters in Northampton.

Her interest in White House history inspired her to ask for a joint resolution by Congress to authorize acceptance of gifts of furniture. She wanted to restore antiques to the building and treat it as a living museum. She also renovated the family quarters, adding a sky parlor to let in more sunlight.

To help preserve the legacy of her husband, she donated materials and memorabilia to the Forbes Library, a public library in Northampton, and made plans to transfer the Coolidge family homestead, where Calvin had been sworn in as president, to the state of Vermont.

Suggested Readings

Ferrell, Robert H., ed. *The Real Calvin Coolidge* 10 (1994). Plymouth, Vt.: This issue of the journal of the Calvin Coolidge Memorial Foundation contains essays on Grace Coolidge, with her poems.

Heller, Milton F., Jr. *The Presidents' Doctor: An Insider's View of Three First Families*. New York: Vantage Press, 2000. A good friend of Grace Coolidge gives his view from the White House.

Ross, Ishbel. *Grace Coolidge and Her Era: The Story of a President's Wife*. Plymouth, Vt.: The Calvin Coolidge Memorial Foundation, 1988. A journalist's view of the 1920's and Grace Coolidge. Good use of original sources.

Stoddard, Gloria May. *Grace and Cal: A Vermont Love Story*. Shelburne, Vt.: The New England Press, 1989. A highly readable story of the two.

Wikander, Lawrence E., and Robert H. Ferrell, eds. *Grace Coolidge: An Autobiography*. Worland, Wyo.: High Plains Press, 1992. A collection of Grace Coolidge's articles published in 1929-1930 in *American* magazine. Her own words are helpful, but she keeps her opinions and feelings to herself.

Cynthia D. Bittinger

Lou Hoover

Lou Henry Hoover

Born: March 29, 1874
     Waterloo, Iowa
Died: January 7, 1944
     New York, New York

President: Herbert Hoover
1929-1933

Overview: Although popular and well-known during her lifetime, Lou Hoover is just beginning to recover from the obscurity that followed her death in 1944. The fact that Herbert Hoover's presidency had ended disastrously following the stock market crash and his unsuccessful reelection bid in 1932 may have contributed to her decline. More likely reasons, however, may be found in her refusal to engage in acts of self-promotion and her disillusionment with the outcome of the election.

A new generation of scholars is rediscovering a vivacious, intelligent, self-confident woman who was dedicated to significant acts of public service.

Early Life

Lou was the first of two daughters born to Charles Delano Henry and Florence Weed Henry. Her parents were typical of the new middle class which emerged in the years following the Civil War. Her mother had taught school, and her father had been preparing for a career in banking when the Civil War intervened. Very little is known of Charles Henry's apprenticeship as a banker, but he had risen to the position of teller with the First National Bank of Waterloo before being asked to participate in the organization of several small banks in Iowa, Kansas, and California. He was then appointed manager of a bank in Monterey, California, in 1890.

Lou Hoover. *(Library of Congress)*

217

Little is known of Lou's childhood and teenage years except for occasional glimpses that have survived in newspaper articles, in some of her school papers, and in her letters to friends and family. She was friendly and well liked, intellectually curious, adventuresome, and a natural leader who was respected by her classmates. Many years later, friends would recall how she organized a working party to clear a vacant lot for softball games. Others remembered her firm insistence that two African American boys be included in the playgroup.

Her personality included generous portions of common sense and practicality combined with an innate friendliness and good humor. These personal attributes, coupled with a keen sense of intellectual curiosity, are evident in letters to her parents and in class writing assignments from her high school and college years. What began as a love of nature and the outdoors expanded into increasingly formal studies of zoology, geology, chemistry, and biology in high school and college.

Marriage and Family

Before the Henry family left Iowa in 1887 in search of a healthier climate for Mrs. Henry, Charles Henry introduced Lou to the joys of camping, hiking, and fishing along the banks of the Cedar River. These excursions became more frequent and far-ranging after they moved to California, first to the brand-new settlement of Whittier in 1887 and then to Monterey. The fact that Florence Henry was often in poor health and could not accompany her husband may help explain why Charles came to prize Lou's company on those extended forays into the mountains. Certainly he could not have wanted a more enthusiastic and observant companion. Years later, having become president of the Girl Scouts of America, Lou would proudly recall that she "had been a girl scout, before the organization existed, when my father took me hunting, fishing and hiking in the mountains."

These outdoor expeditions not only led to a pleasant and rewarding relationship with the Girl Scouts, they eventually led Lou to her life's partner, Herbert Hoover. As did many young women of her class in the 1880's, Lou found the opportunities before her both exciting and frustrating. It was the height of the Victorian age, and there was a definite, exhilarating sense of living on the edge of modern times. It was not, however, an open society in which everyone had an equal chance to take advantage of the new opportunities. Options for women were still limited. A college education helped, but a young woman would soon discover that her professional horizon was limited to teaching, medicine, or working in very routine clerical occupations. Lou, however, was determined to find her niche, that special place in which she could utilize her special gifts for the good of society.

No doubt influenced by her mother's experiences as a teacher, Lou graduated from San Jose Normal School in June of 1893 but, unable to find a teaching position, took an assistant cashier's job in her father's bank. The following spring she was asked to substitute in the Monterey schools. Later that summer, she attended a lecture on geology by Professor John C. Branner, a popular faculty member at Stanford University. She had been fascinated by the dramatic rock formations of the rugged Sierra Nevada, and Branner was an excellent speaker. When he assured her that she could find a career in geologic research, she enrolled for the fall term at Stanford. Soon after her arrival on campus, Branner introduced her to his lab assistant, a shy senior student named Herbert Hoover.

In a letter to a friend, Herbert remarked upon the unusual development of a woman student in the geology department and added that she was "a nice one too." A few days later, his classmates met to decide if their new classmate should join them on field trips. They agreed that if she did not prove an encum-

Herbert Hoover

Unlike most of his predecessors, Herbert Hoover had no consuming desire to become president. His single-term presidency, from 1929 to 1933, was the only elective political office he ever held. Orphaned at the age of eight, he was determined to get an education so he could take care of himself. In four years at Stanford University he became a legendary student leader. Graduating in 1895, during a depression, he could only get work as a laborer in the mines but soon found a position with Louis Janin, a highly respected mining consultant. In 1897, Janin recommended Hoover for a position with a British firm wanting to hire an American engineer to develop their Australian holdings.

Hoover's practical experience as a "pick and shovel" miner enabled him to predict which mines were worth developing and which should be sold. Soon he was offered a junior partnership and sent to perform similar miracles for the Chinese Bureau of Mines. By 1912, Hoover was the foremost mining consultant in the world and a wealthy man. In the process he had discovered that amassing wealth was neither difficult nor fulfilling. He began telling close friends that he was interested in public service but still had not decided on an outlet for his energies when World War I began in 1914.

Hoover's genius for large-scale organization became evident soon after the war began, when he organized the repatriation of forty thousand stranded American tourists. When it became obvious that eight million Belgians were starving, he was asked to establish relief programs for all of the non-combatants in Belgium and northern France. Between 1914 and 1923, he invented the first large-scale relief organization in history and became a world celebrity. His reinvention of the Commerce Department in 1921-1928 added new laurels to his wartime achievements and led to a landslide presidential victory over New York Governor Al Smith in 1928.

During the frenzied stock market speculation of 1925-1929, Hoover had issued repeated warnings, but the public refused to listen. When the market collapsed six months after his inauguration, in October, 1929, he immediately held meetings of state governors and business and labor leaders to mobilize state public works programs, prevent layoffs, and maintain wage levels. At first, he refused to provide direct federal relief, believing that it would lead to widespread dependence on government assistance programs. Limited success with direct federal relief programs in 1931-1932 came too late to prevent his defeat in the election of 1932. Once hated by many, he lived to achieve partial vindication for his views. The importance of getting people off welfare was eventually recognized in the 1960's and became a stated objective of the Bill Clinton administration in the 1990's.

brance, she would be allowed to go on future trips. They were completely unprepared for Lou's athleticism and obvious familiarity with the outdoors. Herbert began to regard her in a new light, as a charming young woman who loved the outdoors and would not shrink from a life as the wife of a mining engineer. By the time he graduated from Stanford in 1895, the young couple had come to an understanding: They would marry when Herbert had proved himself and was able to support Lou.

When Hoover left Stanford in 1895, the economy was still reeling from the Panic of 1893. Jobs were scarce, especially in the mining industry, but he made the best of the situation by taking a "pick and shovel job." This later proved to be a great advantage, for Hoover learned more in a few months in this new classroom than most engineers would learn in a lifetime about predicting a mine's potential and how to manage men in a humane and efficient manner. Less than three years later, he was promoted to a junior partnership in a London firm and was ready to claim his bride. Returning to California by way of Suez and London, he stopped long enough to receive instructions on his new assignment in China. A few weeks later, in late January of 1899, he was back in Monterey.

After a whirlwind shopping tour of San Francisco bookstores, where they purchased every available map and book on China, Herbert and Lou Hoover were married in a simple ceremony in her parents' house in Monterey on February 10, 1899. A few days later, Florence Henry wrote to friends that "we had been prepared not to like him," because he was pl;anning to take Lou off to China. Florence had to admit, though, that they had soon grown to like Herbert as much as Lou did. In commenting on the adventure that Lou was about to undertake, Mrs. Henry correctly predicted that such a life would suit her daughter very well.

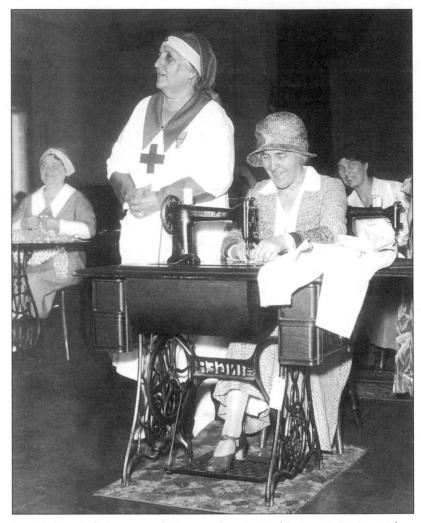

Lou Hoover, in hat, visits Red Cross workers in Washington, D.C., September, 1932. *(Library of Congress)*

Herbert and Lou arrived in China just as growing dissatisfaction with Western control and influence was about to erupt in the Boxer Rebellion of 1900. Trapped in Tientsin with eight hundred Europeans and Americans by approximately forty thousand well-armed Boxer fanatics, the Hoovers' calm fortitude became an inspiration for the international community. Later, during the presidential campaign hyperbole of 1928, Lou modestly attempted to minimize her role, though she did admit to nursing and writing letters for the wounded and managing the settlement's small dairy herd. She failed to mention standing watch during the early morning hours so the men could rest and how, on one of her errands of mercy, the tire of her bicycle was shot out from under her. After the first, small international relief force arrived, Herbert insisted that she leave with the other women and children. She flatly refused; it was the only time she is known to have defied her husband.

In many respects, the siege of Tientsin was the forge in which the partnership of their marriage was tempered. Although there is no evidence that she helped Herbert prepare some of his later field surveys or consulting reports, it is quite likely that she did. She did have a degree in geology and had conducted research for Professor Branner in the British Museum. In China she had accompanied Herbert on field trips and had astonished superstitious miners by going down into several mines. In succeeding years she would follow her husband around the globe five times to such exotic places as Egypt, Siam, China, Australia, Japan, Siberia, New Zealand, and India. When her sons Herbert, Jr., and Allan were born, she waited only a few weeks before joining her husband. This tested her ability to care for her family and helps to explain how she could later remain absolutely unflappable in the face of minor White House "emergencies" that seemed to unnerve everyone but the First Lady.

Another result of this globetrotting lifestyle was to make the Hoovers a close-knit family. Lou took a very intense interest in everything her husband and sons did, even when her terms as Girl Scout president required that she travel to address conferences from Spokane, Washington, to Miami, Florida. Unfortunately,

Herbert and Lou's surviving personal papers reveal few of the intimate details that biographers and historians rely on to assess motives and explain behavior. The information that has survived, largely in Lou's correspondence with family and friends, reveals a remarkably "normal" family trying to remain unaffected by life in the goldfish bowl of public life. When the Hoover family could get away together, they went on family camping and fishing trips. Lou's letters reveal an intense interest in every aspect of her sons' education. She understood the importance of masculine role models for her sons and refused to have them taught by her women teacher friends, regarding them as impractical and overindulgent.

Presidency and First Ladyship
Presidential couples have demonstrated varying degrees of interest in the presidency. Some have pursued it with unseemly ambition, and others have regarded it as an opportunity to serve their country. The Hoovers approached it as both an opportunity for public service and as a sacred duty that they felt honor-bound to accept. To say that Herbert Hoover lacked politi-

Lou Hoover and the Girl Scouts

Lou Hoover's public service activities stretched from the Spanish-American War (1898) through the Boxer Rebellion (1900) and two World Wars. As First Lady, she supported many organizations, but her greatest satisfaction came from working with her beloved Girl Scouts. Her love of the outdoor life began during her preteen years in Iowa. After her family moved to Monterey, California, her father began taking her on extended camping trips up into the Sierra Nevada. Later, when she was president of the Girl Scouts, she delighted in reminding everyone that she had, in fact, "been a girl scout before the movement existed."

Her formal involvement with the movement came in 1917 when Girl Scout founder Juliette Low invited Lou to take over a newly formed troop of girls in Washington, D.C. During the next twenty-seven years, Lou served as a board member, vice president, honorary president, and president. Girl Scout membership exploded during those years, from 27,000 in 1927 to a phenomenal 1.4 million at the time of Lou's death in 1944. Most of that growth came from her success in securing donations of more than $575,000 in the early 1920's to fund the development of an innovative program of activities that girls found irresistible.

cal ambitions is a considerable understatement. His effort to secure the Republican nomination in 1920 failed in part because his friends were not able to persuade him to run a year earlier. For the next three years, he explored the possibility of becoming a part owner of a major newspaper, hoping to turn it into a potent, honest force in the political education of the general public. When this failed to develop as planned, he began to heed the entreaties of his friends, notably Lou.

Although she always respected his wishes, he listened to her and valued her opinions. Although they were very correct in public, their regard and affection for each other was nevertheless obvious to their friends. Lou was devoted to her husband, going out of her way to provide a comfortable environment in which he could relax and escape the pressures of work. During the years when he was commerce secretary, this meant having friends and other stimulating guests as dinner companions almost every evening. There was no letup during the presidency. Although Lou was not enthusiastic about politics or campaigning, she did not shirk her political obligations or any opportunities to assist with the campaign.

Once the election was over, the society page editors were beside themselves. The prospect of an experienced international hostess as First Lady—writers H. G. Wells, George Bernard Shaw, and Rudyard Kipling had been her guests when the Hoovers were in London—was almost too much for them. Lou did not disappoint the papers and took her ceremonial duties quite seriously. Her White House staff was especially impressed with her ability to make newcomers feel welcome, even in sophisticated White House society. White House musicales featured only American artists, and the list of those who performed would later read like a *Who's Who* of emerging operatic superstars. Lou's duties as First Lady limited her Girl Scout activities, but she used her position to promote Girl Scouting.

Legacy

Frequently in the news in her dual role as First Lady and Girl Scout president, Lou Hoover was also the first presidential wife to speak on radio, both during the campaign of 1928 and several times during her husband's administration. She used these occasions to promote the efforts of volunteer relief agencies rather than direct federal doles. The most notable of these radio talks, on March 23, 1931, included an appeal to Girls Scouts everywhere to take an active role in relieving the suffering of families devastated by the Depression. For more than a year, she had conducted her own private relief agency from the White House. When the appeals became too numerous for her staff to handle, she hired another secretary, with her own funds, to direct the relief work. Typically, she insisted that this personal program be kept confidential.

Although the Girl Scouts remained number one in her affection, the former First Lady found many new outlets for her wisdom and energy during the post-presidency. Her patronage of the arts expanded to include ballet, opera, and a variety of concert series in San Francisco and Palo Alto, California. Her involvement in the activities of the Salvation Army led naturally to her role in organizing and promoting a 1940 clothing drive on behalf of British War Relief. Her good deeds ended abruptly on January 7, 1944, while on a visit in New York. Lou had attended an afternoon concert with one of her former secretaries and suggested that they walk back to the Waldorf-Astoria Hotel. Feeling fatigued after a few blocks, she hailed a cab. Back at their apartment, she told her husband that she was going to rest before dinner. When he checked on her later, it was too late for the house doctor to save her. She had suffered a heart attack.

Lou Hoover set a high standard for the First Ladies who followed her. Her rich legacy includes a zest for living, genuine friendliness, intelligence, dedication to her family, and a host of public service endeavors. Although a product of Victorian times, her attitudes and wide range of public service activities clearly mark her as the first of the modern First Ladies.

Suggested Readings

Allen, Anne Beiser. *An Independent Woman: The Life of Lou Henry Hoover*. Westport, Conn.: Greenwood Press, 2000. A scholarly treatment of Lou Hoover's life; thoughtful and very readable.

Mayer, Dale C. "An Uncommon Woman: The Quiet Leadership Style of Lou Henry Hoover." *Presidential Studies Quarterly* 20 (Fall, 1990): 685-698. An in-depth examination of Lou Hoover's pivotal role in the dramatic growth of the Girl Scouts.

_____, ed. *Lou Henry Hoover: Essays on a Busy Life*. Worland, Wyo.: High Plains Press, 1994. A collection of essays based on extensive research of Lou Hoover's personal papers. Includes comments on the significance and nature of her papers by the archivist in charge of arranging them.

Nash, George. *The Life of Herbert Hoover*. 3 vols. New York: W. W. Norton, 1983. The first three volumes in Nash's as yet unfinished multivolume biography of the thirty-first president are generally regarded as the definitive account of Herbert Hoover's life. Each volume contains references to Lou Hoover.

Pryor, Helen. *Lou Henry Hoover: Gallant First Lady*. New York: Dodd, Mead, 1969. Long out of print and lacking footnotes, this account still has much to recommend it. Pryor was a friend of the Hoovers and interviewed many of Lou Hoover's friends for this very personal portrait.

Dale C. Mayer

Eleanor Roosevelt

Anna Eleanor Roosevelt

Born: October 11, 1884
New York, New York
Died: November 7, 1962
New York, New York

President: Franklin D. Roosevelt 1933-
1945

Overview: Eleanor Roosevelt was First Lady during two of the most fearful events in U.S. history: the Great Depression and World War II. Born into the uppermost layer of American society, her union with Franklin D. Roosevelt was based more on intellectual compatibility than the values of the social class from which they came. The White House has seen its share of complex marriages, but few have been as complicated as the Roosevelts' relationship. Franklin's infidelities strained the warmth of the marriage in such a way that when he desperately needed a zone of peace within the White House, Eleanor was unable to provide this. Yet their political partnership would accomplish more than either Franklin or Eleanor could have achieved without the other, changing the United States as well as the nature of the presidency and First Ladyship.

Eleanor Roosevelt, 1933. *(Library of Congress)*

Early Life

Anna Eleanor Roosevelt was born on October 11, 1884. As with all children, her emotional development was shaped by the adults in her life, especially her mother. Eleanor wrote in her autobiography:

> I can remember standing in the door . . . and I can see the look in [my mother's] eyes and hear the tone of her voice as she said, 'Come in, Granny.' If a visitor was there she might turn and say, 'She is such a funny child, so old-fashioned that we always call her Granny.' I wanted to sink through the floor in shame.

Eleanor's mother, Anna Hall Roosevelt, was from an elite New York family whose names are found on one of the first society registers ever published, according to biographer Blanche Wiesen Cook, who describes Eleanor's maternal grandmother, Mary Hall, as strict and adamant. The aloofness Eleanor felt from her mother and grandmother were partially allayed by the warmth of her father, Elliott Roosevelt, who fondly called Eleanor his "little golden hair." The Roosevelts were a distinguished New York family as well. Elliott's brother, Theodore, would become president of the United States in 1901. Elliott was charming and sensitive and had been a dashing figure in New York society when he married Anna. Eleanor wrote, "My father was always devoted to me."

Because of her parents' troubled relationship and Elliott's alcoholism and other excesses, Eleanor's father was often away from his family. The Roosevelts were brought temporarily closer during the building of a summer house in Hempstead, New York. Eleanor was excited because it meant she would spend more time with her father. "Little Eleanor is as happy as the day is long, plays with her kitten, the puppy and the chickens all the time and is very dirty as a general rule," boasted her proud father in 1889.

That year, Anna gave birth to the first of her two sons, Ellie, followed by Hall in 1891. In Eleanor's autobiography she is explicit about her feelings of being left out when her mother was with the two little boys: "I felt a curious barrier between myself and these three." To Eleanor, her mother's sigh and exasperated voice were further proof that only her father understood and loved her. Eleanor's relationship with her father always remained special in the family, in spite of his absences and reckless personal life.

When Anna Roosevelt was almost thirty, she contracted diphtheria, and in December of 1892 she died. "One fact," wrote Eleanor, "wiped out everything else. My father was back and I would see him soon." Eleanor's father was not able to see her until after she and her brothers were installed in Grandmother Hall's house, where it had been decided the children would live. Elliott had not been permitted to come to his wife's funeral.

How much eight-year-old Eleanor knew of her father's alcoholism and brief institutionalization is unclear. She said it was only after her mother died that she developed an awareness that there was something wrong with him. During her years with her grandmother, Eleanor's aunts and uncles lavished attention on her and her brothers. However, it was her correspondence and infrequent visits with her father that most comforted her and encouraged her hopes that one day they would again live together. As much her father doted on her, he could not be consoled when, in 1893, three-year-old Ellie died of scarlet fever and diphtheria. Not allowed to see his surviving children, Elliott dropped further into despair and died suddenly in 1894, apparently after a prolonged drinking binge. His last letter to Eleanor, written the night he died, said, ". . . Kiss Baby Brudie for me and never forget I love you. . . ."

The tragedy of losing her mother when she was eight and her father when she was ten compounded the loneliness Eleanor had felt since her early childhood. She was somewhat shy and uncertain of herself, yet her father had given her the ideals that she tried to live up to all her life: "to be noble, brave, studious, religious, loving and good." When Eleanor was fifteen years old, Grandmother Hall decided it was not good for her to remain at home. "Your mother wanted you to go to boarding school in Europe, and I have decided to send you, child."

A year after Eleanor arrived at the Allenswood school, on the outskirts of London, the headmistress wrote to Mrs. Hall:

All that you said when she came here of the purity of her heart, the nobleness of her thought has been verified by her conduct among the people who were at first strangers to her. I have not found her easily influenced in anything that was not perfectly straightforward and honest, but I often found she influenced others in the right direction. She is full of sympathy for all those who live with her and shows an intelligent interest in everything she comes in contact with.

Eleanor soon developed her own circle of friends, and her years of loneliness were overcome by a budding confidence. The Allenswood years also shaped Eleanor's tastes in literature, music, theater, and the arts, but what made those years among the most important in her life was the influence of the school's headmistress, seventy-year-old Marie Souvestre. Souvestre was at home in the world of high politics and high culture, and her tastes made a great impression on Eleanor. According to Cook, "Eleanor had never before experienced female authority as a freeing rather than a constraining force." Despite the vigor of Mlle. Souvestre's convictions, she insisted that Eleanor and the rest of her students think for themselves and express their own feelings. Intellectual independence and a lively sense of curiosity, she felt, were the most important traits one could possess.

Eleanor, almost eighteen, was a changed person when she returned to the United States in the early summer of 1902. She had grown into a lively, sensitive, and intelligent young woman. She was tall and graceful. The Halls had called Eleanor back to New York to be introduced to society. Eleanor dreaded this uncomfortable ordeal. She was self-conscious about her looks, which first her mother, then an aunt, had told her were unremarkable. Feeling she disappointed her family by not being a "belle," she considered her debut season to be "utter agony." Her agony, though, was in part self-inflicted, as she was invited to all the parties ("Automatically my name was placed on everybody's list," she said) because of her family's position. With courtiers she was cautious and quick to consider them "fresh," but according to Cook, "she was at ease in conversation, especially with older people . . . . She appeared to be years older than her contemporaries."

Eleanor wrote to her brother, Hall, at school nearly every day, wanting him to know he belonged to somebody. While living in New York City, she joined the Junior League and asked to be assigned to work at the College Settlement on Riverton Street, where young girls were taught calisthenics and dancing. Eleanor noticed that the poor on the Lower East Side stood together to claim their rights, and it was part of her education in the realities of social change. She was finding a role she felt comfortable with, and she worked diligently at the settlement house.

Eleanor quickly emerged as one of the leaders of the Junior League, which worked as part of a network of reform organizations which included the Public Education Association, the Women's Trade Union League, and the Consumers League. These activities exposed her to a wide range of social issues. One of the League's major goals was to obtain legislation that would prohibit child labor and the cruel "sweating systems" where children worked in slum conditions. Eleanor was finding a vocation and a role, and she applied herself with scrupulous diligence to the settlement tasks and social problems she encountered. Later in life, she would go on to teach and serve as administrator at the Todhunter School for Girls in New York City and found an experimental furniture factory for the needy at Val-Kill, New York.

Marriage and Family

Even though she still often felt awkward and did not enjoy the social events of her coming out, Eleanor had many admirers, including some whose interest was serious. They had missed their chance, however. A young man who knew his mind had asked for her hand,

Franklin D. Roosevelt

Born in 1882 in Hyde Park, New York, the only child of an affluent family, Franklin Delano Roosevelt enjoyed an early life of comfort and success. Educated at Harvard University, he was working toward a career as an attorney when he married Eleanor Roosevelt, his fifth cousin, in 1905. Franklin entered public service when he was asked to run for the New York state senate in 1910. In 1912 he was reelected for s second state senate term, which was interrupted by his appointment as assistant secretary of the Navy. He became a candidate for U.S. vice president in 1920.

At age thirty-nine, Franklin was tall and lean and was noted for his charm, leading one society matron to call him "one of the beautiful young men of his time." His political career looked promising in spite of the loss at the polls in 1920. However, in 1921 he was stricken with polio and lost the use of his legs. The disease confined him to a wheelchair but did not stop his career. In 1928 Roosevelt was elected governor of New York and, four years later, was elected president in a landslide vote.

He was the longest serving president in U.S. history, elected to four consecutive terms. Moreover FDR, as he was affectionately known, served during some of the most critical moments in U.S. history. Upon assuming office in 1933, he was faced with the staggering burden of the Great Depression. His New Deal programs, such as the creation of Social Security, public works projects, and other experimental economic and social relief initiatives, were reviled by the wealthy establishment from which he came. His policies, though, helped bring the United States out of economic disaster. In Eleanor Roosevelt's autobiography, she described the "letters that came in such numbers" after Franklin's death: "Touchingly people told their stories and cited the plans and policies undertaken by my husband that had brought about improvement in their lives. In many cases he had saved them from complete despair."

By the end of the 1930's Roosevelt was faced with a new nemesis, the specter of fascism in Europe and world war. After the Japanese surprise attack on Pearl Harbor on December 7, 1941, Roosevelt announced the entrance of the United States into World War II. He guided Americans through war and planned for world peace by envisioning a United Nations and what would become the Marshall Plan for rebuilding Europe. Buoyed by the success of D day, the amphibian invasion of France on June 6, 1942, he announced that he would accept the nomination for an unprecedented fourth term as president. He then went on a Pacific inspection trip to bases in Hawaii and Alaska. The president was victorious, but the strain of the war was evident.

One month before Germany surrendered to Allied forces, Roosevelt died of a cerebral hemorrhage on April 12, 1945, at Warm Springs, Georgia. He had established a rehabilitative facility there for polio patients. He is remembered as one of the United States' greatest presidents.

and she had become secretly engaged. Franklin Delano Roosevelt's most fateful action as a charming young man was to pick his fifth cousin, shy, plain Eleanor Roosevelt, to be his wife. He was a junior at Harvard University when he encountered Eleanor after she returned from Allenswood. They spent hours talking, and he often accompanied her as she went about her settlement-house work. The poverty he witnessed on those excursions, Eleanor wrote later, had a lasting effect on him.

They were married on March 17, 1905. President Theodore Roosevelt, Eleanor's uncle, gave the bride away. Franklin was the only child of Sara Delano Roosevelt, a widow, and his mother never felt Eleanor was good enough for him. Sara repeatedly intervened in Eleanor and Franklin's marriage, choosing their home and furnishings and even who would raise the Roosevelt children. In 1906, Franklin and Eleanor's first child, Anna, was born, followed by James in 1907, Franklin in 1909 (he lived a few months), Elliott in 1910, another son they named Franklin in 1914, and John in 1916. In later years, Eleanor regretted that she had let her mother-in-law make so many decisions for her. She wished she had insisted on caring for her children herself, instead of hiring nurses. She realized too late that both she and the children would have been happier.

Other problems of adjustment were exacerbated when Franklin would not intervene in disagreements between his mother and his wife. He was not inclined to let Eleanor share her frustrations with him. Likewise, if he disappointed her, such as forgetting an anniversary, she did not speak about it. Instead, she withdrew into heavy silence. Franklin loved and admired his wife but was puzzled by her moods and wished she would speak up. He wanted to live up to her expectations and was aware of his shortcomings.

There were other differences. Eleanor went to church regularly, but Franklin often skipped Sunday services to play golf. When he neglected his duties or forgot promises, Sara or Eleanor would square things for him. Whether gladly or not, Eleanor accepted the role of manager in family affairs.

In 1910 Franklin was asked to run for a seat in the New York senate. His chances were slim, but he went forward with confidence. Eleanor was delighted. He was elected state senator, and the family moved to the state capital. There, Eleanor found herself the wife of Albany's most talked-about young politician. Out from under her mother-in-law's thumb, her initiation into official life was swift and sudden. Eleanor, with her gift for making alliances, was clearly a political asset to her husband. Their friends considered them an exemplary and happily married couple. While Eleanor insisted that politics was a man's domain, she was ambitious to improve society, in an era when women's abilities were seldom valued or encouraged. By working, as she said, on her husband's behalf, she was able to share his career. She met hundreds of new people, coped with new situations, and discovered that she could manage—and she liked it.

In January of 1913, Franklin was appointed assistant secretary of the Navy, and the Roosevelts moved to Washington, D.C. The move brought new challenges, and Eleanor responded by continuing to grow in her development as a politically savvy spouse and social activist. When the secretary invited members of the cabinet and their wives to join him at a naval target practice, a young officer asked Eleanor if she would like to climb the skeleton mast. She put on a suit of dungarees, boldly climbed to the top, and had an excellent place to view the firing.

On March 18, 1917, German submarines torpedoed three American vessels, and soon afterward the United States entered World War I. Eleanor became deeply involved in the war relief effort. She organized the canteens the Red Cross set up in Washington; when she was not at a canteen, she visited sailors in Navy hospitals. She gave out wool to knitters and collected the finished products, to be sent to servicemen.

In 1918 Eleanor discovered that a romance was going on between her husband and Lucy Page Mercer, who had been her social secretary for the previous four years. Eleanor was humiliated; Franklin had made little effort to conceal the affair from their many friends, and Eleanor felt she had been deceived under her nose in her own house. She offered her husband his "freedom," but a divorce would have meant the end of Franklin's promising political career, something he found difficult to contemplate. With the help of his strong-willed mother, a truce was arranged, mostly on Eleanor's terms. Franklin was banned from his wife's bedroom permanently, their sons James and Elliott later claimed.

The shy, primly correct society matron who had earlier marveled over attracting the handsome Hudson River scion also vanished forever, to be replaced by a disillusioned woman who was determined whenever possible to go her own way. Many biographers believe her husband's affair had exhumed her childhood feelings of abandonment: Franklin's infidelity triggered all the sadness Eleanor felt for her charming but dissolute father. She also decided she would not repeat her mother's mistake of further damaging her marriage by remaining aloof.

Out of the Roosevelts' pain a bond was formed which fortified their relationship, and Eleanor emerged from the ordeal a different woman. Ended was the subordination to her mother-in-law; emergent was the realization that to build a life and interests of her own was not only what she wanted to do but what she had to do. The Roosevelts forged a working partnership that endured their increasingly separate private lives. Both Eleanor and Franklin stayed in the public eye after World War I. When he received the Democratic nomination for vice president in 1920, he asked her to accompany him on the campaign trail, and she agreed.

Franklin was not elected vice president, and the following year he was stricken with polio. Supremely confident and outgoing before the paralysis, Roosevelt was dealt what appeared to be a blow from which neither he nor his political career could recover. The illness confined him to a wheelchair; during subsequent public appearances he donned heavy leg braces and gave the appearance of walking.

His diagnosis further shaped the nature of the Roosevelt marriage and further influenced Eleanor's growing independence and confidence. Franklin's mother wanted him to discontinue his political career and retire at their beloved Hyde Park home, Springwood. Roosevelt himself was temporarily defeated as well. However, Eleanor both nursed her husband and helped him through the ordeal. She insisted that he maintain his vital interest in politics, and daily she brought newspapers as well as friends and associates to his bedroom. She also kept his political career alive by continuing her activism in Democratic and New York politics through a number of activities.

Eleanor's encouragement and campaigning to keep the Roosevelt name in the public mind helped Franklin make a comeback in 1928, when he was elected governor of New York. It was she who had encouraged him to accept the nomination, even though she was unsure what effect his return to public life would have on her new-found independence. She had by then emerged as a political force in her own right, and some of the hats she wore were those of columnist, public activist, and associate principal of the Todhunter School for Girls. In deference to her husband's governorship, she resigned her official post as editor of the *Women's Democratic News* and turned down several public speaking engagements.

Presidency and First Ladyship

Eleanor soon found out that Franklin was being urged to run for the presidency. The news plunged her into a depression. Her entire family was thrust into the national spotlight, and she saw the White House as a restrictive environment which would reduce her to a ceremonial figure by the formidable weight of tradition. After Franklin was elected, she again gave up cherished activities, such as teaching and making radio broadcasts, to fulfill the expectations of propriety placed on a First Lady.

By 1933, when Franklin Roosevelt assumed the presidency, the United States was in the throes of the Great Depression. The sense of optimism that took hold of the millions of struggling Americans as they welcomed a new Chief Executive ushered in, as Roosevelt promised, "a new deal for the American people." Social Security had been nonexistent until that time. The administration's plan for government reg-

Eleanor Roosevelt guest-hosts 1930's radio program Hobby Lobby. *(Archive Photos)*

ulation of the economy under New Deal policies included reforms in industry, labor, housing, finance, and agriculture.

These issues had all been incubated during Roosevelt's terms as governor of New York. Then, Eleanor's observations and social activism had influenced her husband's policies. Now, as First Lady, she assertively sought a New Deal for women. At her press conferences, she allowed only women reporters. The number of stories on her in *The New York Times* during her first year in the White House was an astonishing 320. The act of permitting only women to cover her press conferences helped launch the careers of many women journalists and, because Eleanor was so newsworthy, ex-

panded the opportunities for women journalists beyond simply the society pages. There was another consequence of her press conferences: Eleanor's alliances with these grateful reporters assured the First Lady of positive press coverage at their hands.

The woman who would become known as "Eleanor Everywhere" traveled more widely than any former serving First Lady, often by herself and often tied to quasi-official government business. Claiming that her husband needed her as his eyes and ears, hands and feet, she became the most ubiquitous First Lady in history. Eleanor's claim was not entirely true: Franklin was able to leave the White House. Despite his being wheelchair-bound, he was one of the great campaigners of the twentieth century. Some of his most famous speeches were delivered in Boston, Detroit, Chicago, and other bastions of the Democratic Party. Meanwhile, Eleanor hurtled around the country, inspecting everything from prisons to coal mines, speaking in Boston one night and Des Moines the next and Denver the next.

From her notes of these travels, she deluged her husband with reports and requests. She later wrote, "I think I sometimes acted as a spur, even though the spurring was not always wanted or welcome." Historian Geoff Ward said, "She kept at him on issues which he might have, in rush of business, wanted to overlook. He never lost his affection, or his wish to do what he should do because she wanted him to do it."

Eleanor later wrote:

Very often he would bait me into giving an opinion by stating as his own a point of view with which he knew I would disagree. I remember one occasion, I became extremely vehement and irritated. The next day to my complete surprise he calmly stated as his own the arguments that I had given him!

Nonetheless, some have argued that Eleanor traveled so many miles because she herself did not always feel welcome in the White House, or any house, with her husband. Moreover, she felt free to differ with her husband's positions on a wide range of issues. Maintaining that degree of independence from the White House, she kept active in her own endeavors. A circle of close female friends—most of them social activists like Eleanor—supported her throughout her public career.

In the 1920's, Eleanor had established a network of activist women inside the Democratic Party, one of whom was a dynamic social worker named Molly Dewson. Eleanor appointed Dewson as head of the Women's Division of the Democratic Party. Six weeks after

Franklin was inaugurated, Dewson sent Eleanor a seven-page letter listing the names and qualifications of ten women to be considered for jobs. In Roosevelt's first term, more than one hundred women were appointed to jobs which ranged from employees of the National Aeronautics Board to the secretary of labor, Frances Perkins, the first woman to hold a cabinet post. The First Lady compiled a list of women in executive positions in the government and regularly invited them to receptions and dinners. She also played a key part in opening up lesser jobs for women in various federal departments. In the U.S. Post Office Department alone, one historian credits Eleanor with the hiring of four thousand women.

Eleanor championed a host of human rights causes, from women's rights to civil rights to alleviating the plight of the poor. No one expected such candor and activism from a politician's wife in the 1930's. She pursued her advocacy of human rights with a mix of political initiatives, editorials, and other writings as well as the example of her own life. She spoke her mind and talked freely to reporters. In 1936, she began writing her newspaper column titled "My Day," which was published six days a week until 1962. Most of her positions on human rights issues were ahead of their time, and she was one of the first prominent public figures to embrace such a diversity of issues.

Arguably the most forceful civil rights advocate to serve as First Lady, Eleanor spoke out on a number of issues relating to race and lobbied her husband and politicians to promote a civil rights agenda. She fought for an antilynching law, promoted the hiring of blacks both in the White House and in government jobs, and was active in the National Association for the Advancement of Colored People and the National Urban League. She supported Howard University, the nation's foremost black university, and befriended prominent black leaders such as educator Mary McLeod Bethune, whom Franklin made director of the Division of Negro Affairs.

Marian Anderson at the Lincoln Memorial

In 1939, Constitution Hall in Washington, D.C., was sought as a concert venue on behalf of Marian Anderson, the famed contralto from Philadelphia who had been acclaimed throughout her tours of Europe and South America. She was the third-highest box office draw in the United States at that time. The Daughters of the American Revolution (DAR), which owned the hall, refused to accommodate the singer, who was black.

At the time Eleanor Roosevelt, whose ancestors had fought in the revolution, belonged to the DAR. She resigned her membership in protest over the rebuff. "By then," said Nina Gibson, Eleanor's granddaughter, "she had the self-confidence and the strength to stand alone because she knew, in the depths of her soul, that this was wrong." In part, Eleanor's letter of resignation said:

> ...I am in complete disagreement with the attitude taken in refusing Constitution Hall to a great artist. You have set an example which seems to me unfortunate, and I feel obliged to send in to you my resignation. You had an opportunity to lead in an enlightened way and it seems to me that your organization has failed. I realize that many people will not agree with me, but feeling as I do this seems to me the only proper procedure to follow.

The First Lady's action increased the publicity surrounding the incident. Eleanor then helped to arrange a free concert on the steps of the Lincoln Memorial. The event brought attention to both the singer's tremendous talent and the reality of segregation in the capital of the United States. Anderson had the Mall of Washington as her auditorium as seventy-five thousand people of all races gathered for the performance, which took place on April 9, 1939. It was Easter Sunday. Millions listened on their radios. "My country 'tis of thee, sweet land of liberty..." were the opening lyrics she sang.

Eleanor had explained her thinking in her syndicated newspaper column, "My Day," in which she shared her public and private life with millions of readers. The column also served as a forum for her views on social and political issues. Without mentioning the singer in her February 27, 1939, column she wrote:

> ...if you belong to an organization and disapprove of an action which is typical of a policy, should you resign or is it better to work for a changed point of view within the organization? In the past, when I was able to work actively in any organization to which I belong, I have usually stayed until I had at least made a fight and been defeated.... But in this case, I belong to an organization in which I can do no active work. They have taken an action which has been widely talked of in the press. To remain a member implies approval of that action, and therefore I am resigning.

In 1943 the DAR invited Anderson to perform at Constitution Hall for a war relief concert. Both black and white concertgoers attended the event.

During World War II, Eleanor equated the fascism of Europe to the ugly segregation found at home in the American South. Such a position was highly controversial and perhaps the boldest ever taken by a First Lady. It earned Eleanor some of the most brutal criticism she would experience in her life. Newspapers from around the country attacked her comments.

Neither the attacks nor the political fallout that some advisers feared would harm her husband's presidency slowed Eleanor's commitment. To the regular charge that she inappropriately wielded political power, she regularly issued disclaimers to possessing any political clout. Yet, virtually every insider in the Roosevelt White House testified to Eleanor's often relentless attempts to influence her husband. Cabinet officers and other advisers expressed extreme irritation at her many intrusions into their jurisdictions. From Eleanor's legions of conservative enemies came a barrage of denunciation of her progressive causes that portrayed her as a walking, talking menace to the American way of life.

Both Roosevelts would have been happy to leave the White House in 1941. Under ordinary circumstances, Franklin might not have been nominated for an unprecedented third term as president in 1940. "Serious minded people," wrote Eleanor, "were worried about the war" that had erupted in Europe the year before, however. Despite Franklin's "weariness that had already begun, and the desire to be at home," she said, he felt "the desire to see and to have a hand in the affairs of the world during that critical period."

The 1940 Democratic convention demonstrated the standing that Eleanor had attained. In the president's absence, Mrs. Roosevelt's presence was deemed necessary to garner support for Henry Wallace as vice president. Never before had a First Lady addressed a political convention. Eleanor had determined her speech would be brief. As she strode toward the podium, she was struck by how the unruly delegates quieted. She explained to them they had a duty in making the president's job easier by letting him have the running mate he wanted. "You will have to rise above considerations which are narrow and partisan," she told them. Her remarks were wildly cheered—and the delegations agreed to the president's choice of vice president. It was considered a miracle by some.

Roosevelt and Wallace were elected in 1940; the following year the United States entered World War II. In 1943, Franklin sent Eleanor on a tour of the South Pacific islands, where she visited some 400,000 G.I.'s. Admiral William F. Halsey, Jr., reported that in the hospitals, "She went into every ward, stopped at every bed and spoke to every patient. She walked for miles, and she saw patients who were grievously and gruesomely wounded. But I marveled most at their expressions as she leaned over them. It was a sight I will never forget." Upon her return, Eleanor wrote warm notes to the family of each serviceman with whom she had visited.

She kept up her efforts throughout the long years of the war. Her popularity soared. Eleanor, however, had in her husband a partner who was not always a ready source of support. On one occasion Franklin hurt her deeply when she entered his study, where he had been relaxing before dinner, and handed him a stack of briefs. Annoyed, he shook his head and tossed the papers to their daughter, Anna. "Here, Sis, *you* take care of these tomorrow," he said.

Eleanor's energy was so boundless, she failed to recognize how tired her husband had become. By the end of Franklin's third term, the war in Europe was nearly won. The success of his campaign for president in 1944 would allow him to direct victory in the Pacific as well, she was sure. Early into that fourth term, Eleanor was busy as ever on April 12, 1945, the day her husband's secretaries summoned her to the White House. There they told her that Franklin had died of a brain hemorrhage in Warm Springs, Georgia.

She sent for Vice President Harry S. Truman. When she gave him the news, his eyes filled with tears and, after a moment, he asked Eleanor if there was anything he could do for her. She turned the question away from herself, asking: "Is there anything we can do for you? For you are the one in trouble now."

During the train trip from Georgia to Washington with Franklin's coffin, Eleanor did not sleep. Looking out at the countryside Franklin had loved, she saw the respectful, sorrowful faces of people who had come in crowds to the railroad stations to pay tribute. "My husband and I had come through the years with an acceptance of each other's faults and foibles, warm affection and agreement on essential values," she wrote. "We depended on each other." Now she was alone. Eleanor would live for seventeen more years.

By May, 1945, one month after Franklin's death, Germany surrendered to the Allied forces. By August the war was over. In 1946 Eleanor was appointed by President Truman as a delegate to the organizational meeting in London for the United Nations General Assembly. She was chairwoman of the United Nations Commission that negotiated and drafted the Universal Declaration of Human Rights, which was unanimously adopted by the General Assembly in 1948. The document reflects her life's work for the cause of human rights.

She traveled widely, continued to support the Democratic Party, and campaigned for Democratic candidates. She cofounded the liberal group Americans for Democratic Action, had her own television discussion show, continued her newspaper column, and wrote many books, including her autobiography, originally published in three volumes. Eleanor died in 1962 at age seventy-eight.

Legacy

What was unique about Eleanor Roosevelt was the scope and variety of the causes and issues she embraced and the tenacity with which she pursued them, not only with her husband and his administration but with her own network and contacts. Eleanor worked tirelessly to promote an impressive array of issues, such as unemployment insurance, social security, civil rights, women's rights, and trade unions. Throughout her political life, three projects were of particular interest to her, each of which also helped her cope with the confinement of being a public figure: She taught government and English literature at the Todhunter School, invested herself in the Val-Kill factory, and maintained a relationship with the Democratic Women's Committee.

She was the longest serving First Lady in U.S. history. More importantly, she had what she called "this horrible sense of obligation which was bred in me, I couldn't help it." Nor could she help being her husband's sometimes nagging conscience. He had used her as his eyes and ears, and she reported to him what had to be done, whether he wanted to hear it or not.

Whenever it was suggested that she run for public office, Eleanor declined, knowing that she would not have been as effective if she had to worry about politics. The Roosevelts served during times of crisis: the Great Depression and World War II. Eleanor's relationship with her husband not only stands as one of the most remarkable in American history, it had considerable effect upon its course. It was a partnership between a president who had the power but had to consider political repercussions and a First Lady who had a heart and did not have to answer to the electorate.

Her achievements have to be assessed against her limitations in the private role of loving counselor, companion, protector—in a word, wife. Yet Eleanor Roosevelt's life became an inspiration to women everywhere, and she remains a giant figure in U.S. history. She had wanted to make her father proud of her, and she accomplished more than he could have imagined.

Suggested Readings

Beasley, Maurine H., et al., eds. *The Eleanor Roosevelt Encyclopedia.* Westport, Conn.: Greenwood Press, 2001. Alphabetized entries include people, causes, and issues relating to Eleanor Roosevelt. With photographs.

Collier, Peter, with David Horowitz. *The Roosevelts: An American Saga.* New York: Simon & Schuster, 1994. Filled with drama and anecdotes, it is a soaring tale of triumph over heartbreak and frailty.

Cook, Blanche Wiesen. *Eleanor Roosevelt.* 2 vols. New York: Viking, 1992-1999. The two volumes cover Eleanor Roosevelt's background, activities, and relationships through 1938. Skillfully and engagingly written.

Roosevelt, Eleanor. *The Autobiography of Eleanor Roosevelt.* 1961. Reprint. New York: Da Capo Press, 1992. The author's compelling prose not only tells her own life story but teaches a history lesson of the late nineteenth and early twentieth centuries.

Roosevelt, Elliott, and James Brough. *Mother R: Eleanor Roosevelt's Untold Story.* New York: G. P. Putnam and Sons, 1977. A history of a husband and wife, who, in spite of difficulties, lived as man and wife for more than forty years.

Ward, Geoffrey C. *Before the Trumpet: Young Franklin Roosevelt, 1882-1905.* New York: Harper and Row, 1985. A richly detailed family epic, played out on two continents and full of surprises.

Patricia Foltz Warren

Bess Truman

Elizabeth Virginia Wallace Truman

Born: February 13, 1885
      Independence, Missouri
Died: October 18, 1982
      Independence, Missouri

President: Harry S. Truman
      1945-1953

Overview: Bess Truman became First Lady upon the sudden death of Franklin D. Roosevelt in April, 1945. She was a private person who avoided reporters and felt uncomfortable in the Washington, D.C., political arena. Behind the scenes, however, she was a shrewd and trusted adviser to her husband, and she played a key role in President Harry S. Truman's most important political decisions.

Early Life

Elizabeth Virginia Wallace was born on February 13, 1885, in Independence, Missouri, the oldest child of Margaret (Madge) Gates Wallace and David Wallace. Bess was both an excellent student and an accomplished athlete in high school. She was considered to be the best tennis player in Independence—male or female—as well as an excellent ice skater and horseback rider.

When she was eighteen years old, Bess's life was shattered by the violent death of her father. He was one of the most popular men in town, but his life was deeply troubled. Wallace held a succession of minor political patronage positions that never produced enough income to support his extravagant wife and their five children. Becoming increasingly depressed, Wallace began drinking heavily. On the morning of June 17, 1903, forty-three-year-old David

Bess Truman. *(Library of Congress)*

Wallace committed suicide by shooting himself with a revolver. His death by his own hand profoundly influenced Bess for the rest of her life; after her father's death she became much more reserved, private, and pessimistic.

Marriage and Family

Bess first met Harry S. Truman in 1890, when he was six years old and she was five. Harry was absolutely infatuated with her, but she considered him to be just a friend. In 1906 they began seeing each other more frequently. Bess's mother strongly disapproved of the growing relationship, but Harry was determined to win Bess's hand in marriage. In June, 1911, he finally summoned up the courage to propose, but she refused. Bess knew that her mother was almost totally dependent upon her, which had discouraged other suitors but not Harry. Afraid that he would take Bess away from her, Mrs. Wallace told her daughter, "You don't want to marry that farmer boy, he's not going to make it anywhere." Finally, in 1917, after seven years of courtship and just before Truman joined the Army and was to be shipped overseas, Bess accepted his proposal. She wanted to get married at once, but now Harry refused, telling her that she must not tie herself to a man who might come home a cripple or not at all.

Harry returned safely from World War I, and on June 28, 1919, they were married. They

Harry S. Truman and Bess Wallace on their wedding day, June 28, 1919. From left: Louise Wells, Ted Marks, Truman, Frank Wallace, Bess Wallace, and Helen Wallace. *(AP/Wide World Photos)*

moved in with her mother at 219 North Delaware Street in Independence. Harry and a war buddy, Eddie Jacobson, opened a men's haberdashery in Kansas City, but it went bankrupt in 1921. Unemployed and in debt, he decided to try his hand at politics, accepting the support of the powerful Pendergast family, a Kansas City political machine, much to the distaste of Bess. She always believed that her father's lack of success in politics had much to do with his depression, alcoholism, and suicide, and she re-

Harry S. Truman

In 1943, Harry S. Truman was quite content being a U.S. senator. One year before the Democratic National Convention would meet to nominate President Franklin D. Roosevelt for an unprecedented fourth term, there was growing speculation that the president's closest political advisers were pressuring Roosevelt to replace his current vice president, Henry Wallace. Behind closed doors, the Democratic Party bosses were searching for a "safe" candidate, one who would satisfy both the conservative and liberal wings of the party. Many of them were aware that the president's health was declining and that he would probably not live to complete a fourth term. They realized that the man nominated to run with Roosevelt in 1944 would in all probability be the next president.

To Truman's surprise, his name was among the top contenders for the position. Among those being considered, he emerged as a compromise candidate. He had established a reputation as an honest, hard-working senator and a loyal supporter of Roosevelt's New Deal (although the two men barely knew each other), and he was popular with labor unions. Many Democrats simply felt that Truman was the candidate who would do the party's presidential ticket the least harm—hardly a rousing endorsement.

Roosevelt won a fourth term in November of 1944, but, as feared, he did not live very long. When he died on April 12, 1945, Truman had been vice president for only eighty-two days. World War II was coming to an end, and now Truman had inherited the awesome decision of whether to unleash the atomic bomb to hasten the end of the war. The bombs fell in August, 1945, and after the war he would face many more difficult decisions as he struggled to stabilize the postwar American economy and contain the spread of communism abroad. In 1950 Truman authorized the use of U.S. troops in Korea, and in another controversial decision, he fired the popular General Douglas MacArthur, commander of the American forces in Korea, because, he said, "He wouldn't respect the authority of the president."

Truman was a plain-spoken man from the American heartland who rose through the ranks of roughhouse Missouri politics to the U.S. Senate, the vice presidency, and the presidency. In looking back over his seven difficult years as president, he told the American people: "When Franklin Roosevelt died, I felt there must be a million men better qualified than I to take up the presidential task. But the work was mine to do, and I had to do it. And I have tried to give it everything that was in me."

membered the publicity and public humiliation of her family by the press following his death. Bess had no desire to be a politician's wife.

Truman was elected county judge of the eastern district of Jackson County in 1922, but he was defeated in 1924. This setback placed a considerable strain on their marriage, as Margaret Truman, their only child, was born at home on February 17, 1924. In 1926, after a few unsuccessful business ventures, the Pendergast machine agreed to support Harry for presiding judge of the county court. Truman easily

won the election. Quietly and behind the scenes, Bess worked to aid her husband, but she kept a low profile in public. Her husband and daughter were her top priorities; she had no desire for public attention or acclaim.

Truman earned respect as a county judge, and soon there was talk of him as a candidate for governor of Missouri. He was, however, passed over for the nomination and was certain his political career was over. Missouri political boss Tom Pendergast did have plans for Harry, though: a run for the U.S. Congress.

Bess did not approve. Concerned about her ailing mother, she was not eager to leave Missouri for Washington, D.C. Meanwhile, Pendergast had changed his mind and picked another candidate. Harry was dejected, but a few weeks later he received some astonishing news: Pendergast had chosen him to run for the U.S. Senate.

Bess supported her husband's decision to accept the nomination but was not certain she could endure the personal and political attacks sure to come their way. Truman waged a relentless campaign across the state of Missouri, often speaking as many as sixteen times in a single day. She would frequently appear with him on the platform but never said a word on his behalf. Political speeches, she told Harry, were not her style. He won an overwhelming victory in the November, 1934, election, and in the following January, Harry and Bess, along with their ten-year-old daughter and Mother Wallace, boarded a train for Washington. Bess enrolled Margaret in Gunston Hall, a private school for young girls, where she would spend the school year and then return home for the summer.

Whenever they could, Bess and Margaret stayed in Independence. Harry missed them, but he understood Bess's homesickness. Although she preferred to stay home as long as possible, she realized that he was relying on her more and more. Senator Truman called his wife a genius at handling reporters, and she became his favorite speechwriter. When Bess was away from Washington, Harry constantly kept her informed of events in the Senate, and she, in turn, was his eyes and ears at home. He often used his letters to her as an opportunity to clarify his thoughts.

By Truman's second term, Bess had become such an important partner—and their finances were so low—that he put her on the Senate payroll as his secretary. As his work on the Truman Committee required frequent travel to visit arms factories and military installations, Bess became more involved in the daily operation of the office. Truman was quite content being a senator, but by the summer of 1943, rumors about his possible vice presidential candidacy began to circulate. "I don't want to be the vice president," he said, "the vice president simply presides over the Senate and sits around hoping for a funeral…. It is a very high office which consists entirely of honor and I don't have any ambition to hold an office like that. And besides," he added, "the Madam doesn't want me to do it."

Presidency and First Ladyship

Privately, many of the Democratic Party bosses knew President Franklin D. Roosevelt was dying and their choice for vice president would very likely become Roosevelt's successor. Truman knew perfectly well what his nomination meant. A reporter remarked to him that as vice president he might "succeed to the throne." Truman replied, "Hell, I don't want to be president." He was concerned about Bess and Margaret's privacy, and he knew the fact that his wife was on his Senate office payroll would surely surface. Additionally, Bess very much feared that her father's suicide, which had so strongly affected her as a young girl, would become public.

On the convention floor, the momentum was building for a Truman vice presidential nomination, although Harry continued to insist that he was not interested in the job. On the afternoon of July 19, 1944, he was summoned to a hotel room where the party bosses were waiting. They had Roosevelt on the phone, who said, "You tell the senator that if he wants to break up the Democratic Party in the middle of the war, that's his responsibility." A stunned Truman replied, "Well, if that's the situation, I'll have to say yes."

Bess was very unhappy about the sudden turn of events. After delivering his brief acceptance speech, Truman and his wife made their way to a waiting car through a crush of reporters and photographers. As they got into the car,

Bess glared at Harry and asked, "Are we going to have to go through this for the rest of our lives?"

Truman tirelessly campaigned for Roosevelt in 1944, traveling thousands of miles around the country. Throughout most of the campaign, Bess had remained so obscure that reporters knew virtually nothing about her. At one point her job as Truman's Senate secretary was made an issue, but Truman vigorously defended his wife, telling the press that it was no secret Bess was on the Senate payroll. "She's a clerk in my office and does much of my clerical work," he said. "I need her here and that's the reason I've got her there. I never make a report or deliver a speech without her editing it. . . . There's nothing secret about it." This would be the only time during the campaign that the press would scrutinize Bess. To the Trumans' immense relief, nothing was said about the death of her father.

On April 12, 1945, at the beginning of his fourth term as president, Roosevelt died of a massive brain hemorrhage. That evening, Harry S. Truman took the oath of office as the thirty-third president of the United States. Bess and Margaret stood next to him as he solemnly took the oath. Later Bess recounted that she spent most of the night thinking about how her and Harry's life would be changed. "I was very apprehensive," she admitted. "The country was used to Eleanor Roosevelt. I couldn't possibly be anything like her."

A few days later, the new First Lady held her first press conference which, she announced, would also be her last. A reporter asked, "Mrs. Truman, how are we ever going to get to know you?" She quickly replied, "You don't need to know me. I'm only the president's wife and the mother of his daughter."

During Harry's first years as president, Bess held no press conferences, made few public appearances, and expressed few personal opinions. "People don't warm up to her easily," one article said. "[They] respect her integrity and recognize her determination to measure up to

A Missed Opportunity

In her first autumn in the White House, Bess Truman uncharacteristically became entangled in controversy.

In October of 1945, the Daughters of the American Revolution organization (DAR) wanted to give a tea in her honor in Constitution Hall. Seeing no reason not to accept, Bess thanked them for the invitation. It then came to light that Hazel Scott, one of the leading nightclub entertainers of the time and wife of New York Congressman Adam Clayton Powell, a prominent Democrat, wanted to give a concert in Constitution Hall but was turned down by the DAR because she was an African American. The day before Bess was to attend the tea, Powell sent her a telegram urging her not to attend. "I can assure you," he told her, "that no good will be accomplished by attending and much harm will be done."

Mrs. Truman wired back: "May I call your attention to the fact that the invitation was extended and accepted prior to the unfortunate controversy which has arisen. . . . In my opinion, my acceptance of the hospitality is not related to the merits of the issue which has since arisen. I deplore any action which denies artistic talent an opportunity to express itself because of prejudice against race origin."

Bess attended the tea, and Powell called her the "last lady." From that day until Harry Truman left office, Powell was never invited to the White House, even for the annual receptions for members of Congress.

the requirements of her position, but they do not enthuse about her."

In private, Bess's Washington friends found her warm and kind, and they were extremely fond of her. She was said to be considerate of others, a gracious hostess, and an entertaining conversationalist, although she almost never discussed public affairs. Old friends from Independence or members of the White House staff who saw her on an almost daily basis would speak warmly of her.

The newspaperwomen who had the run of the White House during Eleanor Roosevelt's regime were incredulous and enraged at Bess's public silence. The First Lady flatly refused to be interviewed. Finally, after months of trying, Washington women reporters persuaded Mrs. Truman to answer a series of written questions in 1947. Her extremely brief, written, penciled replies were read aloud by two White House secretaries.

Longtime White House servant J. B. West, who served in the Truman White House, said, "Bess guarded her privacy like a precious jewel, yet within that privacy played a prominent role far exceeding what any but a few suspected. She did advise Truman on decisions. And he listened to her." To the American public, though, Bess remained a mystery. It would take some time for her to warm up to the press and the public.

Bess's role in the hard-fought presidential campaign of 1948 was considerable. Harry called her his "chief adviser," and she was. Virtually every decision he made was discussed with her. "She was a one-woman Gallup poll and audience-reaction tester," *Newsweek* magazine reported, "keeping a sharp watch on the crowds which listened to her husband's oratory. She was also the careful censor of the President's occasional lapses into humorous over-exuberance." She accompanied her husband by train on the famous whistle-stop campaign across the country. Newsmen told of seeing her sitting at a window of the train, busily blue-penciling Harry's speeches. At every stop the routine was the same: They would appear together on the rear platform of their private car, Harry would deliver a few words and then introduce Bess as "the boss," and then Margaret as "the boss's boss." This homespun display of family solidarity helped to portray Truman as a decent and devoted family man to the small-town crowds of the American heartland and was considered by many to be a decisive factor in Truman's election victory in 1948.

The final two years of Truman's administration, as the Korean War raged, were the most difficult of his entire presidency. Yet early in 1952, he was still toying with the idea of running for another term. Bess feared that Harry could not survive another four years as president, and she did not think that she could survive either. She reminded him that he would be seventy-three years old at the end of another term. On March 29, 1952, Truman announced to the American people what most had already suspected: He would not be a candidate for president. Bess was happy and relieved.

Legacy
After the inauguration of President Dwight D. Eisenhower, Bess and Harry returned to Missouri to live much as they had before they had left for Washington—as just ordinary citizens. Harry S. Truman died on December 26, 1972, at the age of eighty-eight. Bess continued to live in their Independence home for another ten years. She died on October 18, 1982, at age ninety-seven.

Unlike Eleanor Roosevelt, who preceded her, Bess preferred to remain in the background. She saw her most important role as being the president's sounding board and confidante.

Suggested Readings
Ferrell, Robert H. *Dear Bess*. New York: W. W. Norton, 1983. A revealing and fascinating glimpse of Bess and Harry Truman's relationship, as revealed through his personal letters.

McCullough, David. *Truman*. New York: Simon & Schuster, 1992. The Pulitzer Prize-winning biography of Harry S. Truman's life and times.

Robbins, Jhan. *Bess and Harry: An American Love Story*. New York: G. P. Putnam's Sons, 1980. A sentimental narrative of the Trumans' long life together.

Truman, Harry S. *Memoirs*. 2 vols. Garden City, N.Y.: Doubleday, 1955-1956. Truman's official memoirs of his presidential years.

Truman, Margaret. *Bess W. Truman*. New York: Macmillan, 1986. A detailed and intimate portrait of Bess, written by her daughter.

_____. *Souvenir: Margaret Truman's Own Story*. New York: McGraw-Hill, 1956. Margaret Truman's account of growing up as the president's daughter.

Raymond Frey

Mamie Eisenhower

Mamie Geneva Doud Eisenhower

Born: November 14, 1896
    Boone, Iowa
Died: November 1, 1979
    Washington, D.C.

President: Dwight D. Eisenhower,
    1953-1961

Overview: The last First Lady born in the nineteenth century was Mamie Doud Eisenhower, wife of Dwight D. "Ike" Eisenhower, the thirty-fourth president of the United States. A thoroughly private person who lacked a policy agenda, and thus avoided taking public stands on prominent issues of the day, she supported her husband by performing the considerable range of social duties expected of a First Lady.

Early Life

A native of Boone, Iowa, Mamie was born during the Victorian era, coinciding with the lengthy reign of Britain's Queen Victoria (1837-1901). The behavior of conventional Western society during the Victorian age has been described as reserved and prim, with many dictates as to what was proper conduct for both men and women. Born in 1896, Mamie was one of four daughters of a wealthy businessman.

She spent her early childhood in small towns in Iowa, later moving to Denver, Colorado, and spending many winters in the family's winter home in San Antonio, Texas. She lacked extensive formal education, completing her schooling by attending Miss Walcott's Fashionable School in Colorado. She declined her father's offer to send her to college. In October, 1915, during a visit to San Antonio, Mamie met an Army lieutenant assigned to nearby

Mamie Eisenhower. *(Library of Congress)*

Fort Sam Houston, named Dwight D. Eisenhower, called Ike. They became engaged the following Valentine's Day and were married in Denver on July 1, 1916.

Marriage and Family

Mamie's long life of public service began upon her marriage to Ike. The Army life provided a striking contrast to the comfortable lifestyle to which she had been accustomed. As the wife of a junior officer in the Army, Mamie had to live on an annual income that was a fraction of what her father had earned. Moreover, she had to adapt to the nomadic life associated with military service. During her husband's lengthy Army career, the Eisenhowers relocated twenty-five times; seven of those moves came within one year. On a few occasions her husband was assigned to overseas posts, where she either could not or did not want to accompany him. However, she did go with him to Manila, Philippines, from 1936 to 1939. Ike and Mamie's longest separation was during World War II, when she saw him only once between 1942 and 1945.

Throughout these periods of separation, she sought ways to maintain close ties among her husband, herself, and their children. Their first son, Doud Dwight, lived from 1917 to 1921, when he died of scarlet fever. Their second son, John Sheldon Doud, was born in 1922. Operating on a limited budget and writing her husband lengthy letters every day during extended periods of separation, Mamie steadfastly held together her family and her marriage.

The Eisenhowers bought their first house in 1950—thirty-four years after they were married—in Gettysburg, Pennsylvania. It is not surprising, then, that Mamie viewed the prospect of living for several years in one place, the White House, as comforting in contrast to her often nomadic life as a dutiful Army spouse. By this time Ike had attained the rank of general, and he commanded Operation Overlord, the

1944 D day invasion of Europe across the English Channel. The operation's success made him a national hero; it was he who directed the liberation of Europe during World War II. In 1951 he went to France to assume command of the newly formed North Atlantic Treaty Organization (NATO), returning to the United States the following year to run for president.

Although Mamie apparently enjoyed accompanying her husband on campaign trips, she never wanted to give a speech herself. She enjoyed being introduced and waving to the crowds, viewing her public role in campaigns as that of a supportive wife, appearing at her husband's side, frequently smiling, and applauding his comments along with the crowd. However, during the 1952 presidential campaign, Republican strategists scheduled extensive appearances for her with her husband to draw a stark contrast with his opponent, the Democratic nominee Adlai Stevenson, who had recently been divorced.

Lengthy campaigning did not help Mamie's persistent health problems, which were exacerbated by extensive travel. Her preferred mode of travel was either train or automobile. Although she did travel by aircraft, her lifelong struggle with Ménière's syndrome made flying a difficult task at best. Lightheadedness, caused by a carotid sinus condition when a vein would press against the inner ear, often caused her to stagger in public, which spurred rumors that she had a drinking problem. Although, like many in her generation, she drank alcohol on social occasions, there is no evidence that she had a problem with alcohol consumption. She did, reportedly, suffer from claustrophobia. Because of these recurring health issues, she made fewer public appearances during Eisenhower's second term and declined to accompany the president on major overseas trips in both 1959 and 1960.

The Eisenhowers had a long and happy marriage which survived the difficulties associated with Ike's career as an Army officer: long

Dwight D. Eisenhower

Dwight David ("Ike") Eisenhower was president of the United States during the period following World War II, which was a time of unparalleled American dominance. In the wake of war, the United States was unquestionably the most powerful industrial and military power in the world. A West Point graduate and career Army officer, Eisenhower entered the war as a major and rose through the ranks to command Allied forces during the Normandy invasion (June 6, 1944) and the victory over German dictator Adolf Hitler's forces throughout Western Europe. Eisenhower, having attained the rank of five-star general, capped his career as Army chief of staff and commander of North Atlantic Treaty Organization (NATO) forces in Europe.

Ironically, Eisenhower entered the White House after a successful campaign as a "peace" candidate seeking to end American involvement in the Korean War raging in Asia (1950-1953). He was successful in negotiating an armed truce with North Korean and Chinese forces along a demilitarized zone near where the hostilities had begun. Eisenhower spent much of the remaining years of his presidency dealing with such Cold War issues as building alliances with Western Europe through NATO and working with nations of Southeast Asia through the Southeast Asia Treaty Organization. In addition, crises such as those at the Suez Canal in 1957, in Lebanon in 1958, in Berlin as the Soviet Union began the blockade, and the 1956 revolution in Cuba appeared throughout his presidency.

Eisenhower's most trying moment in foreign affairs likely came in May, 1960, when Soviet forces shot down an American U-2 spy plane flying deep within Soviet Union territory. After initially denying surveillance efforts, Eisenhower was forced to recant his statement when the Soviets publicly displayed the U-2 pilot, Francis Gary Powers.

Eisenhower's domestic presidency was known for its lack of breadth, particularly when measured against the efforts of his predecessors Franklin D. Roosevelt and Harry S. Truman. One burgeoning issue found throughout Eisenhower's presidency was the Civil Rights Movement. Civil rights leaders won a stunning victory in the 1954 Supreme Court verdict in *Brown v. Board of Education of Topeka, Kansas*. A critical factor in the outcome of the case was the role played by Earl Warren, the chief justice of the United States, whom Eisenhower had nominated. The case was the first of a series of important civil rights verdicts rendered by the Warren court. In 1957 the president sent federal troops to Central High School in Little Rock, Arkansas, to enforce a racial integration order. He did so over the strong objections of both a majority in the Arkansas legislature and Governor Orval Faubus.

Eisenhower, after winning presidential elections in 1952 and 1956 by comfortable margins over former Illinois governor Adlai Stevenson, ended his political career with a farewell address warning against the dangers to American society stemming from what he termed a military industrial complex composed of an array of weapons manufacturers and professional military officers.

workdays, frequent household moves, and the sometime requirement of living in cramped, uncomfortable, and even harsh conditions. While such factors would severely strain any marriage, the Eisenhowers overcame occasional disagreements triggered by Ike's career demands and arrived at a mutually acceptable solution. In sum, many of the parameters of their relationship were defined by their goal of meeting the demands of his military career.

Substantial evidence suggests that they had a strong marriage. For example, each of them wrote lengthy and frequent letters to the other when they were apart as well as corresponding

President and Mrs. Eisenhower help to open a First Ladies' inaugural gown exhibit at the Smithsonian Institution, May, 1955. *(Library of Congress)*

with other family members. Many of the surviving letters suggest a close relationship, marked by occasional, but not powerful, disagreements. A rumored affair between Ike and his driver-secretary Kay Summersby was vigorously denied by the general. Overall, the Eisenhowers' personal correspondence, coupled with subsequent accounts from friends and peers, shows that their solid relationship withstood career-based obstacles seldom encountered by their generational peers.

The Eisenhowers' other family relationships supported the strength of their marriage. The couple had a consistently closer relationship with the Doud family than with the Eisen-

howers, and they received nurture and some financial support from the Douds. Significantly, both of Mamie and Ike's sons were heartily loved and given a nurturing and supportive environment.

Presidency and First Ladyship

Unquestionably, Mamie enjoyed being First Lady, but she set her own terms in regard to the position. She viewed her role as First Lady as one of managing family matters and the social obligations of the president and supporting his responsibilities as chief of state.

Although it has been noted that no job exists to prepare anyone to become president of the

United States, few incoming First Ladies were better prepared for the impact of the office on their lifestyle than Mamie. Her lengthy experience as the wife of an Army officer—and particularly the years when her husband served at the highest levels—provided her with the necessary experience in planning and managing large, formal social gatherings. The breadth of her obligations had increased along with Ike's promotions in rank. Generals, particularly those assigned to major commands overseas, were frequently expected to entertain important military, economic, and political figures.

Helping Mamie develop her skills as the hostess for an important figure were her husband's overseas Army assignments, especially to the Philippines in 1936 as an aide to General Douglas MacArthur and in 1951, when Eisenhower was appointed supreme commander of NATO forces in Europe. In both instances, Mamie was put in charge of a large home that also served as the setting for the social events over which she presided, together with an ex-

tensive domestic staff. As her husband's career-related social obligations became progressively larger and more complex, Mamie became increasingly comfortable in giving orders to the staff, supervising the execution of those plans, and making immediate corrections if she thought them necessary.

The NATO assignment in particular provided her with extensive opportunities to plan and carry out large social events, attended by an array of important international guests. The couple lived in a fourteen-room villa at Marnes-la-Coquette, just outside Paris. She often was the hostess for gatherings of more than one hundred guests, including European royalty.

The Eisenhowers had been married more than thirty-five years upon arriving at the White House. Mamie had long before become comfortable with being married to a powerful man. She knew how to deal with those seeking to curry favor with her husband. She also had endured harsh criticism of her husband and

The Mamie Look

According to Susan Eisenhower in her book *Mrs. Ike*, Mamie Eisenhower had closets filled with clothes, and her name appeared more than once on the New York Dress Institute's list of best-dressed women. She was not, however, exempt from occasional criticism of her wardrobe. When, during her White House years, she was lambasted for wearing a flowered dress with a halter top, she responded, "I hate old-lady clothes and I shall never wear them." When the French press decried her lack of style in wearing American clothes, she said, "Imagine paying $800 or $900 for a dress! I'm perfectly happy with those little $17.95 numbers I order from New York newspaper ads."

Designer Arnold Scaasi came to be a fan of the First Lady, for whom he designed gowns which she wore to state dinners with the likes of Soviet premier Nikita Khrushchev and French statesman Charles de Gaulle. Susan Eisenhower quotes Scaasi as expressing surprise,

> . . . at how pretty Mrs. Eisenhower was. Photographs did not capture her exquisite coloring, her wonderful skin, or the remarkable figure she had for a woman in her early sixties. She was not photogenic. Her bangs sometimes looked rather strange in photographs, but in person they were very attractive and looked normal and perfectly right. . . . Mrs. Eisenhower loved pretty clothes—colorful clothes. They weren't "hard chic." She liked clothes that moved well . . . the dresses always had to have lots of movement.

herself from jealous or vengeful rivals. Mamie always had to guard both her public and private actions, to avoid saying or doing anything that could reflect poorly on her husband's career. Instead, she cultivated the art of maintaining a gracious appearance in the background.

On a personal level, she enjoyed living with her family in one location for the longest period of time since their wedding. Although Mamie and the president were the only full-time residents of the second floor of the White House, her mother, Elvira Carlson Doud, lived with them for a time. In addition, their son, John, and his family were frequent guests. The sights and sounds of their four grandchildren playing in the hallways and on the White House grounds were both comforting and uplifting for the president and the First Lady.

One noteworthy activity Mamie undertook as First Lady was to reclaim antique furnishings which had previously been used in the White House. She was particularly interested in acquiring furniture and china. Mamie established a reputation among the White House staff for being the lone person in charge. She was known as a forceful, yet fair, manager who paid great attention to the countless details of overseeing the operation of the White House.

Mamie was much more passive concerning public policy, eschewing politics and avoiding discussion of issues with her husband during their private time together. "It wasn't my business anyway—he was president and I wasn't," she explained to one interviewer. She completely avoided speaking in public or at news conferences and entered the Oval Office only four times during her husband's eight years in the presidency, and only after being invited to do so, she reported.

Aside from attending to personal family matters, Mamie devoted her time as First Lady to planning and carrying out the myriad social obligations expected of a chief of state. She planned each occasion, particularly those held in the White House, down to the smallest detail.

She carefully orchestrated all of the receptions, parties, state dinners, and other social gatherings in the White House. She was by now comfortable in dealing with the nuances of protocol as well as the boundless ego of the occasional public official.

Legacy

Although many incoming First Ladies have encountered difficulty in adjusting to life in the public eye, Mamie Eisenhower possessed several tools for dealing with the challenges. First, she had overcome many more trying times earlier in her marriage: The death of her first son left emotional scars which remained with her the rest of her life. In addition, as the wife of an Army officer, she moved repeatedly and lived in not only Army posts in western and southern parts of the United States but overseas in the Panama Canal zone and the Philippines. Moreover, after her husband became a senior officer during World War II, Mamie was separated from him for most of the remaining three years of the conflict. The White House was the most permanent address she had enjoyed since they were married in 1916.

Another strength Mamie brought with her to the White House was an apparent determination to create what later might have been called an image to support the position of her husband. On one dimension, she was passionately devoted to her family and provided the public with countless images of a caring wife, mother, and grandmother. She also sought to present a fitting picture of a president's wife. Mamie was regularly named to "best-dressed" lists of prominent Americans. Her favorite color was pink, which she wore regularly in a variety of ways. She also popularized bangs to the point that similar hairstyles were referred to as Mamie bangs.

Suggested Readings

Brandon, Dorothy. *Mamie Doud Eisenhower: A Portrait of a First Lady.* New York: Scribner's,

1954. Written while Mamie Esenhower was First Lady, by a contemporary.

David, Lester, and Irene David. *Ike and Mamie: The Story of the General and His Lady*. New York: World Publishing, 1978.

Eisenhower, Dwight D. *Letters to Mamie*. Edited by John S. D. Eisenhower. Garden City, N.J.: Doubleday, 1978. Dwight Eisenhower's letters to Mamie Eisenhower from abroad.

Eisenhower, Susan. *Mrs. Ike: Memories and Reflections on the Life of Mamie Eisenhower*. New York: Farrar, Straus and Giroux, 1996. This portrait of Mamie Eisenhower by her granddaughter contains many photographs.

Hatch, Alden. *Red Carpet for Mamie*. New York: Doubleday, 1978. With illustrations.

Henney, Elizabeth. "Presenting: Mamie." *The Washington Post*, August 2, 1942. Interesting for its contemporaneous view of the general's wife.

Robert Dewhirst

249

Jacqueline Kennedy

Jacqueline Lee Bouvier Kennedy

Born: July 28, 1929
    Southampton, New York
Died: May 19, 1994
    New York, New York

President: John F. Kennedy
    1961-1963

Overview: One of the United States' most compelling First Ladies, Jaqueline Bouvier Kennedy was also one of the most intriguing women of her time. Serving at the height of the Cold War, she and her husband, John F. Kennedy, dazzled the world. Uninterested in policy and ambivalent about her role, Jackie nevertheless played her part magnificently. In her renovation of the White House she demonstrated the importance of a First Lady having a proper project and positioned the presidential spouse as a key public relations partner in the media age.

Jacqueline Kennedy. *(Library of Congress)*

Early Life

Like Jack Kennedy, Jacqueline Bouvier was raised in a world of wealth and elegance that emphasized appearances over integrity. Born to John Vernon Bouvier III and Janet Norton Lee Bouvier in 1929, Jacqueline Lee was the oldest of two sisters. The Bouviers' marriage was an alliance between her father's social standing and her mother's newer money. Jackie's parents divorced when she was eleven.

Especially after her mother married the wealthy Hugh D. Auchincloss, Jackie lived amid great splendor yet somehow felt deprived. She was educated at Miss Porter's School for Girls, Vassar College, and spent a year at the Sorbonne before graduating from George Washington University. These schools drilled her in the fine points of gracious living and honed her considerable intelligence.

Jackie could be haughty (her classmates nicknamed her "Jacqueline Borgia"), but she could also be saucy, rebellious, and funny. In June, 1947, Jacqueline vowed in her senior yearbook "not to be a housewife," but she was thrilled when gossip columnist Igor Cassini named her "Queen Deb" of 1947. Cassini described the Vassar freshman as "a regal brunette who has classic features and the daintiness of Dresden porcelain." Jackie was flirtatious yet prim; a breathy and little-girlish way of talking masked her intelligence. She received her bachelor's degree in 1951, and the following year she was hired as the Washington *Times-Herald*'s "Inquiring Photographer."

Marriage and Family

Jackie met Jack Kennedy in 1951 at a Washington, D.C., dinner party. The thirty-four-year-old congressman invited twenty-year-old Jackie for a drink. Over the next two years, they had "a very spasmodic courtship," Jackie would recall. Jack spent half of each week in Massachusetts campaigning for the Senate. "He'd call me from some oyster bar up there, with a great clinking of coins, to ask me out to the movies the following Wednesday in Washington."

Jack was not about to woo Jackie, or anyone else, too ardently. "He's not the candy-and-flowers type," Jackie would say. Jack asked so many friends whether he should marry Jackie that one suggested he "put the matter before the Senate for a vote." If Jackie was moodier than Jack would have liked, she was at least cultured and intelligent. If Jack was less romantic than Jackie would have liked, he was at least successful and sober. He had money, she had class, and both were Catholic.

About fourteen hundred guests attended the Kennedys' wedding on September 12, 1953. This marriage was made in public. Jackie's private life would be public fodder for the rest of her days. However, the marriage itself was no fairy tale. In their first two years together,

Jackie had a miscarriage and Jack, suffering from Addison's disease, had two spinal operations. He missed the entire 1955 Senate session. "The Deb" demonstrated a gritty resilience. She changed the bandages on Jack's oozing wound, buoyed his spirits, and inspired him to write what became the Pulitzer Prize winning book *Profiles in Courage* (1956).

However, Jackie resented her husband's roving eye and single-minded ambition. The former career girl now dreamed of "a normal life with my husband coming home from work every day at five." Jackie ran Jack's errands, cooked his meals, and begged his secretary to "send" him home earlier.

In 1956 Jack dragged his pregnant wife to the Democratic National Convention, where he made an unsuccessful play for the vice presidential nod. Shortly thereafter, Jackie miscarried again. At the time, the senator was traveling in the Mediterranean.

The birth of their daughter, Caroline, in November, 1957, put an end to the rumors that the Kennedys' marriage was doomed. The next year Jack and Jackie, working as a team, appeared in almost two hundred cities, campaigning for the senator's reelection and for a Democratic Congress. They celebrated their fifth anniversary in Omaha, Nebraska, on the stump. Simply but elegantly dressed, with her trademark three strands of pearls, Jackie refused to give speeches in English but greeted ethnic communities in Spanish, Italian, and French. Staffers noted that when Jackie joined Jack, the crowds doubled.

Reporters also loved Jackie. Most media profiles treated this "lithe brunette with elfin charm" as an aristocratic flower blooming in the Democratic garden. What they failed to mention was that the "lovely senator's lady" was testy. Jackie was known to snap at reporters, aides, and even her husband. She moped in the limousine waiting for Jack to finish speaking, or read Proust in French as Jack waved madly to the crowd from his motorcade. Before one of their joint appearances, one aide reminded the senator to "turn to her with a gesture or a smile." Aides held Mrs. Kennedy's cigarette as she took furtive drags on it.

Jack's landslide reelection to the Senate in 1958 positioned him as a leading presidential contender. It also showed that his poised wife could lure votes; Jackie Kennedy highlighted Jack's most appealing features. Her society background brought class to his wealth, her glamour made him look cool but not cold, her continental ways added a touch of savoir faire to his image. Jackie's presence was particularly important to Catholic voters, who praised Kennedy as a good family man. Nevertheless, this preoccupation with popularity unsettled Jack. "When you run for the presidency, your wife's hair or your hair or something else always becomes of major significance," he said.

Jackie allowed reporters to watch her at home in Hyannis Port, Massachusetts, as she watched Jack's first televised debate against the Republican presidential nominee, Vice President Richard Nixon. She also hosted a meeting of the Women's Committee for the New Frontier. In her living room, Jackie filmed campaign commercials in English and Spanish, alone and with celebrities such as noted author

John F. Kennedy

Despite being the son of an ambitious banking tycoon who would become an ambassador, John Kennedy had no intention while growing up of becoming president. He was too bookish, too mischievous, and too sickly. Besides, his millionaire father was grooming the eldest son, Joe, for the task.

After young Joe's heroic death during World War II, the senior Joseph P. Kennedy pushed Jack into politics. Jack's own wartime heroics on PT-109, combined with Kennedy money, connections, and mystique, launched his remarkable political career. In 1947, when Jack was barely thirty, he was already a congressman. By 1952 he was representing Massachusetts in the U.S. Senate. Four years later he nearly became the Democratic vice presidential nominee; six years later he was reelected to the Senate by a landslide, and in November, 1960, John Kennedy became the first Catholic and the youngest man ever elected to the presidency. He was forty-three. His wife of seven years, Jackie, was only thirty-one.

With the aging Dwight Eisenhower passing the torch, Kennedy's victory became a generational triumph, heralding the rise of the "GI Joe generation" to power. Moderate, pragmatic, even cautious, Kennedy was also eloquent, charismatic, and inspiring. During the Cold War, he hovered on the brink of nuclear disaster in Cuba and Berlin, while also generating great hopes the world over through his idealistic programs such as the Peace Corps.

Kennedy's symbolic power took on a life of its own. Although he kept the ideas fuzzy, he revitalized liberalism. Millions believed with him "that things can be improved." "Negroes are getting ideas they didn't have before," Kennedy's black adviser Louis Martin warned in 1962. "Where are they getting them?" Kennedy wondered. "From you!" Martin replied. "You're lifting the horizons of Negroes."

Kennedy's tragic death in November, 1963, initially saved him from disappointing the millions who believed in him and his ideals so intensely. Ironically, his death also allowed his successor, Lyndon Johnson, to transform Kennedy's poetry into legislative prose. Volcanic, populist, and manipulative, Johnson was able to push through Congress a Civil Rights bill in 1964 and a host of Great Society welfare programs in 1965 that revolutionized the United States. Nevertheless, Kennedy is the one most often hailed as both a great liberal and an inspiring president.

Dr. Benjamin Spock. She also granted some television interviews. While she grimaced at the reporters' questions and resented their lights and wires, at least she was at home and away from mobs.

Presidency and First Ladyship

The new First Lady at once boosted and undermined the president's respectability. Her poise and her interest in the arts gave the administration a sophisticated sheen. If her youth and growing celebrity had its share of political disadvantages, anxieties about relying on an untested leader in a treacherous age drowned in a sea of celebrations welcoming the new generation to power. "Jacqueline Bouvier Kennedy will bring youth, beauty and babies to the White House," one conservative weekly gushed during the transition. Barely three weeks after her husband's victory, Jackie gave birth to John F. Kennedy, Jr., called John-John.

While insisting she only wanted to be a good wife and mother, Jackie revolutionized the role of First Lady. Rather than playing to America's matrons, she played to the cameras and the middle-class masses. She reflected a well-bred woman's interest in philanthropy, the arts, and entertaining combined with a suburbanite's zeal for home improvement and PTA meetings. "If you bungle raising your children, I don't think whatever else you do well matters very much," she said.

At the same time, the "Jackie look" swept the United States. Of twenty-three fashion shows mounted in New York City during January, 1961, all but five mentioned the First Lady-to-be. *Photoplay*, the best-known movie magazine, featured side-by-side photographs of Jacqueline Kennedy and actress Elizabeth Taylor on its June, 1962, cover. In bold, the headline screamed: "AMERICA'S 2 QUEENS," promising "A comparison of their days and nights! How they raise their children! How they treat their men!"

For all her popularity, Jackie had little impact on policy. Echoing former First Lady Mamie Eisenhower, Jackie said she talked to the president "about family matters, never about matters of state." She said, "Jack has always told me the one thing a busy man doesn't want to talk about at the end of the day is whether the Geneva Convention will be successful or what settlement could be made in Kashmir or anything like that."

Comparisons with Jackie diminished her predecessors. Mamie Eisenhower was caricatured in the press as a frumpy grandmother. Bess Truman became "American Gothic to the core, stubbornly wearing her orchids upside down, curling her gray hair tight the way she'd always done it in Missouri," according to columnist Dorothy Kilgallen.

Reporters "interviewed Jackie's hairdresser, her pianist, her caterer . . . even . . . the owner of the local diaper service," Helen Thomas of United Press International recalled. Once Thomas called White House press secretary Pierre Salinger at 3:00 A.M. to inquire whether one of Caroline's hamsters had died.

Scrutiny of Jack's weekend activities, Jackie's purchases, Caroline's jokes, and John-John's first steps overwhelmed the White House press office. Salinger "found it impossible to jump from an announcement on nuclear testing to a precise description of Mrs. Kennedy's latest hat." He consigned "all questions involving society, zoology, and millinery" to the East Wing. Forty people now helped the First Lady cope with her public duties, including a press secretary, Pamela Turnure, and a growing correspondence unit. Social secretary Letitia Baldrige supervised the staff and reported to the First Lady.

Public scrutiny was relentless. When Jackie missed Mass, correspondents demanded that she attend. When she went to Mass in slacks, observers chided her to dress appropriately. In *McCall's* magazine, former Congresswoman Clare Boothe Luce chastised the First Lady for patronizing French, not American, designers.

Jackie Kennedy, at Cottage Industries in India, watches a man make pottery, 1962. *(Library of Congress)*

solarium on the third floor of the Executive Mansion "normal."

Jackie tried to separate her official and personal roles. She rejected the title of First Lady as suited to "a saddle horse." She preferred the more democratic "Mrs. Kennedy." The "president's wife should be just that— his wife," she insisted. "People must be as sick of hearing about us and [Caroline's pony] Macaroni as I am," she said. She commanded her press secretary to follow a press policy of "minimum information given with maximum politeness," although the First Lady still sometimes lapsed and lashed out at reporters.

On the other hand, Jack Kennedy and his men indulged the press. They believed that, as author and Kennedy adviser Arthur Schlesinger, Jr., would say, Jack's "coolness was itself a new frontier." Kennedy worried about Jackie's hostility to the press. "Poor Jack," she said. "He thinks if I ignore them he'll be impeached."

At one dinner, the president grabbed the First Lady by the arm, dragged her across the hall and commanded: "Say hello to the girls, darling."

Nonetheless, her greatest contributions were in the realm of public relations. Jackie lobbied for what eventually became the National Endowment for the Arts and the John F. Kennedy Center for the Performing Arts. White House aides said that the Kennedys triggered a "general ferment of excitement and hope for [a] new era of cultural activity on the part of the general public."

Jackie's White House restoration project was a huge success in the eyes of the public. She said she wanted "to make the White House the

"Just as the personal activities of the President can never be dissociated from his role as America's First Citizen, so, too, the personal activities of the President's wife cannot be dissociated from her role as First Lady," Luce lectured, continuing that Mrs. Kennedy's task as First Lady "is to form and lead American taste."

Seeking shelter from all the attention, Jackie established a private school in the White House for Caroline. By 1963, when Caroline entered first grade, it had twenty students in two classes, including children of administration officials and family friends. A tribute to Jackie's desire to be a normal mom, the school suffered. It was hard to consider a school meeting in the first house in the land" because it "belongs to the people of America." Privately, she refused to live in a house that looked like what she called a "dentist office bomb shelter." In endeavoring to make the White House fit for a president—and herself—Jackie organized a Fine Arts Committee, hired a curator, advocated changes in the laws governing income tax deductions for donations, supervised production of a White House guidebook, and raised millions of dollars. She beautified the state rooms and made the Executive Mansion more like a home, installing a private dining room with a small adjoining kitchen and a nursery. The initial printing of 250,000 White House guidebooks sold out in three months. By 1962, the White House averaged 4,560 daily visitors, up from approximately 3,000 before.

The restoration was Jacqueline Kennedy's defense against the vulgarity of politics. When she saw a congressman posing in the Rose Garden with "an enormous bunch of celery," she stormed into Jack's outer office and dictated a memo saying: "I think it is most undignified for any picture of this nature to be taken on the steps leading to the President's office or on the South grounds."

Jackie immersed herself in her project. Once, Civil Rights activist Dr. Martin Luther King, Jr., came to meet the president in the residence. The elevator he was on stopped at the basement level, and Jackie climbed aboard, streaked with soot. "Oh, Dr. King," she gushed, "you would be so thrilled if you could just have been with me in the basement this morning. I found a chair right out of the Andrew Jackson period—a beautiful chair." King sputtered, "Yes—yes—is that so?" Jackie said, "I've just got to tell Jack about that chair." She then caught herself and retreated, saying, "But you have other things to talk to him about, don't you?" As she left, King shook his head: "Well, well—wasn't that something!"

On February 14, 1962, Mrs. John F. Kennedy took Americans in twenty-eight million homes on a televised tour of the White House. In her thin, breathy voice and her upper-class accent, Jackie showed the nation the "mahvelous" colors, and the antique "chaiahs" of the redone mansion.

The White House renovation was Jackie's great gift to Jack; she had proven she could help his career. After so much work had been done, Jackie did not want the White House to be "an empty museum." She wanted to create a democratic Versailles, hosting Nobel prize winners and artists such as Pablo Casals at dinner. Jack preferred James Bond movies and Broadway musicals, but he considered the arts "a part of our arsenal in the Cold War."

The Kennedys jazzed up the White House social life. Shocked society columnists watched as hard liquor flowed, ash trays appeared, and music began before the First Couple arrived. Feeling young, glamorous, and powerful, the Kennedys' guests enhanced the legend of the Kennedy parties. "It was all so gentle, and reassuring, in that lovely house, so well done and so easy," novelist Katherine Anne Porter rhapsodized. "What style they had, those young people! And what looks."

Despite the gaiety, Jackie renounced many of the matronly duties her predecessors had performed. She often begged off from receptions at the last minute. When she announced her second pregnancy in 1963, the president joked, "Now Jackie will have an excuse to get out of things." As Letitia Baldrige said, there was a "civil war" between Jack's people in the West Wing and Jackie's people in the East Wing: "The presidential assistants tried to force decisions affecting Mrs. Kennedy on our office without consulting us."

Jackie escaped from the tension regularly. She shopped in New York, spent weekends at Cape Cod, Massachusetts, and in Palm Beach, Florida, vacationed on the Riviera, and lobbied for assignments to romantic places. Reporters rephrased comedian Jimmy Durante's "Mrs. Calabash" signoff line: "And good night, Mrs.

Kennedy, wherever you are." To justify his wife's travels, the president encouraged her to accept Prime Minister Jawaharlal Nehru's invitation to visit India. Kennedy and the prime minister did not get along, but Jackie had charmed the elderly Nehru, just as she had charmed General Charles de Gaulle in Paris. Jackie would keep American policy evenhanded by also visiting Pakistan. The Kennedys labeled the two-and-one-half-week voyage in March, 1962, a "semi-official" trip, more than a personal tour but not quite a state visit. The nearly 400,000 words of press coverage, and sixty-one broadcasts totaling almost 1,000 minutes during her ten-day stay in India were overwhelmingly positive.

Many Americans were less enchanted. Letters to the White House ran two to one against Jackie's pilgrimage. The most common criticism had to do with the estimated cost of the lavish travel. To millions, Jackie symbolized all that was wrong with the Kennedys—their arrogance, wealth, and dynastic ambitions. Many conservatives who disagreed with Jack politically hated what he and his family represented. The affluent United States which reporters applauded terrified others as too spoiled and too weak. The criticisms worried the president. After seeing pictures of his wife swimming with Gianni Agnelli, the owner of Fiat autoworks, Jack telegrammed: "A little more Caroline and less Agnelli."

The president barely won the 1960 election. Jackie's vacation came just before the 1962 congressional elections. Conservatives such as Arizona Senator Barry Goldwater were making effective attacks on the "headlong national rush for money," the decline of traditional morality, and the growth of federal power. Goldwater was anticipating a 1964 campaign posing his "genuine commitment" to tradition against Kennedy's cynicism. The chorus of disapproval from genteel ladies harmonized with the growing populist conservatism.

Jackie remained defiant. "People told me ninety-nine things that I had to do as First Lady, and I haven't done one of them," she boasted. A month before the 1962 elections, a Gallup poll showed that Mrs. Kennedy remained popular. Respondents most often mentioned her "good looks," her "good personality," and her intelligence. Her actions, however, attracted criticism. Asked "what are the things you like least about her," survey respondents mentioned her travels away from her family, her love of the limelight, her hairdo, her clothes, and her undignified behavior.

In August of 1963, Jackie gave birth five weeks prematurely. She had been vacationing on Cape Cod, and Jack was working in Washington. Jack was with Patrick Bouvier Kennedy when he died two days later at the Children's Medical Center in Boston. In mourning their son, the Kennedys' cool facade cracked. After the burial mass, the president wept on the coffin. "My dear Jack, let's go, let's go," Archbishop of Boston Richard Cardinal Cushing said as he pulled the president away from the casket. "Nothing more can be done." Artist and close friend Bill Walton spent the weekend with the Kennedys. "She hung unto him and he held her in his arms," Walton remembered, "something nobody ever saw at any other time because they were very private people." Hoping that some good could come from such anguish, observers sensed a new tenderness in the presidential couple. Jackie told Jack that, great as this loss was, "the one blow I could not bear would be to lose you."

Two months later, Jackie was off cruising on the Mediterranean aboard the 303-foot yacht *Christina*, owned by the notorious Greek shipping magnate Aristotle Onassis. In the 1950's, Onassis had paid seven million dollars to avert a federal indictment. "Jackie, do you know what you're doing?" Jack asked. "Are you aware of this fellow's reputation?" One Ohio congressman attacked the "impropriety of our First Lady . . . in accepting the lavish hospitality of this international character." A widely circulated photograph showed the First Lady sunbathing in a bikini. "Does this sort of behavior seem fitting for a woman in mourning?" editorialists asked.

When she returned, Jack exploited the length of her absence to get her politicking. Since September, 1962, his popularity had been declining; by November, 1963, only 43 percent of those polled would approve his performance. He feared a showdown with Barry Goldwater; backlash against New York Governor Nelson Rockefeller's divorce and hasty remarriage to a divorced woman boosted Goldwater's standing. Kennedy did not want to lose the moral high ground. Republican National Chairman William Miller wondered what first family life was coming to "with Sinatra types infesting 1600 Pennsylvania Avenue . . . twisting in the historic East Ballroom . . . [and] all-night parties in foreign lands."

Jackie agreed to accompany her husband on a political trip to Texas, to repair their relationship and her reputation. On the morning of November 22, 1963, a rain-drenched crowd greeted President Kennedy in Fort Worth. They had been waiting for more than an hour "to hear him and see Mrs. Kennedy," as Vice President Lyndon Johnson would say. "Where's Jackie?" someone shouted. "Mrs. Kennedy is organizing herself," Jack quipped. "It takes longer, but of course she looks better than we do when she does it." For one last time, Jack played the harried husband, building his wife up while cutting her down.

Jackie's concession placed her in an open limousine by her

husband's side when an assassin's bullet shattered his brain. Her presence in the convertible made her an integral part of witnesses' memories of that day. "It's my husband, his blood, his brains, are all over me," she told doctors as she sat with the dying president.

Legacy

The assassination and the outpouring of public grief that followed retroactively exorcised any public doubts about the Kennedys or their marriage. "The manner of the President and his wife to each other was always simple, courte-

Attending President John F. Kennedy's funeral, November 24, 1963, from left: Senator Edward Kennedy, Jacqueline Kennedy, and U.S. Attorney General Robert Kennedy. In front are Caroline and John Kennedy, Jr. *(CNP/ Archive Photos)*

A Shining Moment

Less than a week after her husband's assassination, Jackie Kennedy summoned the journalist Theodore White for an interview. "I kept saying to [Jack's brother] Bobby, I've got to talk to somebody, I've got to see somebody, I want to say this one thing." With White's editors at *Life* magazine holding the presses at a cost of thirty thousand dollars per hour, and with a thunderstorm battering the house, Jackie remembered Jack's favorite musical, *Camelot*, and how his favorite song cried: "Don't let it be forgot, that once there was a spot, for one brief shining moment that was known as Camelot."

Jackie's interview may have been the most notable action ever taken by a First Lady. Just as she had during the funeral, she helped cement the Kennedy legend. In speaking to White, she offered the defining metaphor for her husband's presidency. *Camelot* had never been associated with Kennedy. In fact, many Kennedy confidants believed that the macho president would have disliked such a fluffy label. However, Jackie's epitaph stuck. Even after scandals stained the Kennedy name, Americans still yearn for what she helped her husband's administration symbolize: what journalist White, prompted by Mrs. Kennedy, would call "a magic moment in American history."

ous and loving, without gestures, without trying," Katherine Anne Porter wrote in the *Ladies Home Journal*, marveling how their life was "lived hourly in love with joy, yet every duty done and every demand fulfilled." Jackie recognized that she was starring in the greatest performance of her life.

Widowhood made Jackie Kennedy the primary keeper of Jack's memory. No longer a thorn in his side, no longer a potential political liability to be neutralized, she guarded Jack's image. Troubled by the meaninglessness of the death—"If it had at least been for his civil rights stand" she mourned—she helped make his death a monument to American idealism.

Just as presidents following Franklin D. Roosevelt would strive to emulate the success of his policies and programs in the Oval Office, all presidential couples who succeeded the Kennedys would strive to be lauded as they were at home. Jackie Kennedy would live out her days as a celebrity, always watched, rarely heard. For all the Kennedys' imperfections, the two would epitomize the great hopes, great faith, and great power Americans felt at the start of the 1960's.

Suggested Readings

Baldrige, Letitia. *Of Diamonds and Diplomats.* Boston: Houghton Mifflin, 1968. Excellent insights from Jackie Kennedy's social secretary and key strategist.

Heymann, C. David. *A Woman Named Jackie.* New York: Lyle Stuart, 1989. The best of the many popular Jackie Kennedy biographies, more authoritative and less breathless than most.

Reeves, Richard. *President Kennedy.* New York: Simon & Schuster, 1993. A superb account of John Kennedy's presidency, offering a sense of how the president and his wife functioned day-to-day.

Schlesinger, Arthur M., Jr. *A Thousand Days.* Boston: Houghton Mifflin, 1965. The memoirs of the former Kennedy adviser evoke the magic of what Jackie Kennedy called Camelot.

Thomas, Helen. *Dateline: White House.* New York: Macmillan, 1975. One of the reporters who covered the Kennedys reflects back on some of her and her colleagues' excesses.

Gil Troy

Lady Bird Johnson

Claudia Alta "Lady Bird" Taylor Johnson

Born: December 22, 1912
Karnack, Texas

President: Lyndon B. Johnson
1963-1969

Overview: An instrumental influence in Lyndon B. Johnson's long political career, from running his congressional office during World War II to campaigning hard for his policies and bids for office, Lady Bird Johnson was an adviser to her husband and also one of the most active of all First Ladies. Known for her program to beautify the United States, she emerged as one of the most prominent advocates of conservation of her time. In addition to her high-profile nationwide campaign to keep the natural environment clean, which resulted in legislation, the First Lady embraced a variety of social issues. She continued her work on behalf of social and environmental causes after leaving the White House, remaining one of the most beloved of all First Ladies.

Early Life

Claudia Alta was born to Thomas Jefferson Taylor and Minnie Pattillo Taylor in the small community of Karnack, Texas. She was the third Taylor child, following two sons: Thomas, Jr., and Antonio. Her father, known to his friends as TJ, was a moderately successful businessman who owned a store and made his money selling land and dealing in a variety of commercial pursuits. The Taylors had been married in 1900 and appear to have suffered some tensions in their marriage, although they stayed together. Minnie Taylor was a cultured woman who loved intellectual and artistic endeavors. She appears to have been somewhat bored with both her marriage and rural Texas.

Lady Bird Johnson. *(Library of Congress)*

In 1918 tragedy struck when Minnie, pregnant with her fourth child, fell down a staircase. The accident caused a miscarriage and ultimately the death of Mrs. Taylor.

Before her untimely passing, Minnie read often to her daughter and imparted to her a love of reading and an appreciation for learning. Lady Bird would always enjoy books and do well in her educational pursuits. She earned her now-famous nickname as a child when the family's cook and nursemaid Alice Tittle commented that the young girl was as pretty as a lady bird. Although as a youngster Lady Bird was not too keen on her nickname, it stuck and she grew to accept it.

The widowed TJ Taylor worried that he would be unable to raise his young daughter by himself, so he invited his deceased wife's sister, Effie Pattillo, to come live with the family. Effie moved from her home in Alabama to the Taylor home in Texas. Lady Bird appears to have missed her mother, and it has often been said that the young girl had a lonely childhood. She found solace in the outdoors, playing in the woods near her home. This fledgling appreciation for nature would later result in landmark environmental programs. Her aunt was not as refined as her mother had been, but as Minnie had, Effie encouraged the young girl's interest in learning, particularly in educating Lady Bird about her natural surroundings. As a girl, Lady Bird learned the names of the trees and flowers near her home and would later remember in vivid detail the Texas bayous, meadows, and wildlife with great admiration.

She attended public schools in Texas and frequently visited her relatives in Alabama, in the company of her Aunt Effie. In 1927, at age fifteen, Lady Bird graduated from Marshall High School and enrolled in St. Mary's, a religiously affiliated school for girls in Dallas. Two years later, in 1930, she entered the University of Texas at Austin, where she majored in history. A good student, Lady Bird wrote articles for the campus newspaper, *The Daily Texan*. She was popular among her peers and enjoyed socializing, although she always had high standards for those she dated. In fact, she made it known that she would only marry a man with ambition who would make something of himself. Lady Bird enjoyed her studies and what the city of Austin had to offer an inquisitive and ambitious young woman. After completing her degree in 1933, she stayed in school for one additional year to complete the requirements for a bachelor's degree in journalism.

As a student, Lady Bird expressed an interest in pursuing a career as a writer or reporter, despite the limited opportunities during the Great Depression. Such ambitions highlight her confidence and high goals. These plans were interrupted on August 31, 1934, when a friend introduced her to a twenty-six-year-old congressional aide named Lyndon B. Johnson. At their initial meeting, the two made quite an impression on each other; Lyndon asked Lady Bird to marry him on their first date. She turned her suitor down, but they continued a long-distance courtship after he returned to the nation's capital. The relationship progressed rapidly in spite of the distance separating them. They exchanged numerous letters and spoke on the telephone. Lyndon's respect for his new love and her intelligence was evident in his choice of gifts for her, which included a book on the rise of Nazi Germany. Soon after meeting, Lyndon and Lady Bird introduced each other to their families; then the relentless Lyndon paid a sudden visit to Lady Bird, driving all the way back to Texas to again propose marriage. This time Lady Bird accepted the offer.

Marriage and Family

The couple decided to marry right away and went to San Antonio, Texas, where they were wed on November 17, 1934. After the wedding, they honeymooned in Mexico, then moved to Washington, D.C. Lady Bird was disinterested in politics but resigned herself to her spouse's career, which she understood to be his driving

Lyndon B. Johnson

Lyndon Johnson was born on August 27, 1908, in central Texas near Johnson City, the community his family had helped settle. The Johnsons were not poor but felt the effects of the harsh rural economy. After high school, Johnson worked his way through Southwest Texas State Teachers College (now University) and taught students of Mexican ancestry.

Johnson was always interested in politics and worked as a congressional aide as a young man. He was first elected to office in 1937, winning a seat in the U.S. House of Representatives. After six terms in the House he was elected to the Senate in 1948, eventually becoming the powerful Senate majority leader during Dwight D. Eisenhower's presidency. In 1960 Johnson was selected as the vice presidential candidate running alongside John F. Kennedy. After Kennedy's assassination in 1963, Johnson finally realized his goal of being president.

Johnson's presidency was one of the most active in the history of the office. His Great Society program extended social protections and supports to a wide cross-section of citizens through a variety of education, medicare, Medicaid, urban renewal, and other economic development and antipoverty programs. Johnson also signed the monumental 1964 Civil Rights Act. In spite of his landslide election in 1964 and these numerous legislative successes, the president was caught in the divisiveness of the Vietnam War, and his support for the war eroded much of his popular support. In 1969, he startled the United States when he suddenly announced that he would not seek re-election. After a brief retirement back at his Texas ranch, Johnson died of a heart attack on January 22, 1973.

passion. In 1935 Lyndon was named director of the Texas branch of the National Youth Administration. Two years later, when one of Texas's incumbent congressmen died, Lyndon decided to pursue the seat. His wife supported his campaign in several ways, including contributing ten thousand dollars she had inherited from her mother's estate. Lady Bird's father donated another twenty-five thousand dollars, enabling Johnson to mount a successful campaign in 1937.

Politics would always define the Johnson marriage, and this became quite apparent to Lady Bird when she became a congressional wife. She involved herself thoroughly in her husband's career, joining him on trips to Washington, touring the sites of the capital city, and helping in his congressional office. All the while, she was developing not only more of an appreciation for politics but also a knack for public service. In 1941, the death of a U.S. senator from Texas presented a political opportu-

nity for Lyndon, who decided to pursue the Senate seat. His campaign was unsuccessful, and, possibly from the stress of political life, Lady Bird suffered more than one miscarriage during this period of their marriage.

Shortly after his failed bid for the Senate, Lyndon departed for naval duty. In 1942 he toured the South Pacific, inspecting World War II naval operations, but decided not to give up his seat in the House of Representatives. Instead, as he would often do in his career when he needed someone dependable, he turned to his wife, who ran the congressional office for him. Lady Bird worked with Lyndon's constituents, many of whom were quite demanding. She wrote letters, answered questions, and handled political issues that arose. She performed these difficult tasks admirably.

On his return from duty, Lyndon found his office functioning smoothly. The postwar period brought the birth of their daughters Lynda Bird in 1944 and Luci Baines in 1947. Later that year, when a senator from Texas retired, Johnson again entered a Senate race. This time his bid was successful, although by only a handful of votes in an extremely tight race. Lady Bird played a visible and prominent role in this campaign, foreshadowing the role she would assume as First Lady. Her efforts might also have made a difference in the campaign's outcome. Overcoming her hesitancy about speaking in public, she helped run the campaign and organized women volunteers. Well liked by Johnson's supporters, she was popular with the crowds.

Throughout the 1950's, Johnson's political star continued to rise. By the end of the decade, he was the powerful leader of the U.S. Senate and a contender for the presidency. Perhaps in recognition of this, and still a bit hesitant about her public appearances, in 1959 Lady Bird enrolled in a public speaking class with the Capital Speakers Club. Later, during Johnson's presidency, she would help edit and provide critical feedback on his addresses.

Politics dominated their family life, but these congressional years were challenging to Lady Bird for another reason: It was hard to live with Lyndon. He was restless and had a quick temper, and his demanding nature was felt by all those around him. He was demanding of his wife; he criticized her in front of others, complaining even about her clothing. She endured his scorn as well as his bouts of marital infidelity. As the couple worked through these difficulties, Lady Bird's influence on her husband's life and career was beneficial. She calmed him, balanced his rashness with her steadfastness, and even expanded his narrow social views and interest in arts and culture. She was one of the few who could command the attention of the headstrong and temperamental politician.

The stress of political life showed itself on Lyndon. His compulsion to work long hours, along with the unhealthy amount of weight he had gained and his excessive smoking, endangered his health. In 1955 he had his first heart at-

tack. It was Lady Bird who encouraged him to cut his dependency on tobacco and to alter his diet. She watched over what he ate, and although she could not get him to reduce his schedule or pace of work, she helped him improve his health.

Lady Bird also brought financial security to their marriage and to his political career. To address the uncertainty and low pay of a career in politics, in 1943 the Johnsons invested money from Lady Bird's inheritance in the purchase of radio station KTBC. Lyndon used his contacts with the Federal Communication Commission to enhance the terms of the purchase, but it was Lady Bird who managed all facets of the enterprise, from hiring employees to soliciting sponsors, balancing the books, and cleaning the offices. She ultimately parlayed a seventeen-thousand-dollar investment into millions. When the station began turning a profit, it prompted her to acquire other holdings, forming the basis of the Johnson media conglomerate.

Lady Bird grew to love the Texas Hill Country surrounding the LBJ Ranch near Austin, which they called home when in Texas. During this period in her life, she continued to develop her love of nature, gardening in the capital city and observing the scenery she passed traveling to and from Washington. The unsightly dumps, billboards, and roadside trash she saw also made an impression on her. Years later as First Lady, she supported a nationwide beautification program which included roadside beautification.

Presidency and First Ladyship

Events of John F. Kennedy's presidential campaign of 1960 provided an indication of the type of First Lady that Lady Bird Johnson would later be. After initially attempting to discourage her husband from accepting the vice presidential spot on the Democratic ticket with Kennedy, which she believed would limit his ultimate goal of attaining the presidency, Lady

Bird assumed an active role in the campaign. She worked hard, particularly in the South, where she campaigned widely for the ticket and proved to be highly effective. She earned rave reviews in Dallas, where, when campaigning, she encountered a group of Nixon supporters who became unruly and aggressive. Lady Bird remained calm and continued speaking undeterred, despite being confronted by hecklers. Her poise impressed media observers.

As a vice presidential spouse, Lady Bird undertook many of the duties that the First Lady, Jacqueline Kennedy, left unfulfilled. Because Jackie Kennedy was disinterested in many formal duties and was raising her young children

during the early 1960's, Lady Bird Johnson became the most active vice presidential spouse in history and one of the most visible. She traveled with the president and vice president across the United States and worldwide, made numerous public appearances, and hosted teas and other socials which benefited her husband's public standing as well as that of the Kennedy-Johnson administration.

After the tragic assassination of President Kennedy in November, 1963, Lady Bird Johnson found herself suddenly and unexpectedly thrust into the First Ladyship. Jackie Kennedy had undertaken a historic, well-received renovation of the White House during her tenure

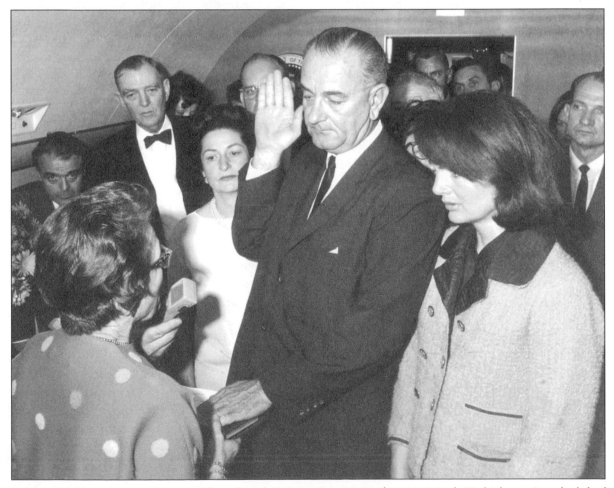

Lyndon B. Johnson is sworn in as president aboard Air Force One, November, 1963. Lady Bird Johnson is to the left of him and Jacqueline Kennedy is to the right of him. *(Lyndon Baines Johnson Library)*

and asked the incoming First Lady to continue her work on the Executive Mansion. Lady Bird took an active role in the Committee for the Preservation of the White House and saw that Mrs. Kennedy's work was carried on during the Johnson administration.

As First Lady, Lady Bird was a partner and adviser to her husband. In this capacity, she read his speeches, provided advice when he solicited it—something he did frequently—and promoted a variety of programs and issues pertaining to her husband's Great Society program. One of the social programs she advocated was Head Start, where she worked closely with Sargent Shriver, the head of the Office of Economic Opportunity. The First Lady visited numerous Head Start sites and often spoke out on the program's behalf. Lady Bird was also an advocate for women's involvement in numerous social issues, holding high profile "Women Doer Luncheons" at the White House in honor of women of distinction. The main goal of Lady Bird's First Ladyship, though, was her effort to make the White House a comfortable place for Lyndon. His health and best interests had been her priority throughout their married life.

However, it was her beautification projects for which her days as First Lady would most be remembered. The word beautification also involved broader conservation initiatives. The 1960's saw a new awareness of the natural world, encouraged by the publication in 1962 of Rachel Carson's landmark book *The Silent Spring*. The Kennedy administration had convened a White House conference on conservation issues and promoted various environmental measures, most of which were pending at the time of Kennedy's assassination. Lady Bird would pick up the cause and carry it forward, far beyond the original intention of the previous administration. In fact, she became the Johnson administration's point person on environmental issues and a nationally recognized advocate of environmentalism. She received

mail from environmentalists and concerned citizens asking her assistance in protecting everything from the Colorado River to the redwoods to neighborhoods. Such causes were natural for the First Lady, who had developed a lifelong appreciation of nature.

Although she held no formal press conferences like those of her predecessor Eleanor Roosevelt, Lady Bird enjoyed good relations with the press corps and female journalists in particular. Lady Bird was also well served by a large staff and press secretary who helped her to publicize and implement her efforts, most notably her beautification project. She also enlisted the support of other public figures who, recognizing her influence and popularity, often sought her support. In 1964 she toured the American West with Stewart Udall, secretary of the interior, who shared her enthusiasm for the outdoors. On the trip she delivered speeches, dedicated a dam, and visited American Indian reservations. The trip raised awareness for such issues and helped spark the First Lady's interest in pursuing a special project related to the outdoors.

By 1965, after Johnson's successful 1964 reelection, the First Lady was ready to embark fully on her beautification initiative. Lady Bird wisely chose to begin her project on a local scale, in the capital city. Initially, she worked on initiatives such as cleaning public parks and planting trees and flowers. She set up advisory boards, enlisted the support of the National Park Service, and involved local civic leaders and youth groups. The local efforts included landscaping and beautifying Capitol Hill as well as poor neighborhoods, where she got black and disadvantaged youths involved in neighborhood and outdoor projects. She established the First Lady's Committee for a More Beautiful Capital, which brought together public, private, and community leaders and ultimately landscaped numerous public areas around Washington. She would also be a driving force behind the Society for a More Beauti-

The Lady Bird Special

A southerner, President Lyndon B. Johnson worried what would become of his political base of support in the South as a result of his support of the 1964 Civil Rights Act. Indeed, many southern whites were strongly opposed to the landmark civil rights legislation, which became a divisive issue in the region. As testimony to his confidence in his wife, the president supported a goodwill trip by the First Lady through several southern states to rally support for Johnson during this critical election year.

Departing from northern Virginia on a four-day whistle-stop tour on a train dubbed the Lady Bird Special, Lady Bird traveled more than one thousand miles through the Deep South, ending in New Orleans, Louisiana. On behalf of the president, she delivered speeches at twenty-eight scheduled stops and met with prominent political leaders in each state she visited. Her message was to remind the audiences of her husband's roots in Texas and ask for their support. The First Lady had to endure many hostile crowds and threats from angry hecklers. She succeeded in impressing observers as well as the press with her calm and articulate defense of the Johnson administration. After the conclusion of this campaign swing, she traveled to Texas, Oklahoma, Kentucky, and Indiana to continue her appeal on her husband's behalf. She is credited with minimizing the defections from the Democratic Party in the South during the 1964 election.

ful Capital, which managed donations on behalf of these efforts.

A major component of her beautification project was highway beautification, an effort to improve unsightly roadsides. In 1965 the Johnson administration promoted the Highway Beautification Bill. The bill included provisions for removing roadside trash, planting trees, and minimizing the number of billboards near scenic roads. Lady Bird was the front person for this bill in the public's mind, and her popularity and credibility on such issues benefited the legislative battle.

Not surprisingly, the initiative encountered opposition from advertisers and businesses located near the affected sites, who saw a threat to their commercial endeavors. Lady Bird also received criticism from politicians, including Congressman Bob Dole of Kansas, who mocked her efforts, even suggesting that the language of the bill be changed to read "Lady Bird's Bill" or "the President's Wife's Bill." She was unwavering in her commitment to the project, however, attending the legislative debates and making a number of public trips and speeches to rally

support for the measure. The First Lady was seen at national parks, hiking among redwoods, and meeting with interested groups. With her help, the Highway Beautification Act of 1965 was passed, marking one of the few times a First Lady's initiatives or activities had resulted in legislation. Only Ellen Wilson and Eleanor Roosevelt had been so directly involved in lobbying for the passage of a law.

The First Lady's influence was felt in the administration's promotion of conservation in a broad sense; the president even discussed the beautification project in his State of the Union address and referred to his wife on conservation matters. She helped to make possible the White House Conference on Natural Beauty in May of 1965. Lady Bird visited national parks and historic sites and embraced such issues as clean air, clean water, and the protection of scenic rivers. For each of these policy issues, she met with organizations, followed legislative debates closely, and delivered numerous speeches for conservation. When speaking, the First Lady sometimes encountered crowds hostile to the president's policies on Vietnam, but she again showed great calm in addressing her audiences, often winning the admiration of her husband's political enemies.

Outside the full official schedule and political demands of living in the White House, Lady Bird managed to carve out some degree of normality for her family during the presidential years. The high points of her First Ladyship included the weddings of both of her daughters during her White House years. She protected her husband's still-marginal health, monitoring his diet and insisting that he take time for relaxation, though the cloud of the Vietnam War loomed over the later years of the Johnson presidency, adding to their stress. She worried about Lyndon's health during the tumultuous 1968 campaign; concern for his well-being caused her to oppose his plans for reelection that year. Ultimately, Johnson shocked the United States when he announced that he would not seek another term in office. She was greatly relieved by his decision to return to private life.

Legacy

As the Johnson presidency was winding down, the couple began giving thought to Lyndon Johnson's presidential library. It was Lady Bird who initiated the development of that project, meeting with architects, visiting possible sites and other presidential libraries, and overseeing plans for the memorial to the Johnson presidency. The Lyndon B. Johnson Library was established in Texas and, throughout her post-White House years, Lady Bird remained active in the organization.

Lady Bird Johnson expanded the role of First Lady, engaging Americans in a consciousness-raising exercise on conservation and initiating enormously successful projects. All subsequent First Ladies have been expected to champion a special cause, in part because of the success and visibility of Lady Bird's beautification program.

Her leadership on these many issues did not end when the Johnsons left Washington. Her post-White House life remained focused on her causes, and she remained in the eyes and hearts of the public. Her active retirement at the LBJ Ranch included continuing with her beautification project, including several local undertakings in and around Austin, and establishing awards for beautification initiatives in her home state. She also continued her interest in politics, supporting women candidates for office and members of the Democratic Party.

Remaining a powerful force and respected public servant long after leaving the White House, the former First Lady served on the board of the National Geographic Society, was a popular member of the Board of Regents of the University of Texas, and was selected by President Jimmy Carter to serve on the Commission on White House Fellows. Among the many recognitions she received for her life of public service were the Presidential Medal of Freedom, presented to her in 1977 by President Gerald Ford, and the Congressional Gold Medal in 1988.

In 1963 she had begun chronicling her years in the White House, clipping articles, jotting down observations, and saving remembrances of those special years. In 1970 she published part of her collection as *A White House Diary*. Another love of hers for which she retained a passion was wildflowers. With donations of her own land, time, and money, Lady Bird founded the now-famous National Wildflower Research Center and sponsored conferences and extensive work on behalf of promoting the national wildflower campaign. In 1988 she coauthored the book *Wildflowers Across America* with Carlton Lees.

Although slowed by a slight stroke in 1993, Lady Bird continued her interest in her many political and social projects. She remains one of the most beloved and admired of all First Ladies. As testimony to her First Ladyship, several subsequent spouses of presidents and presidential candidates have cited her as an inspiration.

Suggested Readings

Carpenter, Liz. *Ruffles and Flourishes*. College Station: Texas A&M University Press, 1992. A detailed account of Lady Bird Johnson from her former staff director, providing valuable accounts of Lady Bird Johnson's First Ladyship.

Gould, Lewis L. *Lady Bird Johnson and the Environment*. Lawrence: University Press of Kansas, 1988. A scholarly assessment of Lady Bird Johnson's role in promoting numerous environmental issues and the lasting significance of her beautification projects.

Middleton, Harry. *Lady Bird Johnson: A Life Well Lived*. Austin: University of Texas Press, 1992. Published on Lady Bird's eightieth birthday, this is a collection of intimate pictures and memoirs, chronicling her life.

Montgomery, Ruth. *Mrs. LBJ*. New York: Holt, Rinehart and Winston, 1964. Written while she was still First Lady, this book looks at the Johnson marriage and at Lady Bird.

Smith, Marie. *The President's Lady: An Intimate Biography of Mrs. Lady Bird Johnson*. New York: Holt, Rinehart, and Winston, 1964. Explores the interests and background of the First Lady, devoting attention to her upbringing and married life. Although dated, it is still a useful study of Lady Bird.

Robert P. Watson

Pat Nixon

Thelma Catherine "Patricia" Ryan Nixon

Born: March 16, 1912
    Ely, Nevada
Died: June 22, 1993
    Park Ridge, New Jersey

President: Richard M. Nixon
    1969-1974

Overview: Pat Nixon had a great capacity for love and compassion. As First Lady, she was a promoter of community service, a goodwill ambassador, and an advocate for women. As the wife of a controversial president, Richard M. Nixon, she maintained her grace and self-respect in the face of protest and demonstration. Finally, she withstood the ultimate indignity as she watched the man she loved driven from office. Through it all, Pat maintained her composure, bolstered her family, and earned the admiration and respect of many Americans.

Pat Nixon, circa 1969. *(Library of Congress)*

Early Life
Thelma Catherine Ryan was born on March 16, 1912, in a miner's shack in Ely, Nevada. Kate Ryan insisted that her daughter be called Thelma Catherine, but her husband, Will, the son of Irish immigrants, was equally firm that his "Babe" celebrate her birthday on St. Patrick's Day. In 1913, Thelma's family purchased a ten-acre farm in Artesia, California, and moved into a small house that had no electricity or indoor plumbing. Survival on the Ryan farm was an all-consuming effort. With her two older brothers, Thelma tended the fields, fed the animals, drove the ox cart, and picked tomatoes and cauliflower.

The Ryan children learned early not to expect much and to be stoic in hiding their feelings. Despite his own violent mood swings, Will Ryan did not accept open demonstrations of emotion. His daughter would grow up to prefer silence to confrontation. Thelma learned about the larger world from her father as well. The escape through books, the love of travel and adventure, and a strong sense of independence became as much a part of her as they were of him. Thelma was a tomboy who loved the outdoors, but reading was her favorite pastime. As she explained, books were "the biggest influence on my life. [They] gave me a horizon beyond the small town we were living in. Somehow I always knew there was more in the world than what we were experiencing then."

When she was six years old, Thelma joined her brothers in the mile-long walk to grammar school. Because she had already learned to read, she was recognized as an exceptional student and skipped second grade. She became a perfectionist about her schoolwork, her appearance, and even her chores. Thelma also excelled at oration, and soon she was asked to speak before local clubs. She gave one speech on behalf of Senator Robert "Fighting Bob" La Follette that was so powerful her father deserted the Democratic Party in 1924 to vote for him.

In her rare moments of free time, Thelma loved to garden and visit the beach. With her best friends, she learned to roll cigarettes. The girls scandalized Artesia by wearing blue jeans. In the summer of 1925, however, thirteen-year-old Thelma had to grow up. Her mother died of liver cancer. In addition to her schoolwork and farm chores, Thelma now had to do all the housekeeping for her father and older brothers. She became convinced that she could do anything if she had to.

Throughout her years at Excelsior High School, Thelma was active in student government and school plays. She was also a superb student who just missed graduating as valedictorian of the class of 1929. During her senior year, Will Ryan developed tuberculosis. Thelma had to add nursing to her list of responsibilities. She dreamed of broadening her horizons and earning a college degree, but the United States was in the middle of the Great Depression, and the Ryan farm had not produced a profit in more than a year. Instead of college, Thelma went to work to pay for her father's hospitalization. He died in 1930, and she changed her name to Patricia in honor of her father's Irish heritage.

Pat began working two or three jobs at a time—as a cleaning woman, chauffeur, stenographer, X ray technician, librarian, sales clerk, model, detective, and movie extra—to pay for her education at Fullerton Junior College and the University of Southern California. In 1937 she graduated magna cum laude with degrees in business and education. She wanted to be a buyer for a department store, but in that time of national economic crisis, when Pat was offered a teaching position, she took it. For eighteen hundred dollars per year, she would teach typing and business courses at Whittier Union High School. The long summer vacations would allow her to pursue her passion for travel.

Pat moved to Whittier, a town of twenty-five thousand people fifteen miles south of Los Angeles, in the fall of 1937. Because of her openness, availability to students, and her compassion for those who had to work their way through school, Pat was a very popular teacher. In addition to her classroom duties, she coached the cheerleaders and directed student plays. Like all Whittier teachers, she was expected to take part in community activities.

Marriage and Family

In February, 1938, Pat auditioned for a role in a play being produced by the Whittier Community Players. Richard Milhous Nixon, the twenty-four-year-old assistant city attorney, was also trying out for a role. From the moment he saw Pat Ryan, he could not take his eyes off of her. He fell in love with her that night. Although not usually impulsive, he told her he was going to marry her. Pat was stunned; they

Richard M. Nixon

Richard Milhous Nixon was one of the most controversial American presidents. His years in office (1969-1974) were marked by great accomplishments and great personal and political failings. Historians have speculated that Nixon's ambition—he had wanted to be president since he was eight years old—caused problems when it collided with his sense of inferiority. Although he had been a congressman, senator, and vice president, he entered the White House doubting that people liked him.

As president, Nixon's biggest problem was how to end the unpopular war in Vietnam. He began to withdraw American ground troops and train the South Vietnamese to fight without U.S. support. Yet Nixon also began sustained bombing of North Vietnam and extended the war to neighboring Cambodia and Laos. Much of the American public was outraged, and the United States and its allies continued to lose on the field. In 1973 Nixon was forced to accept a peace treaty and withdraw all American troops from Vietnam. The United States had lost thirty-five thousand lives, failed to achieve its objective, and lost an important post in Southeast Asia. By early 1975 the Communists had united Vietnam under their rule.

While fighting the North Vietnamese Communists, Nixon tried to improve U.S. relations with other Communist nations. In February, 1972, the president paid an official visit to the People's Republic of China, opening new markets for trade and, in Nixon's words, "bridging sixteen thousand miles and twenty-two years of hostility." In May, 1972, the Nixons traveled to the Soviet Union. There Nixon arranged a favorable trade agreement for the United States, completed negotiations for the first Strategic Arms Limitation Treaty, and initiated scientific and cultural exchanges.

Nixon did not neglect domestic policy. He supported new Social Security benefits, subsidized housing for working class families, championed a minimum family income, and created both the Environmental Protection Agency and the Occupational Safety and Health Administration. Nixon took the United States off the gold standard, basing the dollar's value on the world market rather than the price of gold. He balanced these liberal measures by nominating conservatives to the Supreme Court. He also strengthened the Republican Party in the South by opposing most Civil Rights initiatives.

The last months of Nixon's administration were consumed by scandal. In 1972 Vice President Spiro Agnew admitted taking kickbacks while governor of Maryland and pleaded no contest to charges of income tax evasion. Agnew resigned from office in October, 1973. Ten months later, facing certain impeachment for obstructing justice in the Watergate scandal, Richard Nixon became the first U.S. president to resign from office.

had barely spoken. She returned home and told her roommates she met a man who was "nuts."

Richard, whom many considered Whittier's most eligible bachelor, pursued Pat with single-minded devotion. He learned to dance and ice skate to impress her, helped her grade student papers, wrote poetry for her, and even drove her to Los Angeles for dates with other men. Gradually, Pat realized she had much in common with the young attorney. They were

both shy and detested confrontations. Both had been orators in school and had skipped second grade. They loved to read and to walk the beach at San Clemente. Like Pat, Richard had wanderlust. He wanted to go places and make a difference. As Pat told her amused roommates, "he's going to be president someday."

On the second anniversary of the day they met, Richard wrote: "And when the winds blow and the rains fall and the sun shines through the clouds, as it is now, he still resolves as he did then, that nothing so fine ever happened to him or anyone else as falling in love with Thee—my dearest heart." A month later, he proposed. The Nixons were married on June 21, 1940, in a small family ceremony. After a honeymoon in Mexico, they resolved to save all their money and travel the world. However, World War II intervened. While he volunteered for active duty in the Navy, she worked in Washington and San Francisco in the Office of Price Administration.

After the war ended, Nixon entered politics. He had dreamed of public service since he was a boy, and Republicans in California's Twelfth Congressional District enthusiastically encouraged his candidacy. Pat had reservations about a political life, but she acquiesced: "I could see it was the life he wanted, so I told him it was his decision and I would do what he liked." This reflected a great deal of faith in her husband. The campaign would be financed by the Nixons' carefully accrued savings. Pat was pregnant with their first child.

In the 1946 congressional race, the "Dick and Pat" team was born. He respected and relied upon her advice. While he stumped for votes, she staffed the campaign office, answering mail, doing research, and writing speeches. Six hours after their daughter Tricia was born, on February 21, 1946, Pat was doing research in her hospital bed. Three weeks later she went back to work at the office. As the campaign progressed, Pat was increasingly called upon to go with the candidate to meet voters. She was nervous and ill at ease at first, but her natural grace and charm prevailed. Pat's charisma softened her husband's dour personality and made him seem more human and accessible to voters. The Dick and Pat team campaigned together for his reelection to the House in 1948, the year their daughter Julie was born, and for election to the Senate in 1950.

When General Dwight D. Eisenhower chose Senator Nixon as his running mate in 1952,

Pat stated she would campaign with her husband because "we always work as a team." She handled mail and news releases, attended women's meetings, and made informal, nonpolitical speeches. A party official claimed, "She's the best one on the ticket . . . the crowds just love her." A seasoned campaigner by 1952, Pat was still troubled by the intrusion of the campaign into the family's private life. Reporters and photographers hounded the Nixon girls, inventing stories about them when none were forthcoming.

The most intrusive issue in 1952 was the charge that Richard Nixon had accepted personal gifts from wealthy benefactors. The suddenness and fierceness of the attack and Eisenhower's failure to support his vice presidential nominee shocked Pat. Yet when her husband pondered resigning from the ticket, Pat insisted he fight.

Nixon chose to plead his case on national television. Seated beside Pat, he made a full and detailed disclosure of their personal finances, described their modest lifestyle, and said that instead of fur, Pat wore "a respectable Republican cloth coat." Nixon admitted that he had indeed accepted one gift, a puppy named Checkers whom his daughters loved and he refused to give back. He defused the scandal without answering the most important charges. The speech was a huge success, and three million people wrote in support of Nixon. The Eisenhower ticket went on to victory in November. Pat Nixon, however, remained "scarred for life" by the experience. She would forever find it nearly impossible to talk about the charges or the Checkers speech. The unfairness of the charges, the loss of privacy, and the lingering suspicions wore away at her idealism and enthusiasm for political life.

Nonetheless, Pat became the most involved vice presidential spouse to date. Fulfilling her lifelong desire to see the world, she made frequent goodwill trips with her husband. Pat studied the countries she was to visit and, while traveling, tried to avoid ceremonial functions. She preferred to see schools, public housing projects, and hospitals. In Panama, she was the first dignitary to visit a leper colony. She insisted on meeting women's groups in every country she visited. Pat wanted to bring attention to women's accomplishments as well as their problems, especially in nations where women's status was low. State Department officials and President Eisenhower praised Pat's diplomatic skills. This was especially true in 1958, when the Nixons were targets of death threats and violent anti-American demonstrations in Peru and Venezuela. A Secret Service agent said Pat displayed, "more guts than any man I've ever seen." The press called her "magnificent."

Pat was so popular that when Nixon ran against Senator John F. Kennedy in the 1960 presidential election, the Republicans made her an important part of the campaign. "When you elect a president, you are electing a First Lady whose job is more than glamour," they announced. "The First Lady has a working assignment. She represents America to all the world. Pat Nixon is part of the experienced Nixon team. She is uniquely qualified for the position of First Lady." Pat attended coffees and rallies in her honor and encouraged women to engage in the political process. She described herself as "reflective of women all over America taking an active part not only in political life, but in all activities." Pat also undertook her traditional Nixon campaign role.

Vice President and Mrs. Nixon arrive at a stop during the 1960 presidential campaign. *(National Archives)*

She advised the candidate, answered mail, wrote speeches and position papers, and did research. She joined her husband in fulfilling his campaign promise to visit all fifty states, even when that meant traveling to twenty-five states in fourteen days.

Pat Nixon gave so much of herself in the election of 1960 that she was bitterly disappointed by the outcome. The results were very close: Nixon lost by two-tenths of 1 percent of sixty-nine million ballots cast. Pat pushed for a recount, but Nixon, however, conceded. It was one of the few times in her life that Pat cried. The events of 1960 added to her disillusionment with politics, and even though she regretted losing, she was glad to be out of public life.

Pat had always tried to shield her daughters from politics. She told a reporter, "We are trying to let the girls grow up happily in a good home. I want that more than anything else." Pat refused most requests for pictures of her daughters and entertained political guests in hotels, rather than in the Nixon family home. She agonized over long trips that took her away from Tricia and Julie, and while away, she wrote to her daughters every day. When she was in town, Pat made it a point to be home every afternoon when the girls returned from school. She made them cocoa and cinnamon toast, helped with their homework, and made their home a haven for neighborhood children. She dreaded the day when the girls would be old enough to read the news and see criticism of their father. Their security and well-being was always Pat's first priority.

In 1962, when Richard decided to campaign for governor of California, Pat did not want to disrupt her family's privacy and contentment. Nonetheless, when both Tricia and Julie supported their father's plan, Pat gave in. When he lost the election, the Nixons moved to New York City. Pat rejoiced that they were "out of the rat race." She did not miss politics. From 1963 to 1968, as Richard traveled the country in support of Republican candidates, Pat—for the first time in their marriage—stayed home. She filled her days with reading, swimming, running, and yoga, regaining some of the privacy she had surrendered to her husband's ambition.

Pat was distraught when polls showed Nixon to be the leading Republican candidate for president in 1968. She was still greatly wounded by the Checkers incident and the bitter loss to Kennedy. Yet, in a tumultuous time in American history, with the United States mired in the Vietnam War abroad and antiwar and Civil Rights demonstrations at home, Pat truly believed her husband could make a difference for the United States. In the end, she swallowed her reservations. In a campaign Nixon described as "inordinately difficult for her," Pat worked hard rallying the volunteers. She met with women of all perspectives and carried a message to the candidate: "They want peace." Ignoring the long tradition of the Dick and Pat team in electoral politics, Nixon's staff downplayed Pat's contributions. They barred her from campaign strategizing and failed to introduce her when she made joint appearances with her husband.

Presidency and First Ladyship

During Richard Nixon's presidency (1969-1974), Chief of Staff H.R. Haldeman increasingly excluded Pat from political decisions and appearances. Nonetheless, she was an extraordinarily successful First Lady who made significant contributions to her husband's administration and to the country.

Pat Nixon really loved people, and they responded to her warmth. She received fifteen hundred letters per month. While Pat could not read all of them, she insisted on being informed about the issues addressed to her. She wanted every letter answered within three days because she knew how important a letter to the White House was to people. For the same reason, Pat personally signed everything sent out in her name. People in crisis wrote to the First

Lady, as they had to Eleanor Roosevelt, and Pat did whatever she could to help them through political channels.

As White House hostess, Pat wanted a warm house which was accessible to the public. She was the first First Lady since Florence Harding to come downstairs to welcome tourists. In her first four years in office, Pat met more than a quarter million White House visitors. Some were overcome with emotion at meeting the First Lady, and she greeted them with comforting hugs. She believed the White House belonged to the people, and she opened the place to them in new ways. She gave evening tours at Christmas for working people and opened the gardens during the summer. Pat designed less militaristic uniforms for the guards, narrated a filmed tour of the house, installed ramps for the disabled, and ordered that blind visitors be allowed to touch the antiques.

Pat's love of people also inspired her first project as First Lady. In 1970 she announced plans to recruit a nationwide cadre of volunteers dedicated to community service. She said, "Our success as a nation depends upon our willingness to give generously of ourselves for the welfare and enrichment of the lives of others." During her first tour on behalf of volunteerism, she visited and encouraged programs in the inner cities. She explained that such programs could accomplish things that legislation could not, and she sought out and commended programs for children, migrant workers, and the disabled. Pat belonged to several groups, including the National Center for Voluntary Action, and she frequently conferred with their leaders and attended awards ceremonies. She used the Thanksgiving holiday to put her support of voluntary action into practice. She invited senior citizens and soldiers without families to dinner at the White House. Pat was the first First Lady to issue a Thanksgiving Proclamation encouraging peace and hope amid the antiwar demonstrations taking place in the United States.

Pat's sincerity and warmth enabled her to be an outstanding goodwill ambassador for the United States. In sixty-five months as First Lady, she visited thirty-one nations. On foreign trips, Pat refused to be serviced by an entourage because she thought it was an unfair expense to the taxpayers. In marked contrast to other First Ladies, Pat packed her own suitcases and styled her own hair. Although Secret Service agents forbade it, she would have preferred to fly on commercial airlines.

Pat accompanied her husband on official trips to Vietnam, the Soviet Union, and China. She also made important contributions to U.S. diplomatic relations on solo journeys. Pat's deep compassion for the suffering of others prompted her trip to Peru in 1970. When she learned that an earthquake there had killed 80,000 people and left 800,000 homeless, the First Lady contacted her network of voluntary associations to gather food, clothing, and medical supplies. She then flew to Peru to deliver relief, attend a memorial Mass, and inspect the worst-hit areas. Peruvian President Juan Velasco's policies were anti-American; he sought ties with the Soviets and seized American-owned businesses. Pat's concern for the suffering Peruvians changed this. Velasco's aide claimed that her visit meant more than anything else President Nixon might have done. A Lima newspaper praised her "human warmth" and "solidarity." The Peruvian president awarded Pat the Grand Cross of the Sun, the oldest decoration in the Western Hemisphere.

Another solo jaunt took the First Lady to Africa in 1972. There she was presented with Liberia's highest honor, the Grand Cordon of the Most Venerable Order of Knighthood. She spoke to the National Assembly of Ghana and addressed a crowd of 250,000 in Ivory Coast (now Côte D'ivoire). The nations of postcolonial Africa distrusted the United States, but wherever she went, Pat charmed the people. The president said, "The substitute was doing a much better job than the principal would have

Gifts from China

In 1972 Richard and Pat Nixon made a historic visit to the People's Republic of China. Pat prepared for the trip with her usual curiosity and thoroughness. She studied the Communist Party structure, learned several Chinese phrases, and familiarized herself with the teachings of Mao Zedong, chairman of the Chinese Communist Party.

While her husband attended closed meetings, Pat charmed people and made news wherever she went. At the Evergreen People's Commune, she petted a pig and recalled her own childhood on a farm. She visited a school and spoke about her days as a teacher. The First Lady also talked with workers in a glass factory, watched an acupuncture procedure at a free clinic, and dined on goldfish. Refusing to be drawn into political debates, she simply found elements of Chinese culture to praise. Zhou Enlai, the Chinese foreign minister, was so captivated by Pat that he gave her two rare giant pandas as his personal gift. The pandas' presence at the National Zoo in Washington, D.C., captivated crowds for twenty-eight years, symbols of conservation, friendship, and goodwill.

done." His aide wrote: "Mrs. Nixon has broken through where we have failed. . . . People, men and women—identify with her—and in turn with you."

Chief of Staff Haldeman ignored the First Lady's diplomatic triumphs. He tried to isolate the president and omit Pat from presidential trips. Nonetheless, by 1972 Pat had visited thirty-nine states and more nations than any other First Lady. Although she had become a public figure in her own right, Pat deflected all praise back to the president. To the consternation of Haldeman, Pat advised her husband on television appearances, read issue papers, and attended cabinet meetings and briefings. She believed it was important for women to be politically informed, and she wanted to make women an important part of the administration.

Pat's disillusionment with politics made her glad her that daughters would not be political wives. She had higher aspirations for them. She speculated that Julie might run for office some day and suggested that if she herself was younger, she might consider a political career. Pat's own experience as a working woman made her sensitive to the women in her husband's admin-

istration and to the nascent women's movement. During Nixon's presidency, the number of women in high level appointments tripled, and more than one thousand new women were employed in government. Pat publicly called upon her husband to appoint a woman to the Supreme Court. He considered several but appointed men, leaving Pat disappointed that her advice had not been followed.

Pat considered the newly formed National Women's Political Caucus "wild," but she agreed with their goals of getting more women elected, "even if they were not Republicans." To Pat, a woman who had supported herself, her father, and her brothers, put herself through college during the Depression, and held several jobs at a time, the Equal Rights Amendment (ERA) was important on a personal level. She was the first sitting First Lady to support the ERA. She was also publicly in favor of abortion rights, which her husband renounced.

Although Pat could disagree with her husband on occasion, she strongly supported his policies in Vietnam. This made her a frequent target of protesters. At one public appearance, as confetti fell upon the First Lady, demonstrators shouted, "If this were napalm, you would now be dead." At another event, women dressed as witches cursed her and chanted antiwar messages. When Pat spoke in Boston, thousands of protesters picketed, burned a car, smashed windows, and fought with police. When Pat attended a concert at the Washington Monument, she was booed. Despite her best efforts over the years to protect her daughters from publicity and political demonstrations, Julie had to forgo her graduation ceremony at Smith College because of threatened protest. The First Lady was deeply concerned with the antiwar demonstrators. On her second volunteerism tour, she deliberately scheduled stops on college campuses. Though under a death threat, Pat reached out to the students. One protester said, "She wanted to listen. I felt like this is a woman who really cares about what we are doing. I didn't expect her to be like that." As in the past, Pat softened the president's image and brought unexpected credit to his administration.

Pat Nixon could not, however, save her husband from his greatest political crisis. In June, 1972, the Democratic National Headquarters at the Watergate Hotel in Washington, D.C., was burglarized. Although the break-in received little media attention, two reporters traced the burglars to the Committee to Re-Elect the President. Nixon denied any knowledge of the break-in, and Pat believed him. Nonetheless, the Senate began an investigation. This made the president more and more reclusive, and he isolated the First Lady from his troubles. Pat did succeed in getting the president to fire Chief of Staff Haldeman when testimony revealed he was involved in the break-in. However, witnesses before the Senate also revealed that the president made secret recordings of his conversations in the Oval Office. There was a protracted struggle over release of the tapes.

During that interval, the press hounded the Nixons. They suggested that the president misused public funds. Pat was the first First Lady to have her marriage scrutinized while in office. Reporters charged her with bigamy and ac-

cused the president of having an affair with a communist spy. Rumors of divorce were rampant. False reports claimed that Pat was drinking heavily. As much as this pained the very private woman, she remained fiercely loyal. She told one reporter, "I have great faith in my husband . . . [and] I love him."

In June, 1974, the Supreme Court issued a unanimous decision requiring President Nixon to release the tapes. Pat was shocked when she read the transcripts. As Julie Nixon explained, "the Richard Nixon on those tapes was not the Richard Nixon the family saw every day." Although incomplete, the tapes were very damning. They included the president's ravings against his enemies, anti-Semitic and profane remarks, and his efforts to use federal agencies to harass private citizens. The tapes also proved that Nixon had ordered a cover-up of his role in the Watergate break-in.

In July, 1974, the House Judiciary Committee adopted three articles of impeachment charging Nixon with obstruction of justice. Pat kept working. She was still proud of her husband and remained convinced that the entire scandal was a Democratic plot to destroy him. The president was awed by her strength, and when he realized the only alternative to impeachment was resignation, he could not bring himself to tell Pat of his decision. Julie told her mother the president had to quit. For only the second time in her adult life, Pat cried. Watergate only added to the personal anger and bitterness she developed toward politics during the Checkers incident and the 1960 election. Her hopes and idealism irrevocably crushed, Pat Nixon dried her tears and began to gather boxes for the move back to California. On August 9, 1974, with Pat at his side, Richard Nixon departed the White House as the only president forced to resign from office.

Legacy

In retirement, the Nixons settled in San Clemente, California, on the same beach they had walked while courting. Pat, in deep despair, became a recluse. She refused to give interviews, serve on charity boards, or see her friends. Nonetheless, she remained one of the most admired women in the United States, according to a *Ladies Home Journal* poll. In July, 1976, Pat suffered a stroke that left her partially paralyzed. As she recovered, and resumed reading and gardening, *McCall's* magazine called her the "unsinkable Pat Nixon." She remained bitter about politics but was convinced that her husband would eventually be fully vindicated.

In the 1980's the Nixons moved to the New York City area to be closer to their children and grandchildren. A second stroke in 1983 left Pat in frail health. Although she had never permitted herself to be seen smoking in public, she was a lifelong smoker. In her later years, Pat suffered from lung problems and emphysema. She died of lung cancer on June 22, 1993. She was eighty-one years old and had fulfilled her childhood dreams of seeing the world and making a difference. She would be fondly remembered for her many contributions to her husband's political career, for her sincerity and concern for the American people, and as an ambassador of goodwill in the United States and abroad.

Suggested Readings

Anthony, Carl Sferrazza. *First Ladies: The Saga of the Presidents' Wives and Their Power.* Vol. 2. New York: William Morrow, 1991. Contains a balanced overview of Pat Nixon's tenure as First Lady.

Eisenhower, Julie Nixon. *Pat Nixon: The Untold Story.* New York: Simon & Schuster, 1986. A very comprehensive view of Pat Nixon's life, as told by her daughter.

Nixon, Richard Milhous. *RN: The Memoirs of Richard Nixon.* New York: Simon & Schuster, 2000. The president's autobiography.

Small, Melvin. *The Presidency of Richard Nixon.* Lawrence: University Press of Kansas, 1999. A thorough and scholarly examination of the Nixon administration.

Summers, Anthony, and Robbyn Swan. *The Arrogance of Power: The Secret World of Richard Nixon.* New York: Viking, 2000. Offers a critical journalistic view of Richard M. Nixon's career and marriage.

Mary Linehan

Betty Ford

Elizabeth Ann Bloomer Ford

Born: April 8, 1918
Chicago, Illinois

President: Gerald R. Ford
1974-1977

Overview: Betty Ford is remembered as one of the most outspoken and influential First Ladies of all time. Although she entered the White House during turbulent times, she captivated a nation. Gerald R. Ford's taking office in the aftermath of the Watergate scandal meant that Betty would be subjected to greater scrutiny than most of her predecessors. Fortunately for the country, she did not shy away from the challenge. Her positive attitude, candor, and honesty were refreshing remedies for an ailing nation and set the standard for the modern First Lady.

Early Life

Born to William and Hortense Bloomer on April 8, 1918, in Chicago, Betty was the youngest of three children. Her family moved to Grand Rapids, Michigan, when she was two years old. It was at 717 Fountain Street that Betty would spend her formative years with her mother, father, and two older brothers.

Her childhood appears to have been happy and full of fond memories. From jumping through piles of leaves in the fall to swimming in Whitefish Lake in the summer, Betty was a typical child who enjoyed playing with friends and family. She would later say, "There were few shadows over my childhood."

Betty especially enjoyed spending time with her older brothers, Bill and Bob. She became something of a tomboy while following them around and pestering them to let her play sports with them and the other boys. Betty also joined them on the annual Halloween ram-

Betty Ford, 1974. *(Library of Congress)*

page they called "garbage night." Instead of trick-or-treating, they would tip over garbage cans, whitewash porches, and soap windows in their neighborhood. While under the care of her brothers, Betty also developed a life-long tendency to root for the underdog. When-ever they would fight, she would inevitably get involved by pulling off the guy on top—regardless of which brother happened to be winning. She did not care who won; she just rooted for the individual who happened to be losing at the time.

Despite a generally happy childhood in a loving family, Betty missed being able to spend a lot of time with her father. William Bloomer's work as a machinery salesman kept him away from home much of the time during Betty's early years. When he was home, he showered the children with gifts, which Betty later as-cribed to his "trying to make up for his ab-sences." It is clear that Betty never truly under-stood her father's frequent departures; she swore at an early age that when she was grown she would marry a man who stayed at home.

While William was away, Hortense was her children's primary caregiver—and disciplinar-ian. She was often very hard on Betty. Hortense tended to be very formal and strict with her daughter, scrutinizing the way she dressed, her table manners, even her chewing gum—which could not be done in the presence of others. Hortense was also of the opinion that anything worth doing was worth doing right. After one of Betty's school shows, in which the girl did not perform up to her mother's standards, Hortense said, "If you don't do it well, don't do it at all."

Betty's mother also had a softer side and knew how to make her daughter feel special. From early on, Betty's mother would tell her that she had "popped out of a bottle of cham-pagne." Betty liked the idea. Hortense also knew how to instill a sense of pride in her daughter when Betty was feeling down, as she did once when Betty came home from school

crying because the other children had teased her about a birthmark on her arm. Hortense turned the situation around, stating that be-cause Betty was the only girl with that particu-lar mark, she was a "very special child." That logic allowed Betty to return to school the next day with her head held high, aware that she was unique. The combination of strict formal-ity and loving intuition helped Betty and Hortense to develop a special bond; Betty wor-shiped her mother and wanted to be like her. In later years, Betty would form a similar bond with her own daughter.

When Betty was eight years old, something happened that would influence her life into her early twenties: She discovered dance. At eight, she and a group of other children began taking social dance classes. While all of the kids were doing it, dancing proved to be something spe-cial for her. Despite the fact that her initial re-cital was nothing spectacular—her mother thought Betty was not very good and should give it up—Betty persevered. She continued to study through elementary school, middle school, and high school with the hope of one day becoming a professional dancer. By the time she was fourteen, Betty was giving dance lessons. After high school graduation, she at-tended the Bennington School of Dance in Ver-mont. She loved being able to dance eight hours a day with no interferences. While at the school, Betty became mesmerized by one of the in-structors, the legendary choreographer Martha Graham.

In 1939, at the age of twenty-one, Betty went to New York City to study dance under Gra-ham's direction. While in the city, however, Betty found that she could have fun too. In fact, it appears that life in the city became a distrac-tion and that socializing began to interfere with her dancing. At one point, Graham told Betty to make a choice, saying, "You can't carouse and be a dancer too." After the counseling session, Betty threw herself into dancing but also won-dered whether she had the internal drive to commit to dance completely. Betty's mother also noticed with concern that Betty was enjoying herself in New York. Hortense thought that the city posed a danger to young Betty and that it might be best for her to return home to Michigan. Hortense made a deal with Betty to bring her back to Michigan. She asked Betty to humor her by coming home for six months before deciding whether to continue her dancing career. If, after the allotted time, Betty still wanted to live in New York, Hortense would never speak another word on the subject. When Betty approached Graham with her mother's plan, Graham told Betty that it was probably the right thing to do. With that, Betty returned to Michigan—for good.

Marriage and Family

Betty did not lose touch with New York. Upon returning home, she supported herself by working at Herpolsheimer's Department Store as a fashion coordinator. In addition to organizing fashion shows and window displays at the store, Betty was often asked to go to New York to place orders. She continued to be involved with dancing; when not working, she gave dance lessons to children. She also continued to lead an active social life.

Betty was often wined and dined by local bachelors, but she never felt any particular attraction to any of them, thinking they all tended to be a bit too stuffy. A young man named Bill Warren was different, however. Betty had known Bill for years and had dated him when they were younger. This time around, however, Betty was more attracted to him than she had been in earlier days. Unfortunately, her mother was not nearly as enthusiastic about Bill as Betty was. Betty had to sneak out of the house or lie about whom she was seeing in order to avoid confrontations. Eventually, things got too serious between Betty and Bill for them to hide their relationship any longer. Early in 1942, they announced their engagement and were married in the spring of that year.

Despite her efforts to make the marriage a success, problems arose between Betty and Bill. She had always wanted a husband who would stay at home and provide stability—this desire, of course, stemmed from her disappointment with her father's frequent absences. For three years after Betty and Bill were married, they would bounce from town to town while Bill worked at a variety of jobs, never settling down. Whenever the two would stay put for any period of time, Bill would spend more time at the bars than at home. When, in 1945, Betty finally decided to end their marriage, Bill became seriously ill. Bedridden, he required constant attention, and Betty remained by his side for the next two years in order to take care of him. When he at last recovered, Betty filed for divorce, and Bill raised no objections. In her words, the whole episode was a "five-year misunderstanding." In 1947, Betty was on her own.

In August of that year, a friend convinced Betty to go on a date with a young Grand Rapids lawyer named Gerald Ford. He had recently ended a long-term relationship, and her divorce was not yet final; neither one was looking for a serious relationship. In fact, they agreed to take things lightly and not to take each other seriously. Despite their intentions, they got along famously and began to see more of each other.

The test of their relationship came at Christmastime, 1947. Jerry left for Sun Valley, Idaho, on a skiing trip which would keep him away for three weeks. Because of work, Betty was not able to go with him. This was the first time that they had spent weeks apart since they had begun dating, and Betty knew that she would miss him. It seems that Jerry missed her, too, because he wrote to her every day. Moreover, he bought her a hand-crafted belt. The belt was not important; the significance of the gift was. One of his friends found out about the seemingly innocuous present and responded by saying, "Jerry Ford actually gave a present to a girl? This must be serious." The friend was correct. Despite their initial agreement not to become too serious about each other, Betty and Jerry were deeply in love. In February of 1948, a mere six months after they began dating, Jerry asked Betty to marry him, and she eagerly accepted.

When Jerry proposed, he said they could not get married until the fall. Though he did not tell her why at the time, she soon found out that he was planning to run for Congress. She immediately began to help him with his campaign and also recruited some of the models from Herpolsheimer's, her dancing friends, and anyone else she could corral to assist with the effort. The excitement was contagious as their

friends got wrapped up in the Ford for Congress campaign. While Betty was thoroughly invested in Jerry's cause, the initial excitement eventually gave way to the realization of what her life was about to become.

Jerry won the primary election. Despite Betty's childhood decision to marry a man who would be a permanent household fixture, Jerry would be required to be away quite often. The night of the primary turned into a planning session for the next election. (Betty had thought they could plan for the wedding.) On the eve of their wedding rehearsal dinner, Jerry showed up for cocktails and then left to make a speech when the rest of the family went in to eat. Betty

Gerald R. Ford

As a young man, Gerald Ford was a tremendously gifted athlete, and he used his athleticism to his academic advantage. He attended the University of Michigan, where he majored in economics and political science. His goal was to become an attorney. Upon graduation, Ford was approached by two professional football teams, the Lions and the Packers, but he rejected them both. Instead of playing football, Ford accepted an offer to serve as a boxing coach and assistant football coach at Yale University. He hoped to become an attorney and believed that Yale had one of the best law schools. Eventually Ford was admitted to the Yale School of Law, and he was graduated in the top 25 percent of his class. Along the way, he was given a taste for politics when he worked for a brief time on the presidential campaign of Wendell Willkie.

Ford returned to Michigan and worked as an attorney prior to joining the U.S. Naval Reserve in 1942. He served in the South Pacific until his ship, the USS *Monterey*, was damaged during a storm in 1944. With the ship out of commission, Ford spent the remainder of his military time on dry land until 1946, when he was discharged.

Upon returning to Grand Rapids, Ford again practiced law. However, his overseas experience and work on the Willkie campaign had given him a more international outlook than he had held as a youth, and he decided that isolationism was not an appropriate course for the United States. With the encouragement of his stepfather and local political leaders, Ford set out to challenge the isolationist incumbent Bartel Jonkman for the Republican nomination for the U.S. House of Representatives in Michigan's fifth district. Despite the long odds, Ford won the nomination and eventually went on to represent Michigan for almost a quarter of a century. Ford was elected to Congress twelve times, and he received more than 60 percent of the vote each time. He was looked at by some in the Republican Party as presidential material, but that office was not something he sought.

Ford's true ambition was to become speaker of the House. He never planned on running for the presidency and had no desire to move from the legislative to the executive branch of government. If not for the events of Watergate, Ford would never have entered into the office of president of the United States, and Betty Ford would never have become First Lady.

was at the head of the table all alone until the minister took pity on her and sat in the groom's spot, though Jerry did return in time for dessert. Finally, on October 15, 1948, Jerry was out campaigning and arrived late to their wedding. Betty later told him that if he had not shown up, she would have married someone else. She was kidding of course; she loved him, and his frequent absences would not change that. Jerry was a politician, the Fords were a couple, and together they were about to go to Washington, D.C.

In the capital, Betty began to learn about politics and the legislative process. She attended sessions of Congress and joined several organizations whose members were wives of politicians. Betty also helped Jerry on weekends, doing filing and office work; that was sometimes the only way she could see him during his busy freshman term. During this time, Jerry often attended social functions without Betty. When Betty would run into some of the other congressional wives, they would ask why she had not been in attendance. Apparently, not everyone in town knew that Jerry Ford was married. After Betty had a "chat" with Jerry about the situation, he began informing people around Washington that he was not, in fact, a bachelor. Joint invitations soon followed.

The Ford family began to expand on March 14, 1950, with the birth of their first son, Mike. Two years later, on March 16, 1952, their second son, Jack, was born. About this time, the walls of the Fords' apartment were figuratively closing in on Betty, and she began to lobby for a house. In 1955 the Fords moved to 514 Crown View Drive in Alexandria, Virginia. Not long after settling into the new house, the Ford family began to grow even larger. A third son, Steve, was born on May 19, 1956, and Susan, their only daughter, was born on July 6, 1957. Throughout his children's early years, Jerry was forced to be away on congressional business much of the time, and Betty was left in charge at home.

His time away from home increased when Jerry became the minority leader in the House of Representatives in January, 1965. While Betty was proud of her husband, she once commented, "The Congress got a new minority leader, and I lost a husband." For a time, Jerry was away from home as much as 258 days per year. Betty was forced to assume the role her mother had played during Betty's youth: primary caregiver. Being alone to serve as den mother, as Sunday school teacher, as chauffeur, and in other capacities that went along with raising four children left Betty with little time for herself. Finally, in 1970, she experienced a nervous breakdown from the strain.

With support from a psychiatrist, Jerry, and her children, Betty slowly began to realize that she did not have to be superhuman. Moreover, they made it clear to her that she did not have to do everything for her family, and that it was important for her to take time for herself and to do things that were important to her. One thing that was important was for the family to have more time together and for her to get her husband back from the hold of Congress. Betty and Jerry agreed that he would retire at the end of President Richard Nixon's second term in office.

The Fords believed it was time for them to focus on themselves and their family. While he was still House minority leader, Jerry and Betty began happily contemplating their retirement plans when the resignation of Spiro Agnew as vice president of the United States changed their plans. In Betty's words, "Spiro Agnew upset our applecart."

With Agnew gone, there was speculation that Gerald Ford would be named as successor to the vice presidency, something Betty dismissed, reasoning that Jerry was too important for the Republican Party in Congress. Betty was so certain that Jerry would not be named—she felt it would be former Texas Governor John Connally—that she made a five-dollar bet with her daughter, Susan. Betty lost. While excited for her husband, Betty was inwardly saddened that their retirement plans would be delayed. Though disappointed, she put on her game face and pushed forward. According to Leesa Tobin, an archivist for the Gerald R. Ford Library and Museum, Betty "responded as a true politician's wife." Betty reportedly said, "Well, if they just wind me up and point me in the right direction, I'll be there."

If Agnew's departure and Jerry's subsequent selection as vice president changed their plans, the resignation of Richard Nixon put the Fords—especially Betty—into a tailspin.

Presidency and First Ladyship

The Fords had barely enough time to adjust to the added stress and pressure of the vice presidency when they were thrust onto center stage: Jerry was called upon to assume the presidency following Nixon's resignation in the wake of the Watergate scandal. Gerald R. Ford was sworn in as the thirty-eighth president of the United States on August 9, 1974, a day that Betty described as "the saddest day of my life."

Part of the sadness stemmed from the fact that the Fords and Nixons were friends. Betty was particularly fond of Pat Nixon, who she thought was a "very warm, friendly person." Betty, a caring person herself, hated seeing the pain in the White House as the Nixons were forced to seal themselves off from the media and the rest of the world. Of the protests going on outside, Betty felt that the personal attacks against Pat were particularly cruel and unfair. Betty also felt that it was a sad day for the United States in that one of its constitutional institutions, the presidency, was under attack. The remainder of Betty's sadness came from the nervousness and apprehension that accompany a sudden change.

Betty had been handed her saddest day and was suddenly expected to take on a role that was foreign to her. However, she was a quick study and took to the role of First Lady in a way no one had imagined possible. First and foremost, Betty entered into the office intent on maintaining family relations. To her, family had always been of the utmost importance. Beyond the inherent ties that a mother has with her children, Jerry and Betty were true companions and confidants. President Ford's speech following his oath of office provides some insight into the importance of the partnership that the Fords had developed over the years, despite his frequent absence. When he stated that "I am indebted to no man and only to one woman—my dear wife," it was clear that Betty was much more than a social sidekick.

While she knew that her husband's job pressures would put some strain on the family and that time together would be hard to come by, she set out to maintain stability in any way possible. One seemingly small attempt at normality actually created a minor stir when Betty insisted that she and the president would not be sleeping in separate bedrooms and that they would be bringing their own bed into the White House. She was accused of being immoral, but she did not care. She was perfectly willing to take on the duties of a First Lady but was not about to give up part of herself and the things she cared about in the process, a lesson she had learned from her breakdown in 1970.

It was apparent from the outset that her approach to the role of the First Lady would be direct. In discussing her view of being First Lady, Betty stated, "My approach was: I will just be open and not beat around the bush and answer their questions as best I can." The Ford presidency came at a time when the citizenry was questioning the integrity of government; Betty believed that candor and honesty would be crucial to the healing process. She set the tone for things to come when, at the first full-fledged press conference by a First Lady in more than twenty years, she announced to reporters that she wanted to encourage greater political participation by women. She endorsed the 1973 Supreme Court decision in *Roe v. Wade*, which established women's legal rights to abortion.

Driven by a Cause

Though Betty Ford is remembered for being the champion of very serious causes such as breast cancer awareness and substance abuse treatment, the role that she played in the fight for women's rights is often underplayed. When it came to supporting the Equal Rights Amendment (ERA), she was a vocal advocate and a strong lobbying force.

So powerful was her message that she became the target of lawyer Phyllis Schlafly, one of the primary players in the successful crusade against the passage of the ERA. Schlafly and her organization, called STOP ERA, were so concerned about Betty's impact that they demanded an accounting of how much federal money was being spent on the endorsement through telephone bills, staff time, or salaries of federal officials working on the issue.

Not to be dissuaded, Betty carried on and pushed forward with style. She even had an ERA flag (designed by one of her Secret Service detail) placed on her car. She had jokingly mentioned that while the president and other dignitaries had flags, she had a car with none. She said, "If the president gets flags, why shouldn't the First Lady?" What better way to announce her own motorcade than with a bright red, white, and blue flag emblazoned with ERA?

Betty made speeches in support of the Equal Rights Amendment (ERA) and openly discussed equal rights for women in interviews. She contacted legislators across the United States, encouraging them to vote for the amendment; if they could not openly endorse the measure, she wanted them at least to allow it to come to a vote.

Perhaps Betty's most lasting impact as First Lady came in the area of breast cancer awareness, an issue she had not intended to tackle. She began her monumental fight on September 26, 1974, the day she was diagnosed with breast cancer. When a tumor was discovered, the entire Ford family went into shock. However, despite the very private nature of the situation, Betty made a decision that would have a tremendous social impact: She decided to make her condition known to the public. This decision coincided with her philosophy of an open, honest First Ladyship. Though she could have quietly had the tumor removed and gone on with her life as if nothing had happened, she decided to discuss the uncomfortable issues of breast cancer and mastectomy publicly. While such a decision was undoubtedly difficult,

Betty, being an unassuming and humble person, acted as if she had no choice at all. According to her, "I got a lot of credit for having gone public with my mastectomy, but if I hadn't been the wife of the president of the United States, the press would not have come racing after my story, so in a way it was fate."

Nevertheless, by talking about her cancer and mastectomy, Betty was personally responsible for increased breast cancer awareness, and she became fully aware of the power that the First Lady holds. After she went public to alert as many women as possible to the benefits of early detection, millions scheduled appointments at clinics across the country. According to journalist Lisa Liebman, "Her courage and candor not only removed the stigma from the topic but also saved countless lives." Physicians afterward referred to the "Betty Ford effect" and the number of diagnoses directly attributable to her speaking out.

Of course there were times when the honest, candid approach led to controversy, but Betty stayed the course and never swayed from being as forthright as possible. From her views on abortion rights and the Equal Rights Amendment to her opinions on marijuana, premarital sex, and other socially sensitive issues, Betty was never shy about her position. In the process, she accomplished much and left a mark on the office of the First Lady in a very short time. Because of her presence, First Ladies who followed were held to a higher standard by the public. If Gerald Ford had been reelected when his term expired in 1976, there is no telling what great things Betty might have accomplished.

Legacy

Shortly after leaving the White House, Betty once again found herself the unwitting spokesperson for an illness that people rarely discussed openly. This time, it was alcoholism and addiction. True to form, Betty openly described her problem to reporters and the world, holding nothing back. Once again, her action had a tremendous spillover effect: If Betty Ford could confront this problem, then it was acceptable for others to acknowledge and fight it, too. She brought the topic to the forefront and made it safe for people to discuss addiction and to seek help. She went on to help countless other addicts by cofounding the Betty Ford Center (for alcohol and substance abuse) on October 3, 1982.

Betty Ford continued to oversee the operations of the Betty Ford Center in Rancho Mirage, California, into her eighties. She also remained active in promoting women's rights, health care, and funding for substance abuse, testifying before Congress on numerous occa-

Former First Lady Betty Ford and former health secretary Joseph Califano meet reporters to discuss a report on substance abuse among women, 1996. *(AP/Wide World Photos)*

sions. The range of her activism and social impact was broad. By continuously giving of herself, Betty became the recipient of more than twenty prestigious awards, including the Freedom of Human Spirit Award (bestowed by the International Center for the Disabled), the Hubert Humphrey Inspirational Award (the American Cancer Society), the Gold Key Award (National Council on Alcoholism), and the Presidential Medal of Freedom (awarded by President George H. W. Bush).

On October 27, 1999, she received the Congressional Gold Medal, an occasion she considered one of her proudest moments. Her husband was also a recipient of the Gold Medal that day; those in attendance were effusive in their praise for both President and Mrs. Ford with regard to their collective efforts to heal "a nation in torment" following Watergate. Everything Betty accomplished—both in and out of the White House—led some scholars to assert that Betty Ford was the "bridge" to the modern First Lady.

Suggested Readings

Boller, Paul F. *Presidential Wives: An Anecdotal History*. 2d ed. New York: Oxford University Press, 1999. Boller devotes a chapter to every First Lady from Martha Washington to Hillary Rodham Clinton.

Ford, Betty, with Chris Chase. *A Glad Awakening*. New York: Doubleday, 1987.

_____. *Times of My Life*. New York: Harper & Row, 1978. Betty Ford's insights provide a good look at life inside the White House.

Ford, Gerald. *A Time to Heal: The Autobiography of Gerald R. Ford*. New York: Harper & Row, 1979. Gerald Ford's frank memoir has been described as a seat in the family room of the White House.

TerHorst, Jerald F. *Gerald Ford and the Future of the Presidency*. New York: The Third Press, 1974.

Weidenfeld, Sheila Rabb. *First Lady's Lady: With the Fords at the White House*. New York: G. P. Putnam's Sons, 1979.

Jeffrey S. Ashley

Rosalynn Carter

Rosalynn Smith Carter

Born: August 18, 1927
Plains, Georgia

President: Jimmy Carter
1977-1981

Overview: Rosalynn Carter faced many challenges in her life. As the eldest of four children, she supported her mother emotionally after her father's death. After marriage, Rosalynn helped her husband, Jimmy Carter, run his family's peanut warehouse business. In 1976, before Carter was elected to the presidency, she campaigned with him. As First Lady, she campaigned in his stead because fulfilling his presidential duties was more important to the president than stumping for a second term in office. Following their White House years, the Carters returned home to Plains, where they were active in their community and church as well as in various charitable endeavors.

Rosalynn Carter, 1977. *(Library of Congress)*

Early Life

Rosalynn was the first of four children born to Althea Murray Smith and Wilburn Edgar Smith. She was born in Plains, a small town in central Georgia. Her father owned and operated a small auto repair shop and also drove the school bus. Her mother had gone to college and held a teaching credential but after her marriage had stayed home and taken care of her growing family. The family lost their savings (one thousand dollars) when the Plains bank failed in 1926.

Because there were no other girls in town her age, Rosalynn had a somewhat lonely childhood. She loved reading and enjoyed books such as *Heidi*, *Hans Brinker, or The Silver Skates*, and *Robinson Crusoe*. She also played games with her brothers and their friends, such as kick the can, cops and robbers, and war. Sometimes they hiked to Magnolia Springs and swam in the spring-fed pool. All the children in the family had chores. Rosalynn's chores were making beds, churning their cow's milk into butter, sweeping the porch, and washing and drying the dishes.

Church activities were very important to the Smith family. Rosalynn participated enthusiastically in church services, Sunday school, Bible school and Methodist Youth League. Another important part of her life was the town school. Rosalynn did well in school, often making all A's on her report cards. She tried to do well in all her subjects. In her seventh-grade class, a young teacher encouraged the students to read and bring articles to class about the events in Europe that year, 1939. Rosalynn searched the newspapers and found many interesting people and places far away from Plains, Georgia, but the events of 1939 were also frightening to the young girl, and sometimes she would lie in bed at night worrying about the future and wishing that somehow the problems of the times would "just go away."

The summer of 1939 brought other problems to Rosalynn's family. Her father, Wilburn, whom she adored, went into the hospital for some tests. Soon after that she realized he was very sick. Once, when he had trouble breathing, Rosalynn was told to call the doctor. Instead, she ran to the doctor's house. When she got there she was so breathless, she could hardly tell him why she had come. The doctor understood and they started immediately toward her home. Some time later Wilburn called the family together and told the children:

> I want you all to listen very carefully to what I have to say and be very brave. . . . The time has come to tell you that I can't get well and you are going to have to look after Mother for me. You are good children and I'm depending on you to be strong."

Rosalynn said that her childhood "really ended at that moment.

In the town of Plains, neighbors and friends helped the Smith family during Rosalynn's father's illness. Future president Jimmy Carter's mother, Lillian Carter, was a visiting nurse and came each day to give shots to Wilburn. After a lengthy illness, he died of leukemia at the age of forty-four. Rosalynn's mother was thirty-four and Rosalynn, the oldest child, was just thirteen. Less than a year later, her grandmother Murray died, and Rosalynn's grandfather moved into town to live with his daughter and her children. Everyone leaned on Rosalynn's mother. She now had the responsibility of caring for her four children and her father. They only had her father's insurance of $18.25 a month on which to live, so Rosalynn's mother sewed for people in the community, and Rosalynn helped her. Her mother also found jobs working in the school lunch room, as a clerk in the grocery store, and later as a clerk in the post office.

As the oldest child, Rosalynn felt that her mother depended on her. Her mother asked her help in caring for the younger children and sought her advice on many matters, such as which job she should take and how to keep within the family budget. Rosalynn felt the need to appear strong, but inside she was full of doubts and fears. Her father's death had left her feeling lost and vulnerable. During her father's illness she had prayed fervently for his recovery, and when he died she wondered why God had not answered her prayers.

In reaction, Rosalynn buried herself in her books and schoolwork. Gradually, she began to take an interest in other things. She tried out for and won a place on the girls' basketball team. For a while she worked after school and on Saturdays, giving shampoos at a local beauty shop. The part-time job provided her with some spending money. She also became friends with Ruth Carter, Jimmy's younger sister.

Public schools in Georgia were segregated, and when Rosalynn was in the ninth grade she began to realize the disparities between the separate school systems. An African American woman asked Rosalynn to type her college graduation thesis. Rosalynn was surprised to find that the woman's thesis had serious spelling, punctuation, and grammatical errors. She helped her correct the errors and was later pleased to learn that the woman received a passing grade. This incident led Rosalynn to realize that many black schools of the time were not equal to white schools.

Rosalynn was valedictorian of her senior class. She wrote her speech and spent hours practicing it until she knew it by heart. Although very nervous (her knees were shaking), she delivered the entire speech. The next year she fulfilled her father's dream and entered college, enrolling at Georgia Southwestern College in the nearby town of Americus. She would have liked to attend a school farther from home, but family finances dictated her decision.

Marriage and Family
Ruth Carter, Jimmy's younger sister and Rosalynn's close friend, had a picture of her brother tacked on her bedroom wall. Rosalynn "couldn't keep her eyes off of it." Jimmy was away at the United States Naval Academy in Annapolis, Maryland, and Rosalynn thought he was the most handsome man she had ever seen. He was three years older than she, and at the time they had not even spoken to each other.

When Jimmy came home on holiday, Rosalynn and Ruth plotted different ways they could bring Rosalynn and Jimmy together, but he always seemed too busy. Finally, Ruth called and invited Rosalynn to go with her and Jimmy to clean up the Pond House, a building Jimmy's father had built outside of town. It was used for church picnics and parties. Rosalynn went with the Carters to the Pond House and found, to her surprise, that she could talk easily with Jimmy. They joked and laughed as they were cleaning.

Later in the day, she went to a youth meeting at the church. As she stood outside on the church lawn before the meeting, Jimmy came by and asked her to double date with him and his sister Ruth and her boyfriend. Rosalynn left the church and went off with Jimmy. After the movie, they rode in the rumble seat of the car. There was a full moon, and on the way home, Jimmy kissed her. She was "completely swept off her feet." Jimmy must have been impressed too, because he told his mother, "She's the girl I want to marry."

Because Jimmy had a date the next night, his last night at home, with a girl from a neighboring town, Rosalynn had resigned herself to not seeing him again until Christmas. Ruth Carter talked her into going with the Carter family to the train station at midnight to see him off. Jimmy's mother also encouraged her. Rosalynn knew it was not the proper thing to do, but she just wanted to see Jimmy again. Jimmy was surprised to see her, but Rosalynn did not care. He walked her over to the edge of the train platform and asked her to write him. Then he kissed her good-bye.

While Jimmy was away at Annapolis, he and Rosalynn wrote to each other regularly. In December, when Jimmy came home for Christmas, they saw each other many times. They attended Christmas parties together, went to the movies, and went for long drives in the country. When he asked her to marry him, she turned him down. She had promised her father that she would get a college education. She was just in her first year at Georgia Southwestern. After two years there, she planned to transfer to Georgia State College for Women, where her mother had studied. At seventeen, Rosalynn felt too young and naïve for marriage. Jimmy understood as she explained all this to him. They agreed to wait.

In February she went with his parents to Annapolis on a holiday weekend. He proposed again, and this time she accepted. They were married on July 7, 1946, in what was planned to be a small church service with only a few friends and family members present. Jimmy

Jimmy Carter

James Earl Carter, Jr., grew up on a farm near Plains, Georgia. He held himself to high standards academically in his schooling at Plains and credits some of the teachers there with inspiring him to read and appreciate literature, music, and art. He was accepted at the United States Naval Academy in Annapolis, Maryland. While home on vacation, he met Rosalynn Smith and, within a short time, asked her to marry him. Their first home as a married couple was in Norfolk, Virginia, where Carter was assigned duty testing new navigation radar and communication and gunnery equipment on the USS *Wyoming*. He was then selected for submarine school in New London, Connecticut. Naval assignments then took him to Hawaii. When war broke out in Korea, Carter's submarine was assigned to San Diego, California. Another move took the Carters back to New London, where Carter was assigned to a small new submarine. He later applied for entrance into the nuclear submarine program headed by Admiral Hyman Rickover and was accepted.

When his father became very ill, Jimmy returned home. In long talks with his father, he learned that his father expected him to come back home to Plains and run the family peanut warehouse business and also take care of his mother and younger brother. Jimmy decided to leave the Navy, although Rosalynn did not want to return to Plains. Eventually, she reconciled herself to it, and they settled in to small-town life, participating in various activities. After a rocky start, the peanut business flourished, and Jimmy began to think of politics as a career. He ran first for state senator and won. Then he ran for governor and lost but tried again and was successful. He then decided to run for president. He was assisted by the Peanut Brigade, a group of volunteers, mostly from Georgia, who passed out pamphlets and knocked on doors, encouraging people to vote for Carter. He won the Democratic nomination and narrowly defeated President Gerald Ford, the Republican candidate, in 1976.

Carter's presidency began with high hopes, but he faced numerous obstacles; the economy was always a problem. There was recession and then inflation. To deal with this, he first recommended increased federal spending and lower taxes, but when inflation resulted, he called for spending cuts and delayed the tax reductions. These ups and downs tended to lower business and consumer confidence. Despite Western opposition, he approved new park and forest lands in Alaska. His most stunning success was the agreements which were achieved by bringing together the Egyptian president and the prime minister of Israel at Camp David. His most serious foreign policy problem began with the revolution in Iran, which spurred high oil prices and shortages; then Iranian militants took over the American Embassy and took sixty-five Americans hostage, fifty-two of whom were held for two and one-half years. Carter attempted a military rescue operation, which failed. The hostages were not freed until after Carter lost his bid for a second term. On the day after the inauguration of President Ronald Reagan, Carter flew to Germany to welcome back the newly freed hostages.

After leaving the White House, Jimmy and Rosalynn Carter became active in a number of causes. Jimmy worked to make the Carter Center in Atlanta not only a presidential library and museum but a study center. Both Carters also volunteered their time and talents for Habitat for Humanity, providing homes for people who might otherwise be homeless.

drove to her home to pick her up, and when they arrived at the church, it was packed.

Rosalynn and Jimmy's first home together was in Norfolk, Virginia. Jimmy was assigned duty testing new navigation radar communications and gunnery equipment. He was gone from Monday until Thursday or Friday every week and then had duty on the ship one other night when it was docked. Rosalynn learned to cope with the various problems of being a young Navy wife. She opened their first bank account and handled the bills, dealing with landlords, plumbers, and electricians. She also learned to cook. She soon became pregnant, suffering from morning sickness throughout the first few months of her pregnancy. John William Carter was born on July 3, 1947.

Rosalynn loved taking care of their new son, but Jack, as they called him, was not an easy child to care for. He cried a lot and did not sleep well. Sometimes Rosalynn did not get much sleep herself and was exhausted from taking care of him. Sometimes she cried, although she tried to hide this from her husband because he did not believe people should cry. Instead, he thought, they should make the best of the situation and put on a smile.

When Jimmy was selected for submarine school, he and Rosalynn moved to New London, Connecticut. While living there in the students' quarters, Rosalynn enjoyed the fellowship of the Navy wives and also studied Spanish with a young Peruvian couple. Next, the Carters went to Hawaii for one and one-half years. Their second son, James Earl Carter III, was born in Hawaii. When war began in Korea, Jimmy's submarine was assigned to San Diego, California. Rosalynn and the two little boys flew to San Diego, where they stayed in a rented apartment in a run-down section of town. Another move took them back to New London, where Jimmy was assigned to a small new submarine. He later applied for entrance into the nuclear submarine program headed by Admiral Hyman Rickover. He was accepted, and

the family moved to Schenectedy, New York, where the nuclear submarine's reactor was being built.

At that time Jimmy's father was diagnosed with cancer, and Jimmy went back home to Plains. While in Plains, he listened to people tell of the help his father had given them. He and his father also had a long talk. Jimmy learned that his father was counting on him to look after his younger brother, his mother, and the family peanut warehouse business. Jimmy decided that he should leave the Navy and return to Plains. Rosalynn, who liked being a Navy wife, did not want to return. She later said that she "argued, cried, even screamed at him." However, Jimmy was determined, and his will prevailed.

Rosalynn was very unhappy at first. Because they had so little money, they moved into a government housing project. Rosalynn refused to join the other wives and children in the courtyard of the housing project; she did not want to fit in. Her mother remonstrated, telling Rosalynn that the neighbors worried about her because she stayed in so much. After a while, Rosalynn began to make an effort to talk with the other women. Rosalynn and Jimmy began to attend church again, and they renewed old friendships. In 1954 there was a drought, and the farmers' crops failed so they were unable to repay credit that had been extended to them. Jimmy and Rosalynn were forced to live on a shoestring budget.

In the spring of 1955 Jimmy asked Rosalynn to come down to the peanut warehouse to answer the telephone so he could visit local farmers. Rosalynn went to the warehouse and took her two children with her. Soon she was making out bills for customers, working on the accounts, and paying the business bills. She liked doing it and so continued to work there. She continued to bring the two young boys with her. They climbed on the fertilizer bags and rode in the truck with their father. That year the Carters had a good harvest, and the family worked hard from August to October weighing and grading peanuts, storing them in the warehouse, and loading them on big trucks to be transported out of Plains.

They rented an old house on the edge of Plains. It had barns and other places for the children to play, but it had no central heat and was cold in the winter. With the installation of space heaters, the kitchen and den were comfortable, but the rest of the house was cold. Sometimes the pipes froze and burst. Despite the problems, they loved the old house. The children had pets: dogs, a pony, lizards, and a snake.

Jimmy also was busy with business and the community. He joined the Lions Club and encouraged the townspeople to spruce up the town. The town applied for funds to pave the city streets and received a grant to do so. Jimmy became director of the Chamber of Commerce, the Library Board, the Hospital Auxiliary, and the County School Board. He also was a scoutmaster and a deacon in the Baptist Church.

Rosalynn joined the Baptist Church with him and taught Sunday school. She joined the PTA, the Garden Club, and the board of a small theater group. She was the den mother for a Cub Scout pack. She attended the boys' basketball games and sent them off to swimming lessons, continued helping out at the warehouse, and studied accounting on her own so that she could keep their books. She and her husband also enjoyed golf and dancing, took the family camping, and vacationed in Cuba, New Orleans, Florida, and Mexico.

When the Supreme Court ruled in 1954 that public schools should be integrated, Rosalynn and Jimmy supported integration in their hometown, but they found that their stance was not particularly popular. Their views were shaped by their experiences in the Navy, where they had seen that integration worked, and they felt that their neighbors and friends were not being realistic in opposing its extension to the schools of Plains. Jimmy was invited, indeed pres-

sured, to join the White Citizens Council, but he refused. The Carters were then told that if they did not join, their business would be boycotted. That frightened them, but with the exception of a few individuals, the boycotts did not develop.

Jimmy decided to run for the state senate. Rosalynn managed the warehouse while he went from county to county campaigning. She also worked with friends and relatives, calling people to urge them to vote for her husband. On the day of the primary election, Jimmy found that there were numerous examples of fraud occurring in a neighboring county. When the election results from that county were announced, 430 votes were counted, but only 330 people had voted. Jimmy worked to gather evidence of the voting fraud, and a new election was called, which Jimmy won. When her husband went to Atlanta for the legislative session, Rosalynn received threats from the political boss of the neighboring county where the fraud had occurred. These threats worried her because she feared that their home or business might be destroyed.

When Jimmy decided to run for governor in 1966, the family again pulled together to campaign. Rosalynn traveled across the state of Georgia, campaigning for her husband. Sometimes she was accompanied by her son Jack and her mother-in-law, Lillian. In every town, Rosalynn contacted the newspaper office and the radio and television stations and suggested they might want to interview her. Most of them did. That year, however, Jimmy was defeated.

The morning after his defeat, Jimmy informed his family and friends that he intended to run again. Although he did not officially announce his candidacy, he began making preparations. The Carters recorded the names and addresses of possible supporters. They secured 150 or more phone books from Georgia towns and cities and wrote out standard letters to send. Jimmy began working on speeches.

Rosalynn kept the files and clipped news

Coming up Roses

Rosalynn Carter loved to work with flowers. While her husband, Jimmy Carter, was governor of Georgia, she arranged bouquets every day to decorate the governor's mansion. The grounds were full of flowering trees and formal gardens that were cared for by trustees. In addition to the formal gardens, Rosalynn had a small flower garden of her own, in which she planted pansies, tulips, begonias, and other blooms. At the governor's mansion, the First Lady found that she could work in the garden whenever she wanted: Digging in the dirt with her jeans on, she was not even recognized by tourists walking past.

items she thought he should read. During the two years before the election, he was out speaking somewhere almost every night. Rosalynn resumed campaigning the year before the election, even though it was difficult for her to leave her young daughter, Amy, who was just a toddler. Rosalynn campaigned vigorously. She would get up before dawn to meet with policemen, firemen, maintenance crews, or garbage collectors as they gathered before work. She searched for crowds at football and basketball games, livestock sales, tobacco barns, rodeos, and horse shows. She stood in front of stores, handing out brochures and asking people to support her husband.

She also learned how to give speeches. The first time she was unexpectedly called on to speak, she stammered out something but felt terribly humiliated. After that, she wrote out a small speech and memorized it. She gave that speech at small coffees and receptions. She was very nervous, so much so that sometimes she would throw up on the way to wherever she was supposed to talk. She kept on and eventually got better at it.

Jimmy won the election. The Carters visited the beautiful governor's mansion in Atlanta and attended a conference for newly elected governors in North Carolina. Both of these trips helped prepare Rosalynn for her role as the governor's wife. According to a family story, though, Lillian Carter believed that Rosalynn was not capable of performing the duties of a

First Lady. When Rosalynn and Jimmy moved into the governor's mansion, Lillian went along too, and announced that she would act as First Lady since Rosalynn was not sophisticated enough to do it. Rosalynn simply waited until she and Lillian were alone and then told her mother-in-law that she was welcome to come and visit but that she wanted to run her own household. Rosalynn even suggested that it might be better if Lillian packed up and went home and came back later when things were more settled. After that, Lillian came occasionally for visits, and Rosalynn became known as a gracious and capable hostess and as a woman who was concerned and active in a number of statewide issues.

Rosalynn hired competent staff, a housekeeper, and a personal secretary, and trained prisoners to cook and wait on table. She convinced the state policemen to maintain a less obvious presence at the mansion and to wear plain clothes when they accompanied the Carter family away from home. The governor's mansion was open to tourists four days a week and was also used as a place for special receptions for a number of groups, such as senior citizens, students, mentally retarded children, and garden clubs.

Rosalynn became a member of the Governor's Commission to Improve Services to the Mentally and Emotionally Handicapped. She went to the meetings of the commission and worked one day a week at the Georgia Regional

Hospital. She visited the other state hospitals and reported her findings to the commission. She also worked with the Women's Prison Committee of the Commission on the Status of Women.

When Jimmy decided to run for the presidency, Rosalynn began campaigning for him nearly a year before the primaries. She began in Florida, then visited Iowa, New Hampshire, Vermont, and the remaining New England states. By November, 1976, Rosalynn had campaigned in forty-two states. She went to coffees, teas, receptions, luncheons, and dinners. She answered questions about mental health, education, prison reform, and reorganization of government. She also worked at raising money to finance the campaign, calling potential donors.

She and Jimmy got help from the Peanut Brigade, a group of volunteers, mostly from Georgia, who paid their own way and traveled all over the country, telling voters about Jimmy Carter. For example, they came to New Hampshire a month before the primary election and worked very hard, knocking on doors and handing out campaign brochures. Jimmy Carter won the Democratic primary there. He lost the Massachusetts primary but won in Florida. The Carters found campaigning tiring and frustrating but also very exciting.

They gained enough votes from the primaries to be certain they could win the Democratic presidential nomination. The convention was to be held that year in New York City. A number of earlier contenders called to say they would release their delegates to cast their votes for Carter. The Democratic Convention was followed by three months of campaigning. Rosalynn campaigned on a schedule specifically laid out for her. She was accompanied by her secretary and usually flew in a chartered airplane. They traveled all over the United States. Again, Jimmy won.

In the time between the election and the inauguration, Jimmy invited Democratic sena-

tors and representatives, potential cabinet members, and others to meet with him at his home in Plains. Jimmy met with them, but it was Rosalynn and her mother, her secretary, and two daughters-in-law who made stacks of sandwiches and pitchers of iced tea and lemonade for their guests.

Presidency and First Ladyship

On the day of Carter's inauguration, he rode in a limousine beside President Gerald Ford to the ceremony at the Capitol. Rosalynn and Betty Ford followed in the second car. Following the inauguration and lunch at the Capitol, Jimmy, Rosalynn, and their children broke with tradition and, instead of riding back home in automobiles, got out and walked along the route. Holding hands, with Amy between them or dropping back to walk with her brothers, the Carters walked, waving and smiling at the cheering crowds. Their walk was broadcast all over the United States; it was the beginning of a new administration.

On that first day, after exploring the White House, Jimmy and Rosalynn attended seven inaugural balls and, during the next two days, a series of receptions. Rosalynn found it all exciting but also exhausting. Her hand throbbed from shaking so many people's hands and her feet hurt. Finally she slipped her shoes off while she was still standing in a reception line.

As they settled in at the White House, Rosalynn found that she had many things to discuss with her husband, such as decisions about White House guests, invitations, and answers to letters. Jimmy suggested that she arrange to have lunch with him one day a week; they could take up the matters at lunch, and he would not be faced with them at the end of a long working day, when he had to deal with weightier problems. Rosalynn and Jimmy continued to discuss matters of varied importance. She found that it was easier for her to learn about people's problems than it was for him. He was always surrounded by officials, while she could still meet and talk with individuals about their concerns, whether they were the special problems of the elderly, high fuel costs in the North, or raising children in the inner cities. In her own words, she gave her husband a "firsthand report of the attitudes and needs of people in our country." She and the boys also acted as sounding boards when Jimmy was trying to think through a particular issue.

Rosalynn and Jimmy did argue about political timing. There were a number of instances when she wanted him to postpone addressing controversial issues until his second term, such as the Panama Canal treaties, Middle East policies, or the energy policy. Jimmy would say that it was more important to do what needed to be done than to win a second term as president.

Rosalynn had a staff of twenty-one people to plan and carry out all official and social White House functions. They were responsible for arranging the details of teas, receptions, luncheons, state dinners, ceremonies on the White House lawn, lectures, and briefings by the president, vice president, and cabinet members, and for coverage by the press at these events. They were also in charge of sending out information on the White House and its history.

In addition, Rosalynn and her staff worked on her special projects, such as setting up the President's Commission on Mental Health, putting together a task force to inventory federal programs for the elderly, and making a list of qualified women for federal appointments. Finally, they were responsible for handling the mail addressed to the family. They received nearly eleven thousand letters each month. Rosalynn spent endless hours autographing photographs and always had a stack of photos waiting for her signature at her desk.

She also attended cabinet meetings. Jimmy had suggested that she attend so that she would know what was going on as well as the reasons behind the decisions that were being made. She took notes occasionally if there was something

she wanted to ask Jimmy about, but she usually sat quietly in the background and never participated in the discussions.

In June of 1977, Rosalynn visited seven countries in Latin America. She spent two months preparing for the trip, attending briefing sessions, practicing her Spanish, and reviewing materials on Latin America. Although some members of Congress opposed her going, saying that Latin Americans would not appreciate a woman envoy, she was well received. She was accompanied by State Department representatives, secretaries, and Secret Service agents. Also along were twenty-seven members of the press. Rosalynn spent a number of hours with government leaders at each stop. She presented her husband's policies on issues such as trade, human rights, and arms sales. She took notes on the concerns expressed by those she spoke with and carried those concerns back to her husband as well as the State Department.

Among the many who visited the White House during the Carter Administration, a few guests stand out. When the planned visit of Pope John Paul II to the United States was announced, thousands of people wrote to ask if they could be invited to the reception for him. The guest list kept expanding until it was decided to hold the reception on both lawns outside the White House. It had been cold and rainy, but as the pope arrived, the sun burst through the clouds. Soprano Leontyne Price sang the Lord's Prayer. The president welcomed the pontiff, who replied with remarks calling upon Americans to be leaders in the struggle for peace and human rights in the world. Then the pope moved through the crowds, blessing all he passed.

In September of 1978, other important visitors arrived: Prime Minister Menachem Begin of Israel and President Anwar el-Sadat of Egypt. They had been invited to attend a meeting at Camp David, the presidential retreat in Maryland, in the hope that they might be able to reach an accord between their two nations.

Jimmy hoped that these talks might lead to peace in the Middle East. Rosalynn had become friendly with the two men's wives, who were also invited; it was hoped that including the wives at the meeting would lead to a more relaxed atmosphere. Living accommodations were arranged to facilitate discussions. The Sadats were assigned to one cabin, the Begins to another, and the Carters stayed in a third, all within one hundred yards of one another. Each leader brought his own advisers and secretaries, who stayed in buildings a little farther away.

Rosalynn had worked on an international call to prayer, along with Jimmy's prayer group and press secretary Jody Powell.

> . . . conscious of the grave issues which face us, we place our trust in the God of our fathers, from whom we seek wisdom and guidance. As we meet here at Camp David, we ask people of all faiths to pray with us that peace and justice may result from these deliberations.

Rosalynn was at Camp David during most of the deliberations and was one of the few people with whom her husband could discuss the problems of the meetings. She also represented her husband at a number of scheduled events at the White House, as he was so deeply involved in the Camp David negotiations. When the negotiations were successful in arriving at a peace treaty that the Israeli and Egyptian leaders both agreed to sign, Rosalynn and her staff invited the cabinet members and the Egyptian and Israeli embassies' personnel to the White House for the formal signing of the treaty, ending thirty-one years of hostility between the two nations.

The year after this foreign policy triumph brought international crises. The Soviet Union invaded Afghanistan, and Jimmy led the United States in withdrawing from the coming 1980 Moscow Olympics. He also declared an embargo on shipments of grain to the Soviets.

Also in 1979, Iranian militants invaded the American Embassy in Tehran and captured sixty-five Americans, holding them hostage and demanding the return of deposed Iranian leader Mohammad Reza Shah Pahlavi for trial. After the Iranian revolution, the shah had left Iran to come to the United States for medical treatment. Carter refused the terrorists' demands and imposed sanctions against Iran, which initially won him widespread support in the United States. At that time, he announced his intention to run for reelection in 1980.

Because Jimmy said that he was needed in Washington, D.C., to deal with these crises, Rosalynn tried to fill his place on the campaign trail. She traveled from Washington for two or three days each week to campaign around the country for her husband. It was she who had to face angry farmers in Iowa who feared that the Soviet grain embargo would hurt them. As she campaigned around the United States, she was asked many times about the hostages in Iran. She and her husband were both frustrated by the situation; diplomatic measures had not secured the hostages' release. She met with the families of the hostages, one of whom suggested that people tie yellow ribbons around trees to symbolize their longed-for return. Rosalynn tied one around a tree on the White House lawn. People around the United States also tied ribbons on trees.

Popular opinion was shifting, though: People began to ask why the president was not taking stronger action. When Carter's intelligence information indicated that no release of hostages was in sight, his administration attempted a military rescue operation to free them. The operation failed tragically, with the deaths of eight volunteer rescue team members in a helicopter crash. The hostages did come home; ironically, they were released on January 20, 1981, the day Jimmy's successor, Ronald Reagan, was sworn in as president.

Legacy

Rosalynn opened new paths for future presidents' wives by assuming a major role as First Lady. She was used to acting as her husband's partner, and she frequently substituted for him at ceremonial occasions and advised him on policy matters and political strategy. She served as hostess at the White House, a traditional role, but also as hostess at Camp David during the negotiations between leaders of Israel and Egypt. She was also a major campaigner in all of Jimmy's electoral contests.

Carter's defeat in 1980 was very difficult for Rosalynn to accept, but in subsequent years she and her husband engaged in a variety of activities. They moved back to Plains and remained active in their town and church as well as Habitat for Humanity housing projects. In 1982 the Carters founded the Carter Center in Atlanta, a nonprofit public policy center dedicated to fighting disease and poverty, promoting human rights, and educating people worldwide. Both Jimmy and Rosalynn Carter served on the Center's board of trustees, and both wrote accounts of their lives. Rosalynn's book, *First Lady from Plains*, was well received. More books followed, some written with her husband and others by herself. Looking back at her life, Rosalynn said, "Although we face extraordinary responsibilities and will live a life we never dreamed of, we are first and foremost always Rosalynn and Jimmy Carter from Plains, Georgia."

Suggested Readings

Carter, Hugh. *Cousin Beedie and Cousin Hot: My Life with the Carter Family of Plains, Georgia.* Englewood Cliffs, N.J.: Prentice Hall, 1978. A Carter relative offers a homey remembrance of the childhoods and early lives of President Jimmy Carter and First Lady Rosalynn Carter.

Carter, Jimmy. *An Outdoor Journal: Adventures and Reflections.* Little Rock: University of Arkansas Press, 1994. Interesting outdoor information, comparable to a scout manual, which includes information about the Carter family.

Carter, Jimmy, and Rosalynn Carter. *Everything to Gain: Making the Most of the Rest of Your Life.* Little Rock: University of Arkansas Press, 1995. Warm and unpretentious dual account of the Carters' transition from the White House back to ordinary life; highlights issues such as health care and the Carter Center.

Carter, Rosalynn. *First Lady from Plains.* Boston: Houghton Mifflin, 1984. Rosalynn Carter's candid memories of her life before and during her First Ladyship.

Carter, Rosalynn, and Susan K. Golant. *Helping Someone with Mental Illness: A Compassionate Guide for Family, Friends, and Caregivers.* New York: Times Books, 1998. Cleanly organized discussion of the mental illness issues is interwoven with individual accounts.

Kaufman, Burton I. *The Presidency of James Earl Carter, Jr.* Lawrence: University Press of Kansas, 1993. Author argues that Jimmy Carter's well-intentioned abandonment of Washington protocol hurt his presidency.

Jean M. Choate

Nancy Reagan

Anne Frances Robbins Davis Reagan

Born: July 6, 1921
New York, New York

President: Ronald Reagan
1981-1989

Overview: Nancy Reagan, one of the most controversial First Ladies, was also one of the few to serve two complete terms. Politically, Nancy was solidly conservative, as was her husband. Ronald Reagan's election to the presidency ushered in a new era in American politics. In eight years, Nancy evolved from a political liability to a holder of considerable power in the Reagan administration.

Nancy Reagan, circa 1981. *(Library of Congress)*

Early Life

Anne Frances Robbins was born July 6, 1921, the only child of actress Edith Luckett and Kenneth Robbins, a car salesman. Although she was christened Anne Frances, she was always called Nancy. Shortly after her birth, Nancy's parents divorced. After that, she rarely heard from her father. Edith Luckett continued her work as a stage actress, and Nancy spent her first two years as a "backstage baby."

In 1923, wanting her child to have a normal life, Edith sent Nancy to Bethesda, Maryland, to live with relatives for several years. As a girl, Nancy played with dolls and gave them tea parties on the front steps of the house. Her happiest childhood memories were visits with her mother in New York. Nancy loved to dress up in her mother's costumes, wear her stage makeup, and pretend to be an actress.

Edith Luckett remarried in 1929, and Nancy moved with her to Chicago. Loyal Davis, Nancy's stepfather, was a prominent neurosurgeon and chairman of the Department of Surgery at Northwestern University. His ultraconservative political views may well have shaped Nancy's thinking, but as a girl she disliked politics. She was more excited by their apartment on Lake Shore Drive, which overlooked Lake Michigan. Although initially jealous of the relationship between Edith and Loyal, Nancy came to love the doctor. Secure in a family at last, fourteen-year-old Nancy initiated adoption proceedings and became Nancy Davis.

Through her teens and twenties, Nancy Davis's first love was theater. An average student at the exclusive Girls' Latin School, she acted in all the school plays. In her senior year, she played the lead in *First Lady* by George S. Kaufman. In 1939, Nancy had her debut and entered Smith College. She majored in English and drama. Nancy acted in several college plays, but her real experience in theater came during vacations when she worked as an apprentice in the summer stock theaters of New England. She ran errands, cleaned the dressing rooms, painted scenery, sold tickets, and occasionally performed.

Her first professional role came in 1943, when an old friend of her mother offered Nancy a small part in the traveling company of a play called *Ramshackle Inn* (1943). The show ultimately made its way to New York, and when the run was over, Nancy decided to stay there. She found a fourth-floor walk-up apartment at 409 East Fifty-first Street and acted on the "subway circuit" in the outer boroughs of New York. Eventually, Nancy made it to Broadway. She appeared in *Lute Song* (1945) with Mary Martin and Yul Brynner. A Metro-Goldwyn-Mayer (MGM) scout saw her in a production and asked her to come to Hollywood for a screen test. She was soon signed to a seven-year contract at a weekly salary of $250.

Marriage and Family

Nancy Davis had a short, successful movie career. In her fifth film, *The Next Voice You Hear* (1950), she received top billing. In most of her twelve films, Nancy was cast as a young mother or a pregnant woman. This corresponded with her personal plans. When she signed with MGM, Nancy was asked to fill out a questionnaire for the publicity department. Under "ambition" she wrote: "to have a successful marriage." She always knew she would give up acting "when the right man came along."

In the fall of 1949, Nancy Davis urged a producer to introduce her to Ronald Reagan. She had seen the actor in films and "liked what I saw." When they met, Nancy claimed it was very nearly "love at first sight." She appreciated his sense of humor and felt that, unlike other actors she had dated, Ronald was not obsessed with himself or show business. The courtship proceeded slowly, however, as Ronald was still on the rebound after his divorce from actress Jane Wyman.

Nancy Davis and Ronald Reagan were married in a private ceremony on March 4, 1952. The Reagans' first child, Patti, was born on October 22, 1952. She had two half siblings, Maureen and Michael, from her father's earlier marriage; they lived with their mother but spent quite a bit of time on the Reagans' ranch. On May 20, 1958, Nancy gave birth to a son, Ron. Michael Reagan later described her as an affectionate but demanding and overprotective mother. Nancy wanted her children to be as neat and orderly as she was, but they would, to various degrees, become caught up in the counterculture of the 1950's and 1960's.

In 1954 Ronald was asked to host *General Electric Theater* on television. He introduced each episode and starred in four programs per year. Occasionally, Nancy appeared with him. When the Reagans built a new home at 1669 San Onofre Drive in Pacific Palisades, California, General Electric (G.E.) turned their house into a showcase for its latest electrical appliances. The benefits of the job were many, but, as a corporate spokesman, Ronald was continually traveling for the company. He worked for G.E. for eight years and spent the equivalent of two full years away from home.

While Ron was on the road, the couple communicated through letters between "Daddie Poo Pants" and "Mommie Poo Pants." These letters reflect a deeply emotional love affair. As Ronald wrote in 1955, "I've always loved and missed you but never has it been such an actual ache. . . . I find myself hating these people for keeping us apart. Please be real careful because you carry my life with you every second." These separations were too painful for the couple, and after his G.E. commitments ended, the Reagans were never again apart for more than a few days.

Ronald had gone to work for General Electric in 1954 as a Roosevelt Democrat. Eight years later, he left as a committed Republican. From visiting G.E. plants across the United States and talking to the workers, he became increasingly concerned about government interference in the free enterprise system and in the lives of individuals. In 1962 Ronald officially changed his party identification. For the next two years, while hosting *Death Valley Days*, a Western television series sponsored by the Borax Company, he used his fame to campaign for Republican candidates.

By 1965, the Friends of Ronald Reagan had been formed by a group of California businessmen to encourage his candidacy for governor

Ronald Reagan

Ronald Reagan, born in 1911, was the oldest man to date to be elected president. After a career as a radio sportscaster and actor, he came to politics late in life. He was fifty-five in 1966, when he was elected governor of California, and sixty-nine when he became president in 1981. Reagan grew up a New Deal Democrat, but in the 1950's and 1960's he moved steadily to the right. He championed private enterprise and criticized government social programs. He was also convinced that the Soviet Union wanted to destroy all noncommunist governments.

In his first term (1981-1985), Reagan promised to solve the United States' serious economic problems by cutting taxes and government expenditures. He pushed several tax cuts through Congress. To finance the tax cuts, he asked Congress for heavy reductions in programs to aid the poor, the elderly, and the environment. At the same time, Reagan requested and received record amounts of money for the military. Fueled by his distrust of communism, he sent money and advisers to help the governments in El Salvador, Honduras, and Grenada repel communism. In Nicaragua, he supported the opponents of the communist government.

In his second term (1985-1989), Reagan concentrated on foreign policy. He twice met with Soviet leader Mikhail Gorbachev to discuss arms reduction and cultural exchanges. At the same time, however, he pressed Congress for funds to develop a space-based antimissile shield—the Stratgic Defense Initiative, nicknamed Star Wars—to protect against a nuclear attack by the Soviets. Reagan responded fiercely as Americans became the targets of terrorist attacks. In April, 1986, he ordered air strikes against Libya in retaliation for terrorist acts.

In 1987 the Democrats took control of the Congress. They resisted the president's calls for more funding for the Nicaraguan Contras. The Reagan administration schemed to circumvent Congress. In violation of Reagan's pledge never to negotiate with terrorists, the United States sold arms to Iran in exchange for the return of U.S. hostages. Profits of the sale were diverted, in violation of Congressional legislation, to the Contras. In the midst of this scandal, the value of U.S. stocks plummeted. Reagan's combination of tax cuts and increased defense spending created a massive deficit that exacerbated the economic crisis, and the United States became the world's biggest debtor nation. Nonetheless, Reagan left office in 1989 with an approval rating of 70 percent, making him one of the United States' most popular presidents.

in 1966. Nancy wrote to a friend, "It boggles the mind but maybe it'll get me out of the carpool." Later, Michael Reagan claimed his father had no political ambitions but that Nancy and her father had pushed him into running. Initially, Nancy wanted no part of active campaigning. She was shy, uncomfortable in crowds, and terrified of making speeches. As the campaign progressed, however, Reagan's staff convinced her that in order for the Reagan campaign to cover the large state and win the election, she would have to take a larger role. Nancy obliged and learned to enjoy the give-and-take with voters. She was proud to return home every evening and share their concerns with the candidate. Ronald won the election by a landslide.

When the family moved to Sacramento, Nancy realized the governor's mansion was noisy, dilapidated, and a fire hazard. She refused to live there with her children. Much to the consternation of Ronald's staff, the family moved to an estate in the suburbs. The move out of the inner city provoked charges of racism, and Nancy responded by hiring an MGM publicity agent for her staff.

The Reagans disliked the old mansion so much that Nancy undertook a campaign to build a new home for their successors. To this end, Nancy sought donations of furniture from the public. In 1970, as Ronald Reagan sought reelection, his opponent attempted to make Nancy's furniture collection an issue. He charged that she solicited antiques for her own personal use. In response, she held her first press conference and explained that she was collecting historical pieces which would be given to the state to be used by future governors. She defused the issue, and Reagan was elected to a second term.

As First Lady of California, Nancy Reagan sought an active role for herself. Because of her father's work, she had always been interested in hospitals; as the governor's wife, she made frequent visits to state hospitals. At Pacific State Hospital, Nancy was introduced to the Foster Grandparents Program, which paired older people with children who had special needs. The program, which created many meaningful relationships, was small and poorly funded. With her husband's help, Nancy raised money and saw the program expanded to all state hospitals. She was such an enthusiastic proponent of Foster Grandparents that on a trip to Australia she helped a hospital there organize its own program.

Reagan's tenure as governor of California (1967-1975) coincided with the growing opposition to United States' involvement in the Vietnam War. Nancy believed pulling out of Vietnam would be immoral, but she was sincerely worried about the returning soldiers. She made regular trips to veterans' hospitals and listened to horrific war stories. Nancy also volunteered to call the soldiers' wives and mothers. While on an official trip to Vietnam, she insisted on visiting every hospital where there were wounded Americans. She soon became concerned about the plight of American prisoners of war. Nancy wrote a column for a Sacramento newspaper, answering the questions people sent her as the state's First Lady. All her profits from the column were donated to the National League of Families of American Prisoners and Missing in Southeast Asia. As prisoners were released and processed through California, Nancy invited them all to a private family dinner in her home.

Although she was an active governor's wife, she was criticized for her old-fashioned views on marriage. Reporters mocked "the gaze," the worshipful way she stared at her husband when he spoke. It was called "a kind of transfixed adoration more appropriate to a witness of the Virgin Birth." In the age of women's liberation, Nancy insisted her first priority was providing her husband with a warm and loving home, "a source of comfort and strength." Nonetheless, by the end of Reagan's term as governor, the press and prominent Republicans were suggesting that Nancy had too much power over her husband and his political decisions. She responded with an interview in a woman's magazine where Nancy claimed her "sole joy" was "being Mrs. Ronald Reagan." When asked if she would like to be First Lady of the United States, Nancy responded: "I just want to be Ronald Reagan's wife."

Speculation that Ronald had hopes for the presidency began in 1968. At the Republican convention—and against Nancy's strenuous objections—he allowed his name to be put into consideration for the nomination. He had scant support, and the Reagan boom soon crashed. Never again would he make such a momentous decision without consulting Nancy.

Despite this setback, Nancy encouraged Ronald to challenge Gerald Ford for the Republican nomination in 1976. Against the moderate incumbent, Reagan argued for a strong defense system, school prayer, tax incentives, and the death penalty. He opposed gun control and federally funded abortions. In the primaries, unprecedented attention was given to the "contest of the queens." Both Nancy Reagan and Betty Ford actively campaigned for their husbands. While Betty Ford advocated women's rights, Nancy rallied against "drug pushers in the schools" and the decadence and depravity of American popular culture, especially in films. She also disliked the then-new term Ms., and she decried women wearing pants, saying, "a woman should look like a woman." Unlike her opponent, Nancy rejected the Equal Rights Amendment (ERA), claiming that it was "ridiculous" and not "the best way" to attain equal rights for women. She took credit for her husband's reversal of his previous support of the ERA.

The year 1976 was not to be the Reagans' year. Gerald Ford took the Republican nomination but lost to Jimmy Carter in the general election. The Reagans and their conservative followers spent the next four years preparing for another run for the presidency in 1980.

Nancy Reagan played a critical role in the 1980 campaign. She mediated conflicts that developed among the staff, carefully monitored her husband's schedule, and moderated her views on women's issues. While still opposing abortion and the ERA, she now called for equal pay for equal work. Some later speculated that Nancy was responsible for Ronald Reagan's campaign promise to appoint the first woman to the Supreme Court. Still, both Reagans remained solidly conservative, and their victory in 1980 ushered in a new era in American politics.

Presidency and First Ladyship

Nancy considered 1981 the worst year of her life. It began with published reports that she had asked the Carters to move out of the White House three weeks early so she could redecorate and that she planned to tear down one of the walls in the Lincoln Bedroom. Rumors also swirled that she was wielding tremendous power behind the scenes, vetoing selections for Reagan's cabinet. Perhaps the most criticism was directed at Nancy's wardrobe. Her inaugural ensemble included a donated gown valued at $25,000, a $10,000 mink coat, a fur-lined raincoat, a $1,700 dress, and a $1,500 alligator purse. This apparent excess was hotly criticized at a time when national unemployment was at 8.9 percent. Even before she had a chance to prove herself as First Lady, Nancy Reagan was accused of being obsessed with power and status.

She did not help herself when she immediately began a massive renovation of the private quarters of the White House. Nancy considered the place rundown and shabby. She wanted to make it "magnificent." Returning the $50,000 given to every first family for remodeling, Nancy raised more than $800,000 in private contributions. This created a furor when it was revealed that $270,000 came from oil interests in Oklahoma and Texas just weeks after Reagan had removed controls on oil prices.

Nancy also solicited new china valued at hundreds of dollars per place setting. A new set of dishes had not been ordered since the Truman administration, and she thought it reflected poorly on the United States to serve state dinners on mixed china. The donation of the china, however, was announced the same day the Reagan administration proposed a forty-one billion-dollar cut in welfare programs and the Department of Agriculture declared ketchup to be an acceptable vegetable for school lunch programs. Once again, the new First Lady received a barrage of criticism.

Though people sympathized with Nancy in March, 1981, after the attempted assassination of the president, once he recovered, the censure of the First Lady resumed. That summer, when she attended the London wedding of Prince Charles and Diana Spencer, she took along eighteen attendants, including her personal hairdresser, nurse, and photographer. She presented the couple with a $75,000 glass bowl and wore $250,000 worth of diamonds and rubies. The British press dubbed her Queen Nancy. The mockery soon made it back to the United States, where a caricature of the First Lady in a crown and ermine robes appeared on postcards and posters.

Compounding her problems was the charge that Nancy's acceptance of gowns and other clothing donated by fashion designers constituted a violation of the 1977 Ethics in Government Act, which required the Reagans to report these gifts. Whether Nancy broke the law was never resolved, but much of the public was outraged at the excess of her wardrobe. It was widely reported that just one of her handbags cost more than the annual allotment of food stamps for a family of four. In a country ensnared in the deepest recession in decades, where poor people waited in line for surplus cheese and unemployment hovered near 10 percent, Nancy did not seem to grasp the issue. She blamed the furor over her clothing on other women who were jealous that she wore a size four. Such insensitivity was not lost on the American public. A year-end *Newsweek* poll found 66 percent of the country opposed to Nancy's conspicuous consumption in a time of federal budget cuts and widespread economic hardship. By the end of 1981, she had a higher disapproval rating than any other First Lady of modern times.

While Nancy was mercilessly pilloried as being shallow and supercilious during her husband's first year in office, Ronald's advisers considered her a political liability. They urged her to develop a socially useful project of her own. At first Nancy resisted. She considered her husband to be her "project." When his staff told Nancy that her reputation was hurting the president, she understood. Taking up a cause was just another way to serve and support her husband. She immediately and wholeheartedly engaged in a crusade against drug abuse.

In 1982, Nancy entered this reform as a mother trying to help other parents deal with their children. She was empathetic in her approach and, according to historian Carl Sferrazza Anthony, admitted that her children used drugs. Nancy believed parents were "the answer to it all," and emphasized nonprofit efforts, volunteerism, and the value of testimonies from young people who had overcome their own addictions. In response to criticism of the president's slashing 26 percent from the budget for drug treatment and education, she denied that government action was necessary in the war against drugs and cited Alcoholics Anonymous as a successful, free model.

Throughout the year, Nancy used her position as First Lady to publicize the problem of drug abuse. She hosted a meeting of governors' wives and told them there was a secret war in the United States that was capturing and killing millions of children. She urged them, as women and mothers, to organize and fight back. Addressing a meeting of media, corporate, and civic leaders, Nancy announced a new drug use prevention program. At her urging, the president appointed a drug task force. Nancy visited more than one hundred small towns across the

Nancy Reagan speaks at an antidrug conference at the White House. *(Bettman/CORBIS)*

Madness" music video and honored singer Michael Jackson for his antidrug activities. Nancy also appeared on the popular television sitcom *Diff'rent Strokes*. She spoke to the year's largest television audience during halftime at the Super Bowl and was the first president's wife to appear on a late-night talk show. She cohosted *Good Morning America*, and she narrated antidrug documentaries for public broadcasting.

Committed to volunteerism in the fight against drugs, Nancy prevailed upon civic groups to join her crusade. In 1984, the Girl Scouts created a merit badge for drug-free scouts. The Kiwanis put up two thousand billboards featuring Nancy's face and antidrug message. More than five thousand Just Say No clubs were organized after the First Lady encouraged a child in Oakland, California, to "just say no" if he was approached by a drug dealer.

While crusading for drug abuse prevention, Nancy was careful not to get too political. When she asked audiences what else she could do, many suggested she should try to get federal funding for drug prevention increased. Nancy maintained she raised awareness, not funding. She insisted the president was doing all he could to stop the drug traffic through interdiction and strengthening of the criminal justice system. Nancy also refused to become involved in the legislative process. When a congressman asked her to testify before a House committee—as Rosalynn

country, warning that no area was safe from the threat of drugs. When the Reagans traveled to Europe that summer, Nancy canceled plans to attend society galas and instead visited drug treatment centers.

By 1983, the old image of Queen Nancy had been replaced by that of Nancy Reagan, crusader. As a former actress, Nancy knew how the media worked, and she used it to her advantage. She sang in the chorus of the "Stop the

Carter and Eleanor Roosevelt had done—on the effect of drugs on children, Nancy flatly refused. Nonetheless, by the end of 1984, her popularity rating had reached 71 percent.

Her reputation as an antidrug activist soon reached an international audience. She had a private meeting with Pope John Paul II to discuss drug abuse. In 1985 Nancy hosted an unprecedented session on drug abuse for "First Ladies" from thirty nations. It was the first time an incumbent First Lady addressed the United Nations and the first time so many wives of international leaders had met for any purpose. Nancy's presentation led to new programs in several countries, including the United States.

In recognition of his wife's role in the prevention of drug abuse by children, when the president signed antidrug abuse legislation in 1986, he turned the pen over to the First Lady. It was a sign of Nancy's increasing political influence. That same year, in the first joint address by a presidential couple, the Reagans called for a national crusade against the "cancer" of drugs. Together, they finally promised to push for increased antidrug spending. Nancy Reagan was no longer the sympathetic mother or the nice lady extolling a simplistic Just Say No campaign. She had become a powerful political force in her own right. This was evident in 1988 when she became the first First Lady to address a full body of official United Nations representatives. Her speeches reflected a new strength. She charged: "Each of us has a responsibility to be intolerant of drug use anywhere, anytime, by anybody ... be unyielding and inflexible and outspoken in your opposition to drugs."

The sense of power and mission Nancy experienced as an antidrug crusader led her to take an increasingly active role in her husband's administration. This became particularly apparent in Ronald's second term, as Nancy adopted a role that more than one journalist called "associate president."

In the 1984 presidential campaign, Nancy played a leading role. She traveled widely, reaching out to voters and sharing their concerns with the president. She defended so-called Reaganomics, hotly denying that the Republican Party was the party of the rich. Nancy proved shrewd in precinct organization, phone banks, building coalitions, and the day-to-day operations of the campaign. Once again, she monitored the president's schedule to prevent his overexertion. When he stumbled in the first debate, Nancy dictated how he prepared for his second face-off with Democratic candidate Walter Mondale.

After Reagan won reelection by a landslide, the First Lady openly worked with the White House chief of staff and other advisers to set the agenda for Ronald's second term. She announced her hope that the president would get rid of the "deadwood" in his cabinet. She also began to assert herself in foreign policy. As early as 1983, Nancy decided that the president's hard line against communism was hurting his popularity. Now, she pushed for the historic signing of an Intermediate Range Nuclear Forces Treaty with the Soviet Union, which would end the Reagan presidency on a note of accomplishment and create a legacy that would cast her husband as a man of peace. In conjunction with these plans, as the second term progressed, she advised her husband to limit his appearances at military bases and to cut defense spending. Conservatives called this shift in President Reagan's views Nancyism.

Reporters charged that Nancy Reagan had become the ultimate source of access to her husband, a woman who knew her power and enjoyed using it. This point was highlighted in July, 1985, when the president was diagnosed with cancer and scheduled for immediate surgery. While shielding the public—and her husband—from the truth of his condition, Nancy moved quickly to establish her authority. She announced that she would have "veto power" over any appointments, rearranged the president's schedule for the coming weeks, and controlled all access to her husband. Nancy, rather than the vice president, filled in for Reagan at official functions. As the president recuperated, he acknowledged and praised his wife's powerful role during the crisis. Calling Nancy "my everything" and "my partner," he thanked her on behalf of the American people for her "strength" and "for taking part of the business of this nation."

In 1987 the Iran-Contra scandal broke, and Ronald Reagan was accused of selling arms to the United States' enemies. The president's approval rating plummeted. Nancy took charge, demanding that her husband fire Chief of Staff Donald Regan, Central Intelligence Agency Director William Casey, and conservative Director of Communications Pat Buchanan. The president acceded to his wife's wishes. The press once again became critical of the strong First Lady. *The New York Times* called her "power hungry" and likened her to former First Lady Edith Wilson, portraying Nancy as unelected and unaccountable but controlling the actions and appointments of the executive branch. Regan wrote a book comparing Nancy to the "ruthless" Livia, who ruled the Roman Empire through the manipulation of her hapless husband, the emperor.

Nancy, who had timidly retreated from media censure in 1981, now stood up to her critics. In a speech to news editors, she defended her actions as consistent with the requirements of her position. She stated it was legitimate for a First Lady to look after a president's health and well-being. If that meant advocating the removal of aides who failed to serve the president, she said, she was only doing her job. As for asserting her opinion on policy matters, Nancy commented, "It's silly to suggest that my opinion should not carry some weight with a man I've been married to for thirty-five years. I'm a woman who loves her husband, and I make no apologies for looking out for his personal and political welfare."

Later, she responded in her book *My Turn* (1989) that Donald Regan was more concerned with his own aggrandizement than with serving the president and the country. Public opinion polls showed that the American people supported the First Lady and her definition of her role. She left office in 1989 with soaring approval ratings.

Legacy

The Reagans retired to Bel-Air, California. From there, Nancy continued her antidrug work, under the auspices of the Nancy Reagan Founda-

---

Written in the Stars

Nancy Reagan was devastated by the March 30, 1981, shooting of her husband. When she learned that the assassination attempt had been predicted by a California psychic, Nancy immediately called the woman. That year, Nancy became convinced that through astrology she could have prevented the shooting. From then on, the clairvoyant scheduled all presidential speeches, trips, public appearances, Air Force One take-offs, press conferences, and interviews according to Ronald Reagan's astrological chart. Through the First Lady, all policy decisions and appointments were vetted by psychic readings. Horoscopes even determined the historic Reagan-Gorbachev summits.

The astrologer claimed that Nancy was highly perceptive and had keen insight into the motives of others. When the First Lady engineered the ouster of White House Chief of Staff Donald Regan, he wrote a book exposing her dependence on the psychic. Nancy defended her beliefs, arguing that she was a loving wife "doing everything I could to protect my husband and keep him alive."

tion. In 1994, Ronald disclosed that he had Alzheimer's disease. Some observers believed that Reagan had been in declining health for years, remembering that during his presidency Nancy would shield him from reporters' questions, whispering responses in his ear. From the time of his diagnosis, Nancy devoted herself to Ronald's care and made very few political appearances. In 2001 she wrote a letter to President George W. Bush, expressing her wish that federal funds be made available for controversial research on the stem cells of human embryos. Scientists believed that Alzheimer's disease was among the medical conditions that could be helped from treatments derived from stem cells. A portion of Nancy's letter was paraphrased in the *Washington Post* as saying, "My husband and I believe our legacy should be that no other family should have to go through what our family has been suffering."

No one could question Nancy Reagan's devotion to the president. She proved that a First Lady could be a devoted wife, a skilled hostess, an advocate for social reform, and a wielder of considerable political power. In the end, Nancy saw her most important legacy as the campaign against drug abuse. On leaving the White House, she asked to be remembered as someone who used her position to the best of her ability to help the children of the United States.

Suggested Readings

Anthony, Carl Sferrazza. *First Ladies: The Saga of the Presidents' Wives and Their Power.* Vol 2. New York: William Morrow, 1991. Contains a balanced overview of Nancy Reagan's tenure as First Lady.

Reagan, Nancy. *I Love You, Ronnie.* New York: Random House, 2000. The letters of Ronald Reagan to Nancy Reagan.

_____. *My Turn.* New York: Random House, 1989. Nancy Reagan's account of her years in office and a response to her critics.

Regan, Donald. *For the Record: From Wall Street to Washington.* New York: Harcourt Brace Jovanovich, 1988. An insider's assessment of Nancy Reagan's power.

Wallace, Chris. *First Lady: A Portrait of Nancy Reagan.* New York: St. Martin's Press, 1986. A contemporary journalist's favorable account of Nancy Reagan's life and activities.

Mary Linehan

Barbara Bush

Barbara Pierce Bush

Born: June 8, 1925
New York, New York

President: George Herbert Walker Bush
1989-1993

Overview: After nearly thirty years of living a very public life, including becoming a leading advocate for literacy, a best-selling author, and a popular public speaker known for her quick humor and uncommon frankness, Barbara Bush would still say that simply being a wife and mother had been her life's mission. Nevertheless, the fact that she was the wife of one president and the mother of another will make her one of the most celebrated First Ladies ever, an honor shared by only one other. Unfortunately, Abigail Adams did not live to see her son John Quincy sworn in as president, so Barbara Bush truly made history on January 20, 2001, when she stood on the steps of the west side of the Capitol and watched, with her husband, George Bush, as their son, George W. Bush, became the forty-third president of the United States.

Early Life

Barbara Pierce was born June 8, 1945, to Marvin and Pauline Pierce. She was the third of four children. She was very close to her father, who worked for the McCall's Corporation and became its president in 1946. She wrote in her memoirs, published in 1994, that Marvin Pierce was the "fairest man I knew, until I met George Bush."

She was not as close to her mother, whom Barbara described as a beautiful, talented woman who really did not appreciate the life she had. "My mother often talked about when her ship would come," Barbara wrote. "She had a husband who worshiped the ground she

Barbara Bush, 1989. *(Library of Congress)*

walked on, four loving children, and a world of friends. Her ship had come in—she just didn't know it."

Despite disagreements with her mother, Barbara Bush considered her childhood a happy one, filled with love, friends, security, and lots of books. She first developed a love of reading from many long evenings spent in the family living room, when everyone would be reading a favorite book or magazine. She grew up in Rye, a bedroom community of New York City, where she and her friends could roam the streets freely and everyone knew everyone else and their dog.

During her sixteenth year, while home from boarding school, Barbara met George Herbert Walker Bush at a Christmas dance. The Japanese had bombed Pearl Harbor just a few weeks earlier, but Barbara was oblivious to almost everything except her new beau. "I married the first man I kissed," she once told an audience. "It makes my children sick when they hear that, but it's true."

In the midst of the romance and resulting engagement, George Bush, then the youngest pilot in the Navy at age eighteen, shipped out with his squadron for the South Pacific. Despite their separation, his almost daily love letters left no doubt in Barbara's mind that he would come back to her, as shown in this note that he wrote her shortly after they became engaged: "I love you, precious, with all my heart and to know that you love me means my life. How often I have thought about the immeasurable joy that will be ours some day. How lucky our children will be to have a mother like you."

The romance nearly ended in tragedy when, on September 2, 1944, Bush's plane was shot down while he was on bombing mission near the Japanese island of Chichi-Jima. Although his two crewmates were killed, the future president parachuted out of the plane and was eventually picked up by an American submarine. A number of days, "all of them a complete blur," would pass between Barbara's learning that

George had been shot down and that he had been rescued. They finally married on January 6, 1945, while George was home on leave.

Marriage and Family

Fortunately, World War II ended before George was shipped out again. While George went to Yale University, Barbara had their first child, George Walker Bush. At the time, they shared married student housing with eight other families, including ten children. When George graduated in 1948, the young family made what would become one of many bold, adventuresome moves in their lives to come: They left the protected environment of their families and friends on the East Coast and moved to the dusty oilfields of West Texas.

It did not take long for the young Bush family to realize how different their new life was to be. Their first home, in wind-swept Odessa, Texas, was a tiny duplex, which they shared with a mother and her daughter who seemed to have questionable occupations. The two families shared the one and only bathroom, which became quite a problem at night when the two neighbors entertained their gentlemen callers. The visitors often forgot that when they left the bathroom from their side, they had to unlock the bathroom door that led to the Bushes' side of the duplex.

Her mother was convinced that Barbara had moved to the end of the earth and even insisted on sending her items such as laundry detergent. Nevertheless, George and Barbara Bush thrived in Texas. After working as a supply salesman, Bush quickly moved up the corporate ladder and eventually ventured into the oil business. There were plenty of dry wells along the way but enough successful ones to enable George and his partners to become true pioneers in the offshore drilling business.

They continued to have babies. By 1953 the family included not only George W., but a girl named Robin and a new baby, Jeb. As Barbara wrote in her memoirs, "Life seemed almost too

George Herbert Walker Bush

While flying torpedo bombers in the Pacific, nineteen-year-old George Bush informed his father he would not have time for college when World War II ended. "I'll have to do without, just a job anywhere with a fairly decent salary—lots of people will need a good butler when this is over," the impatient teenager wrote. Obviously, his life took a different path, greatly shaped by his war experience, including his being shot down and losing two crew members. It would be thirty years before he even thought he might be president, much less the father of another president.

After graduating Phi Beta Kappa from Yale University, a still restless Bush headed to the Texas oil fields, where he eventually founded his own oil company. Inspired by his father's public service—Prescott Bush went from town moderator in Greenwich, Connecticut, to the U.S. Senate for ten years—Bush was elected in 1966 to the U.S. House of Representatives and went on to serve as U.S. ambassador to the United Nations, chairman of the Republican National Committee, chief of the U.S. Liaison Office in China, director of the Central Intelligence Agency, and vice president of the United States before he was elected president on November 8, 1988.

As president, Bush was immediately forced to deal with political upheaval in Eastern Europe as the region teetered on the brink of freedom. His main challenge was to guide the process without provoking Soviet extremists and their military. Without a shot being fired, the Cold War ended, the Soviet Union ceased to exist, the Berlin Wall fell and Germany was reunified, and Eastern Europe and the Baltic States all became free. Yet Bush considered his most important accomplishment the liberation of Kuwait after it was invaded by Iraq's Saddam Hussein. Bush put together an unprecedented coalition of thirty-two nations which fought side by side in operation Desert Storm, paving the way for Israel and her Arab neighbors to begin anew their quest for peace in the Middle East.

Domestically, as only the second president to serve a full term without party control in either chamber of Congress, Bush faced even greater challenges. He had a particularly bruising budget battle with Congress in 1990, during which he broke the "No New Taxes" pledge he made during his 1988 campaign. The resulting budget compromise is widely credited today with reducing the federal deficit and putting the economy on more solid footing. Nevertheless, the budget deal was a major contributor to Bush's defeat in 1992, along with the third-party candidacy of Ross Perot. After leaving office, Bush focused his energies on his presidential library, the George Bush School of Government and Public Service at Texas A&M University, and his work with the M. D. Anderson Cancer Center in Houston.

good to be true." However, a short time after Jeb was born, three-year-old Robin was diagnosed with leukemia. While George stayed back in Texas to watch the boys and his oil business, Barbara took Robin to New York to seek the best treatment possible. Robin died six months later, leaving behind her heartbroken parents and bewildered older brother, George, who was six at the time. Barbara told the story of how she finally pulled herself out of her deep mourning. She overheard little George tell his friends that he would not be able to come out and play, as he had to play with his mother. She realized right there and then that it was time she put aside her grief and come back to the family who needed her.

"George and I love and value every person more because of Robin. She lives on in our hearts, memories, and actions," Barbara wrote. Robin's death began a lifelong devotion on the part of both Bushes to the cause of cancer. Barbara would later serve as honorary chairwoman of the Leukemia Society of America and would become involved with Ronald Mc-

Donald House Charities. George served on the board of the M.D. Anderson Cancer Center in Houston, the premier cancer hospital in the United States. They cochaired a national movement, The National Dialogue on Cancer, which seeks to reduce the risk of this dreaded disease.

After Robin's death, three more children followed quickly: Neil, Marvin, and finally, another girl named Dorothy, whom they would call Doro. The family eventually moved from West Texas to Houston, where George's offshore oil business continued to thrive, but his growing interest in politics and public service would soon chart a whole new course for the family.

After losing a bid for the Senate in 1964, Bush was elected to the House of Representatives in 1966. The family packed up and moved to Washington, D.C., not realizing it would be more than twenty-five years before they would move back to Texas for good.

In between, Bush would serve as ambassador to the United Nations, chairman of the Republican National Committee during the Watergate years, the U.S. envoy to China, Central Intelligence Agency (CIA) director, vice president, and finally president. It was an incredible journey during which Barbara, who up until the family moved to Washington had largely been a car pool mom, Cub Scout den mother, and PTA activist, learned the tools of diplomacy, entertaining, media relations, and public speaking. It was not a life she had sought but one at which she quickly excelled.

She never lost sight of what she considered her most important job: making a home for her husband and children. From Houston to Washington to New York to China and back, she lugged family photos, furniture, dogs, and keepsakes, so they would feel at home. She viewed every move as an adventure; by the time they were married fifty years, George and Barbara Bush had lived in thirty different houses in seventeen different cities. Some assignments were more difficult than others. Barbara especially loved their year in China, when the two of them spent a great deal of time together, exploring a very different world. Her least favorite time periods were when her husband was head of the Republican Party during the Watergate scandal in the 1970's and, later, Central Intelligence Agency (CIA) director. For the first time in their marriage, her husband could not come home and share with her what he had done at the office that day. "He knew I was not good at keeping secrets," she confessed.

When Jimmy Carter won the White House in 1976, Bush lost his job at the CIA, and the Bush family moved home to Texas after being gone for ten years. Barbara was thrilled and set about making a home in yet another house, possibly for the last time. Within a few years, however, Bush decided to run for the vice presidency, and Barbara gave up her role as homemaker to become the candidate's wife. When the election was over, her husband was vice president, and Barbara suddenly found herself "Second Lady." Despite keeping a very busy schedule and her budding interest in literacy, it would be eight more years—not until her husband became president—before the spotlight would truly shine on Barbara, and she would establish herself as one of the most beloved women in the United States.

Presidency and First Ladyship
Barbara wrote in her memoirs that the very first thing she did after her husband became president on January 20, 1989, was "to unpack some of our personal pictures to set around on the tables so this great big house would feel more like home."

However, by this time Barbara certainly understood the fact that her plan to simply be a wife and mother was no longer practical. She was now First Lady of the United States, a title that came with no job description and no salary but with enormous potential to do good. She was determined to stay out of her husband's presidency—"They elected George, not me," she said—and decided to take her cue from one of her predecessors and role models, Lady Bird Johnson, who had described the position as First Lady as the best bully pulpit in the world. In her very first staff meeting, Barbara told her East Wing team that she wanted to do something every single day to help others. In her four years as First Lady, Barbara Bush used that bully pulpit in many and diverse ways, often listening simply to her heart.

When she read in the newspaper that Washington, D.C., area malls were banning Salvation Army bell-ringers because they disturbed Christmas shoppers, she immediately went to the closest mall (taking the press with her), found a bell ringer, and made a point of making a donation and talking about how important this Christmas tradition was. The malls changed their minds.

As she learned more about the acquired immunodeficiency syndrome (AIDS) virus and how frightened the American people were, she visited an AIDS residential home in Washington called Grandma's Place, to make the point that all AIDS victims—children and adults—needed love and care. When a young man told her in front of the media that his own mother was too afraid and too ashamed to hug him, she immediately got up and gave the young man a huge hug.

She traveled across the country visiting homeless shelters, food banks, abused women's shelters, Boys & Girls Clubs, schools, hospitals, and orphanages. During the Desert Storm conflict, she focused her time and energy on visiting military bases to comfort families whose loved ones were fighting a war halfway around the world, in the harsh Middle East desert.

When her husband traveled abroad, Barbara went with him and became almost as popular abroad as at home. In addition to the traditional teas and museum tours enjoyed by First Ladies, she made a point of visiting schools, hospitals, and orphanages abroad as well, making friends wherever she went.

Despite all these varied concerns and causes, Barbara devoted most of her time and energy to literacy, which she had adopted as her number one cause. However, with the increased visibility which comes with the White House, she became the true champion of a growing movement to make the United States a more literate nation. For four years, she tirelessly visited literacy programs in nearly every state in the nation, encouraging students, tutors, and professional staff to continue their work. She talked to anyone who would listen about the importance of literacy to the United States' future. She refused to take credit but stood proudly by as her husband signed the 1991 National Literacy Act, which was the first piece of legislation ever enacted specifically for literacy.

She also established the Barbara Bush Foundation for Family Literacy, which continues to thrive and to grow every year, and to date has given nearly eight million dollars to 262 literacy programs around the country. Her foundation's annual "Celebration of Reading," in which best-selling authors are invited to share their work, has become the most successful literacy fund-raiser in the United States.

When asked in a speech why she devoted so much time to family literacy, Barbara said:

> Like the experts, I truly feel that if more people could read, write, and comprehend, so many of our social problems could be solved. If you can read and write, you can learn. If you can learn, you can get a job and support yourself and your family. You will be less tempted to turn to drugs, alcohol, or crime, to drop out of school or get pregnant before you are ready. You will have pride and dignity and will be able to enjoy the best things in life, including a good book or bedtime stories with your child.

While she was promoting her causes, Barbara Bush was earning huge approval ratings as First Lady. When asked why she was so popular, she would scoff and credit her white hair and less-than-perfect figure. However, others would say it was more about her sharp wit, outspoken and down-to-earth nature, and reputation as a gracious hostess.

The public got its first glimpse of the relaxed atmosphere of the White House when Barbara's dog Millie gave birth to six puppies in March, 1989. Millie "wrote" about the puppies and life at the White House in her tongue-in-cheek 1990 best-selling book, *Millie's Book*, which earned more than one million dollars for the Barbara Bush Foundation for Family Literacy. The birth of the puppies, the constant presence of the Bush grandchildren, and Barbara's sense of humor quickly endeared her to the entire country. She loved telling stories about life at the White House, especially if they had surprise endings. One of her favorites took place on a Sunday afternoon when the family was enjoying a relaxing time together. Barbara was swimming in the pool while George played horseshoes nearby. (Barbara swam every day at the White House, rain or shine, wearing a snorkel and mask.)

On this particular day, she had just gotten started when a big rat swam right in front of her mask. She flew out of the pool screaming, bringing every Secret Service agent, security guard, and her husband running. While the Secret Service tried to decide what to do, her husband walked over and, using the pool skimmer, drowned the rat.

Despite this incident, Barbara loved life at the White House, and she and her husband became famous for the many intimate dinner parties they gave upstairs in the private residence, movie parties with popcorn in the White House movie theater, or weekend get-togethers at Camp David, the presidential weekend retreat in the Maryland mountains. Whether entertaining visiting dignitaries such as Mikhail and Raisa Gorbachev or Margaret and Denis Thatcher; celebrities such as Arnold Schwarzenegger and Maria Shriver, Kevin Costner, or the Oak Ridge Boys; or friends and family from back home, both Bushes earned reputations as gracious and fun hosts.

Barbara also became well-known for a determined, quiet resolve. She did not ruffle easily. When Bush became ill during a state dinner in Japan and passed out on international television, the world panicked while Barbara quietly reassured everyone in the room that her husband simply had the flu. When he was hospitalized with heart problems, she once again stayed calm and stuck to her schedule, while

Always with a Twinkle

Barbara Bush was famous for her sharp wit, but there was no one she would rather tell a story about than herself. One of her favorites took place the night of a beautiful state dinner at the White House for Boris Yeltsin, the new president of a newly democratic Russia. His state visit was a historic and exciting moment in history. During dinner, Yeltsin leaned over and through an interpreter asked the American First Lady, "Barbara, I don't know the protocol. What should I do if a lady has her foot on my foot?!"

Barbara looked over at the beautiful woman sitting on his other side, feeling very sorry for her, but before Barbara could answer, Boris lifted his foot, and hers shot upward. She realized she had been grinding his foot into the ground throughout dinner. Yeltsin then told her that in Russia that meant the woman loved the man. She told him that was not true in the United States. The next night, at a Russian Embassy dinner, Yeltsin wrote on Barbara's menu: "Dear Barbara, Remember it was you who stepped on my foot and you knew what it meant. I feel the same, Boris."

other people urged her not to leave his bedside. During Desert Storm, when Americans became fearful of commercial airline travel because of terrorist threats, she gave up her Air Force plane (much to the Secret Service's dismay) and insisted on flying commercial airlines. She always knew how to make a point without making a fuss.

As have all First Ladies, at times she found herself in hot water, usually because of an inadvertent quote she gave a reporter. The only controversy still remembered today occurred in 1991, when Wellesley College invited her to be its commencement speaker. A handful of the graduates protested the selection, circulating a petition that said "Barbara Bush has gained recognition only through the achievements of her husband." Before long, the protest became the rage of newspaper columnists and talk show hosts as the First Lady was forced to defend the life she had chosen for herself, that of wife and mother. The flap ended the day she finally gave her speech, during which she tried to bridge the distance between the two generations of women. She said, in part:

Cherish your human connection, your relationships with friends and family. For several years, you've had impressed upon you the importance to your career of dedication and hard work. This is true, but as important as your obligations as a doctor, lawyer, or business leader will be, you are a human being first, and those human connections—with spouses, with children, with friends—are the most important investments you will ever make. At the end of your life, you will never regret not having passed one more test, not winning one more verdict, or not closing one more deal. You will regret time not spent with a husband, a friend, a child, or a parent.

Barbara Bush reacts as a large balloon falls at the Houston Astrodome after President George Bush accepted the Republican Party's nomination for a second term, August, 1992. (AP/Wide World Photos)

Disappointed by her husband's defeat in 1992 to Bill Clinton, Barbara nonetheless left the White House very much ready to return to private life. She told friends that she and George moved back to Houston prepared to stay out of sight and out of mind. She went back to cooking (admittedly with little success) and to driving a car for the first time in twelve years. She wrote her memoirs (another best-seller), joined the speaking circuit, and devoted more time to her children and grandchildren.

Legacy

Soon after leaving the White House, she composed a letter to her children about the lessons she had learned, which illustrated perhaps better than anything her down-to-earth approach to life and who she was as a person. It said, in part:

> Try to find the good in people and not the bad. Take a lesson from your dad. He says when I remind him that someone has been hateful, "Isn't it better to make a friend rather than an enemy?" He's right.
>
> Don't talk about money—either having it or not having it. It is embarrassing for others and quite frankly vulgar.
>
> Do not buy something that you cannot afford. You do not need it.
>
> If you really need something and can't afford it, for heaven's sake call home. That's what family is all about.
>
> Do not try to live up to your neighbors. They won't look down on you if you don't have two television sets. They will look down on you if you buy things that you cannot afford and they will know it! They are only interested in their possessions, not yours.
>
> Be sure you pay people back. If you have dinner at their house, have them back or take them out. People love to come to your home. Plan ahead and it will be fun.
>
> Value your friends. They are your most valuable asset.
>
> Remember loyalty is a two-way street. It

goes up and down. Your dad is the best example of two-way loyalty that I know.

> Love your children. I don't have to tell any of you that. You are the best children two people ever had. I know you will be as lucky. Your kids are great. Dad and I love them more than life itself. I think you know that about your dad. I do also.
>
> Remember what Robert Fulghum says: "Don't worry that your children never listen to you; worry that they are always watching you."
>
> For heaven's sake enjoy life. Don't cry over things that were or things that aren't. Enjoy now what you have to the fullest. We can always find people who are worse off and we don't have to look far! Help them and forget self!
>
> Above all else, seek God. He will come to you if you look. We, your dad and I, have tried to live as Christian a life as we can. We certainly have not been perfect. Maybe you can! Keep trying.

However, for Barbara Bush, retiring from public life was not to be. In addition to increasing demands as a speaker and her continued involvement with her literacy foundation, a decision by two Bush sons in 1994 kept the family in the spotlight: George W. in Texas and Jeb in Florida followed in their father's footsteps and entered the political arena in 1994, despite their mother's advice not to. ("I just did not want them to get hurt in case they lost," she explained.) Eventually, George W. became governor of Texas, and after losing his first attempt, Jeb became governor of Florida. "Now you know we went to Texas to breed governors," Barbara joked with audiences.

In 2001, with one son as president and one as a governor, Barbara said it is a legacy neither she nor her husband ever sought and refuse to brag about. When asked about her son the president, she simply said, "We are proud of all five of our children." When asked about her incredible life, she referred people to the dedication of her memoirs, which she said explained her life best: "To faith, family, and friends; and to George Bush, who taught me that these are the most important things in life."

Suggested Readings

Bush, Barbara. *Barbara Bush: A Memoir*. New York: Charles Scribner's Sons, 1994. Barbara Bush's memoir gives readers a candid, private look at the more than twenty-five years she and her husband lived in the public eye.

Bush, Barbara. *Millie's Book: As Dictated to Barbara Bush*. New York: William Morrow, 1990. A dog's view of the Bush White House, "dictated" by First Dog Millie Bush.

Bush, George H. W.. *All The Best, George Bush: My Life in Letters and Other Writings*. New York: Scribner, 1999. A collection of letters, diary entries, and memos, beginning with eighteen-year-old George's letters to his parents during World War II and continuing through his post-presidency years.

Grimes, Ann. *Running Mates: The Making of a First Lady*. New York: William Morrow, 1990. Barbara Bush's evolution as George Bush's political supporter and partner.

Kilian, Pamela. *Barbara Bush: A Biography*. New York: Saint Martin's Press, 1992. A biography of the forty-first president's wife.

Parmet, Herbert S. *George Bush: The Life of a Lone Star Yankee*. New York: Scribner, 1997. Award-winning historian gives the first full account of the former president.

Radcliffe, Donnie. *Simply Barbara Bush: A Portrait of America's Candid First Lady*. New York: Warner Books, 1989. Based on interviews with Barbara Bush, her family, and friends, this first biography explores her life.

Jean Becker

Hillary Rodham Clinton

Hillary Diane Rodham Clinton

Born: October 26, 1947
Chicago, Illinois

President: William Jefferson Clinton
1993-2001

Overview: Hillary Rodham Clinton was the most frankly political and controversial First Lady in the second part of the twentieth century. Amid scandals and setbacks during Bill Clinton's administration, she learned from every defeat and emerged in a slightly different incarnation, embracing new ideas and achieving success in other areas, such as her advocacy for children and her speech at the International Women's Conference in China. The vindication of her efforts was her victory in the New York state senate race, the first time a First Lady was elected to public office. She greatly enlarged the scope of the role of the First Lady and guaranteed that those who followed her could have a marked influence on public policy issues.

Early Life

Hillary Diane Rodham was born in Chicago, Illinois, on October 26, 1947. She was the oldest child and only daughter of Dorothy and Hugh Rodham. When Hillary was three years old, her family, which included brothers Hugh and Anthony, moved to suburban Park Ridge, Illinois.

Hillary was a bright, serious child. At Maine East High School, she established herself as one of the top students. At the same time, Hillary became acquainted with Don Jones, a young minister hired to work with the young people at her church. Jones influenced Hillary to read the works of philosophers Paul Tillich and Reinhold Niebuhr. Later, Jones arranged for Hillary and other members of the group to hear a speech given by Civil Rights activist Dr. Martin Luther King, Jr. After Dr. King's speech, the group had the opportunity to meet with him.

Hillary Rodham Clinton. *(Library of Congress)*

317

Many observers feel that Hillary's wide and varied readings and the meeting with King formed the underpinnings of her social philosophy.

Hillary entered Wellesley College in the fall of 1965. She established a reputation as an active, vocal, and strongly opinionated student leader. Two years later, she was elected president of the college government. Her desire for reform was guided by her desire to "do the right thing."

As the Class of 1969 neared graduation, Hillary was named Wellesley's first student commencement speaker. Senator Edward Brooke of Massachusetts, the primary commencement speaker, told the graduates that the United States was strong and the world awaited them. After hearing Brooke's speech, Hillary put aside her carefully written comments and boldly told the senator and other listeners that her generation was tired of promises for change. "The challenge now is to practice politics as the art of making what appears to be impossible possible," she said. Her candid observations earned Hillary a note in *Life*, the first mention of her name in a national magazine.

Hillary left Wellesley changed in one especially important way: She was now a Democrat. The Rodham family was staunchly Republican, and Hillary had been a "Goldwater Girl" in 1964, supporting Arizona senator Barry Goldwater for president, and had worked for the House Republican Conference. She found her political allegiances shifting in 1968 and worked for Democratic presidential hopeful Senator Eugene McCarthy in the primaries. She remained a Democrat in spite of McCarthy's defeat.

Hillary continued her education at Yale University Law School. Once again, her academic accomplishments were impressive, and she served on the board of editors of the *Yale Review of Law and Social Action*. While at Yale, Hillary was influenced by activist lawyer Marian Wright Edelman. Her association with Edel-

man was the basis for a lifelong interest in protecting the rights of children.

Another important consequence of Hillary's years at Yale was meeting fellow law student William Jefferson Clinton. Almost immediately, the two became inseparable. Hillary decided to delay her law school graduation to spend time with Bill and study for an extra year in a law school program devoted to children's rights.

In addition to their romantic relationship, Hillary and Bill seemed to complement each other politically. During the summer of 1972, the two worked for Democratic presidential nominee George S. McGovern in Texas. The couple began to develop a national network of friends and contacts in the Democratic Party. Bill and Hillary both graduated from Yale Law School in 1973.

Marriage and Family

From the beginning of their relationship, Bill had made clear his intention to return to his native Arkansas to run for public office. Clinton kept his promise, taking a teaching position at the University of Arkansas Law School as he planned his first campaign. Hillary's first job was with Edelman's Children Defense Fund in Cambridge, Massachusetts. In early 1974, Washington, D.C., beckoned, and Hillary was hired as a staff attorney for the House Judiciary Committee, which was considering impeachment proceedings against President Richard Nixon. Her employment ended when Nixon resigned the presidency in August, 1974.

While she was dubious, Hillary decided to join Bill in Arkansas and accept a position teaching at the law school. Her friends were aghast; Hillary could become one of the top lawyers in the country. Her prospects seemed unlimited. Hillary herself acknowledged this when she admitted that her family and friends thought that she had lost her mind when she made the decision to follow Bill. She arrived in Fayetteville when Clinton was in the midst of his first congressional campaign. Clinton lost

William Jefferson Clinton

In December, 2000, *The New York Times* wrote that Bill Clinton "has lived more lives than most politicians ever dream of having, and skirting more deaths, only to rise again." Clinton knew the dizzying success of an agreement between Yitzhak Rabin and Yasir Arafat and the dismal days of a Senate impeachment trial. He rose from every defeat to move on to other issues and concerns and took the United States along on his wild ride.

During his 1992 presidential campaign, both Bill and Hillary Clinton advised Americans that they would be getting "two for the price of one." Using the theme "It's the economy, stupid," Clinton defeated incumbent president George Bush in November, 1992. Clinton's intelligence and energy seemed to promise a new vision for the country.

Clinton's troubles started almost immediately upon arriving at the White House with the highly controversial "Don't ask, don't tell" policy regarding gay men and women in the military. That furor paled by comparison to the president's push for universal health care. Though well intentioned, the effort went down in defeat. Clinton believed the defeat of health care reform was his greatest policy failure. One of the results of the debacle was felt on election day, 1994, when Republicans took control of Congress for the first time in forty years. Clinton was determined to work with Republicans, but it was obvious that continuing battles between the two sides over a balanced budget brought about two government shutdowns in 1995.

Clinton was handily reelected in November, 1996, defeating former senator Bob Dole. However, storm clouds were gathering: In March, 1997, the Senate approved an investigation into White House and Congressional fund-raising practices. Two months later, the Supreme Court ruled that Paula Jones could pursue her sexual harassment lawsuit against the president. There was an ongoing investigation of the Clintons' involvement in possible fraud and conspiracy connected with their Whitewater Development Corporation.

The most devastating blow to the Clinton presidency was allegations of a sexual relationship between Clinton and former White House intern Monica Lewinsky. Clinton repeatedly proclaimed his innocence; then, in August, 1998, he admitted that he had lied about the affair. Independent Counsel Kenneth Starr found that there were grounds for impeachment, and on December 19, 1998, Clinton became the second president in United States history to be impeached. A few months later, the Senate acquitted the president.

Even if Americans found Clinton's ethics questionable, they respected the fact that he had helped to strengthen the economy. In spite of the impeachment, the president continued to receive strong job approval ratings. As his time in the White House neared an end, Clinton focused on Social Security, education, and foreign affairs, with special attention to Middle East peace negotiations.

A man who possessed great talents and strengths and was a virtuoso politician and communicator, Clinton is likely to be remembered, however, for promises he was unable to keep and missed opportunities.

the campaign, but the relationship deepened. The couple were married in October, 1975. Hillary decided to retain her maiden name.

Clinton undertook another campaign, and this time he was successful: He was elected attorney general of Arkansas in 1976. Shortly after the election, Hillary was offered a job at the Rose Law Firm, arguably the most high-powered and prestigious law firm in the state at that time. In December, 1977, President Jimmy

Carter appointed Hillary to serve on the board of the federally funded Legal Services Corporation, which had been created under President Lyndon B. Johnson's administration. A few months later, she became chairperson of the board.

Bill Clinton was elected governor of Arkansas in 1978. As the state's First Lady, Hillary devoted her energies to children, families, and education. She founded the Arkansas Advocates for Children and Families and chaired the Arkansas Education Standards Committee. In addition to these responsibilities, she maintained a busy law practice. She became a partner at the Rose Law Firm in 1979. Her daughter, Chelsea Victoria Clinton, was born on February 27, 1980.

Clinton was reelected governor five times. He had always aspired to be elected president and thought his chances looked particularly promising in 1992. Things were going well when Gennifer Flowers disclosed to the national media that she and Bill Clinton had conducted a twelve-year affair. Clinton denied Flowers's allegation. It was an open secret that the Clintons' marriage had been troubled over the years, but Hillary came to her husband's defense. On the television program *60 Minutes*, she told viewers that she supported her husband. She said, "I'm not sitting here because I'm some little woman standing by her man . . . . I'm sitting here because I love him and respect him and I honor what he's been through and what we've been through together, and you know, if that's not good enough, then heck, don't vote for him." People admired Hillary's tough, gritty style and candid response. The Clinton candidacy, which was said to be dead, survived.

Hillary was involved with every phase of the campaign. She was an astute strategist, critic, and campaigner, unafraid to tackle substantive issues. More than any other prospective First Lady, she was quizzed about her own views and her prospective role in her husband's administration. On election day,

Clinton soundly defeated President George H. W. Bush, and the couple who had suggested that the United States would get "two for the price of one" swept into the White House.

Presidency and First Ladyship

Hillary Rodham Clinton had made it clear that she would not be a traditional First Lady, consumed with the ceremonial obligations of her role as presidential spouse. Her office in the West Wing spoke to the activist that she intended to be during her White House tenure. The new president appointed her to head the President's Task Force on National Health Care Reform. Clinton had campaigned on this issue and had suggested that the First Lady would be responsible for reform efforts.

The task force began its work with the goal of bringing major change to health care in the United States. There were almost six hundred people working in subgroups and task forces. The First Lady closed meetings to the media and the public, believing that secrecy was critical to the success of the project. The Association of American Physicians and Surgeons brought suit in federal court to open the meetings to the public. A federal judge ruled that the task force was guilty of misconduct in withholding documents and closing meetings. Later, however, the United States Court of Appeals for the District of Columbia reversed the ruling, and wrote that Mrs. Clinton was a full-time federal official, and the commission was not obligated to open its hearings. It was reasonable, declared the judges, "to treat the President's spouse as a 'de facto officer or employee' of the government."

After months of hard work, meetings, and a bravura performance by Hillary testifying before Congress about her task force's work, the new plan was unveiled. Replete with bureaucracy, regulations, rules and requirements, it appeared that there was something to offend every constituency. Congress, which at first had seemed amenable to change, now balked at the complex plan. Compromises were offered that might have mollified Democrats and Republicans, but Hillary refused to budge, especially on the issue of universal health coverage. Her intransigence and the very nature of the tangled plan marked it for defeat. Though well intentioned, the health care plan collapsed completely in August, 1994. It was a humiliating defeat for both the Clinton administration and Hillary.

Reverberations were felt during the 1994 midterm elections, when the Democrats lost control of Congress. Though it was not the most important reason for widespread Democratic losses, the health care debacle was certainly a factor.

Hillary seemed to take a step back and retrench her involvement in politics. At the suggestion of Bill's senior political adviser Dick Morris, the First Lady faded quietly into the background for a time. She embraced a more traditional stance as presidential spouse, addressing groups and conferences and traveling to Asia with Chelsea. A psychologist suggested that, to try to exorcise her personal demons, Mrs. Clinton have "conversations" with her role model, Eleanor Roosevelt, and vent her spleen about the pressures of being First Lady. The technique is credible and well known in creativity work, but it served as fodder for talk show hosts. Displaying an impish streak, Hillary began speeches at the time by telling audiences, "As I was saying to Eleanor Roosevelt . . ." Later, Hillary followed in Eleanor Roosevelt's journalistic footsteps when she began writing a weekly newspaper column, which she titled "Talking It Over."

The Clintons seemed to move from catastrophe to crisis to emotional precipice. Over the years, the couple had to deal with questions about their Whitewater Development Corporation and a 1978 Arkansas land deal. Allegations included the question of whether Bill Clinton, as governor of Arkansas, had pressured businessman David Hale into making an illegal loan that would have benefitted the Clintons' Whitewater partners, James and Susan McDougal. The disappearance and reappearance of Hillary's billing records from the Rose Law Firm—records that related to work Hillary had done for the McDougals' Madison Guaranty Savings and Loan—resulted in the First Lady being subpoenaed to testify before a grand jury in 1996.

The firings of seven career employees at the White House Travel Office (referred to as Travelgate) and the suicide of Hillary's former partner at the Rose Law Firm and Deputy White House Counsel Vincent Foster also generated public relations headaches for the Clintons, as did Hillary's successful commodities trading and allegations of sexual misconduct by the president levied by Paula Jones and Kathleen Willey. One veteran White House reporter commented that she had never seen a president and First Lady take so many hits.

Hillary scored two victories as she began to reemerge on the national stage in late 1995 and early 1996. The first was a series of four speeches that she gave at the United Nations Fourth World Conference on Women in Beijing, China, in September, 1995. A second victory came in January, 1996, when Hillary published *It Takes a Village: And Other Lessons Children Teach Us.* Drawing on her lifelong interest in children and her experiences as a mother, she wrote about the ways in which children develop and their relationships with their parents and society. The title of the book, taken from an African proverb, suggested that children needed the support of a community of committed adults to thrive. Many critics endorsed the message of the book, while others believed it to be liberal do-gooder drivel. The book enjoyed moderate success, and later in the year the First Lady was presented with a Grammy Award from the Recording Academy for her oral performance of the book.

Hillary comes closest to Eleanor Roosevelt in her mastery of public communication. Inde-

---

Speaking for Women Everywhere

In the dark days after the health care debacle and widespread democratic losses in the 1994 midterm elections, First Lady Hillary Rodham Clinton assumed a more traditional role in her husband's administration. However, Hillary emerged in a different persona when she addressed the United Nations Fourth World Conference on Women in Beijing, China, in September, 1995. There had been a question about whether the First Lady would attend at all because the United States protested the People's Republic of China's poor human rights record, and this had exacerbated tensions between the two governments. Hillary was granted permission to attend the conference and, once in China, lost little time in castigating China, India, Bosnia, and a number of Middle Eastern countries for practices she considered abhorrent, including the murder of female babies, selling girls and women into prostitution, and forced sterilization. She told her listeners, "If there is one message that echoes forth from this conference, let it be that human rights are women's rights. And women's rights are human rights, once and for all."

There was virtually no coverage of the speech in China, but in the United States and around the world it received extensive and enthusiastic coverage. Many delegates to the conference lauded Mrs. Clinton for her remarks. The speech was a defining moment for Hillary Rodham Clinton.

---

pendent of her Senate campaign discourse, it is likely that the First Lady gave between nine hundred and twelve hundred speeches and statements. Hillary had the support of speechwriters, but she was a capable extemporaneous speaker, able to fashion her message at the podium with little more than an outline to reinforce major ideas. Ever careful of the impact of her words, Hillary ensured that especially important speeches were carefully researched, written, and delivered verbatim. Observers, however, noted her adeptness at tailoring her comments to a specific audience. While levity was rare in her discourse, she occasionally used gentle, self-deprecating humor in her speeches. Displaying a quick mind and training as a lawyer, she used language with precision and was able to think rapidly and construct arguments as she faced listeners.

Mrs. Clinton did not experience the same success Mrs. Roosevelt had with the press. Neither Clinton enjoyed a "honeymoon," the period of time after entering the White House traditionally devoid of criticism. There was an uneasy relationship between the First Lady and the press during her White House tenure. For-

mer United Press International White House Correspondent Helen Thomas recalled that during an interview, she reminded the First Lady that she had a reputation of being hostile to the press. According to Thomas, Mrs. Clinton responded, "'No, I don't think that is valid,' but she said it with a smile." Hillary went on to tell Thomas that she championed a free press in her travels around the world.

Her feelings may have been genuine, but for the first three years of the Clinton administration, the First Lady virtually held herself incommunicado; she gave only one press conference, and that was organized because of concerns over her commodities trading. Hillary's staff seemed to feel that press attention to the First Lady was biased and superficial. Reporters generally were not invited to accompany the First Lady on her domestic trips but were given the chance to cover her foreign journeys where she guaranteed press conferences. Few, however, were able to avail themselves of the opportunity because of the prohibitive cost of overseas travel. Two media critics appraising the situation wrote that Mrs. Clinton's press relations "are not so much rocky as they are nonexistent." Things improved over the next few years, and Hillary seemed better able to tolerate the press when she initiated her campaign for the U.S. Senate.

As the Clintons approached the 1996 presidential campaign, Hillary had a disapproval rating of 54 percent and seemed to be the most unpopular First Lady in history. She struggled to regain political momentum and, over time, was successful. This was underscored by protests from Republicans who did not want Mrs. Clinton actively involved in the ongoing national debate about welfare reform. Still, Hillary's speech at the 1996 Democratic National Convention was gentle in tone as she spoke about family rather than politics; hammering the Republicans was left to others. The First Lady traveled throughout the United States, speaking on behalf of Democratic Party office seekers. In November, 1996, Bill Clinton defeated former Senator Bob Dole handily and became the first Democratic president since Franklin D. Roosevelt to be reelected to office.

After the election and through the end of 1997, Hillary visited schools and hospitals in Washington, D.C. She advocated literacy, took part in the President's Summit for America's Future, and avidly endorsed the microbusiness, or microenterprise, movement as a way to encourage self-employment among poor people. She traveled extensively to Africa, Russia, and Central Asia and represented the United States at the funeral of Britain's Princess Diana.

On January 21, 1998, stories suggesting a sexual affair between the president and a White House intern surfaced in the national press. The president angrily dismissed the charges during a news conference at the White House, shaking his finger and telling the American people, that he did not have an affair with "that woman, Miss Lewinsky." The next day, Hillary Rodham Clinton appeared on the *Today* show and told host Matt Lauer that Clinton had been targeted by a vast right-wing conspiracy that sought to discredit him. Her vehemence in defending her husband suggests that Hillary believed her husband's protestations of his innocence.

The president maintained this posture until August, 1998, when he admitted that he had lied to the country, misled his wife, and, in fact, had an affair with Monica Lewinsky. Many of Hillary's supporters were angered when she ostensibly forgave her husband and issued a statement through her press secretary, who said, "[Mrs. Clinton] is committed to her marriage and loves her husband and daughter very much. She believes in the president, and her love for him is compassionate and steadfast."

Clinton's admission set in motion the events that led to his impeachment on December 19, 1998, on charges of perjury and obstruction of justice. He was not convicted of high crimes and misdemeanors in the subsequent Senate trial, but many believe that his presidency and legacy, despite his entreaties and heartfelt contrition, were forever tarnished.

Throughout a sometimes volatile marriage, Hillary not only "stood by her man" but frequently was the strategist charged with solving his problems. As 1999 began, the First Lady considered moving out of her husband's political shadow to run for the U.S. Senate seat being vacated by the retirement of New York's Daniel Patrick Moynihan.

It seemed that Hillary had ruled out the possibility of a run for elective office years before, when she told an interviewer, "I think there are so many ways to serve, and I would be involved in my community . . . but I don't know that I would have pursued an elective [office], no." In the summer of 1999, she nonetheless embarked on a "listening tour" through New York to find out if state residents would support her candidacy. It was the first time that Hillary Rodham Clinton stood alone; she told reporters, "It's a different feeling to be the person who is in the spotlight . . . speaking on my own behalf . . . . I loved what I did. I had a wonderful time."

The results of the tour were encouraging, and in an effort to establish residency in the Empire State quickly, the president and Mrs. Clinton bought a home in Chappaqua, New York, in November, 1999. Two months later, on New Year's Day, 2000, Hillary Rodham Clinton became a part-time First Lady and a full-time campaigner. She officially entered the Senate race in February, 2000, amid hoopla and speeches. Responding to charges that she was a carpetbagger, she told the voters of New York, "I hope you'll put me to work for you. I may be new to the neighborhood, but I'm not new to your concerns."

Hillary's likely opponent, New York City mayor Rudolph Giuliani withdrew from the Senate race in May, 2000, disclosing that he had prostate cancer and had to devote his energies to fighting the disease. Into the breach stepped Suffolk County (Long Island) congressman Rick Lazio, running in his first statewide race. While Hillary would not have to contend with the combative mayor, she faced a formidable challenge, as four out of ten New Yorkers told pollsters they would prefer to vote for anyone but the First Lady.

During the ensuing campaign, Hillary traversed the state, sharing her plans for dealing with the national debt, tax cuts, social security, gun control, and a plethora of other issues. The initial spark of her campaign faded in unending slump speeches: One newspaper wrote that without the president, Mrs. Clinton was just another politico seeking votes.

The First Lady and Lazio, who traded barbs, charges, and counter charges, met in three acrimonious televised debates. Sometimes, however, the opponent was not Lazio. Early in the

A "humbled" Hillary Rodham Clinton accepts the nomination of the Democratic Party for Senate, May, 2000. *(AP/Wide World Photos)*

first debate, moderator Tim Russert asked the First Lady if she could be trusted, in light of the fact that she had gone on national television to defend her husband and point a finger at a vast right-wing conspiracy. Hillary responded, "Obviously I didn't mislead anyone. I didn't know the truth. And there is a great deal of pain associated with that."

Near the conclusion of the same debate, Lazio walked over to Hillary's side of the stage and demanded that she sign a pledge renouncing "soft" campaign money, referring to unregulated campaign contributions which usually take the form of services. The First Lady, who had raised millions in soft money, refused to sign until Lazio would reject the money he was receiving from independently financed advertising. After Lazio's theatrics, Hillary commented, "I admire that . . . that was a wonderful performance." Lazio, who had been warned about his abrasive debate tactics, had given Hillary a needed boost in the polls, and she continued to gather momentum.

In another display, Lazio and the New York State Republican Party intimated in telephone calls to prospective voters that Mrs. Clinton had ties to the terrorists who had blown up the USS *Cole* in Yemen in October, 2000. This brought outraged response from Hillary, who called the telephone calls unacceptable and said, "I believe the Republican Party and Congressman Lazio owe an apology to the families of the sailors who died in the terrorist bombing . . . ." The State Republican Party refused to apologize, and the telephone calls continued. The strategy backfired, and with a little over a week until election day, polls indicated that Hillary was forging ahead of her opponent.

The polls proved correct, and on the morning of November 8, 2000, with the outcome of the presidential race still very much in doubt, *The New York Times* trumpeted Hillary Rodham Clinton's Senate triumph with the headline "First Lady Ends 16-Month Run with Victory." Hillary trounced Lazio, 55 percent to 43 per-

cent. After twenty-four years as a political wife, the first sitting First Lady to be elected to public office was sworn in as a United States senator on January 3, 2001.

Legacy

Hillary Rodham Clinton's eight turbulent years as First Lady were fraught with controversy and scandal but also achievement. Able to take a hit, the First Lady learned from every setback, every misstep, and continued to move forward. Her legacy is twofold. Hillary redefined the office of First Lady, moving away from noncontroversial issues, such as literacy, drug abuse, and mental health, to controversial issues. The president gave his wife executive responsibility and made her the point person on a major legislative initiative. Few questioned Hillary Rodham Clinton's power or importance. She evolved from personal adviser to public spokeswoman to point person on public issues. Future First Ladies may elect to take less public roles, but the opportunity to be actively and publicly involved in discussions of the national agenda is now a viable option.

Hillary further pushed the boundaries of the role of First Lady by running for public office prior to the conclusion of her husband's term in office. No sitting First Lady had previously run for elective office. By taking this action, she decided that she would devote her energies to campaigning, becoming a part-time First Lady. As First Lady, Eleanor Roosevelt had been involved in public affairs; she served as a member of the United States Delegation to the United Nations and chaired its Committee on Human Rights. Mrs. Roosevelt, however, undertook her duties after leaving the White House. Hillary's actions were unprecedented.

Like her husband, Hillary was among the first public figures to live in a relentless media culture that magnified every mistake. As a partner in her husband's presidency, she came to use that media attention to her benefit. Bold, creative, and tenacious, she chose to take a storied institution and give it limitless possibilities. Those who succeed her may not care to follow the trail that she blazed, but that trail, and the potential for accomplishment, will remain.

Suggested Readings

Clinton, Hillary Rodham. *An Invitation to the White House: At Home with History.* New York: Simon & Schuster, 2000. Hillary Rodham Clinton looks at the history, traditions, and workings of the Executive Mansion.

_____. *It Takes a Village: And Other Lessons Children Teach Us.* New York: Simon & Schuster, 1995. Hillary Rodham Clinton discusses child rearing in her award-winning book.

Flinn, Susan K., ed. *Speaking of Hillary: A Reader's Guide to the Most Controversial Woman in America.* Ashland, Oreg.: White Cloud Press, 2000. A collection of essays by friends and foes assessing Hillary Rodham Clinton's life, defeats, victories, and legacy.

Gould, Lewis L., ed. *American First Ladies: Their Lives and Their Legacy.* New York: Garland Press, 1996. Gould's carefully researched article was the first scholarly treatment of Hillary Rodham Clinton's tenure as First Lady.

Milton, Joyce. *The First Partner.* New York: Perennial Books, 1999. A solid, general biography of Hillary Rodham Clinton.

Sheehy, Gail. *Hillary's Choice.* New York: Random House, 1999. Some of the material in this book appeared in *Vanity Fair* magazine. This alternately confusing and enlightening biography attempts to explain Hillary Rodham Clinton's life choices.

Myra G. Gutin

Laura Bush

Laura Welch Bush

Born: November 4, 1946
Midland, Texas

President: George W. Bush
2001-

Overview: Only the second First Lady in U.S. history to be married to the son of a former president, Laura Bush followed in the footsteps of First Lady Louisa Adams, who served in the early 1800's. A reserved school librarian and teacher from a small town in Texas, Laura Bush was a hesitant political spouse who nevertheless proved herself to be a major force in George W. Bush's life and political career, emerging as an admired, competent public figure and nationally recognized advocate of literacy and reading.

Laura Bush. *(AP/Wide World Photos)*

Early Life

Born and raised in the small town of Midland, Texas, Laura was an only child. Her mother, Jenna Welch, and her father, Harold Welch, who worked as a home builder before his death in 1995, gave their daughter a happy upbringing. An otherwise contented home life was briefly shattered when seventeen-year-old Laura was involved in a car accident that claimed the life of her then-boyfriend. She was not seriously injured and recovered emotionally.

During her formative years, Laura developed a love of reading and was a serious student. After finishing high school in Texas, Laura enrolled in Southern Methodist University, near Dallas, where she earned a bachelor's degree in education. She then received her master's degree in library science at the University of Texas at Austin. From 1968 until 1977, Laura pursued a career as a teacher and school librarian with school systems in Austin, Dallas, and Houston.

Although they grew up in the same town in Texas, attended the same junior high school, and, amazingly, lived in the same apartment complex in Houston as adults, Laura Welch and George W. Bush were not acquaintances. After attending public schools in Texas and the same elite private school that his father and grandfather had attended, George went to Yale University in Connecticut. After graduating, he returned to Texas for a stint with the Texas Air National Guard. It was during this period when George and Laura lived in the same Houston apartment complex that they finally met, although it was in their hometown of Midland. The two were introduced at a barbecue by mutual friends who were trying to play matchmaker, even though Laura and George had ex-

pressed reservations about the arranged "date." The spark of a romance was kindled, and Laura and George started dating after that initial meeting.

Marriage and Family

After a three-month courtship, George asked Laura to marry him, and she agreed to do so. They were wed just one month afterward, on November 5, 1977, in Midland. Both bride and groom were thirty-one years old. George would later call the decision to marry Laura the wisest choice of his life. Although they were opposites in many ways, their union was a happy one. Laura's influence on her husband was seen as positive by all who knew the couple. George described his youth and young adulthood as irresponsible; it was not until after marrying Laura and having children that he ap-

George W. Bush

George W. Bush was born in 1946 and grew up in rural Texas, while his father worked in the oil industry. The son of a president and grandson of a U.S. senator, he grew up with politics as part of his family life. As a young man, he witnessed the start of his father's political career, and later he would "cut his political teeth" on his father's presidential campaigns in 1980, 1988, and 1992. As his famous family members had been, he was educated at Yale University. He later earned a master's degree at Harvard Business School.

Much has been said of Bush's recklessness as a young man. After graduating from college, he was somewhat directionless before he chose to work in the oil business in Texas, as his father had done. This career met with mixed success but was followed by a break that would provide him with a high profile in Texas and enable him to launch his successful bid to be governor of the Lone Star State. He became part of a group of investors that bought the Texas Rangers, a professional baseball team, and he emerged as a driving force in the day-to-day operations of the team, helping to turn the franchise's losing ways around.

George W. Bush, known as W, worked on his father's presidential campaigns and gained valuable experience and contacts, which he put to good use during his own bid for the governorship of Texas. He was able to put together his own winning team, with which he defeated powerful incumbent Ann Richards in 1994 to become governor of Texas. The victory, soon after his father had left the presidency, helped heal the pain of the elder Bush's loss to Bill Clinton in 1992. As governor, George W. Bush initiated educational reforms and was known for his bipartisan approach to governing, reaching out to leading Democrats in his state. He asserted himself as his own person in 2000, gaining the presidency in a hard-fought election where, in spite of losing the popular vote, he won the electoral college vote after a prolonged legal process.

peared to develop some direction in his life. She is credited with helping him calm his exuberance and supporting him when he overcame an alcohol addiction.

The newlyweds lived in Midland, and George, having decided to pursue public office, ran for U.S. Congress. Laura was uncomfortable with politics and hesitant about her role in his political career. However, she proved to be a capable campaigner and political spouse. The bid for office was unsuccessful, and George pursued a career in the oil business in Texas, followed by part-ownership of the Texas Rangers, a professional baseball team.

In 1981, after a difficult pregnancy and a bout with toxemia, Laura gave birth to twin girls, Jenna and Barbara, named for their maternal and paternal grandmothers, respectively. Laura participated in the political career of her father-in-law, George H. W. Bush, including his campaigns for the presidency. However, she worked hard to keep the media attention off her daughters in an effort to give them normal childhoods. This became increasingly difficult when her husband ran successfully for governor of Texas in 1994, but she succeeded in fostering a private family life for her children.

As First Lady of Texas, Laura worked hard to promote family literacy programs and reading, much as her mother-in-law, Barbara Bush,

Laura Bush waves to the crowd at a rally for presidential candidate Texas governor George W. Bush in Springdale, Arkansas, July, 2000. *(AP/Wide World Photos)*

had done while in the White House. Laura was successful in establishing the Texas Book Festival as a prominent event in her home state. The festival brought Texas authors from around the state to Austin and raised awareness for the causes of literacy and reading as well as money for libraries around Texas. In 1998 Laura helped develop a program that encouraged parents

Surprising Political Journey

Laura Bush, like her mother-in-law, Barbara Bush, was a viable part of her husband's political career. Although a reluctant political spouse, she emerged as a popular figure and a valuable asset to George W. Bush's presidency. Up until the time of her marriage in 1977, Laura had not demonstrated an interest in politics. Immediately after the wedding, however, she found herself in the role of political spouse when her husband ran for a seat in Congress. So uncertain was Laura about the prospects of a political career that she made George promise not to make her speak in public. The pledge did not last long, as Laura, busy on the campaign trail, found herself making short public speeches. Although her husband's campaign proved unsuccessful, Laura and George would go on to campaign for the elder George Bush during his unsuccessful bid for the presidency in 1980.

As a political spouse, Laura would deliver numerous speeches and make countless public appearances during her father-in-law's eight years as vice president and four years as president as well as during her husband's successful bid for the governorship of Texas. By the time George W. Bush campaigned for the presidency in 2000, Laura had become an integral part of his career, and although she was not well-known outside of Texas, she had established herself as a capable and confident speaker.

Despite her initial shyness and lack of interest in publicity and politics, Laura had made her presence felt in her husband's career. A stabilizing force in the Bush marriage as well as in George's life and work, she was not shy about exerting her preferences and views when she felt she had something to offer. From refocusing the floundering Bush presidential campaign shortly before the election in 2000 to speaking to a worldwide audience at the 2000 Republican National Convention that nominated her husband, it has been a surprising political journey for this former librarian from a small town in Texas.

to read with their children and to prioritize reading at home, which would better prepare youngsters to succeed in school.

Laura also championed social causes as First Lady of Texas, including the Community Partners Program, a nonprofit volunteer organization that worked with the Texas Department of Protective and Regulatory Services. She gave her time to efforts to create an "Adopt-a-Caseworker" program to help fill the need for such services, and she participated in efforts to provide donated clothing and diapers for neglected and abused children.

Presidency and First Ladyship

As had former First Lady Barbara Bush, Laura made the promotion of literacy and reading her special projects as First Lady. During the First Ladyship of her mother-in-law, Laura had be-

gun to work with the Barbara Bush Foundation for Family Literacy, and both the issue and organization found another champion in the East Wing of the White House. Laura also embraced several important social causes during her First Ladyships in Texas and in the White House, including education, breast cancer awareness, promoting abstinence among schoolchildren, and building public support for adoption. She stated that her mother-in-law and another former First Lady from Texas, Lady Bird Johnson, were her personal heroes and tried to model her approach to the office of First Lady on the examples of both these predecessors.

Despite her initial reservation about entering public life, Laura overcame her natural shyness and emerged as a valuable part of the Bush team. George's family had a long record of public service and was as well connected politically as any family in U.S. history. This, along with her mother-in-law, the former First Lady, provided Laura Bush with an abundance of resources upon which to draw during her years in the White House.

Legacy

Six months after becoming First Lady, Laura Bush announced the creation of a nonprofit fund-raising foundation to help school and classroom libraries buy books. The Laura Bush Foundation for America's Libraries was intended to help address the fact that public school libraries nationwide had lost funding in recent years as school districts suffered budget cuts.

"Connecting children with books is a critical step toward instilling the love of reading early," said Laura. She added that her work with other book lovers would ensure that every child in the United States had access to "the building blocks of learning through books."

Along with the foundation's establishment, Laura planned to carry out the legacy she had established as First Lady of Texas by hosting the first National Book Festival at the Library of Congress in September, 2001.

Suggested Readings

Bush, George W., with Karen Hughes. *A Charge to Keep*. New York: William Morrow, 1999. The George W. Bush story from his own perspective, written with the assistance of his longtime media aide and spokeswoman. He speaks to the influence Laura had on his life.

Ide, Arthur Frederick. *The Father's Son: George W. Bush*. Boston: Minuteman Press, 1998. Although published prior to George W. Bush's presidency and before the final stretch of the 2000 campaign cycle, the book examines Bush's early life, influences, and his relationship with his father. There is also some discussion of Laura Bush.

Minutaglio, Bill. *First Son: George W. Bush and the Bush Family Dynasty*. New York: Times Books, 1999. A balanced account of the forty-third president, which devotes attention to Laura Bush's role in calming a wayward young man and the central role she has played in his political career.

Watson, Robert P. *First Ladies of the United States: A Biographical Dictionary*. Boulder, Colo.: Lynne Rienner, 2001. The book offers profiles and biographical information on every First Lady to date, including Laura Bush, and provides comparative facts on all the presidential spouses.

Robert P. Watson

Presidential Partners

Overview: Presidential scholars have long noted that an important asset to any successful president is the president's spouse. First Ladies have been extremely active in campaigning for their husbands and their respective parties' nominees for congressional seats. They have been active in social and charitable causes, either on their own or with the president's policy agenda.

Perhaps the two most notable social hosts of their times were Dolley Madison and Jacqueline Kennedy. Modern First Ladies such as Lady Bird Johnson, Rosalynn Carter, and Hillary Rodham Clinton contributed to the professionalization of the office of the First Lady and its integration with the White House Office. They also championed their own public policy causes, from the beautification of the United States to mental health care awareness to the protection of children at risk. Modern First Ladies have become so involved in the policy process that they have appeared before congressional committees to testify for legislation sponsored by the White House.

History

When one surveys the various roles and functions that First Ladies perform, it becomes clear that the most important role for any First Lady is that of presidential adviser. While First Ladies have no constitutional role, they often see the president upon arising for the day and retiring at night. No other presidential adviser or lobbyist can hope to match this arrangement. Influence is, in part, conditioned by the type of relationship a First Lady has with the president. This type of relationship has changed as society has changed.

The suffrage, equal rights, civil rights, and women's movements have all contributed to a new society for women, and First Ladies have strongly influenced these movements and causes. For example, in the twentieth century, both Pat Nixon and Betty Ford actively supported the proposed Equal Rights Amendment to the Constitution. To understand the relationship between a First Lady and the president, one must explore the types of partnerships First Ladies have developed and the impact of changing societal roles concerning women upon this relationship.

Robert P. Watson, in his book *The Presidents' Wives*, presents a useful typology for assessing partnership. He develops five categories for First Ladies: full partner, partial partner, behind-the-scenes partner, partner in marriage, and nonpartner. This typology is based upon the relationships and interactions between First Ladies and their presidential spouses.

Full partner First Ladies are very active in politics. They are concerned about public policy issues, presidential appointments, political campaigning, and presidential speeches. Because of these interests, they serve as top presidential advisers and their level of activism with both public and private (social and charitable) issues is quite high. The public perceives them to be influential publicly and privately. These First Ladies are active in the careers of their husbands, but many achieve influence in their own right.

First Ladies who are partial partners are also interested in their husbands' careers. They serve as presidential advisers and support the presidents' political activities, from campaigning to appointments. However, they serve as minor rather than major advisers. This type of First Lady supports her husband but is not a major force in his political career. Her role concerning policy is more private and less visible, but she does participate in charitable and social causes.

A First Lady who acts as a behind-the-scenes partner is almost invisible in the policy process. This type of First Lady shies away from the public arena, yet she is extremely supportive of her husband's political activities. Her influence is private and personal in nature. Because this type of First Lady is not as visible as the previous two types, she is not a full partner.

First Ladies who serve as partners in marriage are not political partners. They are more traditional in nature, serving as personal rather than political advisers to presidents. Activity on the part of this type of First Lady is more social or personal in nature. Historians view them more as hosts than advisers.

Some First Ladies can be categorized as nonpartners. This type of First Lady is neither active nor supportive of the president. While all other First Ladies participate in the social aspects associated with the position, nonpartners refrain from such activities. As a result, they cannot achieve any significant influence in the realm of politics nor do they wish to. The nonpartner might, however, advise the president on private and personal matters.

During the last few decades there has been a general evolution from the nonpartner and partner in marriage type of First Lady toward the full partner model, a result of the revolution in women's roles and overall societal changes.

Guests enjoy a ball given by Louisa Adams, far right. Future president Andrew Jackson stands in the center while President John Quincy Adams is at the right. *(Courtesy of Craig Shermer, National First Ladies' Library)*

Role and Activities

As women became more educated and active in the private work force, they simultaneously became more active in the political process. They worked to achieve higher status in society. Writer Gladys Engel Lang presents a few models of women based upon different types of status. A satellite status implies that women are mere appendages of their husbands, with no independent ideas. Sponsored status means that women can achieve notoriety as a result of their relationship with a prominent man. However, they use such a relationship to find or earn their own way. Women who have their own ideas and act independent of their spouses can achieve autonomous status. This type of status resides within them, and their independent accomplishments are examples of this type of status.

Successes, from that of the suffragist movement at the turn of the twentieth century to that of the women's movement in the 1970's, led directly to the evolution of women from satellite status to autonomous status. Just as the general direction for First Ladies points toward a partnership model, the general direction for modern women remains toward achieving autonomous status. There are enormous implications for modern First Ladies in the way they organize their offices, view public policy activism, enter a partnership with their presidential spouses, and integrate their efforts with the White House office.

Watson characterizes both Letitia Tyler and Jane Pierce as nonpartners. President John Tyler inherited the presidency after the death of William Henry Harrison. Tyler's wife Letitia had suffered a stroke two years earlier and either did not wish to or simply could not assume the duties of First Lady. Her daughter-in-law Priscilla Cooper Tyler assumed the duties of a social hostess in Letitia's place. Letitia died during her husband's tenure as president.

Jane Pierce never accepted the Washington, D.C., lifestyle. She disliked being the wife of a congressman. She would avoid her official responsibilities by feigning illness, and these shenanigans continued while she served as First Lady. She was often depressed and secluded. This was especially the case after the death of her son Bennie in 1853. Nonpartner category First Ladies are few, and most had special circumstances. In Letitia Tyler's case, her health was a major concern. For Jane Pierce, failure to cope with the Washington scene and her husband's chosen profession played a major role in her nonpartnership.

Partners in Marriage

Watson characterizes Elizabeth Monroe, Anna Harrison, Margaret Taylor, Julia Grant, Grace Coolidge, Mamie Eisenhower, and Pat Nixon as partners in marriage. These First Ladies have one thing in common: They preferred privacy, and they remained distant from politics. For example, Elizabeth Monroe secured privacy for her youngest daughter's wedding, and this resulted in a strained relationship with the Washington establishment. She refused to court the public's favor, and her obsession with protecting the family's privacy only deepened over time. She left the daily operation of the White House to her husband. Mrs. Monroe's actions place her at the extreme fringes of this category. Anna Harrison resented William Henry Harrison's election to the presidency. She refused to attend his inauguration, but her tenure as First Lady ended with the death of her husband one month after his inauguration. Margaret Taylor also preferred privacy. She did not participate in the Washington social life and became a bit of a recluse by confining herself to her room for long stretches of time.

Other partner in marriage First Ladies participated in their husbands' careers and were active on the social side of White House events. Grace Coolidge always separated politics from social functions. President Calvin Coolidge did not allow her to participate in political decisions, and he did not ask for her advice on matters of policy. He controlled her schedule and dictated her behavior. Grace, however, was an asset to her husband because of her great sense of humor, charm, and outgoing personality.

Julia Grant was also extremely supportive of her husband's career and active on the social side of the ledger. She represents somewhat of a transitional figure because she lobbied President Ulysses Grant for a specific piece of legislation, and she accompanied him on a trip around the world.

Mamie Eisenhower simply did not seek the glare of publicity. She had no social causes to advance. She suffered from a chronic illness that contributed to her desire for privacy. On the other hand, Mamie was responsible for expanding the staff attached to the office of the First Lady to six secretaries and a staff director, demonstrating that even traditional First Ladies have had some impact on staffing.

Pat Nixon served as First Lady during the Vietnam War and the Watergate scandal. Her relationship with her husband appeared warm but traditional. She did not like politics or campaigning, although she reluctantly participated in both. She tended to shun publicity yet traveled widely and acted as an ambassador for the Nixon administration on her various travels abroad. Her main interest lay in increasing volunteerism throughout the United States. She also expanded the fine arts and furniture collection in the White House. Unlike others in this category, Pat served as an effective spokeswoman for President Richard Nixon's agenda.

The category of partner in marriage consists of various degrees along a continuum. It ranges from a strict separation of domestic and social life from politics, as with First Ladies Monroe, Harrison, Taylor, and Coolidge, to a more fluid relationship between social affairs and politics, as with the cases of First Ladies Grant, Eisenhower, and Nixon.

Behind-the-Scenes Partners

Watson has characterized a few modern First Ladies as behind-the-scenes partners. Perhaps Bess Truman represents a weak example in this category. Bess refused to hold press conferences and never developed a working relationship with the press. She had an aversion to publicity and photographs. After President Franklin Roosevelt's funeral, Bess told his secretary of labor, Frances Perkins, "I don't know what I am going to do. I'm not used to this awful public life." Despite this, Mrs. Truman achieved influence with President Harry Truman by the very nature of her role as wife and trusted confidante.

Jackie Kennedy's primary emphasis was on the White House restoration and a dedication to the arts in the United States. She insisted on privacy concerning family matters. While Jackie's interests were decidedly feminine, this should not obscure her private political maneuverings for causes dear to her. It is no secret that she supported President John Kennedy's agenda and monitored his legislation as it passed through Congress. She was not shy about lobbying Congress for her initiatives, as she did to obtain money to save the temple complex at Abu Simbel in Egypt from submersion during the building of the Aswan High Dam.

Nancy Reagan was perhaps the ultimate, and strongest, example of the modern behind-the-scenes partner. President and Mrs. Ronald Reagan were very close. Nancy was a tenacious supporter of her husband, both socially and politically. While other First Ladies worked as active partners in both marriage and politics, what separates Nancy from the others was her intense activity in support of President Reagan, the person: She was extremely protective of him. Mrs. Reagan was influential in controlling the president's appointments schedule, especially after the assassination attempt. She played a role in the firing of White House Chief of Staff Donald Regan and the moving of National Security Advisor William Clark to the Interior Department. Nancy also influenced President Reagan concerning the pursuit of

Nancy Reagan holds an early Christmas present given to her by Ronald Reagan, December, 1985. *(Archive Photos)*

arms control and the de-emphasis of various divisive social issues. While there can be no doubt about Nancy's influence, it was a type of influence exercised for the good and well-being of the president. The marital relationship that the Reagans forged over many years contributed to Nancy becoming the ultimate behind-the-scenes player.

Partial Partnership

According to Watson, Dolley Madison, Edith Wilson, and Lady Bird Johnson exemplify the partial partners category. Dolley Madison was the first and perhaps the greatest social host of the new republic. She was extremely active in social affairs, but she also played a role in politics. She oversaw the refurnishing and restructuring of the White House. She served as the outgoing counterweight to President James Madison's shy and inconspicuous nature. There was a political side to her social maneuverings. Dolley used social gatherings to soften the way for political choices. Many of her dinners and other social gatherings served

to solidify congressional support for President Madison's agenda. The Madison marital relationship was warm and cordial. Dolley served as an informal adviser. Historians generally treat her with respect and view her as a pre-modern First Lady.

Edith Galt was a widow who married President Woodrow Wilson after the death of his first wife, Ellen Wilson. Edith was an independent, self-confident woman devoted to her husband. Their marital relationship was a warm and loving one. World War I politicized Edith. She was active in support of the war effort and accompanied President Wilson on his European trip to present his peace plan, the Fourteen Points. Edith also accompanied him on his train tour of the United States to generate support for this plan. He suffered a stroke during this trip, and she subsequently acted as his chief of staff. All presidential requests went through her. This arrangement, which she termed a "stewardship," gave her a historic opportunity to influence policy. The object of her concern was the health of President Wilson. She shares this characteristic with Nancy Reagan, but Mrs. Reagan was a behind-the-scenes influence, whereas Mrs. Wilson was more overtly active and perhaps even signed presidential orders. There was public concern about this arrangement, as expressed in the newspapers of the day.

Lady Bird Johnson was extremely active in the policy process. Whereas Jackie Kennedy shied away from formal duties as First Lady, Lady Bird substituted for Jackie quite regularly as the wife of then-Vice President Lyndon Johnson. Lady Bird had managed Johnson's congressional office and their Texas radio station. Because of these efforts, she acquired experience in the world of business and the world of political spousehood. She was active not only in social affairs but also in political campaigning during the 1960's. She supported her husband's Great Society agenda.

Her marriage to Johnson was difficult because of his dominating nature and extramarital relationships, but the two formed a professional partnership based upon mutual political respect. Lady Bird gave her husband advice on his speeches, appointments, and campaigns. She served as his trusted political adviser. Lady Bird was interested in the progress made in the president's Head Start program, illiteracy, poverty, civil rights and, of course, beautification. She reinforced the president's natural proclivities toward conservation. President Johnson, in turn, worked toward her goal of beautification.

Lady Bird worked closely with Secretary of the Interior Stewart L. Udall on beautification issues. She received briefings from the White House staff on various issues, and she assembled a network of influential women to help in her beautification campaign. During her fight for highway beautification, she participated in legislative and lobbying strategy sessions with the White House staff, the first presidential spouse to do so. Lady Bird Johnson was, perhaps, the strongest example in the category of partial partner.

Full Partnership

The full partner First Lady is active in politics, social issues, and social affairs. These First Ladies serve as top presiden- tial advisers and are influential publicly and privately. Sarah Polk, Eleanor Roosevelt, and Rosalynn Carter are examples in this category.

Sarah Polk always considered housekeeping duties as secondary to her marital relationship. President James K. Polk accepted this arrangement, which was quite novel in the 1840's. The couple remained childless, and this fostered Sarah's devotion to Polk's political career. She established an influential network of women and men not only to further her husband's political career but also for her own support. This network of supporters valued Sarah's judgement and insight. First Lady Polk openly noted that she would not concentrate solely upon domestic chores. She served as an informal presidential assistant and often read papers and advised her husband on important issues of the day. The Polks' marital relation-

Sarah and James Polk. *(Courtesy of Craig Shermer, National First Ladies' Library)*

ship reflected the deep friendship the two had forged. Yet they did not agree on all issues, for Sarah had an independent nature. Clearly, she was testing the social and moral boundaries of her day and setting the stage for future First Ladies to continue her efforts in the next century.

Most historians credit Eleanor Roosevelt with changing the role of First Lady. More than any other White House occupant up to her time, she defined the role of a modern, activist First Lady. She became the first presidential spouse to speak at a national convention, author a newspaper column, serve as a radio commentator, and hold regular press conferences. While Eleanor did not particularly like to campaign, she did so for her husband. She served as an informal presidential adviser and became the first First Lady to testify before Congress. She was also involved in many issues, such as miners' rights, the plight of the unemployed, women's rights, youth issues, civil rights, and war relief. She exercised a considerable amount of independence from her husband on many of these issues, making her a political force in her own right.

The marriage of Franklin and Eleanor Roosevelt was strained by President Roosevelt's affair with Eleanor's secretary Lucy Mercer. Eleanor was deeply pained by this, but she did not let it interfere with her own political agenda. However, the affair did contribute to her independence on various issues. Thus, the partnership displayed by Eleanor and Franklin was largely professional in nature. Clearly, Eleanor was testing the boundaries between sponsorship status for women and outright autonomy.

The relationship between Jimmy and Rosalynn Carter was a personal and professional partnership. The Carters were best friends and marriage partners. When President Carter announced Rosalynn's trip to Latin America, he noted that she had "long been his partner." The relationship was one of mutual respect and admiration. Rosalynn was a full and essential partner in the Carters' peanut business. As First Lady, she made sure that she was taken seriously by other policy makers. She was active in President Carter's campaigns and served as an influential adviser. She formally lunched with the president once a week. Rosalynn was active in giving her opinions, and she championed various women's issues and causes. She attended formal cabinet meetings and even took notes during negotiations at Camp David, the presidential retreat.

Rosalynn displayed independence from the president on a few issues, such as capital punishment, abortion rights, and the timing of the Panama Canal Treaty. She used her influence and her working relationship with President Carter to help pass the Mental Health Systems Act, becoming the first presidential spouse to testify before Congress since Eleanor Roosevelt. Rosalynn's work involved interactions with the White House staff. The personal relationship of full partnership between the Carters, as well as Rosalynn's experiences as an independent businessperson and advocate of mental health legislation, aided such work.

Significance

These examples demonstrate the importance of First Ladies operating within the partial partner and full partner categories. First Ladies who did so pushed the social and moral boundaries of their times. First Ladies such as Dolley Madison and Sarah Polk set the stage for their modern successors. Modern First Ladies, such as Lady Bird Johnson, Eleanor Roosevelt, and Rosalynn Carter, achieved partnerships with their husbands that allowed them to have a significant impact upon public policy. When comparing the First Ladies of the nineteenth century to those of the latter half of the twentieth century, the movement from satellite to sponsorship to autonomous status becomes apparent. Modern First Ladies who have established good working relationships with the presidents and have significant job experience dealing with issues and are active in the public pol-

First Lady Hillary Rodham Clinton Wins New York Senate Seat

As First Lady, Hillary Rodham Clinton showed a deep commitment toward activism that is reminiscent of Eleanor Roosevelt. This commitment to social issues and causes was formed early in Hillary's life. She was affected by the struggle for civil and women's rights, the Vietnam War, poverty, and children's issues.

Hillary displayed leadership abilities in Wellesley College's student government and was elected president in her junior year. She was eventually graduated from Yale Law School. Later, she wrote about the problems of disadvantaged youth and worked for the Children's Defense Fund, with attorney Marian Wright Edelson. Hillary then served as a staff attorney on the House Judiciary Committee during the investigation into the impeachment of President Richard M. Nixon. After this experience, she took a teaching position at the University of Arkansas. This record of early achievement demonstrates that Hillary developed stands on issues independently and with conviction.

At the White House, Hillary served as President Bill Clinton's closest adviser. In this capacity she worked on political campaigns, lobbied for her initiatives, and testified before Congress. When New York's senior senator, Daniel Patrick Moynihan, announced his 2001 retirement, the New York Democratic establishment recruited Hillary to be his successor. She established New York residency in suburban Chappaqua and ran a disciplined campaign for the Senate. She began her campaign with a "listening tour," which served to introduce her to New York's voters. She successfully rebutted criticisms of her carpetbagger status by emphasizing substantive issues such as education, the environment, and health care. Hillary mastered New York's issues and campaigned in all sixty-two New York counties. Her original opponent, Rudolph Giuliani, the mayor of New York city, quit the race in May of 2000 and was replaced by New York Representative Rick Lazio. Lazio had a difficult time countering Hillary's message and developing rapport with the New York voters. In the end, he could not overcome an overwhelming New York Democratic advantage in voter registration. On November 7, 2000, Hillary Rodham Clinton became the first First Lady to be elected to the United States Senate. She won a hard-fought race against Lazio and received 55 percent of the vote to his 43 percent.

During her commencement speech at Wellesley College, Hillary had challenged her fellow students to use their intellect for the social good. She advised those present that politics was the "art of making what appears impossible, possible." Hillary took the opportunity to follow her own advice while making history in the United States Senate.

icy arena are most likely to operate out of the partial partner or full partner categories. They are most likely to achieve sponsorship or autonomous status.

The partnerships of these modern First Ladies have had an impact not only upon public policy but also upon the office of the First Lady. The activism of the partial and full partner First Ladies has led directly to the increased profes-sionalization in the office of the First Lady. For example, within the office of the First Lady, the number of staff members has increased, and specific office functions are now highly integrated with the White House Office. Staff and assistant pay has increased to professional levels, and staffers are better educated about their responsibilities. Many current staff members have presidential adviser status. All of this has led to a closer working relationship with the White House Office. This relationship will continue as long as future First Ladies have close working relationships with their spouses and a desire to be active campaigners, advisers, and participants in the formulation of public policy with their own support networks. The phenomenon of First Ladies as full partners with their presidential spouses is the wave of the future.

Suggested Readings

Anthony, Carl Sferrazza. *First Ladies: The Saga of the Presidents' Wives and Their Power.* 2 vols. New York: William Morrow, 1990-1991. A unique glimpse at the power and prestige in the evolving role of the First Lady.

Caroli, Betty Boyd. *First Ladies.* Expanded ed. New York: Oxford University Press, 1995. A look at the varying roles each First Lady to date has undertaken, along with vital statistics.

Carter, Rosalynn. *First Lady from Plains.* Boston: Houghton Mifflin, 1984. Rosalynn Carter's candid memories of her life before and during her First Ladyship.

Gould, Lewis L., ed. *American First Ladies: Their Lives and Their Legacy.* New York: Garland, 1996. An informative and objective combination of biographical sketches and histories of the First Ladies.

Gutin, Myra G. *The President's Partner: The First Lady in the Twentieth Century.* New York: Greenwood Press, 1989. Examines the public communications and private personas of twelve First Ladies.

Robertson, S. L. "The First Lady, the First Family, and the President's Friends." In *Guide to the Presidency,* edited by Michael Nelson. Vol. 2. Washington, D.C.: Congressional Quarterly, 1996.

Watson, Robert P. *The Presidents' Wives: Reassessing the Office of the First Lady.* Boulder Colo.: Lynne Rienner, 2000. A statistical and research-oriented assessment of the roles and the long-ranging impacts of the First Ladies as presidential partners.

Anthony J. Eksterowicz

White House Manager

Overview: Despite never being formally or legally designated as an office, the position of First Lady has evolved throughout history into one of managing White House activities. The White House has remained simultaneously the home of the president and the setting for important functions of the chief of state's office. The First Lady's task of White House manager, as slightly redefined by each new occupant, has evolved throughout the past two centuries. On one hand, First Ladies have managed an increasingly large staff responsible for helping them plan and implement an array of formal state functions. Although primarily social in their setting, the management of receptions, dinners, concerts, or balls is laden with political implications.

History

Over the years, the managerial tasks of First Ladies have been focused not only on developing and supervising the public events held within the Executive Mansion but also in maintaining and improving the facility itself. Efforts to improve the White House have been made within one of two areas of concern: refurbishing and redecorating or renovating. The projects have varied as perceived needs changed over time. Moreover, some First Ladies (and their husbands) simply emphasized maintaining and improving the White House, while other First Ladies focused their attention elsewhere. Overall, nineteenth century First Ladies, with a few notable exceptions, tended to place less emphasis on White House refurbishing and redecorating or renovating duties than did their counterparts in the following century.

The White House was designed by James Hoban, an Irish architect and builder living in Charleston, South Carolina, whose entry won a nationwide contest in 1792. However, delays in the construction of the building postponed its occupation until November 1, 1800, when John Adams became the first president to live in the still-unfinished facility.

Major Preservation and Renovation

Since that time, the structure has undergone several major renovations as well as more frequent redecoration efforts. While the exterior of the Executive Mansion remains essentially the same as when President John Adams moved in, the interior has been subject to three extensive restoration efforts. Among the most serious threats to the White House structure were two major fires. The first, and most damaging, blaze occurred in August, 1814, when British soldiers burned the White House, along with much of the U.S. capital, during the closing months of the War of 1812. Only the exterior walls survived the attack, remaining primarily intact. Then, in 1929, an accidental fire damaged most of the offices in the West Wing during Herbert Hoover's administration. In addition to renovations imposed by those emergencies, there have been several efforts to make serious improvements to the facility over the years.

Noteworthy nineteenth century renovation efforts date from 1807, when President Thomas Jefferson and Benjamin Latrobe, surveyor of public buildings, began design work on porticos on the north and south sides of the structure and terraces extending from the east and west

The White House in 1814. *(Courtesy of Craig Shermer, National First Ladies' Library)*

ends of the White House. The completion of those projects, including numerous modifications, continued throughout the century.

In 1815 President James Madison sought to rebuild the burned-out White House to restore the facility and adjacent executive offices to their original state. With this in mind, the Commission of the District of Columbia, recreated to oversee the project, commissioned James Hoban to implement the task. Under Hoban, the commission's first task was to shore up the exterior walls which, thanks to a rainstorm soon after the 1814 fire, had been spared the most intense heat. However, the cold temperatures from the harsh winter of 1814-1815 had taken their toll on the deteriorating inner walls. Hence, extensive removal of parts of the outer walls occurred in 1816.

Work progressed steadily to the point where the new president, James Monroe, could occupy a still-uncompleted White House, beginning in October of 1817. The president and his wife, Elizabeth, at first lived in a few rooms on the second floor, while carpenters and craftsmen worked feverishly to finish the rest of the building around them. The massive restoration and rebuilding task progressed sufficiently for President Monroe to renew the tradition of hosting a public reception at noon on New Year's Day, 1818. Restoration work on the White House and construction of the adjacent executive office wings, in accord with Jefferson's earlier design, was greatly hampered by the Panic of 1819. Work in this phase ended in January of 1820.

In the twentieth century, one of the most important renovations was begun in Theodore Roosevelt's administration with the construction of an important addition to the White House's now-famous West Wing. This addition, which included the Oval Office, was completed in 1909. Roosevelt, and later his successor William Howard Taft, clearly meant the Oval Office to be the main working area for the president. Taft was the first president to use the new facility, moving his base of operations there from the second floor of the White House, where presidents traditionally had their work areas. Many previous presidents had conducted their daily business in the second-floor study and the old Cabinet Room. Taft officially moved into the Oval Office in late October, 1909. The new executive wing, whose final design was by Nathan Wyeth, was connected to the living areas of the White House by a colonnade which, in part, stemmed from the pavilion designed by Jefferson a century earlier. In 1927 the roof of the White House was raised, and a third floor was created in place of the area that had been the attic.

On the other side of the structure, the offices of the First Lady, which had been located in various areas of the White House throughout history, were eventually consolidated in a new East Wing, constructed in 1942. Since that time, most First Ladies have used that area as a base of operations. Their staffs gradually expanded over the years to a peak of about two dozen persons. However, several First Ladies, including Eleanor Roosevelt, Mamie Eisenhower, Jackie Kennedy, and Hillary Rodham Clinton, had offices elsewhere in the Executive Mansion. Despite differences in their personalities and operation styles, most of those First Ladies wanted refuge from the turmoil of the daily operation of the other offices.

The most extensive renovation since the rebuilding of the White House during the Madison and Monroe administrations early in the nineteenth century occurred from 1948 to 1952, during much of President Harry S. Truman's administration. At that time, the interior of the building, with the exception of the third floor, was removed and carefully marked and stored. With the outer walls of the facility left intact, the structure was reinforced with a steel frame, and a deep basement and foundation were installed. Whenever possible, original interior furnishings, such as doors, mantels, or other woodwork, were reinstalled in the renovated interior.

Few could dispute the necessity of undertaking such a massive renovation and restoration project. Soon after moving into the White House, the Trumans had realized that the floors, ceilings, and walls of the structure were literally falling in on them. Engineers determined that the floor of the Oval Study, installed in 1902 in the restoration during Theodore Roosevelt's administration, could support the weight of no more than fifteen people by 1948. The leg of a grand piano in Margaret Truman's bedroom literally sank through the floor, into the ceiling of the room below. Chandeliers in the Blue and East rooms would mysteriously sway, possibly from the shifting weight of someone walking on the floor above.

Engineers discovered that the rooms of the west half of the building were deteriorating the most extensively. Previous renovation efforts had led to the removal of some interior load-bearing walls, and workers had compensated for the loss of that support by installing steel rods, which shifted support of the weight to steel crossbeams overhead. However, these beams were upheld by walls too weak for the task. The weight of the top floors was transferred downward, thereby causing the walls of the lower floors literally to bend and bow outward. Not surprisingly, the Trumans quickly won congressional funding for a massive $5.4 million undertaking.

The subsequent renovation project would be massive indeed. The entire building, except for the third floor, would be carefully removed and what few parts could be reused would be numbered and stored so that they could be replaced afterward. Unfortunately, most of the wood furnishings, such as paneling, molding, and doors, simply had deteriorated too much over the years to be restored. Much of the woodwork in the building came apart upon being dismantled. The subsequent pieces, together with fireplace bricks and occasional surviving square nails, were combined into small "kits" and sold to help finance the project. The first interior stage, during which important delicate furnishings were dismantled, took several months. This was followed by the relatively quick demolition of the remaining beams, flooring, and doors.

Next, an extensive network of freestanding steel beams was installed to support all of the building's interior, independent of the exterior walls, which were left to support only themselves. In all, 660 tons of steel were used to support the White House. Finally, an extensive basement and two sub-basements were dug, encased in concrete, and anchored with concrete piers sunk deep in beds of sand and gravel. The basements were connected to the rest of the house by elevators and staircases. With the restoration work being done during the height of the Cold War, President Truman directed that the concrete walls and ceilings of the bottom sub-basement be made as bomb-proof as possible. The exterior walls remained essentially untouched. In sum, when completed, the restored White House had five lev-

els spanning the two sub-basements, the ground floor, and the second and third floors. The official public entertainment rooms on the main floor were restored to appear as they previously had. However, the modern service areas were largely hidden from public view. The number of rooms in the Executive Mansion increased from forty-eight to fifty-four, with the additional rooms used primarily as service areas.

Work on the three-year project was directed by a six-member commission appointed by President Truman. The chief architect for the renovation was Lorenzo Winslow, a well-known Washington, D.C., architect who had completed virtually all of his designs by the end of 1949. A crucial element of his design, subject to considerable scrutiny before its approval, was his plan for the staircase extending from the second floor to the main entrance foyer serving the front door. The second-floor design, however, nearly replicated the original plan, with modifications made primarily to improve bathrooms and expand closet space. The biggest differences were largely hidden from public view. For example, Winslow added mezzanine levels, primarily housing service areas, at each end of the building. The contractor selected was John McShain, Inc., of Philadelphia.

Tractor Pull

President Harry S. Truman, during the massive restoration and renovation project undertaken by his administration, gave strict orders that the exterior of the White House was not to be harmed. However, plans required the complete removal of most of the interior of the building, the digging of two sub-basements, and constructing an extensive foundation. Needing heavy equipment to complete the task on deadline, engineers dismantled a tractor and carried the pieces into the building through a doorway, then reassembled the machine. Workers then used the tractor to dig downward to create a large, new doorway safely below the original walls, sufficiently large enough to allow passage of trucks and additional tractors with which the rest of the work could be completed.

The subsequent dismantling and demolition work led to the reaming out of the entire White House interior below the third floor. This was followed by the complete restructuring of the interior of the building, roughly following the original plans drafted more than a century before.

Gutted interior of the White House as seen in 1950, when a major renovation was undertaken during the Truman administration. *(AP/Wide World Photos)*

Furnishings for the project were contracted to B. Altman & Company, a Manhattan department store. At the height of the project, more than three hundred workers were known to be toiling feverishly to complete the task in time for President and Mrs. Truman to move back into the White House for Christmas of 1951.

Hence, during much of his presidency, the Truman family lived across Pennsylvania Avenue in Blair House while the Executive Mansion underwent the extensive rebuilding of its interior. Throughout the time of the restoration work, the president and the White House staff continued to work in both the east and west wings of the mansion. The Oval Office itself never was directly affected by work on the project. Despite the Christmas, 1951, deadline,

the Trumans were not able to return to residence in the White House until 6:20 P.M. on March 27, 1952.

Refurbishing and Redecorating

Over the years, First Ladies have played a variety of roles in managing White House refurbishing and redecorating efforts, varying according to their personalities, how they viewed the position of First Lady, what society expected from them at the time, and the expectations of their husbands, the presidents. Hence, the management efforts of First Ladies ranged from being spectators to playing central roles.

While many First Ladies played either a limited role or no role whatsoever in managing White House renovations, they frequently were at the forefront in overseeing redecorating and managing day-to-day activities. Several First Ladies played prominent roles in restoring or refurbishing the White House during their husbands' presidencies. Particularly noteworthy were the efforts of Julia Tyler, Abigail Fillmore, Mary Lincoln, Julia Grant, Caroline Harrison, Edith Roosevelt, Bess Truman, and Jackie Kennedy.

In the 1840's, Julia Tyler made several improvements, both to dress up the building and to make it more liveable. She began by acquiring several pieces of fine French furniture. In addition, she made improvements to the lighting and heating systems in the White House. While the Tylers themselves financed

Millard and Abigail Fillmore established the Library in the White House, shown here in 1900. *(CORBIS)*

these improvements, the Fillmores in the early 1850's persuaded Congress to appropriate two thousand dollars to buy books to create the first White House library in the second-floor Oval Room. Abigail Fillmore also had installed in the White House plumbing and other improvements to the kitchen and bath areas, including an iron range and a bathtub.

However, the continuing extensive use of the White House increasingly strained the maintenance of the facility. By the time of Abraham Lincoln's presidency in the 1860's, Mary Lincoln sought primarily to dress up the decorative setting of the mansion rather than improve the facility structurally. She replaced many of the decorative furnishings in the White House. However, at the time her tastes were thought to be exceptionally expensive,

and the private sources she found to finance the endeavor ignited a scandal and caused her husband political headaches.

Perhaps learning from the problems of the Lincolns, Julia Grant won congressional funding in the decade following the Civil War to redecorate the Blue and East Rooms on the main floor. The funds also allowed for china and artwork for the facility. Also of note, she added gates, complete with guards, around the building.

Perhaps the most ambitious renovation and remodeling effort by a First Lady during the late nineteenth century was undertaken by Caroline Harrison in the early 1890's. Appalled by the deterioration of the building, Mrs. Harrison initiated a public relations campaign, featuring detailed guided tours of the facility, to convince both public and congressional visitors that the White House needed extensive repairs. She made a complete inventory of the building's contents and hired an architect to design wings extending from the east and westsides of the White House. Her efforts were rewarded with the replacement of many deteriorating floor areas in the building. Finally, marking the nature of the times, Mrs. Harrison oversaw the installation of electric lights in the Executive Mansion.

However, her efforts were soon to be surpassed. Shortly after the start of the new century, Edith Roosevelt began one of the most extensive restoration efforts in the history of the White House. When completed several years later, her work affected most areas of White House operation. First, seeking to recapture much of the historical setting of the facility, she persuaded Congress to finance an extensive refurbishing project. The effort included a campaign to purchase dining, art work, and home furnishings used in the White House by previous administrations. Second, with the guidance of a prominent architectural firm, Mrs. Roosevelt redecorated the White House in a way consistent with its eighteenth century origin, while also continuing the modernization efforts begun by Caroline Harrison and further improving the building's electrical and plumbing fixtures. These remodeling efforts encompassed the family's living quarters upstairs as well as the public rooms on the main floor.

Mrs. Roosevelt also had noteworthy improvements made to the official areas of the White House. She had the office area enlarged and improved. Her efforts included the State Dining Room and the Cabinet Room, which were each expanded to better meet the official demands placed upon them.

The next noteworthy restoration project was undertaken in the early 1960's, by Jackie Kennedy. Reminiscent of Edith Roosevelt and her restoration philosophy, Mrs. Kennedy worked for establishing the White House Historical Association. She then began collecting historic art and furnishings important to the history of the presidency, the White House, and the nation as a whole. To assure the continuity of her efforts, Mrs. Kennedy won approval to establish a curator and commission to protect and preserve the building and its contents. Furthermore, the new preservation policy forbade future presidents from giving away, removing, or selling White House furnishings.

Mrs. Kennedy made history in 1962 when she led an unprecedented televised tour of the White House, introducing each room and its contents and history to a large nationwide audience, most of whom had never visited the mansion.

Significance

The White House has come to mean many things to Americans. It is a national symbol, museum, and residence of the United States' chief executive. For more than two centuries, government officials and citizens alike have worked to preserve the classic building for following generations. First Ladies and presidents have tended to take an active leadership in such efforts. Their work has had to contend with the frequently conflicting goals of maintaining a building which is a national treasure, yet has to meet such contemporary needs as being a family residence and site for formal state events, frequently of international importance.

Suggested Readings

Aikman, Lonnelle, ed. *The Living White House.* 10th ed. Washington, D.C.: White House Historical Association, 1996. Brief history of the White House, including anecdotes of visitors, events, and first families.

Freidel, Frank, and William Pencak, eds. *The White House: The First Two Hundred Years.* Boston: Northeastern University Press, 1994. Eleven papers from distinguished scholars reflect on the changing public role of the First Lady, among other topics.

Seale, William. *The President's House*. 2 vols. Washington, D.C.: White House Historical Association, 1992. Young adult history of the White House includes its construction, reconstruction and renovations.

Watson, Robert P. *The Presidents' Wives: Reassessing the Office of First Lady*. Boulder, Colo.: Lynne Rienner, 2000. A statistical and research-oriented assessment of the roles and the long-ranging impacts of the First Ladies as presidential partners.

White House Historical Association. *The White House: An Historic Guide*. Washington, D.C., 1995. The history and use of each room in the White House is discussed. Contains good photographs.

Robert Dewhirst

Nation's Social Hostess

Overview: First Ladies have presided over everything from formal state dinners for dignitaries and diplomats to casual teas for community and civic groups. By custom that dates to the very first presidential spouse, the First Lady has been responsible for social entertaining in the White House. This role has been institutionalized within the office to the extent that the First Lady not only is expected to host White House functions but also is seen as the United States' social hostess.

History

The tradition of presidential spouses presiding over social affairs on behalf of the president and nation dates to Martha Washington, the first presidential wife. Lady Washington, as she was called, was uncertain of the role she would assume as the wife of the new president. Indeed, while much uncertainty remained regarding the specific functions of the president, even less certainty surrounded the duties of his wife. The Constitution was completely silent as to the nature of the roles or duties of the president's spouse.

George and Martha Washington contemplated the protocol that would define the inaugural presidency. This was an important undertaking because the social protocol would help define the essence and image of the new experiment in popular governance. Several European powers were doubtful about the prospects of the upstart nation, and there was the need to assert the legitimacy of the new government. This would be accomplished by the Washingtons, in part, through state social affairs. Although it was George who made the decision to hold a weekly social reception hosted by the president and a weekly levee over which Mrs. Washington would preside, it was Martha who hosted the events and established the tone for the nation's social affairs.

Another challenge for the Washingtons, in addition to the many questions surrounding the nature of presidential social functions, was attempting to balance the competing need to develop social affairs fit for dignitaries from the courts of Europe with the need to appease the popular taste for democratic simplicity. The new country opposed anything that even remotely resembled the court politics of the old European monarchies, such as titles, royalty, and the pageantry of high society. In spite of the challenge, the first couple somehow managed to walk this tightrope, setting a social tone befitting both the importance of the office and the principles upon which the country was founded.

Martha's levees were well attended by curious citizens eager to meet the president and his lady and see their government in action. In permitting such a democratic affair, the Washingtons made a strong symbolic statement and distinguished the new nation from European powers, where such access was unattainable for the citizenry. Where George Washington was somewhat formal and aloof, Lady Washington was warm and approachable, which further highlighted the democratic image they were establishing. At the same time, she and the president started the practice of hosting members of Congress at the president's residence, which effectively blended the social realm with the political realm, again demonstrating the importance of these early social affairs.

Martha Washington, by and large, received positive reviews for her social events. With each action, she was literally establishing precedents for the office and framing the role of social hostess for the First Lady, a duty that has remained to the present time.

John and Abigail Adams were the first to live in the newly constructed White House, moving into the "President's House" in late 1800, only months before the end of his single term in office. Abigail Adams, who often joined Mrs. Washington at her levees, sitting at her side, continued her predecessor's social practices. However, unlike the Washingtons, John and Abigail Adams had been to Europe and had firsthand familiarity with the social customs and practices of the ruling class.

By the time of Thomas Jefferson's presidency, the presidential spouse's role in hosting social functions was well established. However, Jefferson was a widower, his wife, Martha, having died long before his presidency, and he was disinterested in promoting an active social calendar while president. Nevertheless, the role of social hostess remained, as official Washington favored having social affairs. Jefferson asked his oldest daughter, also named Martha, to preside over his state affairs. Martha shared this duty with Dolley Madison, the wife of Jefferson's secretary of state. Although the president preferred simplicity, abandoning protocol, formality, and the recognition of rank, and held a limited social agenda, social hosting would be a centerpiece of the next administration.

Dolley Madison would be remembered as perhaps the most gifted and successful social hostess in the history of the White House. Arguably the most famous woman of her time, Dolley's socials were the toast of the town. They were so well attended that they were actually referred to as "Mrs. Madison's Crush."

Dolley used these socials to not only accommodate the social interests of official Washington but also to further her husband's agenda and political standing. Blending politics and socializing in a way that resembled art, Dolley succeeded in charming her guests, bringing to-

Designed for Success

Dolley Madison was the first to undertake a renovation of the White House. The second presidential spouse, Abigail Adams, had been the first to actually reside in the newly completed building. She found it barely livable, as only a few rooms had been completed and little thought had been given to practical matters such as doing laundry. Dolley found a mansion lacking in design for such functions as social entertaining. With the assistance of famed architect Benjamin Latrobe, she redesigned the "President's House" to serve as the political and social capital of the new nation.

Mrs. Madison and Mr. Latrobe designed a state dining room, parlor rooms, and interior spaces to enable the building to host social affairs and better accommodate crowds and guests. The First Lady also selected ornamental furnishings, fabrics, and silver pieces befitting the type of mansion she envisioned. She also promoted the United States through her choice of art for the building and furniture, much of which was painted or manufactured by Americans. The newly designed mansion enabled her to host her famous and crowded "drawing room" socials and "Mrs. Madison's Wednesday Nights," which commenced in 1809. So crowded were these functions that they were actually nicknamed "crushes." However, Dolley's celebrated social parties and future social affairs would not have been possible had she not had the vision to design the White House to serve its important social function.

gether political opponents, fostering viable political discussions, and obtaining valuable political information from her guests, all at her social affairs. In hosting such important and popular functions, she also enhanced her own social and political standing. She became a recognizable power in Washington during the Jefferson and Madison presidencies and, later in life after her husband's passing, she returned to the capital city and to her former status. In fact, noted orator and politician Daniel Webster proclaimed Dolley "the only permanent power in Washington, all others are transient."

The elaborate affairs and her popularity earned Dolley the nickname "Queen Dolley." Yet she succeeded, as did George and Martha Washington, in balancing the tastes of Europe with the tastes of the new nation. Through these famous social events, Mrs. Madison became a fashion trendsetter, another facet of the contemporary First Ladyship. Dolley was given to excess in her tastes, showcasing the very latest in French fashions, elaborate jewels and gowns, layers of makeup, and her signature peacock feather plumes and turbans. Women of Washington society wanted to see what Dolley was wearing, and she ushered in new fashions.

Dolley Madison's successes institutionalized the role of social hostess for all subsequent First Ladies. First Ladies following her would be held to her standard. The events helped her husband politically, by bringing the leading figures on the political scene together at the

President John F. Kennedy, front left, gestures as he stands with Mrs. Kennedy and a group at a White House reception, October 10, 1961, for the Supreme Court and federal judges. *(AP Photo/Bob Schultz)*

White House, and personally, by countering his rather subdued personality and small physical stature with her vivaciousness and charm. These events provided the First Lady with an ideal venue for showcasing her formidable social skills. At Dolley's funeral in 1848, President Zachary Taylor was moved to state: "She will never be forgotten because she was truly our First Lady for a half-century."

Role and Activities

Because of the success of Dolley Madison and precedents set by other early First Ladies such as Martha Washington and Abigail Adams, First Ladies serving ever since have been expected to fulfill similar social duties. In fact, this role is so associated with the office that many First Ladies have developed identities as host-

Culture as a Fixture

Jacqueline Kennedy's First Ladyship is remembered for her historic renovation of the White House. However, the First Lady was also one of the foremost promoters of American culture. Through her social affairs, Mrs. Kennedy sought to put American culture on equal footing with U.S. military and economic might.

Her focus was on the country's cultural heritage, and the White House became an international stage to showcase arts and culture. The First Lady offered an array of performances, including the American Ballet Theater and the National Symphony Orchestra. She also hosted international artists and Shakespearean theatrical performances. Her interest in promoting American cultural heritage resonated with Mrs. Kennedy's extensive historic renovation of the White House, bringing antiquities and period furnishings to the mansion. Her actions promoted American history and culture in the eyes of the world and contributed positively to the Kennedy image.

esses apart from their identity as the wife of the president. The duty has also come to be expected of them. In considering the role of social hostess, modern First Ladies are, to a degree, being asked to step back in time and fulfill a social obligation established long before any women's movement.

Such a role was not designed for the First Lady. Rather, it developed in part from the sex-role norms of an earlier time. Because early presidents had no budget, few resources, and yet were expected to provide a social calendar for official Washington, foreign dignitaries, and the nation, such a duty naturally fell to their wives to fulfill. Social affairs of this nature were within the feminine realm. Before women's suffrage, the only avenues to political participation and power were through marriage and presiding over such social functions. That such affairs were so political and important is an ironic twist to the story of how the role evolved. Even in more recent times, when public funds have been made available to cover such functions (early presidents were expected to pay for social events out of their own pockets, an expense that nearly bankrupted such presidents as Thomas Jefferson and James Monroe) and the first couple is served by a staff of trained ushers, butlers, chefs, and social sec-

retaries, the First Lady remains as the social hostess ultimately responsible for all social gatherings in the Executive Mansion.

Social hosting involves many roles and activities. The First Lady must oversee a variety of social events, from state dinners for hundreds to protocol-laden diplomatic gatherings to entertainments and casual receptions. Today, she has at her disposal an extensive staff of experts on every facet of protocol and entertaining as well as a budget to assist her in organizing such events. The first presidential spouse to benefit from a staff member on the federal payroll was Edith Roosevelt, who was assisted by Isabelle "Belle" Hagner, who had been reassigned from the War Department.

Many modern First Ladies have promoted culture by showcasing the arts. White House performances are well known and have attracted internationally renowned singers, musicians, and artists as well as operas and musicals. Some First Ladies have featured American culture in their social agendas. For instance, Jacqueline Kennedy promoted American performers, as did Pat Nixon, Rosalynn Carter, Hillary Rodham Clinton, and other First Ladies. Mrs. Carter had the Public Broadcast System carry these performances, and Nancy Reagan had the artistic performances shown as a televised series dubbed *In Performance at the White House*. Dolley Madison even solicited recipes from women around the United States and then featured them at White House dinners in an attempt to promote the United States to both her American and her foreign guests.

First Ladies have also used these social functions to enhance their husbands' popularity and to promote their own visibility, power, and influence. Social events remain an opportune way to enhance the president's image. Rarely is the news coverage of such affairs negative, and most guests come away touched by the majesty of their visit to the White House. Mindful of image, Edith Roosevelt and Nancy Reagan were known to screen photos of White House social events, selecting those to be released to the media and public. Many First Ladies were conscious of the image portrayed through the guest lists, which have often been

announced in social publications in the capital city. Dignitaries from Mark Twain, Charles Dickens, and Booker T. Washington to relatives of Napoleon and several kings and queens have been guests at White House affairs. The process for receiving such guests at White House socials is itself molded by tradition and protocol. Guests' names are called as each enters to her or his own introduction, and receiving lines allow guests to meet the president's party. Some early First Ladies such as Martha Washington and Julia Tyler even received their guests while seated on thronelike chairs on raised platforms. Yet the White House has been and remains accessible to a broad cross-section of its citizens. Frances Cleveland held socials for working women, even accommodating their work schedules. Lady Bird Johnson held her "Women Doer Luncheons" to honor achievements of women, and Julia Grant invited both

Prime Minister Jawaharlal Nehru of India shakes hands with President Dwight Eisenhower at the White House, with Mrs. Indira Gandhi and Mamie Eisenhower, 1956. Pat Nixon is in the background. *(Library of Congress)*

celebrities and common folk to her events.

Many First Ladies have held one or two formal dinners a week, one or two evening or afternoon receptions, and perhaps one large party per month. However, ample discretion exists for each First Lady to tailor her events to her own liking. It is a time-honored custom to throw a large party on July 4 in honor of the United States' birth, and it used to be customary to hold an open house for the general public every New Year's Day—something that attracted thousands and was ended in 1933 by the Hoovers. Abigail Fillmore wanted to curtail her social calendar but compromised on offering receptions on Friday evenings and Tuesday mornings and dinner parties on Thursdays. Like Mrs. Fillmore, most First Ladies have felt obligated to accommodate the public and maintain a full social schedule.

White House social events have reflected the style and tastes of the First Ladies. Nancy Reagan preferred formality, while Rosalynn Carter preferred informality in her social events. Mrs. Carter reduced her social calendar and the number of dinners in a symbolic effort to reduce costs on behalf of taxpayers. She also ended the practice of printing the White House menus in French.

First Lady Julia Tyler, on the other hand, hosted parties for up to three thousand guests while surrounded by her court of female attendants. She required female guests to wear hats, male guests were forbidden to smoke or wear swords or guns at her events, and the White House staff was ordered to don white gloves for these regal and popular affairs. Lady Bird Johnson was the first to host a barbecue cookout, and she also entertained guests at her family's LBJ Ranch in Texas, where she featured the tastes of the region's cuisine. First Ladies have offered dinners in the White House Rose Garden, on the South Lawn, and even atop the roof in summer.

Not all of the functions associated with the early First Ladies remain. One of the early customs was to call, whereby guests would visit and leave a calling card. First Ladies were expected to return the call promptly. The practice occupied too much time, and First Ladies such as Martha Washington complained about its impracticality. Elizabeth Monroe eventually ended the practice, in part because of her poor health, but she was criticized for doing so. Similarly, it was customary for women to visit the White House only when the wife or presidential hostess was present or presiding. Mrs. Monroe often declined to appear at her husband's events. As a result, many of the women of the capital city felt snubbed by both her nonresponse to their calls and their inability to attend White House functions because of her absence. Such a fury was raised that President Monroe was forced to convene a meeting of his cabinet to determine what to do about the dilemma.

Sarah Polk cut back on alcohol served at White House events for religious reasons, as did Lucy Hayes, earning her the nickname "Lemonade Lucy." Sarah Polk even forbade dancing at many affairs, and numerous First Ladies observed the Sabbath, offering no social events or dinners on Sundays. Abigail Fillmore limited her duty of standing in the long receiving lines because of a bad ankle, and several First Ladies, including Eleanor Roosevelt, have complained of afflictions they termed "White House feet" or "White House hand," conditions resulting from standing in endless receiving lines and shaking so many hands of guests. Dolley Madison chose to sit at the head of her dinner table, so as to be able to oversee and manage the conversation of her guests, while Ida McKinley sat next to her husband, so that he might tend to her in the event she suffered one of her frequent epileptic seizures. Such breeches of protocol in seating were met with mixed responses.

Significance

Social affairs are an important component of diplomacy and national politics, especially in Washington. Food, drink, and conversation are key components to the body politic. The White House is the center of U.S. national political life, and its social events represent the United States to all guests and the world. Every aspect of state affairs has significance, including the guest list, seating chart, menu, and choice of entertainment. So, too, does a bewildering array of sensitive social etiquette and protocol issues which govern social hosting.

Perhaps no one understood this better than Dolley Madison: The social is the political and vice versa. Dolley embraced the political nature of her social affairs and employed her gift for reading people and her charm, using these talents in political service to her husband. Entertainment and lobbying went hand in hand at the Madison White House, and the political significance of social hosting has continued to the present time.

Social events help lend credibility to new administrations, as they continue the rich tradition first shaped by George and Martha Washington. These affairs provide a nonpolitical setting in which public officials can conduct political business. Louisa Adams hosted an elaborate and high profile social at the outset of the 1824 presidential campaign in honor of Andrew Jackson, an event which was designed to build support for her husband among the key officials in attendance. Several other First Ladies followed this example. Like Louisa Adams, whose husband was entirely deficient in social charm, Dolley Madison, Julia Tyler, Frances Cleveland, and other popular First Ladies used their grace to the benefit of presidential standing.

A Multi-Faceted Role

There have been enormously successful social hostesses in the history of the office, including Dolley Madison, Angelica Singleton Van Buren (Martin Van Buren's hostess), Julia Tyler, Harriet Lane (James Buchanan's hostess), Frances Cleveland, and Edith Roosevelt, to name a few. There have also been those First Ladies who were not as successful in discharging the duty.

Jane Pierce, grieving from the recent death of her last surviving son, curtailed not only her social calendar but her appearances at her husband's events. Mary Lincoln was a gracious and capable hostess and a well-intentioned one as well. However, her attempt to provide credibility for the Union and her husband's presidency by hosting regal social affairs backfired. Even though she saw such social events as a form of enhancing political power, the public and her husband's many critics saw her efforts as too extravagant. Her purchases of expensive gowns and china service, her decision to redecorate the White House, and her extensive dinner menus only provided ammunition for a country in the midst of a devastating war.

Some First Ladies, such as Dolley Madison, Julia Tyler, Julia Grant, Helen Taft, and Mamie Eisenhower, have thoroughly enjoyed functioning as hostess, while others, such as Elizabeth Monroe, Margaret Taylor, and Eliza Johnson, attempted to avoid the duty. Some spouses were unable to fulfill the full range of social duties because of poor health. In such instances, young daughters, nieces, and daughters-in-law often assisted in meeting the social demands of life in the White House.

The role of social hostess has allowed First Ladies to enhance their popularity and serve issues larger than the particular social affair at hand. For instance, Edith and Theodore Roosevelt saw their grand socials as a way of complementing the president's internationalist and imperialist view of the United States. To their minds, a grand nation with ambitions of being a military and political world power ought to have grand social affairs. Caroline Harrison recognized the deteriorating condition of the White House and even had plans drawn up to build a new White House, expanding upon her role as social hostess. Mrs. Harrison also used her talents as an artist to design her own china service, which featured scenes celebrating natural America, and in so doing promoted the country while serving food.

The importance of social events is such that only in times of war, severe economic crisis, or a death in the presidential family have they been drastically curtailed. The First Lady has, since the inaugural presidency, functioned as the White House's and the United States' social hostess. Most First Ladies have discharged this responsibility with grace and dignity, even though they have had little formal training to prepare them for events of this magnitude, and, in doing so, fulfilled a vital component of the presidency and offered a necessary service to the nation.

Suggested Readings

Anthony, Carl Sferrazza. *First Ladies: The Saga of the Presidents' Wives and Their Power.* Vol. 1. New York: William Morrow, 1990. A unique glimpse at the power and prestige in the evolving role of the First Lady.

Caroli, Betty Boyd. *First Ladies.* Expanded ed. New York: Oxford University Press, 1995. A look at the varying roles each First Lady to date has undertaken, along with vital statistics.

Diller, Daniel C. *The Presidents, First Ladies, and Vice Presidents: White House Biographies, 1789-2001.* Washington, D.C.: CQ Press, 2001. Contains biographies and images of presidents, vice presidents, and first Ladies through the George W. Bush administration.

Gould, Lewis L., ed. *American First Ladies: Their Lives and Their Legacy.* New York: Garland, 1996. An enjoyable, informative, and objective combination of biographical sketches and histories of the First Ladies.

Gutin, Myra G. *The President's Partner: The First Lady in the Twentieth Century.* New York: Greenwood Press, 1989. Examines the public communications and private personas of twelve First Ladies.

Mayo, Edith P., ed. *The Smithsonian Book of the First Ladies: Their Lives, Times, and Issues.* New York: H. Holt, 1996. Contains a short biographical chapter on every First Lady through Hillary Rodham Clinton.

Truman, Margaret. *First Ladies.* New York: Random House, 1995. A colorful yet warm glimpse into the changing roles of the First Lady, as seen from the author's own experiences as a president's daughter.

Watson, Robert P. *The Presidents' Wives: Reassessing the Office of First Lady.* Boulder, Colo.: Lynne Rienner, 2000. A statistical and research-oriented assessment of the roles of the First Ladies.

Robert P. Watson

First Ladies and Social Causes

Overview: Among First Ladies of the United States were many women to whom nineteenth century social mores would not dictate virtual invisibility. Some First Ladies moved into their quarters in the White House and stayed there; some appeared dutifully at official functions, but it was never a consideration for them to publicly express their thoughts regarding issues. Other First Ladies were exceptions. Then, during the twentieth century, the position of First Lady evolved into one consisting of partnership and activism. Not only does the modern First Lady advise the president on policies and appointments; she also serves as a visible advocate for a wide range of social causes.

History

Most First Ladies have been able to avoid the inherent dangers of an aristocratic style of behavior. Along with their husbands, they have readily recognized the pitfalls of offending the American public with anything that smacked of snobbishness. Over the years, it has been a fundamental societal expectation in the United States that women should be agreeable and charming. This perception has evolved and been significantly modified in recent years. Consequently, a number of First Ladies have felt comfortable using the symbolic power of their position to perform some active crusading in order to address national problems or for the purpose of correcting social injustices nationwide.

Human Rights Advocates

First Ladies have played an essential role in advocating human rights throughout the years. Although they have not necessarily been high profile leaders in a variety of human rights causes, they have oftentimes been involved in the front lines of battles being waged in their time. First Ladies have taken up the social causes of civil rights and child welfare laws and have served as outspoken advocates of national and international peace. They have also served as proponents of aid for the poor, hungry, disenfranchised, and homeless.

First Lady Ida McKinley was an advocate for peace as an opponent of the Spanish-American War. Rosalynn Carter was considered to be an outspoken champion of international human rights. Edith Roosevelt played a high-profile role in assisting President Theodore Roosevelt in his efforts to negotiate a peaceful resolution to the Russo-Japanese War. She attended peace talks attended by representatives of Russia and Japan and assisted in efforts designed to decode highly confidential messages that were being transmitted by countries involved in the conflict. Theodore Roosevelt would later receive the Nobel Peace Prize for his role in the peace talks.

In 1999, President Bill Clinton's administration announced the formation of massive efforts to provide disaster relief for Latin American countries that had been ravaged by earthquakes and hurricanes. First Lady Hillary Rodham Clinton was responsible for announcing the launching of this huge humanitarian effort. She played a key role as a visible leader of the effort to raise funds and deliver aid to the affected nations.

First Ladies have long championed the cause of disabled veterans and soldiers who had been hospitalized or were incapacitated by their wounds. During the Civil War, Caroline Harrison often appeared at her husband's troops' camps in Kentucky and Tennessee. She frequently provided assistance in mending uniforms and performing day-to-day chores. In addition, she worked closely with the Ladies Patriotic Association and Ladies Sanitary Committee in her efforts to organize public food drives. She also assisted in gathering food, clothing, and medicine for soldiers.

Barbara Bush was an advocate of universal literacy. First Lady Grace Coolidge taught deaf children prior to living in the White House, and she returned to efforts on their behalf after she returned to private life. Hillary Rodham Clinton was actively involved in working with the Children's Defense Fund, along with renowned children's rights activist Marian Wright Edelman, prior to becoming First Lady. Hillary continued to champion this cause during the Clinton administration. Perhaps the most visible example of these efforts can be seen in her authorship of *It Takes a Village*, a best-selling book on children's welfare.

Grace Coolidge enrolls the president in the American Red Cross, 1925. *(Library of Congress)*

Civil Rights Activists

Frances Cleveland was highly active in raising public awareness of the need for civil rights. She worked toward the creation of a charitable organization dedicated to assisting poor and orphaned black children. However, her efforts in this regard were unsuccessful, as she was unable to solicit sufficient public and financial support for the project. She was, however, a highly influential member of the Colored Christmas Club. This organization donated funds to needy African Americans in Washington, D.C., during the holiday season. Frances opened White House reception areas as well as her Saturday receptions to African Americans, becoming perhaps the first First Lady to integrate the White House through these activities.

First Lady Eleanor Roosevelt had a long and illustrious record of serving as an advocate for human rights from 1933 until her death in 1962. Her role as a proponent of human rights beyond U.S. borders earned her the nickname First Lady of the World. She has often been referred to as the leading advocate for human rights in the history of the White House. Eleanor was among the First Ladies who were targets of vocal criticism for allowing African Americans to visit the White House. As a civil rights activist, she openly opposed job discrimination against blacks, favored desegregation of the United States military, and brought to national attention the inequalities in ethnic minority workers' pay. During her time as First Lady, Eleanor convinced Franklin D. Roosevelt and other key members of his administration to support antilynching laws. Eleanor was successful at convincing her husband to do so, in spite of his concerns as to how such advocacy would be perceived in the South.

Eleanor participated in numerous civil rights activities and organizations. She became involved in sit-ins in restaurants, invited black entertainers to perform at the White House, served on the board of directors for the National Association for the Advancement of Colored People, and was named an honorary member of the National Council for Colored Women. When traveling in the South, the First Lady usually defied local segregation codes by sitting in "colored only" areas of public facilities. She also actively supported African Americans in political office.

Eleanor's human and civil rights activism was not limited to the cause of African Americans. She also advocated on behalf of miners and laborers, the poor, women, prisoners, and those who were hospitalized in mental health institutions. In fact, it has been said that she embraced the cause of almost every individual she

considered to be at a disadvantage. Eleanor reported on the conditions she found in various institutions, fought for housing and public aid for the poor, and played an essential role in convincing her husband to appoint Secretary of Labor Frances Perkins, the first woman ever to head a federal department.

First Lady Eleanor Roosevelt was nominated for the American Peace Award for her work on behalf of human rights. She continued in such endeavors after she left the White House. Eleanor was appointed to serve as a United States delegate to the United Nations. She also chaired the United Nations Commission on Human Rights, which produced the highly acclaimed United Nations Universal Declaration of Human Rights.

The mass circulation and availability of newspapers and television served to heighten the visibility of First Ladies as human rights advocates during the twentieth century. Lou Hoover received a great deal of media attention when she hosted Jessie DePriest, wife of the Illinois representative Oscar DePriest, for tea at the White House. That Mrs. DePriest was an African American was not overlooked by the southern press in 1929. As a result of the controversy created by media coverage of this event, Lou Hoover was eventually symbolically censured by the Texas state legislature.

Lady Bird Johnson's personal train, The Lady Bird Special, was used during her efforts to support Lyndon B. Johnson's campaign for president in the South. She was sent by her husband on a whistle-stop tour for the express purpose of minimizing white hostility toward his signing of the 1964 Civil Rights Act. Needless to say, her travels were carefully and meticulously covered by members of the media. Hostile mobs and threats from the Ku Klux Klan in the racially divided South of the early 1960's awaited Lady Bird Johnson's train at every stop along its route. She also was the target of harsh and virulent public criticism by the ultraconservative John Birch Society. Mrs. Johnson firmly held her ground throughout the campaign in spite of this whirlwind of public and media scrutiny and criticism. She would later earn the praise and respect of the more open-minded and objective journalists. As a result of the highly visible and pervasive media coverage of her campaign efforts in the South, the cause of the Civil Rights movement received much national support and further heightened public awareness of the issue.

First Lady Rosalynn Carter was an outspoken advocate of mental health care during her time spent both in the Georgia governor's mansion and in the White House. It was while living in Washington, D.C., that she played a leading role in drafting legislation designed to meet the needs of the mentally disabled. She also served as honorary chairwoman of the presidentially commissioned task force on mental health. Growing up in the rural and segregated South provided Rosalynn with firsthand experiences related to racial prejudice and intolerance. She was quite vocal in her criticism of white Baptist preachers for disallowing blacks to attend their churches or to become members of their congregations.

Barbara Bush would add yet another facet to the multidimensional roles played by First Ladies in advocating civil rights. She delivered the commencement address at Bennett College, a predominantly black school in Greensboro, North Carolina. She was also the first presidential wife to appoint a member of an ethnic minority to a senior position on her official staff through her designation of Anna Perez as her press secretary. (No First Lady before Edith Roosevelt enjoyed the services of staff members paid for by the government.)

Abolitionists

Slavery was a prominent human rights issue for a number of First Ladies. Mary Todd Lincoln was raised in a prominent, slave-holding southern family. However, before and during the Civil War, she was an outspoken critic of slavery and was highly active in support of the war efforts of the Union Army. Her convictions regarding this matter were so strong that not even harsh criticism from the northern or southern press could deter her involvement in this cause. Mary was considered to be a traitor by the South and was not trusted by the North. There were even accusations of treason brought against her.

The Civil War and slavery were deeply personal issues for Mary. She was overcome with grief at the death of several relatives who fought for the Confederacy, but she was also proud of her maternal grandmother, who assisted slaves in their efforts to escape to the North through the Underground Railroad. Mary befriended a free black who was an outspoken abolitionist and supporter of aid for free blacks: Elizabeth Keckley was Mary's close friend and confidante as well as her personal assistant. Mary remained closely tied to Elizabeth, despite strong criticism of the relationship, although the two would eventually have a falling out.

Mary's relationship with Elizabeth perhaps served as a catalyst for her support of the Contraband Relief Association, an organization dedicated to raising funds and support for freed slaves. She delivered numerous speeches in support of providing assistance to blacks and raised money for the relief effort, donating some herself. At the White House, she hosted Frederick Douglass, who at the time was likely the most prominent black leader nationwide. In addition, Mary invited other prominent African Americans to visit the White House, years before such relationships were deemed acceptable. These interactions occurred roughly seventy-five years prior to First Lady Eleanor Roosevelt engaging in the same type of behavior. However, Eleanor was both brutally criticized for these visits and praised for taking such bold steps.

Two other First Ladies who openly opposed slavery were Abigail Fillmore and Jane Pierce. Both women were disappointed by their north-

Martha Washington knits for troops during wartime, with four other women. *(Library of Congress)*

ern husbands' vulnerability to arguments from southern politicians and their subsequent acquiescence to the southern delegation in Congress. Mrs. Fillmore opposed the Fugitive Slave Act, which had the reluctant support of her husband. This piece of legislation would allow the federal government to provide assistance in returning runaway slaves to bondage.

First Lady Fillmore was an opponent of slavery prior to her marriage and to occupying the White House. She taught slaves who were owned by her family to read and write. She would later offer them their freedom. Louisa Adams also despised slavery and publicly supported the abolitionist movement. She became a devotee of the Garrisonians, who at the time were considered one of the United States' most prominent antislavery societies. Not only did she read the periodical *The Liberator*, but she also participated in the dissemination of antislavery petitions in Washington.

Lucy Hayes's husband, Rutherford B. Hayes, had served as a Union officer during the Civil War. She pleaded with him not to permit soldiers serving under him to return slaves to the South. Furthermore, she became a highly visible figure in the abolition movement and was a proponent for the rights of former and freed slaves. Over the years, she has received credit for having a significant influence on her husband's opposition to slavery. Mrs. Hayes was an individual of powerful convictions; she practiced what she preached. She taught Weliza Jane Burrell, a former slave, to read and write. In addition, Lucy developed a friendship with Winnie Monroe, another former slave, whom Lucy hired to serve as a cook in the White House.

Of course, not all First Ladies were leaders on civil rights issues. The issue was considered off-limits by several women. Others, such as Sarah Polk, "employed" slaves while she lived in the White House. Later, First Lady Polk would adhere to a neutral position regarding the Civil War; however, slaves were held on her cotton plantation in Mississippi after she left the White House. Furthermore, she neglected to free her slaves after James Polk's death, even though there was a stipulation to do so in his will. Other First Ladies who owned slaves included Margaret Taylor, who was from Maryland, and Martha Washington, who was from Virginia. Ellen Arthur's family not only owned slaves but also fought for the South during the Civil War.

Activism pertaining to human rights issues on the part of First Ladies ranged beyond the geographic borders of the United States to international concerns during the second half of the twentieth century. Pat Nixon traveled with her husband to Africa in 1972, while First Lady Hillary Rodham Clinton joined President Bill Clinton on a similar journey in 1998. The International Women's Year Conference in 1977 featured First Ladies Lady Bird Johnson, Betty Ford, and Rosalynn Carter in attendance. First Lady Hillary Rodham Clinton delivered a keynote speech at a similar meeting nearly twenty years later.

Women's Advocates

Betty Ford was an outspoken proponent of women's rights on an international level. She also championed the cause of universal literacy and was a strong advocate of the Equal Rights Amendment, lobbying the United States Congress on behalf of the measure.

One of the pioneers for women's rights was Lucy Hayes. Her husband was elected president in 1876, in a contentious campaign following the Civil War. The Democrats won the White House by approximately half a million popular votes. Southern states, which were still under military occupation, were allegedly bribed by Republicans to oppose the Democrats. Hayes won the election by one electoral vote. Needless to say, the outcome hardly reflected a national consensus. Hayes entered the White House as a president disdained by more than half the voters. As a result, Lucy Hayes' role as First Lady became significant during her husband's administration. She was the first First Lady to hold a college degree and was more than prepared for the challenges that faced her during her years in the White House.

Lucy served as a catalyst for hope being instilled in the minds and hearts of many women who were starting to develop a resentment toward their separate but not quite equal status in American life. The Cincinnati Wesleyan-educated First Lady was viewed as being the em-

Lemonade Lucy

Lucy Webb Hayes is perhaps best known as the First Lady who banned alcohol from the White House. Although the official decision was made by her husband, Rutherford B. Hayes, it earned her the nickname of Lemonade Lucy. The liquor ban was not a decision made by the Hayeses in haste or on impulse. They were well aware of the potential risks involved in doing so and took those risks because they were concerned that the United States of 1877 was in danger of drowning in alcohol. It took a great deal of courage for Lucy to support the decision. As White House hostess, she was the target of most of the criticism for the ban. However, both she and the president wanted to send a message to the American people about their opposition to alcohol, which they felt needed to be conveyed in light of the large amount of usage that was occurring at the time.

bodiment of the New Woman, one who wanted to receive equal pay for equal work and to have the right to enter the workplace and the political sphere. For some women, Lucy Hayes was like a creature with divine powers.

Women's rights was an extremely unpopular issue during the late 1800's. Lucy was acutely aware that her husband was in no position to run the risk of having a politically controversial spouse. As a consequence, instead of joining the women's rights movement or the women's temperance movement, Lucy became the honorary president of the Women's Home Missionary Society, an organization that campaigned for the betterment of the lives of the poor in the appalling slums of nineteenth century American cities. This cause was beyond

Literacy advocate Laura Bush shares a hug with third-grader Shanel Adams at a Washington, D.C., elementary school, 2001. *(AP/Wide World Photos)*

criticism from all areas of the political arena.

Lucy was a politically astute and tremendously popular First Lady. Although her husband was the target of constant criticism, few people (other than those in opposition to the temperance movement) had anything negative to say about Lucy. She was praised in verse by the well-known poet Henry Wadsworth Longfellow and by Supreme Court Justice Oliver Wendell Holmes. Journalist Ben Perley Moore declared her to be the most influential First Lady since Dolley Madison.

Advocates for the Needy and the Poor

Another pioneering First Lady launched a crusade that sent a message to the president almost forty years after Lucy Hayes left the White House. Woodrow Wilson's first wife, Ellen Axson Wilson, achieved this during the brief time span of eighteen months that she served in the White House. Born in Savannah, Georgia—the segregated South—Ellen Wilson did not consider herself to be a crusader for radical reform. Instead, she believed that all Americans possessed certain basic rights. Although this message was a central theme of her husband's foreign policy, the Wilson administration, which was dominated by conservative southerners, was ironically negligent in its dealings with domestic racial injustice.

Upon Wilson's election to the presidency, many progressive whites and blacks had high hopes for the role he might play in significantly changing the Jim Crow practices that permeated the federal government. Instead, by the summer of 1913,

An Example for Americans

In addition to the Alley Bill, which sought improved housing for blacks who lived in alleys in Washington, D.C., Ellen Wilson took up the cause of working conditions of women and blacks in government office buildings. She was appalled by the lack of light and air as well as the deplorable restroom facilities. Soon Ellen became an outspoken advocate of reform for these workers. As a result of her involvement in these causes, she became known as a noble woman who had set an example in advocating for black Americans that other white women would follow.

Against her doctors' advice, she remained an active proponent of these issues throughout her struggle with Bright's disease, a fatal kidney disorder for which there is still no known cure. Regrettably, the Alley Bill became stalled by segregationists and obstructionists in Congress just prior to her death. On her deathbed, she indicated to her husband that she would pass away more peacefully if the Alley Bill was passed by Congress. Word reached the Capitol, and the Senate immediately passed the bill.

merely six months after his inauguration, segregation in all departments of the federal government had actually increased. Subsequently, a petition was signed by more than twenty thousand angry black Americans from thirty-four states, urging the president to change this policy.

During her brief tenure in the White House, Ellen met Charlotte Wise Hopkins, a force in the District of Columbia branch of the National Civic Foundation, whose objective was to improve living conditions for the poor, regardless of race. Hopkins blamed segregation, which made it impossible for African Americans to buy homes in most areas of Washington, for the substandard housing in which many people lived. Her solution to the problem was to construct model homes, which could be built inexpensively, with plumbing and electricity.

Within a week after her initial encounter with Hopkins, Ellen visited the fetid alleys of Washington. She informally talked to the residents without identifying herself as the First Lady. Soon thereafter, she became a stockholder in the Sanitary Housing Company, the organization that was responsible for erecting the model homes. Before long, Ellen became the honorary chairwoman of the women's depart-

ment of the National Civic Foundation. Word of her involvement in this cause spread swiftly throughout Washington. A group of fifty prominent citizens drafted an "Alley Bill" that proposed the clearing of the slums and the construction of model homes in their stead. This piece of legislation was later passed by Congress.

Social Activists

First Ladies have become closely identified with their particular social causes. Barbara Bush was best known for her support for adult literacy, while Lady Bird Johnson advocated conservation and beautification of the outdoors. To a great extent, the First Lady can be seen as the country's "first volunteer." Lucy Hayes visited many prisons, schools, and asylums as part of her efforts to improve their conditions. Frances Cleveland participated in making clothing for the poor.

Ida McKinley made slippers for charities. Caroline Harrison supported several Washington charities and was a benefactor of the Garfield Hospital. Helen Taft sponsored the planting of cherry trees throughout Washington. Lou Hoover supported a variety of needy causes, including the Lyceum Club, Friends of the Poor, the League of Women Voters, the Campfire Girls, and the Girl Scouts.

Lady Bird Johnson was perhaps the exemplary advocate of social causes among First Ladies. Her support for conservation extended beyond mere beautification. She was aware of the close relationship between quality of life and the physical environment. She lobbied for the removal of unsightly billboards and advocated planting wildflowers, preserving scenic rivers, and enhancing national parklands. She was successful in gaining the passage of the Highway Beautification Act of 1967, known as "Lady Bird's Bill." She later became an active member of President Lyndon Johnson's progressive Head Start program.

Significance

The office of the First Lady is, by its form and substance, highly political. It has evolved over the years to become an essential component of the American political process. Many First Ladies have been passionate in advocacy of their causes and were highly successful in their efforts to gain support for their positions. Their sphere of influence extended beyond the walls of the White House. They were effective spokespersons in bringing about significant changes in attitudes, behaviors, and legislation in the United States.

Suggested Readings

Boller, Paul F. *Presidential Wives: An Anecdotal History.* 2d ed. New York: Oxford University Press, 1999. Boller devotes a chapter to every First Lady from Martha Washington to Hillary Rodham Clinton.

Caroli, Betty Boyd. *First Ladies.* Expanded ed. New York: Oxford University Press, 1995. A look at the varying roles each First Lady to date has undertaken, along with vital statistics.

Gutin, Myra G. *The President's Partner: The First Lady in the Twentieth Century.* New York: Greenwood Press, 1989. Examines the public communications and private personas of twelve First Ladies.

Rosebush, James S. *First Lady, Public Wife: A Behind-the-Scenes History of the Evolving Role of First Ladies in American Public Life.* Lanham, Md.: Madison Books, 1987.

Truman, Margaret. *First Ladies.* New York: Random House, 1995. A colorful yet warm glimpse into the changing roles of the First Lady, as seen from the author's own experiences as a president's daughter.

Watson, Robert P. *The Presidents' Wives: Reassessing the Office of First Lady.* Boulder, Colo.: Lynne Rienner, 2000. A statistical and research-oriented assessment of the roles and the long-ranging impacts of the First Ladies as presidential partners.

Lawrence J. Rifkind

First Ladies and Presidential Campaigns

Overview: The president of the United States serves a unique dual role in the conduct of U.S. business. The president is the head of state responsible for making major appointments, along with assuming a significant and decisive role in the development and passage of legislation. The president also presides over ceremonial functions. In many other countries, these two roles are played by two separate individuals. The American president often relies on substitutes to preside over ceremonial functions. This individual is frequently a member of the household, typically the First Lady. The same strategy has been frequently employed during political campaigns.

It was unusual for presidential candidates to campaign for office publicly during the first one hundred years of United States history. In contrast to contemporary practice, most of the posturing and positioning that occurred leading up to a presidential election took place in private, frequently behind closed doors. Historically, the campaign season for the presidency itself was quite brief, generally not extending beyond the actual nominating conventions. The high-profile style of campaigning that occurs today began to unfold during the latter part of the nineteenth century.

Presidential campaigns, as practiced in contemporary times, are, to a great extent, a twentieth century phenomenon. With the increasing popularity of television, the mass media, and an ever-growing campaign season, presidential campaigning has evolved into a highly public series of events. The advent of presidential campaigns as we know them today came in

Herbert Hoover, Republican nominee for president, waves to the crowds on a trip through New Jersey, September, 1928. Lou Hoover is seated next to him. *(AP/Wide World Photos)*

366

the late twentieth century. In 1880, Lucretia Garfield assisted her husband with his presidential campaign strategy and decision making. The role of the First Lady in the presidential election process has assumed a growing significance since then.

The election process has served as an arena through which the candidates' wives could move to the forefront of their husbands' campaigns and into a position of prominence. Although until the twentieth century it was considered inappropriate for women to campaign openly, the groundwork for such participation was laid much earlier. Because presidents must seek a popular mandate instead of the approval of their own political party's caucus (as is the case for the position of prime minister in other nations), they cannot rely on established contacts and trust that has been built up over years of working closely with colleagues. Instead, the American president must rely heavily on the support of the general population for election to public office.

It is often the case that a stand-in campaigner is generally useful and enjoys certain advantages over the candidate. In advance of Jimmy Carter's receiving the 1976 Democratic Party nomination, Rosalynn Carter ventured off on her own in a concerted attempt to gain support for her husband, fourteen months prior to the Democratic National Convention. This ef-

fort proved especially valuable for the candidate, because his wife had the popularity and skills needed to reach out to the general population. Lady Bird Johnson traveled and campaigned on her own through several states in 1964. She was confident that chivalry in the South still existed and that she would be accorded certain courtesies not available to her husband. Mrs. Johnson referred to campaigning as one of the bills that a politician's wife must pay for the position being sought by her husband.

President Lyndon Johnson waves from behind his wife and daughter Lynda, right, as Lady Bird Johnson's campaign train prepares to leave the station, October, 1964. *(AP/Wide World Photos)*

One Thousand Miles

The White House years of Jackie Kennedy, Lady Bird Johnson, and Patricia Nixon coincided with the onset of the feminist movement, which redefined the role of women nationwide. There arose a tendency toward less tolerance of women who viewed themselves primarily as supporters of their husbands' accomplishments. The growing sense of political awareness among women provided the catalyst by which campaign strategies were redesigned, resulting in entire families being drawn into the election process to assist in the creation of a favorable image of the candidate's suitability for election to public office.

Over the years, First Ladies have played active roles as spokespersons for their husbands' presidential campaigns. Such was the case in Lady Bird Johnson's extensive travels aboard the eighteen-car train frequently referred to as the Lady Bird Special. This whistle-stop tour traversed the South in an attempt to enhance support for Lyndon Baines Johnson during his bid for reelection. The strategy was to become an integral component of the Johnson campaign's efforts to build support among those individuals in the South who were upset with his support of the Civil Rights Act of 1964.

Lyndon Johnson suggested that his wife, who was very popular nationwide, should travel throughout the South in order to minimize his losses among conservative, segregationist southerners. Lady Bird Johnson's train left Washington, D.C., on October 5, 1964. It spent four days traveling through Virginia, North Carolina, South Carolina, Georgia, Florida, Alabama, Mississippi, and Louisiana. The tour covered a distance of approximately one thousand miles.

Along the way, Mrs. Johnson made forty-seven speeches in as many appearances. She called upon southern governors, senators, and representatives in each of the states she visited to support her husband's candidacy. As she traveled from state to state, the First Lady encountered hostile, threatening crowds. Throughout her journey, however, she held her own against what at times appeared to be insurmountable opposition. Lady Bird's whistle-stop campaign is credited with having minimized Republican gains in the South.

Earlier in his political career, Lyndon Johnson's election to the United States Senate was in large part attributable to his friendship with Speaker of the House of Representatives Sam Rayburn. This close relationship, in turn, was due to the influence of Lady Bird. Rayburn had become very fond of her during her husband's term in the House of Representatives. Often Rayburn would bestow attention on both Lady Bird and her little daughter, Lynda, who was born in 1944. Rayburn and Lady Bird spent many a serious evening discussing political issues, and the Texas congressman's wife increased her already extensive knowledge of domestic and international topics under the tutelage of "Mr. Sam." He later wrote Lady Bird that their friendship had been the most heartening thing in his life.

Front Porch Campaigning

Front porch campaigning marked what many consider to be the first formalized and concerted role for candidates' wives during presidential campaigns. This approach began during the late 1800's and early 1900's. It was so labeled because the candidates literally sat on the front porches of their respective homes and invited prospective voters and supporters to visit them. Many presidential candidates of this time, including James Garfield, Benjamin Harrison, and Warren Harding, employed this strategy. As a consequence, members of the voting public were provided with an opportunity to meet and have a dialogue with the candidates and their wives. Thus, spouses'

Dolley Madison and Scandal in Washington

It has been widely believed that Dolley Madison's claim to fame stems mainly from having introduced ice cream to Americans. Ice cream is considered by some, however, to have been the contribution of Thomas Jefferson, who recorded the recommended recipe for the sweet dessert, to which he was first introduced in France.

Dolley Madison did possess unusual political influence. For almost fifty years she served as a pivotal player in Washington politics, demonstrating an uncanny talent for using special occasions to her husband's political advantage. She established her political role during the Jefferson administration. Throughout his two terms in office, from 1801 to 1809, the widowed Thomas Jefferson relied heavily on Dolley to help him entertain guests. Later, when James Madison succeeded Jefferson as president, Dolley served two additional terms in office, from 1809 to 1817, solidifying her popularity among both politicians and the general public. After her husband retired from politics, she continued to serve as an unofficial mentor and tutor to a variety of young White House hostesses. Dolley Madison made her last celebrated appearance in the White House during the Polk administration in 1849.

Dolley Madison's physical attractiveness and close personal relationship with Jefferson became a catalyst for a firestorm sex scandal. From the onset of their friendship, gossip suggested that Dolley was, in fact, Jefferson's mistress, since she and her husband had lived in the White House with President Jefferson for a brief period of time before she and James moved into their own home. Although Dolley had her defenders, rumor and innuendo were widely spread through the print media during that period. The Madisons were childless, which fueled the allegations.

Dolley was very hurt by these rumors. Among the more vicious charges were claims that Dolley had engaged in relationships with Democrats that were designed to gain electoral votes for her husband and that she and her sister Anna were pressed into service to form relationships with foreign diplomats and heads of state in order to gain support from European nations.

Dolley wrote her husband and informed him that she would forever resolve not to allow other men into her room unless they were entitled by age and long acquaintance. Her sister Lucy wrote the Federalists that the lies being circulated about them could not injure or harm them. Thomas Jefferson reacted to the scandalous rumors with amused shock. He thought that his age and ordinary demeanor would have made him immune from such discussions. James Madison would go on to win his party's nomination and the presidential election against Charles Pinckney, who claimed that he was beaten by Mr. and Mrs. Madison. He would later muse that he might have had a better chance for success if he had campaigned solely against Mr. Madison.

role in the presidential campaign became more formalized.

Caroline Harrison was not at all enamored of the immense amount of public attention that was focused on a presidential campaign. However, she was nevertheless an active participant in her husband's 1888 bid for the presidency. She endured a seemingly endless flow of guests to their home during the election campaign, which was actually labeled the "front porch" campaign. As a result of this open-house approach to the campaign, Caroline endured a large number of inappropriate requests for housing, a loss of privacy, and damage to their home and personal belongings as well as the theft of the fence surrounding their home.

Florence Harding participated in her husband's 1920 campaign in an openly public manner. As a result, her considerable political acumen and abilities were put to a constructive use in Warren G. Harding's presidential campaign. Florence managed the campaign for him, yet another historical first for a First Lady. The presidential election of 1920 marked the first presidential election in which a candidate's wife invited women's political organizations to meet with her to discuss their potential support for his election to office. A political advertisement that appeared during the campaign proclaimed, "Women! For Your Own Good Vote the Republican Ticket."

Use of the "Trophy Wife"

The 1892 campaign of Grover Cleveland featured the image of his popular, young, and attractive wife, Frances, on campaign paraphernalia, including buttons and cards. Her likeness appeared above her husband's image, as well as that of his running mate. During William McKinley's 1896 run for the presidency, Ida McKinley's hometown, Canton, Ohio, organized the Women's McKinley Club, which produced campaign buttons featuring Ida McKinley's picture. None of these items contained any pictorial representation of William McKinley.

During that same year, a biography of the prospective First Lady was published by the McKinley campaign. This marked what was in all likelihood the first time that a biographical sketch of a presidential candidate's wife was produced. In addition, Ida McKinley maintained an active role in support of her husband's campaign by participating in various pre-election ac-

tivities. During this time frame, the involvement of Caroline Harrison, Frances Cleveland, Ida McKinley, and other aspiring First Ladies marked the onset of a concerted and organized effort to have the candidates' wives play an active role during the election campaign.

The Primary Campaigner

Eleanor Roosevelt was a highly gifted political campaigner. Franklin Roosevelt relied quite heavily on her to travel to and represent him at public events throughout his presidential campaigns because he suffered from paralysis. Quite often, she journeyed by herself, serving in place of her husband. This type of active, hands-on campaigning by prospective First Ladies made them and their husbands the objects of much criticism.

Eleanor, Franklin, and son Elliott Roosevelt are surrounded by supporters at a campaign stop, 1932. *(Archive Photos)*

In Eleanor's case, her activism and independence throughout Franklin's presidential campaigns invited significant criticism on the part of the opposition Republican Party. For example, they utilized campaign buttons that read, "We don't want Eleanor either." This practice continued to be employed during the 1940's and 1950's. Bess Truman was significant in Harry Truman's bid for the presidency. She participated in her husband's highly publicized, high-profile whistle-stop train campaign, and she usually received a warm welcome from people, with crowds often cheering as much for Bess as for Harry.

Lady Bird Johnson emerged as a key player during her husband's political campaigns. Her contributions exceeded mere participation in campaign trips. Instead, her donation of ten

thousand dollars and her father's twenty-five-thousand-dollar contribution provided much-needed financial support for Lyndon Johnson's initial political campaign. The Republican Party developed a "Pat [Nixon] for First Lady" program during the 1960 presidential campaign of Richard Nixon. They also included an event titled Pat Week, which was designed to serve as a rallying point for female supporters of Nixon.

The Reluctant Campaigner

Some wives of presidential candidates have preferred to maintain a low profile during their husbands' campaigns. Usually these individuals have found the physical and emotional demands of extensive travel and intrusions on their privacy to exact too great a toll on them

Bess Truman, left, and daughter Margaret Truman await the big moment of the 1944 Democratic National Convention, when Senator Harry S. Truman will be nominated vice president. *(AP/Wide World Photos)*

The Bachelor President

In 1857 James Buchanan became the only president who was unwed during his time in office (1857-1861). He continued the tradition of placing a female family member in the position of White House hostess by asking his twenty-seven-year-old niece, Harriet Lane, to serve in that capacity. He had assumed her guardianship upon her mother's (his sister's) death when she was ten years old. The press would come to refer to her as the Democratic Queen, and in many ways she performed like a member of royalty. A United States cutter was named for her, and necklines went down in accordance with her own fashion preference.

In the 1850's it had not yet become accepted fashion to have female relatives participate in political campaigns. However, Harriet played an integral part in her uncle's campaign. For example, she met with an influential Pennsylvania Democrat for the purpose of securing his support for Buchanan. Her youth, girlish innocence, and, perhaps, her unmarried status seemed to render the meeting politically acceptable. Subsequently, the Pennsylvanian became so smitten by her that he announced his support for Buchanan's candidacy. Such incidents illustrate why Harriet Lane was viewed as the perfect combination of deference and grace.

When Buchanan left office, Harriet had left her own mark on Washington. She had become a considerable source of influence and decorum during her uncle's term of office. One southern congressman's wife viewed Harriet's White House as having the highest degree of elegance. At times, it was suggested that the capital had never been happier or livelier than it was during Harriet Lane's years in the White House, despite the specter of the Civil War looming on the horizon.

selves and their families. In particular, Bess Truman would have preferred not to participate in the extensive travel and considerable loss of privacy that resulted from her husband's whistle-stop campaigns.

Because of his enormous success as Supreme Allied Commander during World War II, Dwight Eisenhower enjoyed a great deal of popularity in the eyes of the American people as he began his presidential campaign. His wife, Mamie, had been successful in her attempts to avoid the limelight and public attention that accompanied this fame. That quickly changed when she began to play a significant and active role in her husband's campaign in spite of her personal preferences. *The New York Times* suggested that Mamie Eisenhower was worth fifty electoral votes herself. In addition, she wrote an article for *Good Housekeeping* magazine during the campaign titled "Vote for My Husband or for Governor Stevenson, but Please Vote."

Jacqueline Kennedy was another hesitant participant in her husband's bid for the presidency. The former journalist wrote a newspaper column during the 1960 presidential campaign titled "The Candidate's Wife." These articles depicted her own experiences on the campaign trail. They also generated some highly favorable press and subsequent publicity for John Kennedy's candidacy. Yet in spite of her enormous popularity with the American public, Jackie Kennedy was considerably reluctant to make public appearances during the campaign. Her pregnancy at the time made her somewhat self-conscious in public, and she was physically unable to withstand the demands exacted upon her during the campaign as a result of a significant amount of travel that might adversely affect her health. Evidently, Jackie was grateful for her condition, because it provided her with a legitimate excuse not to participate in many aspects of the presidential campaign. In some ways, having a young, attractive, and intelligent wife who was coincidentally pregnant was as much of an asset for the Kennedy campaign as it was a liability.

The Television Age

The coming of the television age gave a new dimension to political campaigns. No longer was the job of First Lady primarily private and ceremonial. Instead, it had moved into the public arena, along with other matters affecting both domestic and foreign policy. This phenomenon was especially the case with respect to highly visible presidential races. Both Mamie Eisenhower's maternal persona and Jackie Kennedy's youthful attractiveness provided visual images well received by television viewers nationwide. Such images enhanced the presidential candidacies and corresponding efforts designed to gain public support.

Television increased the visibility of First Ladies and served to draw them into the public eye. Jackie Kennedy's tumultuous reception while visiting Paris during her husband's term in office resulted in President Kennedy's introducing himself as the man who accompanied her. Lady Bird Johnson learned different techniques for coping with demonstrators on any trip she took. She could often hear the protesting chants of anti-Vietnam War demonstrators as she tried to sleep at night in her White House bedroom. Pat Nixon would learn to walk stoically through showers of confetti accompanied by similar jeers.

Pat Nixon was instrumental during Richard Nixon's campaigns in expanding the base of support for her husband's candidacy. In the eyes of millions of television viewers, she came to represent the values and family traditions of the 1950's. Both Richard Nixon and Dwight Eisenhower took full advantage of this image. Their campaigns produced television advertisements that featured their wives performing tasks as homemakers and mothers. This practice would be employed in subsequent campaigns by most candidates for public office.

It is not unprecedented for a wife to be called upon to assist in the defense of her husband's credibility and reputation against allegations of marital infidelity. There has been ample precedent for the presidential candidate's wife to be called upon to deflect the potential damage created by such charges by appearing on national television and seeming not to care or not to have been hurt if the candidate chooses to acknowledge other liaisons. Such images conjure up memories of Lee Hart's dejected appearance as she talked about Senator Gary Hart's 1987 boat trip with Donna Rice, or Joan Kennedy's grim appearance as she appeared in public with Senator Ted Kennedy after his automobile crash on Chappaquiddick Island in 1969.

Hillary Clinton assumed a more difficult role during her first opportunity for national attention in early 1992, when the Clintons responded to charges of marital infidelity on the part of Bill Clinton that were made by an Arkansas woman, Gennifer Flowers. Hillary assigned herself the dubious task of speaking for herself on national television as she sat beside her husband while he answered questions about the charges. It seemed essential to the success of the Clinton campaign for the presidency that the entire matter be put to rest. Conducting the interview was considered to be a risk worth taking.

The interview was scheduled for the entire broadcast of *60 Minutes* on January 26, 1992. The program followed the Super Bowl football game, which had attracted an audience of nearly 100 million viewers. People tuned in, looking to see if there were any visible signs of discomfort on Hillary's part or any evidence that Bill was not being truthful. However, years of appearing in front of television cameras and numerous public speaking engagements paid off in significant dividends for the Clintons. Bill Clinton seemed to fidget and squirm slightly. He carefully chose his words as he admitted to "bringing pain" to his marriage without actually confessing to what he had done. On the other hand, Hillary Clinton forged ahead in a direct manner. In a final act of defiance, which was unmatched by her husband, Hillary challenged the voters to take into account what the Clintons represented. Then, if they did not care for what they were considering, they should not vote for Bill Clinton. This strategy of full disclosure and candor was quite effective in countering the allegations.

Hillary Clinton modified her role during the presidential campaign of 1992. She began to be less vocal. At the Democratic convention, she participated in a cookie bake-off, sponsored by *Family Circle* magazine, that placed her recipe for chocolate chip cookies against First Lady Barbara Bush's recipe. In addition, as if to emphasize her domestic role, Hillary allowed her twelve-year-old daughter, Chelsea, who had previously been protected from the public view, to appear on the cover of *People* magazine. This image was designed to highlight Hillary's role as a mother rather than a political candidate. In an attempt to make her persona appear more feminine, she dressed in softer clothing and began smiling more frequently. As a consequence, beginning with her husband's acceptance speech delivered at the Democratic National Convention, Hillary's image moved toward the supportive images conveyed by Pat Nixon, Barbara Bush, and Nancy Reagan.

Significance
Most First Ladies have played significant roles in their husbands' pursuit of the presidency. In many instances, the president publicly acknowledged his appreciation for his wife's ef-

forts. Unfortunately, much of the impact of First Ladies on presidential campaigns has gone undocumented and unnoticed, since much of their effort took place off the record. Nevertheless, these women were quick learners who demonstrated a natural aptitude for the task that lay ahead of them.

Suggested Readings

Anthony, Carl Sferrazza. *First Ladies: The Saga of the Presidents' Wives and Their Power.* 2 vols. New York: William Morrow, 1990-1991. A unique glimpse at the power and prestige in the evolving role of the First Lady.

Boller, Paul F. *Presidential Wives: An Anecdotal History.* 2d ed. New York: Oxford University Press, 1999. Boller devotes a chapter to every First Lady from Martha Washington to Hillary Rodham Clinton.

Caroli, Betty Boyd. *First Ladies.* Expanded ed. New York: Oxford University Press, 1995. A look at the varying roles each First Lady to date has undertaken, along with vital statistics.

Gutin, Myra G. *The President's Partner: The First Lady in the Twentieth Century.* New York: Greenwood Press, 1989. Examines the public communications and private personas of twelve First Ladies.

Watson, Robert P. *The Presidents' Wives: Reassessing the Office of First Lady.* Boulder, Colo.: Lynne Rienner, 2000. A statistical and research-oriented assessment of the roles and the long-ranging impacts of the First Ladies as presidential partners.

Lawrence J. Rifkind

First Ladies and Policy Issues

Overview: The notion of presidents' wives being involved in the public policy process is a phenomenon isolated to the latter part of the twentieth century. In the past, the lack of voting rights and educational opportunities for women contributed to a societal belief that women were not qualified to comment on political matters. The twentieth century brought with it women's suffrage, increasing standards of education for women, and substantial numbers of middle-class women entering the work force. As the role of women in society changed, the role of the First Lady changed as well.

History

Given the scant resources of the earliest First Ladies, it is not surprising that their role in shaping public policy was limited. This does not mean that the early First Ladies were inactive; rather, their roles were restricted to sponsoring charities and advising their husbands on policy decisions and political appointments. Historian Laura Holloway places the responsibility for this role with Martha Washington. She notes that:

> Her sphere was limited entirely to social occupations, and possessing wealth and position, she gratified her taste. Had her character been a decided one, it would have stamped the age in which she flourished, for, as there never was but one Washington, so there will never come a time when there will be the same opportunities as Mrs. Washington had for winning a name and individuality.

Because Martha Washington did not seek to expand the role of the First Lady, it remained limited for a substantial time thereafter.

There are large differences in personalities and marital relationships among First Ladies as well as variations in their political and social environments. The participation of First Ladies in the governmental process can be classified along two dimensions: their level of policy involvement and their level of independence from their spouses (the presidents). These distinctions enable us to separate First Ladies who were sources of influence and support for their husbands but had no interest in public policy from First Ladies who pursued more far-reaching agendas. The level of policy involvement will divide First Ladies into two groups: those who were involved in policy issues and those who were not. Non-policy issues are defined as charities or causes that are not controversial, whereas policy issues are substantive and more controversial. Issues such as children or mental health care advocacy are viewed as causes rather than policy issues because no one opposes children or aiding the mentally ill. Non-policy issues also include administrative matters such as presidential appointments, because these disputes often revolve around personalities rather than policies.

First Ladies will also be classified according to whether they pursued interests that were dependent on their husbands' agendas, or outside of the scope of their husbands' agendas. First Ladies who lobbied their husbands to

First Ladies and Policy Issues, Causes, or Charities

First Lady	Policy Issues, Causes, or Charities
Martha Washington	Revolutionary War veterans
Abigail Adams	No specific charities; education of girls
Dolley Madison	Easter Egg Roll; rebuilding of the White House; orphans
Elizabeth Monroe	Redecoration of the White House
Louisa Adams	No specific charities or causes
Letitia Tyler	No specific charities or causes
Julia Tyler	Texas annexation; states' rights
Sarah Polk	Expansionism
Margaret Taylor	No specific charities or causes
Abigail Fillmore	White House library; literacy
Jane Pierce	No specific charities or causes
Mary Todd Lincoln	Wounded Civil War soldiers
Eliza Johnson	No specific charities or causes
Julia Grant	No specific charities or causes
Lucy Hayes	Temperance; women's suffrage; living conditions for the impoverished; anti-immigration
Lucretia Garfield	No specific charities or causes
Frances Cleveland	Women's Christian Temperance Union; music; African American children's charities; women's education and professional employment
Caroline Harrison	Women's equality
Ida McKinley	No specific charities or causes
Edith Roosevelt	First Ladies portrait collection
Nellie Taft	Education for women; beautification and public works; *Titanic* memorial; First Ladies gown collection
Ellen Wilson	Indigenous crafts; housing and recreation facilities for the poor; child labor and truancy; neglected children; adult education; mental health care

First Lady	Policy Issues, Causes, or Charities
Edith Wilson	War-related charities
Florence Harding	Disabled veterans; women's equality
Grace Coolidge	Deaf education; child welfare
Lou Hoover	Women's equality; Girl Scouts
Eleanor Roosevelt	Civil rights; women's rights; worker's rights; child welfare; housing; youth employment; United Nations
Bess Truman	No specific charities or causes
Mamie Eisenhower	Cancer and polio; American Heart Association; United Nations
Jacqueline Kennedy	Historic preservation; the arts
Lady Bird Johnson	Beautification and the environment; urban renewal; promotion of Great Society programs
Pat Nixon	Volunteerism; Equal Rights Amendment
Betty Ford	Equal Rights Amendment; abortion rights; civil rights; the arts; cancer; special needs children
Rosalynn Carter	Mental health care; the elderly; community activism and volunteerism; Equal Rights Amendment
Nancy Reagan	Drug awareness
Barbara Bush	Literacy; homelessness; acquired immunodeficiency syndrome (AIDS); single working mothers; cancer
Hillary Rodham Clinton	Child welfare; health care
Laura Bush	Literacy

adopt a particular course of action are considered independent because their views evolved separately from those of their husbands.

These two dimensions divide First Ladies into four categories. First Ladies who engaged in no policy activity and were dependent on their husbands' agendas are "domestic partners." These First Ladies may have been good hostesses, campaigned with their husbands, and raised funds for charitable causes, but they were either not interested in public policy, or they did not wish to rock the boat.

Other First Ladies had little interest in public policy, but they did attempt to influence their husbands' political appointments and alliances. These First Ladies are "administrative specialists." Other First Ladies have made their policy beliefs public, in most cases expressing views that support their husbands' agendas. These are the "policy supporters."

For a First Lady to be a policy adviser, she must have her own beliefs on a wide range of issues and must seek to gain support for her beliefs. She may lobby her husband, testify before Congress, and even grant media interviews to discuss her agenda. This type of First Lady is a "policy proponent." She is different from other First Ladies because her views have evolved independently of her husband's agenda; they are truly *her* beliefs and concerns. Additionally, they are issues of major political import, where serious political disagreement is possible.

Domestic Partner

The "domestic partners" category contains the largest number of First Ladies and spans the longest period of time, ranging from Martha Washington to Barbara Bush. Given the limited public role permitted women through even the later stages of the twentieth century, it is not surprising that most First Ladies restricted their activities to charitable work, noncontroversial causes, and private support for their husbands' agendas. Martha Washington set the precedent by acting as a gracious hostess and promoting charitable organizations for veterans. Dolley Madison used her position to draw attention to the plight of orphans, and Abigail Fillmore promoted literacy and libraries. Lucy Hayes worked for the cause of temperance, and Caroline Harrison promoted women's education. Nellie Taft brought Japanese cherry trees to Washington, D.C., and Ellen Wilson promoted rural American crafts and the causes of poor and neglected children and the mentally ill. Grace Coolidge took a special interest in the education of deaf children, drawing from her past experience as a teacher of the deaf. Mamie Eisenhower was concerned about cancer and polio and assisted the Red Cross in blood drives. Jacqueline Kennedy embarked on a major historical restoration of the White House, producing a variety of books and documentaries, and establishing a permanent curator. Pat Nixon advocated volunteerism, and Barbara Bush promoted literacy. The vast majority of First Ladies have been associated with charitable interests and political causes. A handful, including many early First Ladies as well as Ida McKinley and Bess Truman, did not commit to any specific, identifiable charity or cause but contributed more generally wherever the assistance of a First Lady was needed.

Some First Ladies advised their husbands on appointments and policy decisions. First Lady historian Carl Sferrazza Anthony suggests that while James Madison confided to his wife "the conversations of cabinet meetings, congressional reports, military maneuvers, and diplomatic dispatches," Dolley Madison remained discreet and took no public position on policy issues. Instead, she aided her husband's agenda through invitations to dinners and social events and the cultivation of personal relationships with potential political allies.

Dolley Madison also had a reputation for patronage, and friends relied on her influence to help them gain government appointments. In this sense, it may appear that she is better represented by the "administrative specialist" category than the "domestic partner" category. However, Mrs. Madison's lobbying efforts do not show evidence of independence of her husband's agenda, making her different from First Ladies such as Nancy Reagan, who sought to undermine her husband's preferred political advisers. Dolley Madison is also different from other domestic partners in the zeal and energy with which she helped to advance her husband's career.

Sarah Polk also assisted her husband in such ways as clipping articles on topics she deemed important. Like Dolley Madison, however, she had no independent policy agenda and kept her influence private. Jane Pierce also served as an assistant to her husband, Franklin Pierce. In this role, she opposed his signing of the Kansas-Nebraska Act and disagreed with him on the feasibility of war if the South seceded from the Union. Because their policy disagreements remained private, however, Jane Pierce cannot be categorized as more than a domestic partner. If she had been more outspoken, she may have become the first policy advocate.

Other First Ladies led more private lives. Little has been written about Elizabeth Monroe; she fulfilled the traditional hostess duties, but her schedule was restricted by illness. Like Elizabeth Monroe, Louisa Adams suffered from poor health, and her activities were quite limited. Letitia Tyler is believed to have advised her husband when he became president, but she was in ill health and died after having made just one public appearance. Margaret Taylor assumed a similarly subdued role, refusing to even pose for a portrait. Eliza Johnson suffered from tuberculosis, and while she did advise her husband, she made few public appearances. Lucretia Garfield's husband was shot after four months in office, and died soon after.

Administrative Specialist

First Ladies in the administrative specialist category are those who stretched the role of personal adviser to play a more active role in their husbands' administrations. While these First Ladies were not always in the public eye, they exercised independence from the president in expressing their views on his advisers and political alliances. Consequently, they may have influenced public policy, although only indirectly.

Abigail Adams probably originated the role of administrative specialist. Her role as a personal adviser to her husband is well known. Her letters to friends and family demonstrate intimate knowledge of the workings of government, including information that today would be considered classified. John Adams trusted his wife more than his formal advisers, and it is generally assumed that she influenced his personnel decisions and alliances.

Mary Todd Lincoln publicly boasted that she planned to help her husband select his cabinet once he was elected. In addition to submitting requests for patronage to the president, there is evidence that Mrs. Lincoln made appointments without his consent by using War Department stationery and signing her own name, with the words "by order of the President through the War Department." She lobbied for the dismissal of Secretary of State William H. Seward and Secretary of the Treasury Salmon P. Chase, although she did not succeed. She recommended the promotion and dismissal of various military leaders throughout the Civil War and even ordered military supplies, in addition to her charitable work with injured soldiers and former slaves.

Like Mrs. Lincoln, Julia Grant had great interest in her husband's appointments; she demanded to know of his plans and attempted to influence his choices whenever she had the chance. Consequently, he occasionally went to great lengths to keep his plans from her. Similarly, Nellie Taft pressured her husband to pursue the presidency. Mrs. Taft managed her husband's schedule and had some influence over his appointments and political allies until her disabling stroke early in his term.

Woodrow Wilson's second wife assisted him in his day-to-day activities beyond the usual scope of involvement for a First Lady because of her husband's health problems. During World War I, Edith Wilson helped her husband decode secret military messages. After the war, Wilson had a stroke and the scope of Mrs. Wilson's assistance expanded. She became a gatekeeper between Wilson and the rest of the world, including his personal advisers. Those she disliked, such as the president's secretary Joseph Tumulty, had difficulty gaining access to the president. Mrs. Wilson also refused admission to Lord Edward Grey, an ambassador sent from Great Britain to aid Wilson in obtaining Senate approval for membership in the League of Nations. Grey eventually returned to London in disgust, and U.S. membership in the League was never ratified. Mrs. Wilson was not opposed to the League; it is widely believed that she had no agenda outside of her

Florence Harding, center, receives the wives of a Philippine delegation seeking the recognition of complete independence of the islands, 1922. *(Library of Congress)*

husband's. However, she did object to jokes told by Grey's assistant about her premarital involvement with the president and, as a result, Wilson's commitment to world government was permitted to suffer.

Similar to Mary Lincoln, Florence Harding played an active role in her husband's administration, and Warren G. Harding openly acknowledged his wife's position as a full partner. She went on the campaign trail and assisted in speech writing. Like Mrs. Lincoln, she advised her husband on political appointments. However, in the case of Florence Harding, the advice was not always sound, and individuals whom she had helped to promote were found to have swindled large sums of money from the federal government. When her husband died unexpectedly, she destroyed numerous government documents related to the scandal, perhaps to preserve his memory or to save herself from further investigation.

Nancy Reagan was also active in matters of personnel administration. Like Florence Harding and Mary Lincoln, Mrs. Reagan was concerned with the loyalty of her husband's advisers. She was influential in the dismissals, resignations, and reassignment of countless presidential advisers and cabinet secretaries. Nancy's overriding concern was her husband's public image and his popularity. Many historians believe that image maintenance, rather than substantive policy concerns, were the motivating factors in Nancy's behind-the-scenes personnel maneuvers.

According to most accounts, Nancy had little interest in influencing public policy. Her major cause, drug awareness, was remarkably bereft of any policy implications. While she promoted drug awareness, President Ronald Reagan cut federal funding for drug treatment programs. Mrs. Reagan did not support the passage of specific drug-related legislation.

Nancy's concern for her husband's image is an element common to all First Ladies in the administrative specialist category. Such First Ladies usually had strong partnerships with their husbands, and were so concerned about the loyalty of their husbands' advisers that they went to great efforts to influence who those advisers were. Policy issues played a minor concern and became important only if personnel issues were viewed as hampering the president's policy agenda.

Policy Supporter

Many First Ladies promote causes that are noncontroversial, such as Nancy Reagan's antidrug campaign and Barbara Bush's advocacy of literacy. These are not issues in the true sense of the word because they do not contain multiple and competing positions—few Americans can be said to be pro-drug abuse or pro-illiteracy. First Ladies in the policy supporters category are those who took public positions on controversial issues to promote their husbands' agendas. They risked public criticism for not "knowing their place"—a place that had been defined for them by decades of First Ladies who chose not to venture into the policy arena. Most examples of policy supporters have been fairly recent, although the first instance of policy support by a First Lady occurred in one of the earliest presidential administrations.

President John Tyler's youthful second wife, Julia Tyler, had a reputation for hostessing that rivaled Dolley Madison's, although Julia's stay in the White House was brief. Like Mrs. Madison, Julia handled patronage requests and used her social skills to advance her husband's agenda. Julia differed from Dolley in that she was the first president's wife to publicly profess support for a controversial policy issue—the annexation of Texas. She lobbied members of Congress, distributed pamphlets, and witnessed the critical vote from the visitors' gallery of the House. She was the first president's wife to be the subject of an issue-based political cartoon, and she received the pen used by the president to sign the annexation papers.

In her role as a policy supporter, Julia Tyler was not necessarily more powerful than First Ladies who played the role of domestic partner, such as Sarah Polk. What makes Mrs. Tyler different from the other First Ladies of her era is that her activities in support of her husband went beyond hostessing, and were in the public eye. By contemporary standards, Julia Tyler's policy advocacy is not unusual; however, for her time, Mrs. Tyler's activity was unique. It captured the attention of the press, and it was more steeped in controversy than traditional behind-the-scenes maneuvering of politically interested First Ladies.

Lou Hoover was also active in supporting her husband's policy agenda. Like other First Ladies, she had many charitable causes and served as a political adviser to her husband. Before Herbert Hoover was elected president, Lou Hoover had been more outspoken and independent in her policy agenda. Once he was elected, she toned down her rhetoric and played the role of supportive wife. The Great Depression began a mere eight months after Herbert Hoover took office, and because Hoover did not believe in government-sponsored programs to alleviate economic dislocation and poverty, Lou's public appearances promoted private charity and encouraged housewives to be frugal in their households and generous with those less fortunate.

Lou became embroiled in controversy when she invited the wife of an African American congressman to tea. Other congressional wives had routinely been invited to social events at the White House, but Representative Oscar DePriest's wife had not. The Hoovers decided to remedy the oversight and perhaps set an example at the same time. Mrs. DePriest was invited to tea, along with other congressmen's wives who supported the Hoovers' views on racial fairness. As a result, Lou and her husband were widely criticized by the white press in the South, and the Texas legislature passed a resolution chastising Mrs. Hoover. While other First Ladies supported racial equality in private, Lou was the first to take a public position in an era when her actions would inevitably generate much public debate.

Like Lou Hoover, Rosalynn Carter's tenure as First Lady was marked by poor economic conditions. Like the Hoovers, the Carters integrated the presidency with their marriage. Early in his term, President Jimmy Carter asked his wife to visit the leaders of seven Central and South American countries to persuade them to support the American Convention on Human Rights and to make Latin America a nuclear-free zone. She noted that while the leaders she visited were generally receptive to her, the press was not always so friendly. She recalled one critic saying: "You have neither been elected by the American people nor confirmed by the Senate to discuss foreign policy with foreign heads of state. Do you consider this trip an appropriate exercise of your position?" Rosalynn's response is an example of how a policy supporter views her position: "I am the person closest to the president of the United States, and if I can explain his policies and let the people of Latin America know of his great interest and friendship, then I intend to do so." Mrs. Carter made a similar visit to Thailand in 1979 to examine the problem of Cambodian refugees at her husband's request, culminating in a successful lobbying effort for United Nations relief.

Policy Advocate

Several twentieth century First Ladies took public positions on controversial issues. Policy advocates differ from policy supporters in that they advance policies that do not originate with their husbands. They may persuade their husbands to support their agenda, but the initiative for the policy is theirs. Given the limited role of the First Lady historically, policy advocates often find themselves criticized in the media for failing to conform to social expectations about how active the president's wife should be.

The most notable First Lady in this respect was Eleanor Roosevelt. President Franklin Roosevelt's polio necessitated that Eleanor take center stage in a variety of political activities. She traveled extensively as an adviser to her husband, visiting sharecroppers' shacks in the South and soldiers' tents in Guadalcanal. She wrote detailed reports complete with policy recommendations after each visit. She and President Roosevelt seldom traveled together, making her more visibly independent than other First Ladies, including those who were her successors. Eleanor's activities went beyond the mere promotion of her husband's agenda. She was truly an independent actor. Her charitable causes were extensive, and she was not afraid to find herself at the center of a political controversy by promoting racial integration and the rights of working women.

Eleanor's policy-making activities were numerous and included affordable housing for the poor, expansion of political and economic opportunities for African Americans in the South and elsewhere, and youth employment. Biographer Joseph Lash claims that Eleanor was the driving force behind many of President Roosevelt's New Deal programs. She was more radical than her husband and more willing to pursue innovative projects in the face of partisan criticism. Lash views Franklin as the conservative and politically savvy member of their partnership, whereas Eleanor was the liberal conscience who pushed her husband to embark on social reforms. Sometimes Mrs. Roosevelt was successful, and on other occasions, the president had to refuse her requests.

Mary McLeod Bethune, president of Bethune-Cookman College, and Eleanor Roosevelt speak before a National Youth Administration meeting, circa 1940. *(Library of Congress)*

Unlike her predecessors, Eleanor had many public forums through which to espouse her views. She wrote a syndicated daily newspaper column, contributed to women's magazines, made weekly radio addresses, and was a popular speaker on the lecture circuit. Eleanor Roosevelt was a tough act to follow for many reasons. Her children were grown, giving her time to pursue her interests. She was well educated and confident of her abilities. She found the traditional daily demands of her position unsatisfying, although such demands often overwhelmed later First Ladies who had larger personal staffs. Eleanor also had a husband who did not mind her being thrust into the spotlight; rather, he created opportunities for her to work and encouraged her efforts.

It took thirty years before another First Lady with her own policy agenda emerged on the political scene. Betty Ford's husband was an unelected president, and her time in office was short. During Gerald Ford's term, Betty campaigned tirelessly for the passage of the Equal Rights Amendment, became a spokeswoman for breast cancer prevention after she was diagnosed with the disease, and spoke out on controversial issues, such as civil rights and gay rights. Consequently, she was the target of political criticism and was even picketed by demonstrators outside of the White House gates. Given her brief time in the White House, Betty could never begin to match the accomplishments of Eleanor Roosevelt.

Few First Ladies were ever in Eleanor Roosevelt's position. The First Lady who most resembles her, in fact, cited Eleanor Roosevelt as one of her role models. Hillary Rodham Clinton's time as First Lady resembles that of Eleanor on many levels. Like Eleanor, Hillary had political causes she brought to the White House with her, gleaned from her experience as a governor's wife. For her era, Hillary was well educated, and like Eleanor, she had a husband who was supportive of her agenda and provided her with the resources necessary to carry it out.

The most visible aspect of Hillary Rodham Clinton's policy advocacy occurred early in her husband's administration, when she headed a task force on health care reform. After President Bill Clinton's failure to get their plan through Congress and the criticism of Hillary that the plan provoked, she engaged in less controversial projects, such as child welfare. Mrs. Clinton became more outspoken and independent once she decided to run for the Senate, but at that point her role could no longer be defined as a First Lady; rather, she had become a political candidate in her own right.

It may also be appropriate to classify Lady Bird Johnson as a policy advocate, although historians seem to view her as a more traditional, less controversial First Lady. Most scholars agree that Lady Bird had an independent policy agenda: beautification. However, viewing Mrs. Johnson's efforts merely as attempts to make cities more attractive is to miss the broader focus of her agenda. During Lyndon Johnson's administration, Lady Bird lobbied Congress to limit the billboards and the thousands of junkyards that lined highways in the United States. Such legislation was opposed by business owners and some members of Congress, and Lady Bird was lampooned in political cartoons which derided her efforts.

Significance

When we place First Ladies into this typology, some definite patterns emerge. First, the active involvement of a First Lady in promoting her

Hillary Rodham Clinton and daughter Chelsea Clinton are greeted by U.S. land mine detection team members in Tuzla, Bosnia, March, 1996. *(AP/Wide World Photos)*

husband's policies or advocating her own personal agenda is rare. Most First Ladies, past and present, have been content to play the role of domestic partner. Earlier First Ladies were somewhat more dependent and less policy-oriented. This is not surprising, given the restricted public lives led by women throughout most of American history. As women have attained more rights, higher levels of education, and better conditions of employment, First Ladies have become more active and more powerful.

Education and a more liberal society are not sufficient, however, to create First Ladies who are active in public policy. Even among the more recent First Ladies, we find many domestic partners. Women such as Grace Coolidge may have taken on more active roles had their husbands permitted them to make public appearances and been willing to solicit their political advice. Additionally, women such as Pat Nixon may have been more influential had her husband's advisers not actively labored to limit her public appearances and her access to the president. The policy activities of the next First Ladies will depend on their own willingness to be involved and the cooperation of the presidents.

Suggested Readings

Anthony, Carl Sferrazza. *First Ladies: The Saga of the Presidents' Wives and Their Power.* 2 vols. New York: William Morrow, 1990-1991. A unique glimpse at the power and prestige in the evolving role of the First Lady.

Boller, Paul F. *Presidential Wives: An Anecdotal History.* 2d ed. New York: Oxford University Press, 1999. Boller devotes a chapter to every First Lady from Martha Washington to Hillary Rodham Clinton.

Carter, Rosalynn. *First Lady from Plains.* Boston: Houghton Mifflin, 1984. Rosalynn Carter's candid memories of her life before and during her First Ladyship.

Holloway, Laura Carter. *The Ladies of the White House: Or, In the Home of the Presidents.* Reprint. New York: A. M. S. Press, 1976. Further subtitled *Being a Complete History of the Social and Domestic Lives of the Presidents from Washington to the Present Time, 1789-1882,* this book includes twenty-five leaves of plates.

Lash, Joseph P. *Eleanor and Franklin.* New York: W. W. Norton, 1971. Joseph Lash, secretary and confidant to Eleanor Roosevelt, won a Pulitzer Prize for this biography.

Valerie Sulfaro

First Ladies and Legislative Activism

Overview: The Constitution is silent regarding her role, but the First Lady is a prominent public figure who can and does use close proximity and indirect power to influence the president's political decisions. On occasion, First Ladies have developed legislation, testified before congressional committees or subcommittees, and communicated directly with lawmakers or their personal staff to promote points of view. The extent and effects of interaction with the legislative process are numerous and complex, some of them entwined with the willingness of the First Lady to shoulder a public role, and some with the wide latitude left to the chief executive to freely choose his advisers.

History

Early presidents' wives principally entertained at receptions and dinners, called on the wives of lawmakers in the U.S. capital, and oversaw the White House domestic staff. In an unusual instance, Dolley Madison, when her husband was ill, acted as his secretary for a few days, forestalling a congressional committee requesting to see her sick husband. In private, however, First Ladies such as Helen Taft often attended House and Senate debates and discussed them with their husbands. Others, such as Mary Todd Lincoln and Ida McKinley, advised their husbands on presidential appointments. Hints of modern development appeared in the nineteenth century when Edith Roosevelt began to hire her own staff to answer mail and reporters' questions instead of relying on the president's staff.

By the twentieth century, First Ladies had emerged as active political partners, selecting their own undertakings rather than simply responding to public pressure to champion their husbands' causes. Before her death, Ellen Wilson lent her name to slum-clearance projects and invited reformers to meet members of Congress at the White House. Using official vehicles to transport observers around Washington, D.C., she showed the decrepit and inadequate housing located near Capitol Hill. Wilson quietly lobbied legislators for legislation to demolish slums and build new housing with federal money. Her association with this cause became so popular that on the day she died in 1914, the Senate passed a housing bill in her honor.

Eleanor Roosevelt was the first presidential wife to testify before a congressional committee; the first to hold a government office (as assistant director of the Office of Civilian Defense); the first nominated to a post requiring Senate confirmation (as a U.S. representative to the United Nations General Assembly); and the first to promote or oppose legislation through newspaper columns and radio addresses. Citing her husband's partial paralysis, she became the president's "eyes and ears," traveling into almost every state and congressional district.

Claudia Taylor (Lady Bird) Johnson tackled the legislative side of civic and highway beautification. She and her staff sponsored and partly wrote a law that President Lyndon B. Johnson

Ellen Wilson, shown with President Woodrow Wilson, lobbied to improve slum housing in Washington, D.C. Her alley bill was passed by Congress as she lay dying in August, 1914. Never before had a First Lady been so closely associated with legislation. *(Library of Congress)*

and conservation in his 1965 State of the Union address and submitted a host of proposals to Congress pertaining to beautification and conservation. Lady Bird's work initiated or at least supported a variety of important natural and environmental policies enacted in the late 1960's, including the National Historic Preservation Act, the Clean Rivers Restoration Act, the Air Quality Act, the National Trail Systems Act, and the Wild and Scenic Rivers Act.

Rosalynn Carter spoke to and lobbied lawmakers on behalf of her own interests, which included mental health education, the Equal Rights Amendment, and the plight of refugees. After persuading President Jimmy Carter to appoint a National Commission on Mental Health, she worked closely, as honorary chairwoman, with professionals on the commission gathering data, making recommendations, and devising legislation to improve mental health programs at the local, state, and national levels. Late in her husband's administration, Rosalynn went before the Senate Resources subcommittee to testify in favor of increased federal spending for mental health programs, tangling with then-chairman Edward M. Kennedy of Massachusetts over what constituted a satisfactory federal health budget. Mrs. Carter also championed legislation to reform Social Security, extend the mandatory retirement age for federal workers, and

submitted to Congress, to eliminate the proliferation of junkyards and billboards along U.S. highways. Lady Bird personally oversaw the White House lobbying for the bill, making numerous calls herself and, despite criticism from such opponents as then-Representative Robert J. Dole of Kansas, was successful in passing the Highway Beautification Act of 1967, known as Lady Bird's Bill, and advancing a proposal to landscape Capitol Hill. As a result of her efforts, President Johnson advocated beautification improve medical services for the elderly in rural areas.

Transcending the traditional role of First Lady, Hillary Rodham Clinton spearheaded the Clinton administration's health care reform efforts on Capitol Hill in 1993 and 1994. In that role, she traveled around the United States, meeting with health care professionals, interest groups, and other citizens to hear their views on the nation's health care system. She regularly attended policy strategy meetings, consulted with members of Congress, and testified before congressional committees on the president's plan. The cochairperson of the Congressional Caucus for Women's Issues, then-Representative Patricia Schroeder of Colorado, credited the "Hillary factor" with pushing through thirty bills affecting women and children in the final days of the 103d Congress (1993-1994).

Congressional Reaction

In an age when husbands and wives increasingly share professional interests, the presidential spouse's role becomes an issue to lawmakers who prefer a more traditional First Lady: one who exercises influence behind the scenes, rather than in public. A notable paradox about First Ladies is that the greater their perceived political and policy influence, the more they are scrutinized by members of Congress because of their unelected and unconfirmed status.

Republican lawmakers, for example, viewed Mary Todd Lincoln as high-handed, untruthful, and untrustworthy. Some thought she had covered up financial irregularities in both her personal and White House accounts. Others were skeptical of her loyalty to the Union itself; she was a Kentucky native whose family members were largely Confederate sympathizers, and she had brothers serving in the Confederate Army. In this contentious atmosphere, President Abraham Lincoln's State of the Union address, while still in draft form, was obtained and printed by a New York newspaper reporter who was known to be a close friend of the First Lady. Questioning Mary's patriotism, and mindful of what later generations would regard as national security leaks, the House Judiciary Committee pondered issuing a subpoena for Mrs. Lincoln,

Rosalynn Carter testifies before Congress about increasing funding for government mental health programs, 1979. *(CORBIS)*

the suspected source of the leaked speech. A popular anecdote, which first appeared in print in 1905, told the touching story of President Lincoln, hat in hand, appearing before a congressional committee to defend his wife. In light of the fact that Mary Todd Lincoln had ties to the Confederacy during the Civil War, it is not surprising that she came under congressional criticism.

Scarcely a year into her husband's first term, President Ulysses S. Grant's wife, Julia Grant, was besieged with questions about political impropriety and ill-gotten profits in the "Black Friday" attempt to corner the gold market. To determine just what Julia knew, House Democrats wanted to hear from her and from the president's sister, to whom Mrs. Grant wrote about gold speculation. For a month in 1870, the House Committee on Banking and Currency, headed by future president James A. Garfield, conducted the Gold Panic Investigation. Its purpose was to look into the causes of the unusual and inordinate fluctuations of gold in New York City during the last months of 1869. House Republicans—of the same party as President Grant—deftly defrayed the First Lady's obligation to testify by protesting that such a request was unseemly and undignified. The Grant presidency also suffered from many scandals among its cabinet members. Therefore, it is not surprising that the Democrats in Congress scrutinized his administration so closely. More important, Democrats, who were known as the Party of the South because the Republican Party was seen as the instigators of the Civil War, had a strong motivation to embarrass the president, who had been the general of the army that defeated them.

In modern times, Eleanor Roosevelt, Rosalynn Carter, and Hillary Rodham Clinton were criticized for their unique legislative activism; all three pushed presidential power to new limits. Eleanor Roosevelt provoked congressional scrutiny by speaking out on matters which many on Capitol Hill preferred to avoid, agitating their constituents and challenging their assumptions about a woman's traditional role, and by running a parallel administration alongside her husband. Capable of charming and exasperating many lawmakers with her unconventional behavior, northern liberals applauded her as an ally, while southern conservatives objected to her civil rights advocacy. Republicans often suspected her motives, some calling her "Lenin in skirts"; Democrats sometimes regarded her as a cross to bear. Mrs. Roosevelt made a special effort to aid women members of Congress, inviting Republicans and Democrats alike to the White House. Representative and future Senator Margaret Chase Smith of Maine respected and admired Mrs. Roosevelt for her intelligence and active leadership and also because, in whatever circumstances, she was a lady. Mrs. Roosevelt encouraged Democratic Representative Helen Gahagan Douglas of California to run for office and bolstered other women's congressional careers. During her last years in the White House, Mrs. Roosevelt's support for civil rights legislation triggered acerbic attacks from Senator Theodore Bilbo, a Democrat from Mississippi. He concluded one Senate speech by asserting: "If I can succeed eventually in resettling the great majority of the Negroes in West Africa—and I propose to do it—I might entertain the proposition of crowning Eleanor queen of Greater Liberia." The galleries, however, hissed at these remarks.

Rosalynn Carter's assistance to her husband was so apparent that it aroused animosity in many lawmakers who felt that an unelected First Lady had no business doing as much as she did. Hillary Rodham Clinton's very public activism in crafting President Clinton's national health care reform encouraged Republican members of Congress to scrutinize her actions. The Republican-controlled Congress investigated the Clintons' Whitewater real-estate venture dating from 1978 and Hillary's role in the 1993 firings of seven White House Travel Office employees. Many Republican lawmakers pushed hard for these investigations because they believed that the president, and especially Mrs. Clinton, acted illegally in both cases. Thus, the increasing activism of First Ladies, embodied in their testifying to Congress, has caused the office to be treated in a different light and often more scrutinized.

Going to the Heart of the Lawmaking Process

U.S. president and political scientist Woodrow Wilson observed over a century ago that the committee system is the very heart of the lawmaking process in the United States. "Congress in session," commented Wilson, "is Congress on public exhibition, whilst Congress in its committee rooms is Congress at work." This adage continues to describe the business of Congress today. Although the U.S. Constitution provides no mandate for a congressional committee system, Congress has long organized itself into committees to perform a broad range of functions for the legislature as a whole: preparing groundwork for legislation, bringing public issues into the spotlight, and whipping legislation into shape. Committees offer Congress the potential of increased efficiency and expertise. In them, lawmakers make their most effective personal contributions to public policy; pursue constituency interests; develop strong relationships with political advocates, executive officials, and other participants in the political arena; and produce measures that can stand up on the floor of each chamber. Given this capacity to enable a legislature to engage actively in a nation's governance, testifying before these bodies provides more access points and potential influence for First Ladies to contribute to the presidency.

First and "second" ladies have testified sixteen times before Congress. Three presidential spouses testified while their husbands were in office, and two testified after their husbands left office. Second spouses testified seven times during their husbands' vice presidencies. As First Lady, Eleanor Roosevelt made two trips to Capitol Hill, Rosalynn Carter two as well, and Hillary Rodham Clinton testified five times. In 1991 Elizabeth (Betty) Ford made an appearance after leaving the White House: She testified before the House Select Committee on Aging about alcoholism treatment coverage restrictions under health insurance. Mrs. Carter also appeared on Capitol Hill in 1991, when she addressed the House Committee on Appropriations on health and welfare programs. Ford and Carter later joined forces in 1994 before the Senate Committee on Labor and Human Resources to speak about the Health Securities Act. In 1995 Nancy Reagan went before the House Committee on Government Reform and Oversight to speak about national drug control strategy, drug abuse, and drug trafficking. Joan Mondale, wife of Vice President Walter Mondale, testified both on Capitol Hill and in field hearings in support of the arts. Marilyn Quayle, the spouse of Vice President Dan Quayle, pointed to the need for women's health and breast cancer research. Tipper Gore, wife of Vice President Al Gore, went before the Senate to advocate mental health care.

In general, such testimony involves friendly interrogation, with questions that build up character and competence. In most cases First Ladies offer their comments on a policy initiated by others. As the United States' "number one migrant," Eleanor Roosevelt was invited to address select committees in 1940 and 1942 on nonpivotal issues such as discrimination against migrant workers, against women, against African Americans, and in employment and training practices. Calling for improving the living and working conditions of migrant labor, Mrs. Roosevelt noted to committee members, "If you are living under conditions which are poor, sleeping conditions that are bad, if you have overcrowding, medical health conditions that are very poor, you are not going to do your job as well nor are you going to produce as much." "Well, Mrs. Roosevelt, you speak my language," commented Chairman John Tolan, a Democrat from California. In the 1950's Mrs. Roosevelt scorned the anti-Communist investigations of Republican Senator Joseph R. McCarthy of Wisconsin. She testified before other, more congenial committees, lending her stature to House and Senate hearings on strengthening the United Nations (1955), raising the minimum wage (1959), improving conditions for migrant labor (1959), regulating the price of hearing aids (1962), and ensuring equal pay for equal work (1962).

An Unprecedented Architect

At the start of her husband's administration, Hillary Rodham Clinton made a series of unprecedented treks to Capitol Hill to testify before key committees to consider the Health Security Act of 1993, the Clinton administration's proposal to provide for comprehensive reform of the health care system. Unlike her predecessors, Mrs. Clinton was the first spouse of a president to testify before congressional committees as the architect of a social policy plan. Although the hearings represented the first time that Mrs. Clinton appeared publicly before Congress, her responses to members' questions made it clear that she knew many of the lawmakers well. Her testimony took place before five committee hearings, each scheduled to last about two hours, although several ran on for nearly three. In the House, she appeared before the Ways and Means, Energy and Commerce, and Education and Labor committees. In the Senate she testified before the Finance Committee and the Labor and Human Resources Committee. Many members seemed unsure of exactly how to treat the First Lady. Many of those who disliked the Clinton plan seemed to separate the plan from Mrs. Clinton, praising her work but disparaging the president's proposal, as if she had little to do with it. In the absence of precedent, lawmakers fell back on the ceremonial idiom of formal congressional occasions, in which they customarily praise one another's work before tearing it

to shreds. "No individual has contributed more to the development of the president's plan than our witness this morning," declared Senator Edward M. Kennedy in his opening remarks before the Senate Committee on Labor and Human Resources. "I have served here with five different presidents," added Democratic Senator Howard M. Metzenbaum of Ohio, "but I remember the record of many other presidents as well, and I don't remember any other president, and certainly no other presidential spouse, that was as fully involved and fully knowledgeable about a legislative program as the two of you are."

Beneath the polite comments, the praise, and the quips, was an elaborate dance between Congress and Mrs. Clinton as White House emissary. Each side signaled its needs to the other. Congressional attention varied. Those Democrats who supported the Clinton proposal lofted easy questions that enabled Mrs. Clinton to explain how the proposed plan worked to the scores of reporters in attendance. Democratic Senator Max Baucus of Montana asked about rural health care, providing Mrs. Clinton the opportunity to explain that the plan aimed to tie rural Americans into urban medical centers. Other members simply sought clarification or information. Democratic Representative Richard Edmund Neal of Massachusetts, for example, wanted to know whether the Shriners hospital in his hometown would be affected by all regulations.

Hillary Rodham Clinton's testimony was fundamentally different from that of her predecessors. Not only did she bring attention to the issue of health care, she articulated a plan to solve the problem. Prior to testifying, Mrs. Clinton consulted health care advocates, medical groups, and business representatives in an effort to hammer out the issue in its complexity, dealing with the give-and-take of different powerful interests. Her approach to the problem eventually failed to muster a winning bloc of votes. The three committees in the House of

Representatives responsible for reporting on a health care plan had very different experiences: The Committee on Commerce did not report a bill, the Committee on Education and Workforce reported a bill more expensive than the Clinton proposal, and the Ways and Means Committee reported a bill more closely resembling the Clinton plan.

The testimonies of Roosevelt, Carter, and Clinton all sought to achieve policy goals that were for the common good, such as improving working and health conditions of migrant workers, finding solutions to the energy crisis, and increasing health coverage for the uninsured and for mental health care. These issues were very serious problems at the time of each First Lady's testimony. The fact that the First Lady provided testimony brought increased attention to these issues. More importantly, these hearings served the agendas of the chairmen of the committees that heard the testimony. For example, Senator Kennedy was known to be a strong supporter of increasing coverage for mental health and health care for all Americans when he chaired the Senate Committee on Labor and Human Resources.

Additionally, presidents ask First Ladies to testify on issues that are either particularly pressing in society or are priorities in their administrations. Eleanor Roosevelt, for example, testified about migrant workers, a direct result of the Great Depression, while Rosalynn Carter testified about the energy crisis, one of the factors that led to the economic recession of the late 1970's and which contributed to the election of Ronald Reagan. Health care coverage and mental health coverage have been pressing issues in society since President Harry S. Truman attempted to nationalize health care.

Significance

The position of First Lady has evolved over the years in response to changing social attitudes and the efforts of a succession of women. The job has gradually come to include direction of a project or cause complementary to the president's agenda but separate from it. This is, in part, because public expectations of the First Lady have changed. Americans now anticipate that the First Lady will take up some social problem as her own and work for its solution. Indeed, the consequences of having no program can be serious. Contemporary presidential spouses, therefore, are increasingly distinct as political figures in their own right with their own special issues. In short, the modern First Lady completes any president's administration. She can largely shape the role of the First Lady to her needs, yet it is clear that a set of imprecise, yet definite, expectations about her role has emerged. The First Lady must satisfy them if she is to be successful and an asset to the president. Too much involvement, however, can raise suspicion and even congressional censure.

Congress is inherently slow as an institution in response to change. Characterized by structure and routine, the legislative process follows established traditions. Not surprisingly, most members remain unsure of exactly how to deal with the First Lady when she testifies and to know the authoritative capacity with which she speaks. Time and familiarity may change this. The gradual evolution from ceremonial hostess to symbol surrogate, issue highlighter, campaign worker, and political adviser reflects the impact of certain activist presidential wives, the changing role of women in society, increased power in the executive branch, and the increased public and press attention focused on presidential politics and personalities.

Contemporary lawmakers appear more sympathetic to First Ladies taking a more active role in politics than their predecessors. At one time, the idea of a First Lady testifying before a congressional committee was inconceivable. Eleanor Roosevelt blazed the trail to Capitol Hill for First Ladies, speaking to lawmakers twice in twelve years. Hillary Rodham Clinton was a transitional First Lady, taking on a new, broader role. As more presidential spouses arrive at the White House fresh from careers in business, they may be more prominent and more visibly political than their predecessors. Like Eleanor Roosevelt, Mrs. Clinton may have been the first of a new generation that will expand the possibilities and responsibilities of the office of the First Lady. At least anecdotally, the more receptive contemporary congressional environment will continue to provide more access points to First Ladies. Whereas in the past First Ladies could influence business on Capitol Hill by discreetly lobbying lawmakers with whom they enjoyed close relationships, future First Ladies might routinely and openly participate in the dance of legislation.

Suggested Readings

Anthony, Carl Sferrazza. *First Ladies: The Saga of the Presidents' Wives and Their Power.* 2 vols. New York: William Morrow, 1990-1991. A unique glimpse at the power and prestige in the evolving role of the First Lady.

Burrell, Barbara. *Public Opinion, the First Ladyship, and Hillary Rodham Clinton.* New York: Garland, 1997.

Feinberg, Barbara Silberdick. *America's First Ladies: Changing Expectations.* New York: Franklin Watts, 1998.

Gould, Lewis L., ed. *American First Ladies: Their Lives and Their Legacy.* New York: Garland Press, 1996. An informative and objective combination of biographical sketches and histories of the First Ladies.

Gutin, Myra G. *The President's Partner: The First Lady in the Twentieth Century.* New York: Greenwood Press, 1989. Examines the public communications and private personas of twelve First Ladies.

O'Connor, Karen, Bernadette Nye, and Laura Van Assendelft. "Wives in the White House: The Political Influence of First Ladies." *Presidential Studies Quarterly* 26, no. 3 (1997): 835-853.

Simonton, Dean Keith. "Presidents' Wives and First Ladies: On Achieving Eminence Within a Traditional Gender Role." *Sex Roles* 35, no. 3/4 (1996): 309-336.

Van Zwaluwenburg, Pamela J. "First Partner: First Ladies and Their Roles." In *Presidential Frontiers: Underexplored Issues in White House Politics*, edited by Ryan J. Barilleaux. Westport, Conn.: Praeger, 1998.

Watson, Robert P. "The First Lady Reconsidered: Presidential Partner and Political Institution." *Presidential Studies Quarterly* 27, no. 4 (1997): 805-818.

Winfield, Betty Houchin. "Madame President: Understanding a New Kind of First Lady." *Media Journal Studies* 8 (1994): 59-71.

Colton C. Campbell

Family Life in the White House

Overview: The lives and lifestyles of presidential families have changed considerably since the inauguration of George Washington in 1789. Through the years, traditions have evolved and family members have been forced to adopt a much more public presence. Much of this has been due to increased perception of the first family as public symbols, and the increased role of the First Lady as an integral component of the official machinery of the White House. Nonetheless, the most significant influences on family life continue to be the individual dynamics of each first family and the degree of politicization allowed by the president and First Lady.

History

The families who have lived in the White House have been quite varied. Presidents have surrounded themselves with groups that have ranged from only immediate family members to extended circles including presidential parents, cousins, nieces, nephews, and assorted other relatives. Some presidents were widowers or, in the case of James Buchanan, a bachelor, and hence had to appeal to relatives to assume social duties. Other first couples were childless but brought either adopted children or grandchildren to live at the White House.

In spite of the differences through the years, several common trends emerged which have defined family life in the White House. First, most first families have been smaller than contemporary averages. While Anna Howard Harrison had 10 children, the average number of children in first families is just 3.5, and many first couples had only 1 child. James and Sarah Polk had no children; Warren and Florence Harding had no children together nor any who lived with them; and the bachelor James Buchanan was also childless. In addition, it should be noted that the children of Martha Washington, Dolley Madison, and Edith Wilson came from previous marriages, and many first couples had adopted children. Even Buchanan was the legal guardian of his niece and nephew when he entered the White House. Second, since the average age of First Ladies upon entering the White House was forty-seven, it has been very common for the first family to include grandchildren. Thomas Jefferson had seven grandchildren living with him, including James Madison Randolph, who was the first of ten presidential grandchildren born in the Executive Mansion through the twentieth century. Third, although the First Lady has no formal constitutional function, tradition and practical utility have meant that many First Ladies have involved themselves deeply in politics as formal or informal advisers to their husbands or as advocates for various causes, including their husbands' political fortunes. When both spouses have been politically involved, family life has been affected in a variety of ways, which range from lack of private time together to the unwanted politicization of private matters. Fourth, and finally, presidents have often turned to members of their extended family to serve in both social and official capacities in the White House. Buchanan and the widowers Jefferson, Andrew Jackson, Martin Van Buren, and Chester A. Arthur all turned to relatives to fulfill the functions of First Lady. This often brought extended families into the White House.

The Public Side of Family Life

In many ways, the Washingtons were atypical of American first families and as such did not reflect later patterns. George and Martha Washington had no role models or guidelines to follow, so codes of conduct had to be invented or adopted from nonpolitical models. The Washingtons initially resisted interaction with the public and were perceived as aloof.

One pattern did emerge which would be consistent throughout later presidencies: the public's fascination with the first family and the details of their lives. George and Martha had no children together, but Martha had two grandchildren, Nellie and George Custis, living with them. During Washington's tenure and stay in the initial two national capitals, New York and Philadelphia, the press reported on the intricacies of the first family in great detail. Reporters followed the presidential grandchildren when they attended a circus or private functions.

The intrusiveness of the press was a problem with which successive first families have wrestled. Throughout the nineteenth century, presidents generally tried to prevent public discussion of the first families. Nonetheless, as family members often assumed official and unofficial posts in government, they were routinely the targets of press scrutiny. From Bartholomew Dandridge, the nephew of Martha Washington who served as a secretary and accountant for George, to Hillary Rodham Clinton's role as adviser to her husband on health care, most presidents have employed family members in some capacity. The sons of John Quincy Adams, John Tyler, Martin Van Buren, Andrew Johnson, Ulysses S. Grant, Millard Fillmore, Rutherford B. Hayes, Franklin D.

Roosevelt, Dwight D. Eisenhower, and Jimmy Carter all served as secretaries or aides for their fathers, while the daughters of Jefferson, James Monroe, Tyler, Zachary Taylor, Fillmore, Andrew Johnson, Benjamin Harrison, William Howard Taft, Franklin D. Roosevelt, Eisenhower, Richard M. Nixon, and Gerald R. Ford served as hostesses or aides to the First Ladies. The 1978 "Bobby Kennedy Law" prevents presidents from formally hiring members of their family into government service, but family members continue to serve in unofficial or nongovernmental positions. For instance, the sons of Ford and George H. W. Bush served in their fathers' reelection campaigns.

While many first families have gone to great lengths to guard their privacy, others have actively sought public attention for a variety of reasons. In some cases, members of the first family have been used to bolster the political fortunes of the presidents. This has resulted in media and public access to the intimate life of those who have occupied the White House. For instance, anecdotes of Benjamin Harrison's close relationship with his grandchildren were used to counter the popular perception that the president was stiff and reserved. For the first time in American history, the public was able to view photographs of the grandchildren in their private nursery and other aspects of family life. Grover Cleveland used his marriage to Frances Folsom to counter his image as a stodgy bachelor. Dwight Eisenhower also utilized his grandchildren in the 1952 election to bolster his grandfatherly image. Once he was in the White House, his grandchildren reinforced the image of the wholesome nature of the first family.

Through the years, First Ladies have also entered or been dragged into the public arena. Political or popular criticism of their husbands often led First Ladies to engage in efforts to defend or advance the interests of their husbands. In addition, criticism of First Ladies and first family members has been used as a mechanism to attack presidents. For instance, Elizabeth

Grover Cleveland was the first president to be married in the White House. He wed Frances Folsom on June 2, 1886.
(Library of Congress)

Monroe's efforts to introduce more rigid protocol in the White House led to charges of "royalism" and "monarchy." Mary Todd Lincoln was accused of Confederate sympathies because of her southern background. In addition, the alcoholism and drug use of two of the sons of John Quincy and Louisa Adams created public scandal, as did the behavior of Dolley Madison's son, Payne, whom the press labeled the "American Prince" and who was known for his gambling and debts. Criticism of her family led First Lady Abigail Adams to openly support press censorship.

As newspapers became more common in the nineteenth century, so did coverage of presidential families and of life in the White House. In 1873 a serial began featuring a regular monthly column on life in the White House, and other magazines, such as *Harper's Weekly*, began running photographs and cartoons of the first family. As media scrutiny intensified in the twentieth century, many presidents and their spouses went to great lengths to protect their families. Both Jacqueline Kennedy and Hillary Rodham Clinton endeavored with moderate success to protect their children from the intrusiveness of the press, even though other first family members actively sought the spotlight.

The public duties of the first family have expanded through the years and reinforced the interplay with the media. Many family members have been involved directly in presidential campaigns, and their presence at the inauguration and other functions is routine. In addition to witnessing the oath of office, spouses have accompanied their husbands to the inaugural receptions, and since 1837, children of the first family have attended the inaugural balls. Fur-

(AP/Wide World Photos)

Egg Rolling

One enduring and popular family tradition at the White House is the Easter Egg Roll, which involves "rolling" a hard-boiled egg across the lawn. After Congress passed a law forbidding egg rolling on the Capitol lawn in 1876, President Rutherford B. Hayes allowed the activity to take place on the South Lawn of the Executive Mansion. Since its inception, the president and First Lady have personally welcomed each egg roller, and often members of the first family participated in the tradition. Presidential grandchildren have been especially prominent participants, and presidential pets often took part. Grover Cleveland's dog Hector often consumed the eggs of unsuspecting rollers while Florence Harding's collie performed tricks for the crowds. The Nixons added the "White House Easter Bunny" and certificates of participation, and Rosalynn Carter gave out ten thousand plastic eggs that contained a personal note from the First Lady. Under the Reagans, autographed wooden eggs were distributed and even Socks, the Clintons' cat, "autographed" eggs as part of the event during the 1990's.

thermore, family members have been involved in the actual ceremony itself. For instance, Lady Bird Johnson initiated the practice of holding the Bible while her husband was administrated the oath of office. Other first families held receptions or intimate lunches for friends and extended family members immediately following the inauguration, distinct from the more formal receptions of that evening. Several presidents, including Grant, built stands so that the public could view the first family as part of the inaugural procession. The practice has now become routine, as first families stand with the new president to review the inaugural parade.

Appearances at public ceremonies and receptions compose the main duties of the first family. For instance, the first family appeared at the public receptions that were held at the White House until the 1930's to celebrate New Year's Day and the Fourth of July. The Tylers held Sunday concerts for the public, and until the 1890's, the South Lawn was open so that the public could view the first family in the gardens. Family members have also long attended diplomatic or other official receptions at the White House, and it has become common practice for presidents to have family members in attendance in addresses to the nation.

The Private Side of Family Life

Family life is constrained by the duality of the president's home serving as both private residence and ceremonial residence of the head of state. This tension is reinforced by the egalitarian nature of American democracy and the fact that with only a few exceptions, the White House has remained open to the public. Early presidential families often had to contend with citizens entering the private areas of family quarters on the second floor. In order to protect their children from public scrutiny, the Clevelands and the Kennedys had private kindergartens established so that their children could interact with other toddlers away from public attention. Increased media examination of first

families in the twentieth century has further eroded the already fragile privacy afforded by the Executive Mansion.

Efforts to get away from the press and pressure of Washington, D.C., led many first families to maintain unofficial residences for vacation purposes. The hot Washington summers contributed to the desirability of such places as escapes from the heat and humidity. Twenty first families had regular second homes, which they retained during their years at the White House. These ranged from Peacefield in Quincy, Massachusetts, used by John Adams and John Quincy Adams, to Walker's Point in Kennebunkport, Maine, used by the Bush family. Other notable homes were the Theodore Roosevelts' Sagamore Hill near Oyster Bay, New York, and Ronald Reagan's Rancho del Cielo in Santa Barbara, California. Franklin D. Roosevelt established a presidential retreat in Maryland, now called Camp David, as a more convenient vacation spot. Later presidents added stables, a golf course, a swimming pool, and tennis courts.

Various first families have also established winter vacation spots. The Hardings preferred Florida, as did later families including the Franklin Roosevelts, the Trumans, the Kennedys, and the Nixons. Georgia was popular with the Eisenhowers and the Carters.

While the first family often attends diplomatic receptions and other official public functions, private celebrations such as birthdays or christenings have generally remained small family affairs. The main exception to this is the president's birthday. Although Washington's birthday was long marked by special ceremonies and eventually its designation as a federal holiday, modern presidential birthdays since Franklin Roosevelt's tenure have become major events. These ceremonies have largely become politicized and exist now mainly as fundraisers or media events designed to engender public goodwill. Birthday parties for presidential spouses and children are traditionally small events, although there have been many notable exceptions.

The White House has also been witness to a variety of other family celebrations. There have been eighteen christenings in the Executive Mansion and five coming-out parties. The presidential home was also the site of Susan Ford's high school prom and numerous high school and college graduation parties. In 1812, Dolley Madison's sister Lucy Payne was married to Supreme Court Justice Thomas Todd in the first of sixteen White House weddings. In 1886 Cleveland became the only president to be married in the dwelling (both Tyler and Woodrow Wilson were married while in office, but not in the White House). In addition to the ceremonies that were actually held in the White House, other marriages of close family members have been celebrated by the incumbent president. In 1992, the first wedding was held at Camp David when Doro Bush LeBlond married Robert Koch. The Grants, Tafts, Hayeses, and Clintons celebrated their silver wedding anniversaries in the White House. In fact, the Tafts' 1911 twenty-fifth anniversary party was one of the largest lawn parties in the history of the White House and included some eight thousand guests. Other prominent anniversaries included that of Dwight and Mamie Eisenhower in 1959, when the couple repeated their wedding vows.

In addition to the presidential funerals, family funerals in the White House have included those of First Ladies Letitia Tyler, Caroline Harrison, and Ellen Wilson; presidential sons William Lincoln and Calvin Coolidge, Jr.; Fred Dent, the father of Julia Grant; and John W. Scott, the father of Caroline Harrison. The support of family proved crucial during these difficult periods following the loss of a loved one. This has been especially true as presidents and First Ladies have coped with the loss of their own parents or children. The premature deaths of Rebecca Van Buren and Patrick Kennedy had tremendous and lasting impact on their respective parents. Several presidents were in office

President and Mrs. Calvin Coolidge at a party celebrating the Fourth of July and the president's fifty-fifth birthday at the Summer White House, Custer State Park, South Dakota, July 4, 1927. *(New York Times Co./ Archive Photos)*

when they lost a parent, as were First Ladies. Nancy Reagan lost both her mother and stepfather. In the case of the Trumans and the Clintons, each spouse suffered the loss of a parent. Members of the first family provide the main social support system for the president, who must continue his duties and balance his personal grief with his responsibilities as the nation's leader.

Successive presidents have gone to great lengths to accommodate and care for ill relatives. William McKinley's devotion to his wife, who had epilepsy, led him to change White House protocol and go to great lengths for her. When First Lady Betty Ford underwent surgery for breast cancer, President Gerald Ford publicly acknowledged his inability to concentrate on matters of state and described the period as the "low" point of his presidency. Con-

versely, various First Ladies, notably Edith Wilson, Mamie Eisenhower, and Nancy Reagan, emerged as fierce protectors of their husbands following illness or, in the case of Reagan, an assassination attempt.

Relationships and dating have always been problematic for presidential children. Many sons and daughters have chafed at both the lack of privacy and the behavioral pressures. From the many nieces and nephews of the Jacksons to the daughters of Wilson and Lyndon B. Johnson, the national media have consistently sought to publicize the private lives of the presidential children. Wilson's daughter Nell's engagement was front-page news after reporters obtained a love letter, and Alan Hoover complained that any time spent with female company resulted in false engagement stories. The

William and Helen Taft at home with their children Helen, Charley, and Robert in Washington, D.C., circa 1909. *(Library of Congress)*

lack of privacy led Buck Grant to study abroad, in Germany. One result of these pressures has been the tendency for many adult children to remain as far from Washington as possible.

Presidents and First Ladies have often gone to extreme lengths to keep their children well rounded and well grounded. Many parents have insisted that their children perform their own chores, such as making their beds or cleaning their rooms. Many children were asked to cook, or at least learn how to cook, their own meals. Calvin Coolidge, Jr., even worked as a field hand on a tobacco farm while his father was president.

Just as the White House is often the scene of joy and intimate celebration, it also is the site of great tragedy and loss. Since William Henry Harrison died in office in 1841, the White House has witnessed the funerals of several presidents, some of whom faced lingering illnesses or slow declines. James Garfield lingered for two months in 1881 after he was shot (in front of his older two sons). The Garfield family had just recovered from a scare caused by First Lady Lucretia Garfield's bout with malaria, and they spent countless hours at the bedside of the president. First Lady Peggy Taylor was so distraught following the death of her husband that she initially refused to allow the body to be embalmed. Equally painful for his family was the gradual demise of Chester A. Arthur, who died shortly after leaving office. The only person to whom he confided about his terminal kidney illness was his son Alan. Woodrow Wilson's family faced similar strains following his stroke. Also traumatic to family members were the sudden deaths of Abraham Lincoln and John F. Kennedy, burdening each family with the loss of husband and father and the resultant dislocation from the White House.

Family Roles and Activities

Each family also brings its own traditions and character to the White House. Historically, the most popular form of presidential entertainment was playing cards. Several presidents and First Ladies were voracious card players. In the twentieth century, Franklin Roosevelt, Truman, and Eisenhower were especially noted for their fondness of poker, while Ida McKinley was also renowned for her affinity for euchre. Fishing has also been a common pastime which brings together first families. John Adams added a billiards table to the White House so that he and his sons could play. Many first families routinely attended the opera or theater. The well-known musical predilection of the Nixons led the American recording industry to donate some two thousand albums and state-of-the-art stereo equipment to the White House. The advent of film and television affected the first families with the same force as the general public. Theodore Roosevelt was the first president to screen films in the White House, but Warren G. Harding had the first real theater built within the dwelling. Since the time of the Trumans, presidential families have also watched television, often together. Both the Eisenhowers and the Reagans often had late meals in their bedrooms while watching television.

More rigorous pastimes have included horseback riding and tennis. Golf and bicycling emerged in the twentieth century as favorite activities. Both Roosevelt families and the Kennedys fancied sailing. Many presidents regularly went hunting with their sons, and both Calvin and Grace Coolidge enjoyed the sport. Jogging has also become a popular physical activity among modern presidents. Jimmy Carter often went running with his wife and son Chip. Many First Ladies enjoyed gardening with their family. For most of the history of the White House, there were greenhouses and gardens on the present site of the West Wing. After the 1902 renovation, the main gardens were located on the south grounds.

Each of the first families has added to, redecorated, or renovated the White House in efforts to make the residence more comfortable and suited to their individual tastes. Additions

White House Zoos

While most first families kept pets, few maintained a menagerie which equaled the Theodore Roosevelts' or that of the Calvin Coolidge family. The Roosevelts had the greatest variety, while the Coolidges' had the greatest number. The Roosevelts had a veritable zoo. There was Algonquin, Archie Roosevelt's calico pony, whom his brothers sneaked into the White House elevator and then Archie's bedroom in an effort to cheer him while he suffered from both whooping cough and measles. Kermit Roosevelt had a kangaroo rat that he hand-fed at breakfast, and Alice Roosevelt kept a green snake, named Emily Spinach, whom she occasionally took to parties in her purse. There was also a parrot, a macaw, a badger, racoons, dogs and cats, and a bear at the White House.

The Coolidges had eleven dogs, seven birds, and three cats. They also possessed a few exotic animals, including two racoons, a bobcat, and a wallaby. The normally reserved Calvin Coolidge was so fond of his pets that he often fed them from the table, even during formal meals.

through the years that were specifically geared toward the first family have included the small schoolroom built for the Hayes children. Seldom was the White House as dynamic as during the tenure of Theodore Roosevelt. The Roosevelt family brought an unparalleled zest and energy to the mansion. They established a zoo, including a bear, and the children engaged in a variety of mischief, often sliding down the staircases on dining trays. During the 1902 renovation of the White House, Theodore Roosevelt had the large staircase in the west hall removed, and the room became the main place for the family to meet and relax. He also added tennis courts. Ford had an outdoor pool installed, and the Clintons added an exercise room in the bedroom suites. A less formal structure was Amy Carter's tree house.

Significance

One of the most important contributions of first families has been their impact on maintaining the mental health and well-being of the president. Although family members have periodically caused embarrassments and even scandal, in general their support and comfort to presidents have far outweighed their negative effects. During times of crisis, the first family is inevitably the main source of strength and cheer.

Martin Van Buren was a widower by the time he became president, but his four adult sons lived in the White House and were his closest advisers. Other presidents, including Fillmore and James Garfield, also relied heavily on their sons for emotional support. Andrew Jackson was lavish with his attention and gifts to Mary Donelson, his great-niece, and to Rachel Jackson, an adoptive granddaughter. In the midst of the Civil War, Tad Lincoln often brought amusement to his father through such antics as firing at the closed door of cabinet meetings with a toy cannon. During the trying days of the Vietnam War and the end of his second term, Lyndon B. Johnson found solace in his grandson Patrick Lyndon Nugent. Playing with the child proved to be highly effective stress release for the president.

Family life in the White House closely resembles family life elsewhere. There are triumphs and tragedies and families both close and estranged. The political and media pressure often draw the families closer together, although many family members have withered under the constant strain. Each first couple continues to exert the greatest influence over family life. The enduring importance of the first family remains its potential as a social support network and source of comfort for the president.

Suggested Readings

Anthony, Carl Sferrazza. *America's First Families*. New York: Touchstone, 2000. A good presentation of family life in the White House, which includes many pictures and little-known anecdotes.

Benson, Harry. *First Families: An Intimate Portrait from the Kennedys to the Clintons*. New York: Bullfinch Press, 1997. A good collection of photographs and engaging behind-the-scenes stories of late-twentieth century first families.

Hess, Stephen. *America's Political Dynasties: From Adams to Kennedy*. Garden City, N.J.: Doubleday, 1966. An intricate examination of the political families who occupied the White House through the Kennedy years.

Kessler, Ronald. *Inside the White House: The Hidden Lives of the Modern Presidents and the Secrets of the World's Most Powerful Institution*. New York: Pocket Books, 1995. An overview of many of the more sensational aspects of modern first families.

Perling, J. J. *President's Sons: The Prestige of Name in a Democracy*. New York: Odyssey Press, 1947. An examination of the lives of sixty presidential sons.

Truman, Margaret. *First Ladies: An Intimate Group Portrait of White House Wives*. New York: Random House, 1996. A good topical examination of First Ladies and their roles.

Tom Lansford

Other White House Hostesses

Overview: Some of the most interesting and influential women who served as First Ladies were not wives of presidents but other family members. From the very first, the position of the president's spouse was viewed as so important that the absence of a wife meant a vacuum had to be filled. In the course of time, daughters, sisters, nieces, and daughters-in-law would be called on to serve, including, in the case of Jane Pierce, her friend and aunt by marriage. This filling of the First Lady's shoes was not always cheerfully done, for Grover Cleveland's sister Rose Elizabeth Cleveland did her share of grumbling, but it was a need all saw as important.

In some cases, the presidents were widowers, such as Thomas Jefferson, Martin Van Buren, Andrew Jackson, and Chester A. Arthur. Some had wives who were invalids, such as James Monroe, John Tyler, and Andrew Johnson. Two were bachelors: James Buchanan and, for one and one-half years, Cleveland. One president, Zachary Taylor, had a wife who refused to act as First Lady and had her daughter step in for her. Among deaths, ill health, and personal inclinations, the role of the First Lady would be seen as one that was necessary, and the vacancy would be filled by a variety of very different but capable women, ranging in age from the eighteen-year-old Mary Abigail Fillmore to the sexagenarian Abby Kent Means. Harriet Lane, James Buchanan's niece, was ranked as the equal of the other First Ladies who were wives, but all the other surrogates would be viewed as either footnotes to the president's administration or secondary to the president's wife.

The Early Years of the Republic (1800-1829)

A widower since the death of his wife in 1782, Jefferson would be able to turn to his two daughters, Maria Epps and Martha (Patsy) Randolph. The women's activities on their own plantations would not allow their being in the newly created Federal City for great lengths of time, however. Maria Jefferson Epps died in 1804, but Patsy, with whom Jefferson had a very close relationship, was able to relieve her father's loneliness when she could. She had a difficult time at home, with an abusive husband and a large family, which took a heavy toll on her health. The red-haired, large-boned Patsy was clearly her father's daughter; she shared his love of reading and nature. Patsy would be her father's closest companion in his last years and would outlive him by only ten years, dying in 1836.

With his daughters' sparse presence in Washington, D.C., Jefferson was fortunate that he could turn to Dolley Madison (1768-1849), the wife of Secretary of State James Madison. One of the reasons Dolley Madison was such a remarkable First Lady in her own right was the years she had been in training, serving as hostess for President Jefferson. She learned her strengths and weaknesses, how to balance her tendency toward flamboyance with her strong political sense, and how to keep a room circulating and to win over friends for her quiet and often overlooked husband and his administration. The eight years serving as a surrogate First

Lady only aided Dolley's capabilities when her husband ascended to the presidency in 1809.

After the departure of Dolley Madison from Washington in 1817, a very different First Lady stepped onto the stage, Elizabeth Kortright Monroe. Seen as haughty and reclusive, Elizabeth faced a number of problems. First, anyone would have found it almost impossible to follow the path of Dolley Madison. Second, and more important, Elizabeth was often and mysteriously ill. The illness she suffered would be whispered about and many speculations made, but the truth was alarming enough. Elizabeth suffered from epilepsy—what then was called the "falling sickness." Few knew, but the many who disliked Elizabeth Monroe did so for her seeming coldness, her refusal to return calls, and her foreign-like elegance. They knew nothing about the real illness behind the mask. To modern minds, Elizabeth's insistence on secrecy seems excessive, but one needs to remember the stigma attached to someone who suffered seizures of any kind. Elizabeth knew this and accordingly paced herself and her slim reserves of energy to be able to do what she could.

Elizabeth also turned over many of her duties to her elder daughter, Eliza Monroe Hay (1787-1840). Educated at Madame Campan's school in Paris, where among her classmates were lifelong friend Hortense de Beauharnais (Empress Josephine's daughter, later queen of Holland) and Napoleon's youngest sister, Caroline Murat, Eliza Hay breathed a more rarified air than most in the young capital. She often offended people with her air of superiority. Secretary of State John Quincy Adams referred to her as "the human fire-brand." While taking over duties for her mother, Eliza often created "situations" for her parents by making receptions exclusive and overly royal in tone. Possibly the biggest offense committed by Eliza was in the matter of the marriage of her younger sister Maria to Samuel Gouverneur in 1820, when no political allies (or enemies) were invited to the White House ceremony. While

Eliza Monroe Hay *(Courtesy of Craig Shermer, National First Ladies' Library)*

Maria had her quiet wedding, Eliza's mistakes created ripples in Washington society that caused no end of damage to her mother's image and her own.

After the Monroes' departure from the White House, which was decorated to reflect their years in Paris, they retired to Oak Hill, Virginia, where Eliza remained close to her parents. By the time of Elizabeth Monroe's death on September 23, 1830, and James Monroe's on the following July 4, Eliza was a widow. She cut ties with the United States and returned to Europe, where she died.

The Antebellum Years (1829-1865)
There is no doubt that death, ill health, and the reclusive views of proper womanhood had a tremendous impact on the roles of the First La-

dies. Death was an ever-present member of nineteenth century families, who could virtually count on losing a number of children, and in some cases, none would survive. Illness and permanent invalidism would also play a dominant role during the years leading to the Civil War. In between the sudden, but not surprising, death of Rachel Jackson after her husband's election in 1828 and the arrival of Eliza McCardle Johnson at the White House in 1865, there was an unprecedented number of surrogate First Ladies. This reflects the society of the 1820's to the 1860's, which saw so much illness among women. In some cases, the illnesses of a president's wife led to death, such as that of Letitia Tyler, or chronic weakness, such as that of Abigail Fillmore, and necessitated a substitute.

Knowing his wife's discomfort in urban society, Andrew Jackson had made it a point to have his secretary, Andrew Jackson Donelson, as close to him as possible. Not only was Donelson the nephew of Jackson's beloved Rachel; he was also married to a Donelson niece, Emily Tennessee Donelson (1807-1836). Both were deeply loved by Rachel Jackson, and Rachel's death on December 22, 1828, meant that Emily Donelson would serve in her aunt's place. This she would do, along with Sarah Yorke Jackson, who was married to the Jacksons' adopted son Andrew Jackson, Jr., for almost the entire eight years of Andrew Jackson's presidency.

Emily's own early death from consumption came in 1836, following a brief banishment from the White House. Only twenty-one when she moved into the President's House, Emily Donelson struck everyone with her beauty, especially her titian-colored hair, piled high, and her poise. Well educated and elegant, Emily was capable of ruling the White House and making life easier for Jackson. She was, however, no easy mark, for she made it clear to the president in his heated defense of Peggy O'Neal Eaton, the wife of the secretary of war,

Sarah Yorke Jackson (*Courtesy of Craig Shermer, National First Ladies' Library*)

that Emily, for one, would not receive Mrs. Eaton, whose reputation was not a good one. (Nor would Floride Calhoun, wife of the vice president, or future First Lady Sarah Polk.) Emily would return to her home in Tennessee, only returning to Washington when wiser heads (Martin Van Buren, for one) prevailed on the stubborn president to send the Eatons to Madrid. In 1834, Emily gave birth to Rachel Jackson Donelson in the White House. Little Rachel and her siblings lightened the lonely life of Andrew Jackson, who would be grieved by Emily's early death.

The beautiful wife of Andrew Jackson, Jr., Sarah Yorke Jackson (? -1887) was from an old Philadelphia Quaker family and was married there in 1831. She spent much of the Jackson years in the White House taking care of her children and the president. "She has been more than a daughter to me," Andrew Jackson later said. Quiet and stately, with dark hair and eyes, Sarah had considerable presence and ability. She would care for Jackson until his death in 1845 and stay on at Jackson's home, the Hermitage, until her own death in 1887.

Martin Van Buren's wife, Hannah Hoes Van Buren, having died in 1819, was so shadowy a figure that her own sons could not remember if her name was Hannah or Anna. A widower for many years, Van Buren had no real need of a hostess; he was so polished in manner and managed all White House details so well that the absence of a hostess was little noted. He did have help from the recently widowed Dolley Madison, whose sharp eye took note of the fact that the president's son and secretary, Abraham Van Buren, was a bachelor. Bringing her cousin, Sarah Angelica Singleton of Charleston, South Carolina, to Washington in 1837, Dolley was able to spark a romance between the two young people. Angelica Singleton had been educated in Philadelphia and had grown very beautiful, with languorous eyes, long black ringlets, and a beautiful smile—all captured in her White House portrait by Henry Inman, considered by Jackie Kennedy to be the White House's handsomest portrait.

Married in 1838, Angelica and Abraham Van Buren honeymooned in Europe and, like Julia Tyler after her, Angelica returned with a severe case of "Queen Fever." Among its symptoms were a desire to sit in a royal velvet purple chair on a dais of three steps and wear ostrich plumes. While not harmful in themselves, these trappings of "monarchial airs" at a time of political unrest would help sweep Martin Van Buren from the White House. While the Whigs delighted in portraying their candidate, William Henry Harrison, as a country fellow, living in a log cabin and swilling hard cider, they also presented President Van Buren as an epicure, eating off gold plates with gold silverware. His image in natty clothes was only reinforced by

Angelica's feathers, royal purple gowns, and her bevy of "ladies in waiting." Though the fact of her having a child in the White House and losing it was forgotten, the image of "Queen Angelica" was remembered. This, along with other issues, ensured the defeat of Van Buren in 1840. Angelica and her husband lived in New York City, and she sympathized with the South in the Civil War, but she remained with her husband in New York. She would lose two of her sons early, but none of the four would carry on the name. She died in New York on December 29, 1878.

Because of Anna Harrison's illness, her husband, William Henry Harrison, chose his widowed daughter-in-law, Jane Irwin Harrison (1806-1846), to accompany him to Washington. She, in turn, asked her widowed aunt, Jane Irwin Findlay (1769-1850), to aid her until Anna would be well enough to join them in the capital. These ladies were, as was Anna Harrison herself, very well educated and viewed the White House without many qualms. They had even ordered dresses from Paris for the social season, which would prove all too brief. Though Jane's marriage to the alcoholic William H. Harrison II had not been long, she was much loved by her in-laws. Strangely enough, her husband's younger brother John Scott Harrison would marry her younger sister Elizabeth, and they would in turn be the parents of future President Benjamin Harrison. The William Harrison White House saw little in the way of entertaining because of the president's illness and death on April 4, 1841. The women would then return with the president's body on the same train which had brought them all south several months before.

When John Tyler received the news of Harrison's death, he was at home in Virginia. There would be no less than four hostesses during his stormy tenure in the White House. Letitia Christian Tyler, the new president's beautiful but frail wife, had suffered a severe stroke in 1839 and had never fully recovered. Making only one public appearance (at her daughter Lizzie's wedding) before her death on September 10, 1842, Letitia Tyler left First Lady duties in the capable hands of her daughter-in-law, Priscilla Cooper Tyler (1816-1889), wife of Robert Tyler. Priscilla was unusual both in terms of her capabilities and her life before her marriage. She had been a Shakespearean actress, whose father also was an actor, at a time when the stage and its celebrities were gaining social acceptance. Priscilla Tyler's entrance into White House history marks the beginning of

Priscilla Cooper Tyler *(Courtesy of Craig Shermer, National First Ladies' Library)*

the House's fascination with actors. Aided by Tyler's daughters Lizzie and Letitia Semple, Priscilla proved to be extremely popular, but she did not willingly turn over her duties (nor would Letitia Tyler Semple) to the younger second Mrs. President Tyler, Julia Gardiner, whom John Tyler married in July, 1844.

The refusal of Margaret Taylor to take on any official duties of the First Lady made President Zachary Taylor turn to his youngest daughter, Mary Elizabeth, called "Miss Betty," who was married to his aide de camp, Col. W. W. Bliss. Mary Elizabeth Taylor Bliss (1828-1909) was educated in Louisiana by nuns and later sent to school in Philadelphia. She married Bliss in 1848. Of her older sisters, Sarah Knox Taylor had married future Confederate president Jefferson Davis against her parents wishes and had died some months later. Betty's sister Ann Taylor Wood would help her during her time in the White House, which ended with their father's death on July 9, 1850. Margaret Taylor died at her son Richard's home in Louisiana in August, 1852. Betty, who married again after Bliss's death, lived until 1909.

Abigail Fillmore was a woman of breeding, education, and intelligence but not one with a great deal of physical strength. Having broken her ankle some years before her husband, Millard Fillmore, became vice president, she was often forced to rest for days before a great dinner or reception. Fortunately for her, if she was not up to the festivities, she could turn to her cultured, multitalented daughter Mary Abigail Fillmore (1832-1854) to take her place. Like her mother, Mary Abigail was of a scholarly bent, and like her mother, she wanted to teach.

She had earned a teaching certificate and in doing so had promised to teach the young of New York, something which she continued even after her father's election to the vice presidency. However, after President Taylor's death in July, 1850, she gave up her plans and moved into the White House to help her mother, the new First Lady. Educated at Miss Sedgwick's in Massachusetts, Mary Abigail spoke Latin and French, read literature, played the piano and the harp, and like her mother and father, read anything and everything. She took her mother's place whenever Abigail Fillmore was not well and helped with the creation of the White House library. For so young a girl (only eighteen when her father became president), she had an enviable reputation for her learning and musical abilities. One of her great joys was to meet Swedish singer Jenny Lind when Lind visited the White House in 1851. Sadly, First Lady Abigail Fillmore died a month after leaving the White House, from pneumonia she contracted at the inauguration of the new president, Franklin Pierce, as she stood in the slushy snow. Mary Abigail Fillmore died in July, 1854, of cholera, at age twenty-two.

The horrible death in a train crash of eleven-year-old Benjamin Pierce, the last to survive of three sons born to Franklin and Jane Pierce, just two months before his father's inauguration (1853) left both parents bereft. Pierce's love for "his dearest Jeanie" knew no bounds, but her obsession in grief, her long hours writing to her dead son, and her inability to face her duties forced the president-elect to find help, which was fortunately not far away. Though older by a generation than Jane Pierce, Abigail Kent had long been a family friend, even before she married Jane's uncle Robert Means. Abigail Kent Means (1788-1857) proved to be a rock of quiet strength to the Pierces, both of whom she loved. She had long been a confidante to Jane and her older sister, Mary Appleton Aiken. During the first two years of the Pierce administration, the president either received the public alone or was assisted by Abby Means. Only occasionally would Jane Pierce make an appearance, though after January, 1855, her appearances became more regular, and Mrs. Means was able to spend some time with her family in Massachusetts. Her presence, however, was still required, and between her help and that of Varina Davis, the second wife of Secretary of War Jefferson Davis (and later First Lady of the Confederacy), the Pierces' last two years, while not glamorous, were certainly more cheerful than the first two. Abigail Means died suddenly in the summer of 1857, some months after the Pierces departed the White House. Jane Pierce grieved that she was unable to be with her at the last, and Franklin Pierce wrote beautifully of her sterling character and personality.

Harriet Lane (1830-1903), President James Buchanan's niece, filled the position of First Lady for her uncle. Buchanan was a lifelong bachelor. Young, blond, blue-eyed, and extremely well versed in social graces, Harriet made a mark on history, especially in that she championed the rights of American Indians, thus making her among the first First Ladies to take up a political cause.

The Gilded Age (1865-1901)

With the departure of Mary Lincoln from the White House on May 22, 1865, the new First Lady, Eliza McCardle Johnson, having suffered from consumption for years, would be unable to fulfill her duties. Accordingly, she turned for help to her eldest daughter, Martha Johnson Patterson (1828-1901), wife of Senator David T. Patterson. Martha was well educated, having attended the Visitation Convent in Georgetown during President James Polk's term. After Martha's marriage to Patterson in 1856, she spent much of her time helping her mother during Andrew Johnson's long absences. Pretty and with fine features, Martha made it clear to acquaintances that they "were just plain folks from Tennessee" and further hoped that "not too much would be expected from them."

Aside from hosting a reception for Queen Emma of the Sandwich Islands and a birthday party for her husband, Eliza Johnson remained out of the public eye.

Martha, aided by her younger sister Mary Stover, proved to be capable, energetic, and a good housekeeper. She dusted off the portraits of Van Buren, Tyler, Polk, Millard Fillmore, and Pierce and had them placed on the walls of the ground level, thrilling her father, who had a deep love of history. The Johnsons' grandchildren had a wonderful time, and tranquillity was maintained even through the tribulations of President Andrew Johnson's impeachment. Martha's husband, Senator Patterson, was able to report to his father-in-law the daily war being waged against him by both the Senate and the House during Johnson's impeachment.

With the death of James Abram Garfield on September 19, 1881, and the departure from the White House of Lucretia Garfield with her children, it was the widower Chester Alan Arthur who assumed the presidency. His wife, Ellen Herndon Arthur, had died in January of 1880, and he mourned her for the rest of his life. He was a cultured, refined man with expensive tastes, but knowing a hostess was going to be needed, he was fortunate to be able to turn to his youngest sister, Mary Arthur McElroy (1842-1917). Educated at Emma Willard's Seminary for Girls, Mary had married John E. McElroy, a businessman, when she was nineteen. She settled in Albany, New York, and became a mother to four. The death of her sister-in-law Ellen in 1880 filled her with grief because they had been friends and had enjoyed a mutual love of music. Mary took her brother's daughter, Nell, under her wing after Arthur's election to the presidency. Mary, called Molly, would spend six months in Washington (three in the fall, three in the spring) and six months in Albany. She was joined by her two daughters, and because she was not regarded as the president's official hostess (as Harriet Lane had been), it was possible for Molly to return calls and make

Rose Elizabeth Cleveland, sister of Grover Cleveland. *(Courtesy of Craig Shermer, National First Ladies' Library)*

private invitations without disturbing Washington's strict forms of courtesy. She loved to surround herself with young faces, and her receptions were always popular. Her last reception, in February of 1885, was attended by thousands, and it would be the largest affair seen at the White House until modern times. With the good wishes of Rose Elizabeth Cleveland, the new hostess, Molly returned to her home in Albany, where she lived until her death in 1917.

Like James Buchanan, Grover Cleveland entered the White House as a bachelor. Knowing his own gruff nature, Cleveland realized he would need a hostess to serve with him at White House receptions. While closer to his sister Mrs. Mary Allen Hoyt, he would actually call on the services of his younger sister, Rose

Elizabeth Cleveland (1846-1918), who was then a teacher and a writer, well versed in Latin and Greek. She had just published a book on the poetry of George Eliot, earning a then-huge sum of twenty-five thousand dollars. Being a well-known lecturer, Rose did not look forward to being a mere ornament at the White House and hoped that her brother would marry soon. Her sister Mary had helped out when Cleveland was governor of New York, but now that he was president, it was Rose's turn. With the publication of her book, her serious state of mind, and her grasp of history, science, Latin, Greek, and rhetoric, Rose was seen at the time as a modern woman, who, it was said, when greeting the public would conjugate Greek verbs in her head. She was a known supporter of temperance and had a great deal of criticism while sitting at any table where wine was being served. She knew the difference, however, between the public and the private roles. After the marriage of Grover and Frances Cleveland in June, 1886, Rose returned to her literary and academic life. She would later say how much she had enjoyed her position and what a unique chance it had been to meet the American people. Later she would live in Italy with another woman, dying there in 1918 from a fever contracted from nursing soldiers in World War I.

Due to the continual ill health of Caroline Harrison, some of the official duties of that administration fell on Benjamin and Caroline Harrison's daughter Mary Harrison McKee (1858-1930). Like her mother, Mamie McKee was musical, artistic, and capable. A young mother of two, Mamie would spend much of the four years with her parents in the White House, visited by her businessman husband, J. R. McKee. After the long illness and death of Caroline's oldest sister, Elizabeth Scott Lord, in early December, 1889, Caroline asked Mamie to receive in her place (out of respect for Mrs. Lord's death) in January, 1890. This started a storm of criticism: It was an insult to the wife of vice president Levi P. Morton and an insult to

Harriet Blaine, the wife of Secretary of State James G. Blaine. The uproar caused Caroline to put aside her mourning and resume her role. This was only the first of a series of sharp rebukes that caused her a great deal of anguish. As Caroline's health gave way, Mamie would be called more and more to the foreground. Having had a good education in Indiana and Pennsylvania, Mamie also gave dancing lessons at the insistence of her mother, who had no patience with the ban on dancing, good Presbyterian as she was. Both Caroline and her daughter delighted in restoring dancing to the White House, which had been banned since 1845. Mamie stayed close to her mother, whose death on October 25, 1892, forced her to take over the First Lady's duties until the end of her father's administration. Her father's remarriage to her mother's niece in 1896 brought a split between father and daughter. Mamie lived in Greenwich, Connecticut, until her death in 1930.

The Modern Age (1901-2001)

The twentieth century brought few examples of surrogate First Ladies, except for brief times during the Taft administration and that of Woodrow Wilson.

In May of 1909, Nellie Taft suffered a massive stroke on board her yacht; it would be a year before she recovered enough to resume her duties as First Lady. At times, her very capable, intelligent, and socially conscious daughter Helen Taft Manning (1891-1987) filled in, aided by Mrs. Taft's sisters from Ohio, Jennie Herron Anderson and Maria Herron. Nellie was too forceful a woman to allow anyone to supercede her. Her own determination and her husband's help had her back in the foreground by 1911. Helen Taft Manning would go on to teach at Bryn Mawr College, of which she later became president.

Between the time of Ellen Wilson's death in August, 1914, and President Woodrow Wilson's remarriage to Edith Galt in December of 1915, Wilsons cousin Helen Woodrow Bones took over some of the duties, helping the president's daughter, Eleanor Wilson McAdoo, whose husband was Wilson's secretary of the treasury. However, since much of the time between Ellen Wilson's death and Woodrow's marriage to Edith Galt was spent in official mourning, there was little in the way of duties that were needed.

For the rest of the twentieth century, aside from a First Lady's illness (such as Florence Harding's in 1922), there was little need for an official hostess other than presidents' wives. It is interesting to note that a real absence was felt when Hillary Rodham Clinton closed up the First Lady's office when she began her Senate campaign in 2000. Chelsea Clinton would step in for her mother, but when Hillary won the Senate race, she returned to her husband's side to assume her duties as First Lady.

Significance

It should be noted that without these "hostesses," a number of presidential administrations would have no representation among the First Ladies, which in turn forces one to reexamine what exactly is meant by the term "First Lady." Looking at the actions of these sisters, nieces, daughters, and daughters-in-law, one realizes they played as important a role as did the wives of the presidents. In the absence of a presidential spouse, these women were forced to step onto the stage of the White House and, in doing so, left their marks on history.

Suggested Readings

Anthony, Carl Sferrazza. *First Ladies: The Saga of the Presidents' Wives and Their Power.* Vol. 1. New York: William Morrow, 1990.

Watson, Robert P. *First Ladies of the United States: A Biographical Dictionary.* Boulder, Colo.: Lynne Rienner, 2001. The book offers profiles and biographical information on every First Lady to date, including Laura Bush, and provides comparative facts on all the presidential spouses.

_____. *The Presidents' Wives: Reassessing the Office of First Lady.* Boulder, Colo.: Lynne Rienner, 2000. Analysis includes bibliographical references and index.

Craig Schermer

Chronological List of First Ladies

President	First Lady	Born-Died	Birthplace
Washington	Martha Dandridge Washington	1731-1802	Virginia
J. Adams	Abigail Smith Adams	1744-1818	Massachusetts
Jefferson	Martha Wayles Jefferson*	1748-1782	Virginia
	Martha "Patsy" Jefferson Randolph**	1772-1836	Virginia
Madison	Dolley Payne Madison	1768-1849	North Carolina
Monroe	Elizabeth Kortright Monroe	1768-1830	New York
J. Q. Adams	Louisa Johnson Adams	1775-1852	London, England
Jackson	Rachel Donelson Jackson*	1767-1828	Virginia
Van Buren	Hannah Hoes Van Buren*	1783-1819	New York
	Angelica Singleton Van Buren**	1816-1878	South Carolina
W. H. Harrison	Anna Symmes Harrison	1775-1864	New Jersey
Tyler	Letitia Christian Tyler	1790-1842	Virginia
	Julia Gardiner Tyler	1820-1889	New York
Polk	Sarah Childress Polk	1803-1891	Tennessee
Taylor	Margaret Smith Taylor	1788-1852	Maryland
Fillmore	Abigail Powers Fillmore	1798-1853	New York
Pierce	Jane Appleton Pierce	1806-1863	New Hampshire
Buchanan	Harriet Lane**	1830-1903	Pennsylvania
Lincoln	Mary Todd Lincoln	1818-1882	Kentucky
A. Johnson	Eliza McCardle Johnson	1810-1876	Tennessee
Grant	Julia Dent Grant	1826-1902	Missouri
Hayes	Lucy Webb Hayes	1831-1889	Ohio
Garfield	Lucretia Rudolph Garfield	1832-1918	Ohio
Arthur	Ellen Herndon Arthur*	1837-1880	Virginia

*Died before her husband took office; **Relative other than wife*

(continued)

President	First Lady	Born-Died	Birthplace
Cleveland	Frances Folsom Cleveland	1864-1947	New York
B. Harrison	Caroline Scott Harrison	1832-1892	Ohio
McKinley	Ida Saxton McKinley	1847-1907	Ohio
T. Roosevelt	Edith Carow Roosevelt	1861-1948	Connecticut
Taft	Helen Herron Taft	1861-1943	Ohio
Wilson	Ellen Axson Wilson	1860-1914	Georgia
	Edith Bolling Wilson	1872-1961	Virginia
Harding	Florence Kling Harding	1860-1924	Ohio
Coolidge	Grace Goodhue Coolidge	1879-1957	Vermont
Hoover	Lou Henry Hoover	1874-1944	Iowa
F. D. Roosevelt	Anna Eleanor Roosevelt	1884-1962	New York
Truman	Bess Wallace Truman	1885-1982	Missouri
Eisenhower	Mamie Doud Eisenhower	1896-1979	Iowa
Kennedy	Jacqueline Bouvier Kennedy	1929-1994	New York
L. B. Johnson	Claudia "Lady Bird" Taylor Johnson	1912-	Texas
Nixon	Thelma Catherine "Pat" Ryan Nixon	1912-1993	Nevada
Ford	Elizabeth "Betty" Bloomer Ford	1918-	Illinois
Carter	Rosalynn Smith Carter	1927-	Georgia
Reagan	Anne Frances "Nancy" Davis Reagan	1921-	New York
G. H. W. Bush	Barbara Pierce Bush	1925-	New York
Clinton	Hillary Rodham Clinton	1947-	Illinois
G. W. Bush	Laura Welch Bush	1946-	Texas

*Died before her husband took office; **Relative other than wife

Chronological List of Presidents

President	Years of Presidency	Party
George Washington	1789-1797	No/Fed
John Adams	1797-1801	No/Fed
Thomas Jefferson	1801-1809	D-R
James Madison	1809-1817	D-R
James Monroe	1817-1825	D-R
John Quincy Adams	1825-1829	D-R
Andrew Jackson	1829-1837	Dem
Martin Van Buren	1837-1841	Dem
William Henry Harrison	1841	Whig
John Tyler	1841-1845	Whig
James K. Polk	1845-1849	Dem
Zachary Taylor	1849-1850	Whig
Millard Fillmore	1850-1853	Whig
Franklin Pierce	1853-1857	Dem
James Buchanan	1857-1861	Dem
Abraham Lincoln	1861-1865	Rep
Andrew Johnson	1865-1869	Rep
Ulysses S. Grant	1869-1877	Rep
Rutherford B. Hayes	1877-1881	Rep
James A. Garfield	1881	Rep
Chester A. Arthur	1881-1885	Rep
Grover Cleveland	1885-1889; 1893-1897	Dem
Benjamin Harrison	1889-1893	Rep
William McKinley	1897-1901	Rep
Theodore Roosevelt	1901-1909	Rep
William Howard Taft	1909-1913	Rep
Woodrow Wilson	1913-1921	Dem
Warren Harding	1921-1923	Rep
Calvin Coolidge	1923-1929	Rep
Herbert Hoover	1929-1933	Rep
Franklin D. Roosevelt	1933-1945	Dem
Harry S. Truman	1945-1953	Dem
Dwight D. Eisenhower	1953-1961	Rep
John F. Kennedy	1961-1963	Dem
Lyndon B. Johnson	1963-1969	Dem

(continued)

President	Years of Presidency	Party
Richard M. Nixon	1969-1974	Rep
Gerald R. Ford	1974-1977	Rep
Jimmy Carter	1977-1981	Dem
Ronald Reagan	1981-1989	Rep
George Bush	1989-1993	Rep
William Jefferson Clinton	1993-2001	Dem
George W. Bush	2001-	Rep

NOTES: Fed = Federalist; D-R = Democratic Republican; Dem = Democratic; Rep = Republican

Libraries, Museums, Historic Sites, and World Wide Web Sites

EDITOR'S NOTE: *Among the following are homes of First Ladies or presidential couples, before or after their years in office. Many of these places are mentioned in the text of* American First Ladies, *and all are open to the public. Each of the first four listings contains information on all or most of the presidents or First Ladies; the sites listed thereafter are president-specific and appear in alphabetical order by president's name. All Web sites were visited by editors of Salem Press in April, 2001.*

General Resources on Presidents and First Ladies

National First Ladies' Library
331 Market Avenue South
Canton, OH 44702
Ph.: 330.452.0876
Fax: 330.456.3414
www.firstladies.org

National Archives and Records Administration Presidential Libraries Web site:
www.nara.gov/nara/president/address
.html
The Presidents of the United States Web site:
www.netcolony.com/news/presidents/
index.html
Contains links for each president that include *First Lady and Family* and *National Historic Sites/State Historic Sites/Places to Visit*. The latter link includes libraries and museums.
The American Presidents Web site:
www.americanpresidents.org/places
Includes links to presidential places for each president.

John Adams and John Quincy Adams

Adams National Historic Site tour
Visitors Center
1250 Hancock Street
Quincy, MA
Ph.: 617.770.1175
southshoreserver.com/birthplace
(Includes home of John and Abigail Adams)

Adams National Historical Park
135 Adams Street
Quincy, MA 02169
Ph.: 617.773.1177
Ph.: 617.770-1175 - visitor information
Fax: 617.472.7562
www.nps.gov/adam
E-mail: ADAM_Visitor_Center@nps.gov

Massachusetts Historical Society
1154 Boylston Street
Boston, MA 02215
Ph.: 617.536.1608
Fax: 617.859.0074
www.masshist.org
E-mail: masshist@masshist.org
E-mail: adamspapers@masshist.org
(Contains the Adams Papers Collection)

James Buchanan
James Buchanan Home
1120 Marietta Avenue
Lancaster, PA 17603
Ph.: 717.392.8721
Fax: 717.295.8825
www.wheatland.org
(Wheatland: Home of James Buchanan and
    Harriet Lane)

George H. W. Bush
George Bush Presidential Library and
    Museum
1000 George Bush Drive West
College Station, TX 77845
Ph.: 979.260.9552
Fax: 979.260.9557
www.bushlibrary.tamu.edu/home.html
E-mail: library@bush.nara.gov

Jimmy Carter
Jimmy Carter Library
441 Freedom Parkway
Atlanta, GA 30307
Ph.: 404.331.3942
carterlibrary.galileo.peachnet.edu
E-mail: library@carter.nara.gov

Jimmy Carter National Historic Site
Contact:
300 North Bond Street
Plains, GA 31780
Ph.: 229.824.4104
Fax: 229.824.3441
www.nps.gov/jica
E-mail: JICA_Site_Supervisor@nps.gov

Grover Cleveland
Grover Cleveland Birthplace, National Park,
    and Museum
207 Bloomfield Avenue
Caldwell, NJ
Ph.: 201.226.1810
caldwellnj.com/grover.htm

William Jefferson Clinton
Clinton Presidential Center
www.clintonpresidentialcenter.com

Calvin Coolidge
Calvin Coolidge Memorial Room, Forbes
    Library
20 West Street
Northampton, MA 01060
Ph.: 413.587.1011
www.forbeslibrary.org/coolidge.html

President Calvin Coolidge State Historic Site
Plymouth Notch, VT
Contact:
Calvin Coolidge Memorial Foundation, Inc.
P.O. Box 97
Plymouth, VT 05056
Ph.: 802.672.3389
Fax: 802.672.3369
E-mail: info@calvin-coolidge.org
www.state.vt.us/dca/historic/Coolidg.htm

Dwight D. Eisenhower
Eisenhower National Historic Site
97 Taneytown Road
Gettysburg, PA 17325
Ph.: 717.338.9114
Fax: 717.338.0821
www.nps.gov/eise
E-mail: eise_site_manager@nps.gov
(Home of Dwight and Mamie Eisenhower)

Dwight D. Eisenhower Library and
    Museum
200 Southwest Fourth Street
Abilene, KS 67410
Ph.: 785.263.4751
Ph.: 877.RING.IKE
Fax: 785.263.4218
www.eisenhower.utexas.edu
E-mail: Library@eisenhower.nara.gov

Millard Fillmore
Millard Fillmore Museum
24 Shearer Avenue
East Aurora, NY 14052
Ph.: 716.652.8875
rin.buffalo.edu/c_erie/comm/cult/muse/
    mfh.html
(Home of Millard and Abigail Fillmore)

Gerald R. Ford
Gerald R. Ford Exhibit
Gerald R. Ford Conservation Center
1326 South 32d Street
Omaha, NE 68105
www.nebraskahistory.org/conserve/
    exhibit .htm

Gerald R. Ford Library
1000 Beal Avenue
Ann Arbor, MI 48109
Ph.: 734.741.2218
Fax: 734.741.2341
www.ford.utexas.edu
E-mail: ford.library@nara.gov

Gerald R. Ford Museum
303 Pearl Street NW
Grand Rapids, MI 49504
Ph.: 616.451.9263
Fax: 616.451.9570
www.ford.utexas.edu
E-mail: ford.museum@nara.gov

James A. Garfield
James A. Garfield National Historic Site
8095 Mentor Avenue
Mentor, OH 44060
Ph.: 440.255.8722
Fax: 440.255.8545
www.nps.gov/jaga
E-mail: jaga_interpretation@nps.com
(Lawnfield: Home of James and Lucretia
    Garfield)

Ulysses S. Grant
U. S. Grant Home State Historic Site
500 Bouthillier Street
Galena, IL 61036
Ph.: 815.777.0248 - voice phone
Ph.: 815.777.3310
www.state.il.us/HPA/sites/galena01.htm

Ulysses S. Grant National Historic Site
7400 Grant Road
St. Louis, MO 63123
Ph.: 314.842.3298 - visitor information
Ph.: 314.842.1867 - headquarters/recorded
    message
Fax: 314.842.1659
www.nps.gov/ulsg
E-mail: ULSG_Site_Manager@nps.gov
(White Haven: Home of Ulysses and Julia
    Grant)

Warren G. Harding
The Harding Home
380 Mt. Vernon Avenue
Marion, OH 43302
Ph.: 614.387.9630
Ph.: 800.600.6894
www.ohiohistory.org/textonly/places/
    harding
(Home of Warren and Florence Harding)

Benjamin Harrison
The President Benjamin Harrison Home
1230 North Delaware Street
Indianapolis, IN 46202
Ph.: 317.631.1888
www.surf-ici.com/harrison
E-mail: harrison@surf-ici.com
(Home of Benjamin and Caroline Harrison;
    includes research library)

William Henry Harrison
Berkeley Plantation
12602 Harrison Landing Road
Charles City, VA 23030
Ph.: 804.829.6018
www.jamesriverplantations.org/Berkeley
    .html
(Ancestral home and birthplace of William
    Henry Harrison)

Grouseland
3 W. Scott Street
Vincennes, IN 47591
Ph.: 812.882.2096
www.americanpresidents.org/places/09.asp
(Home of William Henry and Anna
    Harrison)

Rutherford B. Hayes
Rutherford B. Hayes Presidential Center
Spiegel Grove
Fremont, OH 43420
Ph.: 800.998.7737
www.rbhayes.org
E-mail: admin@rbhayes.org
(Spiegel Grove: Home of Rutherford and
    Lucy Hayes)

Herbert Hoover
Herbert Hoover National Historic Site
(Contact:)
110 Parkside Drive, Box 607
West Branch, IA 52358
Ph.: 319.643.2541
Fax: 319.643.5367
www.nps.gov/heho
E-mail: HEHO_Interpretation@nps.gov
(Includes presidential library and museum)

Andrew Jackson
Andrew Jackson State Park
196 Andrew Jackson Park Road
Lancaster, SC 29720
Ph.: 803.285.3344
www.travelsc.com/cgi-bin/parks/StatePark
    Detail.cfm?ID=3
(Includes Waxhaws Museum)

The Hermitage
4580 Rachel's Lane
Hermitage, TN 37076
Ph.: 615.889.2941
Fax: 615.889.9909
www.thehermitage.com
E-mail: hermitage@mindspring.com
(Home of Andrew and Rachel Jackson)

Andrew Jackson's family cemetery at The Hermitage in Tennessee. The burial site of Andrew Jackson and his wife, Rachel, is marked by the dome. *(AP/Wide World Photos)*

Thomas Jefferson
Monticello
931 Thomas Jefferson Parkway
Charlottesville, VA
Ph.: 804.984.9822
Ph.: 804.984.9800 - recorded message
www.monticello.org
(Home of Thomas and Martha Jefferson)

Andrew Johnson
Andrew Johnson National Historic Site
(Contact:)
P.O. Box 1088
Greeneville, TN 37744
Ph.: 423.638.3551 - visitor information
Ph.: 423.639.3711 - headquarters
Fax: 423.638.9194
www.nps.gov/anjo
E-mail: ANJO_Superintendent@nps.gov
(Includes home of Andrew and Eliza
    Johnson)

President Andrew Johnson Museum and
    Library
67 Gilland Street
Greeneville, TN
(Contact:)
P.O. Box 5026, Tusculum College
Greeneville, TN 37743
Ph.: 423.636.7348
Ph.: 800.729.0256 x 348
www.tusculum.edu/pages/ajmuseum/index
    .html

Lyndon B. Johnson
Lyndon Baines Johnson Library and
    Museum
2313 Red River Street
Austin, TX 78705
Ph.: 512.916.5137
www.lbjlib.utexas.edu

LBJ Museum at San Marcos
120 West Hopkins, Suite 200
San Marcos, TX 78666
Ph.: 512.396.3247
www.sanmarcostexas.com/lbj-museum

Lyndon B. Johnson National Historical Park
P.O. Box 329
Johnson City, TX 78636
Ph.: 830.868.7128 x244
Fax: 830.868.7863
www.nps.gov/lyjo
E-mail: LYJO_Superintendent@nps.gov

Lyndon B. Johnson State Historical Park
P.O. Box 238
Stonewall, TX 78671
Ph.: 830.644.2252
Ph.: 800.792.1112
www.tpwd.state.tx.us/park/lbj/lbj.htm
(Includes bus tours of LBJ Ranch, home of
    Lyndon and Lady Bird Johnson)

John F. Kennedy
John Fitzgerald Kennedy Library and
    Museum
Columbia Point
Boston, MA 02125
Ph.: 617.929.4500
Ph.: 877.616.4599
Fax: 617.929.4538
www.cs.umb.edu/jfklibrary
E-mail: library@kennedy.nara.gov

Abraham Lincoln
Ford's Theater National Historic Site
900 Ohio Drive, SW
Washington, DC 20024
Ph.: 202.426.6924
Fax: 202.426.1845
www.nps.gov/foth
E-mail: NACC_FOTH_Interpretation@nps
.gov
(Includes museum)

Lincoln Home National Historic Site
413 South Eighth Street
Springfield, IL 62701
Ph.: 217.492.4241 x 221
Fax: 217.492.4673
www.nps.gov/liho
E-mail: lincolnhome@nps.gov

Lincoln-Herndon Law Office
6th and Adams Streets
Springfield, IL 62701
Ph.: 217.785.7289
www.state.il.us/HPA/Sites/
LincolnHerndon.htm
(Includes presidential library)

The Lincoln Museum
200 E. Berry Street
Fort Wayne, IN 46802
Ph.: 219.455.3864
Fax: 219.455.6922
www.thelincolnmuseum.org
E-mail: TheLincolnMuseum@LNC.com

William McKinley
McKinley Memorial Library and Museum
40 North Main Street
Niles, OH 44446
Ph.: 330.652.1704
Fax: 330.652.5788
www.mckinley.lib.oh.us
E-mail: mckinley@oplin.lib.oh.us

Saxton-McKinley House
331 Market Avenue South
Canton, OH 44702
Ph.: 330.452.0876
Fax: 330. 456.3414
www.firstladies.org/SXHSINT.HTM
(Ancestral home of Ida Saxton McKinley;
home of William and Ida McKinley; site
of National First Ladies Library)

James Madison
The James Madison Museum
129 Caroline Street
Orange, VA
Ph.: 540.672.1776
www.jamesmadisonmuseum.org

Montpelier
11407 Constitution Highway
Montpelier Station, VA 22957
Ph.: 540.672.2728
www.montpelier.org
(Home of James and Dolley Madison)

Todd House
Independence National Historical Park
Visitor Center
3d and Chestnut Streets
Philadelphia, PA
Ph.: 215.597.8974
www.nps.gov/inde/todd-house.html
(Home of Dolley Payne Todd before she
married James Madison)

James Monroe

Ash Lawn-Highland
1000 James Monroe Parkway
Charlottesville, VA 22902
Ph.: 804.293.9539
Fax: 804.293.8000
monticello.avenue.org/ashlawn
E-mail: ashlawnJM@aol.com
(Home of James and Elizabeth Monroe)

James Monroe Museum and Memorial
Library
908 Charles Street
Fredericksburg, VA 22401
Ph.: 703.899.4559
Ph.: 540.654.1043
www.jamesmonroemuseum.mwc.edu
E-mail: jmmuseum@mwc.edu
(Home of James and Elizabeth Monroe)

Richard M. Nixon

The Richard Nixon Library and Birthplace
18001 Yorba Linda Boulevard
Yorba Linda, CA 92886
Ph.: 714.993.3393
Fax: 714.528.0544
www.nixonfoundation.org

Franklin Pierce

The Pierce Manse
14 Penacook Street
Concord, NH
Contact:
P.O. Box 425
Concord, NH 03302
Ph.: 603.224.5954
Ph.: 603.225.2068
www.newww.com/free/pierce/pierce.html
(Home of Franklin and Jane Pierce)

James K. Polk

The James K. Polk Ancestral Home
301 West 7th Street
Columbia, TN 38402
Ph.: 931.388.2354
www.jameskpolk.com/presite.html
E-mail: jkpolk@usit.net

Ronald Reagan

The Reagan Exhibit
Eureka College
300 E. College Avenue
Eureka, IL 61530
Ph.: 309.467.3721
Ph.: 888-4-EUREKA
reagan.eureka.edu/Legacy/exhibit.html
E-mail: reagan.eureka.edu/Legacy/exhibit
.html

The Ronald Reagan Presidential Library
40 Presidential Drive
Simi Valley, CA 93065
Ph.: 805.522.8444
Ph.: 800.410.8354
www.reagan.utexas.edu
E-mail: library@reagan.nara.gov

Springwood, Franklin D. Roosevelt's family home in Hyde Park, New York. *(Richard Cheek/Home of Franklin D. Roosevelt)*

Franklin D. Roosevelt
Eleanor Roosevelt National Historic Site
4097 Albany Post Road
Hyde Park, NY 12538
Ph.: 845.229.9115
Fax: 845.229.0739
www.nps.gov/elro
E-mail: ROVA_webmaster@nps.gov
(Val-Kill Cottage, home of Eleanor
    Roosevelt)

Franklin D. Roosevelt Library, Museum and
    Digital Archives, an online resource
www.fdrlibrary.marist.edu

Home of Franklin D. Roosevelt National
    Historic Site
4097 Albany Post Road
Hyde Park, NY 12538
Ph.: 845.229.9115
Fax: 845.229.0739
www.nps.gov/hofr
E-mail: ROVA_webmaster@nps.gov
(Springwood, family home of Franklin D.
    Roosevelt)

The Museum of the Franklin D. Roosevelt
    Library
4079 Albany Post Road
Hyde Park, NY 12538
Ph.: 800.337.8474
www.fdrlibrary.marist.edu/dh.html

Roosevelt Campobello International Park
New Brunswick, Canada
Contact:
Executive Secretary
P.O. Box 97
Lubec, ME 04652
Ph.: 506.752.2922
Fax: 506.752.6000
www.nps.gov/roca
E-mail: info@fdr.net
(Summer home of Franklin and Eleanor
    Roosevelt)

The Little White House State Historic Site
401 Little White House Road
Georgia Highway 85 Alt.
Warm Springs, GA 31830
Ph.: 706.655.5870
www.gastateparks.org/dnr/parks/ppage2
    .cgi?linkval=littlewhite
(Franklin Roosevelt's residence in Georgia)

Theodore Roosevelt
Sagamore Hill National Historic Site
20 Sagamore Hill Road
Oyster Bay, NY 11771
Ph.: 516.922.4447
Ph.: 516.922.4788
Fax: 516.922.4792
www.nps.gov/sahi
E-mail: sahi_information@nps.gov
(Home of Theodore and Edith Roosevelt)

Theodore Roosevelt Birthplace National
    Historic Site
28 East 20th Street
New York, NY 10003
Ph.: 212.260.1616
Fax: 212.677.3587
www.nps.gov/thrb
E-mail: MASI_Superintendent@nps.gov

Theodore Roosevelt Collection
Houghton Library
Harvard University
Cambridge, MA 02138
Ph.: 617.495.2449
Fax: 617.495.1376
hcl.harvard.edu/houghton/departments/
    roosevelt.html
E-mail: wfdailey@fas.harvard.edu

William Howard Taft
William Howard Taft National Historic Site
2038 Auburn Avenue
Cincinnati, OH 45219
Ph.: 513.684.3262
Fax: 513.684.3627
www.nps.gov/wiho
E-mail: WIHO_Superintendent@nps.gov

Sagamore Hill, home of Theodore and Edith Roosevelt near Oyster Bay, New York. *(AP/Wide World Photos)*

Harry S. Truman
Harry S. Truman National Historic Site
223 North Main Street
Independence, MO 64050
Ph.: 816.254.2720
Ph.: 816.254.9929 - visitor information
Ph.: 816.254.7199 - visitor information
Fax: 816.254.4491
www.nps.gov/hstr
E-mail: HSTR_Superintendent@nps.gov

Harry S. Truman Library and Museum
500 W. U.S. Highway 24
Independence, MO 64050
Ph.: 816.833.1400
Ph.: 800.833.1225
Fax: 816.833.4368
www.trumanlibrary.org
E-mail: truman.library@nara.gov

John Tyler
Sherwood Forest Plantation
Contact:
P.O. Box 8
Charles City, VA 23030
Ph.: 804.829.5377
Fax: 804.829.2947
www.sherwoodforest.org
E-mail: KTyler@SherwoodForest.org
(Home of John and Julia Tyler)

Martin Van Buren
Martin Van Buren National Historic Site
1013 Old Post Road
Kinderhook, NY 12106
Ph.: 518.758.9689
Fax: 518.758.6986
www.nps.gov/mava
E-mail: MAVA_info@nps.gov
(Lindenwald: Estate of Martin Van Buren)

George Washington
Mount Vernon Estate and Gardens
Mount Vernon, VA
Contact:
P.O. Box 110
Mount Vernon, VA 22121
Ph.: 703.780.2000
www.mountvernon.org
(Home of George and Martha Washington)

Woodrow Wilson
Woodrow Wilson Birthplace and Museum
18-24 North Coalter Street
Staunton, VA 24402
Ph.: 540.885.0897
Fax: 540.886.9874
www.woodrowwilson.org
E-mail: woodrow@woodrowwilson.org

Woodrow Wilson House Museum
2340 S Street, NW
Washington, DC 20008
Ph.: 202.387.4062
www.nthp.org/main/sites/wilsonhouse
.htm
(Home of Woodrow and Edith Wilson)

Bibliography

Adams, Abigail. *Letters of Mrs. Adams, the Wife of John Adams.* Edited by Charles Francis. 2 vols. 4th ed. Boston: Little, Brown, 1848. The first edited selection of Abigail Adams's letters, published by her grandson.

Adams, Louisa Catherine. "Adventures of a Nobody." In *The Adams Papers.* Boston: Massachusetts Historical Society, 1755-1889. Papers are owned by the Adams manuscript trust and deposited in the Massachusetts Historical Society. Her memoir gives testimony to her depression during her White House years.

_____. "Diary." In *The Adams Papers.* Boston: Massachusetts Historical Society, 1755-1889. Louisa's diary covers the period in her life from December, 1819, to January, 1824.

_____. "Narrative of a Journey from St. Petersburg to Paris in February, 1815." In *The Adams Papers.* Boston: Massachusetts Historical Society, 1755-1889. Contains a foreword by Brooks Adams, Louisa's grandson, and chronicles her treacherous trip.

Aikman, Lonnelle, ed. *The Living White House.* 10th ed. Washington, D.C.: White House Historical Association, 1996. Brief history of the White House, including anecdotes of visitors, events, and first families.

Akers, Charles. *Abigail Adams: An American Woman.* Boston: Little, Brown, 1980. An accessible, detailed portrait, which examines the status of women and situates Abigail Adams's life in the social context of her times.

Allen, Anne Beiser. *An Independent Woman: The Life of Lou Henry Hoover.* Westport, Conn.: Greenwood Press, 2000. A scholarly treatment of Lou Hoover's life; thoughtful and very readable.

Ammon, Harry. *James Monroe: The Quest for National Identity.* Charlottesville: University Press of Virginia, 1990. The definitive biography of James Monroe, with a large amount of material on his life with Elizabeth Monroe.

Anderson, Judith Icke. *William Howard Taft.* New York: Norton, 1981. Includes a valuable chapter about Helen Taft.

Anthony, Carl Sferrazza. *America's First Families.* New York: Touchstone, 2000. A good presentation of family life in the White House, which includes many pictures and little-known anecdotes.

_____. *First Ladies: The Saga of the Presidents' Wives and Their Power.* 2 vols. New York: William Morrow, 1990-1991. A unique glimpse at the changing role of the First Lady.

_____. *Florence Harding: The First Lady, the Jazz Age, and the Death of America's Most Scandalous President.* New York: William Morrow, 1998. Biography portrays Florence Harding as a thoroughly modern woman.

Arnett, Ethel S. *Mrs. James Madison: The Incomparable Dolley.* Greensboro, N.C.: Piedmont Press, 1972. Arnett, a regional historian skilled in research, offers reliable coverage of Dolley Madison's early life.

Arthur, Chester A. *Chester A. Arthur Papers.* Washington, D.C.: Library of Congress, 1959. The papers include not only his presidential papers but also letters and many other manuscripts predating his presidency. Biographical information about Ellen Arthur is contained in the biography by John

W. Herndon; includes miscellaneous Herndon notes about her.

Baker, Jean H. *Mary Todd Lincoln: A Biography.* New York: W. W. Norton, 1986. A largely sympathetic biography that looks at Mary Lincoln's life from her perspective.

Baldrige, Letitia. *Of Diamonds and Diplomats.* Boston: Houghton Mifflin, 1968. Excellent insights from Jackie Kennedy's social secretary and key strategist.

Bauer, K. Jack. *Zachary Taylor: Soldier, Planter, Statesman of the Old Southwest.* Baton Rouge: Louisiana State University Press, 1993. An account of Zachary Taylor's career with perceptive consideration of Margaret Taylor as First Lady.

Beasley, Maurine H., et al., eds. *The Eleanor Roosevelt Encyclopedia.* Westport, Conn.: Greenwood Press, 2001. Alphabetized entries include people, issues, and causes relating to Roosevelt. With photographs.

Bell, Carl Irving. *They Knew Franklin Pierce (And Others Thought They Did): A Sampling of Opinions About the Fourteenth U.S. President Drawn from His Contemporaries.* Springfield, Vt.: April Hill, 1980. Includes descriptions of Jane Pierce by historian Elizabeth Ellet and Jessie Benton Fremont, the wife of John C. Fremont.

Benson, Harry. *First Families: An Intimate Portrait from the Kennedys to the Clintons.* New York: Bullfinch Press, 1997. A good collection of photographs and engaging behind-the-scenes stories of late-twentieth century first families.

Bergeron, Paul H. *The Presidency of James K. Polk.* Lawrence: University Press of Kansas, 1987. Has been called the best available one-volume history of James Polk.

Boas, Norman F. *Jane M. Pierce (1806-1863): The Pierce-Aiken Papers: Letters of Jane M. Pierce, Her Sister Mary M. Aiken, Their Family, and President Franklin Pierce, with Biographies of Jane Pierce, Other Members of Her Family, and Genealogical Tables.* Stonington, Conn.: Seaport Autographs, 1983.

_____. *Jane M. Pierce (1806-1863): The Pierce-Aiken Papers Supplement.* Mystic, Conn.: Seaport Autographs, 1989.

Boller, Paul F. *Presidential Anecdotes.* 2d ed. New York: Oxford University Press, 1996. A collection of concise historical chapters on the presidents and their families.

_____. *Presidential Wives: An Anecdotal History.* 2d ed. New York: Oxford University Press, 1999. Boller devotes a chapter to every First Lady from Martha Washington to Hillary Rodham Clinton.

Brabson, Fay Warrington. *Andrew Johnson: A Life in Pursuit of the Right Course.* Durham, N.C.: Seeman Printery, 1972. Includes biographical material on Eliza Johnson.

Brandon, Dorothy. *Mamie Doud Eisenhower: A Portrait of a First Lady.* New York: Scribner's Sons, 1954. This biography is illustrated.

Brant, Irving. *James Madison.* 6 vols. Indianapolis: Bobbs-Merrill, 1941-1961. Standard biography of the president; the last four volumes include the most authentic information about Dolley Madison in the context of American and European history.

Brodie, Fawn M. *Thomas Jefferson: An Intimate History.* New York: Norton, 1974. Provides personal insights into the social and family life of the third president.

Brooks, Noah. *Washington in Lincoln's Time.* 1895. Reprint. Chicago: Quadrangle Books, 1971. Edited revision includes new commentary by Lincoln Biographer Herman Mitgang.

Burke, Pauline Wilcox. *Emily Donelson of Tennessee.* 2 vols. Richmond, Va.: Garrett and Massie, 1941. With illustrations and bibliographical notes.

Burrell, Barbara. *Public Opinion, the First Ladyship, and Hillary Rodham Clinton.* New York: Garland, 1997.

Bush, Barbara. *Barbara Bush: A Memoir.* New York: Charles Scribner's Sons, 1994. Barbara Bush's memoir gives readers a candid, private look at the more than twenty-five years she and her husband lived in the public eye.

———. *Millie's Book: As Dictated to Barbara Bush*. New York: William Morrow, 1990. A dog's view of the Bush White House, "dictated" by First Dog Millie Bush.

Bush, George. *All the Best, George Bush: My Life in Letters and Other Writings*. New York: Scribner, 1999. A collection of letters, diary entries, and memos, beginning with eighteen-year-old George's letters to his parents during World War II and continuing through his post-presidency years.

Bush, George W., with Karen Hughes. *A Charge to Keep*. New York: William Morrow, 1999. The George W. Bush story from his own perspective, written with the assistance of his longtime media aide and spokeswoman. He speaks to the influence Laura had on his life.

Butt, Archibald Willingham. *Taft and Roosevelt: The Intimate Letters of Archie Butt, Military Aide*. 2 vols. Port Washington, N.Y.: Kennikat Press, 1971. This correspondence often recounts conversations between Helen and William Howard Taft during their White House years.

Butterfield, L. H., et al., eds. *Adams Family Correspondence*. 6 vols. Cambridge, Mass.: Harvard University Press, 1963-1993. Intended to be the most complete published collection of Abigail Adams's letters, with additional volumes planned.

Caldwell, Mary French. *General Jackson's Lady*. Nashville, Tenn.: M. F. Caldwell, 1936. The first full-length biography of Rachel Jackson includes previously undocumented anecdotes.

Caroli, Betty Boyd. *First Ladies*. Expanded ed. New York: Oxford University Press, 1995. A look at the varying roles each First Lady to date has undertaken, along with vital statistics.

Carpenter, Frank. *Carp's Washington*. New York: McGraw-Hill, 1960. Contains information based on a prominent journalist's interview with Caroline Harrison.

Carpenter, Liz. *Ruffles and Flourishes*. College Station: Texas A&M University Press, 1992. A detailed account of Lady Bird Johnson from her former staff director, providing valuable accounts of Lady Bird Johnson's First Ladyship.

Carter, Hugh. *Cousin Beedie and Cousin Hot: My Life with the Carter Family of Plains, Georgia*. Englewood Cliffs, N.J.: Prentice Hall, 1978. A Carter relative offers a homey remembrance of the childhoods and early lives of President Jimmy Carter and First Lady Rosalynn Carter.

Carter, Jimmy. *An Outdoor Journal: Adventures and Reflections*. Little Rock: University of Arkansas Press, 1994. Interesting outdoor information, has been compared to a scout manual; includes information about the Carter family.

Carter, Jimmy, and Rosalynn Carter. *Everything to Gain: Making the Most of the Rest of Your Life*. Little Rock: University of Arkansas Press, 1995. Warm and unpretentious dual account of the Carters' transition from the White House back to ordinary life; highlights issues such as health care and the Carter Center.

Carter, Rosalynn. *First Lady from Plains*. Boston: Houghton Mifflin, 1984. Rosalynn Carter's candid memories of her life before and during her First Ladyship.

Carter, Rosalynn, and Susan K. Golant. *Helping Someone with Mental Illness: A Compassionate Guide for Family, Friends, and Caregivers*. New York: Times Books, 1998. Cleanly organized discussion of the mental illness issues is interwoven with individual accounts.

Clark, Allen C. *Life and Letters of Dolly Madison*. Washington, D.C.: W. F. Roberts, 1914. While not up to modern editorial standards, provides a large selection of letters by and about Dolley Madison, her family, and friends, with interesting appendices.

Cleaves, Freeman. *Old Tippecanoe: William Henry Harrison and His Time*. New York: Charles

Scriber's Sons, 1939. Focuses primarily on William Henry Harrison's experiences in Indiana and early history of the region.

Clinton, Hillary Rodham. *An Invitation to the White House: At Home with History.* New York: Simon & Schuster, 2000. Hillary Rodham Clinton looks at the history, traditions, and workings of the Executive Mansion.

———. *It Takes a Village: And Other Lessons Children Teach Us.* New York: Simon & Schuster, 1995. Hillary Rodham Clinton discusses child rearing in her award-winning book.

Coleman, Elizabeth Tyler. *Priscilla Cooper Tyler and the American Scene: 1816-1889.* University: University of Alabama Press, 1955. Details the life and times of President John Tyler's daughter-in-law, who served as hostess in the White House from 1841 to 1844.

Collier, Peter, with David Horowitz. *The Roosevelts: An American Saga.* New York: Simon & Schuster, 1994. Filled with drama and anecdotes, it is a soaring tale of triumph over heartbreak and frailty.

Comer, Lucretia Garfield. *Strands from the Weaving.* New York: Vantage Press: 1959. Family reminiscences from Lucretia and James Garfield's granddaughter.

Cook, Blanche Wiesen. *Eleanor Roosevelt.* 2 vols. New York: Viking, 1992-1999. The two volumes cover Eleanor Roosevelt's background, activities, and relationships through 1938. Skillfully and engagingly written.

Corbertt, Katherine. "Louisa Catherine Adams: The Anguished Adventures of a Nobody." In *Women's Being, Women's Place: Female Identity and Vocation in American History,* edited by Mary Kelley. Boston: Houghton Mifflin, 1979.

Crook, William H. *Memories of the White House: The Home Life of Our Presidents from Lincoln to Roosevelt.* Boston: Little, Brown, 1911.

Cutts, Lucia Beverly. *Memoirs and Letters of Dolley Madison, Wife of James Madison, President of the United States.* Boston: Houghton Mifflin, 1886. Edited by her grandniece.

David, Lester, and Irene David. *Ike and Mamie: The Story of the General and His Lady.* New York: World Publishing, 1978.

Davis, Varina. *Jefferson Davis, Ex-President of the Confederate States of America: A Memoir by His Wife.* 2 vols. New York: Belford, 1890. The future First Lady of the Confederacy was a confidante of Jane Pierce.

DeGregorio, William A. *The Complete Book of U.S. Presidents.* 4th ed. New York: Barricade Books, 1993. A detailed compilation of brief family and political histories of the presidents.

Diller, Daniel C. *The Presidents, First Ladies, and Vice Presidents: White House Biographies, 1789-2001.* Washington, D.C.: CQ Press, 2001. Includes bibliographical references and index.

Dyer, Brainerd. *Zachary Taylor.* Baton Rouge: Louisiana State University Press, 1943. Solid account of Zachary Taylor's career.

Eckenrode, Hamilton J. *The Randolphs.* New York: Bobbs-Merrill, 1946. Story of Martha "Patsy" Jefferson's husband's family in early Virginia.

Eisenhower, Dwight D. *Letters to Mamie.* Edited by John S. D. Eisenhower. Garden City, N.J.: Doubleday, 1978. Dwight Eisenhower's letters to Mamie Eisenhower from abroad.

Eisenhower, Julie Nixon. *Pat Nixon: The Untold Story.* New York: Simon & Schuster, 1986. A very comprehensive view of Pat Nixon's life, as told by her daughter.

Eisenhower, Susan. *Mrs. Ike: Memories and Reflections on the Life of Mamie Eisenhower.* New York: Farrar, Straus and Giroux, 1996. This portrait of Mamie Eisenhower by her granddaughter contains many photographs.

Ellet, Elizabeth F. *Court Circles of the Republic: Or, The Beauties and Celebrities of the Nation, Illustrating Life and Society Under Eighteen Presidents, Describing the Social Features of the Successive Administrations from Washington to Grant.* Philadelphia: Philadelphia Publishing, 1872. The "first historian of American women" discusses Abigail Fillmore.

Farrell, John J. *Zachary Taylor, 1874-1850, and Millard Fillmore, 1800-1874: Chronology, Documents, and Bibliographical Aids*. Dobbs Ferry, N.Y.: Oceana, 1971. Guide for further research.

Feinberg, Barbara Silberdick. *America's First Ladies: Changing Expectations*. New York: Franklin Watts, 1998.

Ferrell, Robert H. *Dear Bess*. New York: W. W. Norton, 1983. A revealing and fascinating glimpse of Bess and Harry Truman's relationship, as revealed through his personal letters.

_____, ed. *The Real Calvin Coolidge* 10 (1994). This edition of the Journal of the Calvin Coolidge Memorial Foundation includes essays on Grace Coolidge, with her poems.

Fields, Joseph, ed. *Worthy Partner: The Papers of Martha Washington*. Westport, Conn.: Greenwood Press, 1994. A collection of all of Martha Washington's known letters, with an informative overview of her life.

Fillmore, Millard. *Millard Fillmore Papers*. Edited by Frank H. Severance. 2 vols. Buffalo, N.Y.: Buffalo Historical Society, 1907. Millard Fillmore mentions his wife in his description of his early years and in other papers.

Flinn, Susan K., ed. *Speaking of Hillary: A Reader's Guide to the Most Controversial Woman in America*. Ashland, Oreg.: White Cloud Press, 2000. A collection of essays by friends and foes assessing Hillary Rodham Clinton's life, defeats, victories, and legacy.

Ford, Betty, with Chris Chase. *A Glad Awakening*. Garden City, N.Y.: Doubleday, 1987. This memoir is illustrated

_____. *Times of My Life*. New York: Harper & Row, 1978. The former First Lady's insights provide a good look at life inside the White House.

Ford, Gerald. *A Time to Heal: The Autobiography of Gerald R. Ford*. New York: Harper & Row, 1979. Gerald Ford's memoir has been de-

scribed as a seat in the family room of the White House.

Frederick, Richard G., ed. *Warren G. Harding*. Connecticut: Greenwood, 1992. Biography of the twenty-eighth president also covers foreign and domestic policies of the 1920's.

Freeman, Douglas Southall. *George Washington*. 7 vols. New York: Scribner, 1948-1957. This multivolume work is widely considered to be the definitive account of the United States' first president.

Freidel, Frank, and William Pencak, eds. *The White House: The First Two Hundred Years*. Boston: Northeastern University Press, 1994. Eleven papers from distinguished scholars reflect on the changing public role of the First Lady, among other topics.

Garfield, James A. *The Diary of James A. Garfield*. 4 vols. Edited by Harry J. Brown and Frederick D. Williams. East Lansing: Michigan Sate University Press, 1967-1981.

Geer, Emily Apt. *First Lady: The Life of Lucy Webb Hayes*. Kent, Ohio: Kent State University Press, 1984. Well-researched, balanced portrait of Lucy Hayes.

Gelles, Edith B. *First Thoughts: Life and Letters of Abigail Adams*. New York: Twayne, 1998. Gelles treats a limited number of periods in Abigail Adams's life, which were best documented by her personal letters, thereby revealing Adams's personality and character in her own words.

_____. *Portia: The World of Abigail Adams*. Bloomington: Indiana University Press, 1992. Gelles takes a critical view of the "Abigail industry" and seeks to define Adams on her own terms.

Goebel, Dorothy. *William Henry Harrison: A Political Biography*. 1926. Reprint. Philadelphia: Porcupine Press, 1974. Originally published as part of the Indiana Library's Historical Collection. Includes bibliography.

Gould, Lewis L. *Lady Bird Johnson and the Environment*. Lawrence: University Press of Kansas, 1988. A scholarly assessment of Lady

Bird Johnson's role in promoting numerous environmental issues and the lasting significance of her beautification projects.

_____. *The Presidency of William McKinley.* Lawrence: Regents Press of Kansas, 1980. A scholastic account of the twenty-fifth president.

_____, ed. *American First Ladies: Their Lives and Their Legacy.* New York: Garland, 1996. An enjoyable, informative, and objective combination of biographical sketches and histories of the First Ladies.

Graf, Leroy P., Paul Bergeron, et al., eds. *The Papers of Andrew Johnson.* 16 vols. Knoxville: University of Tennessee Press, 1967-2000. The full collection of Johnson's correspondence, including some letters sent to Eliza Johnson and references to her.

Grant, Jesse R. *In the Days of My Father, General Grant.* New York: Harper and Brothers, 1925.

Grant, Julia Dent. *The Personal Memoirs of Julia Dent Grant (Mrs. Ulysses S. Grant).* Edited by John Y. Simon. Carbondale: Southern Illinois University Press, 1975. Julia Grant's insightful memoir shows the romance in her relationship with Ulysses S. Grant.

Grant, Ulysses S. *Personal Memoirs of U.S. Grant.* Introduction by James M. McPherson. New York: Penguin Books, 1999. Considered one of the best autobiographies of any major military leader; focuses mainly on his military career.

Grayson, Cary T. *Woodrow Wilson: An Intimate Memoir.* New York: Holt, Rinehart and Winston, 1960. Recounts the life and times of the twenty-seventh president.

Green, James. *William Henry Harrison: His Life and Times.* Richmond, Va.: Garrett and Massie, c. 1941. Illustrated.

Grimes, Ann. *Running Mates: The Making of a First Lady.* New York: William Morrow, 1990. Barbara Bush's evolution as George Bush's political supporter and partner.

Gutin, Myra G. *The President's Partner: The First Lady in the Twentieth Century.* New York: Greenwood Press, 1989. Examines the public communications and private lives of twelve First Ladies.

Hagedorn, Hermann. *The Roosevelt Family of Sagamore Hill.* New York: Macmillan, 1954. A lively narrative of Edith and Theodore Roosevelt's growing family, primarily before and during the White House years.

Halstead, Murat. *Life and Distinguished Services of William McKinley.* Chicago: M. A. Donohue, 1901. Available at most libraries; Halstead was the foremost author of historical accounts at the turn of the twentieth century.

Hamilton, Holman. *Zachary Taylor.* 2 vols. Indianapolis: Bobbs-Merrill, 1951. The most detailed work on Zachary Taylor, which also contains the most complete account of Margaret Taylor's life.

Hatch, Alden. *Edith Bolling Wilson: First Lady Extraordinary.* New York: Dodd, Mead, 1961. With illustrations.

_____. *Red Carpet for Mamie.* New York: Doubleday, 1978.

Heald, Edward Thornton. *Condensed Biography of William McKinley.* Canton, Ohio: Stark County Historical Society, 1964. An overview of William and Ida McKinley.

Healy, Diana Dixon. *America's First Ladies: Private Lives of the Presidential Wives.* New York: Atheneum, 1988. A close look at presidential wives and other women who have served as U.S. First Ladies.

Heller, Milton F., Jr. *The Presidents' Doctor: An Insider's View of Three First Families.* New York: Vantage Press, 2000. A good friend of Grace Coolidge gives his view from the White House.

Helm, Katherine. *Mary, Wife of Lincoln.* New York: Harpers, 1928. An engaging biography that includes family perspectives on Mary Lincoln.

Hess, Stephen. *America's Political Dynasties: From Adams to Kennedy.* Garden City, N.J.: Doubleday, 1966. An intricate examination of the political families who occupied the

White House through the Kennedy years.

Heymann, C. David. *A Woman Named Jackie*. New York: Lyle Stuart, 1989. The best of the many popular Jackie Kennedy biographies, more authoritative and less breathless than most.

Holloway, Laura Carter. *The Ladies of the White House, Or: In the Home of the Presidents*. Reprint. New York: A. M. S. Press, 1976. Subtitled *Being a Complete History of the Social and Domestic Lives of the Presidents from Washington to the Present Time, 1789-1881*, this book includes twenty-five leaves of plates.

Hoogenboom, Ari Arthur. *Rutherford B. Hayes: Warrior and President*. Lawrence: University Press of Kansas, 1995. Author of the first new biography in fifty years makes the case of appreciating Hayes' limited options and the choices he made.

Hoover, Irwin Hood. *Forty-two Years in the White House*. Boston: Houghton Mifflin, 1934. A former White House chief usher recalls his experiences.

House, Edward. *The Intimate Papers of Colonel House*. Boston: Houghton Mifflin, 1930.

Howe, George Frederick. *Chester A. Arthur: A Quarter-Century of Machine Politics*. Reprint. New York: Easton Press, 1987. This biography first appeared in 1935 and is the first scholarly biography of Chester A. Arthur, which contains a little information on Ellen Arthur.

Hunt-Jones, Conover. *Dolley and the "Great Little Madison."* Washington, D.C.: American Institute of Architects Foundation, 1977. The best succinct treatment of Dolley Madison's life, lifestyle, and material culture, with full illustrations of fashions in costume, art, and furnishings at Montpelier and the White House.

Ide, Arthur Frederick. *The Father's Son: George W. Bush*. Boston: Minuteman Press, 1998. Although published prior to George W. Bush's presidency and before the final stretch of the 2000 campaign cycle, the book examines Bush's early life, influences, and his relationship with his father. There is also some discussion of Laura Bush.

Jefferson, Thomas. *The Family Letters of Thomas Jefferson*. Edited by Edwin Betts and James A. Bear. Columbia: University of Missouri Press, 1966. Insights into the lives of Thomas and Martha Jefferson, through Thomas Jefferson's correspondence.

Kaufman, Burton I. *The Presidency of James Earl Carter, Jr*. Lawrence: University Press of Kansas, 1993. Author argues that Jimmy Carter's well-intentioned abandonment of Washington protocol hurt his presidency.

Keller, Rosemary. *Patriotism and the Female Sex: Abigail Adams and the American Revolution*. New York: Carlson, 1994. A study of Abigail Adams's views on women, republicanism, and the role of women in the new republic.

Kessler, Ronald. *Inside the White House: The Hidden Lives of the Modern Presidents and the Secrets of the World's Most Powerful Institution*. New York: Pocket Books, 1995. An overview of many of the more sensational aspects of modern first families.

Kilian, Pamela. *Barbara Bush: A Biography*. New York: Saint Martin's Press, 1992. A biography of the forty-first president's wife.

Klapthor, Margaret Brown. *The First Ladies*. 9th ed. Washington, D.C.: White House Historical Association with the cooperation of the National Geographic Society, 1999. Brief biographies and portraits of the First Ladies through Hillary Rodham Clinton.

_____. *Official White House China, 1789 to the Present*. Washington, D.C.: Smithsonian Institution Press, 1975. Detailed descriptions and illustrations of various administrations' official White House china.

Lash, Joseph P. *Eleanor and Franklin*. New York: W. W. Norton, 1971. Joseph Lash, secretary and confidant to Eleanor Roosevelt, won a Pulitzer Prize for this biography.

Leech, Margaret. *In the Days of McKinley*. New York: Harper & Brothers, 1959. Probably the most entertaining account of the McKinleys.

Leech, Margaret, and Harry J. Brown. *The Garfield Orbit: The Life of President James A. Garfield*. New York: Harper and Row, 1978. A highly readable biography with special insights into the Garfield marriage.

Levin, Phyllis. *Abigail Adams*. New York: St. Martin's Press, 1987. Provides an overview of Abigail Adams's life, largely organized around her marriage and family.

Link, Arthur S. *Woodrow Wilson: A Brief Biography*. New York: World Publishing, 1963. A brief biography of Woodrow Wilson, written by the editor of *The Papers of Woodrow Wilson*.

Lynch, Denis Tilden. *An Epoch and a Man: Martin Van Buren and His Times*. 1929. Reprint. New York: Kennikat Press, 1971. Includes a brief account of the life of Hannah Van Buren.

McAdoo, Eleanor Wilson, ed. *The Priceless Gift: The Love Letters of Woodrow Wilson and Ellen Axson Wilson*. New York: McGraw-Hill, 1962. The love letters since the beginning of Woodrow and Ellen's courtship, up to the time Ellen died.

McCombs, Charles Flowers. *Imprisonment of Madame de Lafayette During the Terror*. New York: The Library, 1943. Information on Elizabeth Monroe's role in freeing Madame Lafayette.

McConnell, Burt, and Jane McConnell. *Our First Ladies*. New York: Crowell, 1969. Profiles the lives of White House hostesses through Pat Nixon.

McCullough, David. *Truman*. New York: Simon & Schuster, 1992. The Pulitzer Prize-winning biography of Harry S. Truman's life and times.

Mayer, Dale C. "An Uncommon Woman: The Quiet Leadership Style of Lou Henry Hoover." *Presidential Studies Quarterly* 20 (Fall, 1990): 685-698. An in-depth examination of Lou Hoover's pivotal role in the dramatic growth of the Girl Scouts.

———, ed. *Lou Henry Hoover: Essays on a Busy Life*. Worland, Wyo.: High Plains Press, 1994. A collection of essays based on extensive research of Lou Hoover's personal papers. Includes comments on the significance and nature of her papers by the archivist in charge of arranging them.

Mayo, Edith P., ed. *The Smithsonian Book of the First Ladies: Their Lives, Times, and Issues*. New York: H. Holt, 1996. Contains a short biographical chapter on every First Lady through Hillary Rodham Clinton.

Means, Anne M. *Amherst and Our Family Tree*. Boston: privately printed, 1921. This history of Jane Pierce's family includes descriptions of her in their letters.

Middleton, Harry. *Lady Bird Johnson: A Life Well Lived*. Austin: University of Texas Press, 1992. Published on Lady Bird's eightieth birthday, this is a collection of intimate pictures and memoirs, chronicling her life.

Milton, Joyce. *The First Partner*. New York: Perennial Books, 1999. A solid, general biography of Hillary Rodham Clinton.

Minutaglio, Bill. *First Son: George W. Bush and the Bush Family Dynasty*. New York: Times Books, 1999. A balanced account of the forty-third president, which devotes attention to Laura Bush's role in calming a wayward young man and the central role she has played in his political career.

Montgomery, Ruth. *Mrs. LBJ*. New York: Holt, Rinehart and Winston, 1964. Written while she was still First Lady, this book looks at the Johnson marriage and at Lady Bird.

Morris, Sylvia Jukes. *Edith Kermit Roosevelt: Portrait of a First Lady*. New York: Coward, McCann & Geoghegan, 1980. The definitive biography of Edith Roosevelt.

Moser, Howard D., et al., eds. *The Papers of Andrew Jackson*, 5 vols. Knoxville: University of Tennessee Press, 1981-1996. The first five volumes include correspondence to and from Rachel Jackson through 1824; more are planned.

Murray, Robert K. *The Harding Era: Warren G.*

Harding and His Administration. Minneapolis: University of Minnesota Press, 1969. Includes bibliographical references.

Nagel, Paul C. *The Adams Women: Abigail and Louisa Adams, Their Sisters and Daughters*. New York: Oxford University Press, 1987. An interesting comparative study of the first generations of Adams women.

Nash, George. *The Life of Herbert Hoover*. 3 vols. New York: W. W. Norton, 1983. The first three volumes in Nash's as yet unfinished multivolume biography of the thirty-first president is generally regarded as the definitive account of Herbert Hoover's life. Each volume contains references to Lou Hoover.

Nelson, Anson, and Fannie Nelson. *Memorials of Sarah Childress Polk*. New York: A. D. F. Randolf, 1892. Reprint. Spartanburg, S.C.: Reprint Company, 1974. This book was reprinted from the 1892 edition in the Tennessee State Library and Archives in Nashville.

Nevins, Allan. *Ordeal of the Union: Fruits of Manifest Destiny, 1847-1852*. New York: Charles Scribner's Sons, 1947.

Nichols, Roy Franklin. *Franklin Pierce: Young Hickory of the Granite Hills*. 1931. Rev. ed. Newton, Conn.: American Political Biography Press, 1998. Jane Pierce is mentioned throughout this comprehensive biography of her husband.

Nixon, Richard Milhous. *RN: The Memoirs of Richard Nixon*. New York: Simon & Schuster, 2000. The president's autobiography.

O'Connor, Karen, Bernadette Nye, and Laura Van Assendelft. "Wives in the White House: The Political Influence of First Ladies." *Presidential Studies Quarterly* 26, no. 3 (1997): 835-853.

Oland, Emily A. *Running Mates: A Biographical Study of First Ladies and Official Hostesses of Maryland*. Baltimore: University of Maryland, 1996.

Olcott, Charles, *The Life of William McKinley*. 2 vols. New York: Houghton Mifflin, 1916. A thorough and accurate examination of William McKinley's life and accomplishments and his life with Ida McKinley.

Parmet, Herbert S. *George Bush: The Life of a Lone Star Yankee*. New York: Scribner, 1997. Award-winning historian gives the first full account of the former president who led the United States through the end of the Cold War.

Peacock, Virginia Tatnall. *Famous American Belles of the Nineteenth Century*. Freeport, N.Y.: Books for Libraries Press, 1970. A general portrait of Harriet Lane.

Perling, J. J. *President's Sons: The Prestige of Name in a Democracy*. New York: Odyssey Press, 1947. An examination of the lives of sixty presidential sons.

Polk, James K. *The Diary of a President*. Edited by Alan Nevins. New York: Longmans, Green, 1952. Annotated, with bibliographical notes.

Pringle, Henry F. *The Life and Times of William Howard Taft*. New York: Farrar & Rinehart, 1939. An exhaustive biography of the president, with extensive coverage of Helen Taft.

Pryor, Helen. *Lou Henry Hoover: Gallant First Lady*. New York: Dodd, Mead, 1969. Long out of print and lacking footnotes, this account still has much to recommend it. Pryor was a friend of the Hoovers and interviewed many of Lou Hoover's friends for this very personal portrait.

Radcliffe, Donnie. *Simply Barbara Bush: A Portrait of America's Candid First Lady*. New York: Warner Books, 1989. Based on interviews with Barbara Bush, her family, and friends, this first biography explores her life.

Randall, Ruth Painter. *Mary Lincoln: Biography of a Marriage*. Boston: Little, Brown, 1953. Based on excellent research, Randall's book discusses the Lincoln marriage with sympathy and understanding.

Reagan, Nancy. *I Love You, Ronnie*. New York: Random House, 2000. The letters of Ronald Reagan to Nancy Reagan.

_____. *My Turn*. New York: Random House,

1989. Nancy Reagan's account of her years in office and a response to her critics.

Reeves, Richard. *President Kennedy.* New York: Simon & Schuster, 1993. A superb account of John Kennedy's presidency, offering a sense of how the president and his wife functioned day-to-day.

Reeves, Thomas C. *Gentleman Boss: The Life of Chester Alan Arthur.* New York: Knopf, 1975. A sensitive biography of Chester A. Arthur, with the fullest treatment of Ellen Arthur of any published source.

Regan, Donald. *For the Record: From Wall Street to Washington.* New York: Harcourt Brace Jovanovich, 1988. An insider's assessment of Nancy Reagan's power.

Remini, Robert V. *Andrew Jackson.* 3 vols. Baltimore: Johns Hopkins University Press, 1977. Reprinted in 1998 with new introduction. The definitive biography of Andrew Jackson, with significant insights into Rachel Jackson and their marriage.

Robbins, Jhan. *Bess and Harry: An American Love Story.* New York: G. P. Putnam's Sons, 1980. A sentimental narrative of the Trumans' long life together.

Robertson, S. L. "The First Lady, the First Family, and the President's Friends." In *Guide to the Presidency,* edited by Michael Nelson. Vol. 2. Washington, D.C.: Congressional Quarterly, 1996.

Roosevelt, Eleanor. *The Autobiography of Eleanor Roosevelt.* 1961. Reprint. New York: Da Capo Press, 1992. The author's compelling prose not only tells her own life story but teaches a history lesson of the late nineteenth and early twentieth centuries.

Roosevelt, Elliott, and James Brough. *Mother R: Eleanor Roosevelt's Untold Story.* New York: G. P. Putnam's Sons, 1977. A history of Eleanor and Franklin Roosevelt, who, in spite of difficulties, lived as husband and wife for more than forty years.

Rosebush, James S. *First Lady, Public Wife: A Behind-the-Scenes History of the Evolving of First Ladies in American Public Life.* Lanham, Md.: Madison Books, 1987.

Ross, Ishbel. *The General's Wife: The Life of Mrs. Ulysses S. Grant.* New York: Dodd, Mead, 1959. Includes bibliography.

_____. *Grace Coolidge and Her Era: The Story of a President's Wife.* Plymouth, Vt.: The Calvin Coolidge Memorial Foundation, 1988. A journalist's view of the 1920's and Grace Coolidge. Good use of original sources.

_____. *Power with Grace: The Life Story of Mrs. Woodrow Wilson.* New York: G. P. Putnam's Sons, 1975. Includes index, bibliography, and illustrations.

_____. *The Tafts: An American Family.* Cleveland, Ohio: World Publishing, 1964. Generations of one family's public service; includes information on Helen Taft's early and later years.

Sadler, Christine. *Children in the White House.* New York: G. P. Putnam's Sons, 1967.

Saunders, Frances Wright. *First Lady Between Two Worlds: Ellen Axson Wilson.* Chapel Hill: University of North Carolina Press, 1985. A complete biography of Ellen Axson Wilson.

Sawyer, Susan. *More than Petticoats: Remarkable Tennessee Women.* Helena, Mont.: Falcon, 2000. Written for young adults, primarily an account of Rachel Jackson's divorce and remarriage.

Scarry, Robert J. *Millard Fillmore.* Jefferson, N.C.: McFarland, 2001. The first comprehensive biography to draw upon Fillmore family papers long believed to have been lost.

Schlesinger, Arthur M., Jr. *A Thousand Days.* Boston: Houghton Mifflin, 1965. This Kennedy adviser's memoir evokes the magic of what Jackie Kennedy called Camelot.

Schreiner, Samuel A., Jr. *The Trials of Mrs. Lincoln: The Harrowing Never-Before-Told Story of Mary Todd Lincoln's Last and Finest Years..* New York: Donald A. Fine, 1987. Includes index.

Seager, Robert. *And Tyler Too: A Biography of John and Julia Tyler.* New York: McGraw-Hill,

1963. A lengthy but detailed look at the lives and times of John and Julia Tyler.

Seale, William. *The President's House*. 2 vols. Washington, D.C.: White House Historical Association, 1992. Young adult history of the White House includes its construction, reconstruction and renovations.

Sellers, Charles G. *James K. Polk: Continentalist, 1843-1848*. Princeton, N.J.: Princeton University Press, 1966.

_____. *James K. Polk: Jacksonian, 1795-1843*. Princeton, N.J.: Princeton University Press, 1957.

_____. "Polk, Sarah Childress." In *Notable American Women*, edited by Edward T. James, et al. Vol. 3. Cambridge, Mass.: Harvard University Press, 1974. Biographical dictionary profiles well-known and obscure women who contributed to American society.

Shaw, John, ed. *Crete and James: Personal Letters of Lucretia and James Garfield*. East Lansing: Michigan State University Press, 1994. The story of the Garfield marriage, as told by James and Lucretia's correspondence written between 1853 and 1881.

Sheehy, Gail. *Hillary's Choice*. New York: Random House, 1999. Some of the material in this book appeared in *Vanity Fair* magazine. An alternately confusing and enlightening biography which attempts to explain Hillary Rodham Clinton's life choices.

Shelley, Mary Virginia, and Sandra Harrison Munro. *Harriet Lane, First Lady of the White House*. Lititz, Pa.: Sutter House, 1980. This is juvenile literature but is the only modern book on Harriet Lane.

Shepherd, Jack. *Cannibals of the Heart: A Personal Biography of Louisa Catherine and John Quincy Adams*. New York: McGraw-Hill, 1980. A helpful biography of Louisa Adams's life, including her public role as First Lady.

Sievers, Harry Joseph. *Benjamin Harrison*. 3 vols. Indianapolis: Bobbs-Merrill, 1968. An accurate biography of Benjamin Harrison;

contains details illustrating Caroline Harrison's political acumen.

Simon, John Y., ed. *The Papers of Ulysses S. Grant*. 24 vols. Carbondale: Southern Illinois University Press, 1969. The set, in which Grant's own words show his humor, pathos, and unique personality, contains all known correspondence written and received by him.

Simonton, Dean Keith. "Presidents' Wives and First Ladies: On Achieving Eminence Within a Traditional Gender Role." *Sex Roles* 35, nos. 3/4 (1996): 309-336.

Small, Melvin. *The Presidency of Richard Nixon*. Lawrence: University Press of Kansas, 1999. A thorough and scholarly examination of the Nixon administration.

Smith, Gene. *High Crimes and Misdemeanors: The Impeachment Trial of Andrew Johnson*. New York: William Morrow, 1977. A detailed account of the Johnsons during the months of the impeachment trial.

_____. *When the Cheering Stopped: The Last Years of Woodrow Wilson*. New York: William Morrow, 1964. Well researched; describes Wilson's life and work as well as his stroke, his last days, and his disillusionment.

Smith, Margaret Bayard. *The First Forty Years of Washington Society*. New York: Ungar, 1965. A reporter who was a friend of Thomas Jefferson and his daughter Martha Randolph provides an account of their presidential years.

Smith, Marie. *The President's Lady: An Intimate Biography of Mrs. Lady Bird Johnson*. New York: Holt, Rinehart, and Winston, 1964. Explores the interests and background of the First Lady, devoting attention to her upbringing and married life. Although dated, it is still a useful study of Lady Bird.

Stoddard, Gloria May. *Grace and Cal: A Vermont Love Story*. Shelburne, Vt.: The New England Press, 1989. A highly readable story of the two.

Stoll, Stasz Clarice. *Female and Male: Socialization, Social Roles, and Social Structure*. 2d ed.

Dubuque, Iowa: W. C. Brown, 1978.

Summers, Anthony, and Robbyn Swan. *The Arrogance of Power: The Secret World of Richard Nixon*. New York: Viking, 2000. Offers a critical journalistic view of Richard M. Nixon's career and marriage.

Taft, Helen (Mrs. William Howard). *Recollections of Full Years*. New York: Dodd, Mead, 1914. Helen Taft's autobiography, written after William Howard Taft's presidency and before his Supreme Court appointment. It is the first memoir of a First Lady to have been published.

Taylor, Lloyd C. "Harriet Lane: Mirror of an Age." *Pennsylvania History* 30 (January-October, 1963): 213-225. This is the best article of historical value that has so far been written on Harriet Lane.

TerHorst, Jerald F. *Gerald Ford and the Future of the Presidency*. New York: Third Press, 1974. Includes index and bibliography.

Thane, Elswyth. *Washington's Lady*. New York: Dodd, Mead, 1954. One of the very few works on Martha Washington; lacks citations.

Thomas, Helen. *Dateline: White House*. New York: Macmillan, 1975. One of the reporters who covered the Kennedys reflects back on some of her and her colleagues' excesses.

Thomas, Lately. *The First President Johnson: The Three Lives of the Seventeenth President of the United States*. New York: William Morrow, 1968. Includes insights into the relationship of Andrew and Eliza Johnson.

Trani, Eugene P., and David L. Wilson. *The Presidency of Warren G. Harding*. Lawrence: Regents Press of Kansas, 1977. Includes index and bibliography.

Trefousse, Hans L. *Andrew Johnson: A Biography*. New York: W. W. Norton, 1989. This scholarly, full-length biography of Andrew Johnson includes insights from the Johnson papers.

Truman, Harry S. *Memoirs*. 2 vols. Garden City, N.Y.: Doubleday, 1955-1956. Truman's official memoirs of his presidential years.

Truman, Margaret. *Bess W. Truman*. New York: Macmillan, 1986. A detailed and intimate portrait of Bess, written by her daughter.

_____. *First Ladies*. New York: Random House, 1995. Margaret Truman, a "first daughter" herself, interviewed Lady Bird Johnson, Betty Ford, Nancy Reagan, Rosalynn Carter, Barbara Bush, and Hillary Rodham Clinton for this book. She had known First Ladies from Frances Cleveland to Edith Wilson and Eleanor Roosevelt.

_____. *Souvenir: Margaret Truman's Own Story*. New York: McGraw-Hill, 1956. Margaret Truman's account of growing up as the president's daughter.

Turner, Justin, and Linda Leavitt. *Mary Lincoln: Her Life and Letters*. New York: Knopf, 1972. Although Mary Lincoln's letters continue to surface, this compendium serves as an excellent introduction to her life.

Van Zwaluwenburg, Pamela J. "First Partner: First Ladies and Their Roles." In *Presidential Frontiers: Underexplored Issues in White House Politics*, edited by Ryan J. Barilleaux. Westport, Conn.: Praeger, 1998.

Wallace, Chris. *First Lady: A Portrait of Nancy Reagan*. New York: St. Martin's Press, 1986. A contemporary journalist's favorable account of Nancy Reagan's life and activities.

Ward, Geoffrey C., ed. *Before the Trumpet: Young Franklin Roosevelt, 1882-1905*. New York: Harper & Row, 1985. A richly detailed family epic, played out on two continents and full of surprises.

Washington, George. *The Diaries of George Washington*. Edited by Donald Jackson and Dorothy Twohig. 6 vols. Charlottesville: University Press of Virginia, 1976-1979. Washington's meticulous and dry diaries, which read somewhat like a farmer's almanac.

Watson, Robert P. *First Ladies of the United States: A Biographical Dictionary*. Boulder, Colo.: Lynne Rienner, 2001. The book offers profiles and biographical information on every First Lady to date, including Laura Bush, and provides comparative facts on all the presidential spouses.

_____. "The First Lady Reconsidered: Presidential Partner and Political Institution." *Presidential Studies Quarterly* 27, no. 4 (1997): 805-818.

_____. *The Presidents' Wives: Reassessing the Office of First Lady.* Boulder, Colo.: Lynne Rienner, 2000. A statistical and research-oriented assessment of the roles and the long-ranging impacts of the First Ladies as presidential partners.

Weidenfeld, Sheila Rabb. *First Lady's Lady: With the Fords at the White House.* New York: G. P. Putnam's Sons, 1979. Illustrated.

Weinstein, Edwin A. *Woodrow Wilson: A Medical and Psychological Biography.* Princeton, N.J.: Princeton University Press, 1981.

Wharton, Anne Hollingsworth. *Martha Washington.* New York: Charles Scribner's Sons, 1897. A lively, if somewhat romanticized, account of Martha Washington.

_____. *Social Life in the Early Republic.* Philadelphia: J. B. Lippincott, 1902. Describes the activities of Abigail Fillmore and her daughter during the Millard Fillmore administration.

Whitcomb, John, and Claire Whitcomb. *Real Life at the White House: Two Hundred Years of Daily Life at America's Most Famous Residence.* New York: Routledge, 2000. Includes new information about the Harrisons at the White House.

White House Historical Association. *The White House: An Historic Guide.* Washington, D.C.: 1995. Describes the mansion's history, architectural significance, and contents. With bibliographical references and index.

Whitton, Mary Ormsbee. *First First Ladies, 1789-1865.* Reprint. Freeport, N.Y.: Books for Libraries Press, 1969. Biographical chapters on the early First Ladies give a detailed sense of the environments in which they lived.

Wikander, Lawrence E., and Robert H. Ferrell, eds. *Grace Coolidge: An Autobiography.* Worland, Wyo.: High Plains Press, 1992. A collection of Grace Coolidge's articles published in 1929-1930 in *American* magazine. Her own words are helpful, but she keeps her opinions and feelings to herself.

Willets, Gilson. *Inside History of the White House.* New York: Christian Herald, 1908. A good source for information on Letitia Tyler and her daughter Letitia Tyler Semple.

Wilson, Edith Bolling. *My Memoir.* Reprint. New York: Arno Press, 1981. Part of this work was originally published in *The Saturday Evening Post* under the title "As I Saw It." With illustrations.

Winfield, Betty Houchin. "Madame President: Understanding a New Kind of First Lady." *Media Journal Studies* 8 (1994): 59-71.

Withey, Lynne. *Dearest Friend: A Life of Abigail Adams.* New York: Free Press, 1981. A biography which highlights the relationship of Abigail and John Adams.

Wooten, James E. *Elizabeth Kortright Monroe.* Charlottesville, Va.: Ash Lawn-Highland, 1987. A slim biography of Elizabeth Monroe.

American First Ladies

Index

Page numbers in boldface type indicate an article devoted to the person or topic.